The American Indian in Western Legal Thought

The Discourses of Conquest

ROBERT A. WILLIAMS, JR.

New York   Oxford
OXFORD UNIVERSITY PRESS

119951

Oxford University Press

Oxford New York Toronto
Delhi Bombay Calcutta Madras Karachi
Kuala Lumpur Singapore Hong Kong Tokyo
Nairobi Dar es Salaam Cape Town
Melbourne Auckland

and associated companies in
Berlin Ibadan

Library of Congress Cataloging-in-Publication Data
Williams, Robert A., 1955–
The American Indian in western legal thought :
the discourse of conquest / Robert A. Williams, Jr.
p. cm. Bibliography: p. Includes index.
ISBN 0-19-505022-3
ISBN 0-19-508002-5 (pbk)
1. Indians of North America—Legal status, laws, etc.—History—Sources.
2. Indians of North America—Government relations—History—Sources.
3. Indians of North America—Tribal government—History—Sources.
4. Racism—United States—History—Sources.
1. Title. KF8205.W547 1989 346.7301'3—dc 19 [347.30613] 88-37260

9 8 7 6 5 4 3 2

Printed in the United States of America
on acid-free paper.

*The American Indian
in Western Legal Thought*

For Joy

Acknowledgments

Many friends have generously helped me in writing this book. My wife, Joy Fischer, and my friend James Henderson deserve special thanks. Milner Ball, Rennard Strickland, and Lloyd Weinreb read the entire manuscript and offered invaluable advice and suggestions. Michael Kenyon, Sybil Kisken, and Jean Collins assisted me in proofreading the manuscript and other related tasks. I am grateful to them all.

I have benefited from many other types of support in writing this book. I thank especially the library staff at the University of Wisconsin Law School and at the University of Arizona College of Law. I also thank Barbara Clelland, Maria Campos, Rosie Gallegos, Norma Kelly, and Angie Valenzuela, all of whom helped me produce the manuscript for this book. Their patience and caring could never be replaced by a personal word processor. The American Council of Learned Societies, The Ford Foundation, The National Endowment for the Humanities, and The Smongeski Fellowship program at the University of Wisconsin have extended to me grants that greatly aided the completion of this book. I gratefully acknowledge their invaluable support.

Tucson   R. A. W.
March 1989

Contents

Introduction, 3

Part I   The Medieval and Renaissance Origins of the Status of the American Indian in Western Legal Thought

1. The Medieval Discourse of Crusade, 13

Truth: Papal Discourse, 15
  The Church Universal, 15
  Reform Discourse, 18
  Civilian Discourse, 26
Power: Crusading Discourse, 29
  Holy War, 29
  Urban's Spanish Crusade, 32
  The First Call to Crusade, 34
  The Instruments of Crusade, 37
Knowledge: Humanist Discourse, 41
  Secular Humanism, 42
  Innocent's Synthesis, 43

**2. The Perfect Instrument of Empire:
The Colonizing Discourse of Renaissance Spain, 59**

The Lithuanian Controversy, 59
  The Intra-European Crusade of the Teutonic Knights, 60
  The Constance Debates on the Rights of Infidels, 62
The Iberian Crusades in Africa, 67
  The Portuguese Appeal to Conquer and Convert the Canary Islands, 67
  The Papal Response: *Romanus Pontifex*, 71
The Spanish Bulls, 74
  The New World's First Entrepreneurs, 74
  The Discovery Era's First Contract for the Conquest of the New World, 78
Instruments of Empire, 81
  Governor Columbus, 81
  The *Encomienda*, 83
  The Dominicans in the New World, 85
  The Laws of Burgos, 86
  The *Requerimiento*, 88
Victoria's "On the Indians Lately Discovered," 93
  The Inquisitions into Indian Capacity, 93
  Franciscus de Victoria, 96
  Victoria's Lecture, 97
  A Guardianship over the Indians, 103

Part II   Protestant Discourses

3.   The Protestant Translation of Medieval and Renaissance Discourses on the Rights and Status of American Indians, 121

The English Reformation, 122
  The Reformation's Transformation of English Society, 122
  A Prefatory Colonizing Discourse, 126
The Elizabethan Restoration, 131
  Laissez-Faire Discourse, 132
  Perfecting Colonizing Praxis: The Merchants' Foray, 134
  Elizabethan Colonialism: Elizabeth's Irish Wars, 136

4.   The Elizabethan Wars for America, 151

The First Protestant Crusade to America, 151
  Sir Humphrey Gilbert: Elizabethan Terrorist, 151
  The Early Colonizing Efforts of Sir Humphrey Gilbert, 157
  Early New World Colonizing Discourses, 160
  The New World Crusade of Sir Humphrey Gilbert, 162
Appropriated Discourses, 163
  Cantabrigian Calvinism, 163
  Peckham's "True Reporte," 165
  The Black Legend of Spanish "Cruelties" in the New World, 173
The Second Elizabethan Crusade to America, 174
  Sir Walter Raleigh: The First Great Puritan Hero, 174
  The Virginia Venture of Sir Walter Raleigh, 177

5.   The English Conquest of Virginia, 193

The Bridge Builders Between the Medieval and the Enlightenment Visions
    of the American Indian in Western Legal Thought, 194
  Alberico Gentili's Oxonian Discourse, 194
  Sir Edward Coke and the English Common Law Presumption
    of the King's Right to Wage War Against Infidels, 199
The Invasion of America, 201
  The Virginia Company's Tactics and Strategy, 201
  The Jamestown Venture, 205
  The War for America, 212
  A Discourse of Conquest, 218

Part III   The Norman Yoke: The American Indian and the Settling of United States Colonizing Legal Theory

6.   The Norman Yoke, 233

Discourses of Containment: The Old Northwest
    and the Proclamation of 1763, 233

An Indian Reserve on the Frontier, 233
The Proclamation of 1763, 235
The Imperial Plan of 1764, 238
Discourses of Resistance, 241
The Crown and the Colonists' Competing Discourses on and Claims
    to the Indian Frontier, 245
Locke's Theory and the Indians' "Wastelands," 246
Locke's Theory Applied: The Colonial Radicals' Praxis
    on the Indian Frontier, 249
The Norman Yoke Applied to America, 251
The American By-products of the Norman Yoke, 255
Benjamin Franklin: Syndicalist, 256
The "Suffering" Traders, 259
The Vandalia Colony, 262
Thomas Jefferson: Revolutionary, 265
Discursive Chaos on the Frontiers of American Colonizing Discourse, 271
Chaos in the Continental Congress, 271
Camden-Yorke, 275

7. **The Colonists' War for America, 287**

The Patriots' Discourses, 288
The Players and the Play, 289
The "Plain Facts" of the "Public Good," 292
The Norman Yoke Revived to Decide the Rights and Status
    of American Indian Tribes, 305
Johnson v. McIntosh and United States Colonizing Legal Theory, 308
Fletcher v. Peck: A Dangerous Contest Compromised, 308
Daniel Webster for the Plaintiff, 309
Defendant McIntosh's Rebuttal, 310
Chief Justice Marshall's Discourse of Conquest, 312

Conclusion, 325

Bibliography, 335

Index, 343

*The American Indian
in Western Legal Thought*

The conquest of the earth, which mostly means the taking it away from those who have a different complexion or slightly flatter noses than ourselves, is not a pretty thing when you look into it too much. What redeems it is the idea only. An idea at the back of it; not a sentimental pretence but an idea; and an unselfish belief in the idea—something you can set up, and bow down before, and offer a sacrifice to. . . .

JOSEPH CONRAD,
The Heart of Darkness

The settler makes history and is conscious of making it. And because he constantly refers to the history of his mother country, he clearly indicates that he himself is the extension of that mother country. Thus the history which he writes is not the history of the country which he plunders but the history of his own nation in regard to all that she skims off, all that she violates and starves.

The immobility to which the native is condemned can only be called in question if the native decides to put an end to the history of colonization—the history of pillage—the history of decolonization.

FRANTZ FANON,
The Wretched of the Earth

Introduction

In August 1246, an assembly of the loyal subjects of the greatest empire the world had known—even greater than that of Rome in its Imperial Age—gathered on a plain in Central Asia. One of the few Westerners to witness this gathering of the Mongol Empire, Friar John of Plano Carpini, a pupil of Francis of Assisi, recorded a partial roster of those in attendance: "Duke Jerozlaus of Susdal in Russia and several chiefs of the Kitayans and Solangi, also two sons of the King of Georgia, the ambassador of the Caliph of Baghdad, who was a Sultan, and more than ten other Sultans of the Saracens."[1] Besides these, John noted the presence of at least 4,000 additional envoys from throughout the Mongol Empire, all carrying tribute and gifts of gold.

This throng had gathered under a gigantic tent, "supported by columns covered with gold plates and fastened to other wooden beams with nails of gold,"[2] to witness the coronation of the newly elected Great Khan of the Mongols, Guyak, grandson of Genghis Khan. As ruler of the Mongols, Guyak would be sovereign over a vast empire stretching from the shores of the Pacific in China, across all of Central Asia including India, to the Baltic and Black seas, the very borders of Western Christendom.

Imagine the awe and trepidation in the mind of Friar John as he gazed on this awesome spectacle. He himself had witnessed the "many skulls and bones of dead men lying on the ground like dung,"[3] marking the long and gruesome trail to Guyak's camp. In his travels eastward across Europe and into Mongol-ransacked Russia, John had collected horrifying accounts of the barbaric practices of the Khan's armies. One such tale related that after a great battle on the River Kalka on the southern steppe, the Mongols laid the defeated Mstislav, prince of Kiev, and the other Russian princes under huge wooden boards. The victors feasted on top of the boards while the Russian princes suffocated to death. Even more horrifying was the fact that the Mongols considered such a brutal but bloodless execution to be a mark of distinction, reserved for special enemies of noble birth. Mongol priests taught that blood contained the individual's spiritual essence, and thus to spill a noble's blood would be to defile the ground on which it fell. Death by suffocation, or drowning, therefore, was the privileged form of execution among the Mongols. For instance, disloyal members of the Khan's own family (of either sex; the Khans did not discriminate) were rolled up in carpets and then thrown into a nearby body of water to drown. Sometimes, to add emphasis to some particular point, more elaborate measures were devised. Guyak himself, shortly after his election, executed one of his principal adversaries, the sorceress Fatima, by sewing closed all her bodily orifices, wrapping her in a sheet of felt, and throwing her into a river.[4]

The horrors that Friar John had seen and heard about on his journey must have weighed heavily on his mind as he contemplated his portfolio as ambassador on behalf of Western Christendom. The sixty-four-year-old Franciscan missionary spoke no Oriental languages and possessed little international diplomatic experience. Yet he had been selected by the new pope in Rome, Innocent IV (1243–1254),[5] for a most important mission. He was to deliver two "gifts" in the form of letters written by Innocent to the Great Khan of the Mongols.

These letters, at least in the mind of their papal author, who had been a canon lawyer of significant repute before he assumed St. Peter's chair, contained messages of utmost import to both the Christian and the Mongol empires. Christian Europe had grown increasingly alarmed at the rapacious westward advance of the Khan's armies. First Moscow, then Kiev—in fact, virtually all of Christian Russia—had fallen under the yoke of Mongol domination and tribute. Worse, the Mongols had launched brief but devastating forays into European Christendom: Poland, Moravia, even as far west as Austria and Hungary. The Mongol advance had been halted only by the death of Ugedy Khan, Guyak's predecessor, and subsequent rivalry among the Mongol princes over the question of succession. Guyak's election, however, had ended the distracting dissension in the empire. Genghis Khan's unfulfilled dream of a world empire could now be singlemindedly prosecuted by his grandson, Guyak, supreme *khaghan* (khan of khans) of the Mongols.

Pope Innocent was especially concerned about a united Mongol military renascence. In the summer of 1244, he had been forced to move the papal seat from Rome to Lyons following the invasion of Italy by the excommunicated Hohenstaufen emperor, Frederick II. This conflict was the latest extension of a debate between the papacy and the Holy Roman Empire that had been carried on since the investiture controversy of the eleventh century. The Germanic imperial successors of Charlemagne refused to accept the doctrine proclaimed by popes since Gregory VII (1073–1085) that the successors of St. Peter exerted universal rule over all of Christendom, including emperors and kings. Frederick II's grandfather, Frederick Barbarossa, had gone to war against the papacy over the issue of Rome's secular jurisdiction, and now Barbarossa's grandson was following the Hohenstaufen tradition.[6]

Innocent, well aware that Western Christendom was particularly vulnerable at this time owing to this internal dissension, had sent Friar John to discover the Great Khan's plans. The papal letters carried by the ambassador-priest were quite blunt in asking Guyak his intentions toward Christendom. What must have worried John even more was the boldness with which the pope expressed his own intentions toward the Khan and his subjects.

The first of Innocent's letters[7] sought to instruct the Mongol Khan in the rudiments of enlightened Christian doctrine. God, the Father of all men, with "unutterable loving-kindness," Innocent wrote to the Mongol, had sent from the lofty throne of heaven down to the lowly region of the world "His only-begotten Son," Christ the Savior. Consubstantial with God himself, this Son had been "conceived by the operation of the Holy Ghost in the womb of a fore-chosen virgin" and had revealed himself in a form visible to all men.

As explained by the canon lawyer–pope, the purpose of this strange and miraculous assumption of a human form by God was to make possible the Son's sacrifice "as a victim for the redemption of mankind." After dying on the cross, but before "rising from the dead and ascending into heaven," this Savior-Son designated a vicar on earth. To this vicar, Peter, had been "committed the care of all souls." Innocent as pope was now the divinely appointed successor to Peter's vicariate. According to Innocent, the Son of God bequeathed to Peter

the keys of the kingdom of heaven by which he and, through him, his successors, were to possess the power of opening and of closing the gate of that kingdom to all. Wherefore we, though unworthy, having become, by the Lord's disposition, the successor of this vicar, do turn our keen attention, before all else incumbent on us in virtue of our office, to your salvation and that of other men.

Having informed the Khan that Innocent, as pope, was bound "to lead those in error into the way of truth," this first papal letter concluded by introducing its bearer, Friar John, who would further inform Guyak of the truths of the Christian faith.

The second letter delivered by John on behalf of Innocent reproached Guyak and the Mongol armies for "stretching out your destroying hand to more distant lands" and thereby violating the divine natural law. This natural law, wrote Innocent, united all men, even "irrational animals," with the "very elements which go to make up the world machine." The pope enjoined the Khan to desist in this "breaking the bond of natural ties" by ceasing his persecution of Christians and to "conciliate by a fitting penance the wrath of divine Majesty." Innocent concluded his epistles with a dire warning:

[N]or should you be emboldened to commit further savagery by the fact that when the sword of your might has raged against other men Almighty God has up to the present allowed various nations to fall before your face; for sometimes He refrains from chastising the proud in this world for the moment, for this reason, that if they neglect to humble themselves of their own accord He may not only no longer put off the punishment of their wickedness in this life but may also take greater vengeance in the world to come.

Fortunately for Friar John, the Mongols' notions of international law extended immunity to an ambassador of a foreign nation. Upon his return to the see of St. Peter, John reported that Guyak had listened intently to the pope's message and had asked only that John deliver a return response. The Great Khan's letter[8] asked the pope to "come at once to serve and wait upon us. At that time, I shall recognize your submission." As for Innocent's argument that he as pope was God's representative on earth, Guyak retorted that "the eternal God has slain and annihilated these lands and peoples, because they have neither adhered to Genghis Khan, nor to the Khagan, both of whom have been sent to make known God's command." According to the Khan's view of things, how could Innocent be certain he was God's agent on earth? The Mongols' successes at war, Guyak argued, could not have occurred if "contrary to the command of God."

This response might have indicated to Innocent that perhaps his own arguments needed refinement. But in a followup letter to Guyak, Innocent warned that he as pope was now even more upset about the condition of the souls of the Khan's subjects, for they could no longer claim ignorance of the true faith on Judgment Day, having been visited by the pope's priestly envoy. As God was losing patience with the Mongols, he was likely to inflict his wrath on them at any moment.[9]

But history records that neither man ever was able to test his respective vision of truth on the field of battle with the other.[10]

As Pope Innocent's letters to the Great Khan of the Mongols signify, the "West" has sought to impose its vision of truth on non-Western peoples since the Middle Ages. In seeking the conquest of the earth, the Western colonizing nations of Europe and the derivative settler-colonized states produced by their colonial expansion have been sustained by a central idea: the West's religion, civilization, and knowledge are superior to the religions, civilizations, and knowledge of non-Western peoples. This superiority, in turn, is the redemptive source of the West's presumed mandate to impose its vision of truth on non-Western peoples.

This book arose out of a desire to retrieve and reconstruct the emergence of this idea of the West's mandate to conquer the earth, and to examine its inaugural applications in the New World. My basic argument throughout the book is that law, regarded by the West as its most respected and cherished instrument of civilization, was also the West's most vital and effective instrument of empire during its genocidal conquest and colonization of the non-Western peoples of the New World, the American Indians.

The West's conquest of the New World was a many-faceted enterprise. Gold, sugar, religion, and innumerable other reasons motivated Europe's invasion of the Americas beginning in the late fifteenth century. But above all, commencing with Christopher Columbus's royal contract with the Spanish Crown to discover a westward spice route to the Indies,[11] Europe's conquest of the New World was a legal enterprise. The archives of Western colonialism in the Americas reveal a profusion of laws that were drafted, enacted, obeyed, ignored, or defied in pursuit of Europe's will to empire in the New World. While the colonizing nations of Europe interpreted and applied their presumed mandates in the New World in radically divergent ways, each assumed that law was an appropriate instrument of empire in imposing its particular vision of truth on the American Indian.

It is in this context of a profusion of laws legitimating, energizing, and constraining the Europeans' will to empire in the New World that the American Indian emerges as a distinct problem in Western legal thought. The many laws and legal documents promulgated by Europeans to regulate their conquests in the New World reveal the existence of a similar profusion of legal discourses about the American Indian. These discourses of conquest are traceable in commonly grouped and constantly supplemented statements and themes focused on the problem of defining the American Indian's rights and status under European colonizing law. The colonizing legal discourses were deployed by rival European colonial nations, the contending forces within those nations, and the European colonists. All sought power over the vision of truth that would be imposed in the New World. All relied on law as a vital supplement to their respective visions of empire in the Indian's America. In the Europeans' conquest and colonization of the American Indian, law and legal discourse most often served to redeem the West's genocidal imposition of its superior civilization in the New World.

In analyzing the relation of Western law and legal discourse to the West's conquest of the American Indian, I have limited my study to the principal New World colonizing nations: Spain, England, and the United States. Because these three nations are primarily responsible for tribalism's near-elimination from the Americas, I have sought to focus on the important roles played by their laws and legal discourses of conquest in imposing the West's vision of truth in the New World.

Given the narrow scholarly training that a lawyer receives and the broad task of understanding more precisely the role of law and legal discourse in the West's conquest of the American Indian, I have employed several other strategies of limitation. I have constructed the book's narratives of the history of the New World's three principal colonial powers and their colonizing laws and legal discourses by relying largely on the more widely cited secondary sources for a particular period. Further, the principal story in each of the three parts of the book focuses on the early period of contact, during which the question of the legal rights and status of the American Indian was most vigorously debated and contested in the respective processes of Spanish, English, and United States colonization.

I have no doubts that the selective nature of the sources and periods studied has resulted in inadequate commentary on certain nuances of interpretation for a particular historical event or personality, neglected scholarly debates, missed documents, and other certain flaws. But my intent has not been to describe the total history of Western law and colonialism in the New World.[12] Rather, I have merely sought to situate the role of Western law and legal discourse in the West's will to empire in the New World. For such purposes, a moderately reliable narrative framework is all that I required for deciphering the traces of the emergence and descent of central motifs in the separate, nationalized laws and legal discourses of Spanish, English and United States New World conquest.

The book's tripartite discussion of the central organizing ideas of Spanish, English, and United States legal colonizing thought also illuminates the tracings of broader themes and strategies. Power, in its most brutal mass-mobilized form as will to empire, was of course far more determinate in the establishment of Western hegemony in the New World than were any laws or theoretical formulations on the legal rights and status of American Indians. But the exercise of power as efficient colonizing force requires effective tools and instruments. As this book argues, law and legal discourse were the perfect instruments of empire for Spain, England, and the United States in their colonizing histories, performing legitimating, energizing, and constraining roles in the West's assumption of power over the Indian's America.

The legitimating function of law and legal discourse in the major Western colonial powers' conquests in the New World extended far beyond providing passive defenses and apologies for the exercise of colonizing power. The immunizing function of law and legal discourse also served as an effective tool for dismissing or deflating demands for further justifications or examinations of the colonizing enterprise.[13] In Western colonizing discourse, the thin veneer of law and legal argumentation does not obscure so much as add value to what otherwise might be regarded as an underlying baseless substance.

In addition to its usefulness in legitimating the exercise of colonizing power, law and legal discourse can affect the exercise of colonizing power, at times arguing effectively for its mobilization, at times arguing effectively for its restraint or its channelization toward the hierarchical goals of a sovereign will. Law's capacity for energizing and constraining social conduct was amply appreciated by the colonizing sovereigns who desired America. Colonization of the New World was presumed by the West to be subject to the rule of law. The question in Western colonizing theory (at least before the twentieth century) was rarely whether power ought to be exercised over savage tribes. Rather, debates almost always focused on which power center within the Western colonizing polities would control that power. These debates and the ways in which law served to energize and constrain the exercise of power in the New World are the principal objects of study in this book.

Again, these legitimating, energizing, and constraining roles of law and legal discourse are only tentatively suggested at various points throughout the book. A more elaborate, refined theory of the relation between law and power manifested as a will to empire awaits articulation on the foundations of a knowledge of colonizing discourse that has barely begun to emerge out of a non-Western history of decolonization. If this book changes, alters, or adjusts ideas about the need for constructing a new hermeneutical foundation for the interpretation of the American Indian's rights and status in Western legal thought, if it destabilizes beliefs about the ultimate justice of the West's present-day hegemony over the Indian Nations of the Americas, then the idea behind it has been redeemed. For this book is but a small part of the global effort on the part of indigenous peoples to bring into existence a different vision of the West's will to empire in the New World, a vision that emerges out of the end of the history of the Indian's colonization in Western legal thought.[14]

NOTES

1. *The Mongol Mission: Narratives and Letters of the Franciscan Missionaries in Mongolia and China in the Thirteenth and Fourteenth Centuries* 62 (C. Dawson ed. 1955) [hereinafter cited as *The Mongol Mission*]. St. Francis personally sent John to establish the Franciscan order in

Saxony in 1221. Active as a founder of monasteries and schools, John probably served as protonotary at the papal curia immediately prior to his mission to the Mongols. I. de Rachewiltz, *Papal Envoys to the Great Khans* 89–91 (1971).

2. *The Mongol Mission, supra* note 1, at 63.

3. *Id.* at 58.

4. I. de Rachewiltz, *supra* note 1, at 100–101. On the Mongol Empire, *see generally* H. Martin, *The Rise of Chingis Khan and His Conquest of North China* (1971).

5. Dates following the names of popes throughout the book are for papal regnal years and can be found in W. Ullmann, *A Short History of the Papacy in the Middle Ages* 367–71 (1972).

6. I. de Rachewiltz, *supra* note 1, at 84–88. On the conflict between the papacy and Frederick II, *see* E. Kantorowicz, *Frederick the Second, 1194–1250*, 578–91, 618–24 (E. O. Lorimer trans. 1957); R. W. & A. J. Carlyle, 5 *A History of Medieval Political Theory in the West*, 6 vols., 293–317 (1903–1936); C. Van Cleve, "The Crusade of Frederick II," in 2 *A History of the Crusades, the Later Crusades, 1189–1311*, 458–68 (R. Wolff & H. Hazard eds. 1969).

7. The letters are reprinted in full in *The Mongol Mission, supra* note 1, at 73–76, from which all quotes are taken.

8. Guyak's response is reprinted in full in *id.* at 85–86, from which all quotes are taken.

9. J. Muldoon, *Popes, Lawyers and Infidels* 44–45 (1979).

10. Guyak died less than two years after his coronation. His successors diverted their attention from western Europe and pursued campaigns into the Moslem East and Mesopotamia. *See* I. de Rachewiltz, *supra* note 1, at 101, 144–59.

11. *See* Chaper 2, text accompanying notes 61–63, *infra.*

12. *See* M. Foucault, *The Archaeology of Knowledge* 3–39 (1972).

13. *See* J. Habermas, *Theory and Practice* 12 (1973).

14. *See* Conclusion, note 14, *infra.*

Part I

The Medieval and Renaissance Origins of the Status of the American Indian in Western Legal Thought

1

The Medieval Discourse of Crusade

At the dawn of Renaissance Europe's discoveries in the New World and conquests of the American Indian, Europeans already enjoyed the singular advantage of possessing a systematically elaborated legal discourse on colonization. This discourse, first successfully deployed during the medieval Crusades to the Holy Land, unquestioningly asserted that normatively divergent non-Christian peoples could rightfully be conquered and their lands could lawfully be confiscated by Christian Europeans enforcing their peculiar vision of a universally binding natural law.[1]

The emergence of this medieval discourse of crusading conquest and colonization of non-Christian peoples can be traced in the archives of the Roman Catholic Church. Numerous Church documents attest to the seamless web of connections between the Crusades undertaken by Christian armies from 1096 to 1271 to recover the Holy Land from the infidel Saracen and the West's colonizing conquests in the New World during the Renaissance era of discovery. The most famous and influential Crusading-era discussion of the rights and duties of pagan nations under natural law is contained in Pope Innocent IV's mid-thirteenth-century legal commentary on an earlier papal decretal by Innocent III, *Quod super his*.[2] Innocent IV, author of the two letters to the Great Khan cited in the Introduction, was once described by the English legal historian Francis Maitland as "the greatest lawyer that ever sat upon the chair of St. Peter."[3] Discovery-era legal theorists, including Franciscus de Victoria and Hugo Grotius, the leading systematizers of the European Renaissance vision of a Law of Nations, cited and relied on Innocent's commentary in their discussions and holdings on the legal rights and status of normatively divergent non-Christian peoples under international law.

Innocent's influential commentary on *Quod super his* focused on the central legal problem raised by the medieval Crusades and Christian warfare against non-Christian societies: Under what circumstances might Christians legitimately dispossess pagan peoples of their *dominium*—that is, their lordship and property?[4]

While conceding that normatively divergent non-Christian peoples possessed the same natural-law rights as Christians to elect their own leaders and to exercise *dominium* over property, Innocent argued that these rights were qualified by the Roman papacy's divinely instituted Petrine mandate. As vicar of Christ's universal Christian commonwealth on earth, the pope had been entrusted by Christ through St. Peter, the first pope, with the care of the spiritual well-being of all the souls of Christ's human flock, including infidels and heathens. Therefore, Innocent reasoned, the papal office necessarily reserved an indirect right of intervention in the secular affairs of all the Church's subjects, actual and potential. Christ's command to Peter, "Feed my sheep," was obvious proof that the pope's divine mandate necessarily included pagan nonbelievers. According to Innocent, these non-Christian peoples "belong to Christ's flock by virtue of their creation, although the infidels do not belong to the sheepfold of the Church." Thus the pope, who possessed jurisdiction "over all men and power over them in law but not in fact," was responsible for infidels, even though they might deny his lawful authority.[5]

Innocent limited the exercise of this broadly conceived, suprajurisdictional papal authority over infidels to those instances where it was clearly necessary for the pope to intervene in order to protect the infidels' spiritual well-being. Such necessary instances included situations in which infidels clearly violated natural law but their rulers refused to punish them, as required by God's divine law. "[T]hrough this power which the pope possesses I believe that if a gentile, who has no law except the law of nature [to guide him], does something contrary to the law of nature, the pope can lawfully punish him."[6] Deluded peoples who rejected the dictates of natural law and the pope's divinely inspired message of salvation demonstrated their need for remediation, according to Innocent's reasoning. Avoiding any extensive deliberation on the content of the natural law that bound the infidel sheep of Christ's flock, Innocent indicated that sexual perversion, as just one example, would necessitate papal intervention and punishment. The worship of idols would also constitute a serious violation of natural law. Innocent argued that such idolatry, if left unchecked, required papal intervention, for "it is natural for man to worship the one and only God." Thus the pope could also "order infidels to admit preachers of the Gospel in the lands that they administer."[7]

As for the sanctions that the pope could impose, Innocent stated simply, "If the infidels do not obey, they ought to be compelled by the secular arm and war may be declared against them by the pope and not by anybody else."[8] In other words, the pope could declare a Crusade against the infidels, directing Christian princes to lead armies of conquest into their territories. The Church's missionaries, of course, were to accompany these Crusading secular armies into infidel lands. Innocent was careful to point out, however, that an infidel, such as a Muslim missionary, could not be accorded reciprocal rights to preach in Europe, "because they are in error and we are on a righteous path."[9]

Innocent's formulation of Crusading-era Christianity's duty to enforce its own normative conceptions of natural law upon non-Christian societies provided European medieval legal discourse with a broad legitimating mandate for wars of conquest and colonization in the lands of other peoples. Just as important, this thirteenth-century canon lawyer–pope's theorizations on the status and rights of infidels exerted a profound, directive influence on future Western colonizing legal thought and discourse.[10] Innocent's central themes of unity and hierarchy, represented in a universally conceived, papally directed

Christian commonwealth guided by Eurocentric norms of natural law, continued to energize Christian Europeans in their colonization of the Americas in the fifteenth century and beyond.

Truth: Papal Discourse

The Church Universal

The idea of the Church as a universal Christian commonwealth, by which all people were united and hierarchically directed by God's chosen vicar, the pope in Rome, exercised a profound influence on medieval legal thought. The idea's animating influence and energy can be found at work in the great historical events of the Middle Ages: the conversion of the barbaric tribes of western Europe; the investiture controversy; the Norman Conquest of Britain; and, of course, the Crusades to the Holy Land. And as Europe emerged from its medieval era, the notion of the pope's supreme jurisdictional authority over all the sheep of Christ's universal flock was carried forward into Renaissance Europe's Age of Discovery. The universal right asserted by popes and Christian princes to enforce Chsitianity's vision of "civilization" and natural law legitimated and dignified the conquest, dispossession, and enslavement of non-Christian peoples throughout the non-European world.

Such a powerful, history-shaping concept could not have been manufactured whole cloth in order to fit the immediate needs of Europe's sudden, dramatic emergence onto the world stage in the fifteenth and sixteenth centuries. The basic idea of the Church as a universal body, uniting all peoples in Christ and hierarchically directed by the pope, God's appointed representative on earth, can be traced to the earliest history of Western Christianity. Its scriptural sources include the famous Pauline allegorical text of the *corpus mysticum Christi*, the Church as the mystical body of Christ:

Christ is like a single body with its many limbs and organs, which, many as they are, together make up one body. For indeed we are all brought into one body by baptism, in the one Spirit, whether we are Jews or Greeks, whether slaves or freemen, and that one Holy Spirit was poured out for all of us to drink. A body is not one single organ, but many. Suppose the foot should say, "Because I am not a hand, I do not belong to the body;" but it does belong to the body none the less. God appointed each limb or organ to its own place in the body, as He chose. . . . Now you 'are Christ's body, and each of you a limb or an organ of it. Within our community, God has appointed, in the first place apostles, in the second place prophets, thirdly teachers.[11]

These central Pauline notions of unity (the community of Christ's body) and hierarchy (the ordering of places appointed to each limb of the body) assumed material significance at an early point in the institutional history of the Western Church. The Emperor Constantine had first granted religious toleration to the Roman Empire's previously persecuted Christians in A.D. 313. By the end of the fourth century, imperial decrees had established Christianity as the official religion of the empire. Imperial recognition of Christianity, however, also entailed certain costs respecting institutional autonomy. Under the Roman constitution, the emperor retained jurisdiction to intervene directly in the affairs of any recognized religious body.

The Roman Church resisted, in theory and in fact, the exercise of the imperial monopoly. Resistance was made easier by the fact that the imperial prerogative was asserted from the new, more distant seat of the empire in Byzantium. The nexus that linked together the Roman Church's arguments against any broadly defined secular right of interference in ecclesiastical affairs was the institution of the Roman papacy. By virtue of the papacy's asserted history, origins, and mandate (according to scripture, Christ had declared: "Thou art Peter, and on this rock I will build my Church"[12]), the Roman pontiff represented the one institution within the Church that could conceivably assert any type of primatal claims in opposition to imperial prerogatives. As St. Peter's divinely elected successor, the pope was posited in early Church legal and political discourse as possessing a universally recognized supreme position in the spiritual life of all Christians within the empire.

The papacy's asserted Petrine origins and mandate quickly assumed centrality in the Roman Church's legal discursive practice. As early as A.D. 494, Pope Gelasius I (492–496), in the most strident Petrinological terms, challenged the support given by Emperor Anastasius I of the Eastern Roman Empire to the schismatic Byzantine patriarchs of Constantinople. Gelasius's letter to the emperor argued that while two powers ruled the world, ecclesiastical and secular, each with its separate sphere, the sacred authority of the priesthood was ultimately placed by God over the royal power:

Of these [powers] the responsibility of the priests is more weighty in so far as they will answer for the kings of men themselves at the divine judgment. You know, most clement son, that, although you take precedence over all mankind in dignity, nevertheless you piously bow the neck to those who have charge of divine affairs and seek from them the means of your salvation, and hence you realize that, in the order of religion . . . you ought to submit yourself rather than rule, and that in these matters you should depend on their judgment rather than seek to bend them to your will. . . . [I]f the hearts of the faithful should be submitted to all priests in general who rightly administer divine things, how much more should assent be given to the bishop of that see which the Most High wished to be pre-eminent over all priests. . . . As your Piety is certainly well aware, no one can ever raise himself by purely human means to the privilege and place of him whom the voice of Christ has set before all, whom the church has always venerated and held in devotion as its primate.[13]

Gelasius's letter gratuitously conceded limited priestly obedience to the secular power, as long of course as the emperor conceded the Church's hierarchical position respecting the spiritual sphere. "For if the bishops themselves . . . obey your laws so far as the sphere of public order is concerned lest they seem to obstruct your decrees in mundane matters, with what zeal, I ask you, ought you to obey those who have been charged with administering the sacred ceremonies?"[14] Gelasius's magnanimous recognition of secular imperial prerogatives was wise political practice, given the fact that too aggressive an assertion of papal primatial authority would throw the Roman Church's constitutional theory into a perilous open conflict with Byzantium's assertion of imperial rights.[15] Gelasius's concessionary dualism reflected an acknowledgement of the papacy's inability to enforce fully its Petrinological thesis and to impose its spiritually hierarchizing logic on the empire during this early period in the Church's institutional history.[16]

The Church's precarious constitutional position within the empire explains in large part why the early popes forcused so much of their energies on the task of enforcing the Petrinological hierocratic viewpoint within the institutional Church itself. The principal enforcement tool of the early popes was the decretal. Inspired by Roman imperial models, decretals were issued by the papacy as binding juristic decisions in Church-related controversies to bishops in Spain, Gaul, and northern Africa. The papal law embodied in the decretals served a centralizing, institutional role in the Roman pontiff's jurisdictional conflict with the Eastern empire.[17]

The missionary activities directed by Pope Gregory I (590–604) to the distant barbaric regions of Spain, Gaul, and Britain also can be seen as part of Rome's distancing strategy for realizing the full implications of its hierocratic pretensions beyond the reach of immediate concern by Byzantium. Converts in these regions were taught by the missionary monks of Gregory's own order, the Benedictines, that the papacy held a divinely willed position of preeminence charged with carrying out St. Peter's commission from Christ to care for all the souls of God's human flock.

An important by-product of this missionary movement directed away from the East was a virtually unmediated integration of the Roman Church's influence and ecclesiastical organization deep into the secular components of an emerging and distinctively western European world view. The great dynastic military order that Charlemagne sought to establish with his papal installation as Holy Roman Emperor in A.D. 800 is but one early instance of the process by which the West and its self-understood historical destiny became inextricably intertwined with the Roman Church's own hierocratic claims to primacy within an as yet unrealized universal Christian commonwealth.[18] As the East's disintegrating power ceased to exercise influence in the western part of the empire, the Church itself was enabled to define a separate civilization energized by the central themes of the unity and hierarchy represented in the Church universal. The German historian Otto von Gierke has described the ineradicable imprints of the patterns imbued in medieval western European legal and political discourse and thought by the Church's dominant themes of unity and hierachy:

Throughout the whole Middle Ages there reigned, almost without condition or qualification, the notion that the Oneness and Universality of the Church must manifest itself in a unity of law, constitution and supreme government, and also the notion that by rights the whole of Mankind belongs to the Ecclesiastical Society that is thus constituted.[19]

The will to empire expressed in this central vision of a universal order established through law and lawgiving is a distinctive feature of the West's colonizing discourses of conquest. Interestingly enough, the emergence of this imperial vision of one right way of life for all humankind, realized on earth under the supreme lordship of the Roman pontiff, can be found articulated in the legal discourse of an institution whose founder reportedly preached the rewards of a nonworldly empire.

Reform Discourse

The Leontine Reform Pontificate

The vision of a unitary Christian society directed by God's vicar, the pope, experienced its most robust elaboration as a theory of the practice of an absolutist government during the investiture crisis of the Middle Ages. The question of whether the institutional Church or secular lay rulers ought to control the nomination and investiture of high Church officers assumed critical import in medieval legal discourse following the demise of the Carlovingian dynasty in the ninth century. The former Frankish empire's imperially conceived centralizing authority was replaced by the rapacious chaos of numerous feudal military suzerainties. The resulting parcellation of sovereignty throughout the western half of the European continent proved disastrous for the institutional Church. Lay military lords indiscriminately seized the estates and offices of secular as well as priestly rivals within their claimed territorial jurisdictions. A feudal lord's unilateral assumption of the role of protector for the abbey or bishopric under his suzerainty transformed Church estates into his personal fief. Feudal responsibilities and services were thereby attached, and the clerical officeholder became subject to the lord's jurisdiction or whim.

This dark era for the West engendered the widespread corruption of the Catholic clergy so often associated with the medieval Church. Wealthy bishoprics and other offices were bartered or sold as fungible commodities by lay lords and kings who demanded the right of investiture for important ecclesiastical positions under their territorial jurisdiction. Many priests pursued their spiritual responsibilities with far less vigor than their worldly appetites, marrying or openly consorting with their concubines. Nepotism and bribery most often determined the succession to episcopal estates.

The pontificate of Leo IX (1049–1056) witnessed the first significant steps toward institutional reform within the post-Carlovingian Church. Leo, like all the other Church reformers of this era, saw clearly that secular control of spiritual offices undermined the supposedly transcendent goals of the universal Christian commonwealth.

Leo had been placed on the papal throne by his kinsman, the German emperor Henry III. With the emperor's support, Leo instituted a series of dramatic ecclesiastical reforms throughout the western European Church. He called and personally attended synods in Rome and councils throughout France and Germany. Decrees were promulgated condemning what the advocates of Church reform regarded as the principal institutional cancers of the age: clerical marriage; concubinage; and, most important, simony, the selling and buying of ecclesiastical offices. All these problems combined in the minds of the reformers to weaken the autonomy of the Church. Bishops bought their sees from the feudal lord. Indemnification was received, in turn, by sale of lesser Church offices to inferior secular nobles who sought sinecures for themselves or kin. Clerical marriage furthered the corruption of the system, as those who had bought Church offices and the attached estates would seek to ensure that their descendants succeeded to the benefice, regardless of qualification, marital status, or loyalty to Rome. From Rome's perspective, clerical marriage and simony thus combined to work against centralization of its authority in Church affairs. From the German imperial perspective of Henry III, the temporal possessions being accumulated by the archbishops throughout western Europe often made them the equals of any rebellious secular noble. When such archbishops combined with their secular feudal allies, the potential for disruption of the emperor's own centralizing will to power became doubly intolerable. Both Leo as pope and Henry as emperor, therefore, had an interest in Church reform.

The decrees of the Council of Rheims called by Leo in 1049 provide a representative example of the form that the papacy's rejuvenated legal discourse assumed during the Reform era. The council's most important decrees were directed against the abuses associated with simony. No one, it was decreed, should be advanced to the rule of a church without election by clergy and people. The buying and selling of ecclesiastical offices and churches were condemned. No layman should hold an ecclesiastical office or church.[20]

The decrees themselves were an attempt by the reformers in the College of Cardinals brought to Rome by Leo to reinstate the separation between secular and priestly functions that had been eroded by medieval feudalism. Leo's close relationship with the German emperor, however, meant that such reforms would never be strenuously asserted against the imperial prerogatives claimed by his kinsman. It was Henry III, after all, who had placed Leo on the papal throne. With Leo's death in 1056, however, the radical implications of his reform movement were more fully elaborated by the extreme hierocratic lawyers and canonical scholars of the Roman curia. Unlike Leo, many of these reformers professed an undivided loyalty to the Church and an undisguised contempt for any secular prerogatives in ecclesiastical affairs, even those claimed by the emperor.

Foremost among the radical party of reformers at Rome was the influential theorist Humbert of Silva Candida. Humbert's radical discourse sought to reinvigorate the universalized, hierarchical themes of Church political and legal discourse that had been suppressed and rendered immotile by medieval feudalism. To Humbert, the parallelism dictated by Pope Gelasius's fifth-century equation of two separate spheres of worldly power, secular and spiritual, could no longer be regarded as tenable in light of the evils engendered by lay investiture. Reason demanded a hierarchical ordering of functions if the papacy was to pursue its Petrine mandate to shepherd all the souls of God's human flock. This ordering of spiritual over lay power had been intimated by Gelasius himself in his letter to the Eastern emperor: "The responsibility of the priests is more weighty in so far as they will answer for the kings of men themselves at the divine judgment."[21] Like most of the radical reformers, Humbert believed that the time had come to explore more fully all the implications of this underemphasized aspect of the Gelasian equation.

Humbert recognized clearly that the Church reformers' will to autonomy required the dissolution of the equal partnership between pope and emperor conceded by Gelasian dualism. A skilled lawyer, Humbert went beyond the mere contention that a bishop who had received his office by simony could not receive episcopal orders. Humbert's hierarchizing logic attacked lay investiture, the practice that made simony possible. He declared flatly that a bishop who had not been canonically elected and approved by the metropolitan (the archbishop in charge of the respective province) was not a bishop at all. "Rather he is to be called a pseudo-bishop":

[M]en promoted in this fashion are not to be regarded as bishops, for the manner of their appointment is upside down; what ought to be done first is done last and by men who should not be concerned in the matter at all. For how does it pertain to lay persons to distribute ecclesiastical sacraments and episcopal or pastoral grace?[22]

Extreme papal hierocrats of the Reform era, such as Humbert, saw the universe ordered according to a divinely inspired, hierarchical logic.[23] According to their view, all grace came from God through the mediating institution of the papally directed Church, which then advised the earthly body led by the king. Lay investiture subverted this divinely mandated and inspired constitutional order. Papal hierocratic constitutionalism required that the grace conferred on a bishop be sanctioned by the mediating authority of the Church. Without this authority, no one could be a bishop at all. Humbert's reformed legal discourse, in subordinating all secular functions to spiritual ends, clearly implied a constitutional principle that in the universal Christian commonwealth, the pope was, of necessity, above the emperor.

Any question that Humbert's hierarchical configuration of the two powers, pope over emperor, reflected the majority position of the College of Cardinals in Rome was dispelled by the legislation of 1059.[24] Enacted during the brief pontificate of Nicholas II (1059–1061), the legislation placed the election of the pope directly in the College of Cardinals, thereby ignoring the traditional imperial right. In addition, this set of laws clearly prohibited lay investiture of any Church office, directly attacking traditional feudal rights of the lay lords. The legislation also prohibited priestly marriage and concubinage.

It was clear to the reformers that enforcement of such radical decrees, particularly canonical election of the pope, required military support. It is not surprising, therefore, given the models available to it, that the papacy seized on feudal discourse to defend its claims to primatial authority in the universal Christian commonwealth. Shortly after the reform decrees of 1059, Pope Nicholas II entered into feudal alliance with the ascendant southern Normans, led by Robert Guiscard.[25] The form of the alliance was of value to both parties. Guiscard sought legitimation of his recent seizure of lands in southern Italy from Saracen armies and pirates. The Church, seeking to distance itself from

Germanic imperial hegemony, reqired a nearby ally capable of defending the Papal States and of providing military support during papal vacancies. In exchange for papal recognition of his right in and to lands in the southern Italian region (which arguably were under the titular jurisdiction of the German Holy Roman emperor), Guiscard agreed to hold these territories as a fief of the Church. In addition, the Norman assumed personal obligations of military vassalage to his new feudal overlord, the pope.

Whatever practical or cynical reasons Guiscard might have had for accepting papal enfeoffment, he defended the legality of the alliance and his feudal grant from the pope by relying on the strident themes of reformist legal discourse. In rejecting German imperial claims to southern Italy, the Norman declared:

In order to obtain God's help and the intercession of Sts. Peter and Paul, to whom all kingdoms of the world are subject, I have subjected myself with all my conquered land to their vicar, the pope, and have received it from the hand of the pope, so that, by God's power, he might thus guard me from the wickedness of the Saracens and I might overcome the insolence of the foreigners. The Almighty has given me victory and subjected the land to me. This is why I must be subject to Him for the grace of the victory, and I declare myself to have the land from Him.[26]

The xenophobic references to the Saracen "foreigners" by Guiscard, a member of feudal Europe's warring caste, would come to assume a prominent place in Church colonial discourse a generation later, during the Crusades. The incantatory phrasing of Guiscard's assignment of responsibility for his military victories to the grace of God, while not novel, again presages a more comprehensively elaborated theme of the Crusading era. The assertion that spiritual grace made possible and legitimated lordship in the secular sphere would come to pervade Crusading-era literature in support of the legal proposition that heathens and infidels lacked rights to property. But the most important aspect of this text in terms of the development of Church discursive practice during the Reform era can be found in the manner in which the papacy had seized on the political and legal forms of feudal practice to its own temporal advantage. In a stroke of tactical brilliance, the papacy had secured the military support required to dissolve the feudal constraints that were choking the institutional Church by inverting the feudal logic that had so long suppressed it. Rome itself now assumed the paramount position in the feudal chain that the reformers had already implied it rightly and necessarily deserved. This singular innovation would eventually assist the pope in assuming the position of the largest feudal potentate in medieval Europe, a fortuitous and obviously welcome byproduct of the reformers' radical, absolutist discourse of unity and hierarchy. The seizure of feudal forms would also provide the legal architecture for Rome's later Discovery-era assertion of jurisdictional authority to assign the New World lands of the American Indian to Renaissance Spain's monarchs. This benefit, of course, could not have been anticipated by the medieval hierocratic reformers. The notion that the pagan nations of the Americas should also be subservient to Rome's jurisdictional authority, however, would certainly have harmonized with their eleventh-century absolutist legal vision.

The Gregorian Irruption

This discursive alchemy by which papal hierocratic and feudal themes were fused so successfully was largely the work of one man, the Archdeacon Hildebrand, who later succeeded to the papal throne as Gregory VII (1073–1085). Much has been written about this most important of the medieval popes, who brought on the most important political and legal irruption of the Middle Ages, the investiture controversy.[27] Gregory was the youngest and longest-surviving of the reform cardinals brought to Rome by Leo IX, and was by far the most zealous and energetic. As archdeacon of the Roman Church early in his ecclesiastical career, Hildebrand-Gregory's duties included military defense of the Papal States. It was in this capacity that he assumed principal responsibility for the negotiations and ultimate alliance in 1059 with Guiscard and the southern Normans.

While there were slight irregularities in Hildebrand-Gregory's 1073 canonical election to the papacy, Henry IV, the German monarch, was at the time dealing with the more pressing problem of a rebellion in Saxony. Given that the young king could ill afford to make an enemy of the new pope, Henry acquiesced to this usurpation of his traditional prerogatives respecting the pontifical office.

In 1075, however, the brief period of détente was ended by Pope Gregory's renewal of the old reform decrees prohibiting any secular interference in the naming of ecclesiastical officers. Henry, having finally quelled the Saxon revolt, openly defied the new pope and sought to name his own candidate to the bishopric of Milan.

Gregory first tried subtle persuasion in asserting his hierocratic position that the pope was above the emperor. In one letter to Henry, Gregory reiterated the Petrinological origins of papal authority, drawing heavily on familiar hierocratic reformist themes:

It would have been becoming to you, since you confess yourself to be a son of the Church, to give more respectful attention to the master of the Church, that is, to Peter, prince of the Apostles. To him, if you are of the Lord's flock, you have been committed for your pasture, since Christ said to him: "Peter, feed my sheep" (John 21:17), and again: "To thee are given the keys of Heaven, and whatsoever thou shalt bind on earth shall be bound in Heaven and whatsoever thou shalt loose on earth shall be loosed in Heaven" (Matthew 16:19).[28]

Henry responded to these Petrine constitutional arguments on the papacy's universal jurisdiction by calling a council of his German bishops. The council dutifully condemned Gregory for various crimes and abuses of papal authority and declared him deposed as pope. Gregory reacted by excommunicating the young king and forbidding him to exercise royal powers.

Although previous popes had threatened to excommunicate and depose a rebellious ruler, no pontiff wielded this potent weapon with so profound an effect on secular political and legal theory and practice as Gregory VII. Being the most serious of all sanctions in a universally conceived, hierarchically structured society, excommunication meant exclusion from participation in the divinely willed Christian commonwealth. All intercourse with an excommunicant was prohibited. Vassals tied by oath to an excommunicated king or liegelord were, in theory, released from their feudal obligations. Unable to issue binding orders to his royal subjects, an excommunicated ruler was denied all means of governance.

Excommunication was thus employed by the papacy as an effective reminder of Rome's hierocratically conceived, absolutist perspective. Pope Gregory used the instrument of excommunication to underscore his own innovative elaboration on the subservience of royal secular power to papal hierocratic goals. Royal authority was useful in the Gregorian cosmology, existing derivatively as a means to the Church's self-proclaimed ends. Secular power could be called on to suppress ecclesiastically defined evil. But secular authority in and of itself possessed no inherent function or aspect. It was only an auxiliary power to be used by the pope in appropriate circumstances and at his sole, divinely inspired discretion.

In Gregorian discursive practice, the pope possessed a "frontierless" jurisdictional authority over the *societas Christiana*, the Christian body politic. The law governing this universal society was contained within the papally pronounced principles of just conduct as articulated in the decretals. And by virtue of the Petrine basis of the papacy, these supreme sources of law were entitled to unqualified obedience. "[T]o the pope every power of the world must be subjected," Gregory insisted. "If the holy and apostolic see, through the principal power divinely conferred upon it, has the right to judge spiritual things, why then not secular things?"[29] Abstracting the principles of divine justice and remitting them in the form of coercive measures, the pope's divinely appointed function, according to Gregory was to superintend the creation of the *ecclesia* as a reality on earth.[30]

Gregory's deposition and excommunication of Henry were welcomed by the many German nobles and bishops who were themselves less than comfortable with the centralizing tendencies of an ascendant Henrician dynasty. They appreciated the opportunity to oppose or weaken the king on legal-theological grounds rather than in open warfare, and embraced Gregory's assertion that the pope possessed the authority to absolve the subjects of unjust men (that is, excommunicates) from their fealty. Unable to issue binding orders to any of his subjects in either theory or practice, Henry was forced to seek absolution in 1077, barefoot, at the snowy gates of Canossa. Left with little choice but to grant absolution to a suddenly humble penitent, the pope released Henry from the bonds of anathema.[31] While Gregory did not restore the king to the throne, Henry's more ardent supporters, who had been neutralized by the ban, grasped the opportunity to repledge their loyalty upon hearing of their liegelord's peace with Rome. Those Germans who had strongly opposed the monarch consequently felt betrayed and, without consulting Gregory, elected their own king, Rudolf of Swabia. For three years Germany was consumed by civil war while Pope Gregory refused to decide which of the two rival kings to recognize. In 1080, when he finally did rule in favor of Rudolf, his second excommunication of Henry failed to work its desired effect. The ban was widely and wisely ignored except by those already steadfastly committed to Rudolf, who was in any event losing the civil war and would be defeated and killed within a few months. Henry thereupon elected an antipope, marched on Rome, and fought Gregory's loyalists in a three-year siege of the city. "Hildebrand, now not pope but false monk,"[32] in Henry's famous words, was forced to flee. The greatest of all medieval popes was never able to return to Rome.

Whatever its ultimate failures, the Gregorian pontificate's significance for the legal and political discursive practices of the West cannot be underestimated. Gregory's words and deeds revealed in stark outline form a wide range of critical problems related to questions of power and knowledge in an evolving western European state system that had yet to free itself from its theological moorings. Gregorian discourse unashamedly deployed themes articulating the possibilities of an unquestioned universal sovereignty to which all secular institutions were subordinated and to which all lay authority was but a supplement. Its universalizing, hierarchical ordering logic easily absorbed opposing discourses and, depending on the political skills of the papal officeholder and on the combination of fortuitous circumstances, had proved itself capable of destabilizing any opposing secular political or legal structures.

The problem for those who would oppose this aggrandizing discourse of papal imperialism was to articulate an autonomous legal and political basis for secular authority in terms that did not accede to Gregory's hierocratic claims of the primacy of spiritual power. In this task the antihierocratic theorists of the Gregorian era would fail. As long as medieval Europeans looked upward in the feudal chain of reasoning determining the trajectory of their political and legal thought there was nothing to stop them from looking well beyond the divine right asserted by their worldly king to the scriptural installation of an ultimate, universal power in the Roman pope.[33]

Gregory himself always anchored his clams to primacy as St. Peter's successor firmly in the scriptural basis of the Word. In a major defense of his militant actions against Henry, Gregory attacked "the madness of those who babble with accursed tongues" against the pope's authority to excommunicate the king "as one who despises the law of Christ."[34] Citing Matthew 16:19, in which Christ installed Peter as the head of the Church with the words "Thou art Peter, and on this rock I will build my Church. . . . And I will give thee the keys of the kingdom of heaven," Gregory asked rhetorically how kings could be excepted from this divine grant of Petrine power to bind and loose in heaven as well as on earth:

[A]re they not of the sheep which the Son of God committed to St. Peter? Who, I ask, thinks himself excluded from this universal grant of the power of binding and loosing to St. Peter unless, perchance, that unhappy man who, being unwilling to bear the yoke of the Lord, subjects himself to the burden of the Devil and refuses to be numbered in the flock of Christ? His wretched liberty shall profit him nothing; for if he shakes off from his proud neck the power divinely granted to Peter, so much the heavier shall it be for him on the day of judgment.[35]

Gregorian discourse could thus always appeal to a normative centering text, the Bible, in articulating the ancillary constitutional principles of its hierarchical reasoning. Christ himself had instituted the Petrine officeholder's privileged role of explaining the Bible's divinely inspired reason to all people. A pope could easily undermine any claim to autonomy asserted by the secular sphere simply by denying its accord with papally interpreted divine reason. In Gregorian discourse, in fact, the assertion of such oppositional claims by a secular or priestly rival ruler indicated an unnatural, intolerable, and ultimately evil divergence from the papally prounounced norms of the universal Christian commonwealth. The delegitimating economy of Gregorian papal hierocratic discourse debased any opposing discourses simply by denaturalizing them. This denaturalizing strategy was amply appreciated by Gregory himself, who cited opposition to the papal will to power as evidence of demonic inspiration:

Who does not know that kings and princes derive their origin from men ignorant of God who raised themselves above their fellow men by pride, plunder, treachery, murder—in short, by every kind of crime—at the instigation of the Devil, the prince of this world, men blind with greed and intolerable in their audacity? If, then, they strive to bend the priests of God to their will, to whom may they more properly be compared than to him who is chief over all the sons of pride?[36]

What form of "pitiable madness," asked Gregory, could make someone doubt that a father should rule his son; a master, his pupil; or the priests of Christ, kings and princes?[37] Anyone who acted contrary to the natural ordering of things in the universe must be possessed by the devil. As between the City of God and the City of the World, there could be no doubt that the rule of men lacked all legitimacy according to divine reason.

In short, all good Christians, whosoever they may be, are more properly to be called kings than are evil princes; for the former, seeking the glory of God, rule themselves rigorously; but the latter, seeking their own rather than the things that are of God, being enemies of themselves, oppress others tyrannically. The former are the body of the true Christ; the latter, the body of the Devil. The former rule themselves that they may reign forever with the supreme ruler. The power of the latter brings it to pass that they perish in eternal damnation with the prince of darkness who is king over all the sons of pride.[38]

Gregory's discourse on difference as evidence of demonic possession in effect sought to exorcise any lay ruler who challenged the papacy's universal authority. Such a challenge reflected "intolerable pride," the sin for which Satan was expelled from heaven. Gregory argued that if an exorcist-priest could be granted power to cast out demons, then he obviously possessed superior power to those subject to demons, such as the prideful "princes of this earth." For Gregory, his excommunication of a prideful prince from the *societas Christiana* for resistance to papal will was the anthropomorphic equivalent of the exorcist's casting out of demons from the body of a possessed individual.[39]

This image of the exorcist casting out the demons of normative divergence from the Church's universalized vision of truth captures the essence of medieval papal hierocratic discursive strategy. Difference from the papal vision required remediation if the universal Christian commonwealth was to be preserved. Gregory's contribution to papal discursive practice was to economize this image of difference exorcised from the *societas Christiana* by debasing all conceptualizations of power and knowledge that were in conflict with the absolutist claims of the papal constitutional vision. Untrue discourses of difference were labeled demonical forms of "madness," to be cast out into darkness and eternal damnation.

Difference mandating remediation thus emerged as a central category in Western legal and political thought and discourse as early as the medieval investiture controversy. Normative divergence from the Church's vision of truth and knowledge signified, not the incomplete nature of all interpretations, but intolerable demonic delusion. When applied within the boundaries of Western Christendom, the Gregorian discourse of difference ignited revolt and the dissolution of an empire. That it would soon also sustain a two-centuries-long Crusade against the normatively divergent peoples of the Holy Land is but one testament to the significance and power of this discursive strategy of difference in the West's will to empire.

Civilian Discourse

While Gregory was prevented by Henry from realizing the full implications of his reformist, absolutist discourse, Gregory's discursive legacy of resistance to secular imperial power continued to inform and direct Western legal and political development through the Middle Ages. The lines of the battle waged between Rome and the secular princes of Europe following Gregory's death were drawn on familiar turf: competing claims for sovereignty and jurisdiction between the imperial and the papal seats over issues such as control of Rome and Italy; the limits and extent of papal legislative authority; and, as always, the papal sanctions that could be imposed on recalcitrant temporal leaders.

Rome's tactical position in this battle was significantly aided by an event that would permanently alter the discursive political and legal practices and styles of the West: the reception of Roman civil law in the twelfth and thirteenth centuries. The Church itself was the immediate and principal intended beneficiary of the interest in ancient Roman law inaugurated in 1084 by Irnerius's lectures at Bologna shortly after the demise of the Gregorian pontificate. Several centuries would pass before the intellectual effusions of this central event ultimately removed the Church from any prominent role in the development of Western legal and political discourse. Until that time of Renaissance, however, the Church itself seized on Romanized civilian discourse to carry out the immense rationalizing project for its own canon law.

The crowning intellectual achievement of the medieval Church's appropriation of civilian discourse is represented by the publication of Gratian's *Concordia discordantium canonum*, or simply the *Decretum*, as it came to be called. The Camaldolese monk Gratian compiled the *Decretum* in the middle of the twelfth century at Bologna, the center of European study of civil law since Irnerius's lectures half a century earlier. As its full title literally states, the book was a "concord of discordant canons," and it cited or referred to virtually every document, writer, and event of any significance in the first thousand years of Church history. Gratian's signal innovation was to arrange these texts dialectically around a disputed issue in canon law. In the style of a running commentary, all the texts in favor of one solution would be marshaled against all the texts favoring the opposing solution. Gratian then attempted to either reconcile or distinguish the texts, or simply to argue why one view was better reasoned than the other.

The profound impact of the *Decretum* on European medieval legal discourse and thought can be attributed in part to the fact that until Gratian's groundbreaking work, no satisfactory method had been developed to systematize the numerous Church legal texts that had accumulated over the centuries of papal legislation. Pope Urban II in the late eleventh century had first suggested that distinctions between papal legislative texts could be drawn by comparing those which contained norms of an "immutable character" and those which were drawn up to meet the exigencies of a particular situation. Other late-eleventh-century Church legal theorists such as Ivo of Chartres attempted to further develop the Urbanian notion of the *distinctio*, but it was Gratian, influenced by his Bolognese legal training, who truly perfected the method in his *Decretum*. Imbued with Roman patterns and influences, his systematizing textual strategy provided the medieval Church with a formalized, rationalistic legal program for the governance of its intended universal empire.[40]

The *Decretum* gained rapid prominence throughout Europe as an authoritative compilation of existing Church law. As Brian Tierney has noted:

[T]he use of such a single, universally accepted code of canons made possible an unprecedented growth of administrative unity in the Church. . . . New legal procedures, often borrowed from Roman law, were adopted in order to facilitate appeals to Rome, and as the appeals flowed in by thousands from every corner of Christendom the necessary apparatus of papal courts, bureaucratic administrators, and delegate judges was developed to cope with them.[41]

Thus Gregory VII's enervated hierocratic claims of an imperial, lawgiving papacy were revived and carried forward a few decades after his death in an even more robust form by the fusion of papal hierocratic theory with Roman civilian jurisprudence.

The *Decretum*'s greatest appeal to the advocates of an imperial papacy in the post-Gregorian age was to be found in its more refined hierocratic elaboration of the constitutional principles of papal jurisdiction. A main departure point for the hierocratic commentators on the *Decretum* who sought to formalize the subordination of secular power to spiritual authority according to natural and divine law was the following Gregorian-inspired *distinctio* contained in Chapter 1 of Gratian's text:

The Roman church established the dignities of all other churches of every rank, the eminence of each patriarch, the primacy of metropolitans, the sees of bishops. But she herself was founded and built on the rock of the dawning faith by Him who conferred simultaneously on the blessed key-bearer of eternal life the rights over a heavenly and earthly empire.[42]

In this brief paragraph, Gratian captured perfectly the cautious but pregnant ambiguity marking the centuries-long development of the Church's absolutist

theory of universal papal jurisdiction. The Petrine basis of the papacy's unquestioned authority over the ecclesiastical empire is clearly asserted in this
passage. But the papacy's rights to jurisdiction over the "earthly empire" are
just as clearly implied. For those hierocratic canonists offering subsequent
commentaries on the *Decretum*, the relevant issue raised by Gratian's *distinctio*
was whether the emperor received his imperial power from the pope and, if so,
whether the pope might depose the emperor and assume directly the imperial
office's temporal jurisdiction. The issue was of more than passing academic
interest, for the decades immediately following the publication of Gratian's
work found the papacy in continuous ideological battles with the Hohenstaufen line of German emperors.[43]

The most influential commentary on Gratian's *distinctio* on the nature of
papal power was written by Rufinus of Bologna in 1157. Rufinus wrote at a
time of intense, hostile relations between Pope Hadrian IV (1154–1159) and the
German Hohenstaufen emperor Frederick Barbarossa. Citing the last line of
Gratian's *distinctio*, Rufinus speculated as follows:

Rights over a heavenly and an earthly empire. He calls the heavenly milita, that is, the
whole body of the clergy and the things that pertain to them, a heavenly empire. He
calls secular men and secular things an earthly empire or kingdom. From this it seems
that the supreme pontiff, who is vicar of the blessed Peter, holds rights over the earthly
kingdom.[44]

In further clarifying the nature of the pope's "rights over the earthly kingdom,"
Rufinus's commentary stressed the relevance of two concepts borrowed from
Roman jurisprudence, "authority" and "administration." Authority, Rufinus
wrote, was the inherent right to direct the exercise of power. Administration was
similar to the right "of a steward, for he has the right to administer but he lacks
the authority to rule." The pope "holds rights over the earthly kingdom as
regards authority."[45] The emperor, who has the duty of administering secular
things, is confirmed by the authority of the pope through the consecration
ceremony. Therefore, argued Rufinus, the pope has direct as well as indirect
forms of authority. He possesses direct authority in spiritual matters and indirect
authority administered through the imperial office in secular matters.[46]

Rufinus's commentary indicates that the theory of universal papal jurisdiction assumed a bifurcated posture in the legal discursive practice of the post-
Gregorian hierocratic commentators on the *Decretum*.[47] In spiritual matters,
the pope directly translated God's divine will to the universal Christian commonwealth. In secular affairs, the pope reserved a right to intervene only when
secular rulers by their conduct threatened the spiritual welfare of Christians.
Of necessity, therefore, the papacy ought to have the right to appoint the most
important secular ruler, the Holy Roman emperor, whose duty was to administer a worldly empire conceived as the instrument of the pope's transcendent
spiritual mandate.

The most famous papal bull of the Middle Ages, *Unam sanctum*, issued by
Pope Boniface VIII in 1302, simply restated the core papal discursive themes of

unity and hierarchy developed over nearly a millennium and crystallized by the post-Gregorian hierocratic canonists in the wake of the constitutional crisis brought on by the investiture controversy.

Certainly anyone who denies that the temporal sword is in the power of Peter has not paid heed to the words of the Lord when he said, "Put up thy sword into his sheath" (Mathew 26:52). Both then are in the power of the Church, the material sword and the spiritual. But the one is exercised for the church, the other by the church, the one by the hand of the priest, the other by the hand of kings and soldiers, though at the will and sufferance of the priest. One sword ought to be under the other and the temporal authority subject to the spiritual. . . .[48]

Boniface concluded *Unam sanctum* with the stark declaration "that it is altogether necessary to salvation for every human creature to be subject to the Roman pontiff." This principle, which was of prime constitutional significance in the universal Christian commonwealth, required an unquestioned and divinely sanctioned universal jurisdiction belonging to the Roman pontiff. Only by the pope's implementation of a Christian government on a world scale, using Christian princes and their armies, would the ecclesiastical society, the representation of humankind's transcendent end on earth, be finally realized. This, of course, was the idea of the Crusades, grounded in the universal Church's assertion of a divine right to enforce its vision of truth in all lands and cultures, Christian and non-Christian alike.

Power: Crusading Discourse

Holy War

As has been seen, the medieval theory of universal papal jurisdiction vested a legal responsibility in the pope to realize the vision of the universal Christian commonwealth. As God's vicar on earth, the pope necessarily possessed unquestioned legal authority to declare the divine truth and exorcise the confounding demons of difference.

An important contribution of the Reform-era papacy was to supplement the Church's traditional vision of unity and hierarchy in opposition to divergence from divine law with the practical tools of papal administration derived from feudal and Roman legal discourse. But an even more significant extension of the theory of universal papal jurisdiction was achieved by the Reform-era papacy's refinement of a discourse of holy war. The idea of a divinely mandated war fought by papally directed Christian princes against the infidel first emerges in Western colonizing discourse in the Reform-era papacy's discourse of Crusade.

The additional instrument of a papally declared holy war against radical difference within the universal Christian commonwealth had first been suggested in the early fifth century by St. Augustine. Thus the distinctive legitimating vision of Western colonial conquest of other peoples' lands as the fortuitous by-product of a crusade against normative divergence traces its descent to the earliest teachings of Western Christendom.

St. Augustine, who had argued that the need for civil authority and the state arose from man's sinful nature, similarly taught that war was another by-product of human wickedness. Nonetheless, the saint conceded the possibility of a *bellum justum* ("just war").[49] A war could be just on only one side, and only self-defense or recovery of stolen property justified hostilities against the perpetrators of such crimes.

Significantly, Augustine's concept of *bellum justum* was originally restricted to the civil sphere, and did not comprehend the notion of a war of religion waged on behalf of the rights of the Church itself. It was only in his role as a North African bishop fighting the Donastic schism that Augustine was forced to consider the possibility that a war could be legitimately waged by the secular arm at the behest of the Church against its enemies.

Donatism had divided the Christian Church from an early period in its history. The schism resulted from the Donatists' efforts to link the validity of sacramental power with the priest's moral state. Donatism thus usually accompanied the calls for clerical reform that echoed frequently throughout the Middle Ages. But Donatism's core radical thesis that spiritual grace determined the qualifications for worldly office attacked the institutional structure of the Church itself, threatening dissolution of doctrinally contentious congregations into various sects led by those thought to be sinless.

St. Augustine was the first great thinker of the Church to deal with the destabilizing implications of Donatism in both theory and practice. His intellectual assault against the Donatist schismatics of the Church in North Africa consisted of carefully crafted arguments contending that the validity of sacramental action was unrelated to the administering clergy's moral state. However, the Donatists and their allies, the Circumcelliones, were not deterred by Augustine's considerable intellectual weapons. They continued to wage an aggressive military campaign throughout the region as self-proclaimed soldiers of Christ. As bishop of Hippo, Augustine had little choice but to ask the state to supply the military force necessary to persuade the schismatics to cease in their unreason and rejoin the fold.

In defending these actions, Augustine considerably extended his own theories on just war to include the idea of a holy war "sanctioned by God" to enforce internal discipline within the Church and the Christianized state. The scriptural command "Compel them to come in" (Luke 14:16–24) justified a holy war against heretics and schismatics who had fallen away from the Church but were nonetheless subject to its discipline.[50]

This Augustinian gloss on a holy war intended to defend the rights of the Church remained essentially intact, although relatively unexplored, through the Middle Ages. The radicalized Reform-era advocates of papal power in the eleventh century, however, found Augustine's idea of a holy war "sanctioned by God" immensely useful in their various campaigns against the enemies of Rome and the Church throughout the universal Christian commonwealth.[51]

Not surprisingly, it was the most radical of all the reformers, Hildebrand–Pope Gregory, who most effectively deployed the underdeveloped Augustinian discourse on holy war in justifying Rome's increasing military adventurism during the Reform era. As archdeacon of the Roman Church prior to assuming the chair of St. Peter, Hildebrand not only designed the feudal architecture of the southern Norman military alliance[52] but also played an important role in securing papal sponsorship for a number of secular armed colonizing ventures. These secular campaigns of conquest were denominated by Rome as "holy wars" in defense of the rights of the Church. In 1063, for example, Archdeacon Hildebrand negotiated a treaty with the French Count Ebolus of Roucy, who planned to cross the Pyrenees to fight a holy war against the Muslims in Spain. The count's treaty with Rome stipulated that all lands captured from the infidels would be held as a fief from the pope.[53]

Ebolus's colonizing campaign was one of several, in fact, sponsored or encouraged by Rome as part of the so-called *reconquista* of the Iberian Peninsula during the decade of Hildebrand's archdeaconite. These "holy wars" of reconquest against the infidel Moors who had wrongly usurped Rome's ancient ecclesiastical rights on the peninsula all proudly received "the banner of St. Peter" from the papacy. Additional papal support was provided in the form of specified spiritual favors for the warriors pledged to fight in the *reconquista* campaigns. The Christian combatants received a general benediction, and the slaying of infidels in the *reconquista* wars was specifically excepted from the Church's normal prohibitions on homicide. During the pontificate of Alexander II (1061–1073), the roster of spiritual privileges was significantly extended by the unprecedented papal grant of a remission of the penance required for sins.[54]

Pope Alexander's grant of this "signal spiritual privilege," as the medievalist James Brundage has called it,[55] represents the first instance of note during the Middle Ages in which the papacy fully exploited its ecclesiastical authority to forgive sins in order to further directly the goals of a secular military campaign led in defense of the rights of Christendom. Although the announcement was Pope Alexander's, the innovation undoubtedly belonged to his principal advisor throughout his pontificate, Archdeacon Hildebrand. Hildebrand's close supervision of the Spanish campaign and his later frequent abuses of this same privilege when he served as pope echo his clear innovating voice in the announcement of this new recruitment incentive.

As Alexander's archdeacon, Hildebrand was also directly responsible for the negotiations by which William of Normandy received the papal banner in connection with his conquest of England in 1066. Through the archdeacon's lobbying efforts, Pope Alexander recognized the Norman claims to England; excommunicated Harold, the British king who had resisted Rome's asserted ecclesiastical privileges in the island; and legitimated the Normans' invasion as a holy war in defense of the rights of the Church.[56]

Such were Hildebrand's innovations in the decade prior to his ascension to St. Peter's chair as Pope Gregory VII in 1073. Under Hildebrand's stewardship as archdeacon of the Roman Church, Reform-era papal discourse articulated far more clearly the Augustinian notion of a holy war fought in furtherance of the papacy's universal mandate and hierarchical rights. The secular motivations of campaigns such as the Spanish and British conquests were supplemented by Rome and translated into spiritual terms. Even aside from the important legal sanctioning authority recognized in the papacy throughout Western Christendom at this time, Christian rulers found the mobilizing potential of papal legitimation of their political and territorial ambitions convenient, if not irresistible.

It is not surprising, therefore, that once in the papal chair, Gregory-Hildebrand sought to draw directly on this mobilizing potential in order to situate Rome itself as the inaugurating force in defining Western Christendom's political and territorial ambitions pursued in holy wars against the infidel enemies of the Church. In the first months of his pontificate, Gregory sought to initiate a military campaign to save Eastern Christianity, then under seige by the Seljuk Turks. Acting on the request of the Greek Emperor Michael Dukas for military aid, Gregory called on a papal feudatory to raise an army for the "service of St. Peter."[57] Gregory himself offered to lead this force in aid of the "oft-beset Christians" of the East.[58] He promised any Christian knight who might participate in this expedition "a double-rather, a multiple-reward,"[59] and issued general appeals to all those who "wished to defend the Christian faith and serve the heavenly kingdom. Hitherto you have fought bravely for passing rewards, fight more bravely now for the praise and glory that surpasses all desire."[60]

Gregory's plans for his military expedition to the East contemplated raising an army of 50,000 fighting men, all prepared "to lay down their lives . . . by defending the law of Christ."[61] Apparently, Gregory also had designs on Jerusalem and the recapture of the Lord's sepulcher after his armies had liberated the East from Turkish control.[62]

Here, then, was the idea of the medieval Crusade in its embryonic form. The pope was to lead a holy war in defense of Christendom's rights against the infidel usurpers of the East. The ultimate military objective of this Crusade was the recapture of Jerusalem. Of course, the investiture controversy and Gregory's removal by Henry terminated what would have beeen Christian Europe's first great holy war of conquest and colonization of the Holy Land. Gregory, however, had succeeded in articulating the major themes of a discourse of Crusade, by which the Church could energize and legitimate Western Christendom's military colonizing ambitions in infidel-held lands.

Urban's Spanish Crusade

When Urban II (1088–1099) ascended the papal throne in 1088, just three years after Gregory's death, the basic elements of a discourse of Crusade were thus virtually in place. Gregory himself had developed the central thematic of a holy war fought by Christian knights under a grant of papal indulgence against the pagan usurpers of the Eastern Holy Land. Urban only had to put into practice the idea of a crusade for Levantine conquest and colonization. Furthermore, the new pope was a self-proclaimed disciple of Gregory who claimed fidelity to Gregorian policy goals. These goals included the aboliton of lay investiture, the assertion of the papacy's Petrine mandate to shepherd and care for the souls of all God's flock, the extension of the actual boundaries of the papacy's theoretical "frontierless" jurisdiction, and the continued exercise of the asserted papal right to intervene in secular affairs where the spiritual welfare of the *societas Christiana* was implicated.

As pope, therefore, Urban was certainly not averse to the idea of a holy war in defense of Christendom, the cornerstone of Gregorian hierocratic militarism. The problem for Urban, however, was in continuing Gregory's militarized Reform movement inside a rapidly evolving European state system led by absolutist-minded monarchs. That the papacy was far too weak militarily to carry out the Gregorian-inspired reforms inside Europe was made particularly evident to Urban by his own embarrassing situation. At the time of Urban's election to the Roman papacy, the effective seat of his office, the Lateran palace, and most of Rome as well, were still controlled by the supporters of Henry's antipope, Clement III. Urban, therefore, was able to sojourn in Rome for only brief periods in the early years of his pontificate. He moved frequently between northern Italy and France. He also visited the friendly Normans in southern Italy. He did not return permanently to Rome until 1096, a year after he proclaimed the First Crusade in Clermont, France. Thus while he was a disciple of Gregory's hierocratic militarism, Urban realized perhaps more poignantly than anyone else that application of the Gregorian papal imperial idea within Christian Europe had failed and, if continued, could fatally weaken the Reform movement. It is no wonder that his mind turned toward outward application of the Gregorian colonizing idea in the years of wandering that marked his early pontificate.[63]

At the time of Urban's ascension to the papal throne, the Iberian Peninsula was not yet a secure part of Western Christendom. Urban's first efforts at application of the Crusading idea focused on making it so. The militant advancement of Christianity on the peninsula had been a basic papal theme since the inception of the Reform movement in the middle decades of the eleventh century. A decisive victory by the Moors in 1086, however, effectively stalled Christianity's colonial advance. Urban took it upon himself early in his pontificate to reinvigorate this colonizing campaign. Tarragona, a Spanish port city on the Moorish frontier that had earlier been made papal property, was totally depopulated at the time Urban became pope. He issued strong appeals to the bishop of Toledo and the knights of Catalonia to support efforts to rebuild the city and reestablish the archbishopric. Urban's appeals offered those who engaged in the enterprise "forgiveness of your sins."[64] This was but a continuation of the Reform papacy's practice of using spiritual privileges for essentially political-colonial purposes.

More important, Urban counseled

those who in the spirit of piety and penance desire to go as Pilgrims to Jerusalem or some other place to turn all the costs and efforts of such a journey towards the restoration of the church at Tarragona, so that . . . an episcopal seat may exist there in safety and so that the city might stand as a wall and bulwark of Christianity against the Saracens.[65]

Urban promised those who supported the Tarragona crusade the same indulgence that would have been gained by a pilgrimage to Jerusalem.

Two critical points stand out in Urban's appeals on behalf of Tarragona. First, Urban urged the Tarragona reconquest a full five years before his Clermont declaration of the First Crusade to the East. Early in his pontificate, Urban had clearly formed in his mind the vision of furthering Christianity through colonization and fortification of strongholds in hostile pagan territories. The planned reconquest of Tarragona represented the practical extension of the Gregorian universalizing jurisdictional mandate in its most aggressive form. Second, Urban also clearly realized the utility of the Church's traditional pilgrimage indulgence in achieving this colonizing goal. By equating a Jerusalem pilgrimage with the papally initiated colonial war in Spain and promising an identical indulgence, Urban forged a critical innovation in Church legal discourse respecting the idea of Crusade.

It had long been accepted by the Church that a pilgrimage to a holy place— and in Christian cosmography no place was more holy than Jerusalem—was a pious work meriting forgiveness of sins. To the reformers in Rome whose principal concern was to actualize the papacy's hierocratic claims to spiritual as well as secular universal jurisdiction, the energies and wealth expended on these long journeys must have seemed profligate superfluities. Urban simply discounted the idea of a pious pilgrimage to Jerusalem without dissipating its motivational potential. From the seat of his own universal authority, Urban as pope unilaterally equated the ancient spiritual privileges associated with a pilgrimage to Jerusalem with the more vital and meaningful goal of Christian colonial expansion in Spain. From this vantage point, the simple but far more powerful synthesis of the pilgrimage idea with a military campaign of Christian expansion toward Jerusalem and the wealth of the Holy Land had clearly entered the realm of possibility in Church colonial discourse. By more efficiently administering a previously undervalued imperial prerogative, Urban transformed the papal pilgrimage indulgence into the lifeblood of the Crusading idea.

The First Call to Crusade

Urban's call at Clermont five years later for a crusade to Jerusalem was thus only a more refined and Eastern-directed application of his Iberian colonizing strategy. The Byzantine emperor at this time, Alexis Comnenus, had appealed to Urban for military assistance against the Turks in early 1095. Urban, then encamped in the northern Italian provinces, was told in graphic terms of the annihilation and devastation visited on the East by the Turks. The emperor described the heathen infidels as being at the very "walls of Constantinople."[66]

Urban pledged full assistance to Byzantium, recognizing that the emperor's request presented a singular opportunity to realize the papacy's long-held desire to reunite Eastern and Western Christianity. As his Clermont call to crusade indicates, he was also clearly aware of the more mundane rewards that such a war offered to those who committed themselves to the campaign of colonizing conquest.

The actual text of Urban's speech proclaiming the First Crusade is not available, but all the surviving contemporary accounts agree on its signal theme: the papacy sought to initiate an armed pilgrimage by Christian soldiers under solemn vow to defend Christendom in the East against the heathen infidel and to recapture the Lord's sepulcher in Jerusalem.[67] Urban reportedly also outlined the various personal benefits accruing to the Crusaders as a supplement to this larger project. The most widely cited account of the speech is that of a supposed eyewitness to the event, Robert the Monk.[68] Robert reported that Urban opened his speech with a solemn declaration:

Distressing news has come to me . . . from the region of Jerusalem . . . news that the people of the Persian kingdom, an alien people, a race completely foreign to God, "a generation of false aims, of a spirit that broke faith with God," has invaded Christian territory and has devastated this territory with pillage, fire, and the sword.[69]

Urban embellished this discourse of racist xenophobia with a gruesome description of the various tortures inflicted on Christians by the heathen barbarian. The predominantly French audience was exhorted to

rise up and remember the manly deeds of your ancestors, the prowess and greatness of Charlemagne, . . . who destroyed pagan kingdoms and planted the holy church in their territories. You should be especially aroused by the fact that the Holy Sepulcher of the Lord our Saviour is in the hands of these unclean people, who shamelessly mistreat and sacrilegiously defile the Holy Places with their filth.[70]

Urban next fashioned a *Lebensraum* argument in support of Eastern colonization, virtually identical in style and tone to the Discovery-era recruitment calls fashioned by later European promoters of colonization in the New World.[71] Suggesting that the land in Europe was overcrowded and inferior in quality to that in the Levant, the pope made a recruitment call:

Because of this you murder and devour one another. . . . Let this mutual hatred stop. . . . Begin the journey to the Holy Sepulcher; conquer that land which the wicked have seized, the land which was given by God to the children of Israel and which, as the scripture says, "is all milk and honey."[72]

Urban concluded by spelling out the particulars of the spiritual benefits for those who agreed to go on this armed Crusade: "Undertake this journey, therefore, for the remission of your sins, with the assurance of 'glory which cannot fade' in the kingdom of heaven."[73] A "vow to God" secured the plenary indulgence for those who desired to make the "holy pilgrimage." Those avowed to this armed Crusade were to wear the Lord's cross on their breast, the legal emblem designating Crusader status. Only after fulfilling the vow could the Crusader return home. At that point, the warrior-pilgrim was instructed to place the cross on his back, between his shoulders. "By this twofold action such men will fulfill that command of the Lord which he uttered in the Gospel: 'He who does not take up his own cross and follow me is not worthy of us.'"[74]

James Brundage, one of the most widely respected authorities on the legal discourse of the Crusades, has stated that the history of Crusade institutions is largely grounded in the history of the Church's ancient tradition of pilgrimage and in the legal apparatus that supplemented it.[75] Prior to Urban's speech, Church canon law had not recognized that pilgrims might bear arms or engage in combat on their journey. In fact, respected canonistic opinion held that militant activities negated any spiritual benefits that might have been derived from the pilgrimage. That Urban could simply discard such prohibitions in articulating this new militant genus of Crusader-pilgrim only serves to underscore the contribution of Gregory VII in preparing the discursive foundations for the Crusades. Gregory's numerous military intrigues and internecine battles with the German emperor had prepared the ground for jettisoning the anachronistic pacifist baggage of earlier canonistic discourse. Gregory, in effect, had succeeded in making the concept of a "holy war" familiar, if not totally respectable, to a large segment of the Church.

In seizing on the pilgrimage tradition as the legal architecture for the Crusades, Urban articulated the first truly colonial-imperialist form of discourse in the West since antiquity in terms designed to appeal to the common people. The idea of religious pilgrimage had already proved capable of motivating men and women toward the completion of sometimes Herculean and almost always risky tasks, at great personal expense. For medieval Christians, the loftier ideals contained in the Church's tradition of pilgrimage, now tied to a divine mandate for a holy war, must have contrasted markedly with the mercenary traditions of previous European feudal warfare. This contrast must account at least in part for the vast armies of recruits with little or no military experience who pledged to sacrifice all in answering Urban's call to crusade.

At least since the Carlovingian era, the Church had been alert to the qualitative difference in motivational potential between a discourse of colonial expansion that was grounded in transcendent goals and one that offered mere earthly rewards. With the declaration of the First Crusade at Clermont, this distinctive feature of transcendence characterizing the history of European colonial expansion attained a mature and robust form.

It should of course be remembered that Urban's reliance on the discourse of pilgrimage addressed only the problem of mass recruitment for the Crusades. There remained the problem of tactical organization of the Crusaders. That knowledge was provided by Europe's feudal warlords and their well-drilled mercenary armies. Urban's speech, which also drew on the Gregorian-inspired notion of the Christian knight engaged in holy war, spoke forcefully and with appealing, legitimating clarity to these members of Europe's military castes. It was from their ranks that Urban recruited the military expertise and capital required for an all-out war against the Saracen menace in the East.

It would thus be difficult to underestimate the class-transcending breadth of the Urbanian Crusading synthesis. While primitive mercantilism and laical colonizing ambitions ultimately usurped many of the papacy's directive functions in later Crusades, Urban's fusion of the Church's tradition of pilgrimage with militant secular adventurism remained the basic energizing ideology that sustained the zeal of most Crusaders for nearly two centuries of recurrent Christian warfare in the East. Not only Marxists but also most moderns in the West may find it hard to acce͵⸱ ͵hat the combinative dynamics of popular religion, a holy war directed toward the conquest of Jerusalem, and the liberation of Eastern Christianity from the infidel—the essential elements of Urban's synthesis—could motivate men to march off to distant wars by the hundreds of thousands. But disbelief is easier to suspend if one considers that the sole surviving parallel institution from the Middle Ages similar in form and function to the Crusading idea, the Islamic East's *jihad*, continues to confound Western sensibilities even today.

The Instruments of Crusade

The manipulability of legal discourse, particularly the facilitating qualities that favor it as one of the indispensable instruments of power deployed by the West's will to empire, can be readily appreciated by examining Crusading-era canonical treatment of the Crusader's pilgrimage vow. Under Church law, pilgrims had always been granted a very specific status, with specific privileges and obligations. Under Urban's call at Clermont, the Crusader was understood to be entitled to all the spiritual and temporal privileges recognized by the Church by virtue of his legal status as a pilgrim. The grant of the plenary indulgence itself represented to the medieval layman "a complete and total wiping out of past misdeeds—an expunging of the record, so to speak—so that the crusader who died was believed to enter immediately, without qualification or post mortem penance, into eternal bliss with the saints in paradise."[76] The indulgence represented an unprecedented legal and spiritual benefit and constituted an almost irresistible inducement to those who were presented with the idea of making an armed pilgrimage to Jerusalem.

The Church was well aware, however, that even its substantial offer of spiritual reward could not overcome the practical problems that confronted the layperson contemplating a Crusading pilgrimage. Land and family would have to be left behind (and in the medieval feudal mind, this order of priority was often established consciously). Legal claims against the Crusader or his estate would have to be delayed or settled. Financing for his party would have to be acquired, but borrowing money required hypothecating property. In a feudal society where land (the majority of which was entailed or in some other manner unalienable) constituted the primary basis of wealth, this might prove difficult, if not impossible.

As an avowed pilgrim, however, the Crusader was entitled to basic rights of protection under canon law (and these rights were considerably expanded by Rome during the Crusades), which could be utilized to circumvent many of these fiscal obstacles. Personal attacks on Crusaders were vigorously punished, often by the papacy itself. Gregory IX (1227–1241) once excommunicated the civic officials of Milan, holding them personally responsible for the restitution of a large sum of money stolen from two Crusaders passing through the city. The papacy might also use the Crusader's privilege of protection to shield a feudal warlord returning from the East whose armies had been decimated in battle. Such a mortally weakened liegelord would have been easy prey in the feudal chaos of medieval Europe, with its merciless savaging of the impotent and maimed.

The general papal practice of extending legal protection to the property and families of Crusaders was especially beneficial to the feudal baron absent on Crusade. The loyal servant of Rome's interests was protected, even though he might have left behind long-unsettled rivalries over boundaries or entire estates. It was also not uncommon for a departing lord to designate an ecclesiastical conservator as guardian of his property.

Legally, the Crusader who sought protection under his Crusading vow had to do so at the proper stage in any judicial proceedings brought against him. Procedural manuals specified the exact forms of the Crusader's plea and indicated that adversaries proceeded against the Crusader at their risk. Even more important, if the Crusader did choose to proceed with the litigation, he enjoyed the *privilegium forti*—the right to an ecclesiastical forum as one protected by the general law of the Church. The privilege vested once the Crusader had taken the cross. The obvious advantages to the Crusader of litigating before the courts of the Church naturally invited resistance by the secular rulers' courts. Compromises between the two jurisdictional authorities gradually facilitated a mutual recognition of certain spheres of competence. One legal treatise writer could declare the state of the law in the thirteenth century:

Whoever has crossed himself with the cross . . . is not required to answer to any secular court if he so chooses in any manner concerning movable property or dwellings. Nonetheless, if the crusader is wanted in a criminal case or an inheritance case, the cognizance of the matter belongs to the secular court. In lesser affairs, the crusader may answer in the secular court if he so chooses.[77]

Any attempt to abridge the *privilegium forti* was checked by the Crusader's privilege of essoin—the right to delay any proceedings to which the Crusader was a party. The secular courts normally acquiesced to this privilege. The famous English jurist Glanvill, who died during a Crusade led by Richard I, set the term of essoin at one year in his *Tractatus* (1189). Roughly a half-century later, Bracton, the most renowned English legal authority of the Middle Ages, delineated with rather precise detail the varieties of essoin in his great treatise on the laws and customs of England. Crusaders participating in a general passage to the Holy Land were recognized by Bracton as enjoying the privilege of essoin without limitation until return or death. Another treatise, written in the last decades of the thirteenth century, agreed with Bracton's basic position that the Crusader's essoin extended to stays of judicial proceedings and even to services due the king![78]

Besides these widely recognized legal privileges, other financial privileges attending the vow of the cross enabled the Crusader to use feudal holdings as security for loans of money regardless of competing rights of his overlord or family. This specific privilege was frequently used by overencumbered lords and contributed to the erosion of several of the more rigid feudal landholding patterns. Furthermore, Crusaders received the privileges of moratoriums on the repayment of debts and exemptions from tolls and taxes. The tax exemption was of particular importance, as both the Church and European monarchs levied numerous direct taxes on the general population to support the many Crusading efforts of the twelfth and thirteenth centuries. Much of the money raised through these taxes was paid directly to Crusaders in the form of subsidies, another important financial privilege bestowed by the Church.

The enthusiasm engendered by an initial proclamation of a Crusade was maintained by the Church's treatment of the Crusader's vow as a binding and permanent obligation with serious legal sanctions attached for nonperformance or breach. The avowed Crusader was legally committed to remain with the Crusade until its goal was accomplished. Punishments for breach of vows ranged from disinheritance of heirs to excommunication. Later refinements in the form of qualifications of the basic Crusading promise indicate the increasing juridicalization of the mechanism. A right of substitution, provisions for escape in the event of unforeseen but legitimate obstacles to fulfillment of the vow, and numerous other contingency clauses gradually destroyed the simplicity of the original promise.

The Church's interest in enforcing the Crusading obligations resulted in the extension of its power through increasingly sophisticated techniques of surveillance. Individual churches compiled annotated lists of those in the parish who had taken the vow, noting how likely each parishioner was to discharge the obligation. Articles of interrogation were drawn up by bishops to keep a more centralized record of the status of avowed Crusaders throughout the diocesan parishes.

These techniques of surveillance complemented an important development in Church canon law, which came to recognize the papacy's power to commute undischarged vows. The pre-Crusade development of the vow had been unable to overcome the religiously grounded construction that a vow created nondispensable natural-law obligations. But Roman civil law, fully renascent in the Church's Crusading-era legal discourse, suggested a previously unrecognized avenue of conceptual escapement. The *Institutes* clearly recognized an imperial prerogative to grant dispensations from the prescriptions of positive law. During the Crusading era, hierocratically inclined canonists vested this and other imperial prerogatives in the papacy as part of their continued development of the canonical theory of universal papal jurisdiction. The pope's *plenitudo potestatis* ("plenitude of power") came to be recognized as an unbounded spiritual sovereignty, which included the power to relax or dispense with votive obligations. The papacy thus jealously guarded its imperially conceived theoretical privilege of commuting vows and exploited the power to its fullest potential. The papal power to commute a vow enabled the papacy to finance later Crusades with professional, well-equipped armies. These armies were paid for by the sale of Crusaders' privileges to those who could not or would not leave Europe. In effect, papal commutation permitted such individuals to fight a holy war against the enemies of the Church by proxy.

By the thirteenth century, in fact, the commutation of Crusading vows was the primary fungible spiritual commodity offered by the Church to induce individuals to finance the implementation of various papal policies. Commutation was used to reward missionaries on Europe's frontiers, the inquisitors combating heresy, and colonists who homesteaded in the Holy Land. Revenues raised by redemptions of Crusade vows enabled later popes to finance their wars against recalcitrant European monarchs, a privilege that Pope Gregory VII never enjoyed in his struggles with the German emperor Henry.

The hierocratic canonists and their Romanized legal methodology complemented perfectly the Crusading-era papacy's own absorptive, imperial goals. Law could be flexibly yet effectively applied to regulate and, even more important, to energize the colonizing zeal of medieval Europeans. As evidenced by their Romanized treatment of the vow, the hierocratic canonists' elaboration of the *plenitudes potestatis* of the papacy proceeded from the fundamental premise that all earthly authority was subservient to Rome, and therefore no power could be denied to the pope.

Alanus Anglicus, one of many British clerics who studied at the Bolognese law school in the post-Gregorian era, advanced perhaps the most extreme and at the same time most influential hierocratic viewpoints on the relation of papal supremacy to earthly rights of *dominium* ("lordship"). Alanus argued that no earthly ruler's power was legitimate unless he believed in the true God and received his power directly from the Church.[79] Thus without question, according to Alanus, the emperor received his sword of earthly jurisdiction from the pope: "This opinion is not invalidated by the fact that there were emperors before there were popes, because they were only *de facto* emperors and none except those who believed in the true God had a right to the sword; nor do infidel rulers have it nowadays."[80]

This passage is significant for a number of reasons. Alanus's argument is based on the extreme hierocratic proposition that before the coming of Christ no ruler on earth had legitimate authority. Upon Christ's birth, however, all true authority (Alanus's term is *dominium*) belonged to the Savior, who unquestionably possessed and exercised both swords, earthly and spiritual. Before returning to his Father, Christ gave the two swords to Peter. Peter's papal successors had, in turn, granted the material sword to the emperor and all other rulers who accepted Christ and his chosen vicar. Alanus relied on familiar medieval anthropomorphic imagery to support his hierocratic, totalizing argument on the papacy's necessary control respecting earthly *dominium*: "The church is one body and so it shall have only one head or it will be a monster."[81]

The medievalist Walter Ullmann has stated that Alanus's systematized refinement of papal discourse's imperial thematics constituted the "turning point in the development of [medieval] canonistic political thought."[82] Alanus's influential assertion that the pope alone possessed sanctioning authority over earthly *dominium* provided a reasoned and concise elaboration of the hierocratic maxim that only Rome could exercise legitimate authority in the universal Christian commonwealth. The emperor's authority was merely derivative of Rome's divinely granted plenitude of power. As for infidel nations, Alanus's Crusading-era legal discourse denied any theoretical legitimacy to their *dominium*. By their rejection of the true God and his chosen vicar the pope, all pagans were presumed to lack rights to property and lordship. The pope held unquestioned universal jurisdictional authority on earth over all the Church's subjects, real and potential. Resistance to that authority constituted resistance to God's law. The papacy possessed the power not only to punish the deluded pagans but also to assume the rule over their territories, which rightly belonged to Rome in the first place.

Alanus's hierocratic thesis that those outside the Church lacked rights to *dominium* presented a new, broader-based foundation for the extension of papal colonial policies. The infidel regions and peoples beyond the Levant were arguably outside the geographical scope of Urban II's initial articulation of the First Crusade as a holy war in defense of Eastern Christianity and the Church's rights to Jerusalem. Alanus's thesis on infidel *dominium*, however, could be cited to legitimate the militant extension of papal law and policies to all the pagan sheep of God's flock throughout the world, whether at peace with Christendom or in a state of perpetual war. As heathens and infidels, such peoples, wherever located, lacked any and all rights to *dominium* in a universally conceived Christian commonwealth hierarchically led by the pope. Thus although the Crusades themselves ultimately failed to reestablish permanent Western hegemony over the Holy Land, the Crusading-era canon lawyers' discourse of *dominium* succeeded in extending the conceptual boundaries of the West's will to empire over the entire non-Christian world.

Knowledge: Humanist Discourse

The central thesis of the hierocratic canonists that the pope was above the emperor in spiritual as well as secular matters was vigorously challenged throughout the later Middle Ages by lay monarchs and their advocates. The proponents of autonomous secular authority themselves discovered the manipulable utility of Romanized legal and political discourse in legitimating resistance to papal hierocratic claims. The great discursive conflict of the later Middle Ages between the Church's unitary vision of papal hierocratism and the ancient naturalistic vision of autonomous secular authority put forward by the advocates of lay power provided an important discursive legacy to the West's later legal and political development. With respect to Western colonizing discourse, the Church's response to the antique-inspired philosophy of the lay publicists and their advocacy of secular autonomy illustrates the capacity of a totalizing discourse to confront, assimilate, and neutralize opposing visions of truth.

Secular Humanism

The turn to Roman-law scholarship by lay publicists in the later Middle Ages was a direct reaction to the extreme ecclesiastical assertions of authority and jurisdiction in secular life. The lay publicists' own Romanized discourse was aimed at constructing a theory of autonomous royal power that had historically been denied by opposing papal hierocratic discourse. Roman law, widely regarded as the "acme of jurisprudential achievement"[83] in the Middle Ages, provided the foundations for European secular legal discourse's own coming Age of Renaissance.

As Alanus Anglicus's extreme hierocratic discourse attests, the Church itself had been the original beneficiary of the renascence of Roman jurisprudence in the twelfth and thirteenth centuries. Gratian's civilian-inspired *Decretum* transformed canonical legal method so as to provide the medieval Church with a formal, rationalized legal program for the governance of its intended universal empire. It was not long, however, until the advocates of secular authority recognized that the ancient texts of the *Digest* and the compilations of Justinian provided secular rulers with their own respected, naturalized, and readily available source of law and legal principles for the governance of a this-worldly, unregenerated human society.

Besides finding Roman law and Romanized systemic principles useful in constructing autonomous secular discourses of law and politics, the advocates of lay power benefited immensely from the West's retrieval of a wider corpus of ancient Greek philosophical texts in the thirteenth century. Greek naturalistic philsophy completed the structural elaboration of Renaissance Humanist legal and political consciousness, combining with civilian jurisprudence to provide a formidably articulated, nontranscendentally oriented world view. Not even hierocratically grounded Church canonists could completely obscure the antique secular origins of critical conceptual terms such as *ius naturale* and *ius gentium*.

In particular, the naturalistic cosmology of Aristotle helped galvanize all secularly oriented political and legal discourse during the later Middle Ages. In texts such as *Nichomachean Ethics*, Aristotle clarified the rules of natural justice as those norms of conduct universally recognized and accepted by all civilized peoples. "Nature," in properly understood Aristotelian terminology, denoted the secular conception of a rationally ordered universe, manifested, but never fully attained, in the actual world.[84]

Stoic philosophy, as filtered through the writings of Cicero, was also studied intensely by the late medieval and early Renaissance theorists. "Nature," in the Stoic sense, referred to the constitution of humans themselves as rational, social beings. The law of nature was thus the sum total of those principles founded on human nature that could be used to determine proper conduct in an individual's rational life and social existence. Cicero's familiar definition of natural law as those principles identical to the morality of a high-minded Roman citizen offered the lay and royal publicists the ideal of a rule of life and civil society discoverable solely by human reason, not by papal decree.[85] It was this humanized vision of natural law as understood in the classical texts that provided Renaissance Humanism with the needed discursive battering ram for its full-scale frontal attack on the crumbling bulwark of the subordinating, ecclesiastically espoused hierocratic edifice.[86]

Innocent's Synthesis

The thirteenth-century papacy recognized clearly the threat to the Church's traditional hierarchical world view posed by the classical revival.[87] As just one example, in 1231 Pope Gregory IX (1227–1241) prohibited the use of any of Aristotle's books on nature in Church educational institutions. Although he acknowledged that the philosopher's works contained "both useful and useless matter," Gregory commanded the Dominicans at the University of Paris that in "examining these books . . . you entirely exclude anything which you may find there to be erroneous or likely to give scandal or offense."[88]

Thus hierocratically inclined Church theorists did not stand idly by while the secular proponents of natural law and philosophy attacked the papally centered world view. In fact, Christian ontological and political speculative thought entered one of its most fruitful periods in the thirteenth century in response to the forceful challenges presented by the naturalized intellectual and political environment.

Thomas Aquinas (1225–1274),[89] who studied and taught at the University of Paris in the mid-thirteenth century and thus would have been well acquainted with the rules of engagement for intellectual battle with Aristotle's works, was without doubt the most successful of the medieval scholastics in harmonizing the "useful" parts of the Aristotelian corpus with the Church's canonistic hierocratic discursive traditions.[90] But even prior to Thomas, a number of Church scholars had devoted themselves with great fervor to the synthesis of ancient pagan and hierarchical Christian speculative thought. Thomas's own teacher, Albert the Great (c. 1200–1280), had lectured extensively on Aristotle at Paris. And, as his letters to the Great Khan of the Mongols attest, Pope Innocent IV (1243–1254), himself a skilled and highly regarded canonical theorist of the generation before Aquinas's, had mastered the naturalistic symbology and phrasings of Humanist-inspired discourse in his hierocratic arguments to Guyak demanding an earthly ruler's submission to the vicar of Rome.[91]

Innocent was well prepared for his role as one of the great lawyer-popes,[92] having served as a renowned canonist and lecturer at the famed University of Bologna, where Irnerius himself had revived the study of Roman law in the late eleventh century. Innocent's writings reflected the eclectic absorption of a wide variety of discursive practices—ancient, scriptural, canonistic, civilian—but the dominant systematizing motifs of all his major texts reflected the increasing pervasiveness of Humanism in thirteenth-century European thought. Particularly among the canonists and theologians who studied and taught at the European centers of legal learning in the mid-thirteenth century, the naturalistically inspired ideas later synthesized by Thomas and subsequent Christian

Humanists were literally in the air. No one with as able and supple a legal mind as Innocent's could have afforded to ignore them. The task, in fact, was to tame them and make them "useful" for the Church. What is so remarkable about Innocent's pontificate is the degree to which he sought to harmonize the theoretical implications of such ideas with a papal practice devoted to achiev- ing the most extreme hierocratic goals.[93] Innocent's pontificate was literally caught between two ages, and an unceasing intellectual effort was required in order to maintain bridges between the theoretical onslaught of the approach- ing Renaissance and the receding glacial style of legal thought fossilized in papal hierocratic discourse.

While Innocent wrote and theorized on a number of topics of vital concern to medieval Church theory, his speculations and pronouncements on infidel rights and status represent perhaps his most enduring contributions to Western legal thought. Innocent was the first great medieval legal theorist who at- tempted to address systematically the questions raised by Christian contact with non-Christian nations. His synthesis of Humanist and hierocratic themes provided European legal theory with a fully elaborated legal discourse for determining the rights and status of pagan peoples. Numerous later legal theorists would elaborate on his influential texts, but it was Innocent who defined the essential terms of debate on the law and legal principles applicable to those normatively divergent peoples that Europe would encounter as it emerged from its medieval period of Crusade to its Renaissance Age of Discov- ery and colonial conquest.[94]

Innocent's most important work on the topic of the legal status and rights of non-Christian societies is contained in his commentary on a papal decretal by an influential predecessor, Innocent III (1198–1216). Entitled *Quod super his*,[95] this earlier decretal addressed the issue of the fulfillment of a Crusading vow and the conditions allowing a commutation or delay.[96] Addressing a collateral issue raised by the vow to go on Crusade only briefly touched on in the original *Quod super his*, Innocent IV asked the question, "[I]s it licit to invade a land that infidels possess, or which belongs to them?"[97] Innocent went on to construct a broad-based defense of the Crusades and the conditions justifying Christian warfare against infidel nations in general.

Innocent's commentary demonstrated his mastery of hierocratic canonical methodology. He began by establishing that the Crusades to the Holy Land were a just war of defense, as the infidel Saracens had wrongly seized the territories in the Levant from the Christian owners. The actions of Pope Urban II and subsequent Crusading popes in authorizing a holy war and indulgences for those who joined the Crusades were in furtherance of Rome's authority and responsibility to defend the rights of Christians in these lands. Innocent then argued that as Christ's life and death had consecrated the Holy Land, his followers, not Muhammad's, should dwell there.[98]

As Innocent must have known, the Augustinian-derived notion that Chris- tians could engage in wars for reconquest of lands seized unlawfully by infidels was regarded as an already settled issue in Church legal theory and practice. Furthermore, since many Crusading princes ventured into regions arguably never occupied by Christians, traditional Augustinian categories could provide only a limited basis for a more general theory of Christian warfare against normatively divergent peoples. Being the good Romanized lawyer that he was, Innocent sought to generate far broader principles from which particular propositions could be deduced and a wider variety of situations could be comprehensively addressed. Innnocent sought to penetrate to the heart of the issue raised by Christian warfare against non-Christian societies: Did infidel societies possess natural-law rights to hold property and to rule themselves, or could Christians legitimately dispossess infidels of their lordship and property on the sole basis of their nonbelief in the Christian God and the papacy's mediating position in relation to that divine power?

The position that infidels, by virtue of their nonbelief, possessed no rights to *dominium* that Christians were required to recognize had been most forcefully articulated by the hierocratic canonist Alanus some fifty years before Innocent's pontificate.[99] The position that infidels possessed the natural-law right to hold property and exercise lordship was the Artistotelian-inspired, naturalistic response to the Alanian position.[100] Innocent's own disposition of the issue was a novel attempt to reach a synthesis between these two polar positions in late medieval political and legal discourse.

The familiar themes of papal hierocratic discourse—unity, hierarchy, and difference—center Innocent's legal commentary on the critical question of the rights of nonbelievers in the universal Christian commonwealth. Deploying these totalizing themes in a style that seemingly conceded the essential naturalistic thesis, Innocent readily accepted that infidels and heathens possessed the same natural-law rights as Christians to elect their own leaders and to exercise *dominium* over property. But while he appeared to reject outright the position of Alanus and the extreme hierocrats that all *dominium* is held through the Church, he qualified the infidel's natural-law rights by reference to the pope's own universalized Petrine mandate. Innocent relied heavily on the previously discussed distinction drawn by Rufinus (and subsequently by Thomas Aquinas) that the pope possessed both direct and indirect authority.[101] Thus the papal office necessarily reserved an indirect right of intervention in the secular affairs of all the Church's subjects, actual and potential. As vicar of Christ's universal Christian commonwealth, Innocent reasoned, the pope had been entrusted by Christ through Peter with the care of the spiritual well-being of infidel and heathen nations. Christ's command to Peter to "feed my sheep" was obvious proof of the proposition that the pope's universal mandate necessarily included pagans and nonbelievers. According to Innocent, these people "belong to Christ's flock by virtue of their creation, although the infidels do not belong to the sheepfold of the Church." Therefore, "the Pope has jurisdiction over all men and power over them in law but not in fact."[102]

Innocent limited Rome's broad, suprajurisdictional authority to those instances where it was clearly necessary for the pope to intervene for purposes of protecting the spiritual well-being of non-Christians. Such necessary instances included situations in which infidels clearly violated natural law and their rulers refused to punish them, as required by divine law. Avoiding any extensive deliberation on the content of these natural-law dictates, Innocent indicated that sexual perversion, for example, would necessitate papal intervention. The worship of idols also constituted a serious violation of natural law that, if left unchecked by infidel rulers, would require papal intervention because "it is natural for man to worship the one and only God."[103] Every "rational creature," argued Innocent, was "made for the worship of God."[104]

Similar normative notions of what is "natural" for humans to do are reiterated throughout the commentary. Innocent's central argument that every rational creature was bound by the dictates of a Christian and Eurocentric natural law which the papacy could enforce as required by divine law represented an attempt to respond to the challenge, both real and theoretical, thrown down by civilian discourse and its denial of the papacy's claims of jurisdiction in the secular sphere. Where humans, Christian or infidel, acted contrary to natural law, the pope's divinely mandated role required him to protect their spiritual well-being.

Innocent's careful blending of hierocratic and naturalistic themes answered another direct challenge to the papal world view. The violent contact with a vast non-Christian civilization in the Holy Land cast obvious doubts on the medieval conception of an essentially universal Christian society. If God, the creator of all, had intended heathens and infidels as sheep of his universal flock, how could their violent rejection of the Christian God and his papally interpreted and revealed divine plan for their salvation be explained?

Innocent, by relying in his text on European-defined normative criteria of reason—that is, on European-defined natural law and on the entailed belief in the monotheistic conception of the Church's own God—attempted to preserve the Church's universalized, hierarchical world view and colonizing imperatives in the face of the destabilizing pagan challenge. A divinely oriented, totalizing epistemology had always provided foundational support for the medieval Church's world view. Divine reason, according to the Church, had revealed the immanence of unity and hierarchy in the world. Humanity's imperfect reason required mediating influences, such as the Church and the office of the papacy, so that this divine reason might be revealed in a comprehensible form. Like all the hierocratic canonists, Innocent held that God's will, interpreted through the pontifical office, expressed a far more perfect rationality than that possessed by imperfect human beings. Those who refused to recognize God's papally revealed plan were obviously irrational and in error. According to Innocent, "There is only one right way of life for mankind, and . . . the papal monopoly of this knowledge makes obedience to the Pope the only means of salvation."[105] The manifest irrationality of heathens and infidels who rejected the pope's message demonstrated their need for papal remediation. They were deluded peoples, according to Innocent, and the pope's divinely instituted Petrine mandate required him to call on Christian princes to raise armies to punish serious violations of natural law by nonbelievers and to order those armies to accompany missionaries to heathen lands for purposes of conversion.[106] "[I]f the infidels do not obey, they ought to be compelled by the secular arm and war may be declared against them by the Pope and not by anybody else."[107] Once more relying on the certitude of his Eurocentric conceptions of reason and truth, Innocent was careful to point out that infidels, such as Muslim missionaries, could not be accorded reciprocal rights to proselytize in Europe, "because they are in error and we are on a righteous path."[108]

Innocent's commentary thus seemingly harmonized the classically inspired naturalistic thesis on man's rational capacity with the hierocratic discursive practices of papal universal jurisdiction. The particular appeal of this colonizing discourse forged by Innocent lay in its prospective as well as retrospective power in structuring the appropriate response by the Church in its relations with normatively divergent peoples. Where willing Christian armies, obligingly licensed by Rome, could simply overwhelm by sheer force of numbers heathen and infidel peoples who were violating natural law, Innocent's discourse authorized conquest and conversion. Power facilitated truth. But, as was the case with the Great Khan and the Mongol armies perched on western Europe's borders, where Rome could not enforce its vision of truth militarily, it could patiently appeal to the heathen enemy's inherent rationality and hope to win him over by the force of the better argument. In such a case, truth facilitated power.

Thus when read in light of Innocent's Humanist-inspired analysis of infidel natural-law rights, the seeming naiveté of the papal letters to the Great Khan[109] actually reveal an insightful recognition of a highly complex pedagogical problem. Unable to call on secular armies at will in an evolving European nationalist state system, Innocent realized the need to call on reason in abating the heathen Mongol menace threatening Western Christendom. In Innocent's two letters to the Great Khan of the Mongols, we see a brilliant lawyer-pope struggling to elaborate the fundamental, architechtonic premises of the Church's subtle discourses of truth and knowledge in a form comprehensible to the heathen Guyak's supposedly irrational and unregenerate mind.

Innocent's first letter to Guyak provides a simplified exegesis of the central mythological tenets of unity and hierarchy structuring Christian belief. The letter presents a series of hierarchical juxtapositions describing humanity's dependent, diminished status in relation to God. Yet despite this diminished status, individuals are united by God's plan to restore humanity to an ascendant position through his Son, who assumed a human form, "visible to all men."[110] Innocent explained to Guyak the epistemological implications of this hierarchically descending union of God and humanity through the mediation of the Savior-Son:

For human nature being endowed with reason, was meant to be nourished on eternal truth as its choicest food, but, held in mortal chains as a punishment for sin, its powers were thus far reduced that it had to strive to understand the invisible things of reason's food by means of inferences drawn from visible things.[111]

This passage represents a critical juncture in Innocent's text, for here the canon lawyer-pope began to draw on the same normatively derived vision of reason that animates his commentary on *Quod super his*.[112] Humanity's powers of reason and understanding are potentially perfect and capable of being nourished on "eternal truth." But humanity's present state of sin prevents individual reason from seeing eternal truth, which is "invisible." Thus the Creator, stated Innocent, "became visible, . . . in order that . . . he might call back to himself the invisible, those pursuing after visible things, moulding men by his salutory instructions and pointing out to them by means of his teaching the way of perfection."[113]

To this point, Innocent had provided a clever exegesis of the subtle interplay between the themes of divine hierarchy and its integral relation to the redemption of humankind's imperfect reason. The divine Savior-Son's own redeeming death, Innocent claimed, lifts humanity "from the shame of servitude to the glory of liberty."[114] This liberty is attained through the perfection of human reason made possible by the Savior-Son's death.

In the next passage of the letter, Innocent boldly reconstituted these mythological themes to assert the papacy's hierarchical universal mandate in bringing this liberating vision of perfected reason to all the world's peoples. Innocent informed Guyak that after his death and sacrifice for humankind's perfection and liberty, the Savior, "rising from the dead and ascending into heaven, . . . left his vicar on earth, and to him . . . he committed the care of souls, that he should with watchfulness pay heed to and with heed watch over their salvation."[115] This vicar, Peter, had been left the keys "by which he and, through him, his successors, were to possess the power of opening and of closing the gate of that kingdom to all."[116] Innocent told Guyak that "having become, by the Lord's disposition, the successor of this vicar," his "keen attention" was turned to securing Guyak's salvation "so that we may be able, with the help of God's grace, to lead those in error into the way of truth and gain all men for him."[117]

Innocent's second letter to the Great Khan, although sterner in tone, employed a Humanist-derived symbology. Innocent began by admonishing Guyak that

not only men, but even irrational animals, nay, the very elements which go to make up the world machine, are united by a certain innate law after the manner of the celestial spirits, all of which God the Creator has divided into choirs in the enduring stability of peaceful order.[118]

Here, Innocent drew on a conception of unity represented by the "world machine." This universal order is hierarchically established by God's "innate law," the embodiment of a totalizing vision of reason by which even irrational animals are bound.

Given the fact of this union of the world machine by God's law, Innocent expressed "amazement" at the Khan's invasion of Christian nations and "laying them waste in a horrible desecration, and with a fury still unabated you do not cease from stretching out your destroying hand to ever more distant lands."[119] Innocent accused the Khan of "breaking the bond of natural ties" uniting humankind. Desiring that "all men should live united in concord of the fear of God," Innocent warned Guyak to desist in his persecution of Christians and "to conciliate by a fitting penance the wrath of Divine Majesty." Finally, the

Khan was warned to pay close attention to Innocent's proselytizing friars and to "make fully known to us . . . what moved you to destroy other nations."[120]

Innocent's *Quod super his* and his two letters to the Mongol Khan articulate thirteenth-century Christian Humanism's *post hoc* legal rationalization for the Church's centuries-long involvement in the Crusades. His recognition of natural-law rights to property and dominion belonging to non-Christian pagan peoples responded to thirteenth-century secular Humanism's most direct and incisive challenges to the medieval Church's subordinating conceptions of human nature. Typically, the medieval Church's traditional discourses of truth and knowledge had narrowly grounded human reason in the privileged interpretations of the priestly caste's transcendent hierarchical world view. Within this world view pagan nations that denied the Christian God and the universal hierarchical authority of his chosen vicar, the pope in Rome, were denied any legitimacy. Their property and lordship could rightfully be confiscated by Crusading Christian armies enforcing the universal jurisdiction of Rome. Innocent's advocacy of a naturalized human reason and its inherent rational capacity to comprehend universalized dictates and norms modified this rigid, hierarchized, descending conception of papal power denying human autonomy in favor of the same appealing Humanist themes that Aquinas would more systematically elaborate as the Christian system of natural law. According to Innocent's Humanist-inspired analysis in *Quod super his*, even infidels shared in a Eurocentrically understood universalized reason. Thus under natural law, they were free and possessed the same rights as Christians. Their lordship and property could not be confiscated by Christians solely on the basis of nonbelief in the Christian God. But as rational beings, infidels, like Christians, were responsible for their conduct under natural law, and excessive breaches of the universalized dictates and norms of this Eurocentric legal discourse indicated a lack of reason requiring remediation. Innocent's novel assertion that the pope could order Christian armies to enforce the rationalized dictates of natural law against deluded pagan peoples under his Petrine responsibility for all the sheep of God's human flock reformulated the legal basis of the Crusades on the naturalistic premises favored by Humanist-inspired Church theorists of the thirteenth century.

For "moderns," such seemingly arcane and desiccated remnants of a once-vital form of legal consciousness might seem to hold little relevance for our examinations of the desacralized fabric of the West's contemporary legal conceptions of American Indian rights and status. But Innocent's efforts at synthesizing the Church's most ancient discursive traditions on the nature of papal power with the ascendant naturalistic discourses of the later Middle Ages would continue to exercise a profound influence on Western colonizing legal thought. Spun from this Old World medieval loom were threads of ideas that came to inform all later European-derived legal thought on the rights and status of the indigenous inhabitants of the New World. Centuries prior to Columbus's transatlantic voyage, the thirteenth-century canon lawyer–pope Innocent IV had discovered for Christendom a new world of legal discourse, premised on the central orienting myth that the Christian European's vision of reason and truth entailed norms obligatory for all peoples. All contrary visions were denied respect. Knowledge and power had been placed in service of each other so that the medieval Crusading idea might not only be legitimized but, more important, be preserved in a form more palatable for Renaissance Europe's will to empire directed at the New World.

NOTES

1. *See* R. Williams, "The Medieval and Renaissance Origins of the Status of the American Indian in Western Legal Thought," 57 *S. Cal. L. Rev.* 1, 11–48 (1983).

2. *Quod super his* was originally published by Pope Innocent III as part of the *Compilatio Terta*, which was completed in 1209 and was the first papally authorized attempt to promulgate an official collection of the ecclesiastical law. *See* J. A. Brundage, *Medieval Canon Law and the Crusader* 76–81 (1969). *Quod super his* dealt with the fulfillment of a Crusading vow and the conditions under which performance might be delayed or commuted. *See* J. Muldoon, "'Extra ecclesiam non est imperium': The Canonists and the Legitimacy of Secular Power," 9 *Studia Gratiana* 551, 572–75 (1966). My discussion of Innocent IV's commentary on *Quod super his* draws heavily on James Muldoon's invaluable research and analysis contained in the two cited sources. Translations of part of Innocent IV's commentary can be found in *The Expansion of Europe: The First Phase* 191–92 (J. Muldoon ed. 1977) [hereinafter cited as *The Expansion of Europe*]; B. Tierney, *The Crisis of Church and State, 1050–1300,* 155–56 (1964).

3. 3 F. Maitland, *Moral Personality and Legal Personality* 310 (1911). For biographical information on Innocent's life and career as a legal scholar and pope, *see* 14 H. K. Mann, *The Lives of the Popes in the Early Middle Ages from 590–1304* (1902–1932); 7 *New Catholic Encyclopedia,* 524–25, *Innocent IV, Pope* (1967); J. Muldoon, *Popes, Lawyers and Infidels* (1979).

4. Innocent framed the question as follows: "[I]s it licit to invade a land that infidels possess, or which belongs to them?" (quoted in *The Expansion of Europe, supra* note 2, at 191–92).

5. The relevant part of the decretal reads:

> [T]he earth is the Lord's and his power is over the entire world and all who live in it . . . [M]en can select rulers for themselves as [the Israelites] selected Saul and many others. Sovereignty, possessions, and jurisdiction can exist licitly, without sin, among infidels, as well as among the faithful. Things were made for every rational creature . . . and because of this, we say it is not lawful for the pope or for the faithful to take sovereignty or jurisdiction from infidels, because they hold them without sin, but we believe rightly, however, that the pope who is vicar of Jesus Christ has power not only over Christians but also over all infidels, for Christ had power over all men. . . . Thus to Peter and his successors he gave the keys to the kingdom. . . . Elsewhere He said, "Feed my sheep." Both infidels and the faithful belong to Christ's flock by virtue of their creation, although the infidels do not belong to the sheepfold of the Church, and so it seems from the aforementioned that the pope has jurisdiction over all men and power over them in law but not in fact. [Reprinted in *id.*]

6. *Id.* at 192. According to Innocent, infidels could not be attacked merely because of their nonbelief in the Christian God. Only specific violations of natural law would justify papal sanctions imposed through intermediaries such as Christian princes. Innocent stated, however, that once Christian armies had ended those practices deemed by the pope to be in violation of natural law, "infidels should not be forced to become Christians, because all should be left to their own free will in this matter" (*id.*).

7. *Id.*

8. *Id.*

9. Quoted in J. Muldoon, *supra* note 3, at 14.

10. *See* J. Muldoon, *supra* note 3, at 348.

11. From the Pauline text, quoted in O. Gierke, *Associations and Law* 145 (1977). Paul's

metaphor appears frequently throughout his epistolary works. *See* Paul, 1 Corinthians 12:12 and 27 and 6:15; Ephesians 4:4, 16, 25, and 5:30.

12. Matthew 16:19.

13. Quoted in B. Tierney, *supra* note 2, at 13–14. On Gelasius and his views on the emperor's position within the Church, *see* W. Ullmann, *The Growth of Papal Government in the Middle Ages* 14–18 (1955).

14. B. Tierney, *supra* note 2, at 14.

15. These tensions were engendered by a metaphysics focused on the problematics of the actual and the ideal, and they can be traced back to Christianity's earliest scriptural origins. While Christianity's founder had stated, "Render to Caesar the things that are Caesar's and to God the things that are God's" (Luke 20:25), he had also declared to Peter, "I will give to thee the keys of the kingdom of heaven. And whatsoever thou shalt bind upon earth it shall be bound also in heaven" (Matthew 16:19). Peter himself, with perfect equanimity, acknowledged the dilemma of the Church's role in the world while providing little in the way of prescriptive guidance toward its resolution with the advice, "Fear God, honor the King" (I Peter 2:17).

16. B. Tierney, *supra* note 2, at 11–13.

Early Church legal and political theorists clearly recognized that such contradiction-laden concessions to secular authority in "mundane" matters deflated the full vigor of the Roman Church's will to autonomy. St. Augustine's *City of God* represents the most influential effort addressed to mediating the apparent contradictions presented by the early Church's actual and idealized situation in the world. *Id.*

Augustine's famous text argued that those who belong to the City of God live by faith, while those of the City of World "seek their peace in the earthly advantages of this life" (*id.* at 11). In defining the Christian's responsibilities to the secular realm, Augustine adopted a pragmatic approach, conceding that the citizens of the heavenly city would of course at times require certain advantages of the worldly city in order "to endure with greater ease, and to keep down the number of those burdens of the corruptible body which weigh upon the soul" (*id.* at 11–12). One of the principal advantages of the worldly city offered to those of the City of God was the "well-ordered concord of civic obedience and rule" (*id.* at 12). Augustine's transcendental orientation, however, viewed such concord in a wholly negative sense, for the sinfulness of human nature had made necessary the existence of this human rule. "The heavenly city," he wrote, "makes use of this peace only because it must, until this mortal condition which necessitates it shall pass away" (*id.* at 12).

According to Augustine, the heavenly city calls citizens out of all nations while it sojourns here on earth, "not scrupling about diversities in the manners, laws, and institutions whereby earthly peace is secured and maintained, but recognizing that, however various these are, they all tend to one and the same end of earthly peace" (*id.* at 12). The Augustinian unity represented by the City of God is maintained in the face of earthly diversity by a hierarchical focus on transcendent ends. The heavenly city "is so far from rescinding and abolishing these diversities, that it even preserves and adopts them, so long only as no hindrance to the worship of the one supreme and true God is thus introduced" (*id.* at 12). Human government, no matter what form it might assume, was ultimately subsumed by the divinely mandated ends of the City of God in Augustinian metaphysics.

Augustine's basic teaching that the state was rooted in human sinfulness dominated Church discourse and thought for centuries. The transcendental orientation of his cosmology placed the spiritual over the secular realm, thus reinforcing the hierarchical claims of the Church to primatial autonomy. At the same time, his system provided an explanation for the fact that the divinely preferred order might not be realized on earth. God's will could be frustrated by human wickedness. *Id.*

The absence of a manifest universal Christian commonwealth on earth would remain a central problem of Church theory and practice throughout the Middle Ages. Augustine, on the theoretical level, and Gelasius, on the level of practice, provided important originary insights toward resolution of this central problem. For Augustine, the Neoplatonic theorist, the unity and hierarchy to be realized by the universal Church existed notionally in a transcendent, potential form. For Gelasius, the practicing pope in conflict with the empire, securing the papal office's relative autonomy in the ecclesiastical sphere without seeming to intrude unnecessarily on imperial prerogatives dictated a strategy of cautious dualism while seeking to distance the Roman Church from Eastern hegemony.

17. B. Tierney, *supra* note 2, at 11. Pope Celestine I (422–427), author of the famous papal hierocratic maxim "The people should be led, and should not lead itself," declared flatly that the law as embodied in the papal decretals "should be our master, and we as its recipients must not try to master, but to serve the law" (quoted in W. Ullmann, *A Short History of the Papacy in the Middle Ages* 16–18 [1972]).

18. The dynamics of the relationship between the medieval Church and the Carlovingian state are more fully elaborated in C. Erdmann, *The Origin of the Idea of Crusade* 22–26 (M. W. Baldwin & W. Goffart trans. 1977). D. Bullough, *The Age of Charlemagne* (1965), and W. Ullmann, *The Growth of Papal Government in the Middle Ages* 44–142 (1970), are also helpful, although several of Ullmann's conclusions regarding the origins and development of the Church's hierocratic theories and structure have been the subject of debate among medievalists. *See* C. Erdmann, *supra*, at p. 22, note 50.

19. O. Gierke, *Political Theories of the Middle Age* 18–19 (F. Maitland trans. 1958).

20. The Rheims decrees are excerpted in B. Tierney, *supra* note 2, at 31–32.

21. Quoted in *id.* at 13–14.

22. Humbert of Silva Candida, "Against Lay Investiture," excerpted in *id.* at 40.

23. The secular power, in Humbert's view, was necessarily subordinate to the ecclesiastical authority. Any correspondence between the two realms could be for no other purpose than that of furthering the higher functions of the spiritual authority. According to Humbert,

> in the existing church, the priesthood is analogous to the soul and the kingship to the body, for they cleave to one another and need one another and each in turn demands services and renders them one to another. It follows from this that, just as the soul excels the body and commands it, so too the priestly dignity excels the royal or, we may say, the heavenly dignity the earthly. Thus, that all things may be in due order and not in disarray the priesthood, like a soul, may advise what is to be done. The kingship in turn, like a head, excels all the members of the body and leads them where they should go; for just as kings should follow churchmen so also layfolk should follow their kings for the good of church and country. [Humbert of Silva Candida, *Priesthood and Kingship*, reprinted in B. Tierney, *supra* note 2, at 1–42.]

The corporatist thematics of Humbert's anthropomorphic imagery and his integrally related notion of an unequal partnership existing between church and state became favored devices of Reform-era hierocratic discursive practice.

24. "Decree on Papal Election" (April 1059), reprinted in B. Tierney, *supra* note 2, at 42–43.

25. *See* "Oath of Robert Guiscard to Pope Nicholas II" (August 1059), reprinted in B. Tierney, *supra* note 2, at 44.

26. Quoted in C. Erdmann, *supra* note 18, at 132.

27. An excellent summary of the significance of Hildebrand-Gregory's contributions to Church discourse is provided in C. Erdmann, *supra* note 18, at 148–81. Also useful are H. Jedin & J. Dolan, *Handbook of Church History* (1969), at Chapters 43 and 44, and W. Ullmann, *supra* note 18, at 262–309.

28. "Letter of Gregory to Henry Complaining of the King's Mistreatment of the Church" (December 1075), reprinted in B. Tierney, *supra* note 2, at 57–59.

29. Quoted in W. Ullmann, *supra* note 18, at 277.

30. Gregory's 1076 Deposition Order of Henry rested squarely on his theoretical assertion that temporal rulership was ultimately subservient to the spiritual and thereby universal authority of the Church and its Petrine head, the pope.

> O blessed Peter, . . . I believe that it is and has been thy will, that the Christian people especially committed to thee should render obedience to me thy especially constituted representative. To me is given by thy grace the power of binding and loosing in Heaven and upon earth.
> Wherefore, relying upon this commission, and for the honor and defense of thy Church . . . through thy power and authority, I deprive King Henry, son of the emperor Henry, who has rebelled against the Church with unheard-of audacity, of the government over the

whole kingdom of Germany and Italy, and I release all Christian men from the allegiance which they have sworn or may swear to him, and I forbid anyone to serve him as king. For it is fitting that he who seeks to diminish the glory of thy Church should lose the glory which he seems to have. ["Deposition of Henry by Gregory" (February 1076), reprinted in B. Tierney, *supra* note 2, at 60–61.]

31. Before the famous scene at Canossa, Henry had agreed to a diet to be held in Augsburg in 1077. The pope would preside in person, and the diet would judge the actions of the deposed and excommunicated king, determining his worthiness to resume the throne.

Just prior to the convocation of the diet, however, Henry utilized the rules of the Gregorian discursive game to execute a brilliant coup. With only a few attendants, Henry crossed the Alps to meet Gregory on his journey northward to the Augsburg diet. He presented himself to the pope as a barefoot penitent at the snowy gates of the castle of Canossa, where Gregory had stopped to rest. A stunned Gregory lifted Henry's excommunication.

32. "Letter of Henry to Gregory Refusing to Recognize Him as Pope" (1076), reprinted in B. Tierney, *supra* note 2, at 59.

33. The more polemical tracts against Gregory and his leading role in the civil war against Henry, such as that circulated by Archbishop Egilbert of Trier in 1080, simply fastened on Gelasian dualistic thematics and bewailed the fact that Gregory had dared to wield both swords, the spiritual as well as the worldly. Other scholars, such as Wenrich of Trier and Peter Crassus, offered more refined arguments against the idea of papal war. Wenrich condemned Gregory's militarism, stating that its wrongheadedness was "self-evident." All men of sense could "judge how poorly this benefits the episcopal, the apostolic, and even the Christian ideal." Peter Crassus's famous pamphlet of 1084 developed the following scholastic's argument as to why papal war was wrong: God desires peace; Gregory wages war in God's name; therefore, Gregory offends God for the sake of God. C. Erdmann, *supra* note 18, at 233–34; *id.* at 234.

The contradiction that the scholastic mind of Crassus found intolerable was most likely dismissed as didacticism by the practical politicians in the papal court. At best, such attacks could only reproach Gregory for disrupting the supposed ancient order of state and society and thereby disturbing the harmonious world order presumably desired by God. *Id.* at 232. But such attacks offered nothing in the way of effective rebuttal to the essential hierarchical logic of the Gregorian program. Papal militarism and hierarchical goals, as Erdmann has noted, were consciously fused in Gregorian discourse. Gregory's totalizing strategy demanded the seizure of secular power in pursuit of spiritually transcendent, more urgent goals. The old order was corrupted. Gregory sought to realize the divine order on earth. *Id.* at 232–34.

34. "Letter of Gregory to Bishop Hermann of Metz" (March 1081), in B. Tierney, *supra* note 2, at 66–67.

35. *Id.* at 67.

36. *Id.* at 68–69.

37. *Id.*

38. *Id.* at 70–71.

39. Gregory was explicit on this point:

All kings and princes of this earth who live not piously and in their deeds show not a becoming fear of God are ruled by demons and are sunk in miserable slavery. Such men desire to rule, not guided by the love of God . . . but to display their intolerable pride and to satisfy the lusts of their minds. Of these St. Augustine says in the first book of his Christian doctrines: "He who tries to rule over men—who are by nature equal to him—acts with intolerable pride." Now if exorcists have power over demons, as we have said, how much more over those who are subject to demons and are limbs of demons! [*Id.* at 70.]

40. B. Tierney, *supra* note 2, at 98, 116.

41. *Id.* at 98.

42. Gratian, *Dist.* 22 c.l. (c. 1140) ed. E. Friedberg, *Corpus Iuris Canonici* (1879), col. 73. B. Tierney, *supra* note 2, at 119.

43. B. Tierney, *supra* note 2, at 117.

44. Rufinus, Commentary on *Dist.* 22 c.1 (1157), reprinted in B. Tierney, *supra* note 2, at 119–20.

45. *Id.* at 120.

46. Two decades after Rufinus, an anonymous commentary on Gratian's text drew on the symbology of the two swords in explaining the papacy's direct and indirect forms of jurisdiction:

> *Rights over a heavenly and earthly empire.* That is, both the material sword and the spiritual sword . . . [T]he apostle . . . has the spiritual sword as regards authority and use, the material sword only as regards authority because, when the emperor is anointed, he is given the power and exercise of the material sword by the apostle. ["Summa inpenatoirae maiestate," Commentary on *Dist.* 22 c.1 (1175–78), reprinted in B. Tierney, *supra* note 2, at 120.]

47. The commentaries of Rufinus and that quoted in note 46 indicate a significant rupture following the Gregorian pontificate in canonistic thought regarding the traditional Gelasian dualistic theme of the two spheres of worldly power, secular and spiritual. Post-Gregorian canonistic hierocratism's dialectial logic had abandoned the untidy dualism of two separate spheres of jurisdiction in favor of the theoretical construct of a direct and indirect authority held by the pope. The pope retained unquestioned power to exercise direct, supreme authority in ecclesiastical affairs. In secular affairs, the pope likewise possessed supreme authority, but required a lay official in the person of the emperor, consecrated by papal authority, to administer indirectly this divinely conferred power.

48. The bull *Unam sanctum* (November 1302) is reprinted in B. Tierney, *supra* note 2, at 188.

49. C. Erdmann, *supra* note 18, at 8.

50. *Id.* at 8–11. *See generally* H. A. Deane, *The Political and Social Ideas of St. Augustine* 154–220 (1963).

51. *See* C. Erdmann, *supra* note 18, at 150–60.

52. *Id.* at 151.

53. *Id.* at 155–56.

54. Alexander, who owed his papal election to his principal advisor, Archdeacon Hildebrand, announced this new inducement in a recruitment letter addressed to French warriors:

> With fatherly affection we urge those who have resolved to go to Spain that they take the greatest care to complete that task which with divine counsel they have set out to accomplish. Let each soldier confess, according to the character of his sins, to his bishop or spiritual father and let the confessor impose suitable penance upon him, lest the devil be enabled to accuse him of impenitence. We, however, by the authority of the holy apostles Peter and Paul, relieve them of their penance and grant them remission of sins, while our prayers go with them. [Reprinted in J. A. Brundage, *supra* note 2, at 24.]

55. *Id.* at 29.

56. C. Erdmann, *supra* note 18, at 150–60.

57. J. Brundage, *The Crusades: A Documentary Survey* 9 (1962).

58. J. Brundage, *supra* note 2, at 26.

59. J. Brundage, *supra* note 57, at 9.

60. C. Erdmann, *supra* note 18, at 167.

61. *Id.* at 167.

62. *See* J. Brundage, *supra* note 57, at 10–11.

63. C. Erdmann, *supra* note 18, at 306–33.

64. *Id.* at 314–18.

65. *Id.* at 315.

66. *Id.* at 325.

67. Various accounts of Urban's speech declaring the First Crusade are summarized in an essay by D. C. Munro, "Papal Proclamation of the Crusade," in *The Crusades: Motives and Achievements* 7–11 (J. Brundage ed. 1964).

68. Reprinted in J. Brundage, *supra* note 57, at 17–21.

69. *Id.* at 18.

70. *Id.* at 18–19.

71. *See* Chapter 3, text accompanying notes 61–112, *infra.*

72. J. Brundage, *supra* note 57, at 19.

73. *Id.* at 19.

74. *Id.* at 20.

75. J. Brundage, *supra* note 2, at 3.

76. *Id.* at 149. The discussion in this section on the instruments of Crusade relies primarily on Brundage's excellent study of medieval canonistic treatment of the Crusader's legal status and privileges. *See id.*

77. *Id.* at 172.

78. *See id.* at 172–73.

79. J. Muldoon, *supra* note 2, at 561.

80. B. Tierney, *supra* note 2, at 123.

81. *Id.*

82. W. Ullmann, *Medieval Papalism* 142 (1949).

83. W. Ullmann, *Medieval Foundations of Renaissance Humanism* 38 (1977).

84. Natural justice, according to Aristotle, is "that which everywhere has the same force and does not exist by people's thinking this or that" (Aristotle, *Nicomachean Ethics* 382 [Great Books of the Western World, 1952]).

85. W. Ullmann, *supra* note 82, at 154–56, states that Cicero was perhaps the most intensely studied and best understood of the ancient writers frequently relied on by the lay publicists. On Cicero, *see generally* L. Strauss, *Natural Right and History* 153–56, 321–22 (1953).

86. Prominent political and legal theorists of the early Renaissance increasingly used classically derived natural-law arguments in defense of secular autonomy. Writers such as William of Ockham, John of Paris, and Marsilius of Padua attacked the doctrinal foundations of papal primatial theory, embracing the radical notion that humans were possessed of a "natural" reason and the capacity to govern themselves independently of the ecclesiastical hierarchy. The state, in theory, had been transformed by the lay publicists into an act of will, a social contract contingent solely on the consent of its constituent members.

Secularized political and legal theory in this instance, however, was following hard on the heels of secularized political and legal practice. Most importantly, Europe's political economy in the thirteenth and fourteenth centuries was undergoing a series of varied and intense transformations. European mercantile activity, within and outside the continent, rapidly expanded. In the cases of the major trading centers of Genoa and Venice, expansion and the initiation of the dynamic processes of capital formation were in part outgrowths of the Crusades themselves. Growth of trade in turn complemented and was complemented by the ascendancy of strong centralizing national monarchies and indigenous administrative and legal systems. *See generally* P. Anderson, *Lineages of the Absolutist State* 15–59, 143–72, 397–431 (1979). Such profound transformations rendered unlikely any attempt at full-scale resuscitation of papal hierocratic thematics in secular political and legal discourse. The Reformation, now in its 200-year-long gestation period, was to be but the completed synthesis of the transformations in Renaissance Humanist political and legal theory and practice brought about by the retrieval of the ancient discourses of knowledge and power. *See generally* O. Gierke, *The Development of Political Theory* 148–63 (B. Freyd trans. 1939); O. Gierke, *supra* note 19, at 38–48.

87. From the early thirteenth century, numerous papal edicts banned the study of Aristotle in Church-supported universities. *See* M. Wilks, *The Problem of Sovereignty in the Later Middle Ages* 84 (1963).

88. *Id.* at 118.

89. For a concise and lucid summation of the natural-law tradition and of Thomistic political philosophy in particular, *see* L. Weinreb, *Natural Law and Justice* (1987).

90. Thomas's synthesis of the "useful" matter from Aristotle's texts and hierarchical Christian speculative thought was achieved by a manipulation of the Aristotelian concept of "nature." While ceding to "nature" a fundamental, notional existence, Thomas only partially submitted to the Humanist-favored naturalistic construct and its inclinations toward a fully secularized, autonomous human existence. Thus Thomas's more careful rearticulation of human nature was grounded in naturalistic theory and discourse, while maintaining fidelity to a core concept of Church hierocratic theory: that individuals could achieve their full, transcendental end only through faith and grace. The scholastic's maxim, "Grace does not do away with nature but perfects it,"

represented the paradigmatic statement of the Thomistic-Aristotelian synthesis. *See* W. Ullmann, *Law and Politics in the Middle Ages* 272 (1975).

This Christian-Humanist synthesis, while respecting the unitary aspects of traditional Christian ideology, acknowledged the more appealing elements of the naturalistic thesis on human nature in a form acceptable to secular and ecclesiastical moderates reluctant to abandon their theocratic moorings. In ceding to the state (and derivatively to an increasingly independence-minded episcopate) a natural and autonomous right of existence, related to but jurisdictionally separate from pontifical authority, the Thomistic synthesis responded to criticisms directed at the most extreme versions of papal hierocratic theory. Thomas's notion of a "double ordering of things," represented by the natural and supernatural, argued that the state "had nothing to do with faith or grace in regard to its origin or operation, but for its better working, grace and faith were necessary complements" (*id.*). The laws of the human state could thus be seen as valid in their own right, but in order to be more perfect (for perfection in all things human was universally recognized in the Middle Ages, even by the secular party, as humankind's ultimate goal), the laws should find their orientation in those traditional tenets of fundamental justice directing civilized—that is, Christian—society.

Thus while the spiritual power, which in Thomistic discourse ultimately referred to the pope, did not possess direct power in secular affairs, papal spiritual authority did imply a regulative, indirect authority over the secular sphere. But it was an authority of limited scope, exercisable only in certain narrowly defined instances:

> The secular power is under the spiritual only in so far as it has been subjected to it by God: namely, in those things that pertain to the salvation of the soul and therefore the spiritual power is, in such matters, to be obeyed rather than the secular. But in those things that pertain to civic good, the secular power is to be obeyed rather than the spiritual. [Reprinted in B. Tierney, *supra* note 2, at 171.]

91. *See* "Introduction," *supra*, at 3–9. Pope Innocent's letters to the Great Khan were delivered by Friar John more than five years before Thomas's Aristotelian-grounded lectures at the University of Paris and more than a decade before the Dominican order had asked Thomas to prepare a basic theological text for Dominican missionaries (his *Summa contra gentiles*) designed to bring infidels to the true faith through rationally presented arguments.

92. *See* F. Maitland, *supra* note 3, at 310.

93. It was Innocent IV who was primarily responsible for frustrating Frederick's efforts to consolidate Germanic imperial power in Italy. *See* sources cited in "Introduction," *supra*, at note 6.

94. J. Muldoon, *supra* note 3, at 348. For biographical information on Innocent's life and career as a legal scholar and pope, *see* H. K. Mann, *supra* note 3; *New Catholic Encyclopedia*, *supra* note 3.

> As a canonist, Innocent IV brought together several strands of legal thought relating to infidels in the first attempt to consider the relations that could exist between Christians and infidels. As pope, Innocent IV initiated the Mongol mission, the first attempt to deal with the Mongol threat to eastern Europe on a diplomatic level, as well as to convert the Mongols to Christianity. The result was the blending of legal theory and papal practice in a single career. It was the union of these two traditions that formed the intellectual background of Vitoria and Las Casas. Innocent IV remains the crucial figure in this development, however, because although many of his successors as pope were also legally trained, none showed both the legal imagination and the personal interest in the problem of the infidels to bring the analysis of the rights of infidels to a more sophisticated level. For three centuries following Innocent IV's death, his thinking influenced the thought of those who wrestled with the problems created when Europeans moved out from Europe itself and encountered people of various levels of culture and civilization. [J. Muldoon, *supra* note 3, 15 348.]

95. On Innocent's commentary on *Quod super his*, *see* note 2, *supra*.

96. *See* text accompanying notes 73–82, *supra*, on the Crusading vow and papal practices of dispensation.

97. Quoted in *The Expansion of Europe*, *supra* note 2, at 191–92.

98. Innocent also justified the Crusades to the Holy Land on the basis of the Donation of Constantine. This document, supposedly discovered deep within the bowels of the papal archives in the late eighth century, attested to the fact that before the Roman emperor Constantine removed the imperial capital east to Byzantium, he donated to Pope Sylvester I (314–325) large regions and islands, specified and unspecified, discovered or yet to be discovered, mostly in the western half of the ancient Roman Empire. Couched in precise, hierocratic phraseology, Constantine's grant of title to and jurisdiction over this large expanse of territory was designed, in the alleged words of the donation, to ensure that

> the supreme pontifical authority may be not dishonored, but may rather be adorned with glorious power greater than the dignity of any earthly empire. [B]ehold we give to the often-minded most holy Pontiff, our father Sylvester, the Universal Pope . . . the city of Rome and all the provinces, districts and cities of Italy and the Western regions, relinquishing them to the authority of himself and his successors as Pontiffs by a definite imperial grant. [Reprinted in *Church and State Through the Centuries* 21–22 (S. Ehler & J. Morrall trans. and eds. 1967).]

This alleged donation by the Roman emperor thus provided a legitimating foundation for papal claims of actual title to and jurisdiction over numerous lands and territories throughout western Europe and the Mediterranean region. *See* M. Wilks, *supra* note 87, at 544–46. Importantly for Innocent's purposes, the Constantinian grant specifically mentioned Judea. The Holy Land was therefore part of the Constantinian-derived papal patrimony. Innocent argued from the donation that the pope, as lawful successor to Sylvester's rights, could call on Christian armies to defend the Holy Land.

Like many other "historical" documents relied on by the medieval Church to bolster its hierocratic claims to secular authority and jurisdiction, the donation was later proved by Renaissance scholars to be a forgery, its text and chronology rife with anachronisms and mistranscriptions. *See Church and State Through the Centuries, supra*, at 15–22; W. Ullmann, *supra* note 18, at 50–74, 177–78. But the "truth" or "untruth" of the donation tells little of its significance in a time when the Church alone possessed the unequaled and unchallenged institutional power to produce, transcribe, or exorcise the components of an entire culture's textual knowledge. The donation added an important and concrete element to the imperial, colonizing character of papal discourse in the later Middle Ages. Innocent, writing in the thirteenth century, had not been the first pope to cite the donation to bolster papal hierocratic claims, nor would he be the last.

99. *See* text accompanying notes 79–82, *supra*.

100. Thomas Aquinas, for instance, writing shortly after Innocent's commentary on *Quod super his*, refuted the position of hierocratic theorists such as Alanus Anglicus that infidel societies could not validly exercise *dominium*. Property was among those things that human reason added to natural law because of its demonstrated utility to human needs. Belief in God therefore was irrelevant to the question of whether infidels could rightly exercise *dominium*.

101. On Rufinus's use of the distinction between the papacy's direct and indirect authority, *see* text accompanying notes 43–47, *supra*. On Thomas's use of the same distinction, *see* note 90, *supra*.

102. Quoted in *The Expansion of Europe, supra* note 2, at 191–92.

103. *The Expansion of Europe, supra* note 2, 15 191–92.

104. *Id.* at 192.

105. M. Wilks, *supra* note 87, at 413–14. Another influential canonist of the Crusading era, Augustinus Triumphus, had made virtually the identical assertion. According to Triumphus, the pope's universal territorial jurisdiction superseded the sovereign rule of earthly princes; even Christians subject to pagan rulers were under the jurisdiction of the pope, as "one could not escape papal jurisdiction by moving to non-Christian territories" (*id.* at 416, note 2).

106. Most papal publicists of the Crusading era adhered rigidly to the hierocratic view that government of non-Christian rulers was contrary to divine law and hence illegal. By the fourteenth century, however, one finds theory tempered by practice. For instance, many writers of the fourteenth century acknowledged *de jure* but not *de facto* papal jurisdiction over pagans. Augustinus Triumphus, *see* note 105, *supra*, in his influential work, *Summa de potestate ecclesiastica*,

noted that it is better for a pagan community to have a pagan ruler than to have no ruler at all. As the sun shines on the just and unjust without distinction, according to Triumphus, pagan government cannot be entirely valueless, but any breach of natural law by a pagan ruler justified the immediate right of papal intervention. M. Wilks, *supra* note 87, at 414–15.

107. *The Expansion of Europe, supra* note 2, at 192.

108. Quoted in J. Muldoon, *supra* note 3, at 14.

109. *See* "Introduction," *supra*, at 3–9.

110. *The Mongol Mission*, at 73. Innocent explained the divinity of the Son and his virgin birth by stating that the Son was "consubstantial with Himself." In the Church's theological discourse, "consubstantiation" referred to the mystery of the sacrifice of the Catholic mass: that the substance of the bread and wine of the Eucharist exists, after consecration, side by side with the substance of the body and blood of Christ but is not changed into it. Thus the reference enabled Innocent to underscore the basic theme of the unity of the Son's divine and human natures, while alluding to the central mythological ritual of the Church: the consecration at the mass. Whether Guyak sufficiently appreciated the subtlety of this representation of the hierarchical relation of God and humankind mediated through the sacrifice of the Son is not recorded by John. One can only wonder, however, about Guyak's reaction to Innocent's explanation of the doctrine of the virgin birth of the Son, following close on the heels of the consubstantiation myth. The Redeemer Son, according to Innocent, "was conceived by the operation of the Holy Ghost in the womb of a forechosen virgin and there clothed in the garb of human flesh, and afterwards proceeding hence by the closed door of His mother's virginity, He showed himself in a form visible to all men" (*id.* at 73).

111. *Id.* at 73.

112. *See* text accompanying notes 95–109, *supra*.

113. *The Mongol Mission, supra* note 110, at 73.

114. *Id.* at 74.

115. *Id.*

116. *Id.*

117. *Id.* Innocent expressed his regret that he himself could not personally deliver the Church's message of salvational responsibility to the Khan. Innocent's excuse was essentially that the pope could not be everywhere at the same time:

> [S]ince we are unable to be present in person in different places at one and the same time—
> for the nature of our human condition does not allow this— . . . we send . . . in our stead
> prudent and discreet men by whose ministry we carry out the obligation of our apostolic
> mission. [Quoted in *id.*]

118. *Id.* at 75.

119. *Id.*

120. *Id.* at 75–76. Innocent's full explanation of the reason that God had not already taken steps to evidence his "wrath" against the Mongols merits elaboration:

> [N]or should you be emboldened to commit further savagery by the fact that when the
> sword of your might has raged against other men Almighty God has up to the present
> allowed various nations to fall before your face; for sometimes he refrains from chastising
> the proud in this world for the moment, for this reason, that if they neglect to humble
> themselves of their own accord he may not only no longer put off punishment of their
> wickedness in this life but may also take greater vengeance in the world to come. [Reprinted
> in *id.*]

It was a commonly expressed belief in Christian Europe that the destruction of the Mongols was inevitable. It is reported, for instance, that the bishop of Winchester once assured Henry III, "Let these dogs destroy one another and be utterly exterminated and then we shall see the Universal Catholic Church founded on their ruins and there will be one fold and one shepherd" (quoted in *id.* at xiv).

2

The Perfect Instrument of Empire:
The Colonizing Discourse
of Renaissance Spain

The Portuguese and Spanish voyages of discovery in the fifteenth century inaugurated the permanent expansion of Europe beyond the Mediterranean world. The emergence of a European world colonizing system necessarily revived legal speculation on the rights and status of the non-Christian peoples that Europe sought to subjugate. Questions that had become peripheral after the cloture of the Crusades and the decline in European colonizing activity in the late thirteenth century resumed prominence in early Discovery-era legal discourse. Law's utility in generating legitimating arguments for the acquisition, maintenance, and defense of colonial spheres of influence was seized on as a principal instrument of empire by the colonizing monarchs of Portugal and Spain. But the story of the Iberian genesis of European expansion reveals that legal discourse served more than this instrumental function. Constructed on the canonically approved Christian Humanist foundations of Pope Innocent IV's medieval speculations on the natural-law rights and obligations of infidel nations, the legal discourses of conquest that emerged out of the Iberian colonization of Africa and the New World both energized and constrained the exercise of imperial power. Responding to the requirements of a paradoxical age of Renaissance and Inquisition, the West's first modern discourses of conquest articulated a vision of all humankind united under a rule of law discoverable solely by human reason. Unfortunately for the American Indian, the West's first tentative steps toward this noble vision of a Law of Nations contained a mandate for Christian Europe's subjugation of all peoples whose radical divergence from European-derived norms of right conduct signified their need for conquest and remediation.

The Lithuanian Controversy

Innocent IV's analysis of infidel rights and obligations provoked little in the way of extended commentary or significant elaboration after the closure of the Crusading movement in the late thirteenth century. It was not until the early fifteenth century, at the dawn of Europe's Age of Discovery, that Innocent's discourse on the legal status and rights of infidels was revived and its canonical

integrity debated and approved in Western legal thought. The formal acceptance of the medieval canon lawyer–pope's positions on infidel rights as the
official doctrine of the Roman Church provided the discursive legitimating
foundations for the first legal discourses of conquest that emerged from the
early colonizing experiences of Portugal and Spain in Africa and the New
World.

The grounding themes of Portuguese and Spanish legal colonizing discourse
were articulated during deliberations associated with the Council of Constance
(1414–1418). This council was the culmination of the Conciliar movement, an
effort by advocates of Church constitutional reform to bring about decentrali-
zation of power and a rejection of papal monarchial themes.[1]

One of the numerous issues debated at Constance involved the rival claims
of the Teutonic Knights and Poland to control over pagan Lithuania. The
Teutonic Knights were one of the most infamous Crusading priestly orders of
the Middle Ages. Their extensive central European empire and territorial
holdings were acquired and sustained on the basis of the medieval hierocratic
doctrine that pagan nonbelievers, such as the Lithuanians, could be attacked
by Christian armies and deprived of their *dominium* (lordship and property) at
the behest of the pope in Rome. The king of Poland, for his part, had entered
into a protective alliance with the Lithuanians to counter the Knights' frequent
raids and assertions of sovereign control over the pagan territory. The parties
submitted their dispute to the jurisdiction of the Constance Council.[2]

Significantly, the Lithuanian controversy raised directly the question of the
legality of the seizure by papally sanctioned Crusading armies of lands held by
infidel peoples solely on the hierocratic basis that pagan nonbelievers lacked
lawful *dominium*. The questions of whether the crusading Knights' claims to
Lithuania would be allowed to stand or the kingdom of Poland could enter
into a protective alliance with the Lithuanians thus raised a host of issues
related to the central concerns of the antihierocratic advocates of Church
reform present at the Constance Council.

The Intra-European Crusade of the Teutonic Knights

The emergence of the Teutonic Knights as a significant colonizing power in
central Europe illustrates the pervasive influence throughout Western Christendom of the medieval traditions of Christian European conquest and colonization of normatively divergent peoples. As the Knights' terrorist activities in
the Baltic region attest, the ancient aggrandizing traditions of the Crusades
were not applied solely to non-European lands and peoples.

German colonial expansion had been a fact of life for the non-Christianized
Slavic peoples of central Europe since the tenth-century Saxon revival of
Carlovingian-style imperial aspirations toward the east. For the next several
centuries, the German emperors launched frequent missionary-*cum*-military
colonizing initiatives to the east, establishing numerous frontier outposts in the
Baltic region.[3]

The German emperors' practice of Christianization by force in the infidel Slavic territories continued throughout the later Middle Ages, legitimated and encouraged by a stridently bellicose style of hierocratic canonical discourse. In the mid-twelfth century, Bernard of Clairvaux, the mystic leader of the Cistercians, a monastic order devoted to ascetic withdrawal from the world, openly encouraged the German princes to destroy the pagan Wends. Bernard argued the extreme hierocratic position that infidels should be killed whenever they presented a menace to Christians. Christ's command to "feed my sheep" clearly meant that "the Lord committed all the sheep to the care of Peter alone, thus commending unity to all in one flock and one Shepherd, according to what is written, 'One, is My dove, My beautiful one, My perfect one' (Canticles 6:8). For where there is unity there is perfection."[4]

The German emperors needed little encouragement from hierocratic mystics such as Bernard to enforce their own unrefined notions of unity and hierarchy inside un-Christianized eastern Europe. The German Crusade against the Wends was fought by "preachers in helmets" who spread the Christian message among the pagans through a campaign of unbridled terror.[5]

During this same era of German eastward expansion, Emperor Frederick II (1194–1250) unilaterally arrogated to himself the authority as head of the Holy Roman Empire to bring the whole world into the Christian faith. To achieve this noble goal, Frederick proclaimed the power to destroy, convert, and subjugate all barbarian nations. The exercise of this power had previously been regarded in canonical doctrine as permissible only with the express sanction of the Roman papacy.[6]

The Teutonic Knights were one of the many militaristic by-products of this jumbled synthesis of papal hierocratic and Germanic imperial discourse. The order was originally established in 1196 in Palestine as a German religious confraternity of monks devoted to good works. Under German imperial influence and benefice, however, the monks were quickly transformed into a military order with a constitution modeled on other Crusading orders such as the Knights Templar.

With the decline of the Crusading movement in the Levantine regions, the Knights abandoned the Holy Land and transferred their colonizing activities to Europe in the early thirteenth century. In 1226 they were expelled from Hungary as a menace after having been invited by the king to assist in the fight against the pagan Kumanians. The Knights thereafter moved their intra-European crusading activities against the pagan infidel into the Baltic region. Imperial and papal recognition of titles to various pagan conquests provided the Teutonic order with ecclesiastical and temporal jurisdiction over large territories in the Baltic area.

The expansion-minded Knights waged continual holy war on their Baltic neighbors, particularly the independent Christian nation of Poland (which was insufficiently Christianized, in the order's opinion) and the pagan kingdom of Lithuania. In 1341 the Knights initiated regular semiannual raids on the Lithuanians. The sacred feasts of the Assumption (August 15) and the Purification (February 2) were chosen by the Knights as appropriate dates for bringing the message of Christianity to the nonbelievers. The Lithuanians suffered devastating casualties and large losses of territory during these prose-lytizing, celebratory forays by the Knights. At one point, the Lithuanians seriously debated abandoning their homeland to the priestly warriors.

Deciding against a diaspora, the Lithuanians chose to negotiate a series of protective alliances with Christian Poland, culminating in the 1383 marriage contract between the Polish princess Jadwiga and the Lithuanian king Jagiello. The price for this permanent alliance was the weaker Lithuanian kingdom's agreement to be converted to Christianity by the Poles. In 1385 Jagiello, accompanied by several Polish bishops, traveled throughout his kingdom, instructing his pagan subjects to follow his lead and accept Christian baptism.

The union was violently opposed by the Knights. From the Crusading order's perspective, the alliance of Poland and Lithuania was a bothersome obstacle to further expansion in the Baltic region. The Knights most objected to Lithuania's sudden Christianization by the near-apostate kingdom of Po-land. The Lithuanians' supposed conversion would deprive the order's frequent aggrandizing raids of the legitimating character of a crusade against the pagan. On the day of Jagiello's coronation as king of Poland, the Knights invaded Lithuania on the pretext that the pagans' conversion was insincere. Many of the converts were slaughtered and their newly constructed churches burned to the ground.

Conflict and tension in the region continued sporadically until 1409, when the Teutonic order launched a direct attack on Poland, which led to the Battle of Tannenburg and the Knights' defeat in 1410. Indemnities and armistices were acquired by the victorious Poles, but the unchastened warrior monks recommenced hostilities almost immediately after the signing of a peace treaty between the two parties. In 1414 a papal legate persuaded the Knights and Poland to submit their long-running dispute over control of Lithuania to the recently announced Council of Constance.

The Constance Debates on the Rights of Infidels

The Constance Council had been called in 1414 primarily to resolve claims to St. Peter's chair by three rival popes. The council was dominated by advocates of the Conciliar movement. The reform-minded Conciliarists' primary concern was with placing all ecclesiastical authority in the hands of a general council of Church prelates and cardinals. These reformers rejected the monarchial pre-tensions of a hierocratically conceived papal office, instead viewing the papacy as the agent of the general council representing the Church. Thus the Lithua-nian question raised issues of central importance to the Conciliarists. A long line of extreme papal hierocratic theorists, most notably Alanus Anglicus and those who adhered to his influential arguments denying infidel *dominium*, had asserted Rome's unilateral right to authorize conquests of pagan territories solely on the basis of nonbelief in the Christian God. The Knights in fact traced their territorial and jurisdictional claims to Lithuania directly to papal Crusading bulls authorizing outright confiscation of the heathens' property and lordship. That the Knights' territorial claims were grounded in an exalted theory of papal paramountcy would not have escaped the Conciliarists' attention.

Besides the Lithuanian question, and the critical issue of the internal constitution of the Church raised by Conciliarism, the Constance Council had agreed to condemn the teachings of the deceased English churchman John Wyclif (c. 1320–1384). Wyclif, the heretical theologian regarded as the spiritual forefather of the English Reformation, had studied and taught at Oxford in the late fourteenth century. In sermons and lectures, Wyclif railed at clerical corruption and its debilitating effects on the Church as an institution of moral authority. In his most notorious work, *De civili dominio* (1376), Wyclif defended royal expropriation of Church property as a legitimate means of attacking clerical corruption. Wyclif defended this radical thesis (which complemented the activities of British leaders, such as John of Gaunt, who sought to check Rome's influence in England) on a doctrinal foundation of apostolic poverty and *dominium* contingent on grace.

The thrust of Wyclif's thesis on *dominium* was expressed in his infamous declaration that "no one is a civil lord, or a prelate, or a bishop, while in mortal sin."[7] Wyclif's views on *dominium* thus revived in a direct and extremely threatening fashion the ancient Donatist heresy that the valid exercise of any secular or ecclesiastical authority depended on the officeholder's spiritual state. St. Augustine himself in the earliest centuries of Christianity had attacked the Donatist heresy that earthly authority was legitimated only by divine grace and that immoral or corrupt clerics could not validly administer the sacraments.[8] Wyclif's novel suggestion for enforcing his Donatist-affiliated thesis against sinful priests extended the heresy one dangerous step further: lay rulers ought to seize the riches of corrupt priests.[9]

It did not take the Church long to respond to this frontal assault on the hierocratic edifice. Pope Gregory XI (1370–1378) condemned Wyclif's opinions as heretical and demanded his imprisonment. The pope's irritation only emboldened an increasingly rebellious English government. Wyclif was allowed to preach his views more widely. He translated the Bible into English, a dangerously regarded innovation attacking the Church's monopoly of power and knowledge. He was permitted to develop further his predestinarian notions on grace; he asserted that the sacraments were not essential for salvation; and he even launched an attack on the whole concept of transubstantiation.

Wyclif had been dead for nearly thirty years at the time the Constance Council was called. English ecclesiastical officials wanted the assurance of having his entire system condemned as anathema by a general council of the Church. The Council of Constance obliged by declaring heretical a number of specific propositions allegedly contained in Wyclif's works. The council was particularly careful to single out Wyclif's heresies linking the validity of secular or ecclesiastical authority to the officeholder's spiritual state.[10]

The council's consideration of the rights of the Teutonic Knights and Poland to control the Christianization of Lithuania thus took place within a highly charged discursive atmosphere, which had already condemned Wyclif's Donatist-linked view that sinful priests lacked valid *dominium* and thus could be deposed of their authority and possessions. Such a view plainly suggested the corollary principle that pagans, who were presumptively not in a state of grace, similarly lacked *dominium* and thus could also be deposed of their property and lordship by righteous Christians. The council, having already comdemned Wyclif's views on priestly qualifications and grace, would naturally have regarded as canonically suspect an assertion by either the Knights or Poland that because the pagan Lithuanians were not in a state of grace, Christians could unilaterally deprive them of their *dominium*.[11] From the Conciliarists' point of view, any such assertion would also have readily recalled the disfavored line of extreme papal hierocratic canonical discourse inaugurated by the English canon-law scholar Alanus Anglicus in the early thirteenth century. Wyclif's fellow Englishman had legitimated attacks on the pagan nonbelievers of the Holy Land on the basis of the papacy's asserted universal jurisdiction over all forms of *dominium*. Alanus's argument that infidels lacked *dominium* because they were not in a state of grace and did not obey God's vicar the pope continued to appeal to hierocratic canonists despite Innocent IV's subsequent commentary in *Quod super his* recognizing the natural rights of pagan nonbelievers.[12] The Conciliarists at Constance, determined to reduce the papal office to less exalted dimensions, would naturally have been inclined to support infidel *dominium*. Their goal at Constance, after all, was to undermine a long and influential line of papal hierocratic canonistic thought that was radically opposed to their own decentralized constitutional paradigm of the Church.

Unfortunately for the Teutonic Knights, their advocate, Johannes Falkenberg, was less than sensitive to the implications of the council's negative views on Wyclif's teachings on *dominium*. Falkenberg's defense of the Knights consisted largely of a polemical, *ad hominem* attack on the Poles and the Lithuanians. He described the peoples of both nations as idolaters, "heretics and shameless dogs who have returned to the vomit of their infidelity." Falkenberg charged that the Poles, as idolaters themselves, could not be trusted with the task of converting the pagan Lithuanians. The Knights were the true defenders of the faith, who had warred on the Lithuanians as infidels and who should be permitted to continue their Crusade, for, as the Knights asserted, the Lithuanians' "rooted insanity and past blindness still show in their daily life."[13] Falkenberg, in other words, based the Knights' rights in Lithuania on the theory that as pagans, the Lithuanians could be deprived of their *dominium* by the Knights and forcibly converted to Christianity, as directed by prior popes.

Poland's advocate before the council, Paulus Vladimiri (d. 1435), a respected canon lawyer and former rector of the University of Cracow, was a Renaissance man in every sense of the word. Schooled in Aristotle and Aquinas as well as in the technicalities of canonical doctrine, he based his arguments in favor of Poland on the same Humanist premises that had earlier structured Pope Innocent IV's discourse on infidel rights and status.

An extremely able lawyer, Vladimiri sought to align the Knights' position as closely as possible with Wyclif's already condemned opinions on *dominium*. He summed up his argument in a paper entitled "Opinio Hostiensis," a brilliant tactical move in itself, as Hostiensis (1200–1271) was the one canonist whose extreme hierocratic opinions on infidel rights as well as on papal paramountcy were widely known. Hostiensis had studied under Innocent IV, but his influential views on papal power more closely followed those of Alanus Anglicus. "Therefore in the order of greatness," Hostiensis declared, "there is only one head, namely the pope."[14]

Hostiensis's own thirteenth-century commentary on *Quod super his* assumed prominence in Western legal thought and discourse as the standard response to Innocent's more naturalistically inspired thesis on the rights of infidels. According to Hostiensis, "It seems to me that with the coming of Christ every office and all government authority and jurisdiction was taken from every infidel lawfully and with just cause and granted to the faithful through Him who has the supreme power and who cannot err."[15]

Hostiensis steadfastly rejected any notion that infidels who did not recognize the authority of the true God and his vicar on earth, the pope, could ever legitimately possess *dominium*. "[W]e assert that by law infidels ought to be subject to the faithful."[16] Thus in accord with Alanus, Hostiensis adhered to the extreme hierocratic view that *dominium* rested on grace, the essence of the ancient Donatist heresy and the more recently suppressed discourse of Wyclif.

Vladimiri's focus on the "opinion of Hostiensis" thus sought to link the hierocratic theologian's views denying the legitimacy of infidel *dominium* with the Teutonic Knights' claim of authority to direct the conversion of the pagan Lithuanians. Through this linkage, in turn, Vladimiri hoped that the council would recognize that Hostiensis's views (and thus the Knights' claims to control pagan Lithuania) were based on a conception of *dominium* too closely akin to the already condemned Wyclifite heresy denying *dominium* to sinful priests. Vladimiri's argument in "Opinio Hostiensis" thus opened with the question of whether infidels could in fact possess *dominium*, for the Knights, he claimed, could justify their rights in Lithuania only by asserting the Hostiensian position that as infidels, the Lithuanians did not possess lawful *dominium*.[17]

Having identified the Knights' position with Hostiensis and (through guilt by ideological association) with Wyclif, Vladimiri urged the council to condemn the Donatist-linked opinion of the medieval hierocrats that lordship was contingent on grace. He asked also that the council adopt the Humanist-inspired position outlined by Innocent IV in *Quod super his* that infidels possessed the same natural-law rights as Christians. Drawing on the texts of Aquinas and Aristotle as supplements, Vladimiri painstakingly elaborated the Innocentian Humanist position on infidel natural-law rights in fifty-two separate statements. All nations belonged to Christ's flock. Therefore, the pope, and only the pope, could authorize Christian princes to invade infidel lands, but only to punish violations of natural law or to facilitate the spread of the gospel. The Knights, argued Poland's advocate, had lied to the pope about the situation in Lithuania. The order sought to wage war only to expand its own empire. The pagan Lithuanians were a peaceful people, and they had in fact been living free of hostilities with their Christian neighbors until unlawfully attacked by the Teutonic order. It was only then that the Lithuanians had exercised their natural-law right to defend themselves. Thus any papal authorizations obtained by the Knights for Lithuanian conquest had been obtained by fraud and were necessarily invalid.

Vladimiri's implied assertion that prior popes had erred in granting the Knights a right to conquer the Lithuanians in itself attacked, by a circuitous discursive route, the Hostiensian line of argument on papal infallibility. The novel thesis that the pope might wrongfully administer his indirect jurisdiction over infidels and that a later council of the Church could correct such a mistake would have appealed to the advocates of Conciliar theory who rejected papal monarchial pretensions.

Vladimiri's argument on the natural-law rights of infidels to *dominium* thus expressly rejected the extreme hierocratic position that only the pope conferred rightful ownership. The pope could interfere with infidel rights only for clear violations of natural law, and, as Vladimiri argued, the Lithuanians had not committed any such unlawful acts. Vladimiri capped his argument by distinguishing the Knights' activities from other, legitimately recognized Crusading campaigns. Unlike Spain, in which papally directed holy wars had been fought against the infidel Moors, Lithuania had never belonged to Christians, so the Knights' cause could not be considered a just war of reconquest. Further, the Knights sought to coerce the Lithuanians to accept Christianity without first providing the opportunity to hear voluntarily the truth of the gospel. Such a course of conduct had been widely rejected by canonistic theory since Thomas Aquinas and his contrary teaching on grace freely accepted as an act of will. Vladimiri argued that only the Poles had proved successful in convincing the Lithuanians to undergo voluntary conversion to Christianity. They should be permitted to continue in this cooperative endeavor. Finally, in an innovative use of Innocentian discourse, Vladimiri called on the pope to protect the Lithuanians' natural-law rights because the Petrine office included the obligation to act as spiritual and temporal protector of the wayward sheep of Christ's flock.[18]

A special commission appointed to settle the Lithuanian controversy issued its report in 1417. Vladimiri's Innocentian-inspired position was upheld in its essential points. Falkenberg, the Teutonic Knights' advocate, was condemned for his "many false, detestable,and damnable [statements] which are against the faith and against good morals." The plain implication of the commission's report was that counselor Falkenberg's "errors of faith" involved his Hostiensian and Wyclifite suggestions that *dominium* depended on grace.[19]

Church doctrine following the Council of Constance was firmly aligned with the position of Pope Innocent IV on the legitimacy of infidel *dominium* under natural law. As James Muldoon, who has written extensively on canonistic treatment of infidel rights in the late Middle Ages, has remarked:

The Council of Constance brought to an end the line of argument about the dependence of *dominium* upon grace. . . . Following the condemnation of Wyclif's opinions, Hostiensis' views on *dominium* were no longer acceptable. In the future, canonists, theologians, popes, and secular rulers who sought to defend the conquest of infidel lands would have to march their troops through whatever loopholes they could find in Innocent's arguments about the natural rights of infidels to possess property and lordship, or they would have to develop new arguments that avoided heresy.[20]

At the dawn of Europe's age of expansion beyond the Mediterranean world, Western legal thought had legitimated a discursive foundation for Europe's will to empire. Conquest of infidel peoples and their lands could proceed according to a rule of law that recognized the right of non-Christian people either to act according to the European's totalizing normative vision of the world or to risk conquest and subjugation for violations of this Eurocentrically understood natural law.

The Iberian Crusades in Africa

The emerging fifteenth-century nation-states of the Iberian Peninsula, Portugal and Spain, were themselves the virtual creations of papally sponsored Crusades against the heathen Moors.[21] It is not surprising, therefore, that these rigorously orthodox Catholic countries readily incorporated the Innocentian position on the legitimacy of infidel *dominium* approved at Constance into their Discovery-era colonizing ventures and legal discourse. Being good proto-capitalists and seeking to eliminate unnecessary risks or distracting obstacles on their respective roads to empire, the Iberians avoided devising any novel legal arguments that might incur bothersome charges of heresy carried to Rome by jealous colonizing rivals. The Lithuanian controversy had provided the lawyers of Discovery-era Portugal and Spain with an easily manipulable legal framework capable of legitimating colonization of pagan peoples on the more liberal basis of a Eurocentrically perceived natural law. As Vladimiri's defense of Poland's rights to Lithuania suggested, there was little need for new and untested legal arguments, given the size of the loopholes that riddled Innocent's legal codification of infidel status and rights under Eurocentrically conceived natural law.

The Portuguese Appeal to Conquer and Convert the Canary Islands

Portugal's history as part of Christian Europe begins with the *reconquista* efforts of the twelfth-century Franks on the Iberian Peninsula,[22] which culminated in the capture of Lisbon from the Moors in 1147. Chroniclers provide testimony of the prominent role played by Church officials in the Lisbon campaign. The archbishop accompanying the Crusaders delivered a speech in which, in precise Augustinian phrasings, he reminded the army of the justness of their papally sanctioned war against the infidels:

Now, as worthy sons of the mother church, repel force and injury; for in law it happens that whatever anyone does in self-defense he is held to have done lawfully. . . . Therefore, brothers, take courage with these arms, courage, that is to say, either to defend the fatherland in war against barbarians or to ward off enemies at home, or to defend comrades from robbers; for such courage is full of righteousness. Indeed, such works of vengeance are duties which righteous men perform with a good conscience. . . . And he who puts wicked men to death is a servant of the Lord, for the reason that they are wicked and there is ground for killing them.[23]

As in all the other European nations that had been Christianized by the Church, the course of early Portuguese political development was significantly shaped by Rome's influence in ecclesiastical and secular administration. In 1179 the papacy accepted the Portuguese kingdom as a fief from King Alfonso Henriques (1139–1185) in exchange for papal, and thereby international, recognition of Portugal's independence from Castile. Rome could therefore usually rely on Lisbon to support most papal policies and edicts.

Given its history of Church-sponsored militant colonialism against the infidel Moors and its strategic location astride the Atlantic overlooking Africa, Lisbon was well situated for initiating European Discovery-era expansion beyond the Mediterranean region. Iberian chronicles of the early Discovery period recognized that the conquest of North Africa would provide useful employment for Iberian Crusaders who had previously made their livings by frontier raids against the infidels remaining on the peninsula. The prospect of establishing military and mercantile outposts closer to the African spice trade and bullion supply also motivated expansion southward. As Immanuel Wallerstein has suggested, the "younger sons" of the Portuguese nobility who lacked land—and therefore a financial base—in their small, feudalized homeland found the prospects of conquest in infidel-held African territories extremely appealing.[24]

Portugal's capture of the African port city of Ceuta, opposite Gibraltar and formerly the bridgehead for the frequent Muslim invasions of the Iberian Peninsula, led to increased knowledge and interest in tribally held lands on the upper Niger and the Senegal rivers. These regions were the sites of an extensive Muslim gold trade. Additionally, the tactical vantage point provided by the Lisbon port facilitated further exploration and penetration of the west African Gold Coast and the islands that lay off it. These island groups included the Canaries (claimed for the Crown by a Portuguese expedition in 1341), the Azores, the Cape Verdes, and the Madeiras.[25]

The kingdom of Castile, Portugal's Iberian neighbor and principal colonial competitor, repeatedly challenged Lisbon's North African interests during the early fifteenth century. Castile sought to enforce its competing claims to control of trade on the North African coast and the nearby islands by repeated attacks on the Portuguese and their fortified African trading posts, called *factorias*. In the Canaries, one of the most strategically located and potentially valuable of the coastal island groups, the conflicting Iberian colonizing desires led to violent attacks on the native populations, some of whom had already been Christianized. In 1434 Pope Eugenius IV (1431–1447), acting at the request of the bishop serving the islands, issued a bull banning all European Christians from the Canaries as a protective measure for the infidel as well as the converted inhabitants.[26]

Eugenius's unprecedented ban on Christian colonizing activities in the Canaries was grounded in principles derived from the Innocentian position on infidel rights affirmed in substance at the Council of Constance two decades earlier. In the Lithuanian controversy, Poland's advocate, Paulus Vladimiri, had urged the novel theory that the papacy could assume an active guardianship over non-Christian pagan peoples who appeared ripe for conversion.[27] Eugenius's bull essentially codified as the law of the Church Vladimiri's construction of Innocent's position on infidel rights and papal protective responsibility.

King Duarte of Portugal (1433–1438), whose sailors had been responsible for the principal incident resulting in Eugenius's assumption of fiduciary responsibility over the Canaries, appealed the papal ban in 1436. The letter of appeal, most likely prepared by Duarte's Crown lawyers,[28] requested that the pope remove the ban with respect to those islands inhabited by infidels so that the Portuguese could continue their conquests on behalf of Christianity.

Besides offering an explanation for the conduct of his sailors, who had attacked the Christian natives (their supply ship from Portugal had been delayed by bad winds, so they had no choice but to descend on the islands), Duarte provided anthropological description to underline the importance of carrying on the vital task of Christian conversion in the islands. The "nearly wild" infidel Canary Islanders, explained the king,

are not united by a common religion, nor are they bound by the chains of law, they are lacking normal social intercourse, living in the country like animals. They have no contact with each other by sea, no writing, no kind of metal or money. They have no houses and no clothing except for coverlets of palm leaves or goat skins which are worn as an outer garment by the most honored men. They run barefoot quickly through the rough, rocky and steep mountainous regions, hiding . . . in caves hidden in the ground.[29]

What later Europeans might have romanticized as a scene of paradise or an original state of nature, Duarte caricatured as evidence of the infidels' animality. The infidel Canarians' lack of the accouterments of Christian European civilization proved that they were barbarians. Duarte's letter contrasted the infidel Canarians, who lived under no form of law (as Christians understood that term), with the Canarians recently converted by the Portuguese. These Christian Canarians had been introduced to civilization and all its benefits. They were now loyal subjects of the Portuguese king, who had provided them with "civil laws and an organized form of society. . . . Where the name of Christ had never been known, Christ is now worshipped."[30]

According to Duarte's letter of appeal, the pope's ban had halted this noble work of Christianization and civilization. Because the Portuguese king had begun the conquest of the islands, "more indeed for the salvation of the souls of the pagans of the islands than for his own personal gain, for there was nothing for him to gain, Your Holiness ought not to be the last obstacle in such a noble cause for one worthy of the help and assistance of Your Holiness."[31]

Duarte concluded his letter by appealing to the pope's sense of the practical realities of the situation and the papal office's own exalted sense of mission and of responsibility for guardianship toward the infidel Canarians. While the Portuguese would continue to obey the pope's ban, could the pope be sure that others, given the strategic location of the Canary Islands, would also leave the natives in peace? Duarte stressed that Portugal possessed the resources and the will to protect the islands and to further the tasks of conversion on the Church's behalf. Portugal had always been a trusted ally of the papacy. Duarte's implication was clear: it was better to have Portugal control this outpost on the frontiers of Christianity than a less cooperative European power that lacked the proper respect for Rome's jurisdictional primacy respecting infidel peoples:

The same most serene prince begs Your Holiness that those islands that he has taken from the hands of the infidels, Your Holiness will grant and give to him out of generosity to that king. If this is done, he will be greatly encouraged to prosecute this renowned work, which is already under way, and lead toward an increased devotion toward Your Holiness. Although many will strive on their own authority to wage war and to occupy the lands of the infidels, nevertheless, because the earth and its fullness are the Lord's who left to your Holiness the fullness of this power over the entire world, whatever is possessed by the authority and permission of Your Holiness is understood to be held in a special way and with the permission of almighty God.[32]

In the two decades following the deliberations at Constance on the Lithuanian controversy, the legal advisors in the royal courts of expansion-minded Christian monarchs had apparently settled on the fundamental legitimating thematics of a colonizing legal discourse deemed acceptable to Rome and Church law. The lawyers who had advised the king in drafting his letter (it is important to recognize that most, if not all, of the king's legal advisors at this time were churchmen—canon lawyers and theologians) had been careful to avoid any implicit justification of Portuguese rights of conquest in the Canaries based on the natives' lack of *dominium*, or natural rights, stemming from their infidelity. Rather, Portugal sought only to prevent the oppression of the natives by other European powers that might not be so solicitous of their rights. As conquest was inevitable, it was preferable that it be carried out under papal guidance and protection. Duarte was therefore respectfully asking that Portugal be appointed as the pope's dutiful servant in administering Rome's responsibility as guardian of these infidel sheep of Christ's flock.

Duarte's letter of appeal also indicated that the Crown lawyers were thoroughly familiar with the less benevolent extensions of Innocentian doctrine respecting infidel rights. According to Duarte's letter, the Canarians would not permit Christian missionaries to land on their islands. Military force would therefore be necessary to protect and facilitate Christian missionary activity. This point was within the clear lines drawn by Innocent in his commentary on *Quod super his*.[33] While Innocent had stressed that infidels should not be compelled to accept Christianity, a refusal to admit Christian missionaries to preach the gospel constituted legitimate grounds for waging war against pagan peoples. Further, as attested by Duarte's anthropological descriptions, the "nearly wild" Canarians were in obvious and continued violation of natural law. Such irrational acts were contrary to the Canarians' spiritual well-being.

Thus, as Innocent had stated, it was within the pope's guardianship responsibility to commission Christian princes who would punish and civilize such lawless people according to Christian norms.

Perhaps the most significant aspect of Duarte's letter is its clear grasp of the importance of the Innocentian dichotomy between the pope's direct and indirect jurisdiction.[34] The essential thrust of the king's appeal was that as a Christian monarch loyal to the pope, he would be the most effective secular agent to fulfill the pope's Petrine guardianship responsibility to care for these wayward sheep of the flock. As a loyal son of the Church, Duarte in fact had already begun "the conquest of the islands, more indeed for the salvation of the souls of the pagans of the islands than for his own personal gain, for there was nothing for him to gain."[35] He now sought only to place this noble task directly under the pope's indirect supervisory jurisdiction in secular affairs in matters pertaining to the salvation of the souls of the pope's universal flock.

The Papal Response: Romanus Pontifex

Despite Duarte's sycophantic pandering to Rome's own indirect imperial pretensions, Pope Eugenius felt obliged to consult his own lawyers respecting the legal issues raised by the king's request. At least two separate opinions were drafted for the pope's consideration by the canon lawyers Antonio Minucci da Pratovecchio and Antonio Roselli. Each opinion opened with an identical statement of the case (probably provided by Eugenius himself): "A certain Catholic prince or King who recognizes no superior wishes to wage war against the Saracens who do not possess or hold lands of that King but who hold lands . . . as if in barbarism."[36]

Both canonists adhered closely to the basic theses on infidel rights outlined in Innocent's commentary on *Quod super his*. Minucci's opinion began with a restatement of the Innocentian position that wars could not be waged against infidels solely because of their nonbelief. The "Saracens" of the Canaries possessed *dominium* under the *ius gentium*, the Roman Law of Nations, embodying the legal norms and practices common to all societies. While infidels did possess *dominium*, however, the papacy maintained a *de jure* form of indirect jurisdiction over their activities, according to Minucci. The pope possessed the authority to deprive infidels of their property and lordship in certain situations, such as those outlined by Innocent: the failure to admit Christian missionaries peacefully or the violation of natural law.[37] As Duarte's letter attested, the conduct of the Canarians, who refused to listen to the gospel and who lived "as if in barbarism," fell within both Innocentian proscriptions. Minucci's opinion therefore could be read as justifying Duarte's continuation of the Crusade against the infidel Canarians.

Roselli's opinion also followed Innocent's basic theses. He cited pagan philosophers, canon lawyers, and Christian theologians in support of the natural-law rights of infidels. Christ's coming could not affect infidel *dominium* under the Law of Nations because such rights never depended on grace. In fact, civil *dominium*, based on the Law of Nations, came about only because of

Adam's fall from grace. Roselli specifically denounced Hostiensis's contrary views on lordship contingent on grace, condemned by the Council of Constance just two decades earlier. But like his fellow canonist Minucci, he recognized that the pope's Petrine responsibility for all the sheep of God's flock might necessitate removing an infidel ruler's *dominium* for a higher good.[38]

The two canonists' Innocentian-derived opinions provided Eugenius with the basic "state of the law" on infidel rights at the dawn of Europe's Discovery era. Although possessing *dominium*, if infidels demonstrated an incapacity to comport their conduct according to natural law, the pope could interfere with their rights under his indirect Petrine guardianship responsibility to shepherd and care for all the sheep of God's flock.

Eugenius's subsequent papal bull, *Romanus Pontifex* (in effect a definitive papal legislative response to the Portuguese appeal backed by the sanction of excommunication for any breach of its contents), simply codified the opinions of his canonists. Eugenius's bull authorized King Duarte to convert the barbarous natives and control the islands on behalf of the papacy. This papal bull of African conquest was reissued several times in the fifteenth century, with each subsequent version significantly extending Portuguese geographical rights on the continent and outer island groups. The most refined version of the papal license of conquest is found in the 1453–1454 rendition of *Romanus Pontifex*, issued by Pope Nicholas V (1447–1455); it not only reconfirmed Portuguese rights in the Canaries but also sanctioned and protected further expansion by Lisbon into the African continent.[39]

Romanus Pontifex[40] provides the modern reader with a precise, juristic synthesis of refined Innocentian-derived papal colonizing discourse at the beginning of Europe's Discovery era. The bull recognized and affirmed Portuguese title to those African "provinces, islands, ports, districts and seas . . . which have already been acquired and which shall be acquired in the future."[41] The opening paragraph of the decree precisely delineated the Petrine source of the papacy's indirect jurisdictional authority over these non-Christian nations:

The Roman Pontiff, successor to the bearer of the keys of the heavenly kingdom and Vicar of Jesus Christ, looking with paternal interest upon all the regions of the world and the specific natures of all the peoples who dwell in them, seeking and desiring the salvation of every one of them, wholesomely orders and arranges with careful consideration those things which he perceives will be pleasing to the Divine Majesty and by which he may bring the sheep divinely committed to him into the one fold of the Lord, and may acquire for them the reward of eternal happiness, and may obtain pardon for their souls.[42]

Whereas earlier hierocratic discourse normally justified the extension of papal territorial jurisdiction in the bellicose tones characteristic of the Crusading movement against the infidel Saracen,[43] *Romanus Pontifex* emphasized the more benign, paternalistic elements of papal suzerainty. The pope authorized the subjugation and colonization of the Africans under his guardianship responsibilities for all the sheep of the Lord's flock. This shift in discursive thematics can be attributed to the Humanist-inspired contributions of theorists such as Innocent and Vladimiri to the West's discourses of conquest. The more

cynical contributions of King Duarte also indicate that eager European monarchs had nobly assumed the burden of carrying Western civilization to the
heathen at an early stage of the Renaissance Discovery era. Unlike that of the
Crusaders, the Portuguese Crown's asserted primary goal was not mere conquest of the Africans. Conquest was a means to the larger declared goal of the
barbarians' conversion to Christianity and civilization. If a portion of the
infidels' lands was taken in the bargain by which the pope established a
guardianship over the natives, so much the better, as the Portuguese had also
come to open up a profitable trade with the Africans, and this required the
establishment of *factorias*. The matrix of relationships for this peculiar type of
colonial enterprise therefore required a less openly militant discursive posture
on the part of the pope and the Portuguese Crown. Papal sanction of Lisbon's
expansion into Africa, grounded in Rome's indirect jurisdiction in secular
affairs, harmonized spiritual *and* secular ends within an evangelically
grounded colonizing mandate. Christian princes could be called on by Rome
(although in practice the princes usually approached Rome first) to bring the
heathen and infidel sheep of Christ's universal flock, living "as if in barbarism,"
to civilization as understood by Eurocentric and Christocentric norms.

That Rome itself was aware of its precise role in providing spiritual legitimacy to the colonizing desires of European feudal potentates in an age of
nationalist expansionism is beyond doubt. Pope Nicholas's understanding of
the symbiotic nature of this evangelical-*cum*-colonial joint venture with the
Portuguese Crown can be deciphered in the wording of *Romanus Pontifex*
itself. From "the plenitude of apostolic power," Nicholas by his bull granted to
the Portuguese Crown full title to any territories in the African region "acquired or to be acquired," along with authority to

freely and lawfully, both now and in the future, make in these territories and concerning
them any prohibitions, statutes and decrees whatsoever, even if they be penal and
include the imposition of any kind of tribute, and may dispose and command concerning them as they would with regard to their own property and their other lordships.[44]

Nicholas granted this plenary authority to establish and enforce lawful trade
monopolies against Europeans and non-Europeans alike so that the Portuguese might, in his words,

be able more keenly to pursue . . . this most pious and noble work [conversion], a work
most worthy to be remembered in every age—which, since the salvation of souls,
increase of the Faith and the defeat of the Faith's enemies are furthered in it, we regard
as a task wherein God Himself, His Faith and His commonwealth, the Universal
Church, are concerned—as they, after the more difficult obstacles have been removed,
shall perceive themselves and shall be fortified in it with favours and privileges granted
to them by us and by the Apostolic See.[45]

The papal promises of favors and privileges were the material reward—the
Portuguese trustee's management fee, as it were—for assuming the administrative
responsibilities of Rome's Petrine fiduciary duties in Africa. European appropriation of other peoples' labor and capital was justified in early Discovery-
era colonizing discourse as the fortuitous by-product of a necessary ele-

emosynary function assumed by Christian Europe for the remainder of the uncivilized world. *Romanus Pontifex* legitimated the origins of the Portuguese trading and slaving empire on the African Gold Coast by reference to the Canarians' radical divergence from Christian norms and the higher transcendent goals of unity and hierarchy contained in the pope's universal Petrine mandate. As for a mundane profit motive, Rome simply took the king of Portugal at his word that his African conquests would be undertaken "more indeed for the salvation of the souls of the pagans . . . than for his own personal gain, for there was nothing for him to gain."[46]

The Spanish Bulls

Perhaps no single historical incident better illustrates the transformations occurring throughout Discovery-era Spain than Queen Isabella's acceptance of Antonio de Nebrija's Spanish *Gramática*, the first-ever grammar of any modern European language. Upon its presentation in the momentous year 1492, Isabella reportedly asked the scholar, "What is it for?" Nebrija answered Her Majesty modestly but with profound prescience and insight respecting the demands of the new expansion-minded age. "Language," he reportedly stated, "is the perfect instrument of empire."[47] For Spanish legal discourse in the Renaissance Discovery era, the demands of empire required that the newly discovered instruments of colonial power be harmonized with the transcendent goals of a universal guardianship elaborated by the Church and the papacy.

The New World's First Entrepreneurs

The papal grants to Portugal of an African conquest and trade monopoly were backed by the sanction of possible excommunication. Church law thus left Catholic Spain with little recourse but to satisfy its imperial aspirations beyond the broad geographic sweep of *Romanus Pontifex*. Spain fortunately found itself better situated than any non-Iberian European nation to extend its trading empire beyond the geographical boundaries of the then-known European world.[48]

After ending a millennium of Moorish hegemony on the Iberian Peninsula with a decisive victory at Granada in 1492, a unified Spanish Crown under Ferdinand of Aragon and Isabella of Castile quickly commenced a xenophobic campaign to solidify cultural and religious unity throughout Spanish society. Muslims and Jews were given the choice of either conforming to the habits and faith of the new Christian order or leaving.

Significantly, Spain's drive for unity in the late fifteenth and early sixteenth centuries did not have to contend with the foreign and civil wars that convulsed most of western Europe during this critical period (the Hundred Years' War and the War of the Roses, to name examples). Nor did it find itself preoccupied with the Turkish advance, as did much of eastern Europe. Thus while other European nations had yet to escape the final vestiges of their struggles toward a "national identity," Spain embarked on its dynastic colonial quests in the late fifteenth century as a united kingdom. At the beginning of Europe's Discovery era, Spain found itself free of any significant civil disunity, with a firmly established territory under Christian hegemony.[49]

Furthermore, Spanish Christianity's long history of fervently nationalistic, papally sponsored warfare against the infidel Moor ensured that the Church's facilitating colonizing discourse of intolerance for normatively divergently peoples would accompany any extension of Spain's imperial aspirations beyond the Mediterranean.[50] For example, the famous secularly promulgated code of the Castilian monarch Alfonso X (1252–1284), *Las Siete Partidas* ("The Seven Parts"),[51] a principal vehicle for the transmission of Roman law throughout Spanish legal culture, proclaimed "the superiority of our religion"[52] and conceded extensive ecclesiastical jurisdiction over all segments of the Spanish laity. Under this code, any Christian who converted to the religion of the Moors could be punished by death.[53]

Thus the tentative reaction of the Spanish Crown in 1485 to Christopher Columbus and his novel yet attractive commercial proposal of a westward spice route to the Indies, which would avoid Portugal's papally granted African monopoly, was perfectly consistent with the traditional theocentric orientation of the Spanish state. The Crown's initial response to Columbus's offer suggests the extent of the intrusive, pervasive role played by the Spanish Catholic Church and its hierocratic discursive traditions in molding and defining Spanish imperial aspirations. Because even cartographical and mercantile questions were regarded as implicating the jurisdiction of the Spanish Church, the king and queen instructed Columbus to submit his proposed westerly "Enterprise of the Indies" to a specially composed junta of priests and canon-law scholars.[54]

The westward trajectory of Columbus's proposal to sail to the Indies can be explained largely by the fact that he was a Genoese, born between the two great ages of Genoese commerce. With the fall of Constantinople and the Byzantine Empire in 1453 to the Ottoman Turks, the rich Levantine trading colonies established by the Genoese merchants during the Crusades were reluctantly abandoned. The chief beneficiaries of this freed-up Genoese capital and mercantile expertise were the Portuguese and their capital city, Lisbon, principal port for the west African trade.[55] Lisbon, not surprisingly, was Columbus's home port during his early maritime career.

Thus Columbus was born and trained as a commercial Genoese sailor at a time when Genoese commerce was moving from east to west, from the Levant to the Atlantic, from medieval-feudal to Renaissance-mercantilist forms. Such monumental transitions of an entire commercial culture are never easily effected. Columbus, like many of his Genoese contemporaries, was forced to adapt to this changing world situation. Columbus did so by looking westward, across the Atlantic. Having sailed on Portuguese trading expeditions, perhaps as far west as Iceland, he was familiar with the farthest chartered reaches of that ocean. He would also have been familiar with the rich overland trade that the emigré Genoese merchants had previously exploited in the Levant as the principal conduit between the Indies in the east and Europe in the west. If

Columbus could convince a royal sponsor to finance a voyage to discover a shorter western sea route to that trade, then the potential riches, as well as discoveries of lands made on the way, would secure for him the wealth enjoyed by many of his older Genoese contemporaries.

The idea of discovery played a crucial, energizing role in the Genoese-defined mercantile sector of the Lisbon economy of the late medieval and early Renaissance period. At the eruption of the European world trading system in the fifteenth century, discovery of new territories meant new markets, new sources of raw materials, and short-term monopoly profits in the volatile Mediterranean trading economy of the early European Discovery era. For a Genoese such as Columbus, discovery was also the route with the fewest obstacles to upward mobility. Columbus was of that generation which had missed out on much of the booty seized by the older Italian captains in the first great rush of Portuguese colonization into North Africa and the coastal islands in the middle decades of the century. This fact must have been doubly apparent to Columbus, whose father-in-law, Perestrello, was one of the many older Genoese captains who commanded trading garrisons for the Portuguese in the Madeira Islands.

Christopher Columbus was not the first to propose the idea of a shorter westward sea route to the East Indies. Many of his contemporaries held the same belief, and some had even acted on it, but with no success. The ancient and medieval cosmographers gave support to the possibility of an alternative route to the East, much shorter than the route around Africa. Columbus himself had come across a statement reportedly made by no less an authority than Aristotle that the Atlantic could be crossed in just a few days. Two books from Columbus's personal library, Pierre d'Ailly's *Imago mundi* and Pope Pius II's *Historia rerum ubique gestarum*, extensively underlined and annotated, contained numerous guesses about the narrowness of the Atlantic. Columbus was fond of quoting Seneca's prophecy in *Medea*: "An age will come after many years when the Ocean will loose the chains of things, and a huge land be revealed." All of this combined with the medieval Christian's faith (a faith professed by Columbus) that the Savior, according to the scriptural prophecy, "shall have dominion also from sea to sea, and from the river into the ends of the earth" (Psalms 22:8).[56]

Columbus, as Samuel Eliot Morison has stressed in his biographical portrait of the Admiral of the Ocean Sea,[57] was by and large a medieval man, rooted firmly in the medieval mercantile traditions of maritime development and crusade.[58] Thus like his Genoese and Iberian contemporaries who had nurtured their colonizing skills in either the Levant or the west African trade, Columbus held the basic medieval belief that the Christian European civilization was superior to any other form of civilization. This in fact was the law taught by the Christian Church, the law that justified the conquistador–mariner captain's colonizing activities in the eyes of God and civilized people. Normatively divergent infidel societies were fit subjects for conquest as long as such conquest was deemed necessary for their conversion to Christianity and Christian civilization. And, of course, since Europeans, wherever they traveled in search of empire, encountered normatively divergent peoples with their own cultures, deities, and customs, conquest and conversion of these peoples were always deemed necessary.

This was the medieval European merchant sailor's truth, and therefore Columbus's truth. When this truth was combined with his knowledge of the colonizing techniques and tactics employed successfully by the Genoese in Africa and the East, Columbus lacked only one element to bring to fruition his own will to conquer and colonize. That element was power, in the form of ships, men, and guns. Truth, knowledge, power—the three pieces of the puzzle whose prize is empire. Already possessing the two most dangerous pieces of this puzzle, Columbus could now bargain for a partner who could supply him with power.

His partner would not be the Genoese merchants of Lisbon or the Portuguese Crown, both of whom he approached in the early 1480s with his proposal for a westward spice route. This was a relatively flush time for Lisbon's economy and merchant sector. The rush of African investment in the years following the Eastern exodus of the Genoese was now turning a profit. It was difficult to convince a merchant to divert capital to a far riskier transatlantic enterprise. Similarly, the Portuguese Crown could see no reason to invest in ships to travel beyond a distant, unchartered horizon. When Columbus approached King John in 1484, "to go and discover The Isle Cypanago [Japan] by this Western Ocean," the Portuguese monarch politely dismissed him. It was only then, from 1485 onward, that Columbus began to lobby other European monarchs, including Henry VII of England through his brother, but particularly the Spanish Crown, Portugal's only serious rival in the Atlantic trade.[59]

Spain, of course, had good reason to listen to the Genoese's plans. The pope's grant to Portugal and subsequent treaties between the two Iberian countries affirming the essentials of the Portuguese papal donation limited Spain's opportunities in Africa. Columbus, who history records was not averse to "puffing" his claims, offered Ferdinand and Isabella the hope of vast new discoveries outside the limits placed on Spanish activities by the papal bulls.

The ecclesiastical commission established by the Crown in 1485 to discuss Columbus's propositions met at the University of Salamanca, a major center of Spanish legal and theological learning. Isabella, who took particular interest in the Genoese's project, appointed her personal confessor, Hernando de Talavera, to head the inquiry. On its initial meeting, the commission could not agree on Columbus's plan but offered a retaining fee as a gesture of good faith. Columbus persisted in his lobbying efforts for the next five years, apparently ingratiating himself even further with the queen. In 1491, after an unfavorable report from the Talavera commission, a second committee was assembled at Isabella's request. This committee approved the feasibility of the plan, declaring that Columbus's ideas were consistent with Holy Writ. According to the commission's reading of scriptural prophecy, all peoples, tongues, and languages would one day be united under the banner of the Savior. The Crown, if it so desired, could finance the Italian navigator's expedition. Over the objections of her royal council, which considered the Genoese's requested remuneration for the venture to be exorbitant, Isabella agreed to sponsor Columbus's venture.[60]

The Discovery Era's First Contract for the Conquest of the New World

Columbus's royal contract for his voyage was based on Genoese legal discursive models and principles developed during the Crusades. Its opening lines stated:

Whereas you, Cristobal Colon, are setting forth by our command . . . to discover and acquire certain islands and mainland in the ocean sea . . . [and] since you are exposing yourself to this danger in our service . . . it is our will and pleasure that . . . after you have discovered and acquired the said islands and mainland . . . [you] shall be our Admiral of the said islands and mainlands . . . and . . . Viceroy and Governor therein. . . .[61]

The first land mass "discovered" by Columbus on his voyage westward was a small Caribbean cay, called Guanahani by its Arawak natives. In the presence of a small band of the island's inhabitants, "with appropriate words and ceremony," Columbus stood on the shore and declared lawful possession of the island. He renamed the island San Salvador and proclaimed it the property of the Catholic sovereigns of Spain.[62] He repeated this procedure throughout his first voyage, claiming each island "discovered" in the "Indies" (actually the Bahamian islands group) for the Spanish Crown.[63]

Columbus apparently based his presumption that he could lawfully claim these "discoveries" for the Spanish Crown on the Arawaks' divergence from European norms of civilization. His description of the Arawaks is markedly similar in tone and content to the description of the Canary Islanders in King Duarte's 1436 letter to Pope Eugenius IV. In that letter, the Portuguese monarch had sought to legitimate his colonizing desires by noting the infidel Canarians' "barbarism."[64] More than five decades later, Columbus gave the following anthropological account of the Arawaks and the seeming backward state of their civilization:

The people of this island and of all the other islands which I have found and of which I have information, all go naked, men and women. . . . They have no iron or steel or weapons. . . .

They do not hold any creed nor are they idolaters; but they all believe that power and good are in the heavens and were very firmly convinced that I, with these ships and men, came from the heavens, and in this belief they, everywhere, received me after they had mastered their fear.[65]

If Columbus was basing Spain's right to his "discoveries" on the Portuguese-derived precedent that lands held by barbarians could be appropriated by a discovering Christian sovereign's agent, then the sequence and scope of his actions raised at least two important legal issues. First, Columbus, a merchant sailor whose knowledge of the state of Church colonizing law was at best rudimentary, lacked prior papal authorization, such as that contained in the

Portuguese bull, *Romanus Pontifex*, for his appropriations of infidel lands. From a legal perspective, Columbus's actions could be interpreted as asserting the right of an agent of a Christian prince to seize territories without papal authorization whenever those territories were occupied by non-Christian peoples living "as if in barbarism." This, in essence, implied a theory permitting secular princes and their agents the authority to interfere unilaterally with infidel rights to *dominium*—a theory well beyond the bounds of Innocentian dogma affirmed at Constance. The lawyers of the papal curia would certainly be alert to testing the canonical integrity of Columbus's actions on behalf of Spain once news of his discoveries reached Rome.

The second legal issue raised by Columbus's "discoveries" related to the claims of Portugal itself to Atlantic territories under papal bulls such as *Romanus Pontifex*.[66] These claims had been confirmed by subsequent treaties, and the Portuguese in fact detained and interrogated Columbus when he anchored in the Azores on his return voyage from the New World. After freely describing the area of his discovery activities, the talkative captain was released. Portugal's King John informed the Spanish ambassador that he would soon reconnoiter his new western possessions, graciously discovered on Lisbon's behalf by the Spanish Crown's agent.

Thus even before Columbus had the opportunity to set foot in Spain, the Spanish Crown had dispatched diplomatic envoys to the papal curia in Rome. Their portfolios included draft documents of title confirming Spain's rights to Columbus's "discoveries." Spain's action in seeking quick papal confirmation of its rights in the "Indies" indicates the importance attached to the legitimating function played by the papacy's hierocratic assertions of jurisdiction over infidel peoples in the international colonizing theory and practice of the Iberian Christian states in the early years of the Discovery period.[67] But even more to the point, Spain's haste can also be explained by the fact that the incumbent pope, Alexander VI (1492–1503), was the Spaniard Rodrigo Borgia. Borgia owed not only his papacy but also much of his family's considerable lucre to the favors of the Castilian Crown. (As just one instance, Borgia's bastard son, the famous cardinal and military leader Caesar, was legitimated by Ferdinand and then granted the immensely profitable bishoprics of Pamplona and Valencia.)[68]

At the Spanish Crown's request, Pope Alexander obligingly issued three successive bulls essentially copying the original petitions drafted by Ferdinand and Isabella's lawyers for confirmation of their titles to Columbus's discoveries. In effect, Alexander's bulls resolved both legal problems raised by Columbus's voyage—the rights of Spain in relation to the barbarous peoples of the islands discovered and the rights of Spain in relation to Portugal—firmly in favor of the Spanish Crown.

The Spanish bulls of 1492 strongly echoed the basic themes of universal papal guardianship first elaborated by Innocent IV in the thirteenth century and then revived in papal legal discourse in the mid-fifteenth-century Portuguese African bulls of donation. The pope, exercising his indirect jurisdictional authority as shepherd of Christ's universal flock, entrusted the heathen inhabitants of the lands newly discovered by Columbus to the care and tutelage of a qualified Christian monarch, in this instance Spain.

The first Spanish bull, *Inter caetera divinai*, issued in May 1493,[69] simply declared that whereas Christopher Columbus had come upon a people "undiscovered by others . . . well disposed to embrace the Christian faith," all the lands discovered or to be discovered in the name of the Spanish Crown in the region belonged legally to Ferdinand and Isabella. By this bull, medieval Church colonizing doctrine was inelegantly stretched to incorporate a new proposition better suited to a world in which previously unknown, distant lands and peoples were rapidly being revealed to Europeans. The pope could place non-Christian peoples under the tutelage and guardianship of the first Christian nation discovering their lands as long as these peoples were reported by the discovering Christian nation to be "well disposed to embrace the Christian faith." It will be recalled that Innocentian doctrine had originally permitted military conquest of non-Christian societies *not* well disposed to accept Christianity—that is, those peoples who idolatrously believed in their own opposed deity or who refused rights of entry to Christian missionaries, and who therefore violated Christocentrically understood natural law. Alexander's first *Inter caetera* thus significantly extended the aggrandizing sweep of Christian legal doctrine on pagan rights and status. Spain's lawyers, who drafted the Crown's proposed bulls, had convinced Rome that random discovery of peaceful non-Christians not in apparent gross violation of natural law permitted the pope to exercise his guardianship responsibilities by placing such peoples under the tutelage and direction of the discovering Christian prince.

Portugal contested any broad reading of this first version of *Inter caetera*, but certainly not on the grounds that it deviated from strict Innocentian doctrine on pagan status and rights. The geography of *Inter caetera I* most concerned King John of Portugal, who believed that a "mainland to the south" of the Canaries existed and was explicitly reserved to Portugal as a field of discovery and colonization.[70] Spain likewise was concerned about the precision of its rights west of the Canaries demarcated in *Inter caetera I*. Spain feared that the bull could be read to affirm title to only a few islands in the region of Columbus's discoveries (Cuba, Hispaniola, and the Bahamas). The Spanish Crown, uncertain about the applicability of *Inter caetera I* to future discoveries, particularly given Lisbon's protests, requested another bull. Alexander obligingly issued a second, predated *Inter caetera*, drawing a line of demarcation (which may have been suggested by Columbus) 100 leagues west of the Azores. Under *Inter caetera II*, Spain took title to all territory west of this line. On the strength of this papal line of demarcation (later adjusted by the 1494 Treaty of Tordesillas between Spain and Portugal to a point 370 leagues west of the Cape Verde Islands), Spain secured virtually all of North and South America, leaving Portugal a fraction of the South American continent now constituting Brazil.[71]

Inter caetera II began with a recounting of Spain's victory at Granada and other Spanish actions that had enlarged and expanded the Catholic Church to the delight of the pope. "We therefore consider it as just and not undeserved by you, that we should concede to you . . . the wherewithal by which you may be able to pursue this your holy and laudable work [conversion], pleasant to immortal God . . . and the expansion of the Christian rule."[72] Combining Columbus's descriptions of the natives' theological disposition with the prose-lytizing thematics of Petrine guardianship earlier delineated in *Romanus Pontifex*, Alexander's bull donating the New World to Spain declared:

[T]hese peoples inhabiting the said islands and lands believe that one God-Creator is in Heaven; they seem to be well fitted to embrace the Catholic faith and to be imbued with good morals; and there is hope that, were they instructed, the name of the Saviour, our Lord Jesus Christ, could be easily introduced into these lands and islands.[73]

Ferdinand and Isabella were praised by the pope for having decided "to subdue the said mainlands and islands, and their natives and inhabitants . . . , and to bring them to the Catholic faith":

[I]n order that you may embark on an enterprise of such importance more readily and audaciously, endowed with the liberality of Apostolic favour, we give, concede and assign to you . . . by the authority of Almighty God bestowed upon blessed Peter and by the Vicariate of Jesus Christ which we discharge on earth—all the islands and main-lands, found or to be found, discovered or to be discovered, westwards or southwards, by drawing and establishing a line running from the Arctic to the Antarctic Pole.[74]

Alexander's liberal bull invested Ferdinand and Isabella with "full, free and integral power, authority and jurisdiction," and forbade any other person to approach Spain's newly recognized possessions or future possessions for pur-poses of trade or for any other reason. The familiar and effective sanction of excommunication backed up the papal grant of title and jurisdiction.

Alexander's papal donation provided Spain with what it considered to be a secure title to Columbus's discoveries in the West. No Christian European monarch, at least in the pre-Reformation era, dared to interfere with Spain's papally conferred rights without risking excommunication. The path was now clear for Spain to carry out its papal mandate to colonize, civilize, and Christianize the "well-disposed" inhabitants of the New World.

Instruments of Empire

Governor Columbus

The first colonizing expedition to the New World was led by Columbus on his second voyage to the "Indies" in November 1493. The men who sailed with Columbus on that voyage were all salaried employees of the Crown, but, like their Italian governor, they carried their own visions of attaining wealth and independent *hidalgo* (landed gentry) status in a land free of the social barriers existing in feudal Spain.[75]

Under the terms of his royal contract,[76] Columbus was to keep one-tenth of the wealth realized in his partnership with the Crown. Upon landing on the

Caribbean island that he had christened Hispaniola, the first European colonial governor in the New World immediately set out to establish the type of
mercantile colonial institutions that had first been perfected ʊ v the Italians in
the Levant and in Africa. Mining and trading for gold were to be the principal
activities of the fortified *factorias* on the island.

Columbus had originally estimated that there was more gold on the islands
"than iron in the Biscay."[77] Spanish technology for locating gold-bearing rock
was primitive, however, so barter was the principal means of obtaining the
mineral during the first years of the Hispaniola settlement. As the food supply
on Hispaniola and surrounding islands failed to meet the needs of the burgeoning Spanish colonial population, Columbus tapped native food sources. This
action, along with the sometimes violent pressures on the "well-disposed"
Indians to provide more gold through barter, led to a breakdown in Indian–
Spanish relations. In February 1495, Columbus violently suppressed an Indian
revolt with 500 conquistadores. As his original estimates of mineral wealth
were proving dismally incorrect, Columbus decided to export the island's only
other worthwhile commodity. Five hundred of the 1,500 Indians captured by
the Spanish were sent to Spain as slaves. To maximize production of what gold
could be found on the island, Columbus instituted a coerced-labor policy,
backed effectively by Spanish arms, cavalry, and dogs. The governor also set
up a feudally inspired tribute system whereby the Indian tribal *caciques* (headmen) were to ensure that each Indian male delivered 25 ducats' worth of gold
on a quarterly basis to the Spanish *factorias*. A line of blockhouses was
established to enforce this system of involuntary tribute.

When significant amounts of gold were finally discovered on Hispaniola in
1499, the ensuing large-scale pit mining created huge demands for manual
labor. Columbus thereupon established a wider-ranging system of forced
labor, "commending" squads of Indians to those Spanish mine owners who
had successfully courted or bought the royal governor's favor. Thousands of
Indians died in resistance or in the mines.

It is worth noting that Columbus, a Genoese merchant sailor well schooled
in Portuguese colonizing techniques, would have been thoroughly comfortable
with the policy of enslaving uncooperative barbarous peoples. Like the *factoria*
institution carried by Columbus from the medieval to the New World, slavery
was also part of the mercantile-colonizing knowledge perfected by the Genoese
during the Crusading era and then brought to Portugal. Italians had been
harvesting sugar with Muslim and other slaves throughout their Levantine
colonies since the twelfth century. The Genoese transferred the institution of
plantation-style slave labor to southern Portugal in the early fifteenth century.
By mid-century the Portuguese colonies in the Azores and Madeiras were
being run by the Genoese using African slaves.[78]

Queen Isabella apparently thought little of Columbus's transatlantic application of these Genoese-Portuguese techniques in her Spanish colonial empire.
Thoroughly incensed by what she considered to be gross arrogations of privilege under the royal contract, the queen terminated Columbus's governorship

in 1500. Reportedly, the queen asked by what right the captain enslaved subjects entrusted to her care by the papacy.[79]

Thus the first great slavemaster sent by the Old World to the New World, the celebrated Admiral of the Ocean Sea, Christopher Columbus returned to Europe in disrepute. He died in ignominy, his contemporaries registering their disapproval by honoring *his* discoveries with the name of another who merely followed him, Amerigo Vespucci. The career of Columbus, in fact, illustrates poignantly the debilitating retrograde impulses of the medieval discourses brought to the New World by the Spanish colonizing experience. Columbus, the medieval man who stumbled upon that world, died thinking he had found a new route to Japan.[80]

The Encomienda

The queen's dismissal of her governor suggests that she recognized that Columbus's actions could have seriously jeopardized Spain's interests in the enterprise of the Indies. If a future pope should ever interpret Spain's actions as inconsistent with the papal bulls of guardianship granting the license to convert the natives to Christianity,[81] Spanish rights of conquest in the region could be suspended. Such an action would not have been unprecedented. Pope Eugenius IV, it will be remembered, reacting to reports of abuse perpetrated by Christian Europeans against the Canarians, banned all further European exploitation of the islands in 1434.[82] The Crown's canon lawyers would surely have been aware of this precedent.[83]

The Crown immediately sent a new governor, Nicolás de Ovando, who arrived on the island in 1501. Ovando's royal mandate included removal of all Indians from Spanish enslavement and the imposition of more centralized control over the activities of the colony. Supervision and a fixed tribute deducted from the Indians' daily wages were to be immediately transferred to the Crown. In attempting to institute these orders, however, the Crown's new governor met intense resistance from Spanish colonists not used to interference from a distant king. The Spaniards in Hispaniola had quickly amassed fortunes from a transplanted feudal system nourished by Indian slaves. Realizing that this new, privileged, managerial class was essential to the success of the colonial endeavor, the Crown withdrew its orders and instructed Governor Ovando to readopt the *encomienda*, the practice of "commending" groups of Indian slaves to worthy Spaniards.[84]

The Crown's lawyers who drafted the royal cedula formally instituting the *encomienda* system justified the enslavement of the Indians by express reference to the terms of Spain's papal grant. The pope's bequest of title in 1493 mandated that the Indians be Christianized and "civilized" by the Spanish Crown. Only by forcibly denying the Indians their freedom and appropriating their labor could the civilizing task of assimilation be carried out. Ferdinand's royal order read in part: "Because of the excessive liberty the Indians have been permitted, they flee from Christians and do not work. Therefore they are to be compelled to work, so that the kingdom and the Spaniards may be enriched, and the Indians Christianized."[85]

This royal order reveals the eruption of a new theme in Iberian colonizing discourse. King Duarte of Portugal, in his appeal to the papacy in 1436 for permission to colonize and convert the Canarians, had apparenlty felt constrained from even suggesting that worldly profit motivated his desire for a papal license to conquer the Canarians. His efforts were intended, he wrote Pope Eugenius, "more indeed for the salvation of the souls of the pagans of the islands than for his own personal gain, for there was nothing for him to gain."[86] Some seventy years later, as Ferdinand's order indicates, the Spanish Crown evidently did not feel inhibited by medieval taboos prohibiting such discussion of a profit motive where Church jurisdiction was implicated.[87] The medieval thesis that infidels could be conquered for unreasonably refusing to be converted had been adulterated by a more modern prejudice, most likely originating in the burgeoning Iberian mercantile discourses. Under the vision of the *encomienda*, coerced labor created the ideal conditions for Christianization and civilization of the Indian. No longer were Christian princes required to suppress discussion of worldly profit when expressing concerns respecting the heavenly salvation of barbarous peoples. The Indians' enslavement for the benefit of a worldly Christian kingdom complemented the goal of the Indian's attainment of a heavenly kingdom. The *encomienda* thus embodied the ironic thesis that in administering the pope's Petrine responsibility to save the Indians, the Spanish Crown had to enslave them.

The *encomienda* system was quickly established throughout the Spanish New World. Usually an *encomienda* consisted of a group of Indian villages "commended" to an individual Spaniard, the *encomendero*. The *encomendero*, in turn, undertook the legal obligations of military service to the Crown, instruction and protection of his Indians, and maintenance of clergy in the villages. The *encomendero* supported his household with tribute from his Indian charges, usually in the form of servile labor. Villages not assigned to individual Spaniards were managed by royally appointed officials. The wage assessments on such villages were paid directly to the Crown. This direct form of tribute came to be legally defined as the *repartimiento*.[88]

From the Crown's perspective, the *repartimiento* was a more politically satisfying and less troublesome arrangement than the *encomienda*. Although both originated in royal prerogative, the creation of individual *encomenderos* served only to institutionalize an archaic and obstreperous feudal mentality in the Spanish New World. Attempts to diminish or abrogate royal grants of privilege always encountered resistance, and the *encomendero* class incesssantly pressured the Crown to make such grants permanent and inheritable.

The elevation of nearly all the Spanish colonists to petty *hidalgo* status by grants of Indian slaves illustrates the nature of the pressures felt by the Crown, despite its own centralizing preferences, to maintain a cooperative and loyal managerial presence in the colony. The extent of that loyalty was directly related to the supply of Indian slaves available to meet both royal and colonial demands for labor in the mines. Conflict between the colonists and the Crown inevitably erupted each time Ferdinand, sole monarch following his wife's death in 1504, either attempted to increase his own share of Indian slaves (estimated at 15 percent of the Indian labor supply) or offered absentee *encomiendas* to political figures in Spain as a means of cementing domestic alliances.[89]

Regardless of the source of demand, whether Crown or colonist, the supply of Indian slaves was diminishing at an ever-quickening rate. Ange Debo has estimated that the indigenous population of Hispaniola alone was reduced from 250,000 to less than 15,000 in the first two decades of Spanish colonial enslavement, as Indians either fled the conquistadores or died in the mines. Similar declines are reported in other regions of Spanish America in the early sixteenth century. On many Caribbean islands entire Indian populations disappeared.[90]

The Dominicans in the New World

It was in response to the rapid declines in Indian population that a quiescent Spanish Church finally awoke to the moral implications of the expanding Indian slave trade in the New World. Religious influence in the Caribbean had been insignificant during the first two decades of Spain's colonizing efforts. The first friary in the New World was not even constructed until 1503, at Santo Domingo by the Franciscans. The first priests who were sent to the islands (there were never more than twenty-five Franciscans in the New World during Ovando's governorship) saw their mission as essentially serving the Spanish colonial population. They in fact avoided any extensive missionary work among the Indians. Some priests even held modest *encomiendas* of a few native slaves to supplement their meager stipends from the Crown.

Furthermore, Ferdinand's refusal to establish an episcopate in the New World until he secured papal agreement to patronage contributed to the absence of evangelical guidance during the early colonization period. It was not until 1512 that the first bishops to the New World arrived in Hispaniola. This was only after Ferdinand had finally secured full patronage through a series of papal bulls brokered in exchange for his military and political support of Rome against France.

Shortly before these bishops were sent, however, Ferdinand had been forced to introduce a highly volatile element into the Caribbean colonial environment: the Dominicans. The Dominicans—the order of Cardinal Torquemada (1420–1498)—had long been regarded as the zealous defenders of religious orthodoxy; theirs was the order most closely associated with the Spanish Inquisition. Ironically, as the order of Aquinas, they were also responsible for transmitting many of the central ideas of Thomistic Humanism in the public discourses of the relatively late-blooming Spanish Renaissance. When reports of widespread heresy among the Spanish New World population reached Castile, Ferdinand had little choice but to send the purifying emetic of fifteen Dominican friars directly to Hispaniola. Arriving on the island in 1510, the Dominicans quickly perceived the debilitating effects of Spanish rule and enslavement on the

Indian population. In that the legal principles governing Christian relations with infidels had been established in Church law by Pope Innocent IV and the Council of Constance, the Dominicans—the order of Aquinas, the Church's preeminent natural-law theorist—found the entire legality of Spain's treatment of the natives highly suspect. As guardians of Church orthodoxy and Thomistic Humanism's recognition of the natural-law rights of all humankind, the order felt bound to inquire into the nature of Spain's rule in the Indies.

The Dominican reform movement in the New World began when Friar Antonio de Montesinos delivered a rancorous sermon to the "best people" of Hispaniola, assembled in his church on the Sunday before Christmas in 1511. Speaking as a "voice crying in the wilderness," Montesinos's Thomistically inspired interrogation excoriated the assembled merchants and *encomenderos* of the island:

[Y]ou are in mortal sin, . . . you live and die in it, for the cruelty and tyranny you use in dealing with these innocent people. Tell me, by which right or justice do you keep these Indians in such a cruel and horrible servitude? On what authority have you waged a detestable war against these people . . . ? Are these not men? Have they not rational souls? Are you not bound to love them as you love yourselves?[91]

The Spaniards on the island were outraged by Montesinos's defense of the natural rights of their slaves. After the sermon, the angry colonists went to the Dominican monastery demanding an apology and disavowal of Montesinos's attack on the king's lordship of the Indies. Pedro de Cordoba, vicar on the island, refused to issue a retraction and stated that Montesinos's sermon represented the feelings of the entire Dominican community. The following Sunday, Montesinos delivered a similar sermon, threatening to withhold confession and absolution from the colonists if they continued to mistreat the Indians.[92]

Upon hearing of the sermon, Ferdinand immediately threatened to return the disruptive Dominicans to Spain "because every hour that they remain in the islands holding such wrong ideas . . . will do much harm."[93] Ferdinand had apparently grasped the essential issue of the entire controversy. The very legality of the Spanish New World enterprise had been called into question by Montesinos and his order, at a time when Ferdinand and his advisors had concluded that the Crown would have to commission new expeditions to other regions of the Caribbean to search for more sources of slave labor for the mines. If the Dominicans persisted in their challenge to the right of Spaniards to enslave the natives, the zealous priests might even be emboldened to take their complaints to Rome, an embarrassing and threatening situation that Ferdinand obviously preferred to avoid.

The Laws of Burgos

Montesinos himself was apparently not intimidated by royal displeasure. Such were the benefits of clergy in the era of inquisition. He voluntarily returned to

Castile to report his order's list of grievances regarding the mistreatment of Indians. His account of the genocidal fury of the Spanish colonists and conquistadores forced Ferdinand immediately to convene a council, composed principally of royalist theologians and canon-law scholars who served the king and his interests. The council met at the Spanish town of Burgos in 1512 and devoted much of its attention to the crucial question of whether the Indians could be saved only by being enslaved.[94]

One of the king's own official preachers, Friar Bernardo de Mesa, was an important participant in the deliberations. He argued that despite the natives' freedom, the Indians' greatest vice was their idleness. The king thus had the duty to "curb their vicious inclinations and compel them to industry." As absolute liberty was injurious to the Indians, Friar Bernardo argued that some form of servitude was a moral necessity. The royal preacher's position was, of course, a defense of the legal basis of the King's existing *encomienda* system.[95]

The licentiate Gregorio was another royal preacher who participated in the council's debates. Like Friar Bernardo, Gregorio argued that the Indians did have to be enslaved in order to be saved. As was common among the proponents of Spanish slave colonialism, the licentiate applied the Aristotelian notion of natural slavery to the Indians. They were of that class of people set aside by nature as slaves to serve that part of humankind (such as the Spanish) destined to be masters.

Besides royalist clerics possessed by the nascent nationalist sensibility of Ferdinand's court, those who usually advanced the idea that the Indians were slaves by nature were those most likely to benefit directly from actualizing the proposition: the Spanish colonists themselves. These émigrés to the New World, in the words of the preeminent English-language historian of the era, Lewis Hanke, had inherited a "distaste for physical labour from their medieval forefathers who had struggled for centuries to free Spain from the Moslems." Hanke illustrates this thesis with the story of the town fathers of Buenos Aires, who "once informed the King that affairs were so bad there that Spaniards actually had to dig in the earth and plant crops if they were to eat."[96]

This negative Eurocentric discourse of difference dominated the discussions of Indian capacity and character at the Burgos Council. Meeting more than twenty times, the council heard extended testimony regarding the Indians' lack of reason, which mandated the diminution of their right to freedom under natural law. Seven basic propositions were drafted to serve as the basis for future Spanish colonial legislation. The propositions recognized Indian "freedom" and the right to humane treatment, but they also stressed the overriding necessity of forcibly establishing conditions whereby the Indians could be inculcated with the virtues of Christianity and civilization.[97]

The actual Laws of Burgos, the legislative code promulgated on the basis of the council's seven propositions, reflected a Eurocentrically determined vision of Indian normative divergence requiring the natives' subjugation and remediation, by peaceful means where possible but by forceful means where necessary.[98] As one section of the Burgos code declared:

Should the natives attempt to oppose the settlement [of a colony], they shall be given to understand that the intention in forming it, is to teach them to know God and his holy law, by which they are to be saved; to preserve friendship with them, and teach them to live in a civilized state. . . . They shall be convinced of this by mild means, through the interference of religion and priests, . . . and if, notwithstanding, they do withhold their consent, the settlers . . . shall proceed to make their settlement . . . without doing them any greater damage than shall be necessary.[99]

The code regulated nearly every aspect of Indian group life. Indian tribal culture was formally relegated to a deficient, diminished legal status, to be reshaped according to Christian European ethical, political, and social norms. Total assimilation of the Indian to the European's truth became the official colonial policy of the Spanish Crown. Affirming the *encomienda* system as being "in agreement with divine and human law,"[100] the Burgos code detailed the responsibilities of the *encomendero*. Indians were to be relocated in new villages closer to the civilizing influence of the Spaniards. The natives' old dwellings were to be destroyed "so that they might lose the longing to return to them."[101] Churches and religious instruction were to be provided, children baptized, marriage encouraged, and nakedness forbidden. Sons of Indian *caciques* were to be entrusted to Franciscan missionaries for four years of intense religious and secular education. All other Indians were compelled to give nine months of service each year to individual Spaniards in order to "prevent their living in idleness and to assure their learning to live and govern themselves like Christians."[102] The laws legitimated outright appropriation of Indian resources and labor as a means to facilitate the overarching goal of assimilation. Because the Indians' normative divergence was proof positive of an irrational incapacity, the Indians' consent to be ruled was logically irrelevant to the drafters of the code. The pope's divinely instituted guardianship administered by Spain over the Indians necessarily excluded the possibility of their capacity to consent or dissent in rational fashion.

The Requerimiento

The deliberations at Burgos in 1512 reopened an issue that the Spanish Crown had considered long settled: the formal basis of Spain's right to conquer and rule in the Indies. As late as 1511, King Ferdinand had firmly indicated the Crown's views on the papal foundations of its just title to the Indies. Ferdinand instructed the governor of Hispaniola to baptize the island's Indians and instruct them in "our holy Catholic faith, for this is the principal foundation upon which we base our conquest of these regions."[103] The Crown had frequently defended the justice of its New World empire on the basis of Pope Alexander's 1493 grant of title. In reprimanding the Dominicans on Hispaniola for Montesinos's sermon, for instance, Ferdinand ordered that the friars be shown the papal donation "in case they had not been informed of the right by which we hold these islands or the justifications by which these Indians not only should serve as they do but also might be held in more slavery."[104]

Ferdinand also adopted the practice of referring to himself as "perpetual administrator by apostolic authority" of the Indies.[105] Isabella's last will and testament espoused similar views.[106]

Naturally, this official consensus on the legitimacy of the papal basis of Spanish title was shared by those who principally benefited from Alexander's papal grant, the Spanish colonists and governing officials. Columbus himself had defended the Crown's claims in the Indies on the basis of the 1493 bulls. In a letter addressed to a rebellious Spanish colonist, Francisco Roldan, Governor Columbus pointed out the need for the Spaniards to avoid mistreating the Indians:

The very ample bull granted by the most holy pontiff Alexander VI to the Catholic Kings to conquer new countries was not given with the intention that the new people should be ill-treated but that they should be well rewarded so as to attract them to the holy faith of Christ the Savior.[107]

The discussions at Burgos, however, had permitted doubts to arise about the precise nature of the Crown's rights under its grant from the pope. The council had met in the same year that Ferdinand had finally ended his long-running feud with the papacy over the critical issue of the right to nominate his own Spanish bishops.[108] The predominantly royalist members of the Burgos Council, all selected by Ferdinand, naturally supported the Crown's position on this vital issue of national sovereignty. The more astute theoreticians at the council perhaps noted the inconsistency of defending the Crown's rights against Rome respecting the issue of Spanish prelatial patronage, while defending the Crown's rights in the Indies on the basis of an unbridled theory of papal paramountcy.

Ferdinand, however, apparently preferred the inconsistency to remain unresolved, in the absence of any other privileged form of legal discourse grounding his imperial rights in the New World. Although the discourse of papal universal jurisdiction had certainly lost much of its authority inside the Renaissance courts of Christian Europe, it retained some usefulness in restraining the aggrandizing aspirations of several European nation-states. Rome's sanctioning power in the early sixteenth century (Luther would not arrive on the European scene with his protest against the selling of indulgences until 1517) still carried considerable weight in intra-European affairs, particularly in Portugal, Spain's neighbor and most serious commercial and colonial rival. Thus, to rebut any legal attacks from inside or outside Spain on his right to rule in the Indies, Ferdinand requested supporting commentaries on the legitimacy of the papal basis of Spain's New World titles from at least two lawyer-scholars loyal to the Crown, the Dominican Matías de Paz (1468/70–1524) and the jurisconsult Juan López de Palacios Rubios (1450–1524).

Paz, the Dominican, was a professor of theology at the University of Salamanca, the center of Spanish legal learning and training in the sixteenth century. Upon receiving Ferdinand's request, he hurriedly composed a scholastic treatise concerning the rule of the king of Spain over the Indies. Commenting on the "doubts which some ecclesiastics have raised concerning the dominion of Our Catholic and Invincible King over the Indians,"[109] Paz's tract relied heavily on papal hierocratic ideology to defend Spain's actions in the New World. According to Paz, the pope enjoyed temporal jurisdiction over all the world, and all powers and rights of dominion held by heathens belonged to the pope, to whom supreme dominion had been delegated by Christ. Spain's title, therefore, unquestionably derived from Pope Alexander VI's grant:

Only by authorization of the Pope will it be lawful for the King to govern these Indians politically and annex them forever to his crown. . . . Once they are converted, it will be lawful, as is the case in all political rule, to require some services from them—even greater services than are exacted from Christians in Spain, so long as they are reasonable—to cover the travel costs and other expenses connected with the maintenance of peace and good administration of those distant provinces.[110]

Paz's uncompromising assertion that all powers and rights of dominion held by heathens belonged to the pope would seem to indicate that the extreme hierocratic thesis on infidel *dominium* condemned a century earlier at Constance had been revived and rehabilitated in Spanish Discovery-era legal commentary. Paz discreetly failed to note a prior generation's negative judgments on the canonical integrity of the Alanian and Hostiensian position denying infidel natural rights. In Renaissance imperial Spain, the court savants apparently did not hesitate to rummage dutifully through the detritus of the medieval legal corpus in order to sustain their monarch's imperial will.

Juan López de Palacios Rubios, one of the most respected jurists of his day, was the other loyal scholar asked by Ferdinand to draft an opinion on the Crown's title. A staunch royalist, López had previously composed the Crown's official apologia for the Spanish conquest of Navarre. The work was thoroughly infused with hierocratic themes, condemning the Navarrese ruler as a rebel against the authority of the pope and the Church. Ferdinand's attack on Navarre was justified on the basis of two papal bulls authorizing the confiscation of all goods seized in the "very holy, very just war." López's most famous work, a set of commentaries on the laws of Toro, was essentially an absolutist tract declaring that to doubt the will of one's prince constituted sacrilege.[111]

López's treatise, "Of the Ocean Isles," sought to remove all doubt about Ferdinand's rights, arguing that Spain's title in the New World was based solely on papal grant. Unlike the more extreme hierocratic thesis put forward by Paz, however, López's argument was based primarily on Innocentian and Thomistic premises. López was at least eighteen years older than Paz, and was therefore closer to the age of Constance and its teachings than to Columbus and the conquistadores. "Of the Ocean Isles" adhered to the canonically correct view of Innocent that infidels possessed natural-law rights to *dominium* but that the pope could withdraw those rights by virtue of his indirect temporal jurisdiction. The pope maintained a responsibility for the care of the infidels' immortal souls—a responsibility that he could delegate to Christian Crusading princes, who then rightfully assumed the duty of subjugation, control, and remediation of the infidels.

López, given his more naturalistic viewpoint, was far more concerned than his younger colleague Paz by the troubling implications of an unmediated theory of pontifical universal sovereignty. López argued that with respect to infidels, the pope possessed the right to insist on punishment only for violations of natural law. The Crown, however, possessed the unequaled right, in López's words, to "enact rules of law . . . by virtue of its supreme power which is inherent in the very marrow of the kingdom."[112]

At a time when Ferdinand was striving to defend other interests of the Crown against papal encroachments, López recognized the corrosive threat to royal autonomy posed by a constitutional theory in which Rome was the sole originating source of legitimacy for every aspect of Spanish rule in the Indies. López thus attempted to limit the reach of papal jurisdiction in the Indies by reserving to Rome only a right to insist on the enforcement of natural law. Constitutionally, only the secular Christian king could enact the positive laws required to punish papally proclaimed violations of natural law—a power that resided in the king alone by virtue of his unquestioned sovereignty over his kingdom.[113]

The learned opinions of Paz and López on the validity of Spain's papally based titles assured the Crown of its legal rights in the Indies. In 1513 Ferdinand convened a group of theologians and scholars to draft regulations for future royal conquests. López was assigned the task of drawing up the formal document of Spanish conquest, entitled the *Requerimiento*.

Unlike López's earlier treatise, the *Requerimiento* did not contain extended discussions of neglected Innocentian subtleties on the nature of papal secular power or the Indians' natural-law rights. The *Requerimiento* was intended as a charter of conquest. Accordingly, it informed the Indians in the simplest terms that they could either accept Christian missionaries and Spanish imperial hegemony or be annihilated.[114]

The *Requerimiento* had to be read aloud to any group of Indians newly discovered by Spanish conquistadores before hostilities could legally be commenced against them. The text of the royal order informing the natives of their natural-law obligation to hear the gospel began with a Christian version of the history of the world, along with an extended discussion of the establishment and Petrine foundations of the Roman pontiff. God had given charge of all the nations of the world to St. Peter, the first pope. He was lord and superior to all humankind, and all should obey him wherever they may live, under whatever law, sect, or belief, for God had given him and his successors the entire "world for his kingdom and jurisdiction." The Indians were informed that the pope was an "Admirable Great Father and Governor of all Men," Christians, Moors, Jews, and gentiles.

The *Requerimiento* next told the Indians that Pope Alexander, one of the great pontiffs who had succeeded St. Peter as lord of the world, had made a "donation" of their territories to the king and queen of Spain. The natives could of course inspect the writings "which passed upon the subject . . . if you wish."[115]

The Indians were then politely asked to take a few moments to ponder this new set of facts. They were also told that they were nonetheless required (hence the title of the document, the *Requerimiento*) "to acknowledge the Church as the ruler and superior of the whole world, and the high priest called Pope, and in his name the king and queen . . . in his place, as superiors and lords and kings" of their countries by virtue of the pope's donation.[116]

If the Indians did not consent and permit the missionary fathers accompanying the conquistadores to preach to them, or if they "maliciously" delayed in doing so, the Spaniards, "with the help of God," would invade their country and make war against them. They were further threatened with subjection to the "yoke and obedience of the Church and of their highnesses":

[W]e shall take you and your wives and your children and shall make slaves of them, and as such shall sell and dispose of them as their highnesses may command; and we shall take away your goods and shall do to you all the harm and damage that we can, as to vassals who do not obey and refuse to receive their lord and resist and contradict him.[117]

The natives were also warned that any "deaths and losses which shall accrue" from the Spaniards' attack on them would be their own fault for failing to heed the *Requerimiento*'s directives, "and not that of their highnesses or of these soldiers."[118]

Theoretically, the *Requerimiento*'s declaration of war following the Indians' refusal to permit missionary priests to enter their lands accorded with the fundamental principles of Innocentian doctrine on infidel rights. Innocent had specifically stated in *Quod super his* that a refusal by heathen peoples to admit Christian missionaries into their countries authorized papal remediative measures exercised through the offices of crusading Christian princes.[119]

In practice, however, the conquistadores' application of this Innocentian principle revealed a frightening gap between law on the books in the Old World and law in action in the New World. Hanke, the English-language authority on the *Requerimiento*, has summarized the history of the required announcement to the Indians as follows:

A complete list of the events that occurred when the Requirement formalities ordered by King Ferdinand were carried out in America, more or less according to the law, might tax the reader's patience and credulity, for the Requirement was read to trees and empty huts when no Indians were to be found. Captains muttered its theological phrases into their beard on the edge of sleeping Indian settlements, or even a league away before starting the formal attack, and at times some leather-lunged Spanish notary hurled its sonorous phrases after the Indians as they fled into the mountains. Once it was read in camp before the soldiers to the beat of the drum. Ship captains would sometimes have the document read from the deck as they approached an island, and at night would send out enslaving expeditions, whose leaders would shout the traditional Castilian war cry "Santiago!" rather than read the Requirement before they attacked the near-by villages. Sometimes Indian messengers were sent to "require" other Indians.[120]

Whether or not the Indians comprehended the alien vision of the *Requerimiento* or the ultimatum it contained, Spain relied on that document as the official legitimating basis of its right to conquer and rule throughout the

Americas. Subsequent papal legislation intended to protect the Indians, given such prominence in the apologias of historians and legal scholars, went unnoted in the jungles of Mexico, Peru, and the other outposts of the sixteenth-century Spanish colonial frontier.[121]

The Italian Humanist Peter Martyr, who served on the Royal Council of the Indies while most of the conquistadores' acts of genocide were being carried out, diagnosed the failure of Spanish Indian policy as follows:

All these instructions have been thought out by prudent and humane jurisconsults and sanctioned by religious men. But what of that? When our compatriots reach that remote world, so far away and so removed from us . . . they find themselves distant from any judge. Carried away by love of gold, they become ravenous wolves instead of gentle lambs, and heedless of royal instructions.[122]

Not until 1556 did the Spanish Crown formally abolish the useless legalisms of the *Requerimiento* and declare the Spanish colonial effort a "missionary enterprise," as opposed to a military conquest. But by that time, of course, as the historian Robert Berkhofer has noted, "The Spanish had conquered most of the major population groups worth exploiting according to their customary methods. Though the kings of Spain espoused a new theory of empire, they never reduced their territorial or jurisdictional claims over the New World or its inhabitants."[123] Law, which Europeans have long revered as their instrument of civilization, became the West's perfect instrument of empire in the heart of darkness that was America.

Victoria's "On the Indians Lately Discovered"

The Inquisitions into Indian Capacity

From a legal perspective, Spain's instruments of empire—such as the *encomienda*, the Laws of Burgos, and the *Requerimiento*—institutionalized and rationalized the papally derived legitimating foundations of the Crown's Indian policy. To radical reformers such as Friar Montesinos and his fellow Dominicans, however, Spain's imperial institutions were "perverse, unjust, and tyrannical,"[124] designed to mask Spanish barbarity. This growing party of dissenters based their opposition to Spanish rule in the New World on the central tenet of Thomistic-Humanist philosophy that all humans possessed the common element of reason. This divine gift gave all individuals, Christians and non-Christians alike, the natural-law right and duty to order their political and social lives by rational means. Spanish colonial law in the New World, however, steadfastly denied the Indians any effective right to self-rule and autonomy. To Humanist-inspired radical reformers, therefore, Spain's colonial regime in the Indies appeared irrefutably opposed to natural and divine law. Dubiously legitimated by papal grant and violently sustained by Indian enslavement, Spain's empire was the subject of intense inquisition by Spanish Humanists in both the New World and the Old.

Many of the principal discursive attacks on Spain's rule in the Indies were voiced by the various missionary orders sent to the New World. Particularly where complaints were voiced by the Dominican order, the vanguard of Catholic orthodoxy and the Inquisition, the Crown had little choice but to appease the missionaries. During the early decades of the sixteenth century, Humanist-minded priests in the Indies prevailed on the king's conscience and obtained orders licensing official inquiries and experiments directed toward reforming the basic character of Spanish colonial rule.

The official inquiries conducted in the New World focused on the Indians' capacity to comprehend the gospel and to order their lives according to "civilized" Spanish norms of conduct. To Spanish Humanist thought of the sixteenth century, both abilities were integrally related, as the habits and usages of "civilization" provided the ideal conditions for the reception of the Christian message. Thus one famous inquiry conducted by the Jeronymite friars in 1517 asked the Spanish inhabitants of Hispaniola the following series of questions respecting the Indian's rational capacity:

Does the witness know, believe, or has he heard it said, or observed, that these Indians, . . . women as well as men, are all of such knowledge and capacity that they should be given complete liberty? Would they be able to live *políticamente* as do the Spaniards? Would they know how to support themselves by their own efforts, each Indian mining gold or tilling the soil, or maintaining himself by other daily labor? Do they know how to care for what they may acquire by this labor, spending only for necessities, as a Castilian laborer would?[125]

The Spanish colonists and colonial officials who most benefited from Indian slavery were of course the most forceful and persistent voices arguing against the Indians' rational capacity in these official inquiries. Their most influential spokesman was the royal officer and official historian of the Spanish court, Gonzalo Fernández de Oviedo y Valdes.

Oviedo had sailed to the New World as a notary and inspector. His official duties included the branding of native slaves. For his efforts on behalf of the Crown, he was paid 1 *tomín* of gold for each Indian branded. In one of his official "Histories" of the Spanish conquest of the Indies, Oviedo described the Indians as naturally lazy, vicious, melancholic, and cowardly. The savages of the New World, in his opinion, were in general a lying and shiftless people and were totally unredeemable:

Their marriages are not a sacrament but a sacrilege. They are idolatrous, libidinous, and commit sodomy. Their chief desire is to eat, drink, worship heathen idols, and commit bestial obscenities. What could one expect from a people whose skulls are so thick and hard that the Spaniards had to take care in fighting not to strike on the head lest their swords be blunted?[126]

Oviedo and other advocates of Indian incapacity relied on Indian slave labor for their livelihoods and bases of power and patronage. Having witnessed how poorly the Indians responded to the civilizing opportunities provided by the *encomienda*, they were convinced by their own experience that they had the better arguments. The Indians were slaves by nature, an empirically proven fact that rebutted the priests' unverifiable faith in a universal human reason. Thus the New World inquisitions into Indian capacity normally ended inconclusively, with each side trading anecdotes and assertions in a political contest of wills over who would possess that part of the Indian deemed most important. The priests sought the Indians' souls; the slavers required only their bodies. A debate proved a poor forum for adjudicating such incompatible possessory rights.

But this was not the only forum in which the capacity of the Indian was analyzed. In order to rebut the self-fulfilling prophecy of the Spanish *encomenderos* that the enslaved Indians were slaves by nature, the missionaries prevailed on the Crown to license various "experiments." These ventures were carried out predominantly by Dominican missionaries to determine the ideal conditions under which the Indian could be civilized to live as a Castilian laborer would. The priests who carried out these experiments normally insisted that the Crown provide isolated areas for their utopian efforts, "far from the sight and sound of Spaniards interested in gold."[127]

The logic of these priestly Humanist-inspired experiments proceeded from the argument that while the Crown justified enslaving the natives because of their unregenerated idolatry and backwardness, the Crown's agents were acting no less barbarously toward them. The Indians were capable of living in a civilized fashion and comprehending the message of the gospel, but not while the Spaniards continued to brutalize them as slaves.[128]

Perhaps the most famous of all the priestly experimenters was the Dominican friar Bartolomé de Las Casas. In 1518 Las Casas, designated by the Crown as protector of the Indians, secured a royal order authorizing the establishment of villages of free Indians in the New World. The Indians were to direct their own affairs in a civilized, "political way like Spaniards."[129] This idea of *reducción*—the establishment of isolated missionary communities to protect the Indians from slavery (and to concentrate and economize proselytizing efforts)—was to become the principal vehicle by which the priestly missionaries pursuing their Church's own peculiar will to empire sought to frustrate the self-fulfilling prophecy of Indian degeneracy that legitimated Spanish American slave colonialism.

The priestly experimenters in their turn failed to resolve definitively the issue of whether the Indians were slaves by nature. Indian indifference or resistance sufficiently frustrated the Humanist priests' efforts to inculcate the religious beliefs and acquisitive values that supposedly motivated the Castilian laborer. Tribal culture, religious beliefs, and social organization could be dismantled by the missionaries, but could never be fully penetrated. Humanism's naturalistic emphasis on individual reason failed to provide many useful insights into the Indians and the radical divergent nature of their tribal existence in the New World.[130]

Like the conquistadores and *encomenderos*, the priests could not view the Indian as other than a supplement to more imperative, European-defined goals. As Hanke has remarked, "Nowhere, during or after these experiments, was there any recognition in official or ecclesiastical circles that the attempt to impose Spanish institutions upon the Indians might be just as deadly to them as the firearms and hunting dogs of the conquistadores."[131] Whether with the worst or best of intentions, and whether through policies of extermination or forced conversions, the Spaniards who brought the burdens of European civilization to the Indians ultimately succeeded only in erasing a multiplicity of cultures and beliefs from the New World. Such was the unseen by-product of a discourse of conquest enforcing a vision of the world focused on one right way of life for all humankind.

Franciscus de Victoria

While the inquisitions into Indian capacity proceeded in the New World, other Humanist-inspired thinkers inside Spain engaged in more formal, theoretical speculations on Indian rights. Throughout Renaissance Spain, the lawyers and theologians who dominated the Catholic universities produced a voluminous, Thomistically inspired literature on a wide range of Humanist topics, especially on the question of the justice of Spanish rule in the Americas. Two themes were central to this newly emergent form of Spanish political and legal discourse: the rejection of papal claims to universal secular jurisdiction and the application of Thomistic natural-law principles to all human relationships, especially relationships between nations.

To the Spanish Renaissance theologian or canon lawyer of the sixteenth century, the two themes were integrally related. Ferdinand's successful struggle with Rome to control patronage and thereby nationalize Spain's episcopate more explicitly harmonized the interests of the Spanish Church and state. The ascendancy in 1519 of King Charles I of Spain (1516–1556) to the position of Holy Roman Emperor as Charles V (1519–1556) intensified the shared resistance of the Spanish secular and ecclesiastical hierarchies to Rome's attempted usurpations of jurisdictional authority inside Spain or its empire.[132] Thomistic Humanism's naturalistic basis provided a ready-made rationalization for the claims of the Spanish Crown and national episcopate to a natural and autonomous right of existence, related to, but jurisdictionally separate from, pontifical authority.

The most important and influential of the Spanish Thomistic Humanist theorists in the early sixteenth-century was Franciscus de Victoria (1480–1546), a Dominican scholar and the first Spanish thinker to apply systematically the full implications of Thomistic natural-law discourse to Spain's treatment of the Indians of America.[133] His lectures on Indian rights are widely recognized as a primary source of the basic principles of post-sixteenth-century Spanish colonial legal theory as well as of the treatment of indigenous colonized peoples under modern international and United States law.[134] Perhaps even more important, in applying Thomistic natural-law discourse to the question of the legal rights of the Indians, Victoria inaugurated the first critical steps toward a totalizing jurisprudence of international order—a Law of Nations intended to regulate all aspects of the relationships between independent states. This singular innovation on Victoria's part initiated the process by which the

European state system's legal discourse was ultimately liberated from its stulti-fying, expressly theocentric, medievalized moorings and was adapted to the rationalizing demands of Renaissance Europe's secularized will to empire.[135]

Victoria held the *prima* chair in theology at the University of Salamanca from 1526 until his death in 1546. He was a noted authority and frequent lecturer on Aquinas and was thoroughly conversant with biblical, canonical, classical, and civilian sources. There were political dimensions to Victoria's position as the leading *Dominican* theologian at the leading center of learning in all of Spain. His opinion on any vital theological or legal issue would carry considerable weight in a culture where sacred and profane truth and knowl-edge had not yet been completely differentiated. Victoria, in fact, was fre-quently called on as an advisor to the Spanish Crown. As just one instance, his opinion was sought by Emperor Charles when King Henry VIII of England sought to nullify the marriage that he had contracted with Charles's aunt, Catherine of Aragon, an action of immense international import.[136]

Victoria's Lecture

Victoria's most important work on Indian rights was a three-part lecture delivered in 1532 and entitled "On the Indians Lately Discovered."[137] This lecture, which was not published until 1557, was the first work by a major Spanish Renaissance writer to embrace the full implications of the Thomistic Humanist idea that a natural-law connection existed between all nations from which arose a system of mutual social rights and duties. From this point of view, international law was conceived of as mutually binding on all nations still in a state of nature by virtue of their sovereignty, and was binding on them in exactly the same way as the prepolitical law of nature had been binding on individuals when they also lived in a state of nature.[138]

In applying this Thomistic idea of a natural-law connection between states to Spain's conquests in the Americas, Victoria developed three fundamental arguments that later Humanist and Enlightenment theorists on international law adopted essentially intact as the accepted European Law of Nations on American Indian rights and status:

1. The inhabitants of the Americas possessed natural legal rights as free and rational people.
2. The pope's grant to Spain of title to the Americas was "baseless" and could not affect the inherent rights of the Indian inhabitants.
3. Transgressions of the universally binding norms of the Law of Nations by the Indians might serve to justify a Christian nation's conquest and colonial empire in the Americas.

Despite the liberative Humanist-inspired impulses contained in his lectures on Indian rights, Victoria was no radical proto-egalitarian seeking ultimately to free the Indian from Spanish Christian hegemony. His discursive practice was thoroughly medieval in its totalizing trajectory, desire for the plenitude of a rationalized world order, and critical focus on the Indians' normative difference. The Dominican's famous defense of Indian rights under natural law did not emancipate the Indians from the guardianship of Christian Europeans. Rather, Victoria's lectures on Indian rights achieved objectives of a larger discursive strategy. Victoria cleansed Spain's will to empire of its non-Thomistic, anti-Humanist vestiges. Having jettisoned the hierocratic papacy's exclusive mediative role in legalizing Crusades against infidels for violations of natural law, Victoria's discourse of conquest reconstructed the legal elements of a possible Spanish title in the Indies on more acceptable Thomistic Humanist foundations. These foundations stressed the autonomy of human reason and the universal obligations of a Eurocentrically constructed natural law. The savage could be conquered and colonized by Christian European nations seeking to enforce or inculcate the rational norms binding on all humankind under a natural Law of Nations.

Section 1: Assertion of the Indians' Natural Rights

In section 1 of "On the Indians Lately Discovered," Victoria drew on Greek philosophical traditions, ancient Roman concepts of natural law (*ius gentium*), Thomistic philosophy, Holy Scripture, and canon law, particularly the canonical tradition derived from Innocent IV's natural-law-based discussion of infidel rights as affirmed by the Constance Council, to argue that the Indians of the Americas were rational beings. As such, the Indians could claim the same natural rights possessed by any Christian European, including rights to property and lordship. By virtue of their natural rights to *dominium*, the Indians were thus "true owners alike in public and in private law before the advent of the Spaniards among them."[139] According to Victoria, "just like Christians, . . . neither their princes nor private persons could be despoiled of their property" without just cause.[140]

In section 1, Victoria dutifully presented the Dominican order's oft-repeated Thomistic Humanist appeal for recognition of formal equality under natural law between the Indian and the Christian European. Specifically attacking the canonical integrity of the revived teachings of Hostiensis and other medieval hierocrats who denied infidel *dominium* on the basis of nonbelief, Victoria grounded Indian property rights on the firm foundation of Christian Humanist doctrine. Repeating the Innocentian and Thomistic thesis on the natural-law rights of infidels,[141] Victoria argued:

[U]nbelief does not destroy either natural law or human law; but ownership and dominion are based either on natural law or on human law; therefore they are not destroyed by want of faith. . . . Hence it is manifest that it is not justifiable to take anything that they possess from either Saracens or Jews or other unbelievers as such, that is, because they are unbelievers; but the act would be theft or robbery no less than if it were done to Christians.[142]

Because natural law rather than grace was the basis of all *dominium*, Victoria asserted that the only just cause that could be advanced for dispossessing the Indians of their lordship or property was an evident lack of reason, since, according to Thomistic theory, "reason is a precondition of capacity for ownership in general."[143] To those colonists and their supporters who vehemently argued that the Indians and their barbarous tribal cultures did not meet European standards of reason as evidenced by their normatively divergent conduct, Victoria responded almost contemptuously: "I for the most part attribute their seeming so unintelligent and stupid to a bad and barbarous upbringing, for even among ourselves we find many peasants who differ little from brutes."[144]

In essence, Victoria's argument in section 1 was based on the fundamental Thomistic Humanist tenet that formal equality among individuals was dictated by natural law. His argument on the legal equality of Indians and Europeans contained in this first section of his lecture has been regarded as his most enduring contribution to Western liberal jurisprudence on Indian rights and status.[145]

Section 2: Rejection of Spain's Papal Title to the New World

In section 2 of "On the Indians Lately Discovered," Victoria considered the arguments for Spain's New World title "which might be alleged, but which are not adequate or legitimate."[146] Victoria tested the adequacy and legitimacy of Spain's possible arguments for title on the basis of the natural-law rights of Indians, which he had established in his opening section.

Title by "discovery" was one obvious and frequently asserted argument for Spain's New World rights. Columbus's discoveries in the Crown's name were based on the presumption, affirmed in its essentials by Pope Alexander's bulls of donation,[147] that Christian European discovery of territory held by infidel or pagan nonbelievers vested title in the discovering European nation. Victoria unhesitatingly dismissed this doctrine, arguing that according to natural law, the Indians whose lands were "discovered" by Spain were free and were therefore "true owners" of the territory they possessed.[148] Victoria's argument dismissing the popular idea of "title by first discovery" theory went as follows:

Accordingly, there is another title which can be set up, namely, by right of discovery: and no other title was originally set up, and it was in virtue of this title alone that Columbus the Genoan first set sail.

Not much, however, need be said about this . . . title of ours, because, as proved above, the barbarians were true owners, both from the public and from the private standpoint. Now the rule of the law of nations is that what belongs to nobody is granted to the first occupant, as is expressly laid down in the . . . [Roman] Institutes. And so, as the object in question was not without an owner, it does not fall under the title which we are discussing. . . . [B]y itself it gives no support to a seizure of the aborigines any more than if it had been they who had discovered us.[149]

Unlike a later generation of Western colonial theorists,[150] Victoria refused to acknowledge convenient legal fictions such as "discovery" as a legitimate basis for European hegemony in the Indians' America. According to natural law, the Indians were free and thus could not be deprived of the countries they rightfully possessed by Europeans under a fictive "doctrine of discovery."

Victoria's boldest attacks on the prevailing legal paradigms supporting Spain's imperial rights in America were directed at the papal bulls of donation themselves. "The pope," Victoria flatly asserted, "has no temporal power over the Indian aborigines or over other unbelievers."[151] The Spanish Crown itself had requested the papal bulls of donation immediately upon learning of Columbus's discoveries in 1493 and since that time had always referred to Pope Alexander's grant of the Indies as the ultimate legal foundation of its colonial rights in the New World.[152] Victoria's assertion that the pope lacked temporal authority over the Indians attacked the entire hierocratic structure of Spain's New World empire and essentially denied the legal validity of the *Requeri-miento*, the Crown's legitimating and enabling legislation authorizing New World conquests. The Dominican missionaries to the Indians had regarded the papal-hierocratically informed *Requerimiento* as canonically corrupt since its installation as the principal instrument of Spanish empire justifying conquest and enslavement of any New World inhabitants unfortunate enough to hear its text.[153]

Victoria argued that any Spanish contentions to title based on the pope's asserted superior rights of dominion, incorporated into Spanish documents of empire such as the *Requerimiento*, were wholly "baseless" according to human, divine, and natural law.[154] Again citing his Dominican predecessor Thomas Aquinas for support, Victoria stated:

[D]ominion must be founded either on natural or divine or human law; but there is no lord of the earth in any of these. . . . [This] is proved, first as regards natural law, by what St. Thomas well says, namely, that by natural law mankind is free save from paternal and marital dominion. . . . [T]herefore no one by natural law has dominion over the world. And, as St. Thomas also says, dominion and preeminence were introduced by human law; they, therefore, were not by natural law.[155]

Concluding this antihierocratic attack on the *Requerimiento* and the papal monarchial pretensions sustaining the legislation, Victoria claimed, "even if the barbarians refuse to recognize any lordship of the Pope, that furnishes no ground for making war on them and seizing their property."[156] As the Indians were free according to natural and divine law, no human law (such as the *Requerimiento*), whether issued by priest or by king, could bind them without their consent. Such a law "would be void of effect, inasmuch as law presupposes jurisdiction. . . . [T]he law could not bind one who was not previously subject to it."[157]

Section 3: The Indians' Duties Under the Law of Nations

Having established the proposition that according to natural law, the Indian was free, Victoria sought in section 3 of his lecture to delineate the constraints that natural law imposed on the Indians' freedom. The thrust of Victoria's argument in this final part of his lecture was grounded in his maxim that all individuals (including the Indians of the Americas), although free, were subject to the binding norms of the Law of Nations, "which either is natural law or is derived from natural law."[158] First partially realized in the colonial law of the Roman Empire, the Law of Nations' rationalistic, universal character made it "clearly capable of conferring rights and creating obligations" through the "consensus of the greater part of the whole world, especially on behalf of the common good of all."[159] The principles and rules of this Law of Nations, as determined by the majority of humankind, would, according to Victoria, unequivocally "have the force of law, even though the rest of mankind objected thereto."[160]

For Victoria, the sources of the binding rules and principles of his Law of Nations derived from a variety of privileged sources, all Western and thoroughly Christo-Eurocentric in their normative orientation. Roman law, Holy Scripture, St. Augustine, classical writers, St. Thomas, and other authorities were all marshaled by Victoria in typical scholastic fashion to support his central thesis that all "civilized" societies recognized a set body of natural-law rules binding their conduct in the international sphere. These rules, if breached, could be punished by other states under the Law of Nations.[161]

Applying this European-derived body of obligatory rules to the Indians, Victoria defined in precise terms the various basic duties imposed by the Law of Nations on the indigenous societies of the Americas. The first duty was that of "natural society and fellowship." Under this duty,

[T]he Spaniards have a right to travel in the lands in question and sojourn there, provided they do no harm to the natives, and the natives may not prevent them. Proof of this may in the first place be derived from the Law of Nations (*ius gentium*). For . . . it is reckoned among all nations inhumane to treat visitors and foreigners badly without some special cause, while, on the other hand, it is humane and correct to treat visitors well.[162]

Victoria cited the Old and New Testaments to lend support to the universal nature of this natural-law obligation on the part of the Indians to accept the Spaniards into their lands:

"Every animal loveth its kind" (Ecclesiasticus, ch. 15). Therefore, it appears that friendship among men exists by natural law and it is against nature to shun society of harmless folk. Also . . . there is the passage (St. Matthew, ch. 25): "I was a stranger and ye took me in." Hence, as the reception of strangers seems to be by natural law, that judgment of Christ will be pronounced with universal application.[163]

Victoria stated that the Indians could not escape the universally binding nature of this scripturally revealed mandate of natural law that a "refusal to receive strangers and foreigners is wrong in itself."[164] Laws passed by the natives denying other nations the right to travel and sojourn in America would be of no effect, for "if there were any human law which without any cause took away rights conferred by natural and divine law, it would be inhumane and unreasonable and consequently would not have the force of law."[165] Under the Law of Nations, then, the Indians had to accept the Spaniards into their midst.

The second duty imposed on all peoples by the Law of Nations, according to Victoria, required the Indians to allow the Spaniards and other civilized nations free and open commerce. Here, Victoria anticipated liberal arguments of the seventeenth and eighteenth centuries on the legitimate exercise of state power. All the major publicists of the Renaissance and the Enlightenment recognized that collective coercion was permissible under the Law of Nations when its purpose was to facilitate commerce.[166] Writing in the sixteenth century, Victoria stated that the Law of Nations secured to the Spaniards the right to carry on trade among the Indians, "as, for instance, by importing thither wares which the natives lack and exporting thence either gold or silver or other wares of which the natives have abundance."[167] According to the Dominican proto-mercantilist theorist,

So long as the Spaniards do no harm to the Indians, neither may the native princes hinder their subjects from carrying on trade with the Spanish. . . . Also, the sovereign of the Indians is bound by the law of nature to love the Spaniards. Therefore the Indians may not causelessly prevent the Spaniards from making their profit where this can be done without injury to themselves.[168]

Victoria regarded the right to engage in commerce and trade as a natural human right. Quoting the Roman Digest, he declared, "'Nature has established a bond of relationship between all men,' and so it is contrary to natural law for one man to disassociate himself from another without good reason. 'Man,' says Ovid, 'is not a wolf to his fellow man, but a man.'"[169]

Victoria had elevated the profit motive to an extremely privileged status in his totalizing discourse of a universally obligatory natural Law of Nations. Mercantile self-interest was conceptualized as binding nations to one another. Not engaging in trade was seen as contrary to the mutual self-interests that all humankind shared. Therefore, such conduct was irrational and contrary to the Law of Nations, and could be punished. Victoria's high regard for trade and commerce in his Law of Nations must have generated immense enthusiasm for his theories in the proto-mercantilist quarters of Discovery-era imperial Spain. The Christian Humanist's desire for a universal world order adapted to satisfying human needs could be realized simply by expanding the merchant marine and by sending in the conquistadores wherever Spanish trade was not welcomed.

Victoria postulated another duty relating to commerce that the Law of Nations imposed on the Indians. "If there are among the Indians any things which are treated as common both to citizens and to strangers, the Indians may not prevent the Spaniards from a communication and participation in them."[170] Columbus had originated the idea that the Indians lacked a conception of privately held property. In his widely circulated letter of 1493, the captain had stated, "I have not been able to learn if they hold private property; it seemed to me to be that all took a share in whatever anyone had, especially eatable things."[171] Amerigo Vespucci, another early Iberian-sponsored explorer of the New World, had further reinforced perceptions that the Indians held all their property in common. Vespucci's widely read *Mundus novus* contained a wildly distorted ethnography on Indian customs:

They have no cloth either of wool, linen or cotton, since they need it not; neither do they have goods of their own, but all things are held in common. . . . They live according to nature, and may be called Epicureans rather than Stoics. There are no merchants among their number, nor is there barter.[172]

Victoria's analysis of Spanish commercial rights in this part of his lecture may have derived from these few simplified and distorted accounts of Indian property-holding patterns so popular among the Spanish intelligentsia. The Spaniards, he argued, might justly appropriate Indian communally held and shared resources, depending on the extent of privileges the Indians granted other nations:

If, for example, other foreigners are allowed to dig for gold in the land of the community or in rivers, or to fish for pearls in the sea or in a river, the natives cannot prevent the Spaniards from doing this, but they have the same right to do it as others have, so long as the citizens and indigenous population are not hurt thereby.[173]

Here also, the Spanish Crown and merchants would have found much to admire in Victoria's desacralized Law of Nations.

Victoria considered all the obligations found in the Law of Nations to be universally binding. European as well as pagan states fell within the dictates and sanctions of this newly declared form of international law:

If the Indian natives wish to prevent the Spaniards from enjoying any of their . . . rights under the Law of Nations, . . . the Spaniards can defend themselves and do all that consists with their own safety, it being lawful to repel force by force. And not only so, but, if safety can not otherwise be had, they may build fortresses and defensive works, and if they have sustained a wrong, they may follow it up with war . . . and may avail themselves of the other rights of war. . . . When the Indians deny the Spaniards their rights under the law of nations they do them a wrong. Therefore, if it be necessary, in order to preserve their right, that they should go to war, they may lawfully do so.[174]

And if the Spaniards still could not safely exercise their rights in the countries of the Indians, "save by seizing their cities and reducing them to subjection, they may lawfully proceed to these extremities."[175] Citing St. Augustine's teachings on "just wars," Victoria supported this aggressive proposition by arguing that "everything necessary to secure the end and aim of war, namely, the obtaining of safety and peace, is lawful."[176] Thus should the Indians refuse to recognize the Spaniards' rights under the Law of Nations, Spain "may enforce against them all the rights of war, despoiling them of their goods, reducing them to captivity, deposing their former lords and setting up new ones."[177]

A Guardianship over the Indians

Section 3 of Victoria's lecture truly broke new theoretical ground for Western colonizing thought. His desacralized analysis of the Law of Nations identified the natural-law sources of Spain's right to rule in the New World. The Indian was to be judged not by a divinely installed papal mediary, but by the humanized, rationally conceived norms of conduct contained within the eclectic but wholly privileged Western corpus of legal, political, and theological ideas that constituted the Christian natural-law tradition. Hierarchical subjugation of the Indian, so repugnant to Victoria and other Humanist theorists when presented in hierocratic papal discourse, was regarded as eminently acceptable when explained as necessitated by the totalizing vision of reason contained in a natural Law of Nations.

That the Indian would be no less "free" according to the Eurocentric discourse of reason embodied in the Law of Nations than he was under medieval
papal hierocratic dogma was indicated by Victoria himself. Thomas Aquinas's
teaching, echoed earlier by Pope Innocent IV,[178] that reason and not grace
conditioned *dominium*, implied that if infidels acted irrationally, they could be
dispossessed of their property and lordship. As Victoria himself, drawing on
Aquinas's text, stated in the first part of his lecture, "Reason is a precondition
for ownership in general."[179] Thus in a lecture supposedly intended to demonstrate that the Indians were free, Victoria offered the following tentative
assessment of the theory that Spanish rights in the Americas could be based on
a Christian nation's guardianship responsibility to civilize backward, barbarous peoples who could not comport themselves according to the rationalized
norms of natural law:

There is another title which can indeed not be asserted, but brought up for discussion,
and some think it a lawful one.
I dare not affirm it at all, nor do I entirely condemn it. It is this: Although the
aborigines in question are . . . not wholly unintelligent, yet they are little short of that
condition, and so are unfit to found or administer a lawful State up to the standard
required by human and civil claims. Accordingly they have no proper laws or magistrates, and are not even capable of controlling their family affairs; they are without any
literature or arts, not only the liberal arts, but the mechanical arts also; they have no
careful agriculture and no artisans. . . . It might, therefore, be maintained that in their
own interests the sovereigns of Spain might undertake the administration of their
country, providing them with prefects and governors for their towns, and might even
give them new lords, so long as this was clearly for their benefit.[180]

Victoria believed there was "some force in this contention" that Spain might
be justified in exercising a benign guardianship over the Indians, "for if they
were all wanting in intelligence, there is no doubt that this would not only be
permissible, but also a highly proper, course to take; nay, our sovereigns would
be bound to take it, just as if the natives were infants."[181] And, as Victoria
argued, the Crown's mandated guardianship responsibilities under the Law of
Nations would include the duty of bringing the message of the civilized Christian faith to the natives:

Christians have a right to preach and declare the Gospel in barbarian lands . . . , for if
the Spaniards have a right to travel and trade among the Indians, they can teach the
truth to those willing to hear them, especially as regards matters pertaining to salvation
and happiness, much more than as regards matters pertaining to any human subject of
instruction. . . . [B]rotherly correction is required by the law of nature, just as brotherly
love is. Since, then, the Indians are all not only in sin, but outside the pale of salvation,
therefore, it concerns Christians to correct and direct them; nay, it seems that they are
bound to do so. . . . [L]astly, because they are our neighbors, as said above: Now the
Lord has laid a command on everyone concerning his neighbor (Ecclesiasticus, ch. 17).
Therefore it concerns Christians to instruct those who are ignorant of these supremely
vital matters.[182]

Without expressing any awareness that he was compromising the intellectual
integrity of his Humanist-inspired, natural-law-based system, Victoria went on
to argue that as the right to preach the True Faith under natural law and the

Law of Nations "concerns Christians," it was appropriate for the pope, given the spiritual nature of his duties, to assign this right exclusively to an appropriately qualified Christian prince. Thus while Victoria had argued strongly that the pope was devoid of temporal authority to grant Spain direct title to the Indies, the Dominican still maintained fidelity to basic medieval doctrine that the pope held an unquestioned responsibility for the salvation of these wayward sheep of Christ's flock:

Although this [conversion] is a task common and permitted to all, yet the Pope might entrust it to the Spaniards and forbid it to all others. The proof is in the fact that, although (as said above) the Pope is not temporal lord, yet he has power in matters temporal when this would subserve matters spiritual. Therefore, as it is the Pope's concern to bestow especial care on the propagation of the Gospel over the whole world, he can entrust it to the Spaniards to the exclusion of all others, if the sovereigns of Spain could render more effective help in the spread of the Gospel in those parts; and not only could the Pope forbid others to preach, but also to trade there, if this would further the propagation of Christianity, for he can order temporal matters in the manner which is most helpful to spiritual matters.[183]

In exercising its papally granted rights to proselytize and trade, Spain could rightfully wage war if the Indians failed in their duty to accept Christian missionaries who would "correct and direct" them. Thus the Indians, Victoria argued, were obligated under the Law of Nations to listen to and provide facilities for the papally licensed Spanish efforts at conversion. If the Indian princes prevented the Spaniards from preaching the gospel, "an obstacle would thereby be put in the way of the welfare of the Indians themselves such as their princes have no right to put there."[184]

Therefore, in favor of those who are oppressed and suffer wrong, the Spaniards can make war, especially as such vitally important interests are at stake. This proposition demonstrates that, if there is no other way to carry on the work of religion, this furnishes the Spaniards with another justification for seizing the lands and territory of the natives and for setting up new lords . . . with an intent directed more to the welfare of the aborigines than to their own gain.[185]

Spain, in other words, could conquer and colonize the Indians of the Americas for refusing to hear the truth of the Christian religion. This justification for the deployment of colonizing power was identical to the Innocentian-derived argument first relied on by Portugal in the early fifteenth century to legitimate invasion of the Canary Islands,[186] and later by Ferdinand's hierocratic lawyers who drafted the *Requerimiento*.[187] Victoria's rearticulation of the Innocentian discourse on infidel rights simply compounded the sources of self-initiated jurisdictional authority capable of enforcing Eurocentric norms in non-Christian territories. The papacy retained the authority to entrust the propagation of Christianity and civilization in different parts of the world to colonizing Christian princes, but Victoria's discourse supplemented this papal power with the recognition that Christians possessed autonomously grounded rights under the Law of Nations to travel, trade, and preach the gospel in barbarian lands without first obtaining a papal license. In Victoria's discourse of New World conquest, reason as well as Rome were granted the right to initiate enforcement of Christian Europe's universally binding norms and values in lands possessed by heathens and infidels.

Victoria's Law of Nations provided Western legal discourse with its first secularly oriented, systematized elaboration of the superior rights of civilized Europeans to invade and conquer normatively divergent peoples. His discourse of conquest, grounded in the Renaissance vision of a universal reason codified in a Law of Nations, exerted a profound impact on the West's legal conceptions of Indian rights and status. The Spanish Crown's royal proclamation of 1573, which denominated all further extensions of empire in the New World as "pacifications" rather than "conquests" and mandated peaceful conversion of the Indians,[188] fittingly illustrates the rationalized nature of the discursive trajectory launched by the Victorian irruption in Western legal thought respecting normatively divergent tribal peoples. In words and tone that would be adopted and proclaimed countless times (even in our own "modern" era) by subsequent self-appointed European and European-derived sovereigns in the New World,[189] the proclamation proudly commanded Spanish explorers to explain the benefits attached to the Indians' acceptance of the "overlordship" of the Spanish king. The king, the Indians were to be told, has

sent ecclesiastics who have taught the Indians the Christian doctrine and faith by which they could be saved. Moreover, the king has established justice in such a way that no one may aggravate another. The king has maintained the peace so that there are no killings or sacrifices, as was the custom in some parts. He has made it possible for the Indians to go safely by all roads and to peacefully carry on their civil pursuits. He has freed them from burdens and servitude; he has made known to them the use of bread, wine, oil and many other foods, woolen cloth, silk, linen, horses, cows, tools, arms and many other things from Spain; he has instructed them in crafts and trades by which they live excellently. All these advantages will those Indians enjoy who embrace our Holy Faith and render obedience to our king.[190]

Only Christian Europeans could offer the Indians a rationalized existence, which the Indians by the Law of Nations were obliged to accept. European domination benefited the Indians by providing them with the civilizing doctrines of Christianity. In the bargain, the Indians gained freedom to travel (until they were forced onto reservations), to engage in commerce (until they were dispossessed of everything worth selling), and to go peacefully about their other "civil pursuits" (until they were killed or imprisoned for resisting violations of their human rights).

The material wealth of Western culture—bread, wine, silk, tools, and arms, as well as instruction in the superior "crafts and trades" of the European— could be attained by the Indians if they simply agreed to accept the West's civilizing religion and the political and legal hegemony of their self-appointed European guardians. To refuse these benefits indicated delusion and a lack of reason, justifying an even sterner, more disciplined exercise of the Europeans' guardianship over the Indians and their New World.

Franciscus de Victoria was the first articulator of a European discourse of conquest founded on secularly rationalizable norms and values. His Law of

Nations justified the extension of Western power over the American Indians as an imperative of the Europeans' vision of truth. In Victoria's system, the Indians might be subjected to Spanish rule for denying the Spanish conquistadores free passage in their territory, preventing Spanish merchants from making their profit, refusing to share communally held wealth, or hindering the propagation of Christianity. Any of these actions by the Indians would constitute transgressions of the Law of Nations for which the Spaniards could wage a just war and assume all the rights of conquest. In Victoria's view, the Indian's consent to this Law of Nations was immaterial, since the majority of the world's civilized states (that is, European Christian states) had already consented by their long-established patterns of conduct to the norms embodied in Victoria's codification of the Law of Nations. Consequently, despite their lack of knowledge or acceptance of the dictates of the Law of Nations, the Indians were bound.

While the normative foundation of Victoria's Law of Nations was constructed according to a secularized, as opposed to an ecclesiastically dictated, vision of reason, it was a vision no less totalizing and hierarchical in its outlook than the medieval response to radical difference. The Renaissance's disruption of all forms of medieval discursive practice accelerated the process of fragmentation and atomization of a previously imagined unitary European Christian commonwealth. Victoria's Law of Nations sought to replace the theoretical universal sanctioning power of the papacy by the fiction of a Eurocentrically and Christocentrically understood consensus of the whole world in harmony with the West's vision of reason and truth.

Thus in a crucial sense, Victoria's articulation of a Law of Nations preserved the vitality of the ancient core values and norms that would sustain the nascent rationalizing spirit that was emerging in Western legal thought as Europe encountered the uncertain prospects of the post-Reformation and Enlightenment. The emergence of a style of legal discourse that spoke of universal norms binding all humankind into a world community provided a reassuring continuity with the West's medieval discursive traditions of unity and hierarchy. Renaissance legal discourse retained a totalizing trajectory, but in a form that trumpeted the ascendancy of man over priest. Moreover, because this ascendant man retained the idealized, transcendent value structure that had grown out of the Christian European discursive legacy, Victoria's rationalized systematization of a Law of Nations constituted a vital theoretical bridge in the history of Western legal thought and discourse. Hierarchical subjugation of the alien and divergent cultures of the New World could proceed on a "modern," desacralized, legal basis, but a basis nonetheless possessed of all the missionary, chauvinistic zeal that had attended Christianity's will to empire in earlier medieval Crusades to distant lands held by unregenerate "barbarians" and "infidels." Although the Indians were free according to the Renaissance's privileged discourse of a Law of Nations, that same discourse of conquest now determined the confining conditions of the Indians' newfound, European-defined liberty.[191] The medieval Christian European vision of one right way of life for all humankind had been preserved in the animating principles of Western legal thought's first secularized discourse of international law: a Law of Nations, an instrument of empire, in the Spanish conquest of America.

NOTES

1. Conciliarism, the Council of Constance, and the significance of the Concilian movement in Church history are discussed in B. Tierney, *Foundations of the Conciliar Theory* (1955); W. Ullmann, *A Short History of the Papacy in the Middle Ages* 298–305 (1972).

2. On the conflict between the Teutonic Knights and Poland, *see* 1 *Paulus Vladimiri and His Doctrine Concerning International Law and Politics*, 2 vols., 45–114 (S. Belch ed. 1965) [hereinafter cited as *Vladimiri*]; *The Expansion of Europe: The First Phase* 105–24 (J. Muldoon ed. 1977); H. Schreiber, *Teuton and Slave* (J. Cleugh trans. 1965).

3. *The Expansion of Europe, supra* note 2, at 105–6; G. Barraclough, *The Origins of Modern Germany* 41–42 (2d rev. ed. 1947).

4. Quoted in B. Tierney, *The Crisis of Church and State, 1058–1300*, 92–94 (1964).

5. *Vladimiri, supra* note 2, at 61. A chronicle of the colonization and settlement of Livonia (in the Gulf of Riga), written in 1261, contained the following recruitment call for German military assistance against the region's recalcitrant infidel peoples:

> We therefore do not doubt that it has come to your attention how much injury we the Brothers and other Christians who dwell in the land of Livonia have received recently in terms of lost horses, arms and other goods. Because of this, the Catholic faith was greatly harmed so that many who had withdrawn from the error of their infidel ways and worshipped the name of the Lord, now spurning that name, became backsliders worshipping false idols.
>
> . . . [W]e propose to draw the Germans to us, with the help of whom we wage the Lord's battle more forcefully. We will grant them fiefs in the lands which were abandoned when the apostate Kurlands had been killed or driven off, where the sea ports are open to them, where they think that settlement will be most suitable. [Reprinted in *The Expansion of Europe, supra* note 2, at 122–23.]

The recuitment call offered a knight or "honest burgher" who brought a "well-armed" charger sixty Saxon hides (a hide equaled approximately 40 to 60 acres). A "doughty squire with a heavy-armed war horse" received forty hides; a serf with horse and armor, ten hides. Any farmer would be allowed to farm "whatever amount of land he wishes" free for six years, at which time he would pay one-tenth of the produce from the lands (*id.*)

It would be difficult to overestimate the attractiveness of this crusading-colonizing inducement. A peasant who moved to the east to fight a war against the pagans received a significant portion of land as a freeman, a virtually unparalleled opportunity in Europe's feudal land economy. See *The Expansion of Europe, supra* note 2, at 106, 122–23.

6. *Vladimiri, supra* note 2, at 74–75.

7. Quoted in J. Muldoon, *Popes, Lawyers and Infidels* 109 (1979).

8. *See* Chapter 1, text accompanying notes 49–51, *supra*.

9.

> [K]ings, princes, or temporal lords can legitimately and meritoriously take riches away from any ecclesiastical community or person that habitually misuses them, even though such riches were confirmed to them by human grants. . . .
>
> For if God exists, the clerical part of the church can misuse riches; and if so, temporal lords can meritoriously take those riches away from them; therefore the conclusion is based on the existence of God. [Reprinted in E. Lewis, *Medieval Political Ideas* 127 (1954).]

10. J. Muldoon, *supra* note 7, at 107–12. The zeal with which the council sought to eradicate the Donatist implications of Wyclif's discourse on *dominium* is indicated by the simultaneous prosecution of the Bohemian John Hus, condemned as a heretic for preaching views only arguably related

to those of Wyclif. In his defense before the council against the capital heresy charge, Hus denied specifically that he had taught Wyclif's doctrine that a "priest in mortal sin does not consecrate." Rather, he pled that he had only claimed that such a priest administers the sacraments unworthily, although not invalidly. This position, however, was too akin to Wyclif's damnable assault on priestly authority. Hus's "pernicious errors" cost him his life at the stake. *Id.*

11. J. Muldoon, *supra* note 7, at 108.

12. *See* Chapter 1, text accompanying notes 95–109, *supra.*

13. Quoted in J. Muldoon, *supra* note 7, at 112–13.

14. Quoted in B. Tierney, *supra* note 4, at 156–57.

15. Quoted in J. Muldoon, *supra* note 7, at 16.

16. *The Expansion of Europe, supra* note 2, at 193. Later canonists in the fourteenth century elaborated the hierarchical themes of this revived style of papal imperial discourse and its core notion that the pope "cannot err." Giles of Rome (c. 1246–1315), the most forceful and influential of the hierocratic theorists following Hostiensis, asserted in his treatise, *De ecclesiastica potestate,* that all infidels were unworthy of *dominium.* Those who did not recognize the Church's authority, Giles reasoned, had no rights to property that a Christian was required to honor or recognize. "There is no lordship with justice, either of temporal things or of lay persons of anything whatever, except under the Church and through the Church" (quoted in E. Lewis, *supra* note 9, at 114).

Despite the clear Donatist implications of his work, Giles's influence and prestige were such that in 1287 his order, the Hermits of St. Augustine, also known as the Austin friars, officially decreed that "all lecturers and students of the order shall accept and defend with all possible zeal every opinion, position or sentence that our venerable master, Brother Giles, has written or shall write" (quoted in A. Gwynn, *The English Austin Friars in the Time of Wyclif* 38 [1940]). Many loyal members of Giles's order taught at Oxford University in the late thirteenth and early fourteenth century. It was there that the Oxford matriculate John Wyclif most likely came into contact with Giles's zealous disciples and their unquestioned adherence to Giles's central tenet that lordship with justice was held only mediately through the Church. Wyclif, of course, went on to modify substantially Giles's position on *dominium* by reasoning that where a prelate himself was corrupt and not in a state of grace, his authority also lacked legitimacy. *See generally* L. Daly, *The Political Theory of John Wyclif* (1962).

17.

> "It is the opinion of Hostiensis," argued Vladimiri, "that at the coming of Christ all jurisdiction, rule, office and lordship was transferred from infidels to the faithful, since, as his opinion states, infidels are entirely incapable of possessing such things." [J. Muldoon, *supra* note 7, at 113.]

18. *See id.* at 113–18; *Vladimiri, supra* note 2, at 86.

19. J. Muldoon, *supra* note 7.

20. Id. at 119.

21. *See* text accompanying notes 52–56, *supra.*

22. *See The Expansion of Europe, supra* note 2, at 47–49. *See also* A. H. de Oliveira Marques, *History of Portugal,* vol. 1: *From Lusitania to Empire* 36–42 (1972); H. V. Livermore, *A New History of Portugal* 44–46 (1967); "Portuguese History," in *Portugal and Brazil* (H. V. Livermore ed. 1953).

23. Reprinted in *The Expansion of Europe, supra* note 2, at 51. The same archbishop's proclamation delivered at the city gates of Lisbon blended the familiar medieval themes of unity and hierarchy within an early Humanist-inspired naturalistic symbology in explaining the justness of the Christian cause to the barricaded Muslims:

> May the God of peace and love remove the veil of error from your hearts and convert you to himself. And therefore have we come to you to speak of peace. For in concord small things grow great, in discord the greatest go to ruin. But, in order that discord may not forever reign between us, we have come hither to you with a message of conciliation. For Nature so begat us from one and the same principle that, by reason of the common bond of humanity and the chain of harmony derived from the mother of all, one ought not to be unacceptable

to another. And, if you will, we have come hither to this city which you possess not to subdue you and drive you out and despoil you. For the inborn kindliness of Christians ever holds to this principle, that, while it seeks its own, it seizes not the property of others. [Reprinted in *id.* at 53.]

The bishop's speech charged that the "realm of Lusitania" had been fraudulently seized by the Moors and demanded that the city be placed under "our law." "Surely," stated the Crusader-prelate, "if a natural sense of justice had made any progress among you, you would go back unbidden to the land of the Moors from whence you came" (quoted in *id.*).

24. I. Wallerstein, *The Modern World-System* 46–47 (1974).

25. C. R. Boxer, *The Portuguese Seaborne Empire 1415–1825* (1969); E. Prestage, *The Portuguese Pioneers* (1967).

26. J. Muldoon, *supra* note 7, at 119–21; *The Expansion of Europe*, *supra* note 2, at 48, 54–56.

27. *See* text accompanying notes 13–18, *supra*.

28. Reprinted in *The Expansion of Europe*, *supra* note 2, at 54–56.

29. *Id.* at 54.

30. *Id.* at 55.

31. *Id.* at 55–56.

32. *Id.* at 56.

33. *See* Chapter 1, text accompanying notes 105–9, *supra*.

34. *See* Chapter 1, text accompanying notes 100–104, *supra*.

35. Quoted in *The Expansion of Europe*, *supra* note 2, at 55–56.

36. J. Muldoon, *supra* note 7, at 124–25.

37. *Id.* at 126.

38. *Id.* at 126–27.

39. The bull *Romanus Pontifex* is translated in *Church and State Through the Centuries* 146–53 (S. Ehler & J. Morrall trans. and eds. 1967).

40. *See id.*

41. *Id.* at 150.

42. *Id.* at 146.

43. *See*, e.g., the papal bull of May 21, 1179, issued also on behalf of the Portuguese Crown, recognizing the king of Portugal's right of title to all territory he might conquer in the Holy Land: "All the regions which you will have rescued from the hands of the Saracens, and where other neighboring Christian princes could not acquire any legal rights, are conceded by us to your Excellency" (quoted in F. von der Heydte, "Discovery and Annexation in International Law," 29 *Am. J. Int'l L.* 448, 451 [1935]).

44. *Church and State Through the Centuries*, *supra* note 39, at 150.

45. *Id.* at 149.

46. *The Expansion of Europe*, *supra* note 2, at 55–56.

47. J. Trend, *The Civilization of Spain* 88 (1944).

48. On the history of Spanish national development through the early Renaissance and Discovery periods, *see generally The Expansion of Europe*, *supra* note 2, at 73–75; R. B. Merriman, *The Rise of the Spanish Empire in the Old World and the New*, 4 vols. (1962); C. Verlinden, *The Beginnings of Modern Colonization* 13–14, 20–21 (Y. Freccero trans. 1970); J. F. O'Callaghan, *A History of Medieval Spain* (1975); R. I. Burns, *The Crusader Kingdom of Valencia*, 2 vols. (1967); J. H. Parry, *The Spanish Theory of Empire in the Sixteenth Century* (1940).

49. *See generally* A. Nussbaum, *A Concise History of the Law of Nations* 62–63 (rev. ed. 1954); L. Hanke, *Aristotle and the American Indians* 8 (1959); C. R. Boxer, *supra* note 25, at 1–8.

50. A. Nussbaum, *supra*, at 62–63.

51. *See* Alfonso X, *Las Siete Partidas* (J. Scott trans. 1931).

52. Quoted in *The Expansion of Europe*, *supra* note 2, at 95.

53. A. Nussbaum, *supra* note 49, at 62–63; *The Expansion of Europe*, *supra* note 2, at 96–97. Under Alfonso's code, Christians were obligated to convert the followers of the prophet Muhammad. *Las Siete Partidas* declared the "foolish belief" of the Moors "an insult to God." Furthermore, any Christian who converted to Islam could be punished by death:

Men sometimes become insane and lose their prudence and understanding, as, for instance, where unfortunate persons, and those who despair of everything, renounce the faith of our Lord Jesus Christ, and become Moors. . . .

Wherefore we order that all those who are guilty of this wickedness shall lose all their possessions and have no right to any portion of them . . . and, in addition to this, we order that if any person who committed such an offense shall be found in any part of our dominions he shall be put to death. [Reprinted in *id.*]

54. A. Nussbaum, *supra* note 49, at 62–63; 2 S. E. Morison, *The European Discovery of America: The Southern Voyages* 27–44 (1974).

55. J. Brundage, *The Crusades: A Documentary Survey* 275 (1962); C. Verlinden, "The Rise of Spanish Trade in the Middle Ages," 10 *Economic History Review* 1, at 44–59 (1940); C. Verlinden, "Italian Influence in Iberian Colonization," 33 *Hispanic American Historical Review* 2, at 199–211 (May 1953); I. Wallerstein, *supra* note 24, at 48–52.

56. S. E. Morison, *supra* note 54, at 27–44.

57. 1 S. E. Morison, *Admiral of the Ocean Sea* (1942).

58. *See id.* at 5–6. *See also* J. Muldoon, *supra* note 7, at 136.

59. S. E. Morison, *supra* note 54, at 31–43.

60. *Id.* at 34–44.

61. S. E. Morison, *supra* note 57, at 121.

62. *Id.* at 301. *See* J. Collis, *Christopher Columbus* 79–88 (1976), describing the first sighting and landing by Columbus. The island itself was only 6 miles long by 3 miles wide with no mountains or hills. *Id.* at 81. Corn and yams and other roots were the principal food sources for the natives, who, according to Columbus's journals, appeared to be skilled at pottery making and cotton weaving. Columbus described their peaceful and hospitable character by noting, "They invite you to share anything that they possess, and show as much love as if their hearts went with it" (quoted in S. E. Morison, *supra* note 54, at 66).

As for the Arawaks' reaction to Columbus's proclamation of title to their island, one historian has speculated that the Indians probably "watched the proceedings without resentment for they had not the least idea what was happening. Having not yet arrived at the conception of property they were unable to conceive the idea of theft" (J. Collis, *supra*, at 81).

63. The term "Indies" had been widely used by fifteenth-century European explorers to denote China, Japan, the Ryukyus, the Spice Islands, Indonesia, Thailand, and everything between these lands and India proper. In 1492, when Columbus reached the Bahamian island of Guanahani, he mistakenly thought he had discovered his predicted short sea route to the East. Columbus used the broad designation "Indies" for the entire area he claimed under royal patent in the Caribbean basin. *See* S. E. Morison, *supra* note 54, at 26–90, for a detailed discussion of Columbus's "enterprise of the Indies." From Columbus's mislabeling came the term "Indian," used to describe all the natives of the New World, with their varied cultures.

Even after subsequent explorations corrected Columbus's error in geography, the Spanish continued to employ *Indios* for all people of the New World, including the Aztec and Inca societies. . . . From the Spanish term came eventually the French *Indien*, the German *Indianer*, the English *Indian*, and similar words in European languages for the New World inhabitant. [Reprinted in R. Berkhofer, Jr., *The White Man's Indian* at 5 (1978).]

64. *See* text accompanying notes 28–35, *supra.*

65. R. Berkhofer, Jr., *supra* note 63, at 6.

66. *See* text accompanying notes 39–46, *supra.*

67. *See European Treaties Bearing on the History of the United States and Its Dependencies* 56 (F. Davenport ed. 1917). *See also* A. Nussbaum, *supra* note 49, at 17–21; F. Von Der Heydte, *supra* note 43, at 451–52.

68. 2 S. E. Morison, *Admiral of the Ocean Sea* 21–22 (1942).

69. Reprinted in *European Treaties Bearing on the History of the United States and Its Dependencies, supra* note 67, at 9–13.

70. *See id.* at 53–55.

71. *See* 2 S. E. Morison, *supra* note 68, at 22–27.

72. *Church and State Through the Centuries, supra* note 39, at 156.

73. *Id.* at 156.

74. *Id.*

75. For background information on the Spanish colonial development in the New World, *see* A. Debo, *A History of the Indians of the United States* (1970); V. Deloria, Jr., *Behind the Trail of Broken Treaties* (1974); T. Floyd, *The Columbus Dynasty in the Caribbean 1492–1526* (1973); L. Hanke, *All Mankind Is One* (1974); L. Hanke, *The First Social Experiments in America* (1935) [hereinafter cited as L. Hanke, *First Experiments*]; J. H. Parry, *The Establishment of the European Hegemony 1415–1715* (3d rev. ed. 1966); J. H. Parry, *supra* note 48; *Indian Land Cessions in the United States*, 18 Bureau of American Ethnology, pt. 2 (C. Royce ed. 1899) [hereinafter cited as *Indian Land Cessions*]; V. Vogel, *This Country Was Ours* (1972); W. Washburn, *Red Man's Land/ White Man's Law* (1971).

76. *See* text accompanying notes 60–61, *supra.*

77. T. Floyd, *supra* note 75, at 24.

78. *See* I. Wallerstein, *supra* note 24, at 43–44. On race and slavery in the Portuguese colonial empire, *see* C. R. Boxer, *Race Relations in the Portuguese Empire 1415–1825* (1963).

79. T. Floyd, *supra* note 75, at 46–47.

80. R. Berkhofer, Jr., *supra* note 63, at 4–6, discusses Columbus's mistaken belief that he had discovered islands among the East Indies and therefore denominated the Arawak tribespeople he "discovered" in the Bahamas *los Indios.* As for Columbus's geographical state of mind respecting exactly what he discovered, most geographical and naval historians who have studied the issue closely have concluded that Columbus died holding firmly to the belief that he had reached Asia. *See* S. E. Morison, *supra* note 54, at 265–66.

An earlier group of historians, perhaps inspired in 1892 by the quatercentenary of Columbus's first voyage, sought to revise the commonly held thesis that Columbus died unaware that he "had discovered a new world distinct from the India and Cathay which had been the original object of his search" (*id.* at 56). *See* J. B. Thacker, *Christopher Columbus: His Life, His Work, His Remains, as Revealed by Original Printed and Manuscript Records* 568, 612 (1904). Samuel Eliot Morison, the leading contemporary United States scholar on Columbus, refutes these efforts at Columbus revisionism:

> [I]t is one of the ironies of history that the Admiral himself died ignorant of what he had really accomplished, still insisting that he had discovered a large number of islands, a province of China, and an "Other World," and of the ocean that lay between it and Asia, he had neither knowledge nor suspicion. [S. E. Morison, *supra* note 54, at 266.]

81. *See* text accompanying notes 64–74, *supra.*

82. *See* text accompanying notes 26–27, *supra.*

83. As Muldoon has noted, the Spanish Crown was "extremely sensitive to the need for legitimating New World quests" (J. Muldoon, "John Wyclif and the Rights of the Infidels: The *Requerimiento* Re-Examined," 36 *Americas* 301 (1980). Much of the discussion in this section relies on this article.

84. Ovando's experiences as governor are detailed in L. Hanke, *The Spanish Struggle for Justice in the Conquest of America* 19–20 (1949). *See also* T. Floyd, *supra* note 75, at 50–68.

85. L. Hanke, *supra,* at 20.

86. *See* text accompanying notes 34–35, *supra.*

87. L. Hanke, *supra* note 84, at 20.

88. L. Hanke, *supra* note 84, at 19.

89. The political use of the *encomienda* system was necessitated by the fact that Ferdinand had been long resented by royal Castilian society for his Aragonese origins. Five difficult years followed Isabella's death, during which the king was required to make strenuous efforts toward consolidating his power in Spain. Finally, with the 1509 Pact of Blois between the emperor Maximilian and himself, Ferdinand secured his title as regent of Castile. His victory over dissident nobles was costly, however, and he accrued considerable political debts in the struggle. Beginning in 1509, Ferdinand issued a number of absentee *encomiendas* in the New World as patronage to allies in Spain.

90. *See* A. Debo, *supra* note 75, at 20; T. Floyd, *supra* note 75, at 89–122.

91. Quoted in L. Hanke, *supra* note 84, at 17. Montesinos's assertion that the colonists were in mortal sin would certainly have raised alarm, particularly given the legacy of the Inquisition in Spain and the role the Dominican order had played in it.

Since the early Middle Ages, the Catholic episcopate had always retained the right to "inquire" into matters of heresy. It was during the pontificate of Gregory IX (1227–1241), however, that the infamous papal Inquisition became formally elaborated. Not surprisingly, the justification for the Inquisition's more infamous methods originated in firm hierocratic doctrine. Heresy was considered to be "high treason" against the monarchic position of the pope because the crime constituted a denial of the papacy's plenitude of power. It was freely admitted that the juristic principles and procedures of the Inquisition, especially in Spain, bore little resemblance to those practiced by the royal courts and even the papacy itself. But heresy, in that it attacked the very foundations of the hierarchical position of the pope and the Church, demanded an immediate and severe response. *See* W. Ullmann, *supra* note 1, at 252–54.

In Spain, the Inquisition proceeded with unrivaled intensity. The infamous Grand Inquisitor, Cardinal Torquemada (1420–1498), and his Dominican order conducted the heresy trials in Spain during the fifteenth century. The frightening legacy of the Spanish Inquisition under Torquemada's direction determined, to a large degree, the cautious tenor of Spanish philosophical and theological speculation well into the sixteenth century. For an extensive examination of the Inquisition, *see* H. Lea, *A History of the Inquisition of the Middle Ages* (1922).

92. L. Hanke, *supra* note 84.

93. *Id.*

94. *Id.* at 23–25.

95. *Id.* at 23.

96. L. Hanke, *supra* note 49, at 13–14.

97. L. Hanke, *supra* note 84, at 23–25.

98. On the Laws of Burgos and their administration, *see* L. Simpson, *Studies in the Administration of the Indians in New Spain* (1934).

99. Reprinted in *Indian Land Cessions*, *supra* note 75, at 540.

100. L. Hanke, *supra* note 84, at 24.

101. *Id.*

102. *Id.* at 25.

103. *Id.* at 26.

104. *Id.*

105. *Id.*

106. *See* L. Simpson, *supra* note 98, at 32.

107. G. Benzoni, *History of the New World* 32 (W. Smyth ed. 1857).

108. *See* text accompanying notes 90–91, *supra*.

109. L. Hanke, *supra* note 84, at 27. *See also* A. Serra, "The Discovery of the New World and International Law," *Toledo L. Rev.* 305 (1971).

110. L. Hanke, *supra* note 84, at 28.

111. *Id.* at 29.

112. *See* A. Serra, *supra* note 109, at 315–19.

113. *Id.*

114. As Muldoon notes, however, the text of the *Requerimiento* was consistent with Innocent's teaching that infidels could be attacked for refusing to admit missionaries. J. Muldoon, *supra* note 7, at 141–42.

115. *The Spanish Tradition in America* 59–60 (C. Gibson ed. 1968).

116. *Id.*

117. *Id.*

118. *Id.*

119. *See* Chapter 1, text accompanying notes 104–8, *supra*.

120. L. Hanke, *supra* note 84, at 34 (footnote omitted).

121. *See, e.g.,* F. Cohen's discussion of the papal bull *Sublimis Deus* (1537) in "The Spanish Origins of Indian Rights in the Law of the United States" 32 *Geo. L. J.* 1 (1942).

122. L. Hanke, *supra* note 84, at 47.

123. R. Berkhofer, Jr., *supra* note 63, at 125.

124. Quoted in L. Hanke, *supra* note 75, at 58.

125. L. Hanke, *supra* note 84, at 43. On the Jeronymite friars and their activities in the New World, *see* L. Hanke, *First Experiments*, *supra* note 75, at 26–39.

126. Reprinted in L. Hanke, *supra* note 84, at 11. For an extended treatment of the many interesting theories propounded by Oviedo with respect to the Indians of the New World, *see* L. Hanke, *supra* note 75, at 40–45.

127. L. Hanke, *supra* note 84, at 58–59.

128. The Spanish Crown agreed that Indian contact with Spaniards was likely to prevent the success of the priests' experiments in civilization and Christianization. In 1516, as just one instance, Ferdinand issued an order forbidding any Spaniard from approaching the Pearl Coast of Tierra Firme, where the Dominicans were preaching. Ferdinand justified the order by noting the friars' "express wish to try to convert the Indians before they have contact with the Spaniards" (*id.* at 59).

129. *Id.* at 61. Las Casas engaged in the famous debate with Juan Ginés de Sepúlveda at Valladolíd in 1550 on Indian capacity. R. Berkhofer, *supra* note 63, at 11–12.

130. The final officially sanctioned experiment on Indian capacity highlights in a poignant fashion the limiting constraints imposed on the Spanish Humanist reform movement in America by its Eurocentric normative orientation. In 1532 an exasperated royal governor, Manuel Rojas, advised the Spanish Crown to attempt one more experiment, for the sake of "the royal conscience," with a select group of Indians. The plan, announced by royal order in December 1533, was to place the Indians in an experimental village, where, after a sufficient period of instruction and observation, they would be allowed to petition for their liberty. If they had demonstrated that they could use their freedom wisely, they would be set free.

That the natives had a deep-seated aversion to leaving their original homes (there had been reports of mass suicides in response to earlier attempts at removals) mattered little to Rojas. Nor did the fact that the supervisor of the experimental village fell ill and left the natives unattended for eight months. He reported to the Crown in 1535 that the Indians were generally incapable of living by themselves and should all be commended to Spaniards. One Indian who did seem capable of living by himself had appeared before Rojas. The governor determined that the Indian's wife "was old and therefore impossible to reform." Accordingly, the man could have liberty, but his wife was to remain in the village. The Indian declined Rojas's offer and did not request liberty again. *See* L. Hanke, *supra* note 84, at 51–53.

131. *Id.* at 53.

132. During the sixteenth century, the Roman curia attempted to increase its influence over an emerging and increasingly independence-minded episcopate outside Rome, primarily by increasing the predominance in Church councils of the Italian bishops, who were for the most part wholly dependent on the Holy See. At one juncture during the century, there were 150 Italian bishops as opposed to 66 bishops from other countries; hence, the papacy effectively controlled the outcomes of the various episcopal councils during the period. The Spanish bishops especially resented what they regarded as papal interference with the independence of their spiritual functions. The conflict culminated with the convocation of a general council of Trent (later moved to Bologna) in 1545. Led by Archbishop Guerrero of Granada, the Spanish prelates denounced the usurpations of episcopal authority by the Holy See and protested that Rome had effectively transformed the bishops into mere vicars-general of the papacy. Guerrero demanded that the pope's abuses be remedied by the restoration to the bishops of all powers and functions that had been usurped by the Holy See. E. Nys, "Introduction," F.Victoria, *De Indis et de Ivre Belli Reflectiones* 73 (E. Nys ed., J. Bate trans. 1917).

133. On Victoria's life and intellectual background, *see* E. Nys, *supra*, at 55–100.

134. *See* F. Cohen, *supra* note 121.

135. While Victoria's extensive contribution to European international law's conception of American Indian rights and status is not in controversy (*see id.*), a lively scholarly debate has long raged over the Dominican's sometimes asserted status as "the real founder of modern international law" (*id.*, at 44). Felix Cohen, the leading twentieth-century scholar on Indian rights and status in United States law (*see* R. Williams, "The Medieval and Renaissance Origins of the Status of the

American Indian in Western Legal Thought," 57 *S. Cal. L. Rev.* 1, 1 n. 1), has cemented permanently in the minds of United States' Indian law scholars the notion that Victoria was principally responsible for providing "a humane and rational basis for an American law of Indian affairs" (F. Cohen, *supra* note 121, at 9-21). Victoria's lectures on Indian rights, however, advocated denying the Indian self-governing rights, albeit according to the Law of Nations. *See* R. Williams, *supra*, at 70-99. Cohen apparently relied on James Brown Scott's favorable assessment of Victoria in asserting that Victoria was "the real founder of modern international law" (Cohen, *supra*, at 44). *See* J. Scott, "Preface" to F. Victoria, *supra* note 132; J. Scott, *The Spanish Origin of International Law* (1934). The extremely influential Scott (1866-1943) served as an official of the Carnegie Endowment for Peace, director of the endowment's Division of International Law, editor (1907-1924) of its publication *The American Journal of International Law*, and general editor of its series of texts (Victoria's included; see F. Victoria, *supra*) entitled *Classics of International Law*. Here is Scott's evaluation of Victoria's role:

> [T]he general editor is unwilling to allow the volume to get to press without a tribute in passing to the broad-minded and generous-hearted Dominican, justly regarded as one of the founders of International Law, and whose two tractates here reproduced are, as Thucydides would say, a perpetual possession to the international lawyer. Victoria's claim as a founder of the Law of Nations must unfortunately be based upon these two readings taken down by a pupil and published after his death, without the professor's revision and in a very summary form. They are sufficient, however, to show that International Law is not a thing of our day and generation or of the Hague Conferences, nor indeed the creation of Grotius, but that the system is almost as old as the New World. [J. Scott, *supra*, at 5.]

On another occasion, Scott wrote of Victoria, "In the lecture of Vitorio on the Indians, and in his smaller tractate on War, we have before our eyes, and at hand, a summary of the modern law of nations" (F. Cohen, *supra*, at 44 n. 34 [quoting J. Scott, *supra*]).

Other scholars' assessments of Victoria's role as "founder" of modern international law (*see*, e.g., A. Nussbaum, *supra* note 49, at 80-81; E. Nys, *supra* note 132, at 96-99) have differed substantially from those put forward by Cohen and Scott. Muldoon has written a bibliographical survey that provides a superb analysis of the various scholarly opinions of Victoria's contributions to Indian law. *See* J. Muldoon, "The Contributions of the Medieval Canon Lawyers to the Formation of International Law," 28 *Traditio* 483 (1972).

136. E. Nys, *supra* note 132, at 71.

137. F. Victoria, *supra* note 132.

138. O. Gierke, *Natural Law and the Theory of Society 1500-1800* 85 (E. Barker trans. 1934).

139. F. Victoria, *supra* note 132, at 115.

140. *Id.* at 128.

141. *See* Chapter 1, text accompanying notes 82-120, *supra*.

142. F. Victoria, *supra* note 132, at 123.

143. *Id.* at 125-28.

144. *Id.* at 127-28.

145. *See*, e.g., F. Cohen, *supra* note 134, at 11-12.

146. F. Victoria, *supra* note 132, at 129. The summary of the argument presented in section 2 of "On the Indians Lately Discovered" provides a concise example of the "scholastic" method. Victoria set out and proceeded to resolve sixteen basic propositions, which constitute the argument on the illegitimacy of the titles for the reduction of the aborigines of the New World into the power of the Spaniards.

147. *See* text accompanying notes 47-74, *supra*.

148. F. Victoria, *supra* note 132, at 138-39.

149. *Id.*

150. *See* Chapter 7, *infra*.

151. F. Victoria, *supra* note 132, at 137.

152. *See* text accompanying notes 61-69, *supra*.

153. *See* text accompanying notes 105-118, *supra*.

154. F. Victoria, *supra* note 132, at 131.

155. *Id.* at 131.

156. *Id.* at 137.

157. *Id.* at 135. Section 2 of "On the Indians Lately Discovered" represents Victoria's intense, Renaissance-inspired effort to drag Spanish legal discourse into the sixteenth century and to demolish any vestiges of medieval hierocratic forms. This effort even extended to challenging his sovereign Charles V's hierocratically grounded claim to rights in the Indies as Holy Roman Emperor. Charles's Germanic predecessors had proclaimed and frequently exercised the hierocratically conceived universal right to conquer or rule infidels. This right of imperial conquest was regarded as a vital and traditional function of the Holy Roman Emperor's office. Victoria denied any right under natural law to the emperor, *qua* head of any universally conceived, transcendentally mandated empire, to dispossess infidels of their lawful rights and *dominium*. See F. Victoria, *supra* note 132, at 129–31.

158. F. Victoria, *supra* note 132, at 151.

159. *Id.* at 153.

160. *Id.* at 153.

161. In an earlier lecture entitled "Concerning the Civic Power," Victoria had stated that this Law of Nations

> has not only the force of a pact and agreement among men, but also the force of law; for the world as a whole, being in a way one single State, has the power to create laws that are just and fitting for all persons, as are the rules of international law. Consequently, it is clear that they who violate these international rules, whether in peace or in war, commit a mortal sin; moreover, in the gravest matters, such as the inviolability of ambassadors, it is not permissible for one country to refuse to be bound by international law, the latter having been established by the authority of the whole world. [Reprinted in J. Scott, *The Spanish Conception of International Law and of Sanctions* 1 (1934).]

162. F. Victoria, *supra* note 132, at 151.

163. *Id.* at 152.

164. *Id.* at 154.

165. *Id.* at 152.

166. In describing the liberal critique of judicial institutions in the England of William Blackstone's day, Duncan Kennedy has stated:

> The liberal argument was that the exercise of state power was legitimate only to the extent that it: (a) facilitated intercourse between individuals in the private sphere of civil society by protecting their rights against one another; or (b) protected those same individual rights against attempts by the state (especially the executive) to establish itself as a private power center. [D. Kennedy, "The Structure of Blackstone's Commentaries," *Buffalo L. Rev.* 205, 234 (1979).]

The paternity of the first strand of the liberal argument described above as outlined by Kennedy can be traced through the works of Grotius, writing in the early seventeenth century, directly back to Victoria. For example, in his 1609 tract "Freedom of the Seas" (*Mare liberum*), later incorporated into his seminal 1624 work, "On the Law of War and of Peace," Grotius cited directly Victoria's argument in "On the Indians Lately Discovered" to support his own contention that under the Law of Nations the Dutch had the right to sail to the East Indies to engage in peaceful trade with the natives. J. Scott, *supra* note 135, at 141, 145, 159–160.

167. F. Victoria, *supra* note 132, at 152–53.

168. *Id.*

169. *Id.* at 153.

170. *Id.*

171. *The Journal of Christopher Columbus* 194–200 (C. Jane trans. 1960).

172. Quoted in R. Berkhofer, Jr., *supra* note 63, at 7–8.

173. F. Victoria, *supra* note 132, at 153.

174. *Id.* at 154.

175. *Id.* at 155.

176. *Id.*

177. *Id.*

178. *See* Chapter 1, text accompanying notes 100–20, *supra*.

179. F. Victoria, *supra* note 132, at 125–28.

180. *Id.* at 160–61.

181. *Id.*

182. *Id.*

183. *Id.* at 156–57.

184. *Id.* at 157.

185. *Id.* at 157–58.

186. *See* text accompanying notes 25–35, *supra*.

187. *See* text accompanying notes 113–23, *supra*.

188. *See* R. Berkhofer, Jr., *supra* note 63, at 125.

189. Consider, for example, John Eliot's statement concerning the Indians whom he had converted to Christianity as a missionary in colonial New England:

> [T]hey began to enquire after baptism and Church Ordinances, and the way of worshipping God as the Churches here do; but I shewing how uncapable they be to be trusted therewith, whilst they live so unfixed, confused, and ungoverned a life, uncivilized, unsubdued to labor and order; they begin now to enquire after such things. And to that end, I have propounded to them that a fit place be found out for Cohabitation, wherewith they may subsist by labor, and settle themselves such a way: And then they may have a Church, and all the Ordinances of Christ amongst them. [Reprinted in E. Winslow, *The Glorious Progress of the Gospel Amongst the Indians in New England* 97 (1649).]

Perhaps the most famous of the seventeenth-century New England missionaries, Eliot established fourteen "praying towns" in Massachusetts where Indians were to be taught English values and customs along with the Englishman's religion.

After the American Revolution, Congress appropriated moneys to the War Department (which then had jurisdiction over Indian matters) "for the purpose of providing against the further decline and final extinction of the Indian tribes . . . and for introducing among them the habits and arts of civilization" (quoted in R. Berkhofer, Jr., *supra* note 63, at 149). The War Department subsequently handed over these funds to various missionary societies to carry out the work of "civilizing" the Indians. The 1823 statement by the Board of Managers of the United Foreign Missionary Society, one of the larger missionary groups, is strikingly similar in its tone and phrasing to King Philip II's 1573 proclamation mandating the peaceful conversion of the Indian:

> Let then, missionary Institutions, established to convey to them the benefits of civilization and the blessings of Christianity, be efficiently supported; and with cheering hope, you may look forward to the period when the savage shall be converted into the citizen; when the hunter shall be transformed into the mechanic; when the farm, the workshop, the School-House, and the Church shall adorn every Indian village; when the fruits of Industry, good order, and sound morals, shall bless every Indian dwelling; and when throughout the vast range of country from the Mississippi to the Pacific, the red man and the white man shall everywhere be found, mingling in the same benevolent and friendly feelings, and fellow-heirs to a glorious inheritance in the kingdom of Immanuel. [Reprinted in *id.* at 151 (footnote omitted).]

190. L. Hanke, *supra* note 84, at 131 (footnote omitted).

191. Robert Wood provides a thoughtful insight into this historical process—a process central not only to the Spanish colonial experience but also to the European colonial movement and the development of the Law of Nations in general:

> The medieval system of unity gave rise in Western culture to the persistent idea that there are transnational norms which cut across and unite the separate political units and positive legal norms which provide domestic integration. . . .
>
> Although the unity of the medieval order had been shattered and fully independent territorial states had emerged, the concept of a universal community which embraced and

cut across those states continued. And although the centralized papal interpreter of the extraterritorial normative sphere had been eliminated, many believed that the concept was still valid. . . .

. . .

. . . The political system was thus seen as individualistic, contractual, limited, and secular in character. Moreover, as the European state was seen as both founded upon and judged by universal norms, it was in effect an archetypical organization—capable of being transplanted in other regions and expanded conceptually and practically on a global scale. In terms of these images, therefore, Europeans were able to define their relationship to each other and to the world. As the European material base expanded, the conceptual foundations were ready for the extension of the European state system beyond its borders. [R. Wood, "History, Thought and Images: The Development of International Law and Organization," 12 *Va. J. Int'l L.* 35, 38–39 (1971).]

Part II

Protestant Discourses

The history of the West's discourses of conquest would present a far less challenging and diverse terrain to wander had the Reformation not completed the destruction of the Church's hegemony in Western political and legal thought. While post-Reformation Europe retained the totalizing vision of a universal normative world order in the form of a Euro-centered discourse of a Law of Nations, Rome's privileged role in interpreting the Christian European's vision of one right way of life for all humankind did not survive the fragmentation of the medieval system. England and the other western European states that broke with Rome in the sixteenth century refused to acknowledge the pope's presumption of jurisdiction over the nationalized pursuit of worldly empire. The intense rivalry among would-be colonial powers to plant their respective visions of civilization around the expanding globe irrupted into a profusion of discourses throughout Christian Europe, each legitimating, energizing, and constraining the seizure of lands from their non-Christian inhabitants.

In Discovery-era England particularly, the Reformation worked perhaps the most profound transformations throughout all discursive domains of society, redefining and crystallizing a vision of national identity and destiny. The West's most potent, aggressive will to empire emerged from the convergence of radical Protestantism's consuming rivalry with Rome and its papal agent in the New World, Spain, and a national economy freed from religious constraints and primed to create surplus national wealth in the world trading system. The story of the first English legal discourse of conquest illustrates law's appropriative capacity for organizing the chaos of a suddenly liberated will to empire into a rationalized, efficient program for carrying the burden of European civilization to the non-European world.

3

The Protestant Translation of Medieval and Renaissance Discourses on the Rights and Status of American Indians

The patents granted by the Tudor king Henry VII (r. 1485–1509) to the Cabots at the close of the fifteenth century inaugurated English interest in America as a possible colonial empire.[1] Although several centuries separated the Tudor dynasty from the heraldic Crusading traditions established by Richard the Lionhearted,[2] Henry's initial 1497 charter of conquest to John Cabot indicates that the medieval discourses of the Catholic Church respecting infidel rights and status still dominated English legal thought and practice a short generation prior to the Reformation. Henry's charter authorized Cabot and his crew to "occupy and possess all such towns, cities, castles and lands" belonging to heathen and infidel peoples discovered during the voyage, "getting unto us the rule, title, and jurisdiction of the same." The king's feudal charter of conquest, however, carefully instructed Cabot to sail only to lands "unknown to all Christians" in the north, west, and east—avoiding Africa to the south, which had already been granted to Portugal by the pope.[3]

Cabot himself, as initiator of the proposed discovery venture, most likely suggested to the Crown the form of the royal letters patent. Having spent the early years of his maritime career in the principal trading ports of the Mediterranean, Cabot had ready access to information about the Portuguese voyages of discovery and conquest to Africa. It is thus not surprisng that Cabot's patent followed the form of similar charters that the Portuguese kings had been granting to their navigators since the early Discovery era.[4]

This Iberian-inspired document by which King Henry speculatively reserved a "fifth part" of all profits for the English Crown was firmly grounded in the hierocratic legitimating discourses of the Crusading-era Church. Henry's limitation of the scope of Cabot's activities away from Africa was most probably a recognition of a prior treaty between England and Portugal. In that agreement, Edward IV had specifically recognized Portugal's papally based title to its west African discoveries. Henry VII continued to enforce the restriction prohibiting colonizing activity in lands under the papally granted sovereignty of the Portuguese Crown in subsequent charters of colonization. A 1502 patent authorizing the first English attempt to establish a settlement in the New World (which eventually came to naught) contained the following restrictions on the English colonists:

[I]n no manner shall they enter upon or hinder those countries, nations, regions or provinces, heathen or infidel, which have previously been found by the subjects of our most dear brother and cousin the king of Portugal, or any other prince, friend, or neighbor of ourselves, and which already are in the possession of the said princes.[5]

Thus the father of the great antipapist Henry VIII delimited his subjects' colonizing ambitions according to the asserted papally based claims of the Catholic kingdom of Portugal and the other Christian princes of Europe. The Reformation of Henry VIII would alter the trajectory of the entire domain of discursive practices throughout England, but nowhere would that alteration be more aggressively evidenced than in English colonizing discourse. The genealogy of the legal discourse of the Protestant crusade against the infidels of America traces a process by which the medieval discourses of the Catholic Church were domesticated and combined with other discursive practices appropriated from a variety of English and non-English sources. The strange fruit of the seeds planted by this careful Protestant husbandry was a discourse of conquest confirming the election of England as the Christian nation chosen by Providence to pursue a divinely mandated destiny in the New World.

The English Reformation

It was not because of his father's patent restrictions on settlement of Iberian-claimed heathen lands that Henry VIII (r. 1509–1547) failed to follow up on the Cabots' New World discoveries. Wars against Christian princes in Europe and his Reformation of the English Catholic Church sufficiently occupied Henry VIII's attentions and talents to push interest in speculative liens on distant New World territories to the periphery of royal concerns. However, Henry's intracontinental rivalries with other European states, and the radical transformations of English economy and society that were accelerated by his Reformation, articulated many of the vital conditions of English conquest of the northern half of the New World over the course of the next two centuries.

The Reformation's Transformation of English Society

Henry VIII was a fortunate son. His legacy from his father included the raw materials of the first modern sovereign state. Henry VII's centralization of royal power following the Wars of the Roses had reined in the more fractious elements of the higher feudal nobility. Regional turbulence in the historically rebellious north and west had been quelled. The Tudor Crown's demesne lands had been significantly expanded, resulting in increased royal income. Legislative measures had been enacted to maximize feudal incidents and customs duties. Overall, Henry VII's reign of fiscal reform had witnessed a tripling of Crown revenues.[6]

The first Tudor king's son thus assumed the throne in 1509 with a treasury reserve of between £1 and 2 million.[7] Aided by his principal deputy, Thomas Cromwell, Henry VIII built on this foundation, further strengthening the administrative apparatus of the Tudor state. Rationalization and centralization of fiscal management, the rise of the privy council as a coordinating organ of government, and other reforms worked toward overall bureaucratic specialization and order.[8]

It has been argued that the administrative "revolution" achieved by this first "modern" state[9] was a concomitant of the greater coordination required by emerging capitalist interests in the English economy.[10] Whatever impetus toward rationalization existed in the private sectors of the English Tudor-era economy, Henry's own political impulses were always oriented by a medievalized feudal, rather than "modern" capitalist, paradigm of expansion. Henry VIII principally thought and acted in terms of placing his ample royal person on the apex of some already existing, more readily exploitable feudal structure of ascending revenues. Building such a structure from the ground up in a savage, uncivilized, and therefore unfeudalized wilderness an ocean away never appealed to the cash-strapped Henry. Throughout his profligate reign, he preferred to squander the material benefits of his modernizing reforms in support of his extravagant feudal ambitions on the European continent. He sought to revive Lancastrian claims to the French Crown, fought to block the Valois absorption of Brittany, and entertained grand designs on both the Spanish succession and the German imperial throne. Large sums were invested in these dynastic ventures, but all came to naught.[11] National capital that might otherwise have been expended on voyages following up the Cabot transatlantic discoveries was instead diverted and absorbed by Henry's retrograde aspirations in the Old World. His shortsightedness in this regard is underscored by the extra-European activities of the similarly imperial- and absolutist-minded monarchs of Spain and Portugal at this time. The Iberians were rapidly expanding the material base of their political economies to meet the requirements of their emerging capitalist interests by investing outside the fiercely contested European theater of battle. While Henry focused England's limited resources almost exclusively on realizing his expensive continental aspirations, the Iberians were acquiring and feudalizing valuable income-producing lands at relatively minor expense. A handful of conquistadores and the *Requerimiento*[12] could capture a vast territory and a servile labor supply at a fraction of the cost of one of Henry's ill-fated European ventures.

Ironically, the revenue drain from his shortsighted European wars finally led Henry to the conclusion that he also needed cheaply acquired feudatory lands and resources outside the fiercely contested European continent. Henry, however, did not look across the Atlantic for new revenues. He instead looked inside England, to the vast territories and resources of the English Catholic Church.

The seeds of Henry's nationalization of the Catholic Church were germinated by the marriage crisis of 1527 to 1528. Pope Clement VII, subservient to the dominance of Hapsburg power in Europe, enforced Emperor Charles V's objections to Henry's divorce of Catherine of Aragon, Charles's aunt. Henry responded to this obstruction of his plan to marry Ann Boleyn by summoning Parliament in 1529 and rallying national support against Rome and the emperor. He asked for and was granted the endorsement for an unprecedented state seizure of the Church.[13]

While revenues realized from his confiscation of Church property permitted Henry to continue with his continental ambitions, an even greater consequence of his Reformation was the more firm alignment of the emerging capitalist interests in his kingdom with his own. As Christopher Hill has stated, Henry's breach with Rome was a profound act of state, with momentous extratheological implications for all of English society.[14] First, the Reformation considerably weakened the Church as an institution with a principal directive role in England's economic and political life. Henry's dissolution and confiscation of the monasteries brought him lands with a net annual income of more than £136,000 and bullion, plate, and other valuable chattel property worth as much as £1.5 million. The significance of the financial windfall created by the Reformation is further highlighted by the fact that Henry's revenues from Crown lands never exceeded £40,000 a year prior to his break with Rome.[15]

Politically, the clerical majority in the House of Lords was reduced to a minority with the removal of abbots from that body. Benefices providing rich endowments to clergy were lost, bishops lacking a feudal base became dependent on the Crown, and the Church's control over patronage benefiting laymen as well as clerics disappeared. Moneys previously siphoned out of the kingdom to Rome, such as the £40,000 a year in first-fruits and tenths, now became part of the regular income of the Crown. Less tangible, but just as significant in terms of indigenous national institutional development, was the fact that Henry's Reformation cut off legal appeals to Rome.[16] Domesticated reason, rather than the papal curia, would become the ultimate source of appeal in English law.

Henry further shifted the balance of power in his favor by making the lay landed class the chief beneficiaries of his largesse with former Church property. By the end of his reign, Henry had alienated two-thirds of the confiscated monastic lands to private individuals. To appreciate the significance of this transfer of national landed wealth (the most desired type of wealth in a feudal landed economy), it is worth noting that before the Reformation the monastic estates had amounted to perhaps a quarter of all the acreage in England.[17] Henry freely granted the former Church lands to peers, courtiers, royal officials, and servants, and at extremely favorable prices. Just as important, he succeeded in reducing the traditional counterbalancing influences of the great feudal families in the kingdom. A large percentage of the monastic estates went to "new men"—aspiring lesser gentry who had worked their way up through royal service and resultant favor and looked askance at the traditional privileges of the nobility. These "new men" were the greatest ultimate beneficiaries of Henry's Reformation in the English political economy. They saw their landed estates and their corresponding political power increase greatly in the kingdom, at the expense of the higher nobility.

For the new landed classes in particular, acquisition of a monastic estate increased opportunities for extracting surpluses from lands previously managed by a different, less profit-oriented set of assumptions. Improved methods of agriculture, conversion of the abbey into a glass factory or worsted manufactory—these were the sorts of local initiatives that contributed to the transformation of an entire economic culture. As a local ecclesiastical estate was converted into a profit-maximizing participant in the regional, national, or even world economy, other large estateholders would frequently awaken to the new, emergent paradigm of property management. Pursuit of self-interest in the countryside accelerated the conversion of large landholdings from casual crop agriculture to more intensive farming and sheepherding techniques. Baronial munificence was replaced by a profit-making mentality. Particularly in the south and east, numerous disruptions were caused by the eviction of copyholders and enclosure of common lands previously farmed and hunted by the lower orders. Long-established social and class patterns were radically altered. The displaced tenantry occupied the new niches created in a transforming economy. Peasant farmers became factory workers in the growing urban areas or went underground as wage laborers in the mines. The yeoman's semi-independence in the countryside was lost as a new English working class emerged out of the coal pits and mills.[18]

Henry's dissolution of the monasteries caused problems for the old aristocracy as well. Old money was naturally inclined to be out of sympathy with Henry's policies. A monastery was a valuable asset to the family that traditionally endowed it. Revenues were realized through the abbot's feudal dependence. In turn, lucrative posts controlled by the monastery were granted to peers and their family members. Just as important, monasteries provided respectable careers for younger sons left landless by feudal primogeniture. And, as John Milton noted, nunneries, also plundered in the Reformation, were handy "stowage" places for "withered daughters."[19] Henry's closing of these religious institutions meant that new niches would be needed for these displaced members of the better families. For "portionless younger sons of good family,"[20] the growth of free enterprise and merchant entrepreneurship would provide many of those new positions.

Henry's Reformation and dissolution of the monasteries also engendered widespread transformations in social attitudes respecting economic life. Holy days on which little or no productive work was accomplished were a commonplace of medieval Catholic society. In Spain, for example, the number of holy days amounted to several months of lost work a year. Protestantism drastically curtailed observance of a large number of these nonproductive holidays. New attitudes respecting work and the indigent also began to take shape. The monasteries ceased to function as an important cog in the social machinery of relief for the poor, and begging became regarded as a social problem, rather than as a holy state or necessity.[21]

On an international scale, Henry's confiscations of church properties financed England's assumption of a new status as a significant military power in Europe, particularly on the sea. The revenues from the sale of monastic lands

helped Henry underwrite his dynastic wars in France and, even more important, the construction of a formidable naval fleet of more than fifty ships.
While the wars ultimately yielded little in comparison to Henry's enormous
capital investments, the navy served as the first building block for the unrivaled
overseas empire that England constructed during the next two centuries.

Thus by the time of Henry's death in 1547, many of the vital material
conditions for English expansion and colonization were in place. There was the
potential in the English economy for surplus private capital that could be
mobilized for financing speculative investments and surplus manufacturing
capacity that could convert cheap raw materials from colonial markets into
finished goods for re-export to those same new markets. There was a growing
surplus labor pool that could be exported to relieve domestic employment
pressures not absorbed by internal economic expansion. The expanded navy
could foster the development of an expanded merchant marine to carry the
new trade and colonists.

But at the time of Henry's death, these elements were dispersed and largely
unsynthesized in the English political economy. They had yet to coalesce to
form the organizing indigenous principles and distinctive patterns that would
later characterize English colonial discourse as an energizing, dynamic force in
the nation's dramatic overseas expansion. A centralized national political
economy could provide the bridgehead for English New World conquest, but it
could not alone provide the discursive materials necessary to construct the
bridge by which the English came to comprehend and realize their errand into
the North American wilderness. A discursive practice that articulated, organized and dispersed the available knowledges of conquest and empire, and that
explained, legitimated, and energized England's colonization of the New
World, constituted the final condition for England to enter its Age of Discovery. Here also, Henry's Reformation easily located the starting points for the
emergence of a distinctively English colonial discourse. Protestant England
found its natural rival in the popish antithesis represented by Catholic Spain.
English colonial discourse in the Tudor age thus possessed the singular advantage of having a highly volatile inaugural point around which it could organize
its major themes. Spanish colonizing theory and practice presented an array of
already-proved discursive models worthy of appropriation by a Protestant
colonial competitor seeking to challenge papist Spain's illegitimate New World
monopoly.

A Prefatory Colonizing Discourse

In 1553, six years after Henry's death, Richard Eden, educated at Cambridge,
servant in the royal Treasury, and (like so many of his class in Tudor Renaissance England) a part-time man of letters, published the first English translation of Amerigo Vespucci's accounts of his New World discoveries.[22] Vespucci,
an Italian (like Columbus), had made several journeys to the New World on
behalf of both Spain and Portugal between 1497 and 1504.

Eden's abridged translation of Vespucci's sometimes fantastic letters reaffirmed the incredible rumors and folklore already circulating throughout Europe of a strange new world inhabited by flesh-eating, barbarous peoples. Vespucci reported that the natives of the New World had no laws, manners, or civilized religion. They engaged in constant warfare (in this they were not very different from the nations of Europe), but "not for the enlarging of their dominions" or "for the increase of riches, because they are content with their own commodities" (here, the English reader no doubt recognized a difference). Rather, the New World's savages fought only to avenge the death of their predecessors[23] (here, the English reader might have been reminded of a distant heritage of blood feud that had once obsessed the northern tribes of Europe that had stocked Britannia).

Elaborating on this fundamental difference in the acquisitiveness and material value structure of the cultures of the New World (a difference that the Spanish Dominican priest Franciscus de Victoria had seized on in constructing his Law of Nations[24]), Vespucci stated that the savages of America "use no kind of merchandize, or buying and selling, being content only with that which nature has left them. As for gold, pearls, precious stones, jewels, and such other things which we in Europe esteem as pleasure and delicates, they set naught by."[25]

Eden followed his small sampler of Vespuccian exotica with a volume that would make a more extensive contribution to English awareness of the New World. In 1555 Eden published an 800-page text entitled *The Decades of the Newe Worlde or West India*.[26] This tome contained abridged translations of the works of two major early-sixteenth-century historians of the Spanish conquest, Pietro Martire of Anghiera and Gonzalo Fernández de Oviedo.[27]

The abridged translations of the Italian Martire's works were based on the first three segments of his eight-part treatise on the history of the New World, *De Orbo Novo Decades*, published in Seville beginning in 1511.[28] Part 1 detailed Columbus's first three voyages to the New World. Martire did not refute Vespucci's assertions of Indian cannibalism; in fact, he was usually more precise respecting details. Martire, however, made sharp distinctions between cannibalistic and noncannibalistic Indians, thereby introducing his readers to a diversity among American tribal cultures. He described the noncannibal Indians as "meek and humane people,"[29] who freely imitated the kneeling posture of the praying Spanish sailors. Martire's description of Columbus's experiences also affirmed Vespucci's observations on the simplicity of the natives' laws, manners, and wants:

Mine and Thine, the seeds of all mischief, have no place with them. They are content with so little, that in so large a country they have rather superfluity than scarceness. So that they seem to live in the Golden World, without toil. . . . They deal truly one with another, without laws, without books, without judges.[30]

Other favorable images of the Indian appeared throughout Martire's narrative of Columbus's adventures. Except for those peoples encountered only occasionally in cannibal territory, the Indians generally entertained the captain and his men with kindness and liberality.

While images of a "Golden World" constituted a major theme of Eden's translation of Martire's history, the second half of Eden's book, the abridged translation of Oviedo's *Natural Hystoria de las Indias*, first published in 1526,[31] presented a far more uniformly negative image of the Indian. Oviedo had served as overseer and brander of the Indian slaves captured for the Spanish gold mines in the early years of Caribbean conquest. The Dominican missionary Bartolomé de Las Casas, the Crown-appointed protector of the Indians, labeled Oviedo "one of the greatest enemies the Indians have had."[32]

Satan dominated Oviedo's descriptions of the savages of America. The devil was active throughout the Indies. He was honored "with sacrifices of the blood and lives of men."[33] He ruled the minds of the natives through the *tequinas*, the Indian priests.

As has been noted, Eden's translations of Martire and Oviedo were abridgments of the original texts. His editorial hand was particularly heavy with respect to Oviedo's narrative. He eliminated several major passages in which Oviedo detailed acts of Spanish butchery against the Indians on Hispaniola. As just one instance, Eden's book did not include the following passage from Oviedo's original text:

Maliciously they [the Spanish colonists] have caused the death of many Indians who could have been converted and saved. Even if those who died could not have been converted, they would have been useful to your majesty and helpful to the Christians. And no part of the island would have been completely depopulated, for from the above cause it is almost uninhabited. Those who have perpetrated those crimes call the uninhabited places "peaceful.' I feel they are more than peaceful; they are destroyed.[34]

Eden had ample reason for exercising editorial discretion regarding this type of "superfluous" (Eden's own word)[35] material. His translation of Martire's text had already discussed several of the abusive practices of Christopher Columbus's gubernatorial administration. Editor Eden may simply have been trying to avoid reiteration in his subsequent Oviedo abridgment. But it should also be remembered that Mary Tudor (r. 1553–1558), Henry VIII's daughter by his first divorced wife, Catherine of Aragon, was England's reigning sovereign at the time Eden wrote. Like her Spanish mother, Mary was a devout Catholic and had not been treated kindly by her father. Upon assuming the English throne, Mary sought to dismantle many of her father's Protestant reforms. At the suggestion of the Holy Roman emperor Charles V, she wed Charles's son, Philip II, prince of Spain. The royal marriage was intended to initiate English rapprochement with Rome and Catholic Europe. The marriage was very unpopular among English Protestants, particularly the more radical clergy. In February 1555, several prominent bishops who had refused to accept certain essential doctrines of the newly reinstated Catholic Church were burned at the stake as heretics. Thus began the legend of "Bloody Mary" and the hagiography of the Marian martyrs.

Eden himself, having matriculated at Cambridge, an institution suspected of housing many Protestant radicals, would have been regarded as politically suspect in Marian England. His translations of the Spanish colonial texts were published at the height of the Marian persecutions. Given the heated climate of the times, he may have chosen to delete repetitious material that dwelled on the darker side of the Spanish Catholic conquests, to which Philip, Mary's husband, was heir. Despite his caution, Eden would find himself charged with heresy in the general purges of 1556. While he did not lose his life, as did many of his Protestant countrymen, he did lose his job in the royal Treasury.[36]

Perhaps Eden's life was spared because of his treatise's prefatory remarks on the valor of "our noble and gracious prince King Philip."[37] His preface unsparingly flattered the genius of Spain and its heroism in spreading the faith to heathen lands, and implored Englishmen to imitate the Spanish enterprise in those parts of America that had not yet received the light of the Christian gospel.

Eden's preface paid particular homage to King Ferdinand of Spain, who had initiated the conquest of America. "God hath fulfilled in him . . . the promises and blessings of Abraham, as to make him the father of many nations, and his seed to grow great upon the earth."[38] (Eden here was perhaps taking an indirect but wholly gratuitous swipe at the infamous and frequent failures of Henry in fathering a male heir. The allusion would doubtless have pleased Philip, Ferdinand's great-grandson, as well as Mary, who probably felt little affection for her deceased father.)

Eden continued his paean to Ferdinand, whose colonizing enterprises had spread the light of Christian reason to the heathen: "He saved not only the bodies but also the souls of innumerable millions of men inhabiting a great part of the world heretofore unknown and drowned in the deluge of error." Ferdinand had planted a "new Israel," an act "whose perfection extendeth to the gratifying of universal mankind."[39]

Eden's prefatory essay also offered an extended defense of Spain's New World conquests, based on familiar medieval Christian principles of natural law. In the Spaniard's "merciful wars against these naked people" (nakedness was an indication of savagery and barbarity to all educated European Christians of the sixteenth century) nothing was taken from the Indians except that which they regarded as "superfluities" (gold and precious stones, for instance). "For the which they recompensed them with such things as they much more esteemed"[40] (such as baubles and trinkets, according to the reports of Columbus in Martire's text as translated by Eden[41]).

As for critics who asserted that the Spaniards "possess and inhabit" regions rightfully belonging to the Indians and enslave them against their will, Eden repeated an already familiar argument in European colonizing discourse that would only increase in its usefulness as Europe further penetrated new regions in the Americas:

They inhabit their regions indeed. Yet so, that by their diligence and better manuring the same, they may now better sustain both, than one before. Their bondage is such as is much rather to be desired than their former liberty: Which was to the cruel cannibals rather a horrible licentiousness than a liberty; and to the innocent so terrible a bondage, that in the midst of their fearful idleness they were ever in danger to be prey to those man-hunting wolves.[42]

Eden elaborated on this familiar, medievally derived theme of the necessity of the savages' conversion and assimilation to European norms as justifying their conquest and enslavement by European Christians. Those Indians who could not be converted and brought to "civility" had been killed. Those who converted were saved. The Spaniards had thus "brought unto these new Gentiles the victory of Christ's death, whereby they, being subdued with the worldly sword, are now made free from the bondage of Satan's tyranny." Thus "this mighty portion of the world hath been added to the flock of Christ's congregation." Rather than chastise Spain, England should praise the fact that God's kingdom had been enlarged, to the confusion of the devil and the Turk.[43]

Nor could England reproach Spain for using force to convert the natives. Israel was permitted to use "all means and policies to build up the walls of earthly Jerusalem." How much more, Eden declaimed, ought men today use all means available to build up the walls of spiritual Jerusalem, "whose foundation is Christ, willing all the nations of the world to be builded upon the same." And as for those righteous-minded individuals who would assert that the Spaniards' desire for gold was the chief object of their conquest, Eden conceded that even if this were so, a man could be a merchant and a Christian at the same time. In fact, these dual motives, Christianity and profit, could well complement each other.[44]

Eden's image of the merchant-Christian bringing civility through "conversation" (his word for "commerce") with the heathen represents an important new peroration in the discursive thematics of European colonizing discourse. In an era when the European world trading system was about to supersede the medieval Crusade as the preferred device for penetrating alien cultures, the iconography of the Christian merchant-adventurer was gradually supplanting that of the Christian warrior knight. Economic, as opposed to military, penetration was privileged in Eden's text as the preferred instrument of European empire in America. Commerce would be the emetic by which the Indians would gradually be purged of Satan's influence and at the same time would quickly be assimilated into European civilization and its mercantile trading system.[45]

[M]ay these barbarians by the only conversation with the Christians (although they were enforced thereto) be brought to such familiarity with civility and virtue, that not only we may take great commodity thereby, but they may also herewith imbibe true religion, as a thing accidental, although neither they nor we should seek the same. For like as they that go much in the sun are colored therewith, although they go not for that purpose, so may the conversation of the Christians with the Gentiles induce them to our religion, where there is no great cause of contrary to resist; as is in the Jews and Turks, who are already drowned in their confirmed error.[46]

The Indian, according to Eden, was like "a smooth and bare table unpainted . . . upon the which you may at the first paint or write what you list, as you cannot upon tables already painted." Thus the savages would be easier lured to the Christian faith, "for that it is more agreeable to the law of nature than either the ceremonious law of Moses, or portentous fables of Mohamet's Alcoran."[47]

Eden wrote a generation after Henry's Reformation. The notion that an individual could be a good merchant and a good Christian at the same time spoke directly to those segments of English society that sought to harmonize the secular acquisitive impulses released by the Reformation with Christianity's traditions emphasizing spiritual over worldly goals. Eden's colonizing discourse elevated merchant trade with the American savages to the level of a divinely mandated imperative, the worldly means by which the Indians' souls would be saved. Such was the genius, according to Eden, demonstrated by Spain's entry into the New World for profit and Christianity. And the English, Eden urged, ought to emulate the genius of Spain by pursuing Christianity's trade-facilitated divine mandate in regions not yet conquered by *that* Christian country: "there yet remaineth another portion of that mainland, reaching toward the north-east, thought to be as large as the other and yet not known but only by the sea coasts, neither inhabited by any Christian men."[48]

Eden asserted that the unclaimed parts of North America "seemeth little inferior to our Europe, if the inhabitants had received our religion. They are witty people, and refuse not bartering with strangers." The Indians, Eden exhorted, are the new gentiles. Would Christ's disciple Paul, "the doctor of the gentiles," have delayed as long as the English had in bringing the light of the gospel to the heathen?[49] "What then think you he [Paul] would do if he were now alive? Is it to be thought that he would not adventure twenty-five days sailing, to come to such a mart of souls, in such readiness to be easily obtained?"[50]

Eden's preface and his abridged translations of Vespucci, Martire, and Oviedo in essence represented post-Henrician England's first promotional tracts advocating English colonization of North America. These translated discourses of discovery and conquest skillfully filtered out the principal themes of Spanish colonizing discourse for eager consumption by an English-speaking audience. In Eden's texts, the Indians appeared as redeemable yet exploitable savages. Their religion and culture were easily corrected aberrations; their capacity to resist English arms and civilization was negligible. As for the gold, silver, and other forms of wealth found in the Indians' New World, these they lightly regarded. In sum, the Indians' own backward state cried out for Christian conquest and conversion at the hands of the English.

The Elizabethan Restoration

The Spaniards zealously guarded their asserted popish New World monopoly from any and all types of European encroachments. As long as the Catholic wife of Philip of Spain sat on the English throne, no English merchant would be allowed to act on Eden's novel ideas and plant English seeds of commerce and Christian faith in the New World. But the desire for "conversation" with the Indians and the wealth of America, for which Eden, like many of the young gentry and rising merchant class of England so yearned, could be held in check only as long as the English Crown recognized Rome's pretentious approval of Spain's New World monopoly. That situation was bound to change, for in the very month that Eden published his popular translations, Philip departed England, disillusioned with his wife, Mary, who apparently shared with her mother, Catherine of Aragon, the inability to bear a suitable heir. What irony was there, for when Mary died without issue in 1558, her half sister, the Protestant Elizabeth (Henry's daughter by his second wife, Ann Boleyn) assumed the throne of England (r. 1558-1603). By virtue of her Protestant religious persuasion, Queen Elizabeth I also assumed the inevitable title of chief rival to Catholic Spain in both Europe and the New World.

Elizabeth's ascension to the throne reinstituted certain critical economic, social, and religious processes of her father's Reformation, temporarily abated by Mary. Like her father, Elizabeth worked to ensure that the rising landed gentry and merchant class had, in Christopher Hill's famous phrase, "a vested interest in Protestantism."[51] A principal fear of this new class during Mary's reign had been the possibility that the monastic lands they had only recently been granted might be restored to the Church. Elizabeth's ascension to the English throne, however, assured this group that the Reformation's realignment of national wealth would remain undisturbed.

The Elizabethan restoration of Protestantism also injected a new force into the dynamics of English social, political, and economic development, which the Catholic Marian persecutions had suppressed. Anti-Catholic sentiment in England was now freed to express itself in virulent anti-Spanish themes, for it was a Spanish monarch who sat as emperor in Europe, who controlled the papacy, who spread the papist religion to the far corners of the globe, and who, perhaps most important, controlled the commerce of the New World's infidel and heathen lands.

Spain, in fact, and to a lesser degree France, had been engaged in extended exploration of the *North* American continent for several decades at the time of Elizabeth's ascension, while England had left virtually unclaimed the advantages of Cabot's earlier discoveries in that region. Elizabeth's ascension to the throne changed dramatically England's relation to Spain and thereby also its deferential stance toward Spain's papally based claims to hegemony in the New World. Upon assuming the throne, Elizabeth set out (as an inevitable consequence of her championing of English Protestantism) to distance England from Spain and its pretensions to imperial dominance in the whole New World.

Laissez-Faire Discourse

The contending legal visions animating sixteenth-century Europe's Law of Nations are indicated by the tripartite treaty negotiations among Spain, England, and France at Cateau-Cambresis in 1559. In the year before Mary's death, Philip had finally convinced his wife to align England with Spain in its running war with the French Crown. The war itself had spilled over into the New World. French corsairs had attacked Spanish shipping in the Indies, and French pirates (mostly Protestant Huguenots) had sacked Puerto Rico and Havana.

Elizabeth, upon assuming the throne in 1558, seized the opportunity provided by the treaty negotiations to press for an end to the war and the extrication of England from the distasteful Spanish alliance. The cost of England's divorce from Spain was dear: Elizabeth essentially surrendered to the French her Crown's claims to Calais. A treaty between France and England was signed at Cateau-Cambresis in 1559. France and Spain came to terms on the following day.[52]

During the negotiations between France and Spain, neither side's ministers could agree on a vital point of interest and international law. The French delegates insisted on the general right of French merchants to trade in the Indies. Spain, relying on its papal title, insisted on maintaining its monopoly rights in the Western Hemisphere. A letter explaining the impasse, written by the Spanish negotiators to their sovereign, Philip, outlined the parties' positions:

We have discussed for a long time the question of prohibiting the French from sailing to India [America]; but we have not succeeded in inducing them to exclude their subjects from such navigation entirely in such a way that they should not be allowed to go to such places which are discovered by us, but are not actually subject to the King of Spain or Portugal. They are willing only to consent not to go to the territories actually possessed by your majesty or the King of Portugal. . . . They allege the ordinary argument that the sea is common and free, while we are relying upon the principles laid down in the bulls of Pope Alexander.[53]

As the Spanish author of this dispatch admitted, the "ordinary" argument of freedom of the seas was no novelty in the diplomatic discourse of Renaissance Europe—half a century prior to Grotius! According to Frances Davenport, the French in fact were relying on legal arguments made by a group of English merchants who had asserted freedom of the seas as a right under the Law of Nations in negotiations with Spain's ally, Portugal, three years earlier. Both Spain and Portugal recognized that the scope of their claims was considerably narrowed by this more secularized, modern vision of international law, and insisted on th medieval precedent of papally recognized title in treaty negotiations throughout the Discovery period. France refused to assent to the popish principle at Cateau-Cambresis, and the result of this clash of medieval Church and secularized Renaissance legal discourses was to exclude the issue of the Indies from the treaty altogether. An oral agreement between the parties limited the application of their treaty of peace to the Old World. In the New World, beyond these stipulated "lines of amity," as Davenport has explained, "might should make right and violence done by either party to the other should not be regarded as in contravention of treaties."[54]

Elizabeth's negotiators would certainly have been privy to the terms of this agreement, particularly as France relied on an English-asserted precedent. Spain's concession in agreeing to declare the New World a "no man's land," in which civilized nations could attack other civilized nations with impunity and without regard to consequences in the Old World, represented a new era in European international law and commerce. The discovery of America had liberated the discursive practices of the European state system from the earlier constraints imposed by Christianity's vision of a universal Christian common-wealth governed by the peace of God. America had become the first great experiment in laissez-faire market economics, without even a prohibition on predatory tactics. The nation-states of Europe and their subjects asserted the right in this new domain to pursue their economic self-interest without any limitation except that imposed by a rival's superior forces.[55] As for the indige-nous inhabitants of the New World, as heathens and infidels they were re-garded by Catholic and Protestant Christians alike as fit subjects for conquest, colonization, and Christianization.

Perfecting Colonizing Praxis: The Merchants' Foray

The Spanish Crown, made wealthy by an initial small investment in a Genoese sailor's grand dream, could finance further conquests of the New World with the gold, silver, and other wealth plundered by its conquistadores in earlier ventures. However, Elizabeth, heir to a pauper's crown, could ill afford to divert precious revenues to speculative overseas investments. The task of colonizing America fell to the new entrepreneurial class that was emerging within the Elizabethan economy. This new class, a by-product of the social and economic forces and new ideas set free by England's own Reformation, desired greater English participation in the world trading system inaugurated by the Iberian discoveries. Its members constituted the expanding merchant and mercantile-minded sector of the English national economy: cloth and wool manufacturers, shipping interests, and the landed gentry adjusting to the new economies of scale in herding and agriculture. The founding members of the English bourgeoisie quickly educated themselves to the dynamic potential of surplus capital and capacity, and they were eager to penetrate new markets and discover opportunities for new types of investments in the New World.

There were also the well-educated younger sons of this emerging mercantile-minded class. Victims of primogeniture, they nonetheless were blessed with the benefits of an Oxford or Cambridge education, which had awakened them to new types of knowledge and opportunities in the European world trading system. They, too, desired expansion into America, as did a revived and radicalized Protestant clergy,[56] anxious to stem the tide of Spanish-dissemin-ated papistry.

While Elizabeth might have felt herself closely aligned with this new coali-tion of interests, any aggressive tendencies in her foreign policy were tempered by the realization that her father's wars had virtually bankrupted the royal Treasury. During the early years of her reign, Elizabeth sought to avoid the possibility of any new and expensive conflicts with European rivals, particu-larly the Spanish emperor.

Another complicating factor in relations between England and Spain was the position of the English merchants themselves. The major mercantile centers, such as London and Bristol, had carried on a prosperous and peaceful trade with the Spanish Empire since Henry's day. A number of English merchants had in fact been granted concessions to trade freely in the African Canaries. England, it was thought by those merchants who benefited from this peaceful barter, should try to gain entry into Spain's New World markets through a similar concessionary process, rather than by force.

Captain John Hawkins launched the first significant effort to penetrate Spain's New World monopoly. In 1562 Hawkins, after apparently brokering an agreement with several Spanish merchants, set sail from England with at least three ships. Copying methods made famous by his father, William, who had pioneered the English slave trade, Hawkins first stopped on the west African coast, where his men captured 300 Africans. The fleet then sailed to the Spanish West Indies, where Hawkins exchanged his human cargo of slaves for hides, ginger, sugar, and pearls from Spanish plantation owners. His successful trading foray necessitated the hiring of two more ships at Hispaniola. Hawkins's three original ships returned to England, and the two hired ships were sent to Lisbon and Seville.[57]

The Spanish government looked with extreme disfavor on Hawkins's interference with its monopoly rights in the Indies. The ship Hawkins had sent to Seville was seized in port. But the cargo that arrived in England, considering the relatively small investment in the "goods" for which they had been traded, returned a handsome profit to Captain Jack and his backers.[58]

Hawkins financed a second, larger slaving voyage, which arrived in the Indies with its African cargo in 1565. Despite the fact that the Spanish colonial officials had been instructed to forbid the English slave trade, Hawkins again managed to sell his captured Africans at a profit, returning to England this time with gold, silver, and other precious New World commodities.[59]

Hawkins's third voyage to the Indies took place in 1567. The two largest ships in this slaving expedition were owned by Queen Elizabeth herself, who would not let notions of legality (Spain regarded the English trade as blatantly unlawful) or moral qualms about the slave trade stand in the way of a good bargain. This time, however, a fleet of twelve ships under the Spanish viceroy had been dispatched to the Indies to enforce the royal monopoly. The Spaniards attacked Hawkins's fleet at anchor in the bay of San Juan de Ulva. Only two of his ships escaped to the open sea. One of these foundered before returning home. The surviving vessel, commanded by Hawkins's subordinate Francis Drake, returned to England with reports of Spanish treachery and the impossibility of dealing "peacefully" with Spain in the New World.[60]

Elizabeth naturally sympathized with her loyal subjects' desire for revenge against the Spaniards and for defeat of the empire's papist claim to control of the New World. She would not, however, permit an officially sanctioned military expedition against Spain's imperial interests in the Indies. She preferred that Drake and his like-minded English sea-dog compatriots engage in piratical acts of profit and plunder on the Spanish Main. The queen could, of course, disavow such acts of piracy in front of the Spanish ambassador, although she might be more than alert to her royal percentage in such schemes. And besides, her own colonizing desires were focused on Ireland, a far more vital and much easier target for her Protestant conquistadores to acquire and exploit.

Elizabethan Colonialism: Elizabeth's Irish Wars

If Elizabeth was not yet ready to challenge Spain's New World empire officially, she nonetheless had a claim on fertile lands separated from England by water, yet within easy reach, whose wild and barbarous peoples were infected by papistry and ripe for Spanish intrigue. Ireland, claimed by the English Crown since the medieval Crusading era although certainly never effectively reduced to English possession, provided Elizabeth's own Protestant conquistadores with a valuable training ground for practicing Spanish-style colonizing techniques among a savage people.

The Elizabethans' colonial wars in Ireland are of critical importance in any investigation of English Discovery-era colonizing discourses. Until England itself could develop a practice of colonization, with the subsequent ruptures in a theory-bound discursive field that praxis inevitably reveals, its colonizing discourses would necessarily remain underdeveloped and derivative. Ireland provided an unparalleled opportunity to test the new practices of empire perfected by the successful Spanish New World enterprise and to articulate them in a peculiarly English discursive style. This same style, blending together medievally derived legal theories on the diminished status and rights of a normatively divergent savage people, anti-Spanish religious and mercantile nationalism, and English innovations of Spanish colonizing practice, would complete the thematic construction of the colonizing discourse later carried by Elizabeth's Protestant crusaders to the New World.

Pre-Elizabethan Precedents

Ireland had been regarded as part of the English realm since the Norman invasions of the island. This sentiment, however, was held only by those on the English side of the Irish Sea. The Gaelic Irish were a constant and rebellious irritant to the English Crown, and Elizabeth, like her Tudor predecessors, regarded the final subjugation of the island as critical to the security of the realm.[61]

The "popery" of its unreformed inhabitants made Catholic Ireland an easy target for destabilizing Spanish schemes and conspiracies in the Elizabethan mind. Ironically, Elizabeth, the most vigorously Protestant of England's monarchs, traced her Crown's legal title to Ireland back to a papal bull, *Laudabiliter*. Issued at the height of the Crusading era in 1155 by Adrian IV (1154–1159), the only Englishman ever to serve as pope, *Laudabiliter* had been requested by King Henry II (r. 1154–1189) for the ostensible purpose of taking title to Ireland in order to bring the renegade church there into conformity with Gregorian reforms.[62]

This medieval papal grant of authority to invade the kingdom and exorcise radical divergence from the Church's newly redefined norms was couched in words not dissimilar to those contained in the Spanish bulls of conquest later issued in the fifteenth century for America.[63] Adrian granted the English king authority to "enlarge the boundaries of the Church, . . . teach rude and ignorant peoples the truth of the Christian faith, and . . . stamp out the plants of evil from the field of the Lord."[64]

England's papally backed conquest of the apostate island failed to achieve its immediately intended orthodox Christianizing purpose. In 1183, nearly three decades after *Laudabiliter* and the nominal imposition of English hegemony, Gerald of Wales, a clergyman associated with the English court, described the recalcitrant Irish as "a filthy people, wallowing in vice. Of all peoples, it is the least instructed. A race more ignorant than all in the rudiments of the Faith."[65] Gerald argued that the Irish, although nominally Christian, met all the requisite tests of "barbarian" status.[66] This, of course, meant that the tribes remained fit subjects for continued efforts at conquest and militant remediation by the civilized English.

Throughout the late medieval era, the English sought to tame the "wild" Irish by arms and by laws. Frequent military campaigns eventually carved out an area of English settlements known as the Pale in the locale of Dublin. The English colonial presence in the Pale served only to provide further contrast to the "barbarous, exotic, and implicitly subversive" character of the Gaelic tribespeople.[67] Influenced by frontier reports from English settlers, England became increasingly belligerent in its efforts to eradicate this difference in culture, or at least to keep its influence in check. By the Statutes of Kilkenny (1366), the stakes for nonassimilation were considerably raised by the English. Protection of life and property was guaranteed only to those of the Irish who spoke and lived like English people. Those who retained their tribal culture were regarded as outlaws, with no recognized right to hold real or personal property. The statutes also imposed strict penalties on any Englishman who adopted Irish customs or married into an Irish clan[68] (a loathsome but apparently not uncommon practice in the Pale[69]).

Despite the English Crown's persistent efforts, the Gaelic tribes remained steadfast in their resistance to England's "civilizing" efforts. By the time of the ascension of the Tudors in the late fifteenth century, large portions of the island had been reclaimed by the "barbarians."

Henry VIII was able to reconquer strategic sections of Ireland in the latter decades of his reign. The problem then arose of effectively supporting the newly constructed garrisons in the reconquered regions. Sir James Croft, an official of Henry's court, suggested establishing permanent plantations of English settlers as a relatively inexpensive means of maintaining royal control. Croft's suggestion may well have been derived from the examples of Spanish colonization of the New World and its barbarous peoples. Such precedents would have been known to the many better-educated Englishmen at court who either read Latin or traveled widely in Europe. As the entire legal foundation of England's rights in Ireland ultimately referred to the medieval Crusading paradigm, it probably appeared to make eminently good sense, even in Henry's Reformation-era court, to apply the most up-to-date improvements to the old model. Several small settlements were eventually established during the middle decades of the sixteenth century as screens for the eastern frontier of the Pale in the territories of Leix and Offaly.[70]

Queen Mary thus inherited the primitive beginnings of an Iberian-influenced English colonial policy for Ireland when she succeeded to the throne in 1553, following her half brother Edward's short reign (r. 1547–1553). She permitted her lord deputy, Sir Thomas Radcliffe, Earl of Sussex, to develop the policy further. Military frontier colonies under government supervision were attempted in the newly created Kings and Queens counties and to the north in Ulster. Sussex's plan in establishing these colonies was to reward English soldiers and officers who participated in Gaelic conquest with large tracts of confiscated land under a feudal paradigm of rights acquired by conquest. While Philip of Spain's precise role in formulating or encouraging this policy (he had recently married the queen and was at court during this period) is difficult to determine, its basic themes would have sounded familiar to any well-born Spaniard or to one knowledgeable in the methods of the Spanish conquistadores.

Notably, several court officials apparently felt that Sussex's methods were not "Spanish" enough.[71] Sussex was called to London in 1558 to defend his Irish colonial policy before the queen. The archbishop of Armagh, George Dowdall, called for a far more vigorous and widespread crusade against the Irish, one

whereby all the said Irish rebels either must be subdued or banished out of the whole realm, and English subjects to be planted in their lands thoroughly, as it was done in the times of the former conquest. I call this a godly way of reformation to subdue and banish these people that be always disposed to naughtiness, as murder, robbery, stealth and deceit, and do not obey God's or Man's laws. And therefore, as it is well written in the Civil Law . . . I do call it holy to plant good men in the stead of evil. And thus was the occasion that moved the pope's holiness to give the king license at the time of the first conquest [a reference to *Laudibiliter*] to take their lands from them.[72]

The historian David Quinn has argued that "Dowdall's approach to the Irish question suggests . . . that the fact that King Philip (Mary's husband) was the ruler of great imperial territories overseas where he had to do with people as 'wild' [as] or, perhaps, wilder than the Irish had something to do with the form in which the archbishop's plea was framed."[73] Dowdall's reference to the papal bull of conquest for Ireland would have been recognized by many at court as an obvious parallel to Alexander's 1493 bull granting America to Spain. The archbishop's mention of "the Civil Law," probably a reference to the Roman *ius gentium*, recalled the basic legal justification for conquest of the American natives framed by Renaissance-era Spanish jurists under the Law of Nations.[74] It is important to remember also that Eden's pro-Spanish translations of Martire's and Oviedo's histories of conquest had been published in 1555,[75] just three years before the archbishop's speech. The impact of this publication on the courtiers of the period, Eden's most likely audience, would probably have been quite lasting, and Archbishop Dowdall's speech raised themes and arguments readily recognizable to the readers of the translations. The incivility of heathen peoples legitimated their decimation by righteous Christians. In sum, Dowdall simply synthesized the medieval perspective on the diminished status and rights of normatively divergent barbarous peoples with secularist Renaissance-era international legal discourse ("the Civil Law") and applied it to the "wild" Irish, with predictable results. Like Spain in the Indies, England had the natural-law right and duty to reform the Irish, who "do not obey God's or Man's laws."[76] The Spanish theologian and lawyer Franciscus de Victoria had already developed the same basic argument from natural-law principles and applied it to Spain's conquest of the Indians of America in his sixteenth-century discourse on the Law of Nations.[77]

Lord Deputy Sidney's Irish Colonization Venture

The lessons taught by Eden's texts on Spanish colonization techniques and theories had an impact beyond the short-lived Catholic reign of Mary and Philip. The major architects of Queen Elizabeth's Irish colonial policy were intimately familiar with Eden's work, as well as with Spanish colonizing practice and theory.

The first Elizabethan official to focus his energies on bringing the wild Irish under control was Sir Henry Sidney, whom Elizabeth named lord deputy of Ireland in 1565. His assigned task was to suppress the rebellion of Shane O'Neill and his followers in the area of Ulster. The new lord deputy was suited to the job by virtue of two prior appointments in service to the Crown. He had served as vice-treasurer in Ireland in 1556 under Mary, so he was familiar with the terrain. He had also served as a member of the English delegation that had visited Spain in 1554 to confirm the marriage treaty between Mary and Philip. While in Spain, Sidney apparently broadened his knowledge of and interest in the Spanish overseas empire. He was also acquainted with Richard Eden, the translator and promoter of New World colonization, who heartily approved of the Spanish methods of dealing with wild and barbarous peoples. Given his résumé and contacts, Sidney would undoubtedly have approached his task of subjugation from a standpoint of familiarity with a tested colonizing methodology and accompanying discourse.[78]

Not surprisingly, therefore, Sidney immediately set out to broaden the English presence in Ireland through Spanish-style techniques of subjugation. His plan to suppress the Irish contemplated establishing plantation colonies by military conquest. Sidney added one critical innovation to the Spanish model. The English Crown, unlike Spain, could not afford to finance conquests of overseas colonies out of the royal Treasury, so Sidney was required to privatize his colonization scheme.

Under Sidney's plan, private entrepreneurs and syndicates of grantees would provide the financial resources to bring English civilization and the reformed faith to Ireland. These investors would finance the planting of colonies in exchange for royal recognition of feudal rights in any Irish territory they conquered.[79]

Sidney's joint-venture Irish subjugation plan represented a considerable advance in both the theory and the practice of early English mercantile colonialism. He sent several emissaries to Elizabeth to defend the concept, and he constantly lobbied his associates back at court for support. In a letter to the influential William Cecil in 1568, Sidney spelled out his arguments for this new direction in Irish policy. It would be "intolerable" for Her Majesty, Sidney wrote, to defend Ulster with soldiers and to "plant it with People at her owne charges." At the same time, some sort of significant English presence was rquired before "reformation or revenue can be looked for."[80] He thus advocated that those "among the nobility, and principal gentlemen of England" should be "induced" to finance a colony of 2,000 or more. There would be "room enough" for such a large number, argued Sidney,

> but they must be so furnished with money, apparell, victual, and means to till the ground, and seed for the same, as if they should imagine to find nothing here but earth. . . . And all these might well be planted in that tract of ground which I left under the Government of Piers and Malbie. . . . In which I am well assured there liveth not 200th [part of the] men which there might well be nourished.[81]

Several points in Sidney's letter merit comment, as they relate to subsequent English discursive practice more fully developed during the mercantile colonization efforts in North America. The twin goals of religious "reformation" and "revenue," first popularized in Eden's preface to *The Decades of the New Worlde or West India*,[82] were by now familiar themes of English colonial discourse. Another theme would come to assume even greater prominence in English colonial discourse: Sidney's reference to Ireland's extensive regions of underutilized land sounded a novel theme of efficiency, which would be reiterated frequently as English colonizers bounded the "vacant" forests of the New World in the next century.[83]

The notion that Ireland contained large, underpopulated regions ripe for English settlement reflected a long tradition of negative English perceptions of Irish culture and society. Since the medieval era, Englishmen had criticized Irish tribalism's herding-based subsistence economy as extremely wasteful of land. England, of course, had historically devoted much of its land base to agriculture. The post-Henrician acquisitive impulses contributing to rationalization of landed economic activity throughout the English countryside further intensified a deep-seated historical bias against Irish subsistence and tribal culture. To an Englishman of the Elizabethan era, land was intended to be devoted either to surplus-oriented agricultural production or, as was the case with the frequent enclosure of common lands during this period, to production-oriented pasturage. Sidney's letter seems to indicate that although the notion had not yet been elevated to a principle of natural law in English colonial discourse, a savage people's perceived underutilization of land was sufficient justification for an English colonial enterprise, obviating further discussion of its morality or legality. In Sidney's discourse, the motive for conquest (abundant land) was subsumed into its justification (the abundant land was underutilized). The historical trajectory of English colonization of other peoples' lands can in fact be traced by simply plotting those points on the globe where this ample motive discovered this ample justification and sublimely conjoined.

Elizabeth apparently appreciated the strength of Sidney's policy arguments. She chartered various private syndicates that sought to establish feudal empires "beyond the Pale in Ireland." Quinn has noted that these feudal charters were "very much in line" with those granted by Spain to the conquistadores in the New World.[84] The grants of rights of conquest in the queen's name contemplated the invasion of Ireland by private armies, the exploitation of native Irish labor (similar to the Spanish *encomienda* system), and the free appropriation of territory by the conquerors, who would be licensed by the Crown to treat the natives as inferior, dependent peoples.

Many Elizabethans in fact compared the efforts of the queen's Irish conquistadores with those of the Spaniards in the New World. The wild Irish were readily likened to the barbarous savages of the Indies.[85] These comparisons focused on the normative divergence of tribally oriented societies and rested self-assuredly on the common medievally derived discursive foundations of Eurocentric crusading colonialism.[86] Significantly, the modernized patterns of this discourse of conquest first become clearly discernible at relatively early and comparable points in the respective Spanish and English Discovery-era experiences.

Sir Thomas Smith: An Elizabethan Armchair Conquistador

The process of refining and adapting Spanish discursive models to fit the particular English-Irish situation accelerated following Sidney's initial formulation of his plan to establish royally chartered, privately financed, plantation-style colonies. A number of the most prominent and talented men in the realm sought and received charters of Irish conquest from the queen and risked their lives and fortunes to the attempt to establish Elizabethan England's first overseas colonial empire. Sir Thomas Smith (1513–1577), for example, dedicated a considerable part of his wealth and energies to perfecting both the theory and the practice of English colonialism in Ireland. Sir Thomas was a Renaissance man in every sense of that term in Elizabethan society. He was a respected scholar in his own right prior to assuming the duties of Elizabeth's secretary of state in 1572. As England's first academic specialist on the history of colonization, from its earliest Roman origins to its most contemporary instances in the European Age of Discovery, he influenced numerous young members of the English nobility and gentry. He was tutor to Richard Eden and undoubtedly inspired the course of the young scholar-translator's studies on Spanish imperialism.

Throughout his academic and governmental career, in fact, Smith was in the forefront of the new enterprises of knowledge and science that characterized the Elizabethan Renaissance.[87] He was involved with the Society for the New Art, an alchemical venture that sought new and unorthodox methods of making money. In his 1565 study of political institutions, *De Republica Anglorum*, he mapped out new terrain in political theory respecting constitu-

tional development. He also fashioned a surprisingly robust and wholly desacralized theory of manifest destiny in a style that any European-derived
imperialist of the late nineteenth or early twentieth century would have found
comfortingly familiar and well reasoned. England, claimed Smith, was superior to all other nations because bondmen had become virtually unknown
within the realm by the sixteenth century. He argued that the Irish should be
subjugated and colonized by England in order to foster their appreciation for
civility so that they could likewise move toward freedom.[88]

Considering the age in which he lived, the man and his intellectual passions
can be measured by his library. As described by Quinn,[89] Smith's library in
1566 contained among its many volumes

Eden's *Decades of the new world or west India* (1555), . . . and his Translation of
Martin Cortez' *The Art of Navigation* (1561) in the introduction to which Eden paid
tribute to his former teacher. Smith had at least three other works on extra-European
geography, Munster's *Cosmographia*, Barros' *Asia* (1552–1563), and the French *Description d'Affrique* (1556) after Leo Africanus, along with several dozen other works
on general or classical geography and topography.[90]

In short, there was probably no better-stocked or more up-to-date library on
European expansion in all of England than Smith's. Among his other interests,
he was familiar with Greek and English linguistic studies, the civil law, natural
science and theology, and the history of the changes in the value of money. As
Quinn notes, "such a man once interested in the problems of colonization of
Ireland would be certain to have valuable things to say, even though his
practice was unlikely to be as striking as his theory. He was, in fact, happiest as
an armchair empire builder."[91]

Smith's theories on Irish colonization were a synthesis of the classical, the
medieval, and the modern. Ancient imperial Rome provided historical antece-
dents; medieval Crusading discourse, the legal precedents; and contemporary
Spanish colonization techniques and practice, the organizational model.

Smith likened England's task in Ireland to that of the ancient Romans who
had brought civilization and law to England when it was a savage land.
"England was as uncivil as Ireland until colonies of Romans brought their laws
and orders, whose moulds no nation, not even the Italians and Romans, have
more straitly and truly kept."[92] His justifications for conquest of the island
derived directly from medieval Crusading traditions. It was according to God's
will, wrote Smith, to "make apt and prepare this nation . . . to inhabitate and
reform so barbarous a nation as that is, and to bring them to the knowledge
and law were both a goodly and comendable deed."[93] Echoing the Spanish
Laws of Burgos,[94] Smith declared that this task of civilization could best be
implemented by educating the Irish "in virtuous labor and in justice, and to
teach them English laws and civility and to leave robbing and stealing and
killing one of another."[95] Educating the Irish, in Smith's mind, meant in
essence enslaving them to require their "virtuous labor"—a policy reminiscent
of the colonizing theories underlying such Spanish colonial institutions as the
encomienda.

Smith's first significant attempt to implement his colonizing theories began in 1571. With his son, Thomas Smith the younger, who was to apply his father's armchair tactics on the ground in Ireland, Smith presented a petition to the queen. Consistent with the legal architecture of Sidney's broadly stated Irish colonization plan, the Smiths' petition requested a royal grant of the Ards and other lands in Ireland. In return, the Smiths offered to conquer at their own expense all territories under the grant (here, Sidney's influence becomes apparent[96]) and "to make the same civil and peopled with natural English men born."[97]

Smith's privately financed colony in the wild was to be manned by between 800 and 900 adventurers, who would pay annual levies to the feudal proprietors in exchange for grants of lands. A church was to be the first building constructed in each parish.

The subjugation of the "wild" Irish formed the justification for the entire scheme. The sole policy to be applied respecting the natives was one of military conquest. Gaelic lords and their more devoted followers were to be driven out of the regions intended for English settlement. Others would be permitted to remain, provided they accepted their servile status under English hegemony (here the influence of the Spanish *encomienda*, by which individual Indians were "commended" to colonial Spaniards for labor service, becomes clearly decipherable[98]): "All Irishmen . . . which commonly be called churles that will plow the grounds and bear no kind of weapon nor armor, shall be gently entertained and for their plowing and labour shall be well rewarded with great provision that no injurie be offered to them."[99]

In other words, if the Irish "churles" agreed to submit to English rule, they would be rewarded with their lives. Those who resisted would be put to the sword. This was also the essential theory and practice behind another infamous Spanish colonial institution, the *Requerimiento*. Under this royal document of Spanish conquest, the savages of America were given the choice of accepting Spain's papally granted hegemony or facing slaughter at the hands of the conquistadores.[100] Smith's plan further forbade the Irish to purchase land, hold office, serve on juries, be called as witnesses in any real or personal action at law, or "be bound apprentice to any science or art that may damage" the queen's subjects.[101]

Elizabeth approved the Smiths' project by royal indenture in October 1571. The preamble to the Crown charter of conquest restated the same basic proto-utilitarian arguments for Irish colonization that had first been articulated by Sir Henry Sidney. Sir Thomas's contract from the queen declared that many areas within the earldom of Ulster "lieth waste or else inhabited with a wicked, barbarous and uncivil people."[102] The Crown had often desired and wished "that some occasion might be offered" to have Ireland "peopled with good and obedient subjects, which should acknowledge the great benefit of God, her highness' royal authority." Colonizing Ireland with loyal English subjects would aid the Crown and its officers in repressing "all rebels and seditious people." By their presence, the English might "bring the rude and barbarous nation of the wild Irish to more civility of manner."[103] That is, in order to save the Irish, the Smiths were given license by the queen to destroy them.

The contract was soon followed by a royal grant to the Smiths of approximately 360,000 acres in the Ards region. All lands conquered by the Smiths' venture were to be held directly from the Crown, with an obligation to pay rent for all territories occupied by September 1576 and to surrender title to lands not occupied by March 1579.

After securing their contract and grant, the Smiths launched what Quinn describes as England's first direct printed publicity drive for an overseas colonizing project.[104] A broadsheet, described as an "offer and order" for subscribers, signed by Sir Thomas Smith, was circulated almost immediately after the royal grant. The advertisement described the lands the would-be adventurers would receive in exchange for their contributions to the enterprise. The Smiths also published a map of the Ards to circulate among potential subscribers.

The Smiths' most elaborate piece of propaganda was published shortly after the broadsheet. It was a sixty-three-page pamphlet that purported to be a letter from a friend of Sir Thomas's praising the Smiths' plan to another friend. The earlier "offer and order" was reprinted at the end of this "letter." The entire package represented a well-thought-out, integrated promotional campaign without precedent in English economic history. Its novelty must account in large part for the Smiths' original success in securing 800 subscribers within six months of its appearance.[105]

The Smiths' "letter" represents an important artifact of Elizabethan Discovery-era colonizing discourse as well. Its central themes and ideas justifying colonization of other peoples' lands would be echoed in the discursive practice of English imperialism for several centuries.

Excess of population in England was set out in the "letter" as a principal reason for acquiring overseas colonies. The excess was assertedly caused by several factors. The Reformation's destruction of the monastic system had eliminated one important pressure valve for population control. Marriages were on the increase among the children of the landed classes, partly because such children would once have been "thrust into abbeys, there to live (an idle life), since that is taken from them must now seek some other place to live in." Primogeniture, "which giveth all to the elder brothers" was pointed to as a principal factor exacerbating a tight land market. Combined with rising food and clothing costs, younger sons unprovided for by their parents' estates most particularly suffered.[106]

According to the "letter," the ready answer to all these problems lay in Ireland, which already belonged to the Crown and which the Smiths now planned to subjugate on behalf of Her Majesty. The island's unpeopled expanses made it ripe for reclamation by Englishmen. Each subscriber to the Smiths' venture was promised at least 300 acres at a rent of 1 penny an acre. Fathers with "many sons, or landed men that have many younger brothers" were pointedly encouraged to participate. How could a caring patriarch "do better" by his landless heirs and siblings than to set them up as participants in such a project?[107]

Agriculture—with labor provided predominantly by the resident Irish and with markets provided by England, France, and Spain—was to be the primary activity of the colony. The "letter" also claimed that the advantages of civilization would be established shortly after the English arrived. Law, justice, and good order would be brought to the backward Irish land, making it "as pleasant and profitable as any part of England, especially when it shall be furnished with a company of Gentlemen and others that will live friendly in fellowship together."[108]

There was no doubt in Sir Thomas's mind that this fellowship among the English colonists was to be sustained by servile Irish labor and by the imposition of a feudal tribute system. In a letter written in 1572 defending the plan, the elder Smith wrote that he "neither sought to expel or destroy the Irish race, but to keep them in quiet order paying a rent to nourish the garrison and colonies."[109]

Smith's vision of establishing an English feudal gentry in Ireland ultimately fell victim to the financing scheme that he proposed for his colony. He sought to raise at least £10,000 by charging each horseman (300 in all) £20 and each footman (400 in all) £10. Investors who wished to supply only money could sign on for roughly £16. For that amount, Smith would equip and support a footman for one year. The moneys raised by subscriptions were managed by a treasurer who would provide for transportation, purchase foodstuffs, arms, and munitions, and take care of other expenses connected with the colonizing enterprise. A second call for another contribution equal to the original subscription could be made on the investors if necessary.[110]

English merchants had pioneered this joint-stock trading company structure during the mid-sixteenth century as a financing vehicle for trading ventures in the Muscovy and west African trade.[111] The basic model had been adapted to other projects, such as mining and industrial ventures, and Sir Thomas believed that it could be utilized for Spanish plantation-style colonization in Ireland as well. Smith's project, however, encountered an additional, unanticipated cost: the hostile and effective resistance of the Irish tribespeople. On the eve of the expedition's departure from England, Crown officials in Ireland warned London that word of Smith's venture had reached the restless Irish natives. On the basis of this warning and fears of a rebellion, Elizabeth delayed Smith's expedition. The delay proved disastrous, as the majority of the 700 adventurers whom the Smiths had assembled at Liverpool refused to honor their subscriptions and abandoned the project.

By the time Sir Thomas prevailed on Elizabeth to permit the expedition to proceed once again, the Smiths could raise only a small force of 100 colonists to set sail for the Ards. The small size of the colony proved ineffective in countering the Irish resistance. The powers of martial law exercised by the younger Smith as governor earned him the enmity of the local "churles." He was eventually killed by Irishmen employed in his own home. A general uprising drove the remaining colonists out of the area, and most returned to England. Sir Thomas undertook to revive his rights under the royal grant in 1574 with 150 men, but this effort too ended dismally. Sir Thomas Smith would never realize his grand vision of colonial empire among the wild Irish.

Other Elizabethans were willing to assume the task that Smith could not complete. Elizabeth, in fact, would continue her military annexation efforts in Ireland until the eve of her death in 1603. Her Irish wars most often focused on regions that had decent investment potential and were populated by large numbers of indigenous Gaelic Irish openly hostile to English rule. Thus the campaigns for the most part were extremely vicious, drawn-out affairs. Even by the lax standards of European warfare, the Elizabethans imposed harsh justice on the stubborn Irish. All who resisted were labeled as rebels. Non-combatants and combatants alike, men, women, and children, were subjected to indiscriminate slaughter. An English chronicler of the Irish wars sought to defend the slaying of noncombatants with a style of reasoning foreshadowing that put forward centuries later by an English-descended government respecting the nuclear annihilation of another enemy race's civilian targets: "through the terror which the people conceived thereby, it made short warres."[112]

Nicholas Canny has argued that the actions of the English in Ireland indicate that the Elizabethan conquistadores believed that "they were absolved from all normal ethical restraints in dealing with the native Irish."[113] Queen Elizabeth herself became so frustrated with the resistance of the wild Irish to her asserted sovereign rights that at one point she commended one of her grantees, Walter Devereux, Earl of Essex, for his part in the massacre of hundreds of inhabitants of Ulster (including noncombatants):

[W]e do perceive that when occassion doth present you do rather allure and bring in that rude and barbarous nation to civility and acknowledging of their duty to God and to us, by wisdom and discreet handling than by force and shedding of blood; and yet, when necessity requireth, you are ready also to oppose yourself and your forces to them whom reason and duty cannot bridle.[114]

The militant refrains of this style of discourse sound familiar medievally derived themes. "Civility" and "duty to God"—the queen's God, of course— legitimated "force and shedding of blood" against those "whom reason and duty cannot bridle." Normative divergence from English notions of "reason" warranted England's brutal subjugation of the barbarous Irish. A lieutenant accompanying one of Elizabeth's Irish grantees on a colonizing expedition to Antrim County in northern Ireland provided a concise English Protestant translation of medieval Crusading legal discourse and its unyielding view that difference legitimated the extermination of normatively divergent barbarous peoples: "[H]ow godly a deed it is to overthrow so wicked a race the world may judge: for my part I think there cannot be a greater sacrifice to God."[115]

Thus even prior to their first attempts at establishing a permanent empire in North America, the Elizabethans had constructed the foundations of an effective, facilitating discourse of conquest to ground their colonizing praxis in tribally held lands. An insular kingdom with a perceived need to expand beyond its borders, a commercial culture primed to invest surplus capital in the European world trading system, and a religious rivalry with the world's greatest imperial power represented the conditions for the emergence of a discourse focused on the normative divergence of a barbarous people whose underutilized lands were to be more efficiently managed under Spanish-influenced colonizing techniques. Nurtured in the soil of Ireland, this discourse and its discriminating, exterminating view of radical difference would be transplanted by England's will to empire in the vast territories of the barbarous tribal peoples of the New World.[116]

NOTES

1. For background information on the Cabot voyages, *see generally* 1 S. E. Morison, *The European Discovery of America: The Northern Voyages* A.D. *500–1600* 157–92 (1971); J. Williamson, *The Cabot Voyages and Bristol Discovery Under Henry VII* (1962).

2. See generally J. Brundage, *Richard Lion Heart* (1974).

3. Reprinted in *Documents of American History* 5–6 (H. S. Commager 8th ed. 1968).

4. *See generally* S. E. Morison, *supra* note 1, at 157–70.

5. Reprinted in F. Von Der Heydte, "Discovery and Annexation in International Law," 29 *Am. J. Int'l L.* 448, 455 (1935).

6. On the reforms of Henry VII, *see generally* P. Anderson, *Lineages of the Absolutist State* 119 (1979).

7. *Id.*

8. On the "Tudor Revolution" in English governmental administration, *see generally* I. Wallerstein, *The Modern World-System* 232–35 (1974); G. R. Elton, *The Tudor Revolution in Government* (1953).

9. *See generally* G. R. Elton, *supra.*

10. I. Wallerstein, *supra* note 8, at 232.

11. P. Anderson, *supra* note 6, at 123.

12. On the *Requerimiento* and Spanish colonizing practice in the early Discovery era, *see* Chapter 2, text accompanying notes 113–20, *supra.*

13. P. Anderson, *supra* note 6, at 120.

14. C. Hill, "Social and Economic Consequences of the Henrician Reformation" 32 in C. Hill, *Puritanism and Revolution* (1958).

15. *Id.* at 32–33.

16. *Id.* at 33.

17. P. Anderson, *supra* note 6, at 124.

18. *See generally* C. Hill, *supra* note 14.

19. J. Milton, 3 *Prose Works* 80 (H. J. Bohn ed. 1848), quoted in C. Hill, *supra* note 14, at 35.

20. *Id.* at 36.

21. *Id.* at 44.

22. H. C. Porter, *The Inconstant Savage* 13 (1979). I have relied extensively on Porter's superb study of sixteenth-century English colonizing discourse in this section as well as throughout Part II of this book.

23. *Id.* at 15.

24. *See* Chapter 2, text accompanying notes 170–73, *supra.*

25. H. C. Porter, *supra* note 22, at 17.

26. *See The First Three English Books on America* [*?1511–1555* A.D.]*, Being Chiefly Transla-*

tions, Compilations, etc. by Richard Eden (Edward Arber ed. 1895) [hereinafter cited as *The First Three English Books on America*].

27. On Oviedo's role in the Spanish conquest of the Indies, see Chapter 2, text accompanying notes 125–26, *supra*.

28. H. C. Porter, *supra* note 22, at 19.

29. *Id.* at 20.

30. *Id.* at 24.

31. *Id.* at 161–62.

32. H. R. Wagner and H. R. Parish, *The Life and Writings of Bartolomé de Las Casas* 53–54 (1967), quoted in H. C. Porter, *supra* note 22, at 161.

33. H. C. Porter, *supra* note 22, at 165.

34. Quoted in *id.* at 164.

35. *The First Three English Books on America*, *supra* note 26, at 241.

36. H. C. Porter, *supra* note 22, at 25.

37. Eden's Preface appears in *The First Three English Books on America*, *supra* note 26, at 49–60.

38. Quoted in H. C. Porter, *supra* note 22, at 25–26.

39. Quoted in *id.* at 26.

40. Quoted in *id.* at 26–27.

41. *See id.* at 21. *See also The First Three English Books on America*, *supra* note 22, at 27.

42. Quoted in H. C. Porter, *supra* note 22, at 27.

43. *Id.* at 27.

44. *Id.* at 27–28.

45. *Id.*

46. Quoted in *id.* at 28.

47. Quoted in *id.*

48. Quoted in *id.* at 29.

49. *Id.*

50. Quoted in *id.* at 127.

51. C. Hill, *supra* note 14, at 44.

52. *See* F. Von Der Heydte, *supra* note 5, at 457–58. 1 *European Treaties Bearing on the History of the United States and Its Dependencies* 219–22 (F. Davenport ed. 1929).

53. *Id.* at 219; F. Von Der Heydte, *supra* note 5, at 458.

54. 1 *European Treaties Bearing on the History of the United States and Its Dependencies*, *supra* note 52, at 219–22.

55. I Wallerstein, *supra* note 10, at 198.

56. *See*, e.g., H. C. Porter, *supra* note 22, at 132–36.

57. *See generally* J. A Williamson, *Sir John Hawkins* 78–91 (1970); W. Craven, *The Southern Colonies in the Seventeenth Century, 1607–1689* 10–13 (1949).

58. *See* sources cited *supra*.

59. *See* W. Craven, *supra* note 57, at 11; J. A. Williamson, *supra* note 57, at 92–116.

60. *See generally* J. A. Williamson, *Hawkins of Plymouth* 100–56 (1949); W. Craven, *supra* note 57, at 12–13.

61. *See generally* K. Bottigheimer, "Kingdom and Colony: Ireland in the Westward Enterprise 1536–1660" 45–64 in *The Westward Enterprise* (K. R. Andrews, N. P. Canny, & P. E. H. Hair eds. 1978) [hereinafter cited as *The Westward Enterprise*].

62. The bull, along with a brief discussion of its history, is reprinted in *Church and State Through the Centuries* 53–55 (S. Ehler & J. Morrall trans. & ed. 1967).

63. *See* Chapter 2, text accompanying notes 67–74, *supra*.

64. *Church and State Through the Centuries*, *supra* note 62, at 54.

65. *Gerald of Wales, The History and Topography of Ireland* 106 (John O'Meara trans. 1951).

66. *Id.* at 103.

67. K. Bittigheimer, *supra* note 61, at 49.

68. *See The Expansion of Europe: The First Phase* 143–46 (J. Muldoon ed. 1977).

69. On the topic of English adaptation to Irish customs, *see generally* N. P. Canny, "The

Permissive Frontier: The Problem of Social Control in Ireland and Virginia 1150–1650," in *The Westward Enterprise, supra* note 61, at 16–44.

70. On sixteenth-century English colonial policy respecting Ireland, *see generally* D. B.Quinn, "Sir Thomas Smith (1513–77) and the Beginnings of English Colonial Theory," 89 *Proceedings of the American Philosophical Society* 543 (1945) [hereinafter cited as "Sir Thomas Smith"]; D. B. Quinn, "Ireland and Sixteenth Century Expansion," 1 *Historical Studies* 20 (1958); N. P. Canny, *The Elizabethan Conquest of Ireland* (1976).

71. D. B. Quinn, *supra*, at 26.

72. *Id.*

73. *Id.*

74. *See* Chapter 2, text accompanying notes 158–80, *supra.*

75. *See* text accompanying notes 22–50, *supra.*

76. *See* text accompanying note 72, *supra.*

77. *See* Chapter 2, text accompanying notes 158–75, *supra.*

78. D. B. Quinn, "Sir Thomas Smith," *supra* note 70, at 544.

79. *Id.*

80. Reprinted in *Id.*

81. *Id.*

82. *See* text accompanying notes 43–50, *supra.*

83. *See generally* W. Cronon, *Changes in the Land* (1983).

84. D. B. Quinn, "Ireland and Sixteenth Century Expansion," *supra* note 70, at 27.

85. N. P. Canny, "The Ideology of English Colonization: From Ireland to America" 30 *Wm. & Mary Q.* 575–98 (Oct. 1973).

86. *See generally id.*; N. P. Canny, *supra* note 70, at 154–63.

87. D. B. Quinn, "Sir Thomas Smith," *supra* note 70, at 545–46.

88. *Id.* at 546.

89. *Id.* at 545.

90. *Id.*

91. *Id.* at 546.

92. *Id.*

93. N. P. Canny, *supra* note 85, at 588.

94. See Chapter 2, text accompanying notes 97–103, *supra.*

95. D. B. Quinn, "Sir Thomas Smith," *supra* note 70, at 553.

96. *See* text accompanying notes 79–83, *supra.*

97. D. B. Quinn, "Sir Thomas Smith," *supra* note 70, at 548.

98. *See* Chapter 2, text accompanying notes 83–89, *supra.*

99. D. B. Quinn, "Sir Thomas Smith," *supra* note 70, at 548.

100. *See* Chapter 2, text accompanying notes 113–20, *supra.*

101. D. B. Quinn, "Sir Thomas Smith," *supra* note 70, at 548.

102. *Id.* at 551.

103. *Id.*

104. *Id.* at 550.

105. *Id.*

106. *Id.* at 552.

107. *Id.*

108. *Id.* at 553.

109. *Id.*

110. *Id.* at 554.

111. *Id.*

112. Quoted in N. P. Canny, *supra* note 85, at 582.

113. *Id.* at 583.

114. N. P. Canny, *supra* note 70, at 121.

115. *Id.*

116. It is often assumed that European racism was the unfortunate by-product of European Discovery-era dynastic contact with non-European cultures. In examining Elizabethan Irish

colonizing discourse, however, it appears that divergent cultural norms, particularly those preserved in subsistence tribalism, and not divergent pigmentation, energized in part England's fierce subjugation of Irish tribes. The legal discourse articulated by the Elizabethans justifying the conquest and colonization of Ireland's recalcitrant "wild" Gaelic peoples manifests a close structural affinity with the colonizing legal discourse relied on by the English crusaders in the New World justifying their brutal subjugation of the American Indians. *See* Chapter 5, *infra.*

4

The Elizabethan Wars for America

The First Protestant Crusade to America

Ireland provided more than just an opportune field for the Elizabethans to articulate more precisely their Spanish-inspired colonizing discourses. It also furnished the practical training ground for subsequent Spanish-inspired efforts by the Elizabethans to colonize the lands of American Indians.

Sir Humphrey Gilbert: Elizabethan Terrorist

Sir Humphrey Gilbert,[1] the first Elizabethan to attempt a colonial settlement in North America, was one of the most highly decorated veterans of Elizabeth's Irish wars. Records indicate that he served in both the Ulster and Munster campaigns of extermination organized by Lord Deputy Henry Sidney. He received his first independent command as military governor of the Munster colony in 1569. His reign was one of unbridled terror against the Gaelic Irish. Noncombatant peasant farmers and herders were slaughtered in order to cut off the food supply to the Gaelic armies. Once Gilbert had conquered a region, he engaged in a gruesome ceremony with the surviving inhabitants, who received a pardon only on marching to Gilbert's tent and pledging loyalty. According to a contemporary, the path to Gilbert's tent was lined with the heads of the rebels who had recently been killed or executed:

So that none could come into his tent for any cause [but] commonly he must pass through a lane of heads which he used *ad terrorem* . . . and yet did it bring great terror to the people when they saw the heads of their dead fathers, brothers, children, kinsfolk and friends, lie on the ground before their faces, as they came to speak with the said colonel.[2]

Gilbert defended his military actions by reference to his interpretation of his queen's absolute prerogatives. In a letter to Sidney, he speculated "that the Prince had a regular and absolute power, and that which might not be done by the one, I would do it by the other in cases of necessity."[3]

Gilbert complemented his Machiavellian excesses with an extremely intolerant disposition toward the normatively divergent Irish tribespeople. He regarded the Irish as subhuman and was reported to have once claimed that he would not even submit his dog's ears to the speech of the most supposedly noble man among the barbarians. And as the gruesome display outside his tent attests, his mania for conformity to proper English norms of behavior became even more exaggerated once the barbarians were brought under control. Fear rather than love, Gilbert opined, was the emotion that the victor should instill in such detestable vanquished peoples.[4] Imagine Genghis Khan supplemented by the lessons of Machiavelli's *Prince*: such was the widely admired character of Sir Humphrey Gilbert, the first Englishman selected by Elizabeth to conquer America.[5]

An Anti-Spanish Discourse of Discovery

Gilbert had served Princess Elizabeth when he was a young boy, fresh from Oxford in 1554 or 1555. When his service to the princess was concluded, he, like so many of the well-to-do sons of the gentry, studied law. He may have been no more than twenty in 1558 when he resided at one of the Inns of Court affiliated with the Middle Temple. From there, he was commissioned in 1562 by Elizabeth, now his queen, to lead an expedition in aid of the French Huguenots in the religious wars of France.

The young Gilbert's contacts with the Huguenots apparently familiarized him with reports of French Protestant filibusters and their piratical harassment of the Spanish Empire in the West Indies. Following his French tour, the inspired young Protestant nationalist returned to England and presented his first anti-Spanish scheme in a petition to his queen. Gilbert's petition sought Elizabeth's sponsorship of a voyage to undertake the "discovering of a passage by the North, to go to Catala, and all other the east parts of the worlde."[6] An accompanying treatise supported his petition's proposal of a fabled northwest passage to the East. Entitled "A Discourse of a Discovery for a New Passage to Catala,"[7] this treatise was an innovative, if somewhat indiscriminate, drawing together of then available authorities and sources on colonizing theory and practices, as well as extra-European geography.[8]

Gilbert's "Discourse" described the various commodities and benefits that might attend the discovery of a northwest passage. He expounded at length on the competitive advantages to be gained over Portugal and Spain by taking a shorter route to the rich countries in the East, "out of both their jurisdictions."[9] His proposal demonstrated a working knowledge of Spanish colonizing techniques and precedents, combined with a sensitivity to Elizabeth's domestic problems. He suggested, for example, inhabiting "some part of the Countries that might be discovered during the voyage, and settle there such needy people of our Country, which now trouble the commonwealth, and through want here at home, are [forced] to commit outrageous offences, whereby they are daily consumed with the Gallows."[10]

Gilbert's suggestion that colonization would relieve English population pressures was already a frequently expressed theme in Elizabethan colonial discourse. Sir Thomas Smith had invoked it in support of his Irish colonization plan in the 1570s.[11] Smith's concern, however, was primarily for the disinherited younger sons of the gentry, who would find abundant opportunities in a wild, underpopulated land. Gilbert's suggestion of populating eastern colonies with the lower, criminally inclined classes represented an innovation. He likewise extended this novel idea to North America, which, he argued, should also be colonized with the unemployed masses displaced by enclosure, eviction, and the other rationalizing tendencies in the Elizabethan economy. An American colony, Gilbert believed, could serve as both a stopover for resupply to the East and a valuable trading post. Gilbert was convinced by his reading of the authorities that the Indians of America much "esteem" English trifles and commodities. The increase in production of these baubles would doubly redound to the English economy by setting "poore men's children, to learn handy craftes. . . . By reason whereof, there should be none occasion, to have our country encumbered with loiterers, vagabonds, and such like idle persons."[12] Even at this early stage of his career, Gilbert demonstrated remarkable insight into the supply-side aspect of imperial mercantile economic theory.

But the best reason, Gilbert argued, for pursuing his plan was that a northwest passage to the East would cause neither legal nor diplomatic problems for Elizabeth. "All these commodities would grow, by following this our Discovery, without injurie done to any Christian prince, by crossing them in any of their used trades, whereby they might take any just occassion of offense."[13]

Gilbert requested Elizabeth's royal sponsorship of his colonization plan and the grant of one-tenth of all the lands discovered during his voyage. The remainder would belong to the queen, with Gilbert himself presiding over the entire territory claimed by England.

Gilbert's proposal was regarded as a sufficient "occasion of offence" to Spanish interests to prompt Spain's ambassador at the English court, Guzmán de Silva, to send the following letter to his monarch, Philip II, in March 1567:

It appears that this journey [Gilbert's] is a difficult one, but so did those made before the discovery of the Indies and as here they have not much commerce, they are always thinking how they can benefit themselves. I shall try to treat with this gentleman and learn his intention, which might be other [than that which I have described], and, if it appears that . . . he has another evil object, I will give notice, as it is very necessary to keep the matters of the Indies in view and to restrain those who may go to other parts.[14]

However, English—not Spanish—competing interests blocked the queen's sponsorship of Gilbert's proposal. The English Muscovy Company held monopoly rights from the Crown to all trade with Asia to the north. Concerns about Gilbert's possible interference with those Eastern rights were apparently voiced to the government by the influential company. There was no further royal consideration of Gilbert's venture. It was at this point in his career that Gilbert temporarily abandoned his interest in colonizing distant lands and followed Elizabeth's call to colonize Ireland. After his infamous tenure in that country,[15] he returned to London in the early 1570s. He was soon knighted by Elizabeth and elected to Parliament.

A Two-Part Subterfuge

Elizabeth had been excommunicated by the pope in 1570. Her court in the 1570s was thus a place of fervid anti-Spanish, anti-Catholic sentiment and Crown-encouraged piratical conspiracies. In fact, Gilbert's return to England coincided with Francis Drake's wondrously profitable raids in the Spanish

Caribbean during 1572 and 1573. Ostensibly undertaken in retaliation for the previous "treachery" against Captain John Hawkins's third slaving voyage,[16] Drake's astonishing success revealed to Elizabeth and her ministers that Spain was overextended in the Indies. Any pretensions to empire in that part of the world were only as convincing as the number of Spanish warships patrolling the Caribbean and American coastal shipping lanes. Drake had demonstrated that England should not be overly impressed.

Even if Spain were to answer increased depredations against Spanish shipping in the Indies with increased patrols, the ultimate benefits of such a tactical move would redound to England. A Spanish warship in the New World meant one less Spanish warship in the Old. In that Philip was engaged in a civil war in the Netherlands, still a part of his empire, and Elizabeth had decided as a part of her more openly hostile stance toward Spain to support the Protestant Dutch rebels there, a diversion in the New World made good political and military sense. If Philip chose not to answer it, English adventurers would have more freedom to establish colonial footholds in the Americas.

In 1577, a sporadically prosecuted anti-Spanish policy was pressed with greater ambition. With the cooperation of several influential members of the privy council, plans were made to outfit an expedition by Drake, with the queen's sponsorship, for the discovery of "Terra Australis incognita" in the Pacific.[17] In reality, the plan was for Drake to sail around the southern horn of South America, enter the Pacific Ocean, and attack the rich port cities on the western rim of the continent, probing the Spanish South American empire for weaknesses. It was hoped that Drake's piracy might then provoke a defensive response, further diverting Spanish naval power from the Atlantic.

At about the same time that Drake departed on what was to be the first circumnavigation of the globe by an Englishman, Sir Humphrey Gilbert, inspired by the convivial anti-Spanish atmosphere at court, drew up another proposal for his queen's consideration. This scheme of November 1577 envisaged an elaborate two-part plan of attack on Spain in the Atlantic to complement Drake's Pacific initiative. The first part, candidly entitled "A Discourse How Her Majesty May Annoy the King of Spain,"[18] proposed striking directly at Spain's Atlantic fishing fleet. Gilbert suggested the following subterfuge, which would permit Her Majesty to disavow any knowledge of or responsibility for such an attack:

[T]he diminishing of their forces by seas is to be done either by open hostility, or by some colorable means, as by giving of license under letters patent to discover and inhabit some strange place, with special provision for their safety whom policy requireth to have most annoyed by which means the doing of the contrary shall be imputed to the executors' fault; your highness' letter patents being a manifest show that it was not your Majesty's pleasure so to have it.[19]

Gilbert naturally offered to execute this exercise in royal obfuscation without charge to Her Majesty. All he sought was a plausibly deniable royal license for piracy against England's most dangerous and powerful rival. He would sail to Newfoundland on the pretext of making some discovery of land there, but in actuality he would raid the Spanish fishing fleet. Gilbert argued that the depletion of the fleet would lessen Spain's revenues and discourage further investment in shipping.

Gilbert's justification for this seemingly scandalous and unholy policy indicates how thoroughly the themes of radical Protestant discourse had been appropriated and absorbed by the nationalist advocates of a vigorous anti-Spanish policy in Elizabeth's court.

I hold it as lawful in Christian policy, to prevent a mischief betime: as to revenge it too late, especially seeing that God himself is a party in the common quarrels now a foot, and his enemy['s] malicious disposition towards your highness, and his Church manifestly seen, although by God's merciful providence not yet thoroughly felt.[20]

Having drawn God and his providence into this quarrel between rival Christian sects, Gilbert was emboldened to extend the enterprise even further in his next interrelated and similarly candidly entitled proposal, "A Discourse How Her Majesty May Meet with and Annoy the King of Spain."[21] This second project was to be financed with the gains made from Gilbert's raid on the Spanish fishing fleets. Sir Humphrey proposed to raise a fleet to sail to the West Indies and to dispossess the Spaniards of their most valuable ports there.

This second proposal opened with another diatribe against the papist Spaniards: "[S]o long as they be of that religion and we of ours there can be between us and them no good friendship."[22] According to Gilbert, the notorious Spanish Inquisition proved the impossibility of reconciliation between the two sects. In all the dominions that Spain ruled, the papists "labour with all diligence to make the people believe that only their religion is the thing that most pleaseth god, and that all other religions be abominable heresies."[23]

Sir Humphrey's proposal charged that the Indians of America were taught by Spain that the English Protestant could be killed with the same impunity as any infidel Turk or Saracen. The Spaniards assured the Indians that in killing Englishmen, "they do god good service."[24] The converted heathen was being recruited to wage a crusading war on the apostate Englishman! This crime against the queen as head of the Church of Christ could not go unanswered, nor would its prosecution go unaided: "It is god's will that men do their best in all good causes and then he will do the rest that they cannot perform to withstand so great enemies, and especially those that be merely against the true religion of god as the Spaniards be."[25]

Gilbert urged his divinely willed plan as a preemptive measure, to demonstrate to the king of Spain that any kind of peace would be better than war with England. He proposed attacking Spain's wealthiest jewels in the West Indies, Hispaniola and Cuba, both poorly defended in his opinion. Once these islands had been seized and secured, England could easily attack Spanish shipping in the Bahama Straits and in the vicinity of Bermuda. Thus Elizabeth would keep the king of Spain busy defending his interests in the New World, and she "shall little need to care for any harm that he can do in these parts."[26]

The First Elizabethan Charter of New World Conquest (and "Notes")

Official records do not indicate whether Elizabeth officially adopted Gilbert's two interrelated proposals, but within six months of their delivery, in June 1578, Gilbert received generous letters patent from the queen to make an expedition of discovery and conquest into vaguely described regions. The royal instructions attached to the grant were similarly imprecise.[27] The queen's lack of precision in describing the areas to be explored and exploited under her royal charter raises a strong possibility that at least some portion of Gilbert's two-part proposed subterfuge had been adopted as Crown policy. The queen's charter empowered Gilbert "to discover, search, find out, and view such remote heathen and barbarous lands, countries, and territories not actually possessed of any Christian prince or people . . . to have, hold, occupy and enjoy to him his heirs and assigns forever."[28] This limited grant of authority to discover only heathen and infidel lands not already possessed by a Christian prince would have provided the Crown with a plausible defense for any actions that Gilbert might commit outside the limits of the patent. This language also closely tracked the medievalized, Crusading-era boilerplated form of discourse used by Elizabeth's grandfather Henry VII in his 1497 patent to John Cabot.[29] Elizabeth could thus respond to any Spanish complaints respecting Gilbert's voyage or actions with the argument that she was only following the practice of her Tudor predecessors.

Gilbert's privileges under the patent were similar to those granted other adventurers who had sought to conquer territories in the name of the Crown in Ireland and the Northlands during the Tudor reigns.[30] If after six years Gilbert had failed to establish a colony in lands he had discovered, all claims under the patent reverted to the Crown. The queen's grant also provided Gilbert the authority to repulse any intruders who attempted to settle within a 200-league radius of any colony he established. All lands occupied were to be held by homage from the Crown. Royalties were to be paid on any gold and silver, and Gilbert was to have full authority to dispose of lands in his feudal demesne, "in fee simple or otherwise according to the order of the laws of England."[31]

In 1578, the same year that these letters patent were issued, the elder Richard Hakluyt, the lawyer cousin of the most famous Elizabethan-era promoter of English colonization of America, the younger Richard Hakluyt, prepared a series of "Notes on Colonization."[32] These commentaries were probably prepared in connection with Gilbert's voyage, although they were not made public until 1582, in the younger Hakluyt's first major documentary collection on New World colonization, *Divers Voyages Touching the Discovery of America.*[33]

Hakluyt's "Notes" contained well-considered advice on establishing a colony in a wild and hostile land inhabited by barbarian tribespeople. Such a colony, Hakluyt advised, should be able to withstand attack not only from the native inhabitants but also from European rivals, particularly Spain and France. Hakluyt's advice on dealing with the colony's "natural inhabitants" urged an initial policy of self-serving amicability as the wisest strategy for achieving ultimate exploitation. The English, he warned, "might not be suffered by the savages to enjoy any whole country or any more than the scope of a City." A small foothold was all that was required, however, for the natives would most certainly desire the trade brought by the English colonists. Other benefits would naturally follow. "[I]f we might enjoy traffic and be assured of the same, we might be much enriched, our navy might be increased, and a place of safety might there be found, if change of religion or civil wars should happen in this realm [England], which are things of great benefit."[34] Hakluyt elaborated the subtle reasoning behind this basic strategy of feigned peaceful intentions:

Nothing is more to be endeavoured with the inland people than familiarity. For so may you best discover all the natural commodities of their country, and also all their wants, all their strengths, all their weaknesses, and with whom they are in war . . . which known, you may work great effects of greatest consequence.[35]

Hakluyt's discourse presumed that although the savages might at first be resistant to English intrusion, the colonists would inevitably establish a permanent hegemony in America. Establishing an initial peace was only a more efficient instrument for attaining the ultimate ends of empire in the New World: "[A]ll humanity and courtesy and much forbearing of revenge to the inland people [must] be used, so shall you have firm amity with your neighbors, so shall you have their inland commodities, . . . and so shall you wax rich and strong in force."[36]

The Early Colonizing Efforts of Sir Humphrey Gilbert

With the lawyer Hakluyt's "Notes" to advise him, Sir Humphrey Gilbert set out on his first voyage to America in November 1578. Adopting the financing model used by the Smiths[37] for their colonizing venture in Ireland, Gilbert had convinced at least forty-four subscribers to contribute capital to his expedition of discovery. The fleet of 7 ships carried 122 guns and more than 400 men. Many of the men on board were common pirates. Gilbert commanded the flagship, the *Anne Aucher* (named after his wife). The *Falcon*, owned by the Crown, was captained by Gilbert's half-brother, Walter Raleigh (also a favorite of the queen and, like Gilbert, a veteran of the Irish wars). The master of the *Falcon* was a Portuguese pilot, Simon Fernández, who claimed to have frequently sailed the Caribbean and American waters for the Iberians.

To what extent Gilbert's fleet had been assembled in accordance with his two-part plan for annoying the Spanish submitted to Elizabeth in 1577[38] is not known, but a close associate of Gilbert and Raleigh, Edward Hayes, reported that the "puissant fleet" had been prepared "to encounter a king's power by sea."[39] Whatever its ultimate objectives (David Quinn speculates that Gilbert intended to establish a well-armed colony close to the West Indies as a base against Spain[40]), the voyage itself ended inconsequentially. The ships were forced to return to England because of debilitating battles at sea, short supplies, or some other difficulty. The privy council, acting on reports that certain ships in Gilbert's fleet might have engaged in piracy against neutral foreign merchant vessels, prohibited any return voyages until Sir Humphrey pledged assurances of good behavior.

After pledging a bond for £500, Gilbert was permitted to send a second expedition across the Atlantic. One ship, the *Squirrel*, captained by the Portuguese pilot Fernández, crossed the Atlantic in the early spring of 1580 to reconnoiter the North American Atlantic coastline. The vessel returned in June with valuable information on a site for Gilbert's intended American colonization scheme.

Shortly after Fernández's return, Drake completed his circumnavigation of the globe. This was the same voyage that had inspired Gilbert's Atlantic scheme of Spanish harassment in 1577.[41] Drake's voyage was a remarkable feat of navigation and bravado, as well as a remarkable success. After leaving England in 1577, he sailed south through the Straits of Magellan, then northward to the Pacific coast of South America. He then plundered the defenseless port cities of Santiago, Chile, and Lima, Peru. After these immensely profitable raids, Drake sailed farther up the Pacific coast, coming ashore in the vicinity of San Francisco Bay and claiming the entire region for the English Crown. He then set sail for the Moluccas. Rounding the Cape of Good Hope, he returned to Plymouth in September 1580. His *Golden Hind* carried treasure worth approximately £800,000. A grateful queen knighted the fabled sea dog, a hero of the people, on the deck of his ship.

Drake's pirating voyage and Elizabeth's bestowal of knighthood for his acts of piracy brought strong protests from the Spanish ambassador, Don Bernardino de Mendoza. He protested not only against Drake's piracy but also against his very entrance into areas claimed under Spanish sovereignty by virtue of the pope of Rome's grants. Elizabeth, already an excommunicate, was unimpressed by Spain's claim to title to any region of the globe based solely on popish caprice. The queen reportedly told the ambassador that she "could not persuade herself the Spaniard had any rightfull title by the Bishop of Rome's donation, in whom she acknowledged no prerogative, much less authority in such cases." At the same time, Elizabeth reserved to her subjects "without breach of the Law of Nations" the right to trade and establish colonies in those parts of the New World which "the Spaniards inhabit not."[42]

By her rejection of the papal basis of Spain's title, Elizabeth asserted the right of her own subjects to establish colonies in any region of the New World not occupied by Spain. In effect, Elizabeth, sovereign monarch and head of her own reformed church, had decentralized and nationalized the discovery and acquisition process. From the Protestant queen's perspective, at least, the intense competition between the European powers for New World wealth had dictated recognition of only two important, secularly based presumptions in European international law and practice. First, all Europeans had the right to establish colonies upon their discovery of territory in the New World. Rome's mediating role in European colonization had been rendered nugatory by the Reformation. Second, effective occupation of these newly discovered territories was to be the sole test of New World rights between European sovereigns. As with Hakluyt's discourse, prepared in connection with Gilbert's New World discovery expedition,[43] Elizabeth's declaration of the Law of Nations, not surprisingly, entirely disregarded the rights of the New World's infidel peoples. According to this new, secularized Discovery-era doctrine of European rights in non-European lands, the Indians and their lands were supplementary elements to the sectarian-fueled, dynastic aspirations of competing Christian princes and princesses.

Drake's return and Elizabeth's belligerent attitude toward Spain spurred enthusiasm for all types of anti-Spanish schemes and exploits. By the spring of 1582, Gilbert had assembled the major pieces of an elaborate North American colonizing scheme. Oddly enough, Sir Humphrey, the formerly rabid antipapist defender of the true Protestant faith, had decided to incorporate a group of recusant Catholics into his American venture. Gilbert's decision to allow a group of Catholics to infect the New World with their papistry was motivated by a lack of cash. The Catholics desperately desired to practice their oppressed creed and were willing to pay to establish a sanctuary in North America under Sir Humphrey's royal patent.

Following Elizabeth's excommunication in 1570, practice of the Catholic religion by English citizens had been made subject to penalties, fines, imprisonment, and even death. Only token efforts at enforcement of these sanctions had been made prior to the 1580s, but as the fears of a Spanish conspiracy intensified, the issue of nonconformity to the Church of England came into sharper focus in the Elizabethan mind. Questions of national security and disloyalty to the Crown were now implicated by continued practice of the popish ceremonies. By 1581, the monthly fines for recusancy, the failure to attend the Anglican Church, had been stepped up from 1 shilling to £20, an amount that effectively transformed the penalty for nonconformity into state-enforced bankruptcy.

The desperate group of Catholics who had arranged to emigrate to America under Gilbert's patent were led by George Peckham and Sir Thomas Gerard. Peckham had only recently been released from prison for violation of the religious laws, and Gerard, similarly hounded by the authorities, had previously investigated Ireland as a possible refuge for English Catholics. The government would naturally have been suspicious of any Catholic participation in Gilbert's venture, but Sir Humphrey's valuable contacts in the government facilitated the incorporation of Peckham and Gerard's group into the American colonization plan. Sir Frances Walsingham, secretary of state, while no friend of English Catholics, knew Gilbert and supported his project. He may also have welcomed an opportunity to export a group of potential coconspirators with the Spanish out of the realm. Walsingham granted a petition enabling Gilbert to devise approximately 2 million acres under his patent to the emigrating papists. Under the terms of the grant, Gilbert was to be lord proprietor and governor of any colony established by Gerard and Peckham. The two Catholic organizers were each to be lords paramount of separate American seignories, with power to assign lands out of their grants from Gilbert at a rent of 1 shilling per 100 acres. A supreme council, of which Gilbert, Peckham, and Gerard were to be members, was to be established, and each of the parties was to hold court for their tenants' disputes. This blending of corporate and feudal forms recalls the basic organizing models pioneered by Sidney and Smith for Irish colonization.[44]

The Spanish ambassador Mendoza, who kept a close eye on Gilbert's plans, was greatly disturbed by the incorporation of a Catholic element into the American venture. Spain opposed any alien settlement in the New World that interfered with its highly profitable, papally granted monopoly rights. An English plan to invade America and at the same time depopulate England of Catholics who would otherwise have been useful in a conspiracy or an uprising against the queen was doubly odious to Spanish imperial interests. Writing to his sovereign in July 1582, Mendoza explained the "prejudicial" advantage thus secured by the Protestant "heretics": "In this way once and for all the small remnant of good blood in this sick body would be drained away."[45]

Mendoza also reported to King Philip that he had tried to dissuade the English Catholics from participating in the scheme by making it known "that those lands belonged to your Majesty, that you had garrisons and fortresses there, and that they would immediately have their throats cut."[46] To further dampen their enthusiasm for Gilbert's project, Mendoza had told the English Catholics that they were "imperilling their consciences by engaging in an enterprise prejudicial to His Holiness [the pope] and that it would be well for them to report the matter to him . . . and learn if they could justifiably make the voyage."[47] Mendoza, having already notified Rome about the matter and Spain's interest in it, was confident that the English Catholics would be told not to travel to America.

Mendoza was apparently successful in bullying several Catholics into backing out of the project. Others, however, persisted. The ambassador reported that many of the stubborn Catholics had convinced themselves

that there is nothing in it against your Majesty because in the map it is marked as Nueva Francia [New France], which proves it was discovered by the French, and that since Cortes fitted out ships at his own expense to make conquests—and he was a Catholic—they could do the same.[49]

Mendoza was apparently referring to, among other obstinate recusants, George Peckham. Peckham had approached John Dee, Elizabethan England's most respected geographer and mathematician, in July 1582, the same month in which Mendoza wrote his letter. Peckham asked Dee for his considered opinion on whether Spain indeed "owned" the North American land intended for English Catholic settlement under Gilbert's patent. Dee assured him that Spain had no rights in the area. The English Catholics could proceed upon their "voyage of conquest," as they called it.[50]

While the stubborn Catholics were preparing for the colonizing expedition, Gilbert sought to raise additional money for his own separate plans. Besides the Peckham and Gerard group, to which he assigned a total of 8.5 million acres under his patent between June 1582 and February 1583, he sold a number of additional tracts to other grantees. Each grant was typically for millions of acres.

Early New World Colonizing Discourses

Gilbert planned to embark for America in the spring of 1583. It was around this time that the younger Richard Hakluyt, Gilbert's close associate, published his *Divers Voyages Touching the Discovery of America.* Probably intended as a promotional tract in connection with Gilbert's project, *Divers Voyages* contained various documents collected by Hakluyt, which he apparently considered important in relation to the colonization of North America. As previously discussed, the collection included his older cousin's "Notes on Colonization" of 1578.[51] It also contained reprints of documents relating to the Cabot voyages, intended as proof of English title to North America by virtue of prior discovery.

Another publication released at the time of Gilbert's planned embarkation appeared under the name of Secretary of State Walsingham's stepson Christopher Carleill. This 1583 pamphlet was entitled "A Brief and Summary Discourse upon the Intended Voyage to the Furthermost Parts of America."[52]

Carleill's connection to the Gilbert enterprise was indirect; his influential stepfather had attempted to have him named captain of several ships contributed by Bristol merchants to Sir Humphrey's expedition. When this idea fell through, Carleill apparently began to search out other parties to finance an American expedition. Such an expedition would probably have violated Gilbert's rights under his royal patent. Walsingham was almost certainly relying on his influence with Gilbert and the government to smooth things over in case of subsequent conflict between Gilbert and his stepson.[53]

The intentional derivativeness of Carleill's "Brief and Summary Discourse" bears witness to the emergence of a distinctively English colonizing discursive practice at a relatively early stage of England's Discovery era. Carleill's pamphlet set out to recapitulate what had already become the oft-stated, fundamental legitimating arguments supporting English colonization of other peoples' lands. His advice differed little from that outlined in the elder Hakluyt's "Notes" or from that of the Elizabethan architects of Irish colonization. Exploitation of the natives was to be the basis of trade. The "country people" were to be shown how to produce wax, honey, and salt in "good quantity." This labor of the Indians for the benefit of the English would be rewarded by "such trifling things they desire of us."[54] Few English merchants would have tolerated the exploitive treatment at the hands of a trading partner that was advocated in "A Brief and Summary Discourse." Carleill, however, held firmly to the paradoxical belief expressed by many of his Elizabethan contemporaries that contact with sharp-dealing Christian merchants, combined with "gentle and familiar entreating," would lead savage tribal people to an understanding of "what is better for them."[55] According to Carleill's reasoning,

It is to be assuredly hoped, that they will daily by little and little forsake their barbarous and savage living, and grow to such order and civility with us, as there may be well expected from thence no lesse quantity and diversity of merchandize than is now had out of Dutchland, Italy, France or Spain.[56]

Carleill's summary of the by-now-familiar arguments touting the economic benefits of North American colonization did include at least one energizing discursive innovation. Always the economizing editor, Carleill combined the Protestant religionists' frequent calls to stem the tide of papistry and bring the true Christian doctrine to the savages of America[57] with the popular pressure-valve theory of overseas colonization. In the 1570s, Sir Thomas Smith, advocate of Irish colonization, had articulated the "high" form of the pressure-valve thematic of colonization, which viewed overseas conquests as providing new feudal outlets for the younger sons of wealthy families.[58] Ironically, while Carleill's influential stepfather, Secretary of State Walsingham, had sought to place his stepson in a position of command on an American colonizing venture, Carleill himself drew on the "low" form of the pressure-valve theory advocated by Sir Humphrey Gilbert[59] and joined it with the zealous Protestant calls to Christianize the savages of the New World:

To those who have any forward minds in well doing to the generality of mankind, I say thus much more, that Christian charity doth as greatly persuade the furtherance of this action, as any other that may be laid before us, in as much as thereby we shall not only do a most excellent work, in respect of reducing the savage people to Christianity and civility, but also in respect of our poor sort of people, which are very many amongst us, living altogether unprofitable, and oftentimes to the great disquiet of the better sort.[60]

Carleill's advocacy of the social benefits accruing to England from overseas colonization illuminates an important point of irruption in the Elizabethan discourses of conquest. Poverty was no longer regarded as primarily a holy state or solely a matter of Church eleemosynary concern in the disrupted economy of Elizabethan England.[61] The potential of a criminalized, unemployable underclass had forced the issue of poverty into the discursive domain of social order and control. The advocates of colonization had quickly grasped the significance of this point of rupture (and the desire to erase its register), proposing a solution to the problem of the unemployed English masses in their own discourse of displacement of the unplaceable to America.

Such was the already intricately elaborated nature of the Elizabethan call to America. On the eve of the first Protestant crusade against the heathen savages of America, the Elizabethans had already mobilized a colonizing discourse to accompany England's will to empire in the New World. A quarter of a century before the settlement of the first permanent English colony at Jamestown, the presumptions that there was an abundance of commodities ripe for exploitation in the New World, that overseas colonies would catapult England into the forefront of the emerging world trading system, that America presented the opportunity for Englishmen to leave their crowded country for an unbounded virgin land, and that the Indians would gladly welcome the English—along with their pilfering trading practices and their civilizing brand of Reformed Christianity—were becoming staples of English colonial promotional literature. The elements of a distinctively English colonizing discourse were becoming more broadly popularized.

The New World Crusade of Sir Humphrey Gilbert

Gilbert himself departed Plymouth on the first Protestant crusade to North America in June 1583. The chronicler of the expedition was the previously mentioned Edward Hayes,[62] longtime associate of Gilbert and captain and owner of the *Golden Hind* (so christened in honor of Sir Francis Drake), one of the five ships under Gilbert's command. Hayes, like many of the other young men who played leading roles in the seagoing ventures of the Elizabethan Discovery era, was a member of the gentry. His family estate was located in Liverpool. He was well educated, a fellow of King's College, Cambridge.[63]

Hayes's report of Gilbert's third ill-fated voyage was published by the younger Hakluyt in 1589.[64] The well-written and detailed narrative described Sir Humphrey's arrival in St. John's, Newfoundland, in August 1583. Gilbert reportedly announced to the fleet of fishing vessels from various European nations anchored in the harbor his intention to claim the territory on behalf of the Crown of England for purposes of advancing the "Christian religion in those Paganish regions."[65] Shortly thereafter, according to Hayes, Sir Humphrey summoned the captains of all the ships, English and non-English alike. His commission from the queen was read and interpreted, "by virtue whereof he took possession in the same harbor of S. John, and 200 leagues every way."[66] In addition to this ceremony, Gilbert "had delivered unto him (after the custom of England) a rod and a turf of the same soil entering possession also for him, his heirs and assigns for ever."[67] Drake had reportedly performed a similar feudally derived ceremony upon landing in the San Francisco Bay region during his circumnavigation of the globe.[68] Gilbert's "possession" ceremony apparently represented the recognized customary procedure, at least among English sailors, for claiming the Crown's sovereignty over lands "not possessed by any Christian prince or people."[69]

Before departing from Newfoundland, Governor Gilbert declared three laws, the first pieces of English legislation in colonial America. The first proclaimed that the public exercise of religion should be according to the rites of the Church of England; the second declared it to be high treason for any individual to prejudice the queen's right of possession to the claimed lands; and the third stated that "if any person should utter words sounding to the dishonour of her Majestie, he should loose his ears, and have his ship and goods confiscate."[70]

Gilbert never returned to England after claiming his colony. His ship was presumed sunk on the return voyage, but whether by a storm or by encounters with pirates or Spanish warships is not known. The first Protestant crusade to America had ended in tragic falure with the death at sea of Sir Humphrey Gilbert, a most noble and brave Elizabethan conquistador.

Appropriated Discourses

Cantabrigian Calvinism

Edward Hayes's ship, the *Golden Hind*, did return from America, docking at Falmouth in late September 1583. It was probably then or soon afterward that he composed his narrative of Sir Humphrey's failed voyage of conquest to the New World.

Hayes's return crossing had provided him with the opportunity to reflect on the arguments, moral as well as legal, supporting the discovery and conquest of America. The long title of Hayes's narrative of the Gilbert voyage suggested the basic foundation of English rights to North America: "A report of the voyage and success thereof, attempted in the year of our Lord 1583 by Sir Humphrey Gilbert knight, with other gentlemen assisting him in that action, intended to discover and to plant Christian inhabitants in place convenient, upon those large and ample countrys extended Northward from the cape of Florida, lying under very temperate climes, esteemed fertile and rich in minerals, yet not in the actual possession of any Christian prince."[71]

According to Hayes, the unquestioned obligation of planting "a Christian habitation and regiment" in the northerly parts of America had been bestowed exclusively on England by virtue of the Cabot discoveries. England, however, had failed to follow up these discoveries, and Hayes, like Richard Eden before him, castigated his countrymen for wasting the opportunity presented by America to increase Her Majesty's territories and revenue. Hayes delivered a further, even more serious charge against this dereliction of Christian duty: "And which is more; the seed of Christian religion had been sowed amongst those pagans, which by this time might have brought forth a most plentiful harvest and copious congregation of Christians."[72]

Hayes, as has been noted, was a Cambridge man, and the notion of the "seed" of Christian faith planted in the human soul was a Cambridge idea. Cambridge had early on been a hotbed of religious radicalism; the austere doctrines of John Calvin on predestination and its relation to grace were worked there into a unique and radical brand of self-righteous theology that would come to be known as English Puritanism. One of the most influential of the Cambridge Calvinists was William Perkins, fellow of Christ College, who taught and wrote at Cambridge in the latter part of the sixteenth century. Faith, Perkins preached, was a tiny seed planted in the soul by the work of God's spirit. The soul's responsibility was to water and cultivate this tiny seed and to nourish it into growth. Human beings can start this labor of regeneration as soon as they begin to sense the desire to be saved.[73]

Perkins was extremely popular throughout Protestant England, and in early colonial America as well. The historian Perry Miller has called him "a superb popularizer" of Calvinist doctrine and one of the outstanding pulpit orators of the century.[74] Hayes may or may not have come into contact with Perkins at Cambridge. Hayes's narrative of the Gilbert voyage, however, with its numerous references to the importance of planting the "seed" of Christian religion and civility as the principal crops of the New World colonizing enterprise, attests that he was certainly familiar with the Calvinist discourse popularized by the preacher. Hayes had simply appropriated and economized early Puritanism's "planting" metaphor and applied it to America: planting colonies of English farmers in America meant planting the seeds of civility and Christian religion. The seeds of commerce germinated by this divinely predestined endeavor were derivative but fortunate by-products of the seeds of faith planted by the English.

Besides the central figure of the "seed" of faith planted by God in the human soul, another important, although rudimentary, theme in Perkins's Calvinist discourse was the idea of the special contractual relationship between God and humankind. This relationship rested on "the covenant of grace." The preacher Perkins defined this covenant as God's "contract with man, concerning the obtaining of life eternal, upon a certain condition."[75]

Hayes, the Puritan explorer, clearly viewed (albeit in primitive terms) English conquest of America in terms of a covenant between God and the English. The English were to bring Christianity to the heathen according to the mysterious will of God, who would eventually reward them at a time chosen by his ultimate wisdom. The failures of others in attempting to plant in North America should not be attributed to God's breach of this covenant: "events do show that either God's cause hath not been chiefly preferred by them, or else God hath not permitted so abundant grace as the light of his word and knowledge of him to be yet revealed unto those infidels before the appointed time."[76] But, Hayes asserted, the planting in America of the seed of true faith was a predestined fact:

But most assuredly, the only cause of religion hitherto hath kept back, and will also bring forward at the time assigned by God, an effectual and complete discovery and possession by Christians both of those ample countrys and the riches within them hitherto concealed: whereof notwithstanding God in his wisdom hath permitted to be revealed from time to time a certain obscure and misty knowledge, by little and little to allure the minds of men that way (which else will be dull enough in the zeale of his cause) and thereby to prepare us unto a readiness for the execution of his will against the due time ordained, of calling those pagans unto Christianity.[77]

Any seventeenth-century New England Puritan worth his theological salt could trace in Hayes's 1583 narrative the emergence of themes that their own preachers constantly declaimed as the Puritans' errand into the wilderness: the colonization of America was the elect's obligation in fulfillment of the covenant of grace with God. Hayes expressly declared that those who pursued the task of American colonization with motives "derived from a virtuous and heroical mind, preferring chiefly the honor of God" and "compassion of poor infidels captived by the devil, could confidently repose in the preordinance of God, that in this last age of the world (or likely never) the time is complete of receiving also these Gentiles into his mercy, and that God will raise him an instrument to effect the same."[78] In Hayes's appropriated Puritan-inspired discourse of conquest, the English will to empire fulfilled in the New World wilderness was regarded as a predestined event.

Peckham's "True Reporte"

George Peckham, the stubborn Catholic recusant who had sought to insinuate a papist presence into Gilbert's New World crusade,[79] heard the news of Sir Humphrey's tragic end from Captain Hayes in October. Peckham had by this time joined forces with Sir Philip Sidney, an assignee of 3 million acres under Gilbert's patent.[80] Peckham and Sidney set down their plans to establish a

North American colony in a document entitled "Articles of Assurance."[81] These articles established an enterprise using the by-now-familiar vehicle of the joint-stock company. As in the earlier Irish colonization schemes,[82] land rights were apportioned according to the size of the individual's stock contribution.

In November 1583, Peckham published a promotional tract in connection with the venture, under the title "A True Reporte, Of the late discoveries, and possession, taken in the right of the Crowne of Englande, of the Newfound Landes: By that valiant and worthye Gentleman, Sir Humphrey Gilbert Knight. Wherein is also briefly set downe, her highnesse lawfull Tytle thereunto, and the great and manifolde Commodities, that is likely to grow thereby, to the whole Realme in generall, and to the Adventurers in particular together with the easiness and shortness of the voyage."[83]

Besides giving a general account of Gilbert's final voyage, Peckham's "True Reporte" provided an extended defense of American colonization, aimed at the "detractors and hinderers of this journey."[84] It is useful in reading Peckham's pamphlet, therefore, to recognize that it was written in response to a number of voices apparently raised in opposition to American colonization. The nature of these opposed discourses can be inferred from the fact that "A True Reporte" focused extensively on the legality of the English invasion of America and on the feasibility of establishing plantations there. The failure of Gilbert's well-publicized voyage had apparently raised doubts about whether Providence had indeed intended the English to dispossess the Indians of America. Even a gentleman-warrior of Sir Humphrey's considerable talents had not been able to overcome the considerable logistic and financial difficulties involved in establishing an English presence in America. Naysayers with an interest in the competing Eastern trade routes, or Catholics cowed by the Spanish ambassador, may well have argued that God had not predestined the English to plant the seeds of reformation and revenue in the New World.

Peckham was, of course, a Catholic. His God had so forsaken him in England that he was seeking exile (and other Catholic subscribers to join him) in a savage wilderness an ocean's distance from Elizabeth's recusancy laws.[85] He was therefore more likely to seek out arguments (as would other Catholics and less Calvinistically inclined Protestants) grounding England's rights to America on a firmer foundation than asserted divinations of God's unfathomable providence. Peckham's widely circulated "True Reporte," one of the most comprehensive discussions of English rights to the soil of America and the corresponding rights of the savages to appear in the Elizabethan era, thus sought to base England's rights on arguments that all people of good sense could recognize as well reasoned. Of course, such arguments had already been developed by Peckham's coreligionists in Spain.[86] It is evident that one of Peckham's goals in "A True Reporte" was to translate the Spanish Humanist discourse of a Law of Nations recognizing the right of Christian Europeans to invade infidel territories for violations of natural law into terms responsive to the unique concerns and prejudices of his fellow English citizens. At the same time, Peckham was required, for obvious reasons, to make sure that the Spanish origin of this discourse was obscured.

Peckham's "True Reporte" deployed a thorough knowledge of the contemporary and ancient sources on discovery and travel. The pamphlet opened with a gloss on Hayes's report of the sad fate of Gilbert. Gilbert's tragic failure provided Peckham with a segue to the major issues raised by the "detractors and hinderers" of the American colonization enterprise: "whether it were as well pleasing to almightie God, as profitable to men? as lawful as it seemed honorable. As well grateful to the Savages, as gainfull to the Christians." [87]

Peckham's text promised to resolve these central concerns raised by the opposing discourses to American colonization:

I will endeavour my self . . . to prove that this voyage, late enterprised, for trade, traffic, and planting, in America, is an action tending to the lawfull enlargement of her Majesty's dominions, commodious to the whole Realm in general. Profitable to the adventurers in particular, beneficial to the Savages, and a matter to be attained without any great danger or difficulty.

And lastly (which most of all is) A thing likewise fitting to the honor and glory of almighty God. [88]

Peckham focused much of his analysis on the asserted rights of the English under the Law of Nations. Under that universally binding law, Peckham argued, the savages of America could not prevent Christians from lawful travel into the New World for purposes of trade. This duty of "mutual society and fellowship between man and man prescribed by the Law of Nations" was binding on all peoples:

who doubteth but that it is lawfull for Christians to use trade and traficke with Infidels or Savages. . . . A thing so commonly and generally practiced, both in these our days, and in times past, beyond the memory of man, both by Christians and infidels, that it needeth no further proofe. [89]

Christians, in other words, had acquired the right to trade with infidels in all parts of the world by prescriptive custom.

Appropriation and Suppression of a Spanish Colonizing Discourse

As was the practice of his Elizabethan contemporaries, Peckham infrequently cited other than biblical authorities in his text. But his argument that the right to trade was secured by the Law of Nations closely paralleled that of the early sixteenth-century Spanish Dominican theologian Franciscus de Victoria. [90] In his 1532 lecture "On the Indians Lately Discovered," Victoria had stated:

I will now speak of the lawful and adequate titles whereby the Indians might have come under the sway of the Spaniards. (1) The first title to be named is that of natural society and fellowship [compare Peckham's "mutual society and fellowship"]. And hereon let my first conclusion be: (2) The Spaniards have a right to travel into the lands in question and to sojourn there. [91]

Victoria (like Peckham) cited as his first "proof" "the law of nations" (*ius gentium*). Victoria's second proof (like Peckham's) relied on historical custom:

"Secondly, it was permissible from the beginning of the world . . . for anyone to set forth and travel wheresoever he would."[92] Peckham's discussion in this part of "A True Reporte" followed the precise sequence of Victoria's first two proofs. Did Peckham have Victoria's text at hand? Written by a Spanish Dominican priest, "On the Indians" would hardly have been embraced as part of the legitimate knowledge of English colonizing legal discourse. As has already been indicated, Peckham himself had been imprisoned more than once under the Elizabethan recusancy laws. His actions were monitored closely by the government. Anything he wrote promoting his Catholic American coloni-zation venture would be published only if he was certain that it would meet with the approving eye and considered opinion of an intolerant, censorious age.[93] Given Victoria's seemingly casuistical defense of Spanish title to the New World, it would have been politically unwise for Peckham to admit the Spanish Dominican's text as an authoritative exposition of the Law of Nations. But Peckham would probably also have recognized the manipulability of Victoria's legal discourse on the rights *and duties* of civilized nations in the New World under his postulated Law of Nations.

The assertion that Victoria's discourse was appropriated, suppressed, and, in essence, colonized by the Catholic Englishman is further proved by Peckham's delineation of the two sorts of New World planting in which Christians have a right to engage under the Law of Nations:

And for as much as the use of trade and traffic, (be it never so profitable) ought not to be preferred before the planting of Christian faith I will therefore somewhat entreat of planting (without which, Christian Religion can take no root, be the Preachers never so careful or diligent) which I mean to divide in two sorts.[94]

While the vocabulary of this argument was borrowed from Peckham's previous gloss on the Puritan Hayes's text—the "planting" of colonies is necessary for the seed of Christian faith to take "root"—its logic and syntax were most certainly translated from Victoria's Spanish colonial discourse. According to Peckham, the natives of North America could always assent to admit Christians to their countries, whereby quiet possession and Christianity were rightfully established. This was Peckham's first sort of "planting." But if the colonists were unjustly repulsed by the savages, Peckham argued, then under the Law of Nations, Christians could use militant force in order to maintain their rights to plant their seeds of commerce and faith. This was the latter of Peckham's "two sorts" of planting. Because both "sorts" of planting of colonies, by assent or by force, led to the establishment of Christian religion, either sort, according to Peckham, "may be lawfully and justly exercised."[95] That colonization in furtherance of spreading Christianity gave an unqualified legal right to a Christian presence in the savages' country was of course a central organizing point of Victoria's lectures on the Law of Nations and the American Indians.

Peckham also apparently borrowed directly from Victoria's text to make the important point that before undertaking to defend their rights to colonize by force, the civilized Christians should take pains to reveal their peaceful intentions and to explain "how they came not to their [the savages'] hurt, but for their good . . . to dwell peaceably amongst them, and to trade and traffic with them."[96]

For albeit, to maintain right and repel injury, be a just cause of war, yet must there hereof be heedful care had, that whereas the savages be fearful by nature, and fond otherwise, the Christians should do their best endeavor to take away such fear as may grow unto them by reason of their strange apparel, armour, and weapon, or such like, by quiet peaceable conversation, and letting them [the Christians] live in security and keeping a measure of blameless defence, with as little discommodity to the savages as may be, for this kind of war would be only defensive and not offensive.[97]

Peckham had simply condensed Victoria's more elaborate proposition on this point. According to Victoria,

It is, however, to be noted that the natives being timid by nature and in other respects dull and stupid, however much the Spaniards may desire to remove their fears and reassure them with regard to peaceful dealings with each other, they may very excusably continue afraid at the sight of men strange in gowns and armed and much more powerful than themselves. And therefore, if, under the influence of these fears, they unite in their efforts to drive out the Spaniards . . . accordingly, the Spaniards ought to defend themselves, but so far as possible with the least damage to the natives, the war being a purely defensive one.[98]

Victoria's lectures of 1532 were published in Latin in Lyons in 1557, in Salamanca in 1565, and in Golstadt, Germany, in 1580. Peckham, writing in 1583, would have had access to at least these three Latin editions.[99] Peckham's erudition and discourse indicate that he had received as fine a classical education as was available to any member of the gentry. This would certainly have included a working knowledge of Latin. The similarity between these two cited passages, as well as others throughout the two texts,[100] strongly supports the conclusion that Peckham had access either to Victoria's "On the Indians" or to some gloss on it, as it was very popular throughout Europe. The Italian Protestant exile Alberico Gentili, for instance, who taught and wrote on the Law of Nations at Oxford during the final two decades of the sixteenth century, was fully conversant with Victoria's work.[101]

Thus Victoria's iconography of a universally binding Law of Nations was appropriated by his co-religionist Peckham for English veneration. Yet in view of the discursive taboos of Protestant Elizabethan England, the Catholic recusant was not being overcautious in obscuring the icon's Spanish origins. A Spanish casuist's well-sculpted notion that the Indians were bound by the Europeans' normative conception of natural law had been smuggled into English colonial discourse.

A Restoration of Rights

Having demonstrated the general right of the English under the Law of Nations to plant in America, and the reciprocal obligation of the Indians to recognize the right or suffer the consequences of war, Peckham then moved on to the claims of other European sovereigns. He focused particularly on Spain, which asserted competing rights to America under the Law of Nations.

Peckham required no Spanish sources in favorably resolving this problem. England's superior rights to North America could be proved using purely local sources of knowledge. Peckham argued that England's claim to North America was not a new assertion of rights, but a restoration of prior rights: "And it is very evident that the planting there shall in time [might] amply enlarge her Majesty's Territories and Dominions (or I might rather say) restore her to her Highnesse ancient right and interest in those countries."[102]

Peckham could point to various sources of this ancient English right to the northern half of the New World. The first source originated in the story of Madoc, Prince of Wales, son of Owen Gwyreth, who had lived during the twelfth-century reign of Henry II.[103] The Madoc legend enjoyed something of a revival in intellectual circles in Tudor England, which was understandable in view of the fact that Edmund Tudor, father of Henry VII and great-grandfather of Elizabeth, was part Welsh.[104] The story of the twelfth-century Welsh prince may have come to Peckham's attention by way of John Dee. Peckham, it will be recalled,[105] had visited Dee in response to Ambassador Mendoza's claim that Sir Humphrey Gilbert's North American patent rights fell within areas belonging to the Spanish Crown.[106] Dee produced a map of North America disproving the claim. On the back of the map, Dee had written that the Welsh prince Madoc "led a colony and inhabited in Terra Florida or thereabouts."[107] The version of the legend that appeared in Peckham's "True Reporte" had Madoc "departing from the coast of England, about the year of our Lord God 1170, arrived and there planted himself, and his Colonies, and afterward returned himself into England, leaving certain of his people there."[108]

According to an "ancient Welch Chronicle" cited by Peckham, Madoc was a New World Adam. He gave Welsh names to islands, beasts, and birds "which yet to this day beareth the same." Peckham gave instances: "a fruit called Gwynethes which is likewise a welch word." There was also a report by an English seaman who had "seen bearded men there, which can not be natural [in that] country, for that the Americans are void of beards." The evidentiary implication of Peckham's argument was that bearded Welshmen had intermarried with the smooth-faced Indians and spread their hairy-faced progeny throughout the New World as signs of English title.

Peckham's "True Reporte" argued that the twelfth-century Madoc discovery and its sixteenth-century significations established "the undoubted title of her Majestie: For as much as no other nation can truly by any Chronicles they can find, make prescription of time for themselves, before the time of this Prince Madoc."[109]

Peckham could offer even further proof of English title to the northern part of America. Peckham cited the letters patent to the Cabots from Elizabeth's grandfather, Henry VII, by which North America was claimed for the Crown (in effect, a superfluity in light of Madoc's prior discovery, but one well worth citing, as it was of more recent memory).[110]

Peckham asserted that while England had failed to act on these previously acquired rights to North America, no nation had interrupted England's claims by subsequent acts of possession. Thus these rights simply waited to be restored to the English Crown.

Peckham's refrain of a restoration of rights would have played well before an Elizabethan Protestant audience. As H. C. Porter has noted, the theme of restoration was frequently invoked by the advocates of Protestantism to support the religious claims of Elizabeth's Reformation. The Church of England, the royalist bishops argued, was "no new Reformation of things lately begun . . . but rather a reduction of the Church to the pristine state of old conformity which once it had, and almost lost by discontinuance of a few later years."[111] The recusant Peckham's parallel use of this theme of restoration to support Elizabeth's claims to North America over those of other European monarchs consciously harmonized English colonizing discourse with the broader religious refrains of Elizabeth's reign.

The Benefits of the Bargain

Having demonstrated the superior rights of England to colonize North America by virtue of first discovering these infidel-held lands, Peckham next discussed the reasons that the Indians themselves would welcome English colonization. The English would bring Christianity and civilization to America.[112] The savages would find these gifts "very beneficial and gainful" and would bless the hour "when this enterprise was undertaken."[113] They would be brought from falsehood to truth, from darkness to light, from superstitious idolatry to sincere Christianity. Although the English would benefit materially from American trade and traffic, no doubt the bargain would ultimately be in the savages' favor. "And if in respect of all the commodities they can yield (were they more) that they should but receive this only benefit of Christianity, they were more than fully recompenced."[114]

Such were the divinely inspired economics of English colonialism. The natives got the better of the bargain by their conquest at the hands of the English, for they would receive not only the Christians' religion but their civilization as well.

This same logic had been relied on by the Iberian monarchs in legitimating their conquests of normatively divergent peoples.[115] Peckham simply domesticated the justification and the proto-utilitarian theory behind it. The savages, argued Peckham, lacked the knowledge to put their vast lands to productive use.[116] The techniques and tools of Christian civilization, however, could enable the savages to use but "the tenth of their land" in providing for their subsistence, thus freeing nine-tenths of the land for use by the invading English. Again, an honest profit was to be had by the conquest of America. "What just cause of complaint may they have? And in my private opinion, I do verily think that God did create land, to the end that it should by Culture and husbandry, yield things necessary for man's life."[117] Shades of John Locke![118]

According to Peckham, "this is not all the benefit which they shall receive by the Christians." The savages would also be taught to abandon their "unseemly customs" and "riotous routs." They would instead turn to the Christians' more civilized practices: "to a well governed commonwealth, and with all shall be taught mechanical occupations, arts, and liberal sciences."[119] Thus "this intended voyage for conquest," as Peckham called it,[120] would redound to the advantage of both the conqueror and the conquered.

Peckham concluded his pamphlet by seeking to assure his readers that the English would most certainly prevail in their voyage of conquest against the American savages. The Iberian princes, wrote Peckham, within less than ninety years, had greatly enlarged their territories and dominions "through their own industry, by the assistance of the omnipotent, whose aid we shall not need to doubt, seeing the cause and quarrel which we take in hand tendeth to his honour and glory, by the enlargement of the Christian faith."[121] Given England's success in suppressing the Irish, who were similarly wild and savage people, "[m]ay it not much encouarge us to hope for good success in the country of these Savages, being a naked kind of people, void of the knowledge of the discipline of war."[122]

Peckham summarized the familiar arguments of the Elizabethan promoters of North American colonization in his peroration:

[S]ince by Christian duty we stand bound chiefly to further all such acts as do tend to increasing the true flock of Christ, by reducing into the right way those lost sheep which are yet astray, . . . Wherefore my deere Countrymen, be not dismayed, for the power of God is nothing diminished, not the love that he hath to the preaching and planting of the Gospel any whit abated. Shall we then doubt he will be less ready, most mightily and miraculously to assist our nation in this quarrel, which is chiefly and principally undertaken for the enlargement of the Christian faith abroad, and the banishment of idleness at home, than he was to Columbus, Vasques Numes, Hernando Cortes, and Francis Pizzaro.[123]

Peckham's "True Reporte" was perhaps the Elizabethan era's most systematized elaboration of the fundamental problematics that American colonization presented to English legal thought. The Catholic recusant silently incorporated the suppressed Victorian-Spanish legal discourse on the Law of Nations in attempting to prove the lawfulness of Elizabethan colonization in America. He asserted the prescriptive basis of England's rights in North America as opposed to those of other European nations. He explained the benefits of Christianity and civilization offered to the savages of America by English conquest, and demonstrated that it would be irrational for the Indians to refuse the bargain. Other Elizabethans had said many of these same things, but Peckham was the first to attempt to articulate them all in an extended and organized fashion. His "True Reporte" contains in essence the first English-language legal treatise on the justice of appropriating the New World from the American Indians—the synthesized by-product of the fusion of opposed, suppressed, appropriated, and indigenous discourses deployed during the Elizabethan era by the aadvocates of English colonization, who argued that the conquest of America would equally benefit the conqueror and the conquered.

The Black Legend of Spanish "Cruelties" in the New World

Peckham, unfortunately, would not participate in the English conquest of America. The Christian God of his sect finally forsook him. In the same month that Peckham's "True Reporte" was published, Francis Throckmorton, under torture, revealed plans for an international Catholic conspiracy to oust Elizabeth in favor of Mary, Queen of Scots. The Spanish Crown, its ambassador Mendoza, and two Catholic English Lords, Northumberland and Arundell, were implicated. In January 1584, Mendoza was expelled, although Elizabeth had wished to try him with his domestic co-conspirators. An opinion requested from the previously mentioned Oxford law professor Alberico Gentili,[124] however, helped convince the queen that Mendoza should merely be expelled, according to the principle of the Law of Nations respecting the immunity of ambassadors. The wave of anti-Catholic suspicion engendered by the plot swept up Peckham, who was arrested, which ended his participation in the colonization project.[125]

A new book circulating throughout London at about this time added fuel to the fire of anti-Catholic, anti-Spanish sentiment, and increased the sense of immediacy attached to pursuit of England's North American mandate. In 1583 a translation of Bartolomé de Las Casas's *Brevisima Relación de la Destruición de las Indias* of 1552 appeared in English. The English title was certain to catch attention: *A Brief Narration of the Destruction of the Indies by the Spaniards*, often referred to as simply *The Spanish Cruelties*.[126]

Las Casas was heir to the Dominican Humanist tradition in Spain, which had advocated more humane treatment of the Indians[127] but which had also always possessed a certain instrumental quality. The priests sought to save the Indians' souls, and that required that their bodies not be in bondage. Men like Las Casas, himself a one-time *encomendero* in the New World who had taken up the cloth to work as a missionary to the Indians, recognized clearly that it was difficult to preach the virtues of Christianity to those enslaved by virtueless Christians.

Las Casas's vitriolic castigations of the Spanish conquest and its methodology provided grist for the mill of English anti-Spanish sentiments. It was from Las Casas's *Spanish Cruelties* that the English reader first learned in detail of the official document of Spanish conquest, the *Requerimiento*.[128] According to Las Casas, the "harmless" Indians, "meek as lambs," were naturally amenable to the true Christian faith. But the conquistadores under the *Requerimiento* prevented the preaching of the faith of Jesus Christ.[129] Las Casas asserted that Oviedo, whose views on the Indians were well known to any Englishman familiar with Richard Eden's 1555 translation,[130] was the first colonial official to use the *Requerimiento*. He once read its declaration that the Indians were to accept the authority of Spain by virtue of the pope's grant to an empty village.[131]

To Las Casas, the *Requerimiento* ritual was a "diabolical and most unrighteous" mockery. His text described a litany of atrocities perpetrated on the

Indians throughout Spain's New World empire. He estimated that 15 million natives had been killed at the hands of the conquistadores. As for the survivors, their fate was "bondage and calamity."[132]

The 1583 English edition of *The Spanish Cruelties* contained an eight-page appendix of Las Casas's famous debate with Juan Ginés de Sepúlveda at Valladolíd in 1550. Sepúlveda was a learned authority on Aristotle and on Christian theory of just wars. He had been asked to make a statement before a council called by the Spanish emperor, Charles, to consider the perennial question of whether the Spaniards' wars against the Indians were just. Sepúlveda asserted in the strongest terms that the wars were just, basing his argument in part on the Aristotelian notion that certain men (such as savages and barbarians) were by nature slaves. Sepúlveda, who had never been to the Indies, argued that the law of nature, represented by the *ius gentium*, was honored and understood only among the wisest and most prudent of the higher races. The Indians did not live by the law of nature, and thus the Indians were by nature slaves. This was indeed a perverted synthesis, combining Franciscus de Victoria's argument on the right of Spain to subjugate the Indians because of their violations of natural law and the Law of Nations with the popular Aristotelian-derived argument that a slave by nature participated in reason enough to apprehend, but not to have reason. Las Casas, however, who had previously dismissed Aristotle as a "gentile burning in hell,"[133] countered Sepúlveda in the debate with the Dominican Humanist-inspired argument focusing on the Indians' rational capacity to apprehend the gospel. Of this Las Casas had firsthand affirmative experience through his extensive missionary work in the Indies.

Besides reading the Sepúlvedian exercise in casuistics and Las Casas's own condemnation of his countrymen's colonizing practice in the Indies, the English reader of the appendix in *The Spanish Cruelties* would have learned that Las Casas estimated the Indians slaughtered at 20 million in the debates, rather than the 15 million estimate found earlier in the text.[134] Whatever the precise figure, the English knew that the papist Spaniards were wantonly oppressing the natives of the New World. Thus was cemented the Elizabethan era's "Black Legend" of Spanish barbarity in America. England's errand into the wilderness not only would save the savages with the true faith but also would liberate them from the bondage of the Spanish cruelties.

The Second Elizabethan Crusade to America

Sir Walter Raleigh: The First Great Puritan Hero

Perhaps no Englishman of the Elizabethan era devoted himself more passionately to countering Spanish imperial influence in both the New World and the Old than Sir Walter Raleigh, the first great Puritan hero.[135] As Wesley Craven has so aptly stated, "Sir Walter is one of the more difficult figures of history to estimate; one repeatedly hesitates for fear of doing him either more or less than justice."[136] Born in 1554, Raleigh took a short residence at Oriel College, Oxford. While in his teens he volunteered, like his half brother Humphrey Gilbert, to serve in the French Huguenot army for an extended campaign. Also like Sir Humphrey, he later served with distinction in the various massacres and conquests of Elizabeth's Irish wars. Upon his return to Elizabeth's court in 1582, Raleigh quickly found himself in the highest royal favor. In fact, the queen refused to release him to participate personally in any of the five voyages to the New World that Raleigh financed.

Christopher Hill has pointed to Raleigh as a significant contributor to the principal changes in English society that first emerged in the Elizabethan era. These transformations, which culminated in the democratizing revolutions of the seventeenth century against the absolutist-minded Stuart kings, included the decline in power of the Crown vis-à-vis Parliament, the pursuit of an aggressive imperialist foreign policy, the extension of economic liberalism, the beginnings of religious toleration, and the triumph of modern science.[137]

Raleigh was conversant with a broad range of topics. As a political theoretician, he was not an innovator, but he served to introduce the ideas of others. His *Prerogative of Parliaments* was useful to the Puritans and other opposition radicals of the 1620s.[138] He favored expediency in politics and advocated a realism which could only be regarded as "saucy" by an absolutist-minded monarch such as James I.[139] Raleigh once wrote: "That any particular government is now *Jure Divino* is hard to affirm, and of no great use to mankind. For let the government of any country where I am subject be by divine institution or by compact, I am equally bound to observe its laws and endeavor its prosperity."[140] The rule of a king for Raleigh was but the rule of one freeman over others. He thus urged the importance of the king's cooperation with Parliament, an institution that Raleigh knew could not simply be wished out of existence.[141]

Raleigh's views of Britain's proper foreign policy were imperialist, aggressively anti-Spanish, and intimately connected with his views on economic policy. He helped refine, synthesize, and popularize many of the primitive nationalistic ideas first articulated by the Elizabethan generation. He was an early mercantilist, and felt that England had lost out to Spain and Portugal in the first great land grab in the infidel-held parts of the world. Stagnation in the cloth industry after a rapid rise in the first part of the sixteenth century had resulted in unemployment, which was now threatening social and political stability. Colonizing North America would not only ease overpopulation (the familiar argument of all the English advocates of colonization) but also provide raw materials for English industries and open up new markets. England could become self-sufficient economically. Pursuit of this expansionist policy, however, was blocked by Spain, which presumptuously claimed the entire New World. War would have to be waged, but England should first secure a base in the New World capable of capturing Spanish ships laden with gold from the Indies. Such a war would be self-financing. And this type of war not only could secure England's economic independence but also could bring the light of the true gospel to the inhabitants of America. This was the essence of the national policy put forward by Raleigh and his small circle of colonization advocates, who deeply enriched Raleigh's own views. The circle included Richard Hakluyt and the several other Elizabethans who were vitally interested in extending English sovereignty over the New World. Their grand scheme, with Raleigh as its most significant and influential leader, offered something for everyone, from the unemployed to radical Protestant religionists, from city merchants to the younger sons of good families. Raleigh was the first great orchestrator of Elizabethan-era colonizing discourse.[142]

Raleigh's appeal to a later English generation lay particularly in his advocacy of economic liberalism. He openly attacked monopolies and advocated other ideas which an Adam Smith could find sound nearly two centuries later. As a member of Parliament, for example, he once argued against a bill that would have required the "sowing of hemp" by English farmers: "I do not like this constraining of men to manure their grounds at our wills," he said, "but rather let every man use his ground to that which it is most fit for, and therein use his discretion."[143] He never hesitated to adopt a seemingly sensible economic innovation, or to abandon seemingly outworn prejudices. As governor of Jersey, for instance, he established a public register of title for real property. He was an advocate of the merchant class, at a time when the landed gentry tended to look down upon trade: "all the nobility and gentry in Europe trade their grass and corn and cattle, their vines and their fruits. . . . The king of Spain is now the greatest merchant."[144] Raleigh advocated lower customs duties and the use of state power to protect merchant interests, to encourage entry by foreign merchants, and to support the growth of home industries. Governments should "allure and encourage the people for their private goals to be all workers and erectors of a commonwealth."[145] England had to take steps toward controlling the seas, as this would lead to controlling the world's trade. All these arguments were novel at the time Raleigh made them. They would become commonplace assumptions among the English within a few decades of his death. In this he was perhaps one of the first notable Elizabethans to appreciate fully the liberating secular aspects of Puritanism's emphasis on individualism and the merits of a worldly calling.[146]

Raleigh was not, however, a Puritan in religious affairs, if by that term is meant a stereotyped attitude of intolerance toward other creeds. If anything, his attitude toward matters of faith looked even farther ahead of his times, to, in Hill's words, the "tolerance born of indifference which finally triumphed in 1689 [the Glorious Revolution]."[147] His interest in science and history urged him to look beyond the divine first cause of events in the world, to "second causes." He quoted his contemporary Francis Bacon on the fundamental laws of human knowledge, which could be tested and affirmed by reason. While he might be called at most "a Puritan without a sense of election,"[148] this was because, at most, he was an empiricist in a time when scientific experimentation, intellectual skepticism, heresy, and witchcraft were very poorly differentiated in common thought.

An empiricist consumed by nationalist sentiment, an entrepreneur and advocate of knowledge and colonization, Raleigh realized that applying a successful imperial policy in the New World required confronting the barrier of Spanish hegemony. Raleigh would naturally have desired the opportunity to pursue his ideas in a bold overseas colonization experiment. The quintessential Elizabethan Renaissance man moved quickly to keep his half brother Sir Humphrey Gilbert's patent rights to America in the family, so to speak. In 1584 Sir Walter Raleigh, promoter of the first English settment in the New World, convinced Elizabeth to let him organize the second Protestant crusade to North America.

The Virginia Venture of Sir Walter Raleigh

Raleigh's 1584 patent from Queen Elizabeth was virtually identical to that earlier given Sir Humphrey. Raleigh's royal charter authorized the initiation of a crusade to claim, conquer, and plant colonies in America in regions not held by any other Christian prince or people.[149]

Shortly after Elizabeth granted him the charter rights to North America, Raleigh sent out two vessels on a voyage of reconnaissance. The leaders of this April 1584 expedition were Arthur Barlow, another veteran of the Irish wars, and Philip Amadas. Simon Fernandez, the ubiquitous Portuguese seaman (who had reconnoitered the American coast for Gilbert in 1580[150]), was head pilot for the voyage.

According to Barlow's report to Raleigh,[151] after sighting land above "Florida" (the Georgia coast), the ships sailed northward, landing on Hatteras Island on the North Carolina Outer Banks. The English took possession of the island in right of the queen's most excellent majesty, "and after delivered the same over to your [Raleigh's] use according to her Majesty's grant, and letters patents."[152] This was done, according to Barlow, "according to the ceremonies used in such enterprises"[153]—probably the same type of feudal ceremony previously employed by both Gilbert and Drake.[154]

Several natives were met on shore, "as mannerly and civil as any in Europe." The explorers traded several items with the natives;[155] a 3-shilling copper kettle was bartered for £18 worth of skins. The English were already benefiting from the bargain of divinely mandated trade with the savages.[156]

On Roanoke Island, the crew was regally entertained and fed in the Algonquin natives' village. The village was enclosed by "sharp trees" that provided protection against the frequent raids by neighboring tribes.[157] Powhatan, the Indian emperor who claimed sovereignty over the territory "discovered" by the English at this time, was only beginning his confederacy of more than thirty tribes ranging over a 900-square-mile region. After six weeks among the Indians, whom Barlow described as the kindest people in the world, the adventurers returned to England with two Indians enticed on board, Manteo and Wanchese.

Richard Hakluyt's "Discourse"

Upon the adventurers' return to England in September with favorable reports, Raleigh presented a treatise to Elizabeth, written at his request by the younger Richard Hakluyt, now chaplain and secretary to the English ambassador in

France. The treatise, entitled "A Discourse on Western Planting,"[158] argued that the queen should support the establishment of North American colonies in order to counter the odious religious and economic influence of the Spanish in the New World. The pious work of planting the seeds of faith and civility in America could be accomplished by planting colonies among the "simple people," leading them out of "error" and "into the right and perfect way of their salvation."[159] Such a colony would greatly benefit England's own worldly interests by making it possible to weaken Spain in the New World. "If you touch him [the king of Spain] in the Indies, you touch the apple of his eye."[160] Hakluyt explained that the treasures from the New World had enabled papist Spain to spread its military influence throughout Europe, yet Spain's territory in the West Indies was distant and difficult to defend. The Indians were enslaved and greatly desired freedom. Philip could therefore be weakened in Europe by attacking the weakest link in his empire, the West Indies. If the English could build two or three strong colonies between Florida and Cape Briton, and could fortify them properly, then these positions could be used as launching points for an allied English–Indian attack against Philip's entire American empire.

Except for the added element of an English–Indian alliance, Hakluyt's plan of colonizing and establishing fortified privateering posts now advocated on behalf of Raleigh was identical to that earlier put forward under his influence by Sir Humphrey Gilbert.[161] If carried out successfully, with the queen's necessary support, the English–Indian alliance would "trouble the king of Spain more in those parts, than he hath or can trouble us with Ireland, and hold him at such bay as he was never yet held at."[162]

Hakluyt's "Discourse" fused two principal energizing and legitimating themes of Elizabethan colonizing discourse—converting the Indians to English Christianity and civilization and weakening the Spanish empire—to form one unified tactical synthesis. The savages would be liberated by the civilizing, Christianizing English, and then would join with their benign Anglo-Saxon conquerors to drive the Iberians and their tyrannizing papistry out of the New World. Hakluyt, however, warned that England had to plant quickly in the New World, as the Spaniards, and even the French, threatened to usurp the prior claims to the area that England had by right of the discoveries of the Cabots.

The final sections of Hakluyt's "Discourse" detailed the various sources of the English claim of right to North America. Hakluyt indiscriminately cited fabulous legends, historical precedents of dubious validity, wholly secular contract principles derived from common law, and medieval hierocratic theology to support England's North American title rights.

Hakluyt repeated the fabled Madoc legend previously relied on by Peckham[163] (the advocates of English colonization of America indeed constituted a small circle) and cited the Cabot voyages, accounts of which Hakluyt himself recovered from the royal archives and published in his 1582 *Divers Voyages*,[164] proving England's title to North America by prior discovery.[165]

Hakluyt's "Discourse" also dismissed the effect on England's title to North America of Pope Alexander's fifteenth-century bulls of donation granting the

Indies to Spain. Hakluyt was the first major advocate of colonization in the Elizabethan Discovery era to offer an extended discussion of this important topic in English legal discourse, and the diffuse nature of his arguments is worth examining in detail.

Hakluyt first argued on pure theological grounds, citing scripture, that the pope's grant to Spain was *ultra vires*. Christ, according to the Gospels, refused to be a judge in the division of an inheritance between two brothers. As the pope is Christ's vicar, the pope should not seek to exercise powers that Christ himself refused to assume.[166] Hakluyt, however, could certainly understand why the pope might wish to usurp such a power:

It is an easy matter to cut large thongs, as we say, of other men's hides, and to be liberal of other men's goods. Neither is it any marvel though . . . the Pope gave all the West Indies of his free grace to the King of Spain, for they never cost him a penny.[167]

One papal donation in particular, however, that of Ireland to the English king Henry II by the twelfth-century papal bull *Laudabiliter*,[168] presented something of an embarrassment to Hakluyt. As a first-rate scholar, he was well aware that England's currently acted-upon right to conquer and colonize the wild Irish rested uneasily on the identical medieval papal foundations as did Spain's rights in the New World. Recognizing the difficulty of condemning the legal foundations sustaining your neighbor's empire when a part of your own stands on an identical ground, Hakluyt argued that the pope's Irish grant was a meaningless superfluity.

If the King [of England] had not by his force more than by their gift, helped himself, the Pope's donation had stood him in small stead: neither did the Kings of Ireland admit and allow of the Pope's donation. If they had, they would never have rebelled so of against the Crown of England.[169]

What mattered, argued Hakluyt, was not whether the popes have "done this or that,"[170] but whether the pope's act was lawful. Hakluyt displayed a subtle appreciation of the obscure distinctions of medieval papal hierocratic ideology,[171] arguing that the popes themselves admitted that their meddling with worldly kingdoms was done by their "indirect" power. "But such indirect dealing is warranted neither by law of God nor men."[172]

Having attacked the general principle of the pope's power to grant territories, Hakluyt next engaged in an extended assault on the particulars of the Spanish papal donation itself. First, the pope had not acted impartially as arbitrator in the division of the world. The Spanish bull had been written by a Spanish pope "called Borgia, and therefore no marvel though he were led by partiality to favor the Spanish nation, . . . though it were to the prejudice and damage to all others." Borgia, claimed Hakluyt, "was beyond all reason carried away with blind affection to his nation."[173]

Having attacked the *bona fides* of the Borgia-Alexander grant, Hakluyt next questioned the wisdom of a grant of the entire New World to Spain. Basing this argument on grounds of efficiency, Hakluyt noted that the Spaniards were far too poor at the time of the grant (they had even turned to Henry VII for aid in their fight against the Moors) to utilize the large expanse of territory granted under the Alexandrine bulls. The Spaniards had not yet been able "to inhabit a third or fourth part of those exceedingly large and waste countries."[174] Thus the pope could have no possible right to exclude other Europeans from enjoying the underutilized "waste" lands of the New World. Hakluyt at least applied the by-now-familiar English arguments on efficient utilization of the soil with equal force to Europeans and to the New World's own inhabitants. Hakluyt, like his queen,[175] asserted that effective occupation alone, not papal donation, proved the true source of European rights in America.

Concluding his attack on the legal sufficiency of the papal grant, Hakluyt in his most forceful argument examined the donation at face value. Hakluyt claimed that even if the pope had indeed desired Spain to convert the Indians and had therefore granted them the New World with the charge to preach the gospel to the heathens, the condition had "been wonderfully neglected."[176] Spain had only enslaved the Indians, sending "such hellhounds and wolves thither as have not converted, but almost quite subverted them." Hakluyt cited the Dominican Las Casas to illustrate this point. Consequently, the pope's condition that the Spaniards preach the gospel to the Indians "not being performed, the donation ought of right to be void."[177]

Hakluyt's richly variegated "Discourse" illuminates the undifferentiated character of English colonizing discourse in its earliest stages of development. Theology, legend, history, medieval political theory, notions of efficiency, common-law contract, and other legally derived principles such as judicial impartiality and conditional breach—all were drawn together in a seemingly indiscriminate fashion in constructing wholesale arguments for English rights in America.

Yet despite its appearance as a rummaging scramble for any and all legitimating arguments for English colonization, Hakluyt's text points toward the secularized trajectory gradually asssumed by various forms of discursive practice in the Elizabethan era. Hakluyt's analysis of the papal bull under secular utilitarian and legal principles underscores the increasingly rationalized character assumed by English colonizing legal discourse the further it moved from its medieval Catholic influences and moorings, and the closer it moved toward a desacralized mercantilist ideology.

The Newfoundland of Virginia

Elizabeth, despite Hakluyt's innovative arguments, did not directly sponsor Raleigh's plan of colonization of America as a royal venture. Her chief concern with Spain at this time was in the European theater, and she had to prepare for war to defend her own shores. Her revenues were already overextended, as were her heavily taxed subjects. While refusing to finance Raleigh's plan, she did act in other ways that benefited her favorite. For the next several years, the queen regularly added to Raleigh's offices. From them, he derived a steady stream of revenues and other perquisites enriching his station and lightening the personal financial burdens he assumed in his subsequent American voyages of discovery and colonization.[178]

Raleigh was named a member of Parliament in November 1584, a month after the presentation of Hakluyt's "Discourse." In January 1585, Raleigh was knighted, and shortly thereafter he received his seal as governor of Virginia, his American colony, named in honor of his Virgin Queen. Sir Walter's plans for his colony included sending a fleet of ships under the command of his cousin, Richard Grenville, another veteran of the Irish wars. A set of anonymous notes "For Master Rauleys Voyage" survives from the time of the planning of the venture.[179] The notes primarily addressed the military issues connected with the establishment of a self-sustaining, Spanish-style plantation colony: the construction of a fort, the number of soldiers and commanders required for the venture, recommendations for personnel to be included on the trip (masons, carpenters, a surgeon, and a chemist).

Advice contained in these notes for the manner of government.to be adopted by the military general of the colony reflected the hard lessons of Elizabeth's bogged-down Irish wars. The colony's general should rule absolutely, but he should prescribe punishments "by order of law."[180] Expeditions "of discovery" outside the fort should contain at least 200 men, accompanied by an officer and treasurer to assure the queen of her fifth part of any gold or silver discovered. A chief officer was to be responsible for any "disorders." A military code of conduct was outlined, similar to those in force in England. Respecting conduct toward the natives, no soldier was permitted to "violate any woman, or to seize any man's goods."[181] No Indian was to be forced to labor, and striking or misusing the natives was strictly prohibited. Heavy penalties, including beating, imprisonment, or "slavery," were to be imposed for breaches of the various provisions relating to treatment of Indians.[182]

Grenville departed Plymouth, England, with a fleet of five ships. The flagship, *Tiger*, was a royal vessel, Elizabeth's personal investment in the venture. There were 250 sailors, 140 soldiers, and 105 colonists on board. On June 29, 1585, the fleet anchored off the strategicially located Roanoke Island, 10 miles long and 2 miles wide, the intended site of the new military, plantation-style colony. Grenville sailed back to England in late August, leaving behind Ralph Lane, Roanoke's military colonial governor, and the remaining colonists.

Poor relations with the local Indians forced the abandonment of the colony in less than a year. Several personal letters and a narrative written by Governor Lane provide firsthand sources of information on the first colony established in America by the English.

Governor Lane was another hardened veteran of the Irish wars. He possessed and acted on attitudes and assumptions typical of an English conquistador familiar with a barbarous and wild people. Lane's correspondence with associates back in England consistently depicted the Indians of Virginia as using their lands inefficiently. In a letter to the elder Hakluyt, for instance, he described the region surrounding the colony as a "huge and unknown greatness, and very well peopled and towned, though savagely."[183] The land contained an abundance of natural produce, "but being Savages that possess the land, they know no use of the same."[184]

Like all the other Elizabethans committed to establishing an English presence in North America, Lane viewed colonization as an honorable entry into America for conquest[185] and anti-Spanish agitation. He once wrote to Secretary of State Walsingham that Her Majesty's greatness would assuredly grow by the addition

of such a kingdom as this is to the rest of her dominions, by means whereof likewise the Church of Christ throughout Christendom may by the mercy of God in short time find a relief and freedom from the servitude and tyranny that by Spain (being the sword of that Antichrist of Rome and his sect) the same hath of long time been most miserably oppressed with.[186]

Lane's narrative of his administration as governor[187] indicated that the Indians regarded themselves as being "miserably oppressed" by the new English arrivals to their land. The governor's account detailed numerous skirmishes with the surrounding tribes, usually over food supplies. The conflict climaxed in a violent preemptive strike on the Virginia mainland against a group of Indians suspected of conspiring against the settlers. The Indians, like the wild Irish, were a treacherous people, not to be trusted by civilized Englishmen.

One other source of firsthand information on Raleigh's first colony exists: Thomas Harriot's "Brief and True Report of the Newfoundland of Virginia" of 1588.[188] Harriot was appointed by Raleigh to serve as the colony's lay missionary to the Indians—the first English missionary in the New World. Harriot had studied at Oxford and had served as a tutor in Raleigh's house. He was described by a contemporary as a "great lover of virtue, and very learned professor of all arts and knowledge."[189]

Harriot served as Raleigh's eyes and ears for recording impressions of America. He provided Raleigh with detailed observations of the Virginia Indians. His narrative of the first Roanoke colony offers some of the best European-generated anthropological material respecting the peoples encountered in America in the Elizabethan Discovery era.

While Harriot was as unprejudiced an English observer as could be hoped for, he still judged the Indians' difference in Eurocentric, negative terms. Like Governor Lane, he thought the Indians underutilized their land.[190] He also reported that the savages lacked letters, tools, and science, and lived in a state of nature: "In respect of us, they are a poor people."[191] Like the other early Puritans involved in the American colonization initiative, Harriot believed that the Indians' rude, savage state was a result of deprivation. However, the natives, in his opinion, possessed sufficient reasoning capacity to recognize the ingenious manner of the English. Once having seen the English way of life, Harriot believed,

the more it is probable that they should desire our friendship and love, and have the greater respect for pleasing and obeying us. Whereby may be hoped if means of good government be used, that they may in short time be brought to civility, and the embracing of true religion.[192]

These tasks of conversion and civility would be easily accomplished, in Harriot's opinion, as many of the savages already believed that the colonists' tools, weapons, and scientific instruments affirmed God's love for his elect, the English.[193] The Indians, Harriot revealed, had once even asked him to pray "to our God of England" to relieve a drought.[194]

Harriot was not able to realize his desire to bring the rude savages to the True Faith and civility. The fact that the Englishmen's God apparently felt little scruple when Englishmen stole Indian corn quickly eroded any prospects of amity with the neighboring tribes. In the same month that Lane had ordered his preemptive strike on the mainland, Francis Drake arrived at Roanoke. He had been pirating in the Spanish West Indies with a fleet of twenty-three ships, and Raleigh's colony was doubtless serving as a rendezvous point for the plundering sea dogs. The colonists, rather than face an impending massacre by Indians, departed Roanoke with Drake's fleet.

In February 1587, shortly after the Roanoke colonists returned to England, Hakluyt published his edition of Pietro Martire's *De Orbo Novo Decades* and a translation of the account of the travels of a French explorer, René de Laudonnière.[195] Each text contained a dedication composed by Hakluyt by which he intended to encourage Raleigh further in an enterprise that had so far killed Sir Walter's half brother and caused him nothing but financial loss and embarrassment. The dedication in the Laudonnière translation urged Raleigh as follows: "Be you of a valiant courage and faint not, as the Lord said unto Joshua, in the conquest of the land of promise."[196] Hakluyt, the good Puritan, believed that the Indians of Virginia affirmed the truth of Elizabeth's Reformation and the necessity of waging a strong battle in the war for souls on this particular front of the anti-Spanish crusade.[197] The enterprise must therefore be continued. According to Hakluyt, England was awash with men returning from the Netherlands civil war who could now be employed in the conquest of Virginia.

[T]hey go idle up and down in swarms, for lack of honest entertainment. I see no fitter place to employ some part of the better sort of them, trained up thus long in service, than in the inward parts of the firm of Virginia, against such stubborn savages as shall refuse obedience to her Majesty.[198]

The Elizabethans were of course engaged in a war with another stubborn savage tribal people, the Irish, who also had refused "obedience to her majesty."[199] Hakluyt's call to war against the savages of America was declaimed in the identical discursive cant utilized by the Elizabethans in their crusade against the wild Irish. The barbarous heathens of Virginia sought to deny England its rightful claim to the vast, underutilized "waste" lands of their country.

Raleigh began planning for another colony, this one to be headed by John White. Raleigh's previous colonization projects had been aimed primarily at establishing a garrison base for privateering against Spanish shipping, so no women had been brought along.[200] The colony to be led by John White would be different. Raleigh would be overlord back in England, but the major capital responsibility rested in the hands of the Virginia colonists themselves, who were to establish a self-perpetuating English community. A privateering base, in Quinn's words, "could grow up as a cheap subsidiary to the colony."[201]

White sailed from England with three ships in May 1587. There were more than 100 colonists on board, including 17 women and 3 children. Upon arrival in Virginia in July, the colonists decided to rebuild the Roanoke fort and cottages rather than establish a new settlement on the mainland. While relations with the Indians were peaceful at first, food supplies once again posed a problem for the colonists. White was sent to England with the three ships to bring back provisions. He reached Southampton in November, and met with Raleigh to arrange for new supplies.

But the England to which White returned in late 1587 was a nation preparing for war with Spain. The Spanish Armada, not colonization of Virginia, occupied the minds of the nation's leaders. A month prior to White's return to England, Elizabeth and her privy council had ordered a general stay of shipping in all English ports because of the Spanish threat. White was only able to arrange for two small ships not needed by Drake, who was directing the naval defenses. These ships did not leave for Roanoke until April 1588. White's ship was attacked by pirates and looted, returning empty to England in late May. The other ship also abandoned the voyage.[202] Raleigh by this time had assumed major responsibilities in the war with Spain and was unable to raise funds for a return voyage until March 1590. When White finally did land at Roanoke in August of that year, he found the English colony deserted. Perhaps the colonists had fled an Indian attack. Perhaps Spanish reconnaissance vessels had discovered the location of the former privateering base (either by chance or by intelligence from London) and had erased it and its inhabitants from the face of the New World. Or perhaps the English colonists had fled into the interior at the sight of a Spanish fleet and its Inquisition. In any event, the colony of Roanoke was lost, leaving few traces for historians who still seek to decipher its fate.[203]

White returned to England. Raleigh, nearly bankrupt from his various Virginia ventures, lost enthusiasm for North American colonization. The failure of his Roanoke colony, however, did not deter Raleigh from pursuing his life's passion: the weakening of Spanish power in the New World. After Roanoke and the Armada, he shifted operations southward and attempted to establish a military raiding base in "Guiana" (northern Brazil). This effort also ended unprofitably.

Despite his many failures in the New World, Raleigh's outlook never wavered. In 1591 he wrote a diatribe against Spain, invoking Las Casas and the "millions" of Indians "wasted" by the conquistadores.[204] In a 1596 work reiterating this basic theme, Sir Walter reminisced on his life's project: "I have therefore laboured all my life, both according to my small power, and persuasion, to advance all those attempts that might either promise return of profit to ourselves, or at least be a let and impeachment to the quiet course and plentiful trades of the Spanish nation."[205]

Raleigh, of course, would become the posthumous hero of the seventeenth-century Puritan revolutionaries.[206] His dream, shared by his half brother Gilbert and so many of his Elizabethan contemporaries, to sow and reap personal and national profit in America and, "at the least," to strike at Spain in the heart of its New World empire, was never fully realized. Raleigh and his Elizabethan contemporaries, however, did elaborate the thematic superstructure for future English colonial discursive practice. The Elizabethans translated the lessons learned from the Spanish colonizing experience into their own Protestant discourses addressing the peculiar concerns of a society seeking to define a distinct national identity in the world system. More so than even Spanish imperial discursive practice, Elizabethan colonial discourse fused nationalist religious fervor with nationalist economic interests to define and energize England's errand into the American wilderness. The individualized thematics of radical Protestantism's predestinarian vision harmonized easily with the invisible hand orchestrating the impulses sensed by a people involved in an emerging capitalist, market-oriented economy.

Raleigh's contemporary Sir Francis Bacon, reflecting candidly on the motives of the early English crusades to America, once stated: "It cannot be affirmed if we speak ingeniously that it was the propagation of the Christian faith that was the [motive] . . . of the discovery, entry, and plantation of the New World; but gold and silver, and temporal profit and glory."[207] But the ingenious innovation of the Elizabethan conquistadores and their circle of promoters of American colonization was their forging of a discourse of conquest that spoke with intense and legitimating passion to their countrymen's own emerging and merging sense of material and spiritual manifest destiny. The Elizabethan could passionately pursue either side of the colonizing equation of religious reformation and imperial revenue, for English colonizing discourse of the early Discovery era confirmed a faith that in pursuing the one goal, the Elizabethan New World crusader also assuredly secured the other.

NOTES

1. On Sir Humphrey Gilbert's life and career, *see generally* D. B. Quinn, "Introduction" to *The Voyages and Colonising Enterprises of Sir Humphrey Gilbert*, 2 vols., 1–104 (D. B. Quinn ed. 1940) [hereinafter cited as *HG*].

2. K. Bottigheimer, "Kingdom and Colony: Ireland in the Westward Enterprise 1536–1660" 51–52 in *The Westward Enterprise* (K. R. Andrews, N. P. Canny, & P. E. H. Hair eds. 1978), quoting Thomas Churchyard, *A General Rehearsal of Wars* (1579).

3. *HG*, *supra* note 1, at 17.

4. *Id.* at 17–18.

5. *Id.* at 17.

6. *See* "Petition from Sir Humphrey Gilbert to the Queen" (1565), reprinted in *id.* at 105.

7. Reprinted in *id.* at 129.

8. *See* the remarks of D. B. Quinn, *id.*

9. *Id.* at 160.

10. *Id.* at 160–61.

11. *See* Chapter 3, text accompanying notes 105–8, *supra.*

12. *HG*, *supra* note 1, at 161.

13. *Id.*

14. Don Guzmán de Silva to Philip II (1567), reprinted in *id.* at 115–16.

15. *See* text accompanying notes 1–5, *supra.*

16. *See* Chapter 3, text accompanying notes 52–60, *supra.*

17. *HG, supra* note 1, at 32.

18. Reprinted in *id.* at 170.

19. *Id.* at 171.

20. *Id.* at 173.

21. Reprinted in *id.* at 176.

22. *Id.*

23. *Id.*

24. *Id.*

25. *Id.* at 177.

26. *Id.* at 180.

27. *See* "Letters Patent to Sir Humphrey Gilbert" (1578), reprinted in *id.* at 188.

28. *Id.*

29. *See* Chapter 3, text accompanying notes 1–5, *supra.*

30. *See,* e.g., the conditions attached to Elizabeth's Irish grant to Sir Thomas Smith, in Chapter 3, text accompanying notes 101–3. *HG, supra* note 1, at 189.

31. *Id.*

32. "Richard Hakluyt, Lawyer, Notes on Colonization," reprinted in *id.* at 181.

33. *See* 1 *The Original Writings and Correspondence of the Two Richard Hakluyts,* 2 vols., 22–31 (E. G. R. Taylor ed. 1935) [hereinafter cited as *RH*].

34. *HG, supra* note 1, at 184.

35. *Id.* at 182.

36. *Id.*

37. *See* Chapter 3, text accompanying notes 109–111, *supra.*

38. *See* text accompanying notes 18–26, *supra.*

39. *HG, supra* note 1, at 390.

40. *Id.* at 45.

41. *See* text accompanying note 17, *supra.*

42. Quoted in M. Lindley, *The Acquisition and Government of Backward Territory in International Law* 127 (1926).

43. *See* text accompanying notes 32–36, *supra.*

44. *See* Chapter 3, text accompanying notes 61–112, *supra.*

45. Don Bernardino de Mendoza to Philip II (1582), reprinted in *HG, supra* note 1, at 278–79.

46. *Id.* at 279.

47. *Id.*

48. *Id.*

49. *See HG, supra* note 1, at 64.

50. *See id.* at 63.

51. *See* text accompanying notes 32–36, *supra.*

52. Reprinted in *HG, supra* note 1, at 351.

53. *HG, supra* note 1, at 76–81.

54. *Id.* at 356.

55. *Id.* at 357. For example, Sir Humphrey Gilbert had stated that the "traffic of Englishmen" would procure the "love" of the Irish tribesmen to the English nation." *See* H. Gilbert, "The Discourse of Ireland" (1572), reprinted in *HG, supra* note 1, at 126.

56. *Id.* at 357.

57. *See,* e.g., H. C. Porter's account of the well-publicized debates between the Protestant divine John Jewel and the English Catholic Thomas Harding in H. C. Porter, *The Inconstant Savage* 132–36 (1979).

58. *See* Chapter 3, text accompanying notes 105–6, *supra.*

59. *See* text accompanying notes 9–12, *supra.*

60. *HG, supra* note 1, at 360–61.

61. *See generally* C. Hill, *Puritanism and Revolution* 43–44 (1958).

62. *See* text accompanying note 39, *supra.*

63. *See* H. C. Porter, *supra* note 57, at 207. Before launching his career as a sailor-merchant-

man, Hayes served as a tutor to the son of Elizabeth Hoby, sister-in-law of the influential William Cecil, Lord Burghley. The subscription rolls of the earlier Gilbert expedition of 1578 indicate that Hayes was an early financial backer of Sir Humphrey's colonization plans and may in fact have sailed on that first voyage. *Id.*

64. Edward Hayes, "Narrative of Sir Humphrey Gilbert's Last Expedition" (1583?), reprinted in *HG, supra* note 1, at 385.

65. *Id.* at 401.

66. *Id.* at 402.

67. *Id.*

68. *See* H. C. Porter, *supra* note 57, at 189–91.

69. *See generally* F. Von Der Heydte, "Discovery and Annexation in International Law," 29 *Am. J. Int'l L.* 448, 452–57 (1935).

70. *HG, supra* note 1, at 402–3.

71. *Id.* at 385.

72. *Id.* at 386. Conversion of the heathen, argued Hayes, "must be the chief intent of such as shall make any attempt" at colonization, "or else whatsoever is builded upon other foundation shall never obtain happy success nor continuance" (*id.*).

73. P. Miller, *Errand into the Wilderness* 57–58 (1964).

74. *Id.* at 57.

75. *Id.* at 58. As Perry Miller has described, the image of the covenant between God and humankind came to assume paramount theological importance in English and early American Puritanism. It played the role in English Puritan discourse of tempering the harsh predestinarianism of an earlier, primitive brand of Calvinism. The covenant was conceived of as unfolding gradually before humankind, whose obligation was to maintain faith in Christ as the son of God. God, for his part, undertook the obligation not only to save those who believed, but also, according to Miller, "to supply the power of belief, to provide the grace that will make possible man's fulfilling the terms of this . . . covenant" (*id.* at 61–62).

76. *HG, supra* note 1, at 386.

77. *Id.*

78. *Id.* at 387.

79. *See* text accompanying notes 43–44, *supra.*

80. *See HG, supra* note 1, at 90.

81. Reprinted in *id.* at 477.

82. *See* Chapter 3, text accompanying notes 77–112, *supra.*

83. Reprinted in *HG, supra* note 1, at 435.

84. *Id.* at 449.

85. *See HG, supra* note 1, at 71–75.

86. *See* Chapter 2, text accompanying notes 158–90, *supra.*

87. *HG, supra* note 1, at 447.

88. *Id.*

89. *Id.* at 450.

90. *See* Chapter 2, text accompanying notes 165–70, *supra.*

91. F. Victoria, *De Indis et de Iure Belli Reflectiones* 151 (E. Nys, ed., J. Bate trans. 1917).

92. *Id.*

93. Peckham's cautious strategy of ensuring the secular canonical integrity of his promotional tract is evident throughout his text, beginning with the introductory dedication to Walsingham, Elizabeth's influential secretary of State. Walsingham had originally facilitated Catholic participation under Gilbert's patent, and Peckham's introduction rendered all the appropriate supplicating rituals to the secretary. Further imprimatur was sought in the various prefatory poems of commendation by England's most widely regarded Protestant conquistadores; upon request, Drake, Hawkins, Martin Frobisher, and other notables had composed laudatory verse for inclusion in Peckham's text. *HG, supra* note 1, at 436–43. It is likely that all had a financial interest in the venture.

94. *Id.* at 450–51.

95. *Id.* at 451.

96. *Id.* at 451. Compare Victoria's passage below to Peckham's cited text:

If the Indian natives wish to prevent the Spaniards from enjoying any of their rights under the law of nations, for instance, trade . . . , the Spaniards ought in the first place to use reason and persuasion in order to remove scandal and ought to show in all possible methods that they do not come to the hurt of the natives, but wish to sojourn as peaceful guests and to travel without doing the natives any harm. . . . [F. Victoria, *supra* note 91, at 154.]

97. *HG, supra* note 1, at 451.
98. F. Victoria, *supra* note 91, at 154–55.
99. *Id.* at 81–83.
100. Compare the passages below, for instance. The first is Peckham's; the second is Victoria's:

For from the first beginning of the creation of the world and from the renuing of the same after Noah's flood, all men have agreed, that no violence should be offered to Ambassadors. That the sea with his Havens should be common. That such as should fortune to be taken in war, should be servants or slaves and that strangers should not be driven away from the place or country whereunto they do come. [Reprinted in *HG, supra* note 1, at 451.]

For if after the early days of the creation of the world or its recovery from the flood the majority of mankind decided that ambassadors should every where be reckoned inviolable and that the sea should be common and that prisoners of war should be made slaves, and of this, namely, that strangers should not be driven out, were deemed a desirable principle, it would certainly have the force of law, even though the rest of mankind objected thereto. [F. Victoria, *supra* note 91, at 152.]

101. *See* Chapter 5, text accompanying notes 1–31, *infra.*
102. *HG, supra* note 1, at 459.
103. On the Madoc legend, *see generally* G. A. Williams, *Madoc* (1979).
104. H. C. Porter, *supra* note 57, at 211–13.
105. *See* text accompanying notes 49–50, *supra.*
106. *HG, supra* note 1, at 459.
107. *See* H. C. Porter, *supra* note 57, at 21.
108. *HG, supra* note 1, at 459.
109. *Id.* at 459–60.
110.

And this may stand for another title to her majesty, but any of the foresaid titles is as much, or more than any other Christian Prince can pretend to the Indies before such time as they had actual possession thereof . . . , and therefore I think it needless to write any more touching the lawfulness of her Majesty's title. [*Id.* at 460.]

111. Quoted in H. C. Porter, *supra* note 57, at 210.
112. Peckham asserted that although the natives lived in "ignorance and idolatry," the reports of explorers agreed that they are "thirsting after Christianity" (*HG, supra* note 1, at 448). The Christians therefore have a duty to quench this thirst by "planting," which will lead to the establishment of the word of God" (*id.* at 467).

113. *Id.* at 467–68.
114. *Id.* at 468.
115. *See* Chapter 2, text accompanying notes 188–91, *supra.*
116. *HG, supra* note 1, at 468.
117. *Id.*
118. In his famous chapter "Of Property," in *The Second Treatise of Government* (1690), John Locke, a seventeenth-century advocate of English colonization of North America, used the ratios of 10 to 1, 100 to 1, and 1,000 to 1 in contrasting the value of lands improved and cultivated by agricultural labor and the unenclosed and uncultivated "waste" lands of the American Indians. *See* N. Wood, *John Locke and Agrarian Capitalism* 64–71 (1984). Locke's contributions to the colonizing discourse of the United States are discussed in Chapter 6, text accompanying notes 50–62, *infra.*

119. *HG, supra* note 1, at 468.

120. *Id.* at 270.

121. *Id.* at 476.

122. *Id.* at 471.

123. *Id.* at 476–77. As always, whenever the Elizabethans set out to demonstrate the necessity as well as the ease of colonizing America, Spain and its conquistadores provided the minimum standards of achievement.

124. *See* text accompanying note 101, *supra.*

125. *HG, supra* note 1, at 93.

126. *See* H. C. Porter, *supra* note 57, at 152–80.

127. *See* Chapter 2, text accompanying notes 90–94, *supra.*

128. *See* Chapter 2, text accompanying notes 113–19, supra.

129. H. C. Porter, *supra* note 57, at 156.

130. *See* Chapter 5, text accompanying notes 26–36, *supra.*

131. Las Casas told his readers that he did not know whether to laugh or cry about these orders to the Indians either to receive the faith and the king of Spain's dominion over them or to die by the conquistador's sword:

> As if the Son of God which died for every one of them had commanded in his law, where He saith Go teach all nations, that there should be ordinances set down unto infidels, being peaceful and quiet and in possession of their proper land, if so be they received it not forthwith, without any preaching or teaching first hand, and if they submitted not themselves to the dominion of a king whom they never saw, and whom they never heard speak of, and namely such a one whose messengers and men were so cruel, and so debarred from all pity; and such horrible tyrants, that they should for that lose their goods and lands, their liberty, their wives and children, with their lives. [Reprinted in H. C. Porter, *supra* note 57, at 158.]

132. *Id.* at 158–60.

133. *Id.* at 170.

134. *Id.* at 169.

135. This discussion of Sir Walter Raleigh's works, ideas, and contributions to English political discourse borrows heavily from Christopher Hill's enlightening chapter on Raleigh's historical significance in his *Intellectual Origins of the English Revolution* 130–224 (1965).

136. W. Craven, *The Southern Colonies in the Seventeenth Century 1607–1689* 39 (1949).

137. C. Hill, *supra* note 135, at 131–32.

138. *Id.* at 149–53.

139. *Id.* at 150–51.

140. *Id.* at 150.

141. Raleigh quoted his contemporary Francis Bacon in support of his basic thesis of the need to limit kingly power: "Monarchs need not fear any curbing of their absoluteness by mighty subjects, as long as by wisdom they keep the hearts of the people" (quoted in *id.* at 153).

142. *Id.* at 154–57.

143. *Id.* at 165–66.

144. *Id.* at 167.

145. *Id.*

146. *See generally* Max Weber, *The Protestant Ethic and the Spirit of Capitalism* 79–92 (1958).

147. C. Hill, *supra* note 135, at 171.

148. *Id.* at 222.

149. Reprinted in *Documents of American History* 6–7 (H. S. Commager 8th ed. 1968).

150. *See* text accompanying notes 37–41, *supra.*

151. "Arthur Barlowe's Discourse of the First Voyage" (1584–1585), reprinted in 1 *The Roanoke Voyages 1584–1590*, 2 vols., 91 (D. B. Quinn ed. 1955) [hereinafter cited as *RV*].

152. *Id.* at 94.

153. *Id.*

154. *See id.* at n. 5.

155. *Id.* at 100–101.

156. H. C. Porter, *supra* note 57, at 226.

157. *RV, supra* note 151, at 106–7.

158. Reprinted in *RH, supra* note 33, at 211.

159. Hakluyt's "Discourse" began by noting that the people of "that part of America from 30 degrees in Florida northward unto 63 degrees (which is yet in no Christian prince's actual possession) are idolaters" (*id.* at 214).

> It remaineth to be thoroughly weighed and considered by what means and by whom this most godly and Christian work may be performed of enlarging the glorious gospel of Christ, and reducing the infinite multitudes of these simple people that are in error to the right and perfect way of their salvation. [*Id.*]

Having considered the problem at some length, Hakluyt had his own suggestion as to the means: preachers must be sent to America. Hakluyt then made the royally directed sales pitch:

> But by whom should these preachers be sent? By them no doubt which have taken upon them the protection and defence of the Christian faith. Now the Kings and Queens of England have the name of Defenders of the Faith. By which title I think they are not only charged to maintain and patronize the faith of Christ, but also to enlarge and advance the same. [*Id.* at 215.]

Merely sending preachers to the New World, however, would not be sufficient if the queen sincerely intended to bring "the sweet and lively liquor of the gospel to the savages." Hakluyt cited the example of Spanish friars who preached in Florida "before any planting" and were massacred by the Indians as proof of the necessity of colonies to the planting of the Christian faith. The Spanish, along with the Portuguese, had been most successful in planting their religion when they had planted colonies.

> Now if they, in their superstition, by means of their planting in those parts, have done so great things in so short space, what may we hope for in our true and sincere religion, proposing unto ourselves in this action not filthy lucre nor vain ostentation, as they indeed did, but principally the gaining of the souls of millions of those wretched people? [*Id.* at 216.]

160. *Id.* at 249.

161. *See* text accompanying notes 31–36, *supra.*

162. *RH, supra* note 33, at 241.

163. *Id.* at 290. On Madoc, *see* text accompanying notes 103–10, *supra.* Hakluyt also related a dubious tale (only briefly mentioned by Peckham; *HG, supra* note 1, at 448–49) involving the Columbus brothers. In 1488, according to Hakluyt, Bartholomeo Columbus, brother of Christopher Columbus, had approached Henry VII. Bartolomeo showed Henry several maps, explained Christopher's proposed "Enterprise of the Indies," and made an "offer" on behalf of his brother. Hakluyt claimed that this offer was accepted by the Tudor king. Unfortunately, Christopher did not receive Henry's answer immediately. Bartholomeo fell in with pirates, and was unable to rendezvous with his brother for some time. In the meantime, Christopher, worried that the Portuguese might preempt his plan, became impatient and approached Spain with his offer. Spain accepted, but only after the same offer had been accepted by Henry. *RH, supra* note 33.

Hakluyt framed an interesting contract argument out of this set of alleged facts. In taking the enterprise out of Henry's hands, "which was first sent to him, and never refused by him," both Columbus and Spain had wronged the English Crown (*id.*). The wrong may or may not have been actionable in the common-law courts of Henry's day. Whether, with pirates menacing the seas and bandits menacing the overland routes of communication, a fifteenth-century European monarch's mailing of an acceptance by way of the offeror's agent created a binding contract is a question not addressed in the legal treatises of the era.

164. *See* text accompanying notes 50–51, *supra.*

165. *RH, supra* note 33, at 293–95. Conceding that merely discovering a country did not suffice to vest rights, Hakluyt claimed that Sebastian Cabot, who had followed up his father's North American discoveries, did "more than see the country, for he went on land on diverse places, took

possession of the same according to his patent" (*id.*). Sebastian Cabot, thus having seen and possessed the mainland of North America prior to any Spaniard, had secured to England the "best rights and title of any Christian" to that country. *Id.*

166. *Id.* at 298–99. "Our Savior Christ himself sayeth to his disciples, that, while they were in the world, they should be brought before kings and political magistrates for his name's sake. So then they should not be judges and magistrates themselves, especially in the divisions of kingdoms" (*id.* at 299).

167. *Id.* at 301.

168. *See* Chapter 3, text accompanying notes 64–67, *supra*.

169. *RH*, *supra* note 33, at 301.

170. *Id.* at 301–2.

171. *See* Chapter 1, text accompanying notes 43–46, *supra*.

172. *RH*, *supra* note 33, at 302.

173. *Id.*

174. *Id.* at 303. The bull itself, Hakluyt argued, was granted under unusual circumstances in that it confirmed Columbus's discoveries after the fact. By the pope's approval "he seemeth to confess that they [the Spaniards] might have pursued that godly action very lawfully without making him privy to their enterprise" (*id.* at 304). As was the case with the papal bull *Laudabiliter*, allegedly granting Ireland to England, the pope's donation of America to Spain was, according to Hakluyt, a superfluity. So many kings, including English kings, had sent numerous voyages to the New World without being excommunicated, as threatened by Alexander's bull, that even Alexander's successors appeared to recognize the injustice of the bull. *Id.* at 310–11.

175. *See* text accompanying notes 41–43, *supra*.

176. *RH*, *supra* note 33, at 308–9.

177. *Id.*

178. D.B. Quinn, *England and the Discovery of America 1481–1620* 294 (1974).

179. Reprinted in *RV*, *supra* note 151, at 130.

180. *Id.* at 136.

181. *Id.* at 138.

182. *Id.* at 139.

183. Ralph Lane to Richard Hakluyt the Elder and Master H———of the Middle Temple, reprinted in *id.* at 207–8.

184. *Id.* at 209.

185. *See id.* at 202–3.

186. *Id.* at 203.

187. "Ralph Lane's Discourse on the First Colony" (1586), reprinted in *id.* at 235.

188. Thomas Harriot, "A Briefe and True Report of the New-Found Land of Virginia" (1588), reprinted in *id.* at 317.

189. H. C. Porter, *supra* note 57, at 236.

190. *RV*, *supra* note 151, at 341.

191. *Id.* at 371.

192. *Id.* at 372.

193. Harriot wrote, "[M]any of them . . . have such opinion of us, as if they knew not the truth of God and religion already, it was rather to be had from us, whom God so specially loved" (*id.* at 376).

194. *Id.* at 377.

195. H. C. Porter, *supra* note 57, at 247.

196. Quoted in *id.* at 248.

197. *See id.* The Indians of Virginia, Hakluyt asserted, "are of better wits than those of Mexico and Peru . . . whereby it may be gathered that they will easily embrace the Gospel, forsaking their idolatry, wherein at this present, for the most part, they are wrapped and entangled" (*id.*).

198. *Id.* at 248–49.

199. *See* text accompanying notes 113–114, *supra*.

200. See *RV*, *supra* note 151, at 497.

201. *Id.* at 498.

202. *Id.* at 556.
203. *See*, e.g., the discussion of the lost colonists in D. B. Quinn, *supra* note 178.
204. H. C. Porter, *supra* note 57, at 174.
205. *Id.* at 175.
206. C. Hill, *supra* note 135.
207. Quoted in K. Knorr, *British Colonial Theories 1570–1850* 31 (1944).

5

The English Conquest of Virginia

Sir Walter Raleigh, Sir Humphrey Gilbert, and the other Elizabethan conquistadores elaborated the foundations of Discovery-era England's colonizing discourse. Their primitive discourses of conquest sought to harmonize the medieval Church's legal discursive legacy on infidel rights, the Reformation's liberated pursuit of worldly wealth, and radical Protestantism's vested interest in countering Spain's New World papist empire.

The Elizabethan advocates of colonization, however, were never able to perfect their colonizing discourses in the forests of the New World. Their narrow financial base was inadequate to the demands of carrying the Protestant crusade to the Indians of America. The Elizabethan age of New World conquest ended a decade before Elizabeth's death in 1603. The initial failures of Gilbert and Raleigh were sufficient deterrents to poorly capitalized would-be successors.

The shifts in discursive formations inaugurated by the ascension to the English throne of a Scottish king, James I (r. 1603–1625), disrupted the thematic continuity of English Discovery-era colonizing discourses. James cared little for prosecuting Elizabeth's Protestant crusade against either Spain or the Indians of the New World. One signal of the discursive shift in emphasis in the public discourses of the early Stuart dynasty was provided by James's treaty of peace with Spain in 1604. Another signal was Raleigh's conviction on a trumped-up charge of treason in the first year of James's reign.

The de-emphasis of the anti-Spanish rhetoric of the Elizabethan conquistadores permitted a sharper focus on New World colonization as primarily a commercial endeavor. Not coincidentally, this Jacobean shift in discursive emphasis occurred at the same time English colonizing activities were tending toward more broadly capitalized trading ventures. These corporations were devoted to the creation of commercial wealth for their shareholders. Religious or even Crown interests might be tolerated, but only as long as they supplemented the profit motive behind the business of colonizing other peoples' lands.

An investigation of the discourse of conquest perfected during the Jamestown venture of the Virginia Company (which established England's first permanent New World colony) reveals in fact a four-decades-long corporate effort at rationalizing the colonization process on grounds of economic efficiency. During this period, English colonizing legal discourse shifted its principal emphases away from religiously grounded and anti-Spanish motifs in justifying war against the American Indians. In the transformed legal discursive formation of England's seventeenth century, the Indians came to be viewed as the dehumanized entry barrier to the lawfully mandated sovereignty of the English over the underutilized, savage lands of the New World. Thus the peculiar utilitarian thematics of the West's legal rationalizations for the exercise of its will to empire in lands occupied by indigenous tribal peoples emerged in its most refined aggressive form as England prepared for its own Age of Reason and Enlightenment.

The Bridge Builders Between the Medieval and the Enlightenment Visions of the American Indian in Western Legal Thought

The discussions of infidel rights and status contained in the writings of Alberico Gentili and Sir Edward Coke illuminate the nature of the conceptual bridges that were being constructed between medieval and modern forms of Western legal thought throughout the Renaissance Discovery era. Gentili and Coke were two of England's most prominent legal theorists in the era spanning the Elizabethan and Stuart reigns. They were in fact two of the principal architects of the process by which reason and enlightenment gradually opened itself up to English legal thought and discourse.

Alberico Gentili's Oxonian Discourse

At about the time that events forced Raleigh to abandon his plans to colonize Virginia (thus closing off the region to other would-be adventurers by virtue of his exclusive patent rights), Alberico Gentili was named Regius Professor of Civil Law at Oxford. The appointment of the Italian Protestant exile had been secured in 1587 by Elizabeth's influential secretary of state, Sir Francis Walsingham.

Gentili was born in 1552 in the town of San Ginesio in northeastern Italy. The Reformation had spread from Germany to Italy in the early and middle decades of the sixteenth century, particularly in the university towns such as Pisa and Perugia. Gentili's father, Matteo, appears to have encountered the radical opinions of the Reformers while a student at Pisa during mid-century and to have passed them on to his son. At the age of twenty, Alberico graduated from the famed University of Perugia as a doctor of civil law, the same university where Bartolus and Baldus had taught. When the Inquisition began focusing on the Gentilis, the family fled Italy and eventually settled in London, a haven for Protestant refugees. In London, the young Gentili was warmly welcomed into the influential circle of Italian refugees connected with members of Elizabeth's court. Battista Castiglione was tutor to Queen Elizabeth; Giglio Borgarucci was physician to the Earl of Leicester, chancellor of Oxford University. In 1581, Alberico Gentili received an appointment to Oxford as a reader in civil law.[1]

In 1584, as has been previously discussed,[2] Gentili was asked for an opinion on the Mendoza affair, which had implicated the Spanish ambassador in a

Catholic conspiracy to depose Elizabeth in favor of Mary, Queen of Scots. While the respected legal scholar's argument on the inviolability of ambassadors under the Law of Nations may have had little to do with Elizabeth's ultimate decision, Mendoza was only expelled, rather than executed, as was urged by many at the court.

After assuming the Regius professorship in 1587, Gentili delivered and published numerous lectures on a variety of civil-law topics. His most important and noted works focused on the law of war. Between 1588 (the year of the Armada) and 1589, he published three books on the topic, which were issued together in 1598 under the title *De iure belli libri tres* ("On the Law of War in Three Parts").[3]

The Catholic recusant George Peckham had surreptitiously introduced the Spanish-refined Christian Humanist discourse of a natural Law of Nations to English colonial theory in his 1583 pamphlet, "A True Reporte."[4] Gentili's academic stature as a civilian-trained jurist and his impeccable Protestant pedigree secured for him the privilege of making the formal introduction of this totalizing system of thought to English legal discursive practice.

Gentili's *De iure belli* represented the first comprehensive treatment by an English jurist of the law of war in the new style—that is, in the style known today as the Law of Nations. One twentieth-century commentator has claimed that "Gentili is the first great writer on *modern* international law, the first clearly to define its subject matter, and to treat it in the way which is on the whole consonant to the conception and practice of our own time."[5] This assessment slights the contributions to the Renaissance discourse of a Law of Nations made by the Spanish natural-law theorist Franciscus de Victoria[6] (whom Gentili often cited in his texts). Besides disseminating in England the basic themes of continental discourse, Gentili performed important spadework on the methodological and structural innovations to the discursive practices of modern international law more fully elaborated by the Dutchman Hugo Grotius.[7]

Each of Gentili's three books on the law of war treated separate aspects of the legal, political, and moral problems arising in connection with the topic. Part 1 of *De iure belli* treated war in general. Gentili discussed who could wage war and for what just reasons. Part 2 discussed the actual conduct of war. Declarations, acts forbidden and permitted, and treatment of the enemy and noncombatants were the major points of discussion. Part 3 concluded the progression by discussing the rights of the conqueror and the negotiation and execution of treaties.

Questions concerning wars with infidels permeated Gentili's text. Many of his arguments cited or referred directly to Victoria's opinions.[8] While Gentili took pains to distance himself from the Spanish priest's conclusions on many points, his approach to the major issues respecting the rights of non-Christian peoples adopted the same Eurocentric assumptions and attitudes that characterized Victoria's texts.

In his chapter on "honorable reasons for waging war," Gentili expressed accord with the fundamental principle put forward by Victoria that Europeans could lawfully wage war against normatively divergent peoples who violated Eurocentrically conceived natural law:

Therefore, I approve the more decidedly of the opinion of those who say that the cause of the Spaniards is just when they make war upon the Indians, who practiced abominable lewdness even with beasts, and who ate human flesh, slaying men for that purpose. For such sins are contrary to human nature, and the same is true of other sins recognized as such by all except . . . brutes and brutish men. And against such men, as Isocrates says, war is made as against brutes.[9]

Gentili invoked St. Augustine's *City of God*, a core text of Catholic metaphysical discourse,[10] in support of his basic proposition that under the Law of Nations, men might punish other men for committing crimes against nature: "If some earthly city should decide to commit certain great crimes, it would have to be overthrown by decree of the human race."[11]

Victoria had maintained this same Augustinian-derived point in discussing the just title of Spain to the Indians' lands.[12] Pope Innocent IV, in his thirteenth-century commentary on infidel rights, had also declared that violations of the law of nature justified wars by outside parties not directly harmed by such sins.[13] The Augustinian notion of a consensus-grounded right to punish violations of universally regarded norms had been a central organizing theme of Christian European natural-law discursive practice throughout the Middle Ages. For Renaissance theorists of the Law of Nations, the consensual thematics of the Christian natural-law tradition provided the systemic bridge to a new, supposedly secularized legal science. This science of a Law of Nations focused on the construction of a world polity governed by universally binding norms in the civil sphere.

Gentili's Protestant Humanism was, however, particularly attuned to exorcising those parts of the Catholic Church's Christian natural-law tradition speaking to the central issue of normative conformity in the religious sphere. While Gentili was in agreement with the central Augustinian claim that normatively divergent peoples could be punished for violations of the Law of Nations, he imposed a novel qualification on one of the most important traditionally asserted reasons for waging a just war under the Law of Nations. Gentili argued that war against idolators was lawful only "if idolatry is joined with the slaughter of innocent victims, for the innocent must be protected."[14] Idolatry had always been regarded as one of the unqualified offenses punishable by "civilized" nations under natural law. Both Pope Innocent IV and Victoria had recognized this basic principle of the Christian natural-law tradition in their discourses on infidel rights.[15] Given Gentili's heretical past in Catholic Italy and the despicable (from the Protestant viewpoint) justifications used by the papist Spaniards for seizing the lands of Indians throughout the New World solely on the basis of nonbelief, *De iure belli*'s novel qualification that idolatry had to be joined with another heinous crime before it could be punished was not surprising. Protestantism asserted a vested interest in challenging the Spanish imperial juggernaut in the New World. If Spain could not yet be effectively countered by the English on the ground in America, the legality under the Law of Nations of Spain's wars on the Americans for their idolatry could at least be attacked in the Protestant universities of the Old World. According to the Oxford professor:

It is true . . . that these principles [justifying wars based on religion] are said to be the invention of the most greedy of men and to be cloaks for their dishonesty; and that there is no religion so wicked as to order an attack upon men of a different belief. In this way King Ferdinand, who was called the Catholic, covered almost all his excesses with a respectable mantle of religion.[16]

Gentili, the eminent realist on this point, recognized that each individual "declares his own war a holy one. Each one insists that his enemies are godless men. Each names his own case righteous."[17] Thus Gentili's effort to exclude idolatry as a just cause of war against infidels under his Protestant version of the Law of Nations sought to remove a too-easily-abused, self-serving justification for Spanish imperial extension. Idolatry, standing alone, did not constitute a just cause of war. Only those peoples who grossly violated natural law, living "rather like beasts than men, being the common foes of all mankind, as pirates are, ought to be assailed in war and adopt the usages of humanity."[18]

For similar reasons, Gentili diverged from Victoria, Pope Innocent IV, and other Christian natural-law theorists who had asserted that war could be waged against those who refused to hear the gospel:

One reason I do not accept, although it is approved by others among the causes of the war waged by the Spaniards against the Indians; namely that it was lawful to make war upon them because they refused to hear the preaching of the Gospel. For this is only a pretext of religion.[19]

Gentili acknowledged the scriptural command of Jesus[20] to teach the gospel to all men, but "it does not therefore follow that any creature which refuses to hear must be forced to do so by war and arms."[21] Gentili specifically condemned the teaching of Pope Innocent IV (whom Victoria had followed) on this point.[22]

There were, however, a number of ancillary points of consensus between Gentili's Protestantized version of international law and the Catholicized formulation. These points of agreement illuminate the overall totalizing thrust of European colonizing legal discourse in the Discovery era, regardless of its sectarian variants.

Like Victoria, Gentili held strongly to the belief that the law of nature binds all people and the Law of Nations binds all nations:

Therefore, since we may also be injured as individuals by those violations of nature, war will be made against them by individuals. And no rights will be due to these men who have broken all human and divine laws and who, though joined with us by similarity of nature, have disgraced this union with abominable stains. In other words, not only is the civil law an agreement and a bond of union among citizens, but the same is true of the law of nations as regards nations, and the law of nature as regards mankind.[23]

The reference point of this type of discursive practice is the same totalizing concept of human nature that animated the discourse of Victoria's Law of Nations. All humankind shares in a universal nature and should therefore be bound by the same universal norms. In defining these norms, the Protestant Gentili, like his Catholic counterpart Victoria, turned without hesitation to the Christian European's totalizing natural-law discourse. Human nature, Gentili argued, is inextricably bound to knowledge of the divine. Thus while it would be unjust to wage war against peoples who practiced idolatrous religions (for even idolatry indicated a recognition of the divine), civilized states could wage war against those who by their conduct acknowledged no religion whatsoever and thereby denied humankind's common nature.[24] Citing Corinthians and St. Bernard's epistles, the Protestant exile declared,

[T]he law of religion is not the same as other laws. Faith is a special gift of God and Jesus Christ is foolishness among the heathen; but natural things are known naturally to all. Some kind of religion is natural, and therefore if there should be any who are atheists, destitute of any religious belief, either good or bad, it would seem just to war upon them as we would brutes. For they do not deserve to be called men, who divest themselves of human nature, and themselves do not desire the name of men, and such a war is a war of vengeance, to avenge our common nature.[25]

Gentili's message was a familiar one to Western legal thought respecting infidel peoples: his discourse of a Law of Nations sought to eliminate radical difference. The full implications of this position become apparent when one considers Gentili's opinion on the religious rights of conquered peoples following the conclusion of war:[26] "But truly if the victor meets with those who are alien to humanity and to all religion, these he may most justly compel to change conduct which is contrary to nature."[27]

Gentili cited three types of individuals whose divergent religious beliefs seemed contrary to nature. Each type presented separate questions as to whether a victor in war should tolerate religious difference: "there are some who deny God. Some are doubtful about his providence. Others follow the rules and superstitions of their forefathers and cannot bear to let their thought go any farther."[28]

Gentili proposed that the victor in war could treat the first two instances similarly, since those who deny God's attributes deny God, and "therefore those who deny the providence of God, or (which is the same thing) who doubt it, deny Him."[29] For these two classes of individuals who denied God, Gentili proscribed persecution. They should not be tolerated, "nor are any others to be tolerated whose religion impairs the security of victory and its laws."[30]

Gentili's point respecting the victor's intolerance of religious difference is again an eminently practical one. Atheists and those who denied God's providence should not be tolerated by the victor, because people without religion pose a threat to the victor's rule. Thus, Gentili argued that his third troublesome group, those conquered individuals enslaved to the perverse religions of their forefathers, should also not be tolerated by the conqueror. Their divergence from the conqueror's religion, if allowed to continue, would make "the conquest less decisive."[31] In Gentili's system, Christian religion was the instrument by which the conqueror ensured the submission of the conquered. It, too, was an instrument of empire, a fact recognized in the Protestant as well as the Catholic Discovery-era discourses on the Law of Nations.

Gentili domesticated Renaissance-era discourse on the Law of Nations for English consumption. The secularized thematics of unity and hierarchy central to Christian European medieval legal and political consciousness were preserved and maintained in his Protestantization of the Law of Nations. Conquest, colonization, and remediation of radically divergent peoples were mandated by a law that appealed to a Eurocentric conception of human reason and by tactics of convenience that viewed a Christianized savage as a safe savage. Gentili's text improved the pedigree of less systematized and less sophisticated Elizabethan conceptions on infidel status and rights, formally integrating the Renaissance's civilian-inspired natural-law discursive traditions with the indigenous vernacular of English colonizing discourse. The Oxford professor's Law of Nations elaborated a rationalized discourse of conquest for England's era of enlightenment.

Sir Edward Coke and the English Common-Law Presumption of the King's Right to Wage War Against Infidels

In 1608 Robert Calvin, a "Scotsman born," appeared before the court of common pleas, Lord Chief Justice Edward Coke presiding. Calvin sought the return "of his freehold in Haggard, otherwise Haggerston, otherwise Aggerston, in the parish of St. Leonard, in Shoreditch," from which he claimed he had been "unjustly and without judgment" disseised by Richard and Nicholas Smith.[32]

In response to the case, William Edwards, attorney for the Smiths, argued that as Calvin was "an alien born" and "out of allegiance of the said lord the King of his kingdom of England" (England and Scotland were not united at this date), he ought in law be barred from having an answer to his writ.[33]

In considering the arguments of the parties, Lord Coke, whose *Law Reports*, first published in 1600,[34] represented the greatest systematizing effort of the English common-law tradition to that date, was led to a discussion of the rights and status of an alien under English law. Coke distinguished between categories of aliens: "Every alien is either a friend that is in league, etc. or an enemy that is in open war, etc. Every alien enemy is either *pro tempore*, temporary for a time, or *perpetus*, perpetual."[35] Coke stated that under the common law, alien friends, "at this time, a German, a Frenchman, a Spaniard," could acquire goods and maintain an action upon those goods in an English court. Such friendly aliens could also maintain an action for a house that constituted their necessary habitation in the realm.[36]

Coke's genius as a systematizer, bringing reason's light to bear on the poorly articulated although inherent principles of English common law,[37] can be gleaned from his terse treatment of an issue not actually before the court in *Calvin's Case*, although the issue was certainly within the ambit of Coke's discussion. The consensus of reasonable minds on this particular issue perhaps seemed so clear and so widely recognized to Coke that he seized the opportunity that *Calvin's Case* provided to embed a presumption in his common law for ease of future reference.

Having outlined the rights and status of "friendly aliens" under common law, Coke distinguished them from aliens regarded as perpetual enemies:

> But a perpetual enemy (though there be no wars by fire and sword between them) cannot maintain any action, or get anything within this realm. All infidels are in law *perpetui inimici*, perpetual enemies (for the law presumes not that they will be converted, that being *remota potentia*, a remote possibility), for between them, as with devils, whose subjects they be, and the Christian, there is perpetual hostility, and can be no peace.[38]

Coke went on to discuss the consequences of a Christian king's conquest of an infidel kingdom. Once brought under subjection, "there *ipso facto* the laws of the infidel are abrogated, for that they be not only against Christianity, but against the law of God and of nature, contained in the decalogue." Upon conquest, therefore, the king, according to Chief Justice Coke, must establish laws among the infidel "and judge their causes according to natural equity."[39]

Coke's assertion of the king's absolute prerogative powers in infidel territories that were acquired by conquest adopted without comment the medieval Catholic Church's Crusading-era discourse on infidel status and rights. As Coke recognized, this discourse diverged from the ancient Roman law of war, which assumed without distinction that a conquered nation could retain its prior laws until they were changed by the conqueror in the exercise of the prerogatives of conquest. Coke's medievally derived discourse in *Calvin's Case* denied this privilege to infidel nations conquered by a Christian king: "there *ipso facto* the laws of the infidel are abrogated, for that they be . . . against Christianity . . . [and] the law of God and of nature."[40]

A later English court would reject Coke's dictum on infidel status by labeling it the "madness of the crusades."[41] Yet, as we have seen, the Oxford law professor Gentili was infected by this same "madness." In his treatise on the Law of Nations regarding war, Gentili had declared that if a conquering monarch assumed sovereignty over peoples "who are alien to humanity and to all religion, these he may most justly compel to change conduct which is contrary to nature."[42] To Coke and his generation of jurists, medieval Crusading-era legal discourse represented not the "madness" but the underlying foundation of the recent attempts at conquest of America. All Coke sought to do was restate for his contemporaries the law of feudal conquest, with its Crusading-era distinctions denying *dominium* and legitimacy to the king's perpetual infidel enemies.

Significantly, while Gentili had only dallied in the corridors of power, Coke was at home there. He wrote from experience, not from Oxford. He knew men of action who had operated on the presumption of perpetual war with infidel peoples and who never speculated about its rightness under the Law of Nations. Coke, after all, was *there* when the English equivalent of the *Requerimiento* was drawn up, the royal charter for the Virginia Company by which the English resumed their war for America.

The Invasion of America

The Virginia Company's Tactics and Strategy

It was Coke's successful prosecution of Sir Walter Raleigh for high treason in 1603, in fact, that resulted in the reversion of Raleigh's rights over Virginia to the English Crown. The Crown now, however, was worn by a Scottish-born monarch, James I, who had succeeded to the throne upon Elizabeth's death in 1603. The new Stuart king had signed a peace treaty with Spain in 1604, and the various interests that wished to assume Raleigh's patent rights bided their time until James's position on invading the New World to plant English colonies could be fully determined.

At least two groups of merchants were lobbying at court for Raleigh's lapsed patent rights to Virginia. London merchants, many of whom had made substantial profits from the burgeoning Eastern trade, now looked toward the West. A group of Plymouth and Bristol merchants also showed interest. While not so financially powerful as the London group, these merchants were politically well connected. Their patron was Coke's predecessor as lord chief justice of England, Sir John Popham. Their advisor was the younger Richard Hakluyt, the former associate and inspirer of Gilbert and Raleigh. In the autumn of 1605, the two groups joined together (the better to persuade a reluctant king) and petitioned James for the grant of a charter.[43] They argued that experience (among them was Raleigh Gilbert, son of Sir Humphrey, named after his uncle, Sir Walter) had demonstrated that no single person could attempt the settling of colonies. Their proposed joint-venture trading company was formed along the innovative lines of the broadly capitalized East India Company. The New World venture was to operate under royal and private control with the consent of Parliament.

The king apparently agreed to the formation of what came to be known as the Virginia Company. The royal charter, issued on April 10, 1606, gave the company "licence to make habitation, plantation, and to deduce a colony of sundry of our people into that part of America, commonly called Virginia . . . not now actually possessed by any Christian Prince or people."[44] In chartering the enterprise, the Crown approved the company's well-intended religious goals in settling America:

We, greatly commending, and graciously accepting of, their Desires for the Furtherance of so noble a Work, which may, by the Providence of Almighty God, hereafter tend to the Glory of his Divine Majesty, in propagating of Christian Religion to such People, as yet live in Darkness and miserable Ignorance of the true Knowledge and Worship of God, and may in time bring the Infidels and Savages, living in those Parts, to human Civility, and to a settled and quiet Government; Do, by these our Letters Patents, graciously accept of, and agree to, their humble and well-intended Desires.[45]

Historians surmise that the likely drafters of this 1606 legal text, by which the first permanent English colony in America was to be established at Jamestown, included the two finest legal minds in England at the time, Lord Chief Justice Sir John Popham, and another principal in the venture, Sir Edward

Coke, this time applying the law of the realm as attorney general to the Crown.[46] Coke's presumption in *Calvin's Case* that the king was at perpetual war with infidels and could thereby initiate a crusade of conquest was here incorporated as part of the royal contract authorizing the English invasion of America.

The Virginia Company's charter established a bifurcated entity. The London part of the company was vested with authority to settle the southern part of Virginia (south of the Potomac). The northern part of Virginia (north of present-day New York City) was under the authority of the Plymouth Company, which represented merchant interests in Bristol, Plymouth, and other cities in the western half of England. The area between the southern and northern jurisdictions was open to settlement by either the London or the Plymouth Company. The administrative center of the entire Virginia Company was in London. The King's Council of Virginia directed the affairs of the corporation. The council's members were to be appointed by King James, who possessed ultimate supervisory control. The council's responsibilities included nominating the members of the governing council for each colony in America. Besides this very limited form of home-rule power, the charter granted the American colonists the normal rights and liberties of any English citizens within the realm.[47]

At about the time the charter was drafted, the records of the Virginia Company[48] indicate that one of the first matters of business considered by the council was a motion "that some form of writing in way of justification of our plantation might be conceived and pass (though not by public authority), into many hands."[49] The unnamed proposer put forward two reasons supporting the motion: first, that such a justification would "give adventurers, a clearness and satisfaction, for the justice of the action, and so encourage them, and draw on others"; and second, that such a justification would demonstrate to "the Spaniard" that the "state would neither fear, nor be ashamed to proceed" in establishing colonies in those areas of America justly claimed under the title of England.[50]

There was apparently strong dissent to the motion to publish a "justification" of the colonizing enterprise to North America. The minutes of the company meeting detailed the reasoning of those who opposed the legitimating motion. First, they argued that there was no need to encourage or incite adventurers to the project, "for they in this point need it not, nor require it"; and second, "there is much a confession in every unnecessary apology." Better not to say anything; "quietness and no doubting" is the preferred course for one who asserts a settled and confirmed right.[51] Further, the king's great seal and the outfitting of a voyage had already given Spain testimony of "the State's good affection to the journey." To publish England's justification for colonization would only invite the Spanish ambassador to "expostulate with his Majesty about this writing, and then it is not conceived how far his Majesty will be pleased to avow it, which may intimate disavowing."[52]

Opponents of the motion also argued that publishing a justification would be likely to incite "pen-adversaries," both Spaniards and "neutral writers, but of Spanish affections," to respond in print. The Spaniards would defend their title "upon the Donation of [Pope] Alexander, which is so grounded upon the principles of their religion that some of their best authors have pronounced it heresy to doubt it." In any event, the English had recourse to their own convincing "arguments" from God, and Nature and Nations" as to their rightful titles in the New World. These arguments were certainly capable of "overthrowing the Donation," but as the English have "no such convincing and obligatory" documents to counter the donation, raising the issue would only cause trouble and controversy. Dissonance ought to be avoided at the outset of such a sensitive undertaking.[53]

As for those English "pen-adversaries" who claimed neutrality in the enterprise but in reality favored Spain, such individuals could cause even more difficulty for the company. Because Spain was already established in the New World and not likely to leave by force of moral argument, these adversaries would feel free to "cast scruples into our conscience" by writing "against the lawfulness of plantation" in America. This type of attack presented the greatest danger, in the opinion of those opposed to the motion to publish a justification of the company's enterprise, for such efforts "must necessarily grow to disputation of so much intricacy, perplexity, and replication, as shall conduce unto their end of slackening us." While any attack on the morality of the enterprise could certainly be countered by the company, the legitimating defense for raiding the New World would require great "subtlety of distinction."[54]

The company, the opponents of the motion of justification argued, should therefore learn from the example of the Spaniards themselves about the unwisdom of inviting moral qualms to be raised respecting colonization of infidel lands.

For when at first discovery of these parts the Spaniard did subject the consideration of it to casuists, and confessors, it became so interminable, that he [the Spanish king] was forced to resolve roundly upon the worst way lest he should have none to prosecute the Indians as barbars and therefore naturally slaves.[55]

In view of the differing opinions put forth by his casuistical priests, the Spanish king had to resolve that the Indians were barbarians and slaves by nature in order to give himself some pretense of secure title. But this solution proved temporary:

When after 50 years his Friars declined him from that severe and unjust course, and he labored by men of all learning to provide him of a more acceptable title, all the reasons which were prepared by him, by men of discourse, from the Indians transgressing the Law of Nature; from his Canonists, by the Donation: and from his Divines, by preparation of religion, were so incoherent and so resisted by one another, as many books written in his defence, were suppressed in his own kingdom.[56]

Besides the attack on the institution of free speech in Spain, the only other result of Spanish investigation into the justice of the king's title, dominion, and property in the Indies was the confusion resulting from the contending discourses of the king's advisors. They could not agree on the legal basis of the king's rights in the Indies. At best, he was theorized as holding a "Magistracy

. . . by which he is allowed to remove such impediments, as they [the Indians] had against the knowledge of religion"[57] (the influence of Victoria and his school on Spanish colonizing theory and discourse were familiar even to the English).

To the opponents of the motion to publish a justification, the example of the Spaniard's troubles was conclusive:

Because therefore, we shall be put to defend our title, not yet publicly quarreled, not only comparatively to be as good as the Spaniards . . . but absolutely against the natural people: some thought it better to abstain from this unnecessary way of provocation, and reserve ourselves to the defensive part, when they shall offer anything against us.[58]

The motion to publish a justification of the English title, "comparatively" as good as that of Spain or "absolutely" as good as that of the natural people of America, failed. Instead, a strategy of silence, in order to suppress the arousal of any contrary discourse, was agreed on. The justice of the company's royally assigned title in America would operate simply on a presumption of English superior rights in America. No argument for English hegemony in America could be expected to answer the pen-adversaries who did not accept the presumption that the English were at perpetual war with the heathen savages of America. Conquest of America itself would prove the superior right of the English to the Indians' America. Coke's dictum in *Calvin's Case*,[59] published three years after the defeat of the motion, may well have been intended as the written legal justification that his partners in the Virginia Company never desired to publish themselves. For Coke had certainly incorporated their legal position on England's presumed right to invade America into his opinion in *Calvin's Case*.

The Virginia Company's strategy of silence and suppression perhaps made good sense in the intensely competitive atmosphere of early-seventeenth-century mercantile Europe. King James himself claimed to be quite in the dark about the details of the Virginia Company's plans in response to Spanish ambassador Pedro de Zuniga's protests of "how much against good friendship and brotherliness it was for his vassals to dare to want to people Virginia, since it is a part of the Indies belonging to Castile."[60] James went on to say, however, somewhat disingenuously, that he "had never known" that the Spaniards had rights to Virginia, "for it was a region very far from where the Spaniards had settled." The king did not bother to say who had told him this particular detail. He only asserted that his peace treaty with Spain of 1604 prohibited English travel to the Indies, but not to other undiscovered parts of the New World. Since the king of Spain's subjects "have discovered new regions," it seemed to James only proper "that his also might," as long as such discoveries were outside the Indies. The king did promise the Spanish ambassador that he would look more closely into the issues raised by his subjects' proposal to colonize Virgnia.[61]

In a subsequent letter to his king, Ambassador Zuniga reported that James, after his further promised study of the issues, had decided that it was not against the terms of the treaty of 1604 for the English to colonize Virginia. To accede to Spain's request and stop the colonization project would, in effect, "seem to him [James] to confirm that Your [Spanish] Majesty is Lord of all the Indies."[62] When Spain's representative to the 1604 treaty was consulted as to what had actually transpired in the negotiations respecting English travel to the Indies, he reported that

when he discussed peace in England he considered that if he specifically tried to exclude the English . . . from Virginia, he foresaw the difficulty that they [the English] are in peaceful possession of the latter for more than thirty years; if it was declared that it [Virginia] was not part of the Indies, a gate would be opened leading to ruin. It was decided to obtain their agreement, as was done, that voyages should be made only to those of your Majesty's kingdoms to which they were commonly made in the old days before the war.[63]

Thus the 1604 treaty had been left ambiguous on a collateral point to the negotiations: Philip of Spain was desirous of peace in Europe; America was not his principal concern. Spain could claim that the treaty tacitly excluded the English from navigating to the Indies, while, in the words of David Quinn, "from the English point of view, they were tacitly permitted to keep on doing what they had been doing; namely sailing to and through the Indies."[64]

Even the Spanish negotiator at the treaty confided the difficulty of maintaining "legally" the assertion "that everything that is contiguous to the Indies is part thereof. . . . [T]he true [i.e., legally valid] act of possession will be [the act] of throwing out those who are in Virginia before they get further reinforcements."[65] By the early seventeenth century at least, Spaniards recognized as well as did the English that legal arguments had little to do with European "rights" in America. The "truth" of the Europeans' rights would be proved by power—the power to prevent other European imperial nations from encroaching on titles acquired and maintained in the Indians' America by the only form of right that could not be denied by moralizing "pen-adversaries" in Spain or in England: the right of conquest.

The Jamestown Venture

Without any moral or legal justification provided by the company and without any guarantee that either Spain or the Indians would recognize their rights under the Law of Nations, 145 colonists left England under the Virginia Company's sponsorship in 1607. The colonists who sought to settle Jamestown did carry a set of instructions from the London council, warning them that in selecting a site for their settlement, they should not trust the Indians:

You must in no case suffer any of the natural people of the country to inhabit between you and the sea coast for you cannot carry yourselves so towards them but they will grow discontented with your habitation and be ready to guide and assist any nation that shall come to invade you.[66]

In exploring the area around the settlement, the colonists were advised by the council to take "great care not to offend the naturals if you can eschew it and employ some few of your company to trade with them for corn and all other lasting victuals."[67] The trading for food supplies was to be done soon after arrival, before the savages perceived that "you mean to plant among them." The colonists also should watch carefully any Indian guides hired for voyages of local discovery. A compass transverse should be employed in case the guides abandoned the English explorers deep in the woods. The Indians should never be trusted to carry English weapons, and only the best of English marksmen should be permitted to shoot in their presence, lest the infidels underestimate the military capabilities of the colonists. Neither should the death or sickness of any of the colonists be advertised, lest the Indians perceive the English as "common men."[68]

The Emperor Powhatan

The Jamestown settlement was located within Chief Powhatan's empire. The great Indian leader's authority extended to more than thirty Algonkian-speaking tribes in the Tidewater region of Virginia. His own seat of government was originally located 15 miles from Jamestown at Werowocomoco on the Pamunkey River, but was subsequently relocated to a more remote village upstream on the Chickahominy River, nearly 100 miles from the English colony.

The Jamestown colonists were initially surprised by the Tidewater Indians' relatively advanced degree of settled habitation of their "savage" country. Tribal villages contained houses and gardens, as well as numerous tools and decorative artifacts. The Indian settlements were scattered throughout the Tidewater region, and while the English had referred to the country as "ill-populated," Powhatan's early-seventeenth-century confederacy may have included as many as 9,000 individuals.[69] The vastly outnumbered English settlers at Jamestown had no choice but to seek peaceful relations and the Indians' agreement to their plantation colony. Shortly after arriving, the 145 colonists gladly purchased the right to settlement by a payment in copper (highly prized by the Indians) to one of Powhatan's tributory tribes, the Paspahegh.[70]

While relations with the Paspahegh tribespeople were initially peaceful, the anxious English settlers had yet to meet "the great emperor" Powhatan, spoken of in awe-stricken tones by the local Indians. Then in December 1607, John Smith was taken prisoner on an exploring expedition on the James River by Opechancanough, the emperor's brother.[71] It was under these less-than-auspicious circumstances that the Englishman Smith met the famed emperor. Powhatan, at Opechancanough's urging, seemed inclined to execute the first white man he had probably ever seen. But according to the legend, Smith's life was allegedly saved by Powhatan's preteen daughter, Pocahontas.

Powhatan at first adopted a policy of accommodation toward the English. The emperor apparently viewed the intruders, with their trade goods and novel but deadly weaponry, as potential allies to be cultivated for the maintenance and extension of his own feudal empire.[72] The English agreed with Powhatan, but with one major difference: their intention was to use Powhatan in the extension of the English empire in Virginia.

These opposing visions on the precise nature of future Indian–English relations fused to the apparent satisfaction of both parties in what can be fairly described as the first-ever formal treaty ceremony between the English and an Indian confederacy in North America. (Although there was no actual writing, all the other normal solemnities accompanied the festivities.)

In September 1608 Christopher Newport, who had captained the *Sarah Constant* on the voyage to Virginia, returned to the colony with instructions from London to perform a "coronation" of Powhatan. To solemnize the ceremony, Newport had brought along a copper crown, European furniture and clothing, and instructions to build the emperor an English house. Newport's mission coincided with the company's massive recruitment drive in England for colonists. The company apparently desired to make Powhatan some type of vassal or minor lord, prior to any large-scale English migration. As Wesley Craven has put it, "By accepting the crown Powhatan might be understood to have conceded the English title, a point of considerable legal importance to the Europeans, while in the offer of it the English gave due recognition, or so presumably it was felt, to the Indians' right in the land."[73] The presumptions of English Crusading-era-derived legal discourse denying infidel *dominium* were yielding to the emperor's superiority respecting forces on the ground in America.

In fact, Powhatan's reaction to the company's proposal, as well as his conduct at the coronation, suggest strongly that the imperial savage viewed the subinfeudation ceremony from a perspective diametrically opposed to English presumptions. Smith was sent upriver to the chief's village. He was to ask the savage to travel to Jamestown for the coronation ceremony performed by the king's agent, Newport. Powhatan, however, reportedly refused to play the role of a supplement to British power: "If your king have sent me presents, I also am a king, and this is my land. Eight days I will stay to receive him [Newport], your father is to come to me, not I to him, nor yet to your fort, neither will I bite at such a bait."[74]

The emperor was apparently not so savage as to misunderstand the importance of standing on ceremony with the newcomers. In order to crown the emperor of the Virginia savages, Newport was forced to travel 100 miles upriver to Powhatan's seat of government. John Smith's "Map of Virginia," published at Oxford in 1612, described the preposterous coronation ceremony as follows:

All things being fit for the day of his [Powhatan's] coronation, the presents were brought, his bason, ewer, bed and furniture set up, his scarlet cloak and apparel (with much adoe) put on him, being persuaded by Namontacke [Powhatan's son or nephew, who had been taken back to England on Newport's 1608 return voyage] they would do him no hurt. But a foul trouble there was to make him kneel to receive his crown, he neither knowing the majesty, nor meaning of a Crown, nor bending of the knee, endured so many persuasions, examples, and instructions, as tired them all. At last by leaning hard on his shoulders, he a little stooped, and Newport put the Crown on his head.[75]

Smith's assertion that Powhatan did not understand the "meaning of a Crown" is belied by the Indian emperor's own speech demanding to be crowned at his own seat of government.[76] Having enfeoffed (in his own way) as many vassal lords of conquered nations as any European rival of his time, the Indian emperor's own discourse of conquest was thoroughly conversant with the universal symbology of the kowtow and the bow. After the ceremony, the chief expressed his appreciation to the English by giving Newport "his old shoes and his mantle."[77] In any typology of Indian tributary gift giving, the value of what Powhatan gave and of what he received adequately testifies to his own state of mind respecting the implications of the ceremony and the superiority of his position in relation to the British.

According to the company's account of the absurd coronation ceremony (released in England as part of a publicity campaign), the "emperor" of Virginia had accepted "voluntarily a crown and a sceptre, with full acknowledgment of duty and submission." According to the company's advertisements, the Indian emperor "hath licensed us to negotiate among them, and to possess their country with them."[78]

That Powhatan and his subordinates did not consider themselves tributaries to the English or under a duty to facilitate the colonists' insatiable appetite for American land or Indian corn is borne out by events that soon followed the coronation ceremony. Smith assumed leadership of the colony between 1607 and 1609. Despite his constant exhortations against the "idleness" of the settlers and his strict military discipline, Smith's colonists remained dependent on the neighboring tribes for a steady food supply, which they obtained by barter.[79] The colonists' dependence on the Indians apparently liberalized Smith's own views respecting Powhatan's skills as a leader and his savage subjects' ability to provide food supplies not only for their own needs but also for trade with the English. In his account of his adventures in Virginia, Smith wrote admiringly that the "barbarous" Indians possessed "such government as that their magistrates for good commanding, and their people for due obedience and obeying, excel many places that would be accounted very civil."[80]

The Virginia Company's New Strategy

The Jamestown colony's continuing dependence on the savages greatly disturbed investors in England, who had assumed that the plantation would not only be self-sufficient but also produce profitable surpluses for the company's shareholders. The company perceived that the floundering enterprise, if it was to turn a profit, required restructuring in Virginia and in London. A second charter[81] was drafted that completely reorganized the Virginia Company. (This new charter, we are told by Francis Maitland, was principally the work of Edward Coke himself, now serving as James's attorney general.[82]) The company, as opposed to the Crown, was granted greater control, and the fourteen-member council was expanded approximately threefold, its members to be selected by the shareholders. It also appears that the company expanded its financial base considerably; more than 50 London companies and 650 individuals (Francis Bacon among them) now had an interest in the venture. A new plan for emigration was also drawn up, calling for up to 1,500 men and women to be settled in the colony by 1610.[83]

Sir Thomas Gates, the new governor of the colony, received his instructions from the council before departing London. These included detailed provisions for dealing with the savages if they failed to assume their advertised roles as tributary vassals to the English.[84] The instructions stated that Christianizing the Indians remained the pious and noble goal of the plantation.[85] To that end, Gates was to attempt to capture the priests of the surrounding tribespeople,

for they [the tribespeople] are so wrapped up in the fog and misery of their [the priests'] inequity, and so terrified with their continual tyranny chained under the bond of Death unto the devil that while they live among them to poison and infect them their minds, you shall never make any great progress into this glorious world, nor have any civil peace or concur with them.[86]

The company authorized Gates to exercise virtually unlimited powers in his dealings with the theocratic leaders of the Indian confederacy:

and in case of necessity or conveniency, we pronounce it not cruelty nor beach of charity to deal more sharply with them and to proceed even to death with these murderers of souls and sacrificers of god's images to the Devil, referring the consideration of this as a weighty matter of important consequence to the circumstances of the business and place it in your discretion.[87]

According to the company's legal analysis as outlined in these instructions, intervention into tribal culture for purposes of corrective mediation had become necessary and just. The goal of converting the Indians to English civility and Christianity was being subverted by religious leaders of the tribe, who practiced idolatry and the worship of the devil. Idolatrous religious practices constituted those same violations of natural law that the medievally derived Christian natural-law tradition of Pope Innocent and the Spanish Dominican Franciscus de Victoria asserted could justly be punished by acts of war.[88]

As for Powhatan, Gates was instructed to do whatever was necessary to "make him your tributary." The governor was encouraged to approach the emperor's own tributary chiefs and promise to "free them all" from the latter's tyranny in exchange for pledges of loyalty to King James and appropriate tribute. Then, having delivered the Indians from the "exactions of Powhatan," the colonists could attempt to induce the savages toward "clearing much ground of wood and of reducing them to labor and trade (for) this rent [that is, English protection] only."[89]

In London the company called on experts to justify and publicize this new, more aggressive business strategy aimed at undermining the heathen leadership of Powhatan and his priests. As part of the massive propaganda campaign launched to raise subscriptions for Gates's planned voyage, the company commissioned several speeches and sermons by prominent preachers and other public figures praising the colonization efforts and encouraging participation in the noble Virginia enterprise.

Apparently contravening its own initial decision to suppress discussion of English rights in America, the company instructed its commissioned encomiasts to elaborate at length on the justice of the company's enterprise in the New World. Powhatan's opposed vision of English–Indian relations had necessitated the articulation of a discourse of conquest legitimating the Virginia Company's superior right to the emperor's territory. A speech by Robert Johnson was solicited and printed in the early spring of 1609, entitled "Nova Britannia." Johnson, well-bred and of considerable means and connections, was a director of the East India Company and an investor in the Jamestown venture. He was also the son-in-law of Sir Thomas Smythe, treasurer and head of the Virginia Company. According to Johnson's speech, England's "just conquest by the sword" could be defended as an honorable effort "to subdue the tyranny of the roaring lion, that devours those poor souls in their ignorance and leads them to hell for want of light." Any Indians who "obstinately refuse to unite themselves unto us" are to be declared "recusant" and "shall be dealt with as enemies of the commonwealth of their country."[90]

Robert Gray, a popular Puritan preacher, delivered a stridently bellicose sermon on behalf of the company in April 1609. Gray, a Cambridge man, published his sermon under the title "A Good Speed to Virginia." Gray relied on biblical exegesis to prove the justice of the English war against the heathen. Joshua had commanded his people to enlarge their borders and destroy their enemies. Therefore, Joshua's children—the elect English—must "destroy those idolators and possess their lands." Citing St. Augustine for support of the proposition that "we might lawfully make war upon the savages of Virginia," Gray argued

That a Christian king may lawfully make war upon a barbarous and savage people, and such as live under no lawful or warrantable government, and may make a conquest of them, so that the way be undertaken to this end, to reclaim and reduce those savages from their barbarous kinds of life and from their brutish manners to humanity, piety and honesty.[91]

Gray's diatribe against the idolatrous infidels of Virginia was written one year after Lord Coke had declared the virtually identical view in *Calvin's Case*. In that case, Coke held that a Christian king could subjugate his lawless perpetual infidel enemies and could then freely establish civilized laws of natural justice and equity among the savages.[92] Gray appears to have adopted Coke's feudal common-law discourse on infidel rights as a central theme of his sermon on behalf of the company's will to empire. The company's carefully selected discursive pieces were all falling into place.

Besides invoking these familiar arguments on the missionary-*cum*-military aspects of England's rights in America, the preacher Gray developed a biblically inspired utilitarian justification for the conquest of America. According to Gray, the Lord had given the earth to the children of men. Thus man could say of himself, "The earth was mine, God gave it to me and my posterity."[93] Now, however, "the greater part of it [is] possessed by wild beasts and unreasonable creatures, or by brutish savages, which by reason of their godless ignorance and blasphemous idolatry are worse than those beasts."[94] Man, according to Gray, committed a sin whenever he permitted the earth to remain in "the hands of beasts and brutish savages, which have no interest in it, because they participate rather of the nature of beasts than men."[95]

Gray's discourse may indeed sound like proto-Lockean utilitarianism raised to a theological imperative. But the well-read preacher's vocabulary and syntax appear to derive from Gentili's popularizing of the Law of Nations in his *De iure belli libri tres* of 1598.[96] The Oxford professor had written that war was just against "brutish" men who practiced "abominable lewdness" and committed other crimes contrary to human nature.[97] "For of a truth," asserted Gentili, in phrasing very similar to that later used by Gray, "those seem to be dangerous to all men who wearing the human form, live the life of the most brutal of beasts."[98]

Gray did in fact appeal directly to the Law of Nations as support for the final argument of his sermon:

Some affirm, and it is likely to be true, that these savages have no particular propriety in any part of parcel of that country, but only a general residency there, as wild beasts in the forest; for they range and wander up and down the country without any law or government, being led only by their own lusts and sensuality. There is not *meum* and *tuum* [mine and thine] amongst them. So that if the whole land should be taken from them, there is not a man that can complain of any particular wrong done unto him.[99]

Gray was wrong, of course, about the Indians' conceptions of *meum* and *tuum*. John Smith himself had remarked that the Indians had a precise knowledge of boundaries demarcating the land of each tribe.[100] The first pictures of America, illustrations by John White drawn during Raleigh's Roanoke voyages, as well as narratives by other colonists, confirmed that the Virginia Indians lived in settled villages, surrounded by agricultural plots, under as firm and absolutist-minded a monarch in Powhatan as England had ever experienced during the reign of the Tudors.

The company itself attempted to sharpen the theologically derived utilitarian arguments declaimed from the pulpits by preachers such as Gray. A pamphlet entitled *A True Declaration of the Colonie in Virginia, With a Confutation of Such Scandalous Reports as Have Tended to the Disgrace of so Worthy an Enterprise*, was published by the advice and direction of the Council of Virginia in 1610.[101] The author (Francis Bacon, in the opinion of some[102]) relied on Powhatan's asserted permission to settle Virginia as providing a degree of legitimacy to the enterprise. But the savage's "composition" could not stand as a boundary to English wants. Both Plato and Aristotle gave license for wars against unreasonable madmen who committed "bloody injuries." "So that if offences shall arise, it can be no more injustice to war against infidels than it is when, upon just occasions, we war against Christians."[103] Echoing the arguments first put forward during the early Elizabethan colonization efforts in Ireland,[104] the pamphlet argued that there was more than ample room for the English and the Indians in Virginia. Only 2,000 inhabitants peopled the extent of 100 miles (this was a gross underestimation). The English could thus rightly possess a share of the Indians' lands. There was, in fact, no better method than "daily conversation" to bring such "human beasts" to "conversion."[105]

The company's original strategy of silence and suppression respecting discussion of its right in America[106] had been abandoned in the face of the savages' resistance to English blandishments. It had been hoped that the Indians' natural reason would recognize the superiority of English civlization and religion and gladly embrace both. Now it appeared that the Indian was rejecting this reasonable, well-intended bargain. In mobilizing for a full-fledged crusade to America, the company sought to demonstrate the irrationality of "human beasts" who refused to cede sovereignty to the English over lands that the wandering Indians did not, according to the English view of things, rightfully own. War in America was imminent, as indicated by the company's new discourse of conquest. This discourse drew its energizing and legitimating power from the West's ancient mandate to exterminate the radical difference presented to its will to empire by normatively divergent non-Christian peoples and their opposed vision of truth.

The War for America

The Virginia Company's full-scale invasion of America was formally inaugu-rated with the departure from London of Governor Gates's fleet of 800 men, women, and children for Jamestown in May 1609. Another fleet, headed by Lord De La Warr left port in April 1610 with 150 passengers and 3 ships. Sir Thomas Dale, named knight marshal of the colony shortly after his arrival, left England with 300 individuals bound for Jamestown in March 1611. Dale wrote back to London that with 2,000 men released from the jails of England he could easily clear Virginia of Powhatan's people, or at least bring them quickly under English subjection.[107]

Dale's confidence reflected the English belief that a foothold had been firmly established in America. In 1613, Pocahontas was kidnapped and a truce arranged with Powhatan by her marriage to a colonist, John Rolfe, the following year. This time, peace was arranged on the colonists' terms. The Tidewater Indians saw that the English settlers, arriving at Jamestown at regular intervals and in increasing numbers, always came well armed and provisioned.

In 1616, a new promotional device was developed to encourage faster and more populous settlement of the Virgnia wilderness. In addition to the normal land dividend paid to shareholders by the company, an additional allowance of 50 acres was granted for every person transported to the colony. Dividends could also be pooled for larger grants of land. Subsidiary joint-stock compa-nies were formed to take advantage of the pooling concept. In 1618, the company provided a grant of 50 acres for every individual who migrated at his own cost. An act establishing a representative assembly for the colonists was passed by the company in the same year. These inducements worked their intended effect. In April 1618, the English population of Virginia had stood at approximately 400 persons. By the end of the year, it was 1,000. Between the spring of 1619 and the summer of 1620, 1,261 persons migrated to Virginia, more than two-thirds of this group at the charge of the company, now under the aggressive leadership of Sir Edwin Sandys.[108]

The numbers do not tell the whole story. The company itself claimed that between 1619 and 1621, 3,570 people had been sent to Virginia in 42 ships.[109]

Despite the success of the promotional efforts in London, however, large numbers of disappointed colonists returned home after spending only a few years in the colony. In March 1621, for instance, the population of the colony stood at around 840, down from the 1,000 of two years before. In the final months of 1621, however, that population of 840 was nearly doubled with the arrival of 800 settlers aboard 9 ships. Like the boatloads before them, this group of colonists pushed the borders of the English settlement farther and farther into Indian territory, into the dominions of tribes who had up to this point remained at peace in preference to warring with the heavily armed usurpers. Besides, trade with the English had been vigorous, and the tribal members who were traders in the surrounding tribes, like any other good merchants, preferred peace to war. Because of their material wealth in a society where influence accrued to individuals who could afford largesse, they had most likely been in part responsible for maintaining the peace.

The Emperor Opechancanough

The death of Powhatan in 1618 resulted in the eventual succession to the head of the confederacy of his more militant brother, Opechancanough. Opechancanough, who ten years earlier had captured John Smith and advocated his execution,[110] had consistently demonstrated contempt for and distrust of the English usurpers. The relative peace of the first decade of English settlement under his brother had not been to Opechancanough's liking. As new head of the confederacy, he committed himself to maintaining a confrontational posture toward the intruders. The new emperor first made frequent challenges and threats to the newly arrived governor of the colony, George Yeardley. He appeared particularly threatening in his complaints against English depredations and assaults against his subjects. In July 1619, for example, Opechancanough's irritation at a Captain Martin was communicated to the General Assembly of the colony. Martin, it was alleged, had sent out a small boat ("shallop") to trade for desperately needed corn. The shallop met with

a Canoe coming out of a creek where their shallop could not go. For the Indians refusing to sell their corn, those of the shallop entered the canoe with their arms and took it by force, measuring out the corn with a basket . . . and . . . giving them satisfaction in copper beads and other trucking stuff.[111]

Yeardley and the colony's legislature took very seriously Opechancanough's demands for justice regarding this offense. Because "such outrages as this might breed danger and loss of life to others of the colony which should have leave to trade in the bay hereafter, and for prevention of the like violences against the Indians," an order was issued requesting Captain Martin to appear before the Virginia assembly and answer the chief's accusation.[112] In less than a week, the assembly passed several laws regulating Indian trade and intercourse, the first such extensive code of laws enacted in Virginia. All but servants were free to "trade with the Indians," but "no man shall purposely go to any Indian towns, habitations or resorts" without the governor's permission. The penalty for breach of this particular ordinance was 40 shillings.[113]

A licensing system was also instituted for those who sought to trade by boat with the Indians in the bay. Security had to be pledged so that no licensed bay trader would "force or wrong the Indians."[114] The legislation also declared that "he that shall take away by violence or stealth any canoes or other things from the Indians shall make valuable restitution to the said Indians, and shall forfeit, if he be a freeholder, five pound; if a servant, 40 s[hillings], or endure a whipping."[115]

During this same period, significant restrictions on the types of goods that could be traded to the Indians were also codified by the colony. No "English dog of quality" could be sold to the Indians, "upon pain of forfeiting 5 s[hillings] sterling." The sale of guns, shot, powder, and any other arms to an Indian savage was declared a treasonous, capital offense "without all redemption."[116]

Barkham's Case

In November 1619 an agitated Yeardley wrote to London that the new Indian emperor refused to enter into a "treaty" with the council. The belligerent Opechancanough "stood aloof" from the colonists' blandishments, notwithstanding all the governor's "Art and endeaver."[117] Opechancanough's strategy of resistance to English injustices and appeasements alike produced at least one other significant concession from Yeardley. In a desperate effort to placate the emperor, Yeardley had apparently agreed sometime during 1620 or 1621 that any future grants to colonists of lands lying outward from English settlements and claimed by the emperor's confederacy had to be approved by Opechancanough. English encroachments on outlying confederacy territory had been one of Opechancanough's most frequently voiced complaints.[118] Yeardley, the official closest to the situation and most familiar with the emperor's disposition and military capacities, was acting prudently in seeking to ensure the safety of any future English grantees in the regions claimed by the confederacy.

The company in London discovered this innovation in land-patenting procedures when a Mr. Barkham appeared before it with a grant from Governor Yeardley. The grant was for certain lands in Virginia lying to the north of the Jamestown settlement "upon condition that he [Barkham] compounded for the same with Opachankano and procured a confirmation thereof from the company."[119] Barkham had obtained Opechancanough's consent, fulfilling Yeardley's condition, and had apparently traveled to England for final confirmation of his deed. The entire transaction greatly troubled the Virginia Company in London, which was now being asked to recognize a savage emperor's authority to control the company's land sales. The company sat as a court in *Barkham's Case*, exercising Crown-created jurisdictional powers over lands within its royal grant.[120] Barkham's petition for confirmation of his deed presented, in essence, the first significant legal case that directly addressed the legal question of the American Indians' rights and status in the lands of America under English colonial law.

As far as the company was concerned, Yeardley's making the grant to Barkham conditional on the savage Opechancanough's permission raised several troublesome issues. As Lord Coke had recognized in *Calvin's Case*,[121] the king's prerogative powers in infidel lands were acquired by right of conquest. Once the infidels were conquered by the king, their laws were immediately abrogated, for those laws, according to the familiar cadences of English colonizing legal discourse, were presumed to be in violation of the laws of God and nature. Any rights the company possessed to grant lands in America, therefore, had to derive from the king's prerogative powers of conquest assigned to the Virginia Company under the king's charter.

But the company, much to its chagrin, had repeatedly failed to bring the king's perpetual infidel enemies in Virginia under subjection. Accordingly, the first problem the Virginia Company was required to confront in *Barkham's Case* was the fact that the king's inchoate prerogative rights in America had not yet formally vested by right of conquest.

The medievally derived presumptions of diminished infidel status and rights embedded in English colonizing legal discourse seemingly could not overcome the New World reality presented by *Barkham's Case*: the savage Opechancanough was a belligerent, effective, and unsubdued military foe challenging the English Crown's asserted rights to the "savage"-held lands of infidel America. But the very term "sovereignty" in English legal discourse gave the company a possible avenue of conceptual escape. The king, by charter, had assigned his prerogative rights as English sovereign to the company to conquer his perpetual enemies and acquire dominion over their lands. In essence, the company had been authorized to extend English sovereignty over America. There was no room in this Crusading-era-derived feudal paradigm of infidel conquest for a competing sovereignty in an unconquered savage ruler. As Coke had declared in *Calvin's Case*,[122] the infidels' laws, and thus their authority as exercised through those laws, were presumed to be contrary to the law of God and nature. To acknowledge a sovereignty in Opechancanough to interpose its weight in the English land-acquisition process in America would mean that Englishmen had come under the authority of a heathen savage whose laws were contrary to those of God and nature. Accordingly, the competing "sovereignty" of the savage was no sovereignty at all, as it was illegitimate under natural law. The savage might indeed assert rights in American lands. The English might, therefore, be initially required to acknowledge the savage's effective occupancy until the English presence had sufficient military reinforcement. But in English colonizing legal theory a savage could never validly exercise sovereignty over land, for sovereignty, by its very definition, was a power recognized to exist only in civilized peoples whose laws conformed with the laws of God and nature.

The Virginia Company first ruled that Yeardley had overstepped his authority in granting lands without its express prior direction. Any grant made without such prior approval could not be considered "absolute." In this way, the company retained sole authority to rule on any grant made by the governor that it had not first ratified and confirmed. In ruling on Barkham's petition, the court went on to declare that "this grant of Barkham's was held to be very dishonorable and prejudicial to the Company in regard it was limited with a Proviso to compound with Opachankano, whereby a sovereignty in that heathen infidel was acknowledged, and the Company's title [acquired by royal charter] thereby much infringed."[123]

The company's legal decision voiding the *ultra vires* grant and establishing the superior sovereign rights of the English Crown in lands discovered and desired by its subjects in America was declared on July 17, 1622. The Jamestown colony had just celebrated its fifteenth anniversary. By that time, the most fundamental principles of English colonial legal theory respecting Indians and their lands had been settled on as law. The Indians' claim to land in America would be recognized only when it had to be, while they were still in effective possession. But the ultimate "sovereignty" in that land, as far as the English were concerned, could only be in an English king whose subjects had discovered and laid claim to that land, which was possessed not by Christian peoples but by infidels, who lacked all rights and status in English legal colonizing theory.[124] It was thus ruled that no English colonist could compound with the "heathen infidel" for a title to territory within Virginia's chartered bounds.

Acknowledgment of Opechancanough's "competing sovereignty" in the lands of Virginia would have done more than undermine the basic principles of English feudal theory and the king's inchoate prerogative rights of conquest in heathen-held lands discovered by English subjects. In practice, Yeardley's concession would also have meant that the Virginia Company's principal source of revenue would have been subject to a condition precedent whereby the surrounding Indian tribes would determine the colony's rate of expansion, and thereby the company's rate of return on its royally granted charter rights. Indeed, Yeardley's concession was most "prejudicial to the Company," for it would have completely undermined its Crown-granted monopoly over the sale of American lands to English colonists.

The company now clearly recognized that until Opechancanough was in fact brought under submission, its Crown-granted monopoly was worthless. The savage's competing "sovereignty," although illegitimate, effectively blocked English expansion. The presumption of a lack of sovereignty in the infidel emperor thus contained its own imperatives for conquest, for conquest was the only method left for effectuating the king's sovereignty over a savage who would not yield his dominion. This mandate for conquest was the unstated legal corollary of the precedent established by the Virginia Company's ruling in *Barkham's Case*.

The Virginia "Massacre" of 1622

News traveled slowly between Jamestown and London. Shortly after its decision of July 17, 1622, in *Barkham's Case* the company learned that four months earlier, on March 22, Opechancanough had come to a similar conclusion respecting the intractable theoretical problems presented by the competing English and Indian sovereignties asserted in America. He had convinced the confederated Tidewater tribes to launch an all-out assault on the scattered English settlements outside the immediate region of Jamestown. Nearly 350 of the 1,240 colonists died in the coordinated surprise attacks.

The Virginia Company released an "official" account of this "massacre" in the autumn of 1622. It was entitled "A Declaration of the State of the Colony and Affairs in Virginia. With a Relation of the Barbarous Massacre in the Time of Peace and League, Treacherously Executed by the Native Infidels upon the English, the 22 of March Last. Together with the Names of Those Massacred."[125] The list of names of those massacred by the "infidels" gave the precise locations of the attacks.[126] The extent of English penetration into outlying confederacy territory is indicated by the fact that more than twenty individuals were killed "at Captain Berckleys Plantation, seated at the Falling Creek, some 66 miles" from Jamestown. Another dozen were killed at Sheffeild's Plantation 3 miles from Berckley's farm at Falling Creek. The settlements at Henrico Island, 2 miles from Sheffeild's, also suffered casualties.[127] In all, more than thirty of the eighty English settlements along the James River sustained loss of life, an indication of the extensiveness of English settlement, of Opechancanough's careful and deliberate planning, and of the message the imperial savage intended to send.

The author of the company's account of the incident was Edward Waterhouse, a high Calvinist lawyer. From his Puritan perspective, the "greatest cause" of the massacre was the colonists' naive belief in the likelihood of their "speedy winning the savages to civility and religion by kind usage and fair conversing among them."[128] The Indians were hopelessly possessed by the devil:

[T]he true cause of this surprise was most by the instigation of the Devil (enemy to their salvation) and the daily fear that possessed them, that in time we by our growing continually upon them, would dispossess them of this country, as they had been formerly of the West Indies by the Spaniard.[129]

According to Waterhouse, the Indians' fears of dispossession were unjustified, as were the hopes of the colonists that the Indians would be converted by good works. Waterhouse reminded his audience that Calvin had taught that faith, not works, was alone sufficient for conversion. God, inscrutable to humans and not bound by the laws of nature, would effect the conversion of the savages "in His good time, and by such means as we think most unlikely."[130] In other words, God's mysterious providence absolved the company of its responsibility to plant the seed of faith among the heathen, as mandated by its royal charter.

In the meantime, until the God of Mr. Calvin so moved, the English were now free to wage war on the "wicked infidels." The Indians of Virginia had in fact now become the presumed perpetual enemies of *Calvin's Case*, at constant war with the king and his instrument of American crusade, the Virginia Company. The savages' treachery demanded an appropriate response:

[O]ur hands which before were tied with gentleness and fair usage, are now set at liberty by the treacherous violence of the savages, not untying the knot, but cutting it: So that we, who hitherto have had possession of no more ground than their waste, and our purchase at a valuable consideration to their own contentment, gained; may now by right of war, and law of nations, invade the country and destroy them who sought to destroy us.[131]

Thus in one sense, explained Waterhouse, the massacre was "for the good of the Plantation. Now their cleared grounds in all their villages (which are situated in the fruitfullest places of the land) shall be inhabited by us, whereas heretofore the grubbing of woods was the greatest labor."[132] Other fortuities arose from the massacre as well:

Because the way of conquering them is much more easy than of civilizing them by fair means, for they are a rude, barbarous, and naked people, scattered in small companies, which are helps to victory, but hinderances to civility: Besides that, a conquest may be of many, and at once; but civility is in particular, and slow, the effect of long time, and great industry.[133]

Backed by Waterhouse's legal analysis, the company declared all-out war against the confederacy on the basis of the Europeans' Law of Nations. Jamestown's governor was instructed from London to set "upon the Indian in all places."[134] All trade with the savages was prohibited. All the prior benign expressions of the civilizing and Christianizing intent of the English toward well-disposed savages were purged from the new legal discursive practice that asserted the company's right of conquest under the Law of Nations.

A Discourse of Conquest

The rapid diffusion of the far more militant and aggressive discourse of American conquest that was inaugurated after Opechancanough's attack on the Jamestown colonists is illustrated by the Puritan preacher Samuel Purchas's publication of *A Discourse on Virginia* in 1625. Purchas's widely circulated account argued that by virtue of Opechancanough's failed war, England now lawfully possessed America by

right natural, right national, right by first discovery, by accepted trade, by possession surrendered voluntarily, continued constantly; right by gift, by birth, by bargain and sale, by cession, by forfeiture in that late damnable treachery and massacre, and the fatal possession taken by so many murdered Englishmen.[135]

True Christians, "such as have the Grace of the spirit of Christ . . . have and hold the world" by a true tenure from the Lord, whereas "Heathens are not capable." They "range rather than inhabite" their "unmanned wild country." Thus they "have only a natural right, by the relics of the Law of Nature left in man." These natural rights, however, had been "confiscated" by reason of their treachery. Such violations of the law of nature and the Law of Nations gave the English a right of "just invasion and conquest." The Indians had become "Outlaws of Humanity," who by their bloody crime against the English had "lost their own natural, and given us another natural right . . . so that England may both by Law of Nature and Nations challenge Virginia for her own peculiar property."[136]

English retaliation against the Virginia Indians under this new, more militant discursive practice was swift and widespread. Numerous Indian villages were destroyed, crops were burned, and a reward was offered for Opechancanough's capture. As historian Nancy Lurie has written, "The tribes were scattered, some far beyond the traditional boundaries of their land, and several of the small groups simply ceased to exist as definable entities."[137]

As late as 1630, the General Assembly at Jamestown ordered "that the war begun upon the Indians be effectively followed, and that no peace be concluded with them." March 22, the anniversary of the massacre, was declared a holy day throughout the colony. Significantly, the holy day was in honor of the colony's "deliverance" from the Indians at the "bloody massacre."[138] The colony had been delivered from any misconceived notions that peace with the infidels was preferable to wars of conquest and more easily acquired lands.

Opechancanough attempted another uprising in 1644. Apparently he had heard of the revolt in England by the Puritans against the tyrannous Stuart king and had concluded "that now was his time, or never, to root out the English."[139] As many as 500 English were killed in this second revolt. The Virginia Indians indeed became the perpetual enemies of the English. The Virginia General Assembly issued the following proclamation:

Whereas the Indians have justly made themselves our irreconcilable enemies by the late bloody massacre . . . Be it therefore by this recent Grand Assembly recorded to posterity. That we will forever abandon all forms of peace and familiarity with the whole Nation and will to the utmost of our power pursue and root out those which have anyway had their hands in the shedding of our blood and massacring of our people."[140]

The English succeeded in their counterattack on Opechancanough's forces, capturing the emperor himself in 1646. He was brought to Jamestown and fatally shot in the back by an unnamed soldier before he could be deported to England for trial.

Immediately after Opechancanough's death, a treaty was signed by his successor, Necotowance. The new chief ceded most of the confederacy's remaining lands to the English by right of conquest (the king's inchoate rights having been finally perfected by the company), reserving only the area north of the River York, which was declared Indian territory. There the tribes would be able to live and hunt without interference from the English. Necotowance was required to acknowledge that his people held this reservation (which was subsequently reduced by continual English "adjustments" to the treaty) from the "King's Majesty of England."[141]

Four decades after the king's issuance of the Virginia Company's North American charter of conquest, the infidel savages who had resisted the establishment of the Jamestown colony had been brought under the yoke of English "sovereignty." That sovereignty was accompanied by a discourse of conquest that interpreted Indian resistance to English hegemony as irrational delusion, punishable under the laws of God and nature and nations. English conquest and subjugation of the perpetual infidel enemy had proved the most effective instrument of empire—the path of least resistance to the Indians' acceptance of England's superior claim to the underutilized wilderness of America.

The English war for America was launched by an invasion of power and law. King Henry VII's 1497 patent to John Cabot to discover and conquer infidel-

and heathen-occupied lands "unknown to all Christians,"[142] Sir Humphrey Gilbert's promulgation of the first English laws in the New World declared at St. John's Harbor in Newfoundland in 1583,[143] and the Virginia Company's 1622 decision in *Barkham's Case*, which denied a competing "sovereignty" in the heathen emperor Opechancanough[144] represent several instances among innumerable others in which law and legal discourse were called on to serve power and England's will to empire.

In its period of emergence during the Elizabethan era, English colonizing thought and discourse had first regarded the Indians of the New World as supplements to England's will to empire. The Indians were to be trading partners, converts, and allies in radical Protestantism's rivalry with papist Spain.

In the initial period of contact in the Virginia colony, when the English had not yet secured the favorable position in the balance of power between the two races, law and legal discourse were relied on frequently as instruments of constraint. One of the Virginia Company's first legal actions in the New World, the crowning of the Indian emperor Powhatan, sought to impose the feudal discourse of lord and vassal on the English–Indian relationship as a means of more effectively securing imperial goals. Lands were purchased by arms-length legal transactions from Powhatan's tributary tribes. Trading laws and prohibitions were promulgated that sought to prevent abuses of the Indians or transfers of technology detrimental to the long-term interests of the colony.[145]

When the Indians were finally forced to reject their supplementary status and resist further English encroachments, the medievally derived presumptions of English feudal law and discourse denying sovereignty to infidels proved extremely useful in legitimating and energizing England's war against the Virginia tribes. Presuming the savage Indians' lack of rational capacity and condemning their normatively deficient use of the "unmanned wild country" of America,[146] English colonizing discourse emerged in the early seventeenth century as a most potent instrument of empire. England, by "right natural,"[147] held the superior sovereignty over the lands occupied by the American Indian.

This discourse of conquest was confirmed by the English Crown itself in 1632, in an answer to a remonstrance of the Dutch ambassadors protesting the English seizure of a Dutch West India Company ship.[148] According to the Dutch complaint, the company's ship, "laden with petries, etc.," was seized by the English on its return to Europe from North America. This act was "contrary to all right and reason," according to the Dutch. England could not prevent Dutch subjects from trading in New World countries still occupied and possessed by Indian tribes. Further, the Dutch had entered into "confederation" with the tribes of New Netherland and had bought properties in the Indians' country. The English seizure violated the Law of Nations guaranteeing "the freedom of trade by sea, and alliances with distant nations, who are not, naturally, the subjects, nor have become the property, of any other person, by conquest."[149]

The English Crown's reply to the Dutch remonstrance simply reiterated the themes perfected and deployed by England's colonizing agents in their war for

America with the Indians.[150] The Dutch had "usurped" lands in the New World under the lawful sovereignty of England. As for the claim that these lands had been "acquired from the natives of the country,"[151] the Crown flatly denied

that the Indians were *possessores bonae fidei* of those countries, so as to be able to dispose of them either by sale or donation, their residences being unsettled and uncertain, and only being in common; and in the second place, it cannot be proved, *de facto*, that all the Natives of said country had contracted with them at the said pretended sale.

And so to what they say in addition, that the said Natives have their residences around them, the truth is, that the English encompass them on the one side and other, as they well experienced heretofore when they attempted to maintain their right against them. But, moreover, the right his Majesty's subjects have in that country, is justified by first discovery, occupation and the possession which they have taken thereof, and by the concessions and letters patents they have had from our Sovereigns, who were, for the above reasons, the true and legitimate proprietors thereof in those parts.[152]

Thus the basic themes of English colonizing discourse were determined within a few decades of the English invasion of America. The Indian was in continual violation of natural law and the Law of Nations and possessed no rights that civilized English monarchs or subjects were bound to recognize. As "Outlaws of Humanity," Indians could be dispossessed of the lands they claimed by a race of cultivators destined by Providence to plant the seeds of a superior civilization in the New World. These grounding themes of the discourse of conquest descending from the early-seventeenth-century English war for America provided a firm and self-assured foundation for pursuit of the English will to empire in the New World through the American Revolutionary era. Just as important, these themes provided a vital legacy for those English-Americans to whom, by virtue of their rebellion against the English Crown, devolved the mandate to civilize the Indian's wild country.

NOTES

1. On Gentili's life and career, *see* C. Phillipson, "Introduction," in A. Gentili, *De jure belli libri tres* 9a–15a (J. Rolfe trans. 1964). *See also* G. van der Molen, *Alberico Gentili and the Development of International Law* 1–63 (1968).

2. *See* Chapter 4, text accompanying notes 124–25, *supra*.

3. *See* A. Gentili, *supra* note 1.

4. *See* Chapter 4, text accompanying notes 89–102, *supra*.

5. *See* A. Gentili, *supra* note 1, at 18A.

6. On Victoria's contribution, *see* Chapter 2, text accompanying notes 133–87, *supra*.

7. Gentili, *supra* note 1, at 18A.

8. *See*, e.g., *id.* at 39, where Gentili cited "the learned Victoria" in support of the argument that war should not be waged for religious motives.

9. *Id.* at 122.

10. *See* Chapter 1, note 10, *supra*.

11. A. Gentili, *supra* note 1, at 122.

12. *See* Chapter 2, text accompanying notes 174–77, *supra*.

13. *See* Chapter 1, text accompanying notes 101–8, *supra*.

14. A. Gentili, *supra* note 1, at 123. Throughout his texts, in fact, Gentili sought to make a clear distinction between wars waged on the basis of natural law and wars waged on behalf of religion.

He argued, for instance, that religion "is a matter of the mind and of the will, which is always accompanied by freedom" (*id.* at 39). Therefore, religion should never be forced on individuals against their will, including infidel peoples at peace with Christian nations, so long as their divergent religious practices did not involve the murder of innocents. *Id.* at 38–41.

15. *See* sources cited notes 12–13, *supra*.

16. A. Gentili, *supra* note 1, at 40.

17. *Id.*

18. *Id.* at 41. In the same chapter, Gentili declared flatly that "war is not lawful against infidels who live at peace with us and do us no harm" (*id.* at 39). Gentili selectively cited both Victoria and Innocent IV approvingly on this point, although both these Catholic theorists had argued that idolatry, standing alone, justified war against infidel peoples. *See* sources cited notes 12–13, *supra*.

19. *Id.* at 123.

20. Mark 16:15.

21. Gentili, *supra* note 1, at 123.

22. *Id.* "I cannot approve Innocent . . . who . . . say[s] that love of God is a just cause of war against the infidels" (*id.*).

23. *Id.* at 124.

24. *Id.* at 125.

25. *Id.*

26. *See id.* at 340–48.

27. *Id.* at 341. Gentili cited approvingly the example of the Hungarians, who were conquered and made Christians, educated to civilization and commerce, "and trained to the other usages which are demanded by the laws of nature, of nations, and of the state, but which before were wholly unknown to them" (*id.*).

28. *Id.* at 342. "[R]eligion comes from nature," Gentili asserted, adding that heaven and earth put religion into people's hearts. Gentili pointed to Thomas More's influential text *Utopia*, which had spoken about a world in a pristine state of nature, where "every religion should be tolerated, except one which is contrary to nature" (*id.*).

29. *Id.*

30.

Man should have no question as to what is due to a superior being or whether he ought to worship God. . . . Atheists and men devoid of religion are worse than Epicureans, since the Epicureans recognized and venerated God, although they believed that he had no interest in human affairs [Gentili's probable definition of God's "providence"]. They believe that the superior nature of the deity ought to be honored. But the Epicureans in their turn are not to be endured, since they seem to accept God in their words but to deny him by their acts. [*Id.*]

31. *Id.* Gentili urged that the conqueror should instead, if feasible, gradually attempt to effect a transition in the religious rites of a conquered people in thrall to the perverse religion of their ancestors.

32. *Calvin's Case* 77 Eng. Rep. 377, 378 (1608).

33. *Id.*

34. Sir Edward Coke, who performed many roles throughout his public life of knowledge and power—lawyer, speaker of the House of Commons, attorney general, lord chief justice—began publishing his *Law Reports* in 1600. His efforts at retrieval of precedents and case law from a prior, largely undifferentiated legal corpus were described by T. F. T. Plucknett: "Urged by a presentiment of the coming conflict of Crown and Parliament, he felt the necessity of curbing the rising arrogance of both, and looked back upon his country's history to find the means . . . . a fundamental law which limited Crown and Parliament indifferently" (T. F. T. Plucknett, 14 *Studies in English Legal History* 30–31 [1983]). *And see* C. Hill, "Sir Edward Coke—Myth-Maker," *Intellectual Origins of the English Revolution* 225–65 (1965). *See also* C. Bowen, *The Lion and the Throne* (1957).

35. *Id.* at 397.

36. *Id.*

37. *See* sources cited, *supra* note 34.

38. *Id.*

39. *Id.* Increasing English mercantile trade with non-Christian nations led later English courts to question and erode the authority of Coke's opinion in *Calvin's Case. See*, e.g., *Omichund v. Barker*, 18 Geo. II (Ch. 538 [1744]), and the discussion of *Campbell v. Hall*, Chapter 7, text accompanying notes 53–72, *infra.*

40. *Calvin's Case*, 77 Eng. Rep. 377, 397 (1608).

41. *Campbell v. Hall*, discussed *infra.*

42. A Gentili, *supra* note 1, at 341.

43. H. C. Porter, *The Inconstant Savage* 275–79 (1979).

44. *See* "The First Charter of Virginia," in *Documents of American History* 8–10 (H. S. Commager 8th ed. 1968) [hereinafter cited as H. S. Commager].

45. *Id.* at 8.

46. F. Maitland, "English Law and the Renaissance," *Select Essays in Anglo-American Legal History* 203 (1907).

47. *See* H. S. Commager, *supra* note 44, at 8–10.

48. *See* The Records of the Virginia Company of London, vol. 3: *A Justification for Planting Virginia* 1–3 (S. M. Kingsbury ed. 1933).

49. *Id.* at 1.

50. *Id.*

51. *Id.* at 1–2.

52. *Id.* at 2.

53. *Id.*

54. *Id.* at 2–3.

55. *Id.*

56. *Id.* at 3.

57. *Id.*

58. *Id.*

59. *See* text accompanying notes 38–39, *supra.*

60. *The Jamestown Voyages Under the First Charter 1606–1609* 118 (P. L. Barbour ed. 1969) [hereinafter cited as *JV*].

61. *Id.*

62. *Id.*

63. *Id.* at 121.

64. *Id.* at 118, 121, n. 1.

65. *Id.* at 121–22.

66. *Id.* at 50.

67. *Id.* at 51.

68. *Id.* at 52.

69. N. Lurie, "Indian Cultural Adjustment to European Civilization," in *Seventeenth Century America* 44 (J. Smith ed. 1959).

70. W. Craven, *The Southern Colonies in the Seventeenth Century 1607–1689* 79 (1949).

71. H. C. Porter, *supra* note 43, at 287–92.

72. N. Lurie, *supra* note 69, at 40–49.

73. W. Craven, *supra* note 70, at 80.

74. "Captain John Smith's Summary: A Map of Virginia," in *JV*, *supra* note 60, at 413.

75. *Id.* at 414.

76. *See* text accompanying note 74, *supra.*

77. *JV*, *supra* note 60, at 414.

78. H. C. Porter, *supra* note 43, 296.

79. *JV*, *supra* note 60, at 440.

80. *Id.* at 369.

81. Reprinted in H. S. Commager, *supra* note 44, at 10–12.

82. F. Maitland, *supra* note 46.

83. H. C. Porter, *supra* note 43, at 303–5.

84. *See* "Instructions from the Virginia Council in London Advocating Christian Conversion of

the Indians, Tributory Status for Powhaton, and Agreement with His Enemies," in *Early American Indian Documents: Treaties and Laws, 1607–1789*, vol. 4: *Virginia Treaties, 1607–1722* 6–8 (W. S. Robinson ed., Alden T. Vaughan gen. ed. 1983).

85. *Id.* at 6.
86. *Id.*
87. *Id.* at 6–7.
88. *See* sources cited notes 12–13, *supra.*
89. "Instructions," *supra* note 85, at 7.
90. H. C. Porter, *supra* note 43, at 340.
91. *Id.* at 354.
92. *See* text accompanying note 74, *supra.*
93. H. C. Porter, *supra* note 43, at 356.
94. *Id.*
95. *Id.*
96. *See* text accompanying notes 3–31, *supra.*
97. *See* text accompanying note 9, *supra.*
98. *See* A. Gentili, *supra* note 1, at 41.
99. H. C. Porter, *supra* note 43, at 357.
100. *See* "Captain John Smith's Summary: A Map of Virginia," in *JV, supra* note 60, at 371.
101. 4 *Tracts and Other Papers Relating Principally to the Origin, Settlement, and Progress of the Colonies in North America from the Discovery of the Country to 1776* 3–27 (P. Force ed. 1947) [hereinafter cited as *Tracts Relating to the Colonies*].
102. H. C. Porter, *supra* note 43, at 357.
103. *Tracts Relating to the Colonies, supra* note 101.
104. *See* Chapter 3, text accompanying notes 61–112, *supra.*
105. *Tracts Relating to the Colonies, supra* note 101, at 6–7.
106. *See* text accompanying notes 48–58, *supra.*
107. W. Craven, *supra* note 70, at 104.
108. *Id.* at 139.
109. H. C. Porter, *supra* note 43, at 458.
110. *See* text accompanying notes 71–72, *supra.*
111. 3 *The Records of the Virginia Company, supra* note 48, at 157.
112. *Id.* at 157–58.
113. *Id.* at 170–71.
114. *Id.* at 172–73.
115. *Id.* at 172.
116. *Id.* at 170–71.
117. *Id.* at 228.
118. *See* N.Lurie, *supra* note 69, at 49–50.
119. "Denial by the Virginia Company in London of the Sovereign Rights of the Indians in the Land," in 4 *Early American Indian Documents, supra* note 84, at 28.
120. *See* "Introduction" to 1 *The Records of the Virginia Company, supra* note 48, at 71–87.
121. *See* text accompanying notes 38–39, *supra.*
122. *See id.*
123. *See* 4 *Early American Indian Documents, supra* note 84, at 28.
124. *See* text accompanying notes 34–41, *supra.*
125. *See* 3 *The Records of the Virginia Company, supra* note 48, at 541–71.
126. *Id.* at 565–71.
127. *Id.*
128. *Id.* at 553.
129. *Id.* at 556.
130. *Id.* at 553–54.
131. *Id.* at 556.
132. *Id.* at 556–57.
133. *Id.* at 457.

134. H. C. Porter, *supra* note 43, at 468.

135. In S. Purchas, 19 *Hakluytus Posthumus or Purchas His Pilgrimes* 219 (1906).

136. *Id.* at 219–25.

137. N. Lurie, *supra* note 69, at 50.

138. H. C. Porter, *supra* note 43, at 513.

139. *Id.* at 515.

140. "Perpetual War Declared by Colony After Massacre of 1644," in 4 *Early American Indian Documents, supra* note 84, at 63.

141. "Treaty of Peace with Necotowance, King of the Indians" (1646), in *id.* at 67–70.

142. *See* Chapter 3, text accompanying notes 1–5, *supra.*

143. *See* Chapter 4, text accompanying notes 69–70, *supra.*

144. *See* Chapter 5, text accompanying notes 116–24, *supra.*

145. *See* Chapter 5, text accompanying notes 111–16, *supra.*

146. *See* Chapter 5, text accompanying note 136, *supra.*

147. *See* text accompanying note 135, *supra.*

148. *See* "English Answer to the Remonstrance of the Dutch Ambassadors," in *Early American Indian Documents: Treaties and Laws, 1607–1789*, vol. 7: *New York and New Jersey Treaties, 1609–1682* 31–32 (B. Graymont ed., A. T. Vaughan gen. ed. 1985).

149. *See* "West India Company to the States General: The Dutch Define Indian Land Ownership," in 7 *Early American Indian Documents, supra* note 148, at 30–31.

150. *See* 7 *Early American Indian Documents, supra* note 148, at 31–32.

151. *Id.* at 31.

152. *Id.* at 31–32.

Part III

The Norman Yoke: The American Indian and the Settling of United States Colonizing Legal Theory

The radical colonists of the Revolutionary era who constructed the discourses of opposition to British power in America liked to think of themselves as descended from the noble blood of the ancient Saxon race. The ancient Saxons' word for "law" was *lagu*, meaning things laid down or settled. If by "law" the Saxons' descendants who colonized North America meant all the rules of conduct established and enforced by the authority, legislation, or custom of a community or state, or if by "law" they meant the condition existing when obedience to such rules is general, then there was no "law" as the radicals of the American Revolution understood that term in their dealings with the frontier Indian tribes.[1]

On the receding boundary of the eighteenth-century colonial frontier, where the North American Indian tribal confederacies and nations confronted, resisted, or accommodated the British invaders, nothing was *settled* or *laid down*. All was either war or politics (the art of war carried on by other means).[2] The expedient pursuit of interest on the frontier—by military arms or by diplomatic art, by economic aggression or by fraudulent inducement—erupted in an effusion of competing discourses, numberless strategic actuations of themes, a random dispersal of statements. But no "law" could be laid down for that emerging discursive formation that was the American wilderness during the Revolutionary era.

British imperial policy for the North American frontier following the empire's victory in the French and Indian War (1754–1763) was certain to incite the resistance of a race of men who preached the canonical integrity of the view that government existed solely for the preservation of life, liberty, and estate—

or what John Locke called by the more general name *property*.³ Since the inauguration of their colonizing enterprises in North America, English Americans had administered their colonies' Indian affairs largely according to their own interests and desires. With respect to acquisition of Indian lands, the colonists had translated the presumptions of early-seventeenth-century English colonizing discourse denying territorial sovereignty to tribal savages into practices that inevitably resulted in frequent wars, outright confiscation, coerced and fraudulent purchases, and dispossession of most of the choice tribal lands to the east of the Allegheny and Appalachian mountains.

The French and Indian War had erupted, in part, because of the frontier tribes' fears of continuing English American encroachments on the hunting grounds beyond the eastern mountain ranges. During the war, the government in London recognized that the colonists' unregulated pursuit of Indian lands was harmful to imperial interests, and prohibited white settlement on the western frontier as the price for Indian alliances against France. After the war, imperial policymakers decided to continue this plan of Indian appeasement by prohibiting white expansion. Seeking to constrain the colonists' predatory pursuit of landed wealth and to prevent costly Indian hostilities, which might threaten the security of the Crown's North American possessions, the royal government in London promulgated King George III's Proclamation of 1763. It declared the territory beyond the eastern mountain ranges reserved to the Indian tribes of the region. This radical departure from past imperial policy of relative indifference toward relations between Indians and colonists, in effect, placed the imperial government in the anomalous position of preventing the English Americans' pursuit of property on the frontier.

The proclamation, and particularly the subsequently announced Stamp Act, the related financing vehicle for maintaining British garrisons on the frontier, therefore, threatened in a direct and most odiously regarded fashion the colonists' own vision of what America and what the government of America ought to resemble. To radical colonists especially, America was envisioned as a New World of abundant and cheap land free of feudal constraints and governed according to the revered, natural-law-inspired principles of an ancient, defeudalized Saxon constitution. The proclamation, Stamp Act, and other dangerously regarded imperial initiatives of the Revolutionary era thus appeared to the radical colonists to be direct threats to their natural-law rights of life, liberty, and estate, for the British imperial government appeared obsessively focused on seizing the property of British Americans. The tyranny of a government devoted to destroying individual property, rather than rightfully preserving it, demanded the fiercest resistance.

In constructing their discourses of resistance to British power in America, radical colonists appropriated themes and concepts from an eclectic array of sources. The Enlightenment-era discourses of natural law and rights; the British Constitution; the mythology of a purer Saxon-inspired legal and political order in the New World freed from the yoke of Norman-derived feudal tyranny; and especially the common-sense view of property as acquired by labor and governments as established to protect property found in the texts of

John Locke—these are some of the most frequently raided discursive formations. What emerged from the discursive chaos of the Revolutionary era was a vision radically opposed to London's view of the law that ought to govern America; it rejected in particular the assertion of the Crown's prerogative power to control the pace and direction of the colonists' acquisition of property on the Indian frontier.

Thus the colonists of the Revolutionary era were required to confront directly the imperial government's legal discourse of Indian status and rights, for the Crown's assertions of prerogative power on the frontier were legitimated by the Norman-derived feudal doctrine of conquest over infidel-held lands. By the middle decades of the eighteenth century, British imperial policymakers had perfected the utilitarian aggrandizing thematics of English colonizing discourse of the early seventeenth century into a pragmatic management tool for Indian policy on the American frontier. Prior justifications for seizing what the English regarded as underutilized "waste" lands from savage tribes had been translated into a subtly articulated, self-interested discourse of empire. This imperial discourse stressed the expediency of maintaining, above all, peaceful relations with the powerful Indian tribes and confederacies of the frontier. As reflected in the Proclamation of 1763, this imperial discourse accepted the necessity of peaceful purchase of frontier Indian lands under strict imperial supervision in order to avoid costly, needless wars. Despite this pragmatic approach to Indian affairs, imperial policy ultimately rested on the ancient legitimating foundations of the superior rights of Christian Europeans in lands held by normatively divergent, non-Christian peoples. The English Crown, by virtue of English discovery of the infidel-occupied lands of North America, asserted the feudally derived prerogative rights of conquest over North America. This Doctrine of Discovery vested in the Crown inchoate rights of conquest and ultimate title to infidel-held territories not yet granted to English American subjects. Thus while imperial policy of the eighteenth century recognized the Indian tribes' rights of occupancy over their lands, under the legal discourse of the proclamation that right was a diminished one. The Crown held the superior sovereign interest in their lands by virtue of "discovery." The Indians could not sell their right of occupancy to whomever they chose. The right could be extinguished only by the Crown's actual conquest of the lands or, preferably, by authorized purchase from the Indians (who always sold cheap).

The colonists, who intensely desired the lands occupied by the tribes, denied the validity of the proclamation's status as settled law and its attempted frustration of their right to pursue Indian lands. On the eve of the Revolution, a profusion of discourses erupted that challenged the Crown's feudalized legal discourse of prerogative power over American lands, as speculative-minded colonists fanned out across the frontier to negotiate direct purchases of large tracts from the Indian tribes. The radicals of the Revolutionary era rejected flatly the proposition that an English king could deny them their right to purchase lands from the frontier Indians. George Washington, the radical eventually selected to lead the new Revolutionary government, was an avid speculator in Indian lands. He directed his surveyor to violate the proclamation because he desired some "good rich land" on the western frontier. He certainly spoke for his constituency when he declared the proclamation "a temporary expedient to quiet the minds of the Indians."[4] But this was virtually the only point of consensus among the radicals, who, despite their unified rejection of the king's feudal prerogative of rights of discovery and conquest over Indian lands, could not agree on the law that ought to govern their pursuit of wealth and power on the frontier.

Virginia claimed the rights to virtually the entire territory beyond the Appalachian Mountains under its vaguely drawn 1609 colonial charter from the Crown (this was the Jamestown colonizing charter issued by James I to the Virginia Company of London).[5] Virginia's speculators were thus provided with a legal head start toward their efforts at acquiring land on the colonial frontier. Virginians, like other colonists from the "landed" colonies with charter claims to the West, deployed a discursive strategy throughout the Revolutionary era that was designed to support their colony's legal right to patent and perfect the land claims of its citizens in the West without the royal proclamation's interference.

The speculators from the "landless" colonies, such as Pennsylvania and Maryland, with no charter claims in the West, naturally found themselves in disagreement with Virginia's and the other "landed" colonies' reasoning on the law governing land purchases from Indian tribes. They could not bring themselves to accept a form of legal discourse that was only slightly less offensive to common sense than the Crown's feudally derived claims of the prerogatives of a fictively claimed conquest of the Indian frontier. Defying the Crown's and the landed colonies' claims to the West, the speculators from the landless colonies swarmed the frontier, purchasing lands directly from the Indians without the sanction of either the Crown or Virginia and the other landed colonies.

It was from within the Revolutionary era's erupting profusion of self-interested discourses that the radicals who cared most about the lands on the Indian frontier debated the legal status and rights of American Indian tribes in those lands. Those who stood to gain the most from a recognition of the Indians' ability to sell their lands to whomever they pleased urged the most radical extension of the liberatory thematics of the colonists' discourses of resistance. The speculators from the landless states with interests purchased directly from the tribes urged the new nation's Congress to recognize the Indians' natural-law right to sell the lands they occupied to white land speculators. They asked Congress to affirm their Revolutionary-era frontier Indian grants. In contrast, the speculators from the landed states, who stood to gain the most from a recognition of their states' rights to prohibit direct purchases from the Indians without state sanction, preferred the thematics of an ancient colonizing legal discourse holding that as "infidels, heathens, and savages," the Indians did not possess the prerogatives belonging to European-derived sovereign powers in the lands of America. Indians could not sell their lands to whomever they pleased. The state with the original Crown charter claim to the lands possessed the right to control the Indian frontier.

The discursive conflict over who was going to control the disposition of the Indian frontier was one of the most divisive issues faced by the Founders in constructing the United States. The conflict was finally resolved only by a political compromise agreed on by the Founders for the good of the new nation. This provided for the cession of frontier claims by the "landed" states to a federal sovereign claiming exclusive rights to extinguish Indian occupancy claims by purchase or conquest.

The Founders' compromise thus necessarily settled the legal status and rights of the American Indian in United States law. Whatever theoretical natural-law rights to sovereignty the Indians might have possessed over the lands they occupied were denied by a political compromise vesting the United States with a superior title and interest in the lands of the western frontier. The "public good," as the Founders came to understand that term in the Revolutionary era, did not require the recognition of the Indians' natural-law rights in the lands of America.

This Revolutionary political-era compromise denying the American Indians natural-law rights to the lands they had occupied since time immemorial and vesting the superior title to those lands in a European-derived government is embodied in Chief Justice John Marshall's opinion in the case of *Johnson v. McIntosh*.[6] This 1823 Supreme Court opinion is regarded as the textual source of the basic principles of modern federal Indian law, but its acceptance of the Doctrine of Discovery and its denial of territorial sovereignty to American Indian nations actually represents a point of closure, not a point of origin, in United States colonizing discourse.

Johnson was the long-delayed day in court of the successors in interest to a group of frontier land speculators from the "landless" states who had purchased large tracts directly from western Indian tribes during the Revolutionary era. The political compromise of the Founders nearly four decades before the *Johnson* litigation had therefore not only sacrificed Indian landed interests to the public good. The landless states' speculators had suffered as well when the Revolutionary-era Congress had refused to recognize the Indians' natural-law right to sell their lands to whomever they pleased.

Marshall's opinion for a unanimous Supreme Court in *Johnson* asserted that the law of the United States acknowledged the medievally derived doctrine that discovery of infidel-held lands by European nations vested the Europeans with superior title in those lands. Marshall's opinion thus merely formalized the outcome of a political contest that the Founders had fought and resolved among themselves some forty years earlier. The acceptance in *Johnson* of the legal discourse of feudal rights of conquest derived from discovery consecrated the sacrifice of those higher principles that supposedly inhered in the Revolutionary era's radical, natural-law-inspired vision of America as a land free of the oppression and feudal burdens of a Norman yoke. Long before Marshall's formal recognition in *Johnson* of the Doctrine of Discovery as the legitimating foundation for the Europeans' superior rights in the New World, a discourse of conquest, emerging out of a Revolutionary-era vision of the public good that did not include the American Indian, had settled the law of America concerning Indian rights and status.

NOTES

1. The etymology can be found in any standard dictionary. *See*, e.g., *Webster's New World Dictionary* (2d College Ed. 1982).

2. *See* M. Foucault, *Power/Knowledge* 90 (1980).

3. J. Locke, *Two Treatises of Government* 393–96 (1963).

4. Quoted in *This Country Was Ours* 57 (V. Vogel ed. 1972).

5. *See* Chapter 5, text accompanying notes 81–82, *supra*.

6. 21 U.S. (8 Wheat.) 503 (1823). As one pair of scholars note, Marshall's opinion in *Johnson* was "to influence all subsequent thinking" in modern federal Indian law. R. Barsh & J. Henderson, *The Road* 49 (1980). On Marshall's jurisprudential background, *see generally* W. E. Nelson, "The Eighteenth Century Background of John Marshall's Constitutional Jurisprudence," 76 *Mich. L. Rev.* 893 (1978). On Marshall's impact on the development of federal Indian law jurisprudence, *see* F. Cohen, "Original Indian Title," 32 *Minn. L. Rev.* 28 (1947); J. Henderson, "Unravelling the Riddle of Aboriginal Title," 5 *Am. Indian L. Rev.* 75, 87–105 (1977); R. Williams, "The Algebra of Federal Indian Law: The Hard Trail of Decolonizing the White Man's Indian Jurisprudence," *Wis. L. Rev.* 219, 253–258 (1986); H. Berman, "The Concept of Aboriginal Rights in the Early Legal History of the United States," 27 *Buffalo L. Rev.* 637 (1978); M. Ball, "Constitution, Court, Indian Tribes," 1 *Am. Bar Foundation Res. J.* 1, 23–34 (1987). F. Cohen, *Handbook of Federal Indian Law* 486–90 (1982).

6

The Norman Yoke

Discourses of Containment: The Old Northwest and the Proclamation of 1763

An Indian Reserve on the Frontier

Historians, for good reason, mark the year 1763 as the beginning of the Revolutionary era in American history.[1] The British American colonies, after a century and a half of conflicts and confrontations with scattered, under-armed, disease-decimated Indian tribes, had been unable to advance their territorial ambitions beyond the several eastern mountain ranges and larger tribal confederacies inland from the Atlantic seaboard. But in 1763, the British Empire concluded a long and rather expensive war to protect its North American imperial interests from rival French ambitions. That war, the French and Indian War, was ended by the Treaty of Paris of 1763. By the treaty, a victorious England gained control of the rights previously asserted by France to colonize the intensely desired lands and trade of the Indian tribes of the Mississippi and Ohio valleys to the west of the mountains that defined the North American British colonial frontier.

By far, the most strategically vital and valuable prize won in the French and Indian War was the Old Northwest, the region bounded by the Great Lakes on the north, the Mississippi River on the west, the Ohio River on the south, and the Appalachian, Allegheny, and other mountain ranges on the east. But having driven the French out of the Old Northwest, Great Britain now had to maintain a military presence in the savagely populated and controlled region. This was required for two reasons. First, forts had to be established to serve as trading posts for the valuable Indian trade in furs, which the tribal hunters gladly exchanged for British manufactured goods such as spun cloth, metal utensils, and muskets. Second, the forts had to be garrisoned by an army capable of stopping encroachments on Indian territory by English American colonists hungry for the cheaper lands beyond the mountains. An Indian on the warpath against encroaching whites would be one less Indian trapping furs for European markets and accepting payment for those furs in overpriced British manufactured goods. Suppressing Indian hostilities with British troops only added to the empire's ultimate losses from its failure to keep peace on the colonial frontier.

These two goals—facilitating the profitable Indian trade and protecting Indian lands to prevent costly hostilities—were viewed as complementary halves of a self-serving colonial policy put forward by mercantilist interests and their advocates in the British Ministry at Whitehall in the 1760s.[2] These interests considered protection and promotion of England's home industries as paramount in fashioning colonial policy. Consequently, they viewed inland expansion by British Americans away from the Atlantic seaboard with considerable consternation. Transportation costs for British manufactured goods rose to prohibitive proportions the farther inland in America such goods had to be moved. The mercantilists in Whitehall feared that westward expansion of the colonial frontier beyond the reach of the Atlantic ports would ultimately lead to the creation of competing inland manufactures, lessening dependence throughout the colonies on British goods and ultimately on the mother country itself.

This mercantilist thesis was most aptly stated in a policy memorandum prepared for the British Board of Trade by either Secretary of State Lord Egremont, a principal architect of British American colonial policy following the French and Indian War, or his principal advisor on colonial policy, Henry Ellis.[3] Entitled "Hints Relative to the Division and Government of the Conquered and Newly Acquired Countries in America,"[4] the memorandum's discourse of containment reflected the view of a significant party among imperial theorists in the Ministry following the French and Indian War:

It might also be necessary to fix upon some line for a western boundary to our ancient provinces, beyond which our people should not at present be permitted to settle, hence as their numbers increased, they would emigrate to Nova Scotia, or to the provinces on the southern frontier, where they would be useful to their Mother country, instead of planting themselves in the Heart of America, out of the reach of government, and where from the great difficulty of procuring European Commodities, they would be compelled to commence manufactures to the infinite prejudice of Britain.[5]

This mercantilist thesis of containment thus made the protection of the home trade the paramount goal of imperial policy. The thesis also conveniently complemented the antiexpansionist views of other influential ministers in the cabinet who were most concerned with the need for fiscal retrenchment throughout the empire brought about by the late and expensive war. Their arguments for containment to protect the public fisc were most aptly stated by Lord Chancellor Hardwicke in a letter to the Duke of Newcastle, First Lord of the Treasury: "There is one thing upon which I have long thought as the Duke of B[edford, another influential member of the Ministry] does . . . that it is possible for England to be overloaded with foreign colonies."[6] Thus despite the continual ruptures of consensus over American policy that characterized British ministerial policymaking during this period,[7] a significant portion of the Ministry could normally be counted on to sustain the policy of maintaining the lately acquired upper Ohio Valley as an exclusive Indian preserve.

The necessity of a definite western boundary line for English settlement in America had been underscored by lessons learned during the French and Indian War. British commanders in the field had sought to secure the unaligned and powerful Iroquois Confederacy and other upper Great Lakes and western Indian nations as military allies against the French and their allied tribes.[8] The terms demanded by the Iroquois and other tribes for alliance with British forces included a promise that the king would secure the tribes' western hunting grounds from white encroachments in the future. British commanders readily agreed to that bargain in the king's name. Whitehall backed the commitments of its American field commanders, sending supporting instructions during the war to colonial governors strictly forbidding encroachments on the western Indian preserve. Governor Fauquier of Virginia, for example, was told by London that the Indians had agreed to cease hostilities and to ally themselves with the Engilsh "solely upon our having engaged . . . not to settle upon their hunting grounds." Stressing that to permit English settlements in the West would be both dangerous and "an open violation of our late solemn engagements" with the Indians, the Board of Trade ordered Fauquier not to tolerate encroachments by Virginians on "any lands upon the waters of the Ohio, until His Majesty's further pleasure be known."[9]

Because the Indian alliances had proved crucial to securing the British victory against the French, London recognized that with the war concluded, securing the West as an Indian preserve was essential to achieving a cheaply maintained peace and Indian trading-based empire in that region. Such considerations were all that the antiexpansionists at Whitehall required to back their arguments that the Crown's pledges to the western tribes should continue in force now that the war had been won. In January 1763, Secretary of State Egremont informed General Jeffrey Amherst, head of British forces in America, that the Ministry was debating a plan to conciliate the Indian nations by affording them protection "from any encroachments on the lands they had reserved to themselves, for their hunting grounds."[10] Egremont, a chief architect of British imperial policy for the western frontier during this critical period, indicated in a letter to the Commissioners of Trade in May 1763 that the basic principles informing the plan under debate had already been agreed on at the highest levels of the government:

[H]is Majesty's justice and Moderation inclines him to adopt the more eligible Method of conciliating the minds of the Indians by the mildness of His Government, by protecting their persons and property, & securing to them all the possessions rights and Privileges they have hitherto enjoyed & are entitled.[11]

The Indians, the secretary wrote, were to be protected against any

invasion or occupation of their hunting lands, the possession of which is to be acquired by fair purchase only; and it has been thought so highly expedient to give the earliest and most convincing proofs of his Majesty's gracious and friendly intentions on this head, that I have already received and transmitted the King's commands to this purpose to the Governors of Virginia, the two Carolinas & Georgia, & to the Agent for Indian Affairs in the Southern Department.[12]

The Proclamation of 1763

Debate within the Ministry on the particulars of this western plan, formally promulgated in October 1763 as King George III's notorious Royal Proclamation, was speeded up considerably by the news that reached London in August of a general Indian attack on the American frontier led by the Ottawa warrior chief Pontiac. Pontiac's rebellion was one of a number of worrisome Indian uprisings that erupted on the colonial frontier after the tide of the French and Indian War shifted decisively toward the British. With French influence removed from the West, the British army commander Amherst had moved quickly to terminate the expensive system of maintaining Indian alliances with liberal gifts.[13] Amherst also established a trading schedule of fixed trading prices at the British forts, ending the wartime policy of paying inflated premiums for Indian furs as a means of buying peace with the tribes. The general also took care not to oversupply the Indians with guns or ammunition, directing his officers to give out only enough for minimal hunting purposes.

Experienced English traders recognized the dangers inherent in Amherst's parsimonious new policy. George Croghan, a trader who knew the Ohio Valley tribes as well as any other English subject,[14] wrote to a friend back east that the Indians

had great expectations of being very generally supplied by us. . . . Undoubtedly the general has his own reason for not allowing any present or ammunition to be given them, and I wish it may have its desired effect, but I take this opportunity to acquaint you that I dread the event as I know Indians can't long persevere.[15]

Croghan, who actually spent a year's worth of his own salary on goods for Indians who had been refused gifts by Amherst, was correct in his predictions. Indian leaders reacted to the new policies with declarations of war. The Delaware prophet Neolin traveled throughout the Ohio Valley Indian country, relating the vision of resistance that he had received from the Master of Life:

What is now to be done, and what remedy is to be applied: I will tell you my friends, hear what the Great Spirit has ordered me to tell you! You are to make sacrifices in the manner that I shall direct. To put off entirely from yourselves the customs which you have adopted since the white people came among us, you are to return to that former happy state, in which we lived in peace and plenty, before the strangers came to disturb us.[16]

The Master of Life had revealed to his prophet Neolin that the Indian nations must revolt against the white usurpers.

Wherefore do you suffer the whites to dwell upon your lands? . . . Drive them away; wage war against them. I love them not. They know me not. They are my enemies, they are your brother's enemies. Send them back to the lands I have made for them. Let them remain there.[17]

Pontiac was a militant disciple of Neolin's discourse of opposition. Speaking to his Ottawa warriors on the eve of their attack on the British-held Fort Detroit, he declared, "It is important for us, my brothers, that we exterminate from our lands this nation which seeks only to destroy us."[18]

Along with Pontiac's successful assault on Fort Detroit, other western tribes—the Shawnees, Delawares, Chippewas, Hurons, Miamis, Potawatomis, and Senecas—seized British frontier outposts at Michilimachinac, St. Joseph, Sandusky, Presque Isle, Le Boeuf, and Verango. The coordinated warfront extended from the western Great Lakes to Pittsburgh. The Indians now controlled the Upper Northwest, only recently wrested from the French at a high cost by Great Britain.

Its promulgation hastened by news of these disturbing developments, the Proclamation of 1763 drew a boundary line along the crest of the eastern mountain ranges, to the west of which no English subject was permitted to acquire or settle on Indian lands without London's approval. The proclamation thus gave formal legal sanction to the *ad hoc* measures that British army commanders had been required to adopt in the field during the late war.[19] The self-interested discourse of containment articulated by the antiexpansionists in London had been accepted as official royal imperial policy.

British military reinforcements from the east and the western tribes' constant difficulties in securing adequate supplies and ammunition on the frontier secured an eventual peace with the warring Indians. Pontiac's discourse of rebellion was effectively suppressed, and British army officers could now cite the proclamation as evidence of the king's good intentions. The Ministry's "plan" as embodied in the proclamation, however, was intended to address problems far greater in scope than future Indian "conspiracies." It was a plan for managing an empire half a continent in size and a wide ocean away. Its discourse was one of interest and expediency as articulated by armchair empire builders in the Old World, who viewed the honoring of promises made to savages in the New World as the cheapest, most "expedient" means of containing both frontier defense costs and inland expansion by British American colonists.

In closing the western frontier to British settlement, the king's proclamation declared:

And whereas it is just and reasonable, and essential to our interest and the security of our colonies, that the several nations or tribes of Indians with whom we are connected, and who live under our protection should not be molested or disturbed in the possession of such parts of our dominions and territories as, not having been ceded to or purchased by us, are reserved to them, or any of them, as their hunting-grounds; we do therefore, with the advice of our Privy Council, declare it to be our royal will and pleasure, that no Governor or commander in Chief, in any of our colonies . . . or plantations in America do presume for the present, and until our further pleasure to be known, to grant warrants of survey or pass patents for any lands beyond the heads or sources of any of the rivers which fall into the Atlantic Ocean from the west or northwest; or upon any lands whatever, which, not having been ceded to or purchased by us, as aforesaid, are reserved to the said Indians.[20]

The proclamation specifically declared that no purchases or settlements on the lands to the west of the eastern mountain ranges reserved to the Indians could be made without "special leave and license" from the Crown. Any British subjects who had "either wilfullly or inadvertently" settled on these lands were ordered to remove themselves immediately.[21]

The proclamation also spelled out the precise methods by which the Crown would acquire western Indian lands in the future. To avoid the frequent Indian complaints of sharp dealings by the colonists, all western land sales would be controlled by Crown officials acting in the king's name:

And whereas great frauds and abuses have been committed in purchasing lands of the Indians, to the great prejudice of our interests, and to the great dissatisfaction of the said Indians; in order, therefore, to prevent such irregularities for the future, and to the end that the Indians may be convinced of our justice and determined resolution to remove all reasonable cause of discontent, we strictly enjoin and require, that no private person do presume to make any purchase from the said Indians of any lands reserved but that if at any time any of the said Indians should be inclined to dispose of the said lands, the same shall be purchased only for us, in our name, at some public meeting or assembly of the said Indians.[22]

To complement this new, formalized Indian land policy in the West, the proclamation also provided the outlines of a new trade policy for the frontier. It proposed greater governmental controls on those colonists engaged in trade with the Indians.[23] Traders would be required to obtain a license and post a bond as security for potential penalties prescribed under new Crown regulations.[24]

In effect, the new policies for the West announced in the proclamation sought to insulate the American frontier from the greed and ambitions of the king's own colonial subjects. The proclamation signaled a substantial departure from prior Crown practice toward the colonies. Historically, London had allowed the colonies a relatively wide degree of discretion and initiative in handling Indian relations. But the French and Indian War had altered London's perspective on American imperial policy. England had fought and won a long and costly war for control of the Old Northwest. The proclamation was the legal installation of the Crown's political control over this newly acquired territory earned by the outcome of its war.

The Imperial Plan of 1764

The proclamation's constraints on Indian land sales and trade provided only the bare theoretical outlines for a plan of imperial management of Indian affairs on the American frontier. The theory of a boundary line delimiting the extent of westward expansion by British subjects had been strongly stated in the proclamation. The actual boundary line would now have to be negotiated with the frontier tribes in a continent-wide series of treaties, and would then have to be vigorously enforced against the colonists. As for trade, the imperial government had adopted the theory that properly licensed British subjects could engage in the Indian trade as long as they agreed to be regulated to ensure fair treatment of the Indians. Now that theory also had to be implemented and converted into reality.

In 1764 the Board of Trade agreed on a plan for specifically implementing the proclamation's policies in North America. Issued as a circular letter to officials in America,[25] the board's plan called for regulating the commercial and political aspects of Indian affairs under one general system of management. Two separate districts, north and south, were to be established. Superintendents appointed by the Crown were to have control over these two districts, and individual colonies were to cooperate with the superintendents in the administration of their duties. Negotiations with the western tribes setting the precise boundaries between the races were to be expeditiously undertaken by these Crown officers through treaty and other negotiations. The plan called for all Indian trade to be placed under imperial regulations and to be conducted in the southern district at specified Indian towns and in the northern district at designated military posts.

As the proclamation had indicated, all traders were to be licensed by their colonial governor and had to post bonds. The plan also proposed the repeal of all colonial laws dealing with the Indian trade. As ordered by the proclamation, any purchases of Indian lands by English subjects without royal approval were strictly prohibited.[26] The two Indian superintendents were granted the power to appoint deputies, who would preside as justices of the peace beyond the negotiated boundary line.

The perceptions of reality contained in the London-originated imperial discourse of the Royal Proclamation of 1763 and the implementing plan of 1764 differed radically from those expressed in the public discourses of America. Both the Indians and the colonists had strong reasons for opposing the centralizing tendencies of imperial administration at Whitehall.

Pontiac's rebellion[27] had already signaled the western frontier tribes' strong opposition to imperial efforts aimed at rationalizing the trade from a narrow-minded English perspective. As to the establishment of a boundary line separating the Indians from English colonists who desired their lands, any attempt by London to dictate the placement of such a line contradicting the tribes' own notions of the geographical extent of their territorial claims would certainly meet with strenuous objections.

Sir William Johnson, selected as the Crown's Indian superintendent for the northern district, had previously served as Indian agent for the colony of New York. Johnson had been instrumental in securing the crucial Iroquois and Delaware tribal alliances during the French and Indian War. Perhaps no other English-descended individual in the New World or the Old was more familiar with the opposing discourse of empire articulated by the Six Nations of the Iroquois, the most powerful indigenous confederacy on the North American continent in the Revolutionary era. In a series of reports to the Board of Trade in London, Johnson offered his assessment of competing Iroquois imperial pretensions in the western territory. He also provided counsel on the extent to which the government ought to respect the confederacy's claims in drawing any boundary line under the proclamation.[28]

Johnson reported that besides their claims as original proprietors of a large portion of upstate New York, the Iroquois tribes asserted the sovereignty acquired by "right of conquest" over all the lands of the major nations of the Ohio country: "the Shawanese, Delawares, Twighties, and western Indians so far as lakes Michigan and Superior."[29] According to Johnson, all these nations had been conquered by the Iroquois during the past century. The great confederacy, however, allowed their subject tribes the "possession of the lands they occupied."[30] Johnson added that the Iroquois claim to the Ohio country had never been effectively disputed by any of their tributary tribes, "who never transacted any sales of land or other matters without their [the Iroquois'] consent."[31] In Johnson's opinion, therefore, negotiating a boundary line with the confederacy

is a very necessary, but a delicate point. . . . I must beg to observe, that the Six Nations, Western Indians, etc., having never been conquered, either by the English or French, nor subject to their Laws, consider themselves as a free people. I am therefore induced to think it will require a good deal of caution to point out any boundary, that shall appear to circumscribe too far.[32]

Besides the opposing discourse of empire practiced by the Indians and related by Superintendent Johnson, Whitehall had to contend with the views of England's own colonial subjects on the appropriate degree of imperial authority administered on the American frontier. The precise method for financing the Ministry's 1764 plan had not been decided on at the time the plan had been submitted to American colonial officials for review prior to Parliament's consideration of the proposal. The plan would obviously require garrisoning a number of forts with royal troops throughout the West—an extremely expensive proposition. But the Treasury had indicated that it would provide a paltry allowance of only £15,000 for any type of imperial system of Indian affairs in North America. This would not be enough, and it was expected that the colonies would have to share in the expense of the imperial plan for the frontier.

The Crown's two American Indian superintendents in the field both advocated a tax on the Indian fur trade to raise the additional monies needed to finance the imperial plan. This tax would not have significantly or exclusively burdened the colonists, as most American furs were exported to English and European markets. The home government, most likely for these very reasons, was reluctant to raise the additional sums required for the imperial plan by this means. In a letter to Superintendent Johnson, the Lords of Trade expressed their skepticism about the use of a fur tax:

Another regulation of great difficulty and delicacy is the settlement of a Tariff of Trade which tho it be recommended both by yourself and the Superintendent for the Southern District yet seems to us doubtful in its principle and difficult in its execution; since it is in its nature inconsistent with and might in its operation be restrictive of that freedom which is one of the first principles of Commerce and cannot either in Justice or Reason be fixed without the mutual-consent of parties having adverse and contradictory interests.[33]

Here was the rub. The turbulent history of the proclamation and its hostile reception in British America must be viewed in light of the volatile, evolving discourses on both sides of the Atlantic respecting "that freedom which is one of the first principles of Commerce."[34]

In its imperial myopia, Whitehall failed to recognize that the English in America were now an ocean's distance from the more rigid strictures of the mother country's economy. British Americans were experiencing firsthand "that freedom which is one of the first principles of Commerce." Distance from England and its still too feudalized economy and mentality; traditions of local self-government, which London had allowed to flourish in the colonies; and the sense of a well-deserved independence derived from taming a wilderness— all these had combined in the British American mind to accelerate in a rapid and radical fashion the thematization of the European Enlightenment's discourses of laissez-faire economic individualism.[35] To the British Americans, the centralizing thematics of the imperial discourse articulated in constraining texts such as the proclamation and the Board of Trade's plan plainly ran counter to their far more liberalized notions of freedom and commerce. Of necessity, they viewed with alarm any restrictions on their freedom to engage in commerce, whether those restrictions were achieved by tariffs or taxes, by prohibitions on purchasing Indian lands, or by a licensing system for Indian trade. These dangerous sources of foreign infection threatened those unique liberties that had blossomed so freely and rapidly in the virgin soil of America.

But to say only that the British government in London did not fully grasp the nature or intensity of the grievances felt by the colonists after 1763 is to miss an important point. After 1763, the English in London and the English in America were no longer speaking precisely the same discourses. This is proved by the formal act by which Whitehall initiated British America's full discursive rupture with the mother country. Rather than a fur tax, Whitehall decided to implement its 1764 plan of imperial management for the American frontier by imposing a *stamp tax* on the colonies, by which the Americans themselves would pay for the policy of containment embodied in the Proclamation of 1763. To the practitioners of empire in Whitehall, the Stamp Act of 1765 represented an implied corollary to the central principle of a discourse of empire assuming the colonies as supplements to imperial interests. However, to the English in the New World—domesticators of a discursive practice originally rooted in the history of their mother country but now focusing increasingly on purely indigenous concerns—the parasitic logic of subordinating American interests to those of a power an ocean away invited the fiercest resistance.

Discourses of Resistance

The fateful decision by the Ministry to finance the 1764 plan of frontier management with a stamp tax on the Americans was based on pure imperial economics and a mistaken assumption that the colonists viewed their interests and those of the empire as one and the same. Treasury's requests for funds to maintain British armed forces in America after the war were approaching nearly £500,000 annually. The empire alone could not afford to finance the supposedly economizing policy initiatives contained in the 1764 plan for the newly acquired territory of the Old Northwest. Great Britain's national debt had risen from a prewar total of £73 million to £137 million after the French and Indian War. The annual carrying charge on that debt alone equaled £5 million, compared with an annual national budget that averaged only £8 million during this period.[36]

Thus when the Ministry considered the practical problems of paying for the policy behind the Proclamation of 1763, it was only natural to look to the colonies themselves to provide the solutions. Relatively speaking, they were in far better financial shape. Parliament had reimbursed them for more than three-fifths of the meager £2.5 million debt they had incurred during the war. The total annual expenses of all the colonial governments in America were a mere £75,000.[37] In the words of Lord Grenville, first lord of the Treasury, who had originally proposed the idea of taxing the Americans to pay for the policy behind the proclamation, "It was but reasonable the colonies should contribute at least to take off that part of the burden from the Mother Country which concerned the protection and defense of themselves."[38] The proposed Stamp Act thus would authorize a tax on the British colonists to pay for a policy that in effect closed the frontier to their frontierless economic ambitions.

The idea of a stamp tax had been applied in England for many years. As applied in America, Grenville's proposed tax would have placed duties on various categories of legal documents such as pleadings (3 pence), probate of a will (5 shillings), bills of lading (4 pence), and land grants (3 shillings and up, depending on the size of the tract). Dice, playing cards, almanacs, and books serving as almanacs were also to be taxed. So were pamphlets and newspapers at varying rates, depending on size.[39]

The colonists, of course, did not see Lord Grenville's stamp tax as "reasonable." Earlier forms of trade restrictions and duties on the British Americans had been resented and resisted,[40] but the Stamp Act represented by far the most odious attack to date on the colonists' perceived rights and liberties—or so the American radicals of the Revolutionary era claimed. Their discursive strategy of resistance focused on the cumulative impact of serial attacks on their rights and liberties as British freemen. Thus even though the Stamp Act radicalized their discursive opposition to British colonial policy as no previous legislation had ever done, each subsequently perceived attack on American rights would demand an even further distancing of the radicals' discursive practice from the centralizing vision emanating from the mother country.

The colonies registered their opposition to the proposed stamp tax in the strongest of terms. Pennsylvania's colonial assembly declared that a stamp duty levied in Pennsylvania would be repugnant to "our Rights and Privileges as Freemen and British Subjects." The South Carolina legislature presented a similar argument stressing that no British subject could be taxed without his consent or that of his representatives. The Virginia House of Burgesses protested the levy of an "internal" tax on the colony, requesting instead to determine the form and method of taxation itself. New York and Massachusetts denied Parliament's right to tax Americans at all and called for joint colonial action.[41]

In London, this Americanized dialect appeared to be an alien departure from the English discourse of empire spoken by the king's ministers. The Board of Trade declared this new discourse of opposition to imperial power as founded on principles of a "most dangerous nature and tendency." The government reacted with firmness and grammatical rigidity. The reports from America of "indecent disrespect" moved the Ministry to reassert Parliament's "right" to execute "an internal tax, that of the Stamp Duty" on the colonists.[42] The enabling legislation passed with minimal opposition in Commons and no dissent in the House of Lords in March 1765.

Reaction in the colonies to the formal passage of the Stamp Act was immediate and intense. Rioting and opposition led several colonial governors to ask the commander in chief of British forces in America, Thomas Gage, for the aid of regular troops. The general, however, was unable to accede to the requests. He wrote Governor Colden of New York that troops were widely dispersed on the western Indian frontier. To remove them to the seaboard would require at least a month and would leave the wilderness virtually undefended.

The militant assaults on Parliament's sovereignty in the streets of Boston and New York were not the only developments that the imperial government found itself unable and unready to suppress. The colonial radicals also intensified and sharpened their discursive attacks on perceived imperial usurpations of American rights and liberties under the British Constitution. Parliament's unilateral imposition of the Stamp Tax led American radicals to reexamine and reaffirm the roots of the relationship between property and self-government assertedly protected by the British Constitution. What they found in their search for roots was that the Enlightenment discourse of natural law and natural rights affirmed their vision of certain immutable principles of government. These principles thus provided a firm legitimating foundation for their asserted self-governing rights as British freemen and therefore also for their resistance to tyrannous attacks on those natural-law rights protected by the British Constitution.

Samuel Adams, a gifted leader of the radical opposition in Boston, drafted a set of resolutions, which were approved by the House of Representatives of Massachusetts on October 29, 1765. They began as follows:

1. *Resolved*, That there are certain essential rights of the British Constitution of government, which are founded in the law of God and nature, and are the common rights of mankind; —therefore

2. *Resolved*, That the inhabitants of this Province are unalienably entitled to those essential rights in common with all men: and that no law of society can, consistent with the law of God and nature, divest them of those rights.[43]

Adams's resolutions argued that Parliament's acts violated the fundamental maxim that "no man can justly take the property of another without his consent."[44] The Stamp Act violated this vital principle of natural law, as well as the British Constitution assertedly embodying this law, by taxing the colonies without granting a concomitant right of representation in Parliament.

Southward, Patrick Henry, a young radical representing Virginia's western frontier in the Virginia House of Burgesses, introduced a series of militant resolutions that indicated the extent to which some colonists were willing to go to enforce their rights under natural law and its supplement, the British Constitution. Only the first four of Henry's seven original resolutions were ultimately put into the record by the House of Burgesses, although all seven were widely circulated in the newspapers. The four relatively uncontroversial resolutions asserted that the Virginia colonists were entitled by their royal charter of 1609 to all the liberties and privileges of any English subjects under the Constitution, and therefore could not be taxed without representation. Such assertions were, given the temper of the times, rather tame. The other three clauses, however, indicate the direction in which radical theorists such as Henry were moving—toward ultimate rupture with the mother country:

Resolved therefore, that the General Assembly of this Colony have the only and sole exclusive right and power to lay taxes and impositions upon the inhabitants of this Colony, and that every attempt to vest such power in any person or persons whatsoever other than the General Assembly aforesaid has a manifest tendency to destroy British as well as American freedom.

Resolved, that His Majesty's liege people, the inhabitants of this Colony, are not bound to yield obedience to any law or ordinance whatever, designed to impose any taxation whatsoever upon them, other than the laws or ordinances of the General Assembly aforesaid.

Resolved, that any person who shall, by speaking or writing, assert or maintain that any person or persons other than the General Assembly of this colony, have any right or power to impose or lay any taxation on the people here, shall be deemed an enemy to His Majesty's Colony.[45]

The radicals in the colonies freely cited the British Constitution, John Locke, and the natural-law discourse popularized by Enlightenment-era continental legal theorists such as Vattel, Grotius, and Pufendorf to support their arguments for self-government. Colonial agents in London meanwhile were working overtime for repeal of the Stamp Act, utilizing a different line of attack. Dennys DeBerdt, agent for the Massachusetts House of Representatives, linked the revenue law directly to Lord Grenville's program for the newly acquired western territories and indirectly to the Proclamation of 1763. By arguing that the colonies themselves, and not London, could and should control the frontier, DeBerdt sought to undermine the perceived need for an outrageously expensive and poorly conceived program of imperial control of the West. Garrisoning English troops in America was "as absurd as it is needless," he argued. With the French eliminated from the western territories, Massachusetts's agent asserted, the colonists could now protect themselves as they had always done in the past without British troops.[46]

Benjamin Franklin, acting as Pennsylvania's agent in London, argued much the same thing in his notorious 1766 performance before the House of Commons urging repeal of the Stamp Act. Royal garrisons were not required to protect North America, Franklin argued. The Americans could do it on their own. The Pennsylvanian went so far as to deny that the French and Indian War had even been fought for the colonies' benefit. It was "really a British war," fought for British commercial interests. As there had never been any need to send British troops to defend the colonies, there was certainly no need for a Stamp Act to finance an unneeded army there now.[47] Several of the appalled members of Parliament vigorously denounced Franklin's contemptuous efforts at historical revisionism. Lord Clare attacked the ingratitude implied by Franklin's Americanized version of the war. "We have fought, bled, and ruined ourselves, to conquer for them," Clare cried, "and now they come and tell us to our noses . . . that they are not obliged to us."[48]

The Crown and the Colonists' Competing Discourses on and Claims to the Indian Frontier

Despite London's outrage over the colonists' ingratitude, a new Ministry under the Marquis of Rockingham pushed the Stamp Act's repeal through Parliament as a matter of political expediency. Rockingham's faction was uncomfortable with the violent opposition in America to Parliament's authority.

London's concession on the Stamp Act, however, did not mean that the Americans had completely liberated themselves from the tryannous usurpations of a distant, nonrepresentative government. The Stamp Act had merely been the financing vehicle for implementing an equally odious policy of sealing off the American frontier to the colonists' natural destiny and ambitions. And London continued to adhere to the proclamation's declared intent of reserving the western frontier as a game preserve for wandering savages.

The proclamation and the imperial plan of 1764 declared in essence that the absolute power of the king's prerogative extended to enclosing the virgin forests of the New World from the colonists' claims and ambitions. Such extensions of the prerogative and imperial power were perceived by the radicals as striking directly at their particular vision of America. The English had come to the New World in search of plentiful and cheap lands free of the feudal burdens that made land dear and unavailable in England. To radical colonists intent on undermining Crown prerogative rights in their country, the proclamation's assertion that the king, not the colonists, ought to control the pace, the direction, and ultimately the price of the disposition of lands on the American frontier seemed contradicted by their sense of history as well as by their "common sense."

As for the radicals' sense of history, they viewed the entire course of their colonial relations with the empire as one long series of attacks by the imperial government on their rights as English freemen under the British Constitution. Particularly detested was the gradual, century-long process beginning with the Stuart kings by which the Crown had brought formerly independent chartered colonies, and thus the property of America, under its direct royal control. By 1775, in fact, only Connecticut and Rhode Island remained as self-governing corporations, and only Pennsylvania, Delaware, and Maryland retained their original status as proprietary colonies.[49]

In practice, the Crown had tempered the theoretical oppositions to its asserted usurpation of American colonial charter rights by permitting the traditional institutions of colonial self-government—the assembly, the governor, and the council—to continue functioning in roughly the same semiautonomous fashion that had been customary prior to the charter revocations. With respect to the vast western frontier, parts of which were claimed under earlier royal charters by all the colonies except Pennsylvania, Maryland, New Jersey, Delaware, and Rhode Island (the "landless" colonies), these traditions of colonial self-government tended to harden into claims of absolute right on the part of the colonial aristocratic hierarchies to determine the pace and direction of their colonies' western land sales. The colonists' charters established their right to self-government, and therefore their right to control all the lands within their chartered bounds. The colonists from the "landed" colonies (Virginia, which claimed charter rights to western lands extending to the South Seas—that is, the Pacific Ocean—was the most prominent member of this group) argued in the strongest terms that the king could not interfere with these self-governing rights by subsequent proclamation under the British Constitution.

Thus the proclamation was viewed, particularly by radicals from the "landed" colonies claiming the west, as a galling reminder of the history of tyrannous usurpation of colonial charter rights. The proclamation's implied attack on customary self-government demanded that the radicals challenge the legitimacy of the king's assertion of prerogative rights in the western lands. The fact that prior usurpations had gone unchallenged meant little to the radicals of the American age of Revolution, who firmly believed that the nature of tyranny was such that claims against it were never time-barred or estopped.

Locke's Theory and the Indians' "Wastelands"

As for the radicals' own "common sense" view of the proclamation's inherent principle that an English king could seize control of the vast potential estates that sat waiting to be carved out of the American frontier wilderness, all one had to do was turn to John Locke's *Second Treatise of Government* for the true and correct exposition on the issue.[50] Locke's famous discussion of natural law and property was regarded as a canonical text in the discursive practice of the American radicals, precisely because of its appeal to the "common sense" of Revolutionary-era Americans. This harmony is attested to by the radicals themselves. John Adams, nearly half a century removed from the passions of the Revolution, told Thomas Jefferson in 1822 that the Virginian's Declaration of Independence contained not a single new idea. Jefferson acknowledged that his text may well have merely represented "a compilation of commonplaces."[51] Jefferson's fellow Virginian Richard Lee raised the objection that the declaration was simply a plagiarism of Locke. Jefferson, acknowledging his debt to the profound impact on his generation of Locke's seventeenth-century discourse of property and natural law, stated simply that it had not been his task to find new principles and argument. He had only wanted "to place before mankind the common sense of the subject." The declaration, he conceded, was but "an expression of the American mind. . . . [A]ll its authority rests thus on the harmonizing sentiments of the day. . . ."[52]

Locke's natural-law discourse was seized upon by the colonial radicals because his theory of society and property both embodied and affirmed the Americans' own "common sense" interpretation of their peculiar relation to a New World wilderness and an Old World empire. Locke's declaration that "in the beginning all the world was America"[53] would certainly have underscored the colonists' own emerging sense of self-reliance and hard-earned independence. With little assistance from the Crown prior to the French and Indian War, British Americans had constructed a society out of a hostile wilderness. They could regard themselves as having been placed in that "state of perfect freedom" described in the opening chapters of the *Second Treatise*, a state in which all persons are at liberty "to order their actions, and dispose of their possessions, and persons as they think fit, within the bounds of the Law of Nature, without asking leave, or depending upon the will of any other man."[54]

In the New World, the English had purchased their security by their labor in the wilderness, transforming what Locke himself had called the "wild woods and uncultivated waste of America" into valuable properties.[55] The king's proclamation struck directly at the ability of English Americans to continue their cheap acquisition of the vast "waste" lands that the Indians desired to sell on the frontier. Thus the "common sense" embodied in Locke's text told the colonists that the proclamation represented nothing other than an attack on their natural rights to acquire and labor upon American land, thereby converting that land into a valuable property.

Locke's argument on labor and its relation to the privatization of property is by now familiar. The fruits of nature were originally held in common by all. But, according to Locke, "Men . . . have a right to their preservation" and therefore have a need to appropriate to themselves the goods of nature for their subsistence. Locke derived the rightful means of individual appropriation from the assumption that "every man has a *Property* in his own *person*. This no body has any right to but himself. The *Labour* of his body, and the work of his hands, we may say, are properly his." Thus the things of nature removed from their natural state by human effort become an individual's property by virtue of combining labor with those natural goods.[56]

Consent from the other commoners is not required to justify this appropriation, "at least where there is enough, and as good left in common for others. If such a consent was necessary, man would have starved, despite God's plenty given him."[57] As C. B. Macpherson has stated in his study on Locke's theory of possessive individualism, "Thus from two postulates, that men have a right to preserve their life, and that a man's labour is his own, Locke justifies . . . appropriation of the produce of the earth which was originally given to mankind in common."[58] The right to acquire property as long as there was "as good left in common for others" was part of natural law. And Locke specifically implied in his text that that law still held force in the "in-land, vacant places of America."[59] On the vast, unenclosed expanses of the American frontier, where the state of nature was experienced as a reality and not as an assumption in service to a theory, denial of this self-preserving right to acquire the Indians' waste lands therefore contradicted not only "common sense" but also natural law. In the virgin wilderness of America, equality of rank was dictated by the abundance of land but labor on that land assisted the laborer in transcending that equal station. Hard work was more than its own reward. It was the *modus vivendi* for asserting rights that would ensure self-preservation. As Locke himself had stated, "*As much land* as a man tills, plants, improves, cultivates, and can use the product of, so much is his Property. He by his labour does, as it were, inclose it from the common."[60]

Locke's discourse thus legitimated the appropriation of the American wilderness as a right, and even as an imperative, under natural law. In a passage that would most certainly have appealed to the common sense of Americans desirous of acquiring the frontier "waste" lands of the Indian, Locke declared:

To which let me add, that he who appropriates land to himself by his labour, does not lessen but increase the common stock of mankind. For the provisions serving to support human life, produced by one acre of inclosed and cultivated land, are (to speak much within compasse) ten times more, than those, which are yielded by an acre of land, of an equal richnesse, lyeing waste in common. And therefore he, that incloses land and has a greater plenty of the conveniences of life from ten acres, thus he could have from a hundred left to nature, may truly be said, to give ninety acres to mankind. For this labour now supplys him with provisions out of ten acres, which were but the product of an hundred lying in common.[61]

Thus the king's proclamation operated in a doubly odious fashion. First, the law prevented English Americans from appropriating the Indians' "waste" lands and increasing "the common stock of mankind." Second, and even worse from the English Americans' "common sense" perspective, the proclamation reserved the western frontier to savage tribes of Indians. Any colonist reading Locke would quickly have recognized the utter lack of common sense in leaving so valuable a commodity as land in the hands of the Indians of America, whom Locke himself described in the *Second Treatise* as

rich in land and poor in all the comforts of life; whom nature having furnished as liberally as any other people with materials of plenty, i.e., a fruitful soil, apt to produce in abundance what might serve for good, raiment, and delight, yet for want of improving it by labor have not one-hundredth part of the conveniences we enjoy. And a king of large and fruitful territory there feeds, lodges, and is clad worse than a day-laborer in England.[62]

In reading this caricature of the Indians as idle wastrels of the vast American wilderness, it is useful to recall that Locke served as secretary to the proprietors of the Carolina colony (he assisted in drawing up the colony's first constitution), as well as to the Board of Trade. He was thoroughly socialized in the cadences and presumptions of late-seventeenth-century English colonizing discourse. Thus two points are worth noting respecting this passage on the poorly fed, lodged, and clad Indian king. First, the utilitarian justifications for dispossessing the American Indians that had emerged in early-seventeenth-century English colonizing discourse had, by Locke's time, hardened into the assumptions of ideological argument. Second, judging by the Revolutionary era's reception of Locke, the continuity in English colonizing discourse of the thematic of Indian deficiency had been completely integrated into the "common sense" of late-eighteenth-century English Americans.

Locke's Theory Applied: The Colonial Radicals' Praxis on the Indian Frontier

From an Americanized perspective, therefore, the proclamation's mandate that the entire unenclosed "waste" land of the frontier was to be reserved for wandering savages would most likely have been seen as at odds with both common sense and the utilitarian-grounded natural-law vision found in Locke's highly regarded text. Seen from this radical perspective, the Proclamation of 1763 demanded the fiercest resistance.

However, there was much more to the colonists' opposition to the proclamation than a desire to correct history or to practice their own common-sense views about their natural rights to acquire frontier lands. Vast sums of wealth, far beyond any colonists' subsistence needs under natural law, were involved in the controversy surrounding the legitimacy of the proclamation. The sale of frontier lands by the landed colonies had proved to be highly profitable for their ruling elites. Prior to the proclamation, the governments of the landed colonies had freely parceled out unsettled frontier lands acquired by purchase or surrender from the occupying tribes. These grants were made under the landed colonies' asserted charter rights. Even if the Crown had assumed control over formerly independent chartered colonies (as was the case in a number of colonies, including Virginia), there were numerous opportunities presented by the colonial land-acquisition process for huge profits, both licit and illicit, to be made by the Americans along the way.

Governors' royal letters of commission might often entitle them to a percentage of the sale on a fee patent as part of the consideration for accepting a post in the colonies. The larger and more favorable wilderness tracts would go to favorites and men of influence. These speculators gladly paid unreported premiums to obliging colonial officials who had set the purchase prices at artificially low levels.

For the not-so-favored individual colonist who merely desired to obtain a decent-sized tract on the unsettled frontier on which he could exercise his natural rights, acquiring land could be a long and expensive process. After receiving the required license from colonial officials, usually purchased at valuable consideration along with the normal bribes, the individual colonist would most often be required to appease the Indian tribe that claimed the same lands. After bargaining for and accepting a satisfactory offer by the head sachem or sachems of the tribe, the colonist returned with the signed Indian deed of release and presented it to colonial officials. After another round of bribes and fees, the colonist might then finally receive confirmation of his purchase and a patent.

There were numerous variations in the procedure throughout the colonies for patenting lands claimed or occupied by Indians. Sometimes an Indian deed was first acquired by a speculator, who then sought confirmation and a patent from colonial officials, who expected and received compensation for such favors. Or tribes would release their land claims directly to the colonial government, which would then simply distribute patents to favored syndicates and individual buyers. Many of the colonies early in their histories passed prohibitory statutes voiding or outlawing any purchase of Indian lands not made in the presence of a colonial official. Unlike the detested proclamation, these statutes were never intended to halt Indian land sales. Such sales were, after all, a primary source of income for the colonial elites. Rather, colonial land laws merely sought to ensure that only colonial officials dealt with Indians for the sale of their lands, thereby bringing some sense of regularity, control, and title assurance to the land-acquisition process. Nonetheless, even these injunctions were more honored in the breach than in the observance. In practice, the laws simply provided an excuse for initiating another round of bribes and graft.

In short, an individual could acquire land on the American colonial frontier in numerous ways, but all these methods ultimately referred back to the legitimating constitutional paradigm that the colonies and their governing hierarchies held the right to administer the sale of Indian lands and therefore the right to receive the profits and petty graft involved at every stage of the colonial land-acquisition process. From an early period in American colonial history, the granting of and profiting from lands on the unsettled colonial frontier had been regarded as an important aspect of colonial self-government, interest, and prosperity. And to a race of individuals whose patterns of legal thinking easily transformed customs and traditions into the force of common law, any interference with their settled expectations arising from their histories was bound to be resisted.

Thus the Proclamation of 1763 struck at the heart of the colonists' expectations that the lands beyond the eastern mountain ranges claimed under their charters would finance their future prosperity. The proclamation, regarded as another tyrannous usurpation of property rights achieved through the king's despised prerogative, and the related attempt by Parliament to impose a stamp tax on the Americans in violation of the English Constitution were therefore viewed as being of the utmost consequence to the colonists. Resistance to the proclamation's boundary line, like resistance to the Stamp Act, was thus part of a larger conflict over who was going to own, and therefore govern, America. Defiance of such sinister schemes—and the Revolutionary generation sensed great conspiracies against their rights and liberties in virtually every proposal emanating from a perceived corrupt Whitehall during this period—became the *sine qua non* of radical Revolutionary praxis.

Virginians in particular, given their long tradition of speculation in the vast western lands asserted as belonging to the colony under its 1609 Crown charter, were naturally inclined to resist the proclamation. Virginia's wealthiest families had long been among the earliest and most prominent land speculators on the frontier.

A notorious example of the radicals' practice of resistance to and diminishment of Crown rights in western lands is provided by the career of George

Washington himself, the Virginian chosen to lead the radicals in their ultimate break with the Crown and its feudally derived imperial discourse. Washington, the mythic icon who as a youth reportedly could not tell a lie about cutting down his father's cherry tree, apparently felt little compunction about engaging in furtive acts intended to undercut his king's claimed rights in the West. Prior to 1776, in fact, Washington devoted a good deal of his time to pursuing and acquiring speculative landed interests on the frontier in blatant disregard of the proclamation.

A letter written by Washington[63] to his associate William Crawford, instructing him to survey some "good rich land" on the western frontier, indicates the disdain in which many radical colonists held the king's efforts to appease the western tribes.

The other matter, just now hinted at and which I proposed in my last to join you, in attempting to secure some of the most valuable lands in the King's part, which I think may be accomplished after a while, notwithstanding the proclamation that restrains it at present, and prohibits the settling of them at all; for I can never look upon that proclamation in any other light (but this I say between ourselves), than as a temporary expedient to quiet the minds of the Indians, and must fall, of course, in a few years . . . any person, therefore, who neglects the present opportunity of hunting out good land, and in some measure marking and distinguishing them for his own (in order to keep others from settling them), will never regain it.[64]

Washington was not alone in the hunt for "good lands" on the western side of the proclamation's line. Many colonists, Virginians and non-Virginians alike, freely pursued their landed desires, knowing that where the king's power could not effectively be enforced, his law did not matter. Hundreds of settlers moved onto western lands following the French and Indian War in utter disregard of the king's will as expressed in his proclamation. In the summer of 1765, for example, reports of widespread encroachments across the mountains threatening a new Indian war moved the privy council in London to issue orders to the governors of Virginia and Pennsylvania. The governors were to take immediate steps to remove the illegal settlers and to punish depredations against the Ohio River Indian tribes. Commander in Chief Gage reported back to London, however, that the government was simply unable to punish the "lawless Ruffians" infesting the frontier. Even if caught and tried, "No jury would condemn them for murdering or ill treating an Indian." The "Reins of Government," in Gage's opinion, "are too loose to enforce an Obedience to the Laws."[65] On the frontier, London could lay down no law that the Americans would feel obliged to obey in pursuing their own interests.

The Norman Yoke Applied to America

In resisting imperial authority over the frontier, the colonists regarded themselves as anything but "lawless Ruffians." Viewing the acquisition of property and the pursuit of self-interest as closely related to their fundamental rights to govern themselves and to be represented in government, the Americans grounded their rejection of London's directives in a higher law. From their natural-law perspective, property and self-determination were synonymous, and any attempt to deny the pursuit of either was seen as an attack on their fundamental natural-law rights. "The great and chief end therefore, of Men's uniting into Commonwealths, and putting themselves under Government," Locke had written, "is the preservation of their property."[66] Thus the future coauthor of the *Federalist Papers*, John Jay, was not being facetious when he stated the maxim that every one of the Founders would have readily agreed was well founded in common sense: "The people who own the country ought to govern it."[67]

In seeking to wrest the ownership and government of America away from the mother country, the colonists invented or appropriated numerous symbols and slogans as they formulated their discourses of resistance to kingly right and parliamentary sovereignty during the Revolutionary era. But because it spoke with such intensity and immediacy to the central issue of who was going to own and therefore ultimately govern America, and because it appealed directly to a like-minded radical opposition in England, the appropriated symbology of the "Norman Yoke" was perhaps the radicals' most powerful and conceptually most integrated expression of meaning of the American Revolutionary experience.

James Otis, a Boston lawyer, was one of the most influential pamphleteers of the early Revolutionary era.[68] He drew on the image of an alien, Norman king's usurpation of true English rights grounded in natural law in his call to resistance against tyranny, "The Rights of the British Colonies Asserted and Proved" (1764).[69] Otis opened his pedagogically constructed pamphlet as follows:

Here, indeed opens to view a large field; but I must study brevity—Few people have extended their enquiries after the foundation of any of their rights, beyond a charter from the crown. There are others who think when they have got back to old *Magna Charta*, that they are at the beginning of all things. They imagine themselves on the borders of Chaos (and so indeed in some respects they are) and see creation rising out of the unformed mass, or from nothing. Hence, say they, spring all the rights of men and of citizens—But liberty was better understood, and more fully enjoyed by our ancestors, before the coming in of the first Norman Tyrants than ever after, 'till it was found necessary, for the salvation of the kingdom, to combat the arbitrary and wicked proceedings of the Stuarts.[70]

What Otis attempted in this tract was to push his reader beyond the normally regarded historical milestones of English political and legal thought. More conservative colonists based their rights on their colonies' charters from the king. Some were more insightful and went back to Magna Carta as the foundation of their liberties. Otis desired that English Americans recognize the emergence of their rights even farther back in history, in a state of nature that the true ancestors of all English people, the freedom-loving Saxons, enjoyed in full simplicity before the invasion of their Norman conquerors. Otis projected his readers back into history, toward a law established by God, which by its radical priority necessarily superseded any act of mere mortals.

To say the parliament is absolute and arbitrary is a contradiction. The parliament cannot make 2 and 2, 5: Omnipotency cannot do it. The supreme power in a state, is *jus dicere* only; —*jus dare*, strictly speaking, belongs alone to God. Parliaments are in all cases to declare what is for the good of the whole; but it is not the declaration of parliament that makes it so: There must be in every instance, a higher authority, *viz.* God. Should an act of parliament be against any of his natural laws, which are immutably true, their declaration would be contrary to eternal truth, equity and justice, and consequently void: and so it would be adjudged by the parliament itself, when convinced of their mistake.[71]

For Otis and the other radicals of the Revolutionary generation, a natural law of "eternal truth, equity and justice"[72] was not an abstraction. The ideal had been virtually realized in history by their true ancestors, the ancient Saxons, prior to, as Otis put it, "the coming in of the first Norman Tyrants."[73]

According to Christopher Hill, the second half of the eighteenth century witnessed revivals of the "Norman Yoke" discourse by radicals in England as well as America; these revivals recalled the spirit of resistance of England's Glorious Revolution of 1688–1689.[74] As elaborated by the influential pamphlet *Historical Essay on the English Constitution*, published anonymously in London in 1771, the theory of the Norman Yoke boiled down to the opinion that before 1066, the Anglo-Saxons of England lived as free and equal citizens under a form of representative government that was inspired by divine principles of natural law and the common rights of all individuals. The Norman Conquest, however, had destroyed this Saxon model of government.[75] But not even the Norman Yoke could destroy the Saxon Constitution's divinely inspired universal appeal to the minds of free English everywhere. The near-pristine natural-law vision embodied in the Saxon model of government, according to the *Historical Essay*, must have been divinely inspired: "If ever God Almighty did concern himself about forming a government, for mankind to live happily under, it was that which was established in England by our Saxon forefathers."[76] As another essayist put it, "This Saxon model of government, when reduced to its first principles, has a strong resemblance to the natural state of things, under which mankind was found to live at the discovery of the New World by Columbus."[77] Thus historical events such as Magna Carta and the English Revolution's overthrow of the "execrable race of the Stuarts"[78] were part of the continual struggle of the English to reestablish their revered and ancient Saxon rights and liberties.

In America particularly, it was thought possible to continue this noble Saxon experiment, temporarily halted by the crushing tyranny of an alien king and his fellow Norman landlords. John Adams, the Boston revolutionary, sensed providence at work in the settlement of America and the realization of a purer English, Saxon-centered constitution that was to be achieved by the colonists.[79] "It was this great struggle that peopled America . . . [A] love of universal liberty, and a hatred, a dread, a horror, of the infernal confederacy [of temporal and spiritual tyranny] projected, conducted, and accomplished the settlement of America."[80] Thomas Jefferson so strongly desired to establish the historical paternity of his own ideas on political liberty that he "painstakingly collected every scrap of evidence to reconstruct the history of his 'Saxon ancestors.'"[81]

The energizing dynamic added to American oppositional discursive practice by incorporation of the discourse of the Norman Yoke cannot be underestimated. Radical Americans saw plainly and without doubt that the king and Parliament's attacks on their fundamental rights were but a continuation of the Norman Yoke. To the Americans, a corrupt Parliament in league with a foreign-born king was once again subverting ancient English rights and liberties, this time in the virtually pristine state of nature that was America.

The American radicals held a firm conviction that theirs was an environment ripe for creating a special preserve for English liberties. Natural law and natural rights would define America's government. The torch of Saxon liberties had passed to English settlers on the far shore of the Atlantic, as the canker of Norman tyranny and degeneracy had fatally infected all levels of English society at home.

British Americans reveled in the reports of corruption in Parliament and the Ministry that boded so ill for liberty in England.[82] Benjamin Franklin reprinted James Burgh's London pamphlet of 1746, *Britain's Remembrancer: Or, The Danger Not Over*, for an eager American audience. Burgh's tract told of a people who wallowed in "luxury and irreligion . . . venality, perjury, faction, opposition to legal authority, idleness, gluttony, drunkenness, lewdness," and on and on—"a legion of furies sufficient to send any state or empire that ever was in the world to pieces."[83]

Franklin himself offered this antidote, should Britain's vices force its dissolution:

[S]hould this dreaded fatal change happen in my time, how should I, even in the midst of the affliction, rejoice if we [in America] have been able to preserve those invaluable treasures, and can invite the good among you to come and partake of them! O let not Britain seek to oppress us, but like an affectionate parent endeavor to secure freedom to her children; they may be able one day to assist her in defending her own.[84]

Charles Carroll, Jr., of the Maryland Carrolls, felt that the corruption of the English government was hastening the British Constitution "to its final period of dissolution." Like many of the American radicals, he advised an English acquaintance to sell his estate and "purchase lands in this province [Maryland] where liberty will maintain her empire."[85]

The king and his ministers, however, by the Proclamation of 1763 and the 1764 imperial plan of western management, were threatening liberty's empire by prohibiting the purchase of the "waste" lands of America. It took little in the way of a leap of the historical imagination to see in the king's arrogation of rights in the western lands an abuse of his prerogative. The proclamation constituted but another instance of the tyranny of the Norman Yoke, this time applied in America. According to the Lockean-inspired natural-law discourse of the Norman Yoke, lands that should have remained free for appropriation by the labor of Americans had been usurped by a tyrannous monarch and made a part of his feudal demesne.

In fact, it was in response to the imperial government's western policies that the Norman Yoke discourse received its most radical elaboration during the

Revolutionary period. If by "radical" we mean to convey the idea of going to the foundation or source of a thing, then certainly Thomas Jefferson's tract *A Summary View of the Rights of British America* (1774)[86] represents the most radical extension of Norman Yoke thematics, as well as the most radical elaboration of colonial insurrectionist discourse prior to the Revolution.

Jefferson's *Summary View* was one of the most influential and popular pamphlets published before the Revolution. In many ways, it can be seen as a trial run for many of the core statements of American political and legal discourse later elaborated by Jefferson in the Declaration of Independence.[87] To set the stage, it is necessary to examine the historical events that led up to Jefferson's radical discourse in *A Summary View*.

The American By-products of the Norman Yoke

As has been mentioned,[88] the British Ministry, itself torn by internal feuding and factionalism, had repealed the Stamp Act in the face of American rioting and opposition. Now, without the tax, the Ministry lacked a source of revenue for enforcing the proclamation's boundary line and regulating the Indian trade under the 1764 imperial plan. It was hoped that if the western frontier was simply declared off-limits and if a few forts were garrisoned at strategic places, the colonists would simply cease in their efforts to acquire Indian lands. That was not to be. As the example of George Washington's defiant correspondence demonstrates,[89] land speculators, particularly those from Virginia, continued to act on the assumption that the right to control western lands reserved to the Indians by the king's proclamation ultimately belonged to the "landed" colonies, whose chartered limits comprehended ownership of the frontier. The Virginians and other speculators from the landed colonies thus responded to the proclamation by accelerating their speculative activities in Indian-claimed western lands, in hopes of preempting any future actions by the Crown that would be contrary to their colonies' interests. As late as 1767, for instance, Governor Fauquier of Virginia answered the plea of the Crown's southern superintendent for Indian affairs for cooperation in the enforcement of the king's boundary line with the contemptuous declaration, "I know nothing of the Proclamation of the 7th October 1763."[90]

The Virginians had good reason to ignore the proclamation, as numerous other speculative-minded colonists interpreted the proclamation as providing an opportunity for them to realize their own desires in the western territories. Influential individuals from colonies such as Pennsylvania, Maryland, and New Jersey—the "landless" colonies whose boundaries were limited by their charters and which thus could claim no western lands—now had cause to hope that the Ministry in London might be persuaded (or bribed) to ratify grants that they might be able to obtain directly from Indian tribes on the frontier. In effect, the strategy of the speculators from these landless colonies was to use the king's proclamation as the instrument for undermining the extravagant claims of the landed colonies to the entire western part of the continent. They sought to convince the government in London that the solution to the western problem was to allow them to establish, in orderly fashion and with the permission of the Indians, colonies carved out of the vast interior wilderness.

Thus the ultimate and wholly unintended result of the Proclamation of 1763 was to accelerate the process of speculation in western lands by colonists from the landed and landless colonies alike in the decade preceding the Revolutionary War. As the fragile consensus on both sides of the Atlantic respecting the locus of administrative power to confirm rights in Indian lands broke down, speculators swarmed the frontier, surveying lands and purchasing any and all claims and interests from willing Indian tribes. The Indians, having suddenly discovered the meaning of the term "sellers' market," gladly auctioned off little-regarded surplus lands or border territories that might also be claimed by a rival tribe.

Benjamin Franklin: Syndicalist

Many prominent colonists were involved in speculative ventures in western Indian lands in the Revolutionary era. Few, however, could rival Benjamin Franklin's tenacious ability at securing, protecting, and advancing at all levels of government his private financial interests in numerous speculative ventures.

The famous Pennsylvanian had been involved in a number of petty schemes during the French and Indian War. The new situation brought about by the proclamation and the evacuation of the French from the Ohio region, however, offered a man of Franklin's persuasive skills and slippery business ethics abundant opportunities for profitable speculation. The proclamation's boundary line essentially meant that London's assertion of control over the West had usurped, or at least stalled, the forward momentum of the landed colonies' absurd claims to the entire region. For Franklin, who served as the Pennsylvania Assembly's agent in London in the late 1760s and early 1770s, the government's seeming opposition to westward expansion by the likes of the Indian-abusing, unruly Virginians meant only that the Ministry had not heard about the benefits of expansion by other, more flexible Americans who were willing to respect the rights of the tribes by purchasing their lands at fair prices.

Numerous speculators in American lands on both sides of the Atlantic, recognizing the value of Franklin's talents and contacts in the government in London, sought to draw him into their schemes. From the Virginians' self-interested point of view, one of the most worrisome frontier land ventures aided by Franklin involved an attempt made by George Croghan, the previously mentioned frontier trader, and the powerful Philadelphia trading house of Baynton, Wharton, and Morgan to secure sufficient land to establish a proprietary colony in the West.

Croghan had lived and traded with the western Indians since his arrival in America from Dublin in 1741.[91] He traveled to London in 1764 to petition the government for restitution for losses that he and other "suffering" traders had incurred on the western frontier, supposedly at the hands of French-allied Indians during the French and Indian War. The Irish backwoodsman was unsuccessful in securing monetary compensation, but Croghan did learn a valuable lesson while lobbying the English government. Thoroughly frustrated with the corruption he saw everywhere around him, Croghan wrote to his close associate in America, Sir William Johnson, the Crown's Indian superintendent for the northern district:

[T]here has been nothing Don Sence I came to London by the Grate ones but squbeling and fighting [to] see who will keep in power[,] the publick interest is neglected to serve privet-intrest and I blieve itt is hard to say wh. party is yr honistist[,], was I to spake my mind I wold say they are all R-g-e-s [Rogues] alicke[.] I am Nott Sorry I came hear as it will Larn Me to be Contended on a Little farm in amerrica if I can gett one when I go back Butt I ashure yr. honor I am sick of London and harttily tier'd of ye pride and pompe of the Slaves in power hear which are to be pitied tho they Dont Deserve itt.[92]

What Croghan had learned while in London was that if a semiliterate Indian trader with a family of half-bloods to feed (Croghan had married an Indian woman, a not infrequent practice among colonial traders seeking entrée and goodwill with potential client tribes) wanted to get "a little farm in America," he should rely on friends in high places. Late in 1764, he returned to Philadelphia, where members of the influential merchant firm of Baynton, Wharton, and Morgan quickly recognized the value of Croghan's unrivaled knowledge of the western frontier and the western Indians.

Croghan and two partners in the firm, George Morgan and Samuel Wharton, formed a land syndicate called the Illinois Company. Its purpose, in Croghan's words, was to purchase "what Ever grants the French was possesse'd of in the Illinois Country," securing title to at least "Twelve Hundred Thousand Acres,"[93] more than enough to establish a proprietary colony under the Crown's approval. The articles of agreement of the Illinois Company, dated March 29, 1766, named ten shareholders in the venture, including the named members of the firm and Samuel Wharton's father and brother, Joseph Sr. and Jr., as well as Croghan.[94] Benjamin Franklin, thought to be "much attended to by the Ministry," was brought into the scheme in May. Franklin promised from London to forward the interests of his partners "to my utmost here."[95]

William Franklin, governor of New Jersey, was also a member of the syndicate, although his membership was not advertised. William had been closely associated with Croghan's earlier efforts in London to obtain compensation for the "suffering" traders. William was also the illegitimate son of Benjamin Franklin. He had studied law while traveling with his father to England in 1756. The Earl of Bute, a powerful figure in ministerial politics during the period, honored Benjamin Franklin by bestowing knighthood on his son and securing his appointment as governor of New Jersey in 1762. The proprietor of Pennsylvania, John Penn, called the whole business a "shameful affair" and an insult to the people of New Jersey.[96] But then William Franklin's father was the London agent of the Pennsylvania Assembly's Quaker majority. As Benjamin's principal task in London was to secure the revocation of the Penn family's proprietorship, Penn would have been highly insulted by the advancement of any Franklin. It is also worth noting that the Pennsylvanian Joseph Galloway, another partner in the Illinois Company syndicate, was

Benjamin Franklin's closest associate in working against the interest of the Penns.

Croghan had thought it better that William Franklin's participation in the Illinois Company's venture not be publicized. Croghan also thought it wise that another shareholder, his close friend and the imperial Indian agent for the northern district, Sir William Johnson, not be identified with the project. The secrecy was required because the syndicate planned to have Governor Franklin and Indian agent Johnson advocate the venture to the home government in their official capacities as loyal servants of His Majesty's interests in America. As Croghan wrote to Johnson, "it's thought you can be of more service by not being thought Concern'd[.] But this is submitted to y'r honor."[97]

His "honor," Sir William, was not above securing a personal profit in connection with his official position as superintendent of Indian affairs in the northern district. Johnson might be excused for his increasing speculative dealings in Indian lands following the French and Indian War. The failure of the British Ministry to decide on the particulars of an Indian policy, or even to secure or authorize an adequate source of funds to enable its superintendents to carry out their duties, often required Johnson to finance his office out of his own pocket. But Johnson's inclination toward opportunistic behavior became evident frequently enough that one guesses his pocket was more than equal to the demands of his office. He had come to America as a young Irish gentleman to develop the wilderness estate of his uncle, Sir Peter Warren. He succeeded well, building a stockaded mansion staffed by a personal physician, a jester-dwarf, a secretary, a tailor, a butler, and other servants. He lived in "feudal magnificence" with the sixteen-year-old Mohawk sister of Joseph Brant, whom he took as his mistress after his first wife died. Thomas Abernathy tells the following story, derived from Sir William's own papers:

He flattered the gullible chiefs and acquired great influence over them. . . . He once ordered from England several suits of clothes, richly laced. One of the chiefs was present when they arrived and admired them inordinately. In a few days he returned and informed the superintendent that he dreamed he had presented him with one of the suits, which Sir William did. Later Sir William dreamed in turn that the chief gave him a very valuable tract of land on the Mohawk, which the chief did, saying "Now, Sir William, I will never dream with you again, you dream too hard for me."[98]

Only someone familiar with Indian notions of gift giving and reciprocity would have known that the chief was not likely to ignore Sir William's dream. Only someone familiar with the white man's notions of the value of land would have dared to dream as Sir William did.

The brain trust of the Illinois Company—the Whartons, the Franklins, Croghan, and Johnson—had devised an intricate piece of chicanery to advance their venality in London. Samuel Wharton and Governor Franklin sent Superintendent Johnson a paper entitled "Reasons for Establishing a Colony in the Illinois."[99] The paper, of course, extolled the many benefits that would accrue to the empire if the Crown approved the Illinois Company's plan to settle a colony on the frontier. Johnson wrote to William Franklin that he would "cheerfully" do all he could to secure the plan "as early as possible." In fact, he had already begun the cumulative process of recommending the proposal's virtues to the home government in his capacity as a disinterested servant of his Majesty's best interests. "I have already hinted the affair in a letter to the Lords of Trade and I am somewhat of opinion it would answer better that I recommend it in Gen'l terms, as an affair I had heard was in agitation."[100]

William Franklin wrote back to Johnson that he would also forward the plan with his official recommendation as governor of New Jersey. As Croghan had advised, the governor also would pretend not to be interested in the scheme. His supposed detachment from the enterprise would lend his favorable opinion "greater weight."[101]

Benjamin Franklin received the syndicate's "Reasons for Establishing a Colony in the Illinois" in London in September 1766. He dutifully passed the pamphlet on to Lord Shelbourne, secretary of state for the southern department. Superintendent Johnson sent the speculators' proposal to the chief secretary of state, Henry Conway. Johnson's cover letter to the secretary explained the benefits of the plan and stated simply that the company's pamphlet had been forwarded to him by "several Gentlemen of fortune and character."[102]

After apparently sampling initial reactions to the plan in governmental circles, Benjamin Franklin became aware of the need for greater liquidity in greasing the wheels of London's political machine. He wrote to his son in New Jersey that while he personally liked the plan, additional members ought to be nominated to join the Illinois Company. In his opinion, the company's proposal envisaged acquiring more than enough land "to content a large number of reasonable people."[103]

Franklin succeeded in lobbying Secretary of State Shelbourne, who, in turn, convinced the privy council's members of the worth of the endeavor. The Board of Trade, however, headed by the antiexpansionist Lord Hillsborough, killed the proposal for settling a colony in Illinois. Franklin wrote that Hillsborough feared "dispeopling Ireland" with inland American colonies.[104] Commander in Chief Gage, probably worried about security on the frontier and the costs of protecting a new and remote colony, had also apparently objected to the Illinois venture.

The "Suffering" Traders

The speculators, however, had been pursuing other options. The Board of Trade's 1764 plan of imperial management for the West called for formalizing the royal proclamation's principle of a boundary line to white settlement by negotiating treaties with the major Indian tribes along the frontier in the north and south. Sir William Johnson's responsibilities as imperial agent for Indian affairs in the north included negotiating the western boundary with the Six Nations of the Iroquois and their tributary tribes in the Ohio River valley.[105] Croghan now called on Superintendent Johnson for assistance in securing compensation for his "suffering" traders, who had yet to receive restitution for the losses they had allegedly incurred at the hands of the western tribes in the

French and Indian War. Croghan's suggested form of compensation was a grant of land to the traders from the tribes of the region, negotiated by Johnson alongside the imperial boundary treaty negotiations with the Indians.[106]

In actuality, the traders were hardly "suffering." Two entrepreneurs, William Trent and John Hughes, had bought up the rights to the claims of the traders who had truly suffered losses at the hands of the Indians during the war. These claims were then transferred to a group whose membership overlapped that of the Illinois Company. Besides Croghan, the "sufferers" now included the Baynton, Wharton, and Morgan firm, the two Franklins, Joseph Galloway, and others. Johnson naturally was a silent participant in this scheme, too.

Johnson raised the subject of compensation for his partners at a conference with the Delawares and the Iroquois Confederacy in May 1765. He had called the meeting to discuss preliminaries to the formal royal boundary negotiations with the affected tribes. Johnson pressed the representatives from the confederated Iroquois tribes either to grant the "suffering" traders a large tract of land or to risk losing their much-desired trade. The confederacy's negotiators apparently agreed "most cheerfully" to grant the merchants a favorable piece of land on the north side of the Ohio River, far from the Iroquois' own territory, "as it was now of no use to them [the Iroquois], for hunting ground."[107]

Now only two obstacles remained. First, Whitehall would have to accept the Iroquois cession negotiated by Superintendent Johnson in favor of the "suffering" traders, even though the lands ceded by the Six Nations were on the prohibited side of the proclamation line. Second, Virginia would obviously seek to derail the tentative deal negotiated by Johnson in the preliminary treaty discussions. The "suffering" traders' grant was in the vicinity of Fort Pitt, an area of significant speculative value claimed by Virginia under its 1609 charter. The Virginians' anticipated efforts to prevent a new colony from being carved out of "their" western territory would have to be countered by the syndicate.

The task of convincing Whitehall to affirm the Iroquois grant was assigned to Benjamin Franklin in London. His instructions by letter from Baynton, Wharton, and Morgan were explicit. "The Indians cannot give us the land," the letter stressed, unless Sir William was empowered to vary the line on the traders' behalf.[108] Franklin understood. He endorsed the firm's letter with a personal note of reminder: "Very important about the boundary to be urged with the Min[istr]y."[109]

Shortly after this correspondence, Samuel Wharton told William Franklin to instruct his father, Benjamin, to stop urging the Illinois Company project before the Ministry and instead devote all his energies to securing the Ministry's approval of the "suffering" traders' Indian grant. As these lands were near Fort Pitt, Wharton believed they could be more quickly sold to settlers for cash than the lands in the more distant Illinois country. The elder Franklin began circulating the rumor in London that an Indian war was inevitable unless the boundary, including the traders' grant, was affirmed as negotiated by Johnson in the preliminary treaty discussions. He also further ingratiated himself with the various London politicos who determined American policy.[110]

The formal northern boundary between the Indians and the English was agreed to at a treaty ceremony with the Six Nations at Fort Stanwix in October 1768. Superintendent Johnson had been instructed from London to draw the boundary line with the Iroquois and western Indians down the Ohio River southward to the Great Kanawha River, where it was to meet the line that was to be arranged by the southern-district superintendent, John Stuart, with the Cherokee Nation. Johnson, however, blatantly violated these instructions at the Fort Stanwix negotiations, extending the boundary line with the Iroquois Confederacy much farther south, down to the mouth of the Tennessee River. The Iroquois exercised no control over this area between the Great Kanawha and the Tennessee. Yet by agreeing to Johnson's extension of the line, the confederacy obligingly and painlessly ceded the entire territory to the English.

The better claim to the region between the Great Kanawha and the Tennessee rivers belonged to the Cherokees. They, however, had refused to cede these valuable lands in their boundary negotiations with the Crown's southern Indian superintendent. This refusal greatly displeased the Virginians, who claimed the preemption rights to the tract by virtue of their colony's Crown charter of 1609. By recognizing the Iroquois' right to cede this valuable area at the Fort Stanwix treaty ceremony, Johnson had in essence denied the Cherokee claim. Virginia now had only to convince Whitehall to confirm Johnson's unilateral actions so that they could be offered for sale to ready Virginian settlers. The fact that the land was beyond the proclamation line had been rendered immaterial, as the rights belonging to Virginia to settle the area had been obtained from the Iroquois in a valid treaty of cession. As for the Cherokees, any complaints they had could be dealt with later.

As Jack Sosin has argued, the events at Fort Stanwix suggest that in exchange for Superintendent Johnson's generous favor to Virginia in accepting an Iroquois cession of Cherokee territory and in effect making that territory more easily available to Virginians, Virginia acquiesced to the "suffering" traders' grant, which of course had also been made a part of the formal treaty negotiated by Johnson.[111] It is highly unlikely that the Virginia commissioner to the treaty, Dr. Thomas Walker, would have agreed to a cession of territory within his colony's chartered boundaries unless Virginia received some form of valuable consideration in return. Walker himself was an agent of the Loyal Land Company of Virginia, a longtime rival of the Ohio Company, also composed of many prominent Virginians. The Indian lands on the north side of the Ohio that Walker permitted to pass to the "suffering" traders under the Fort Stanwix treaty had earlier been claimed by the Ohio Company.[112] In short, Walker, the double agent, had gained a valuable prize for his colony, the extinguishment of the Cherokee claim to the desirable lands between the Great Kanawha and the Tennessee rivers. At the same time, Walker had managed to undermine a principal intracolonial business rival. On the frontier, it was every speculator for himself.

Johnson had also taken bold steps to neutralize London's expected opposition to the traders' grant. The superintendent had persuaded the Iroquois to make their cession to the king of some 2.4 million acres under the treaty conditional on the reciprocal smaller cession to the "suffering" traders. Johnson, in other words, had negotiated a treaty on the Crown's behalf which declared that if the king desired to enjoy the benefits of a freely extended, multimillion-acre land cession by the largest and most powerful Indian confederacy on the American frontier, he would have to acquiesce in the base chicanery of a group of land speculators.

The news of Johnson's final treaty terms, negotiated in blatant disregard of London's instructions, outraged the antiexpansionist Lord Hillsborough, who had assumed Shelbourne's role in controlling American policy following the collapse of William Pitt's ministry in January 1768. Hillsborough saw clearly that Johnson, the Crown's duly authorized agent, had acquired a vast cession from the Iroquois that in truth belonged to the Cherokees as part of a deal to benefit a syndicate of mendacious land jobbers. The Board of Trade condemned Johnson's actions and refused to confirm the "suffering" traders' grant, thus complicating ratification of the remainder of the treaty.

Samuel Wharton, a controlling partner in the syndicate, was now required to go to London to plead the cause of the "suffering" traders and to urge acceptance of all the terms of the Fort Stanwix negotiations. Arriving in 1769 with William Trent, Wharton drew up several petitions requesting the Ministry's confirmation of the Indian grants to the traders. These were to be presented to the government by the syndicate's solicitor, Henry Dagge. The firm of Baynton, Wharton, and Morgan was now in receivership, and the principals, as well as their associates, Croghan and Trent, were in desperate financial circumstances. Samuel Wharton wrote to Croghan from London, "My *All* depends on the Confirmation of the Indian Grant."[113]

The syndicate's lobbying efforts proved only parially successful. Hillsborough, who reportedly termed the process by which the larger grant of lands to the king had been conditioned on the reciprocal grant to the traders "a piece of management,"[114] was forced by the privy council to accept the Iroquois grant of the area between the Great Kanawha and the Tennessee rivers. He was, however, successful in convincing the Board of Trade to put aside the "suffering" traders' grant for future consideration.[115]

The Vandalia Colony

Wharton continued his lobbying efforts. He made valuable contacts throughout London, most likely through Franklin's offices. Wharton's "general knowledge of American affairs" garnered him several valuable dinner invitations.[116] One of the important personages he met was Thomas Walpole, London banker, member of Parliament, Horatio Lord Walpole's son, and cousin to Horace Walpole. In June 1769, Walpole told Wharton that he had recently dined with Lord Chancellor Camden, a highly respected figure in the government. Lord Camden had confided that the entire Ministry thought Hillsborough "mad" for opposing the Fort Stanwix treaty. The cabinet, except for Hillsborough, was unanimous in the feeling that if the Six Nations so insisted, then the boundary treaty should be confirmed "in all its parts" (meaning of course that the "suffering" traders' grant should also be confirmed).[117]

With hopes revived of undermining Hillsborough and saving the syndicate's Indian grant on the northern side of the Ohio, Wharton spent the summer strengthening his ties with "the first ruling characters" of the government.[118] By the end of July 1769, a new company had been organized. Its membership included a number of London luminaries: Thomas Walpole; Thomas Pownall; Lord Hertford, who held the office of lord chamberlain; Lord Camden; Richard Jackson, counselor to the Board of Trade; George Grenville; Lords Gower and Rockford, who both sat on the privy council; Laughlin MacLeane, a member of Parliament and Lord Shelbourne's confidant; John Robinson, undersecretary of the Treasury; Thomas Pitt; Anthony Todd, the postmaster general; Sir George Colebrook, director of the East India Company; and Richard and Robert Walpole. Many other individuals of influence and importance throughout London also held shares in Wharton's newly formed land-jobbing syndicate.[119]

On the advice of the syndicate's solicitor, Henry Dagge, the idea of pursuing the "suffering" traders' grant before the Ministry was dropped. Wharton and his cabal decided to pursue a path of lesser resistance. The interests of the "suffering" traders' syndicate were formally merged with those of the new and far more powerful London Walpole syndicate. Through its various machinations and contacts, the Walpole Company secured the Treasury's permission in 1770 to purchase an area sufficient for a new colony embracing some 20 million acres. The original Iroquois grant to the "suffering" traders was incorporated into the boundaries of the new colony. The colony was to be called, ironically enough, "Vandalia." The boundary of this new interior proprietary colony was to run along a point on the Ohio River opposite the mouth of the Scioto, then south through the Cumberland Gap, there following the Cumberland Mountains to where the Greenbriar flowed into the Kanawha, then to the source of the Greenbriar, and then along the Allegheny Mountains to the western boundaries of Maryland and Pennsylvania.[120]

Several critical issues were raised by the proposed boundary for the new colony. The western boundary of Pennsylvania was in dispute, and the proprietors of that colony jealously guarded all claims. Also, the proposed boundaries comprehended certain tracts on the Greenbriar that had previously been patented by Virginia and were under its claimed jurisdiction.

News of Wharton's London coup and the Walpole Company's proposed new colony of Vandalia in the West was generally poorly received in America. The Penns, of course, sought information about which western lands were encompassed by the proposal. As for the Virginians, they recognized clearly that they had been fleeced. Arthur Lee wrote from London to his brother Richard in Virginia that the Ministry was going to grant *their* lands to a company of speculators.[121] The Lees' Virginia syndicate, the Mississippi Company (which also included George Washington as a member), protested vigorously against the Vandalia project.

Virginia's own agent in London, Edward Montague, filed a caveat against the petition of the Walpole Company. The Ohio Company, represented by

George Mercer, similarly filed a petition of protest. George Washington also belonged to this syndicate, principally representing a group of Virginia soldiers who had been promised lands in 1754 by then Virginia governor Robert Dinwiddie for fighting the French under Washington's command at the outbreak of the French and Indian War.

One by one, Wharton and Walpole sought to buy off or silence the conflicting claims and interests opposed to their Vandalia plan. Mercer, for instance, was permitted to merge the interests he represented into the Walpole group. The Ohio Company received two of the seventy-two shares of the new company. Washington and his soldiers were to receive 200,000 acres under the arrangement, while Mercer himself received one whole share.

Although several of the private Virginia speculating groups had been bought off, the Walpole Company still had not solved the problem of the Virginia colonial government's rooted opposition to the Vandalia colony. Walpole had tried submitting a desperate charge to the Board of Trade against the Council of Virginia, asserting that land speculators within the colonial government itself were primarily responsible for the numerous illegal encroachments north of the Ohio. The implied claim behind this assertion was that such Virginia-encouraged encroachments would cease, as would Indian resentment, once a proprietary colony was established in the region by the well-regarded gentlemen of the Walpole Company, who promised to treat the Indians well. The antiexpansionist Hillsborough, seeking to delay final approval of the Vandalia colony, convinced the board to ask Virginia's government to respond to Walpole's most serious charges against the honor of certain gentlemen in the colony. Walpole's tactical blunder permitted the board to delay final action on the Vandalia colony for two years as it waited for the considered response of the gentlemen of Virginia.[122]

When the Council of Virginia finally did get around to formulating a response to Walpole's charges, it pleaded innocent. Hillsborough's Board of Trade issued a negative report on the planned Vandalia colony in April 1772, citing fears of unease among the western tribes about the establishment of a new English colony in their midst. The Committee of Council for Plantation Affairs, however, was more susceptible to the blandishments of Walpole and his powerful, expansion-minded associates. The committee threatened to go on record against the report of Hillsborough's board opposing Vandalia. In August, Hillsborough finally gave up the fight. He resigned the government to take an earlship in Ireland. Benjamin Franklin wrote triumphantly from London to his son:

[A]t length we have got rid of Lord Hillsborough. . . . [H]is brother ministers disliked him extremely, and wished for a fair occasion of tripping his heels; so, seeing that he made a point of defeating our scheme, they made another of supporting it on purpose to mortify him, which they knew his pride could not bear.[123]

That Hillsborough might have acted out of a strongly held conviction that westward expansion was not in the best interests of the empire was never admitted by Franklin or the craven English politicians and American land speculators who constituted the Walpole Company. Perhaps Lord Hillsborough viewed an earl's coronet in Ireland as a last refuge of dignity, far away from the scoundrels who apparently adhered to the maxim that what was good for the Walpole Company was good for the empire.

The day after Hillsborough resigned, the privy council approved the Walpole petition. Virginia was to receive some protection in the instrument of government for the new colony. In drafting the enabling documents, the Board of Trade was to insert a clause reserving all prior claims within the limits of the Vandalia grant.

But the colony of Vandalia was never to be. Attorney General Edward Thurlow and Solicitor General Alexander Wedderburn, assigned to draw up the final grant to the company, raised various objections to the proposed terms. In reality, both men harbored doubts about the loyalty of syndicate member Benjamin Franklin. Sensing (correctly) that the Philadelphian was closely aligned with the growing radical resistance in America, Thurlow considered Franklin "unworthy" of the favors of the Crown. When the news reached London of the December 1773 tea party in Boston Harbor held by Sam Adams and his terrorist gang of disguised "Mohawks," Wedderburn openly denounced Franklin before the privy council.[124]

Walpole sought to salvage the Vandalia project by asking Franklin to resign from the company. Franklin was secretly to keep his shares, in hopes that his "Posterity reap the Benefits of them."[125] With events spiraling out of control in America, however, the Vandalia colony was removed from the agenda of major imperial concerns. The Ministry became preoccupied with managing the rapidly accelerating chaos in the colonies. Royal troops were evacuated from frontier forts in the West to assist in quelling the unrest on the eastern seaboard. The governor of Virginia, Lord Dunmore, himself heavily invested in various speculating schemes with his fellow Virginians, sensed the unique opportunity presented by the evacuation of imperial troops from the West. He ordered Dr. John Connally and a group of Virginia militiamen to seize the recently abandoned Fort Pitt. Claiming that London had never properly informed him of the Walpole Company's claims on the upper Ohio,[126] Dunmore ordered his deputy to establish a county government for the area. Fort Pitt was renamed Fort Dunmore, much to the displeasure of the Shawnee Indians, who by force of numbers held the strongest Indian claim to the Iroquois-ceded lands intended for settlement by the Virginians. Provoked into attack, the outmanned and outgunned Shawnees, along with allies from the Delaware and Wyandot tribes, were soundly defeated by the Virginia militia in June 1774 in what became known as Dunmore's War. In the absence of any effective imperial military force to contest its claims in the region, Virginia now controlled the upper Ohio, once the intended site of the Vandalia colony.

Thomas Jefferson: Revolutionary

Dunmore's War was but final proof to exasperated policymakers in London that the Americans would never abide by the proclamation line or by an imperial policy closing the West to their landed ambitions. British officials in the field had reported regularly to Whitehall on the impossibility of keeping the Americans out of the western territory.[127] The home government had sought to reform aspects of the land-granting process in early 1774 by adopting a new policy for certain frontier settlements that had been approved by the Ministry before the issuance of the Proclamation of 1763. Under the new policy, surveys were to be required and the governors could sell lands only in small lots at auction to the highest bidder. The Americans blithely violated this odious policy changing the terms of the land-acquisition process on the frontier, just as they had violated the proclamation.

Resigned to the impossibility of enforcing the policy of a closed western frontier, the Ministry reluctantly decided to turn over control of the Northwest wilderness to the Canadians of Quebec. The former French province, which had been captured in the French and Indian War, was still predominantly Catholic, and the French Canadians had been permitted by Whitehall to continue operating according to their alien civil-law customs. Now Whitehall sought to capitalize on this liberality, recognizing that no Englishman would desire ever to come under the Catholic and alien-inspired government of a Canadian-controlled Northwest. The Quebec Act, transferring jurisdiction of the territory to the former French colony, would become law in the summer of 1774.

It was in response to the crisis represented by this intense set of circumstances arising in the early 1770s—the Vandalia fiasco, Dunmore's War, the new terms for acquiring lands dictated by the Ministry, the looming Quebec Act, and the seeming inevitability of open rebellion with the mother country—that Thomas Jefferson's pamphlet *A Summary View of the Rights of British America* appeared in 1774.[128] Jefferson was without doubt one of the most radical members of the American Revolutionary generation. Not long after presiding as intellectual leader over the bloody revolt with Great Britain, Jefferson commented with wry wisdom that an uprising by a group of impoverished backwoods Massachusetts farmers was "nothing threatening." "[I]f the happiness of the mass of people can be secured at the expense of a little tempest now and then, or even a little blood, it will be a precious purchase." The author of *A Summary View* and the Declaration of Independence once called "the blood of patriots and tyrants" the "natural manure" of the tree of liberty. The "spirit" of resistance to government, Jefferson wrote, "will often be exercised when wrong, but better so than not to be exercised at all. . . . I like . . . a little rebellion now and then."[129]

Written on the eve of the first Continental Congress, Jefferson's *Summary View* forthrightly attacked the Crown's tyrannical usurpation of British American rights and liberties. Jefferson framed his insurrectionist discourse of independence using the radical thematics of the Norman Yoke, setting out his opposed views of the colonists' rights "from the origin and first settlement of these countries"[130] as follows:

[O]ur ancestors, before their emigration to America, were the free inhabitants of the British dominions in Europe, and possessed a right which nature had given to all men, of departing from the country in which chance not choice, has placed them, of going in quest of new habitations, and of there establishing new societies, under such laws and regulations as to them shall seem most likely to promote the public happiness.[131]

According to Jefferson's radical mythology, the British Americans' "ancestors," the freedom-loving Saxons, had similarly emigrated from their original homes. Having left northern Europe, the ancient Saxons "possessed themselves" of England, "less charged with inhabitants." Once settled in England, the Saxons established "that system of laws which has so long been the glory and protection" of Great Britain.[132]

The lords whom the Saxons left behind in northern Europe, according to Jefferson, did not dare to claim "superiority" over those freedom-seeking sojourners who migrated to Britain. That noble race had "too firm a feeling" of their rights ever to bow down to such distant "visionary pretensions" of sovereignty.[133]

Having demonstrated that the Saxons had earned their independence by emigrating to England and establishing a polity there, Jefferson simply extended the inevitable trajectory of the parallel implications of his Saxon history:

And it is thought that no circumstance[s] [have] occurred to distinguish materially the British from the Saxon emigration. America was conquered, and her settlements made, and firmly established, at the expense of individuals, and not of the British public. Their own blood was spilt in acquiring lands for their settlement, their own fortunes expended in making that settlement effectual; for themselves alone they have a right to hold.[134]

Jefferson had seized the radicals' Lockean-inspired thematic wedge—a natural-law-based notion of a government formed by autonomous compact and the consent of the governed—to legitimate the American claim for independence from British sovereignty. His discursive strategy deployed the mythology of the restless, freedom-loving Saxons to dramatize the continuity of the Saxon struggle for natural rights now being played out on the American stage. The Americans, inheritors of the Saxon mantle of liberty, had seen their natural-law rights to freedom frustrated by the continual usurpations of the British Crown and its wrongfully asserted sovereign prerogatives over the colonies. This history of usurpation by the Crown, Jefferson argued, should therefore be recognized for what it was; a wrongful continuation of the perversion of Saxon principles of right and justice, traceable to the first imposition of the Norman Yoke in 1066.

According to Jefferson's chronology of events, it was only when the American colonies had become firmly established and had thus become of commercial value to Great Britain that "parliament was pleased to lend them assistance against an enemy [France], who would fair draw to herself the benefits of their commerce, to the great aggrandizement of herself, and danger of Great Britain."[135] Benjamin Franklin's version of the French and Indian War as a conflict waged solely for England's commercial benefit[136] had apparently become part of the discursive canon of radicals. Jefferson sharpened the argument, reasoning that Britain's assistance in the war could not be differentiated from aid given by the king's armies and navy to Portugal and other allied states, "with whom they carry on a commercial intercourse, yet these states never supposed that by calling in her [Great Britain's] aid, they thereby submitted themselves to her sovereignty." Britain's wartime assistance was "doubtless valuable, on whatever principles granted," but it could not, according to Jefferson, "give a title to that authority which the British parliament would arrogate over us."[137]

Having laid out his Saxon-inspired argument for the independent foundation and autonomy of English America, Jefferson launched into a predictable attack on the Stuart kings and their tyrannous usurpations of American colonial charter rights. The country of America, having "been acquired by the lives, the labours, and the fortunes, of individual adventurers was by these princes . . . parted out and distributed among the favorites and followers of their fortunes" and, by an assumed right of the Crown alone, were erected into distinct and independent Crown colonies.[138] To Jefferson, not just these instances of usurpation but the very claims of the Crown to the American continent were grounded in the perversion of Saxon principles of right and justice. And this perversion, claimed Jefferson, was directly traceable to the Norman Yoke's most significant imposition on the natural-law-based constitution of Saxon England, Norman feudalism.

Jefferson's *Summary View* elaborated an intriguing, revisionist-style history of the introduction of Norman feudal law into England and then later America to support the diagnosis that feudalism was the true source of infection of Saxon principles of right and justice:

That we shall at this time also take notice of an error in the nature of our land holdings, which crept in at a very early period of our settlement. The introduction of the feudal tenures into the kingdom of England, though ancient, is well enough understood to set this matter in a proper light. In the earlier ages of the [Saxon settlement] feudal holdings were certainly altogether unknown. . . . Our Saxon ancestors held their lands, as they did their personal property, in absolute dominion, unencumbered with any superior, answering nearly to the nature of these possessions which the feudalists term allodial.[139]

William the Conqueror, however, imposed military duties on the entire Saxon realm, "and the Norman lawyers soon found means to saddle them [the Saxon's lands] also with all the other feudal burthens."[140] The principal tool used by the Conqueror's lawyers formally to install the alien regime's reign of power was the Norman-derived legal fiction of conquest, which declared that all lands in England were held either mediately or immediately by the Crown. But in actuality, according to Jefferson, many of the lands held by the Saxons were never formally surrendered to the Norman:

[T]hey were not derived from his grant, and therefore they were not holden of him. . . . [F]eudal holdings were therefore but exceptions out of the Saxon laws of possession, under which all lands were held in absolute right. These, therefore, still form the basis, or groundwork, of the common law, to prevail wheresoever the exceptions have not taken place.[141]

Thus Jefferson located the emergence of the venerated English common law of property, real and personal, in the ancient Saxon laws of possession. These ancient laws embraced the fundamental natural-law principle that an individual's property was, in Jefferson's words, "held of no superior."[142] The Normans engrafted onto the Saxon laws of possession a foreign and corrupted system of land laws, a system based on a rationalizing fiction of feudal conquest over lands never formally surrendered by the freedom-loving Saxons. Thus these foreign feudal tenures were but the continuation by legal means of the Normans' war on the noble Saxon race, the means by which the Norman reign of power was formally installed throughout England.

Jefferson's *Summary View* thus asserted that feudal tenures based on the fiction of conquest were odiously regarded exceptions to the natural-law-based principles of Saxon land law. It asserted further that that purer land law prevailed wherever true Englishmen had freed themselves from the tyranny of the Norman Yoke. As "America was not conquered by William the Norman, nor its lands surrendered to him, or any of his successors," according to *A Summary View*, the lands acquired by English colonists in America were held under the Saxon-derived common-law principles of free tenure. Jefferson's assertion that the English had carried their Saxon-derived natural law across the Atlantic with them and acquired lands under it free of the stifling Norman feudal exceptions led him to the obvious conclusion that tenures held by Englishmen in America "are undoubtedly of the allodial nature."[143] The Norman fiction of conquest by which the Crown asserted prerogative rights did not apply in America, although the Crown might will it.

Inspired by the Glorious Revolution's intellectual inheritance of a purer Saxon common law expressive of a natural reason and uncontaminated by the Norman Yoke, Jefferson had performed an impressive feat of historical retrieval. His summary view of the arguments supporting American separation from the feudal prerogatives of an alien tyrant was the most radical extension of the Norman Yoke mythology placed in service of the colonists' radical cause.

The English Crown had historically based its privilege to charter colonies and control the lands of North America on the theory that its Norman-derived prerogative rights of conquest attached immediately to infidel-claimed territories discovered by English subjects. As Lord Coke had clearly articulated in *Calvin's Case* in the early seventeenth century, the Crown was presumed to be at perpetual war with infidels, who were, in turn, presumed to be incapable of conforming their laws or conduct to natural law.[144] Thus English discovery of infidel-held territories amounted to a declaration of war on the Crown's perpetual enemies and imposed on the Crown the duty to subjugate the infidels and provide them with the Christian faith and civilization. Recall that the colonial charters granted by Elizabeth I and James I in the early Discovery era had authorized the conquest and settlement of non-Christian territories in the Crown's name for the express purpose of spreading Christianity and civility among the heathen peoples of the New World.[145]

In the feudal discourse of infidel conquest, the fact that actual "conquests" might not occur for many years following discovery did not work to limit the Crown's feudal prerogatives over the infidel-held lands. The Crown's rights remained inchoate until actual conquest occurred. The medieval Normans, for instance, invaded England in the eleventh century and then Ireland in the following century on the theory that the rightful rule of the indigenous inhabitants had been forfeited by their failure to conform to the dictates of the Roman Church.[146] As Jefferson pointed out with respect to England,[147] and as has been seen with respect to Ireland,[148] many regions in the two realms had never been formally surrendered to the Normans, yet the fiction of conquest and subsequent feudal prerogative claims were extended to both islands. A long delay prior to actual conquest would in no sense have altered the legal validity of the Norman claims under the papal banner declaring the illegitimacy of either indigenous Saxon English or Celtic Irish rule.

These same basic feudal principles, *sans* the medieval papacy's legitimating function in defining the trajectory of the Norman Yoke, had been applied by England's Protestant monarchs to North America. Jefferson's *Summary View* dismissed this Norman-derived theory of the Crown's prerogative rights of conquest in the infidel-held lands of America acquired by mere discovery for what it was, a legal fiction. The king had never formally conquered the Indians' America, just as the Normans had never formally received the surrender of all Saxon-held lands in England. The Norman Yoke was as illegitimately applied in the New World as it had been in the Old. But unlike the situation in a corrupt England, it was not too late to throw off this yoke in America.

Like all the other colonial radicals, Jefferson held strong loyalties to the English Constitution and common law. His grounding arguments in *A Summary View* were ultimately conservative and nonsubversive of those vaunted natural-law-inspired institutions. He sought a return to a purer, Saxon-derived legal vision for America, which required a radical confrontation with the oppressive but only recently felt reality of Norman tyranny in America. But how could Jefferson explain the fact that the Crown had frustrated the flourishing of Saxon common-law principles in America, extending its feudal prerogatives over the colonists virtually without challenge? Could it not be argued that the colonists had perhaps consented to the imposition of the Norman Yoke in America?

Jefferson, the revolutionary theorist and strategist, answered confidently that no freedom-loving Saxon-descended American colonist would ever knowingly have consented to such feudal nonsense had they understood the full legal implications of the feudal fiction of conquest:

Our ancestors, however, who migrated hither, were farmers, not lawyers. The fictitious principle that all lands belong originally to the King, they were early persuaded to believe real; and accordingly took grants of their own lands from the Crown. And while the Crown continued to grant for small sums, and on reasonable rents; there was no inducement to arrest the error, and lay it to public view.[149]

Jefferson, now assuming the role of the radical legal theorist, urged the rapid abandonment of this false legal consciousness in America. The threat to Saxon liberties was increasing daily, as the various steps recently taken by the Crown demonstrated. New imperial policies for the West rendered acquisition of abundant lands on the frontier even more difficult and costly. America's

population and thus its continued greatness would be checked by blind obei-
sance to the fictions of Norman feudal theory. Action had to be taken soon
against the tyranny of a foreign-born king and his corrupt ministers. Americans, the true Saxons, had nothing to lose but their reifications:

> It is time, therefore, for us to lay this matter before his Majesty, and to declare that he
> has no right to grant lands of himself. From the nature and purpose of civil institutions,
> all the lands within the limits which any particular society has circumscribed around
> itself are assumed by that society and subject to their allotment only. This may be done
> by themselves, assembled collectively, or by their legislature, to whom they may have
> delegated sovereign authority; and if they are allotted in neither of these ways, each
> individual of the society may appropriate to himself such lands as he finds vacant, and
> occupancy will give him title.[150]

Jefferson's appropriation of the Norman Yoke discourse and its noble Saxon
symbology made it possible to join the radicals' vision of a natural law realized
in reason and history with the better Lockean-derived view on the American
law of land tenures. By reason and by history, the Saxon law of free tenures,
and not the Norman Yoke of feudalism, ought to reign in the wilderness of
America. In recognizing that detested feudal legal principles lay at the base of
the king's claimed prerogative powers of conquest over western lands, Jefferson's *Summary View* harmonized the colonists' resistance to royal authority
and their self-interested pursuit of frontier lands with the higher ideals of
Saxon-derived natural law and the Lockean-inspired pursuit of life, liberty,
and especially property in the forests of the New World.

Discursive Chaos on the Frontiers of American Colonizing Discourse

Chaos in the Continental Congress

As Jefferson was well aware, the western lands claimed under Virginia's charter
were not vacant and ready for allotment by Virginia, the Crown, or anyone
else. They were occupied and fiercely defended by the Indian tribes of the
region, who had proved time and time again that they would surrender their
territorial claims only for valuable consideration or after costly wars. But the
temporary obstacle presented by Indian occupancy of the lands desired by
British Americans was not the point, as far as Jefferson and all the colonists
were concerned. The real issue was who would control the pace and direction
of the acquisition of Indian "waste" lands on the frontier. Would the Americans' colonial governments acquire the Indians' vast claims to the West for
resale at their discretion to emigrating colonists? Or would the Crown from
London dictate the rate at which America would grow and prosper by asserting its Norman-derived right to extinguish the Indian claim on the frontier and
grant preemption rights to colonists at its sole discretion?

This choice—colonies or Crown—of course did not exhaust all the possible
options. As previously described,[151] a number of speculatively minded individual colonists had invested large sums of money in direct purchases of frontier

lands from western tribes. In effect, their actions extended even further the radical implications of the arguments that Jefferson derived from the discourse of the Norman Yoke. These speculatively minded American radicals in fact were poised to jettison all vestiges of the false legal consciousness inscribed in Norman feudal landholding principles applied to the Indian frontier.

Jefferson had argued in the strongest terms that the English who had emigrated to America had freed themselves from Norman feudal tyranny and established a purer Saxon constitution of nonfeudalized, "allodial" tenures. It should be emphasized that Jefferson's *Summary View* was widely praised and trumpeted by American radicals. The fact that the post-Revolutionary state governments usually moved quickly to abolish many of the remaining feudal incidents of tenure[152] attests to the responsive chord that Jefferson struck in *A Summary View*. But taken to its logical limits, Jefferson's argument could be read as supporting the extreme antipositivist position that neither the king nor Virginia (for Virginia, it could be argued, derived any rights it had from the king's 1609 charter) ought to have the feudally derived right to control the disposition of Indian-occupied lands. If America was a land where property was unencumbered by Norman-derived feudal incidents, then why could not Saxon-descended Americans purchase land on the frontier directly from the Indians, without the intermediary sanctioning authority of a Norman tyrant *or* his chartered colonial government? For did not Virginia and the other colonies with land claims under their charters ultimately derive their political and legal legitimacy directly from the king's fictively maintained prerogative right of conquest as derived from discovery to grant inchoate rights in American lands?

Such explosive questions impelled the widespread and freewheeling activities of the frontier speculators themselves. Even the most respected of colonists were purchasing tracts of land directly from the western tribes at substantial prices on the eve of the Revolution. According to the antipositivistic thematics of the speculators' radical discourse of opposition to the Crown's prerogative powers on the frontier, Americans exercised their natural-law rights as free men when they purchased, without a government intermediary, lands held by the Indians. Concomitantly, the Indians, as free, unconquered nations (for the Indian tribes of the Old Northwest were fiercely independent at this time), exercised their natural rights by freely alienating that which they occupied and held as their own under natural law to whomever they pleased. The Indians' willingness to enter the colonists' land market was proof positive of their rational capacity to act in their own best interests as far as the speculators were concerned.

This self-serving inclusion of the Indians within the speculators' natural-law discourse energized the laissez-faire discursive practice adopted by many of the land-jobbing colonists on the frontier in the years immediately prior to the Revolution. Suddenly, even the most hardened land-market capitalist assumed the mantle of zealous advocate of the Indians' natural-law right to engage in unregulated real-estate transactions. Neither the king nor the landed colonies "owned" the lands on the frontier, argued these speculators. The Indian tribes occupied these lands as free and sovereign peoples. By natural law, the Indians could therefore sell their rights to the land to whomever they pleased, the Proclamation of 1763 and the landed colonies' charter claims notwithstanding.

Few colonists better appreciated the implications of including Indians within that class of peoples protected in their landholdings by natural law than the Philadelphia merchant Samuel Wharton. Wharton, a central figure in the derailed Vandalia project,[153] returned to America on the eve of the Revolution with certain extremely novel views on Indian rights. Wharton was one of the many speculating colonists who, just before the Revolution, shifted the focus of his activities to America and the recently convened Continental Congress in Philadelphia. The Pennsylvania merchant was among that prescient group of speculators who recognized that the spirit of growing independence in the colonies would probably encompass the demand by British Americans for resumption of control over the western frontier's acquisition and settlement. Working behind the scenes at Philadelphia with his brother and partner Thomas, Samuel Wharton sought to convince the more influential members of the new Continental Congress to pass a definitive resolution "expressive of the validity and sufficiency of a title to lands, fairly bought of the Aborigines and held under Grants (only) from them."[154]

In seeking the Continental Congress's affirmation of the Indian's natural-law rights to the West, Wharton naturally sought the assistance of his reliable old partner Benjamin Franklin, also recently returned from Europe. Franklin was in attendance at the Congress and wielded apparent influence, although Wharton himself did not think him capable of asserting too strenuous an effort on behalf of his speculating partners. Referring to the anticipated difficulty of convincing the Congress to confirm the Vandalia cession made to Wharton's syndicate by the Iroquois Confederacy at Fort Stanwix in 1768, Wharton wrote to his brother Thomas that Franklin had

grown old. . . . [He] is not so active as he was twenty years ago, and however well disposed, as I know he is to establish in America, the rights of the Six Nations etc. to their territories, and all fair grants obtained from them, yet will be necessary for you . . . with *his* concurrence, to take an active part with the other members of the Congress.[155]

Samuel authorized his brother to make a present to each of eight delegates to the Congress of half a share in a speculative venture organized to pursue the Vandalia scheme anew in America. Wharton's plan was to get the Congress to affirm "the rights of the Six Nations etc. to their territories, and all fair grants obtained from them"—specifically, the Iroquois grant obtained by Sir William Johnson at Fort Stanwix for the benefit of the "suffering" traders. With this affirmation, Wharton intended to establish an interior colony under the Congress's authority—indeed a most radical proposal.

Thomas Wharton had been given generous license by his brother to bribe select members of the Continental Congress to favor the Indians' natural rights to their lands. Thomas discovered, however, that a number of the most influential delegates at Philadelphia already agreed with the radical proposition that the Indians of the West had all the sovereignty necessary to grant their lands to whomever they pleased.

One of Thomas's encouraging reports to his brother related news of a breakfast with an extremely impressive gentleman, Patrick Henry, who was representing Virginia at the Congress. The Whartons of course were most concerned about Virginia Governor Dunmore's recent war against the Shawnees in the area of the "suffering" traders' grant and the colony's seizure of Fort Pitt.[156] Thomas described a conversation in which Henry voiced his opinion on Governor Dunmore's ultimate designs in prosecuting his Indian war in the vicinity of the proposed Vandalia colony:

As I am on the subject of Vandalia, I cannot help but give you a detail of a very singular anecdote I was yesterday favored with by Mr. Henry, one of the delegates from Virginia, attending the Congress. He is a man of the highest character, an Eminent Lawyer, and man of greatest activities. . . . [I] put some leading questions to discover if possible the real intentions of Dunmore for prosecuting this unjust war. . . . He replied that he was well acquainted with the Secret Springs of this affair and knew it would ultimately tend in the greatest happiness of the proprietors of Vandalia. . . . [H]e said that he was at Williamsburg with Ld. Dunmore when Doct'r Connally [Dunmore's deputy] first came there . . . and informed Dunmore of the Extreme rightness of the land which lay on both sides of the Ohio, that the prohibitive orders which had been sent him relative to the land on the heathen side [the northern shore, site of the proposed Vandalia colony] had caused him to turn his thoughts to the opposite [southern] shore, and that as his Lordship was determined to settle his family in America, he was really pursuing this war in order to obtain by purchase or treaty from the natives a tract of territory on that side.[157]

Thus Virginia's governor, Lord Dunmore, at least according to Henry, had engaged in that time-honored Tidewater planter's practice of waging war on the Indians in order to force a land cession.[158] Fortunately for the Whartons and their syndicate, Dunmore's landed desires as related by Henry were confined to the southern side of the Ohio, an area not in competition with the Vandalia proprietors' claim. But how was Dunmore to acquire these lands for himself, Thomas Wharton had asked Henry, when only a few months earlier the Board of Trade had flatly rejected the governor's petition for an individual grant of 100,000 frontier acres to "settle his family in America"? Henry answered this question for Thomas also, telling his breakfast partner that Dunmore intended to purchase the Ohio lands directly from the natives, bypassing the imperial government's interference. Dunmore, said Henry, "was convinced from every authority that the law knew that purchase from the natives was as full and ample a title as could be obtained; that they had L[o]rd Camden and Mr. Yorke's opinions on that head."[159] Henry further informed Thomas Wharton that he too had "some prospect of making a purchase of the natives."[160] This confession indicated to Thomas that Henry, like Dunmore and a number of other speculating colonists, believed that the Indians possessed a natural-law right to pass titles to their lands to whomever they pleased, without governmental interference.

Thus Patrick Henry, the radical backwoods Virginia delegate; Lord Dunmore, a Crown-appointed governor of patrician descent; and a number of other prominent men in the colonies—all apparently agreed with the natural-law-based principle that a "purchase from the natives was as full and ample a title as could be obtained."[161] The lack of consensus on the western frontier respecting the legitimacy of any form of governmental control over Indian land sales had infected the discourses emerging in Philadelphia on the eve of the Revolution. Certain Saxon-descended radicals of the Revolutionary era had apparently recognized the terminal point of the antipositivistic trajectory of their own natural-rights-based discourses arguing for American independence and denying the Crown's authority to interfere with their self-interested pursuit of life, liberty, and property. All vestiges of the Norman Yoke ought to be obliterated in America, according to this most radical, natural-rights-based discourse of the Revolutionary era. Norman feudalism's denial of the Indians' rights to the lands they occupied and controlled on the American frontier was as opposed to natural law and common sense as was the Crown's attempt under the Proclamation of 1763 to prevent the colonists from purchasing those intensely desired lands.

Camden-Yorke

The opinions of Lord Camden and Mr. Yorke on Indian titles referred to by Patrick Henry in his discussion of the "secret springs" of Lord Dunmore's Indian war figure prominently in the Revolutionary-era discourses on the Indians' capacity to pass valid land titles. The *Camden-Yorke* opinion,[162] as it came to be called, was part of the discourse of opposition to royal prerogative power that came to dominate the English political formation in the decades following the Glorious Revolution of 1688–1689 and the installation of parliamentary sovereignty. It is no wonder, therefore, that speculatively minded Americans appropriated *Camden-Yorke*'s broadly stated limiting principles with a vengeance in asserting their rights to acquire frontier lands, the king's prerogative notwithstanding.

Written in 1757 by Attorney General Charles Pratt (later Lord Camden) and Solicitor General Charles Yorke, the opinion addressed issues connected to the king's rights and the applicability of English laws in foreign lands acquired by English subjects by either conquest or contract. Lord Coke in *Calvin's Case*[163] had clearly established in the early seventeenth century the fundamental feudal principle that the king held both the title and the rights to government over lands that his subjects acquired by conquest in his name. As already explained, this feudal doctrine of conquest was the central legitimating premise of the Crown's political and legal authority in England and in its infant North American empire as well. Yet this foundational premise of the entire royal Norman-derived feudal structure lost much of its aural quality as a source of Crown prerogatives following the radical realignments in British politics in the decades following the Glorious Revolution of 1688–1689. Instead, as the advocates of parliamentary sovereignty formalized their ascendancy under the British Constitution after the revolution, the principle can be discerned re-emerging in legal discursive practice as a source of limitations on the Crown. Particularly in the administration of colonial affairs, when so many members of the privy council, their placemen, and Parliament invariably held secret interests or outright shares in the great overseas trading ventures, delimiting the Crown's rights to interfere with the new forms of property and wealth being created throughout the empire appeared to be a self-evident, self-preserving necessity.

The English lawyers who elaborated and formalized the legal discourse of diminishment of royal prerogatives worked subtly and circumspectly in installing the new regime of limitations on their monarchs. In their cautiously drawn commentary on the rights of the East India Company prepared for the privy council in 1757, Lord Camden and Yorke carefully insulated the property rights of the company in lands that it had acquired by purchase in India from any rival Crown prerogative property claims:

[R]elative to the [Company's] holding or retaining fortresses or districts already acquired or to be acquired by Treaty, Grant or Conquest, we beg leave to point out some distinctions upon it. In respect to such places as have been or shall be acquired by treaty or grant from the Mogul or any of the Indian Princes or Governments[,] your Majesty's Letters Patent are not necessary, the property of the soil vesting in the Company by the Indian Grants subject only to your Majesty's Right of sovereignty over the settlements and over the inhabitants as English subjects who carry with them your Majesty's protection by virtue of your Royal Charters. In respect to such places as have lately been acquired or shall hereafter be acquired by Conquest the property as well as the Dominion vests in your Majesty by virtue of your known prerogative and consequently the Company can only derive a right to them through your Majesty's Grant.[164]

By the time of the *Camden-Yorke* opinion, the root feudal principle that the king controlled the property as well as the right of government in lands acquired by conquest functioned as a more precisely delineated formal principle of limitation in British constitutional theory respecting colonial acquisition of land. According to *Camden-Yorke*, real property acquired by a colonial venture outside the feudal paradigm of conquest was held free of the king's prerogative property claims. Individual Englishmen could purchase lands from indigenous foreign rulers without authorizing letters patent from the Crown. Yet by virtue of the royal charter authorizing the colonial enterprise, these lands were at the same time entitled to "receive your Majesty's protection." The king had no direct right of property in the corporate colonizers' lands acquired by peaceful means; they belonged to the individual purchasers. The king did, however, have a responsibility to defend and protect such lands, according to *Camden-Yorke*.

The original *Camden-Yorke* opinion discussed only the rights of the East India Company regarding its specific situation in India. By the time the American speculators got hold of *Camden-Yorke*, however, it had gone through some predictable material revisions. The version that circulated throughout the American colonies and on the frontier among the speculators during the 1770s had been slightly redrafted so that the grants of territory made by American "Indian Princes or Government" were incorporated into the opinion's holding. This American version of *Camden-Yorke* read in full as follows:

In respect to such places, as have been or shall be acquired by Treaty or Grant from any of the Indian Princes or Governments, your Majesties Letters Patents are not necessary[,] the property of the Soil vesting in the grantee by the Indian Grants, subject only to your Majesties Right of Sovereignty over the Settlements, as English settlements, and over the Inhabitants, as English Subjects, Who carry with them your Majesties Laws Wherever they form Colonies and receive your Majesties protection, by Virtue of your Royal Charters.[165]

This "true copy" of the *Camden-Yorke* opinion was compiled in London in April 1772 by William Trent, partner to Samuel Wharton.[166] Both Wharton and Trent were in London in April 1772, awaiting Hillsborough's Board of Trade report on the proposed Vandalia colony.[167] Trent's transcription of *Camden-Yorke* conveniently omitted several important details. Trent's "true copy" deleted all references to the East India Company and "Indian Moguls." Any such reference would have implicitly limited the opinion's application to the situation in India and the Far East, as American Indian leaders were seldom, if ever, referred to as moguls.[168] Apparently, all that mattered to the American speculators was that the respected opinion of Lord Camden and Yorke held that the king's letters patent were not necessary if an Englishman desired to purchase lands from "Indian Princes or Governments," whether located in the East or the West. Americans could acquire titles to Indian land directly, without royal license or approval, according to their "true copy" of *Camden-Yorke*.

In the colonies in particular, Lord Camden's opinion on any important legal or political matter would have garnered significant attention and respect. He was often cited by colonials for his salutary views on virtual representation in Parliament and his fearless condemnations of ministerial corruption.[169] In a well-publicized speech in the House of Lords in 1770, Camden openly accused the Ministry "of having formed a conspiracy against the liberties of their country"[170]—sweet music to the ears of the American radicals, who believed that the Proclamation of 1763 and its policy of sealing off the frontier was part of a conspiracy by the Ministry against their liberties.[171]

Camden-Yorke's popularity in America was never higher than at the time Jefferson composed his thematically similar discourse of opposition to the Norman Yoke. Jefferson's *Summary View*, constraining the king's feudal Norman prerogative to only those lands actually acquired by conquest, was but the rhetorized elaboration of *Camden-Yorke*'s more highly refined legal discourse of constitutional limitation. Even if Jefferson was unaware of *Camden-Yorke*'s more systematized confinement of the Norman Yoke, this would only demonstrate how widely the basic refrains of antifeudal theory were dispersed throughout the colonial discursive formation.

Samuel Wharton, however, was certainly very familiar with the *Camden-Yorke* opinion. He may well have been one of the first Americans to appreciate its potential applicability to the situation on the frontier. While in London in the 1770s, Wharton corresponded frequently with the Indian trader George Croghan (the initiator of the "suffering" traders' syndicate) back in America. Croghan had set up a private land office in the vicinity of Fort Pitt in the winter of 1770–1771 to sell off sections of frontier grants that he had obtained from various Iroquois chiefs. He found a number of takers at £10 per 100 acres, title guaranteed. Samuel Wharton, who had been encouraging Croghan from London all along, wrote in July 1771 that he rejoiced over the fact that purchasers on the frontier "are as cheerfully disposed" to take title to Croghan's Indian lands as they would be from the Crown or the Penn proprietors. The "good sense" of the settlers demonstrated "that they reason naturally and justly upon the subject." Wharton declared that from the lowest to the highest counselor and personage throughout London, "It is not pretended, the King can have, or has any Degree of Rights to lands, which he has not bought from the natural original proprietors."[172] Wharton told Croghan to obtain the "best price" he could for his Indian lands. Wharton would return to America with "the ablest and most learned Counsellors' Opinions in this Kingdom, in favor of your and our rights."[173]

One of those able and most learned counselors would obviously have been Lord Camden, one of the earliest backers of the Wharton syndicate.[174] It had been Lord Camden who had informed Thomas Walpole of the antiexpansionist Hillsborough's shaky status among his fellow Ministers as a result of his obtuseness respecting the Iroquois' cession to the "suffering" traders at Fort Stanwix.[175] Walpole had passed along this valuable information to Wharton. It provided the effective stimulus to Wharton and Walpole's eventual expansion of the "suffering" traders' syndicate into the Vandalia Company.

Other correspondence between the speculators during the early 1770s provides further evidence of the widespread dissemination of the defeudalized discourse of "learned" men throughout England and English America recognizing the natural rights of the Indians and the legal sufficiency of Indian-derived titles. Wharton wrote Croghan from England in the summer of 1771 on behalf of several "Gentlemen of Weight, Dignity, and Fortune in this Country" about the feasibility of forming a company in which Croghan would act as agent, purchasing lands on the Ohio directly from the Six Nations. Wharton expressed utmost confidence in the security of title of any such lands Croghan purchased. Everyone in London except Hillsborough and his underlings laughed, or so Wharton claimed, "at the idea of coming to England to get a title of lands." The Indians were, after all, "the rightful independent and natural owners" and had proved more than willing to sell for a fair price. What need was there of London's interference in the American frontier land market? Croghan wrote back from America that there were indeed "many gentlemen of fortune" in the colonies who also were fully convinced of the sufficiency of titles from the independent tribes of Indians and were themselves contemplating making major purchases from the natives.[176]

Croghan himself was a central cog connecting the spokes of many a land-speculating scheme on the frontier in the Revolutionary era. He was probably the source of many of the rumors that circulated throughout the American wilderness respecting the opinions of "learned" men on Indian rights and titles. Croghan apparently boasted that he had spoken directly with Lord Camden and Yorke during his 1764 visit to London on behalf of the "suffering" traders[177] and that they had "personally confirmed" to him that grants from Indian tribes were sufficient to vest a title in an English purchaser. In normal times, of course, Croghan's boast that he had met and heard the opinions of these great counselors of English law would probably have been dismissed out of hand. But these were not normal times in America, and people's views on what the law was or ought to be on the American frontier were far from settled. The word of a semiliterate Indian trader of Irish descent who bragged of questioning the king's prerogative with the king's own attorney general and solicitor general may well have been sufficient to start a chain of title running in the forests of America.

Wharton and Croghan were not the only speculators who were privy to the opinions of "learned" men on the validity of Indian-derived titles. As has been noted, Patrick Henry asserted that Lord Dunmore had launched his Indian war on the basis of *Camden-Yorke*.[178] Henry himself apparently entered into a venture to acquire Indian lands shortly after admitting knowledge of the opinion. Washington, an unrivaled and tireless collector of Indian land claims, actually pasted a copy of the abbreviated *Camden-Yorke* opinion on the first flyleaf of his diary for 1773. He probably received the inspirational text from his acquaintance Governor Dunmore.[179] Judge Richard Henderson, the notorious North Carolina frontier land speculator, also knew of the opinion. He organized the Transylvania Company around an audacious plan to buy lands directly from the Cherokees and declare independence from the king if London failed to recognize his Indian-derived title.[180]

It should be noted that by interest as well as by ideology, many Americans were prepared to challenge the imperial government's assumption of control over Indian land sales on the frontier, with or without *Camden-Yorke*. As indicated by the popularity of Jefferson's tirade against the Norman Yoke in *A Summary View*, Americans such as Wharton, Dunmore, Franklin, and Washington were more than ready by the early 1770s, the eve of their Revolution, to pursue their self-interest directly with the Indians without the troubling mediatory prerogative of an alien-born king.

The fact that so many groups of speculators spent large sums of money to purchase lands directly from the frontier tribes on the basis of the entirely novel theory that Indians had the natural right to alienate their territory indicates the proportions of the crisis in colonial legal thought brought about by the Proclamation of 1763, the Stamp Act, and other attacks on English American liberties by a foreign-born king and a corrupt Ministry. England's assault on the colonies had opened up a new field of discourse—a field in which the colonists avidly sought to protect and promote their own interests on the frontier. The most widely divergent theories and discourses on the rights of English Americans *and* Indians thereby proliferated and flourished. In the state of nature that was the American frontier, no law was laid down or settled.

The speculators in Indian land grants never regarded themselves primarily as crusaders for a racially neutral form of American egalitarianism that demanded recognition of the Indians' title to their lands. To the colonists who formed the syndicates opposed to Virginia's and the other "landed" colonies' charter-based claims to the frontier, London's feeble, long-distance attempts to control the West invited widespread doubts about the need for any feudal intermediary institutions for acquiring the most valuable of all commodities in America—land. Thus in the chaos of the Revolutionary era, Indian land rights became a fungible commodity, regulated only by the laws of supply and demand. The Indians' natural-law rights to their lands were highly valued by those who stood to gain the most by a recognition of the savages' natural-law ability to alienate their estates. Those who stood to lose the most by acceptance of the proposition that natural law applied to all human beings, even savages, in turn placed little value on land titles acquired directly from the Indians. Seldom has the dynamic relationship between American racism and the dominant racial caste's economic interests been so clearly revealed within the normative fineries of American legal discursive practice. In the Revolutionary-era debate on the status and rights of Indians in their lands, white interests and expediency, not the rule of law or even the opinions of learned jurists, would ultimately determine whether the Indians enjoyed the same rights as white men in America.

NOTES

1. *See* M. Jensen, *The Founding of a Nation* 3–35 (1968).

2. *See* C. Alvord, 1 *The Mississippi Valley in British Politics* 45–47 (1959), for a concise and informative discussion of prevailing mercantilist attitudes in eighteenth-century thought in Great Britain and its specific application to the Old Northwest.

3. J. Sosin, *Whitehall and the Wilderness* 56–57 (1961). Many of the major points developed in this section draw heavily on the invaluable research and insights of Sosin's book.

4. Reprinted in "Notes and Documents: Hints Relative to the Division and Government of the Conquered and Newly Acquired Countries in America," 8 *Miss Valley Hist. Rev.* 373 (V. Crane ed. 1922).

5. *Id.* at 371.

6. J. Sosin, *supra* note 3, at 13, n. 15.

7. *See* C. Alvord, *supra* note 2, at 19–43.

8. George Washington himself had learned from bitter experience the military value of Indian alliances. He had led a Virginia regiment to defeat in 1754 at Fort Necessity, the battle that inaugurated the French and Indian War. "Indians," Washington argued, "are only match for Indians, and without these, we shall ever fight on unequal terms" (quoted in W. Robinson, *The Southern Colonial Frontier, 1607–1763,* 209–10 (1979).

9. J. Sosin, *supra* note 3, at 44–45.

10. *Id.* at 51.

11. 7 *Documents Relative to the Colonial History of the State of New York* 520–21 (E. B. O'Callaghan ed. 1856) [hereinafter cited as *Documents of New York*].

12. *Id.* at 521.

13. *See* A. Volwiler, *George Croghan and the Westward Movement 1741–1782* 159–64 (1926).

14. *See id.* at 23–24.

15. G. Nash, *Red, White and Black* 261 (2d ed. 1982).

16. *Id.*

17. Quoted in *id.* at 261–62. *See also* A. F. C. Wallace, *The Death and Rebirth of the Seneca* 118 (1970); H. Peckham, *Pontiac and the Indian Uprising* (1947).

18. Quoted in G. Nash, *supra* note 15, at 262.

19. J. Sosin, *supra* note 3, at 52–53.

20. *Documents of American History* 48–49 (H. S. Commager 8th ed. 1968) [hereinafter cited as H. S. Commager].

21. *Id.* at 49.

22. *Id.*

23. *Id.* Abuses of Indians by frontier traders are the stuff of legend in American colonial frontier history. Contemporary sources, both official and unofficial, confirm the basic fact of frontier life that the typical trader regarded the Indian as an object of profit and plunder, not of ethical or moral concern. *See* W. Jacobs, *Dispossessing the American Indian* 31–40 (1972). Robert Rogers's popular play of 1756, *Pontiach: Or the Savages of America, a Tragedy*, related the ethical code of one fictional trader in a scene that, as contemporary real-life accounts support, captures the attitudes of British subjects engaged in the frontier Indian trade. In the play, M'Dole (many of the traders were of Irish and Scotch descent, which only confirmed their incorrigible rascality to British officials and policymakers) is the experienced hand at the Indian trade; Murphy is the initiate. This first-act scene takes place in an Indian trading house.

> *Murphy*: I'm unacquainted with your Indian Commerce and gladly would I learn the arts from you,
> Who're old, and practised in them many years.
>
> *M'Dole*: As you are a friend, I will inform you of all the secret arts by which we thrive, which if all practis'd, we might all grow rich,
> Nor circumvent each other in our gains.
> What have you got to part with to the Indians?
>
> *Murphy*: I've Rum and blankets, Wampum, powder, bells, and such like trifles as they're wont to prize.
>
> *M'Dole*: 'Tis very well: your articles are good. But now the thing's to make a profit from them, worth all your toil and pains of coming hither. Our fundamental maxim then is this, that it's no crime to cheat and gull an Indian.
>
> *Murphy*: How! Not a sin to cheat an Indian, say you? Are they not men? Haven't they a right to justice as well as we, though savage in their manners?
>
> *M'Dole*: Ah! If you boggle here, I say no more; This is the very Quintessence of Trade, and ev'ry Hope of Gain depends upon it; None who neglect it ever did grow rich, or ever will, or can by Indian Commerce. By this old Ogden built his stately House, Purchased Estates, and grew a little King. He, like an honest Man, bought all by weight, and made the ign'rant Savages believe that his right foot exactly weighed a pound. By this for many years he bought their furs, and died in quiet like an honest dealer. [*Id.* at 38–39.]

Numerous laws and regulations were passed by the colonial governments seeking to regulate the abuses of individual traders. The abuses, however, occurred on a distant frontier, where laws were difficult to enforce. In general, the colonies' trade regulations were regarded as being of little use in controlling the conduct of the traders. Since no respectable, law-abiding gentleman would leave his comfortable estate to pursue a career in the forests trucking with savages, the trader's life was the stereotyped preserve of the lower rungs of the colonial American economy: Scots, Irishmen, fugitives from debt. Such rogues had come to America in desperate pursuit of the livelihood that the feudalized economies, monopolies, and guilds of old Europe had denied. They were not about to let colonial officials, either in America or, particularly, an ocean away in London constrain them in pursuing their self-interest in the frontier wilderness of the Indian back country. *See id.* at 1–90.

24. H. S. Commager, *supra* note 20, at 49.

25. "Plan for the Future Management of Indian Affairs," in *Documents of New York, supra* note 11, at 637.

26. *See id.* at 637–41.

27. *See* text accompanying notes 13–18, *supra*.

28. On the life and career of Sir William Johnson, *see* J. Flexner, *Lord of the Mohawks* (1979).

29.

> As original proprietors, this Confederacy claim the Country as their residence, South of Lake Ontario to the great Ridge of the Blew Mountains, with all the Western part of the province of New York towards Hudson River, west of the Caata Kill, thence to Lake Champlain, and from Regioghne a Rock at the East side of said lake to Osswegatche or La

Gattell on the River St. Lawrence (having long since ceded their claim North of said line in favour of the Canada Indians as Hunting ground) thence up the River St. Lawrence and along the South side of Lake Ontario to Niagara.

In right of conquest, they claim all the Country (comprehending the Ohio) along the great Ridge of Blew Mountains at the back of Virginia, thence to the head of Kentucke River, and down the same to the Ohio above the Rifts, then Northerly to the South end of Lake Michigan, then along the eastern shore of said lake to Missillimackinac, thence easterly cross the North end of Lake Huron to the great Ottawa River, (including the Chippawae or Mississagey Country) and down the said River to the Island of Montreal. [Reprinted in *Documents of New York, supra* note 11, at 572–73.]

30. *Id.* at 372.

31. *Id.* at 573.

32. *Id.* at 665.

33. *Id.* at 636.

34. *Id.*

35. *See,* e.g., C. B. Macpherson, *The Political Theory of Possessive Individualism* 194–262 (1962).

36. These figures are provided in J. Sosin, *supra* note 3, at 79–83.

37. *Id.* at 83.

38. Quoted in M. Jensen, *supra* note 1, at 63.

39. H. S. Commager, *supra* note 20, at 53–55.

40. *See,* e.g., the pamphlet of Stephen Hopkins, "An Essay on the Trade of the Northern Colonies," reprinted in *Tracts of the American Revolution 1763–1776* 3–17 (M. Jensen ed. 1967). [hereinafter referred to as *Tracts of AR*].

41. *See* J. Sosin, *supra* note 3, at 86–87.

42. *Id.* at 87.

43. Quoted in B. Wright, *American Interpretations of Natural Law* 72 (1931).

44. *Id.*

45. Reprinted in H. S. Commager, *supra* note 20, at 56.

46. J. Sosin, *supra* note 3, at 93.

47. *Id.* at 94.

48. *Id.* at 94–95.

49. M. Jensen, *The Making of the American Constitution* 10–16 (1964).

50. J. Locke, *Two Treatises of Government* (1963).

51. *See* J. Habermas, *Theory and Practice* 87–88 (1973).

52. *Id.*

53. J. Locke, *supra* note 50, at 343. *See generally* W. Cronon, *Changes in the Land* 55–80 (1983).

54. J. Locke, *supra* note 50, at 309.

55. *Id.* at 336.

56. *Id.* at 327–29.

57. *Id.* at 330–37.

58. C. B. Macpherson, *supra* note 35, at 201.

59. J. Locke, *supra* note 50, at 335.

60. *Id.* at 332.

61. *Id.* at 336.

62. *Id.* at 338–39.

63. Quoted in *This Country Was Ours* 57 (V. Vogel ed. 1972).

64. *Id.*

65. J. Sosin, *supra* note 3, at 108–09.

66. J. Locke, *supra* note 50, at 395.

67. Quoted in M. Jensen, *The Articles of Confederation* 4 (1940) [hereinafter cited as *Articles of Confederation*].

68. *See* B. Bailyn, *The Ideological Origins of the American Revolution* 176 (1967).

69. Reprinted in *Tracts of AR, supra* note 40, at 20.

70. *Id.* at 20–21.

71. *Id.* at 32–33. Otis's authority for his statement that an act of Parliament against the Constitution was void was Lord Coke's opinion in *Bonham's Case*. On Otis's use of Lord Coke, *see* B. Bailyn, *supra* note 68, at 176–78.

72. *Tracts of AR*, *supra* note 40, at 32–33.

73. *Id.* at 20–21.

74. C. Hill, *Puritanism and Revolution* 94 (1958). *See also* J. Pocock, *The Machiavellian Moment* 506–52 (1975).

75. C. Hill, *supra*, at 95.

76. *Id.*

77. Quoted in *id.*

78. B. Bailyn, *supra* note 68, at 81.

79. *Id.* at 20.

80. Quoted in *id.* at 82–83.

81. C. Hill, *supra* note 74, at 94.

82. B. Bailyn, *supra* note 68, at 85–91.

83. Quoted in *id.* at 86–87.

84. Quoted in *id.* at 89.

85. *Id.* at 91.

86. Reprinted in *Tracts of AR*, *supra* note 40, at 256.

87. M. Jensen, *supra* note 1, at 399, 485.

88. *See* text accompanying notes 48–49, *supra*.

89. *See* text accompanying notes 63–64, *supra*.

90. C. Alvord, *supra* note 2, at 294.

91. *See* text accompanying notes 13–14, *supra*.

92. T. Abernathy, *Western Lands and the American Revolution* 24 (1959).

93. *Id.* at 31.

94. *Id.* at 29–33; J. Sosin, *supra* note 3, at 140–42.

95. J. Sosin, *supra* note 3, at 141.

96. T. Abernathy, *supra* note 92, at 22–23.

97. *Id.* at 29; 5 *The Papers of Sir William Johnson*, 8 vols., 128–30 (J. Sullivan & A. Flick eds. 1921–1933).

98. T. Abernathy, *supra* note 92, at 16.

99. Reprinted in *Illinois Historical Collections: The New Regime 1765–1767* 249 (C. Alvord & C. Carter eds. 1916) [hereinafter cited as *New Regime*].

100. *Id.* at 318–19.

101. J. Sosin, *supra* note 3, at 141.

102. T. Abernathy, *supra* note 92, at 30.

103. *Id.* at 30.

104. *Id.*

105. *See* text accompanying note 28–32 for Johnson's discussion of the Iroquois tributory tribes of the Northwest.

106. Johnson's services on behalf of the syndicate led by the Baynton, Wharton, and Morgan firm went beyond secretly representing the "suffering" traders' interests at strategically vital imperial treaty negotiations with Indian tribes. A letter of March 1766 to Johnson from the firm of Baynton, Wharton, and Morgan expressed warmest thanks "for the detail, you are pleased to afford us—respecting the boundary." But Johnson had apparently agreed to provide other services on behalf of the firm. The firm's letter indicates that Johnson received as an enclosure "our most cordial acknowledgements" for the "expectation, you are so good, as to give us," relative to a purchase of supplies from the firm. In other words, Superintendent Johnson received a kickback for ordering from the firm goods for the Indian trade as one of his functions as imperial Indian agent. But this was not all:

> If at any time, there are Curiosities of necessarys—which your Honour would incline to have,—whether they be, the Produce of this Province or foreign Parts;—It will be very

flattering to us—if you will be so kind, as to mention them, as we assure you, it is a high gratification to us, to evidence a sensibility of favors.

Along with the letter, Johnson received a few Spanish chestnuts, a delicacy that was no doubt appreciated. *See New Regime, supra* note 99, at 207.

107. T. Abernathy, *supra* note 92, at 31.

108. *Id.* at 32.

109. J. Sosin, *supra* note 3, at 146. Contemporaneous to these events, the firm wrote to its partner, William Franklin, that all were pleased to hear that the governor's father

has by no means deserted two very principal objects, that we have long had in view, *viz.* the settlement of Illinois, and a restitution for the Indian losses—with infinite pleasure we discover, that Gentleman has these matters much at heart; and we are persuaded, an Exertion of his great ability's, join'd with his usual application, will in time mature them into a happy Execution. [Reprinted in *New Regime, supra* note 99, at 364.]

The firm had decided "not to shackle him [Benjamin Franklin] with any positive instructions, but leave him entirely at his liberty, to act for us in such manner, as he may judge may conduce most to our interest" (quoted in *id.*).

110. T. Abernathy, *supra* note 92, at 33. In addition to these efforts, the traders sought to lobby—or to bribe, if all else failed—Lord Shelbourne's trusted assistant, Laughlin MacLeane, appointed undersecretary of state in December 1766. The Baynton, Wharton, and Morgan firm wrote to William Franklin that MacLeane was a "fortune hunter"; but more important, they regarded him as "a sensible fellow and very sanguine, as to American schemes," who might prove "very useful, in Our Land Affairs." The firm sought to initiate the relationship by having Benjamin Franklin offer MacLeane a seventh part of any profits in return for using his influence with Shelbourne to obtain for the firm a supply contract for the royal garrisons in the Illinois Company. J. Sosin, *supra* note 3, at 147. MacLeane rejected what he himself called Franklin's "Bribe," but in discussing the proposal with Shelbourne, he nonetheless recommended the merchants' plan as being advantageous to the government. *Id.*

111. *Id.* at 176–77.

112. T. Abernathy, *supra* note 3, at 38.

113. J. Sosin, *supra* note 3, at 184.

114. *Id.* at 184.

115. T. Abernathy, *supra* note 92, at 44–45.

116. J. Sosin, *supra* note 3, at 185.

117. *Id.*

118. *Id.*

119. T. Abernathy, *supra* note 92, at 45.

120. *Id.* at 45–46.

121. *Id.* at 47.

122. The delay also allowed Virginia's new governor, Lord John Dunmore, ample time to maneuver against the Walpole syndicate's western interests. Having previously served as governor of New York, Dunmore readily identified the precise locus of power and reward inside the colony. He quickly joined ranks with Virginia's most prominent land speculators and adopted their determined opposition to the Vandalia colony. Shortly after assuming his post, Dunmore blatantly ignored direct orders from Whitehall prohibiting frontier land sales and began freely granting western lands claimed under his colony's ample charter to several Virginia speculators.

As just one example of Dunmore's pattern of dealings as governor of Virginia, he sought to curry favor with George Washington by promising that he would take whatever steps were necessary for securing title to certain lands on the upper Ohio River for Washington's Virginia soldiers. Both Dunmore and Washington knew that these same lands had been ceded by the Iroquois in the Fort Stanwix agreement of 1768 and that the Walpole associates intended to locate their colony of Vandalia in this area. It is not clear whether Dunmore knew that Washington and his men had been incorporated into the Vandalia scheme and that Washington may have been covering all his bets, as a wise speculator should. In any event, while informing Washington that he could not guarantee an "absolute and bona fide title" to the upper Ohio lands, Dunmore made the grant anyway. The Council of Virginia approved the governor's action in 1773. Washington immediately advertised offers to sell his surveys in the upper Ohio valley, confidently guaranteeing title "notwithstanding the unsettled counsels respecting a new colony [Vandalia] in the region." *See* J. Sosin, *supra* note 3, at 222–23.

123. T. Abernathy, *supra* note 92, at 51.

124. J. Sosin, *supra* note 3, at 208–10.

125. *Id.* at 210.

126. *Id.* at 228.

127. *See* text accompanying notes 64–65, *supra.*

128. *See* text accompanying notes 86–87, *supra.*

129. Quoted in J. Kaminski & H. Miller, "Jefferson Had Some Doubts, We the People: The Constitution 200 Years Ago Today," *Wisconsin State Journal*, April 19, 1987, Section S, p. 1.

130. *Tracts of AR, supra* note 40, at 258.

131. *Id.*

132. *Id.* at 258–59.

133. *Id.* at 259.

134. *Id.*

135. *Id.*

136. *See* text accompanying notes 46–48, *supra.*

137. *Tracts of AR, supra* note 40, at 259–60.

138. *Id.* at 260.

139. *Id.* at 272.

140. *Id.*

141. *Id.* at 273.

142. *Id.*

143. *Id.*

144. *See* Chapter 5, text accompanying notes 34–40, *supra.*

145. *See* Chapter 3, text accompanying notes 27–31, *supra*; Chapter 5, text accompanying notes 44–46, *supra.*

146. *See* Chapter 1, text accompanying note 56, *supra*; Chapter 3, text accompanying notes 61–64, *supra.*

147. *See* text accompanying notes 140–44, *supra.*

148. *See* Chapter 3, text accompanying notes 61–69, *supra.*

149. *See Tracts of AR, supra* note 40, at 273.

150. *Id.*

151. *See* text accompanying notes 88–91, *supra.*

152. *See Hawaii Housing Authority v. Midkiff*, 104 S. Ct. 2321, fn. 5 (1984); 3 J. Kent, *Commentaries on American Law*, Part 6: *Of the Law Concerning Real Property*, Lecture 53: *Of the History of the Law of Tenure* 501–10 (5th ed. 1844).

153. *See* text accompanying notes 105–26, *supra.*

154. A. Volwiler, *supra* note 13, at 298.

155. *Id.*

156. *See* text accompanying notes 124–27, *supra.*

157. T. Abernathy, *supra* note 92, at 114.

158. *See* Chapter 5, text accompanying notes 124–41, *supra.*

159. T. Abernathy, *supra* note 92, at 114.

160. *Id.* at 115.

161. *See* text accompanying note 160, *supra.*

162. Reprinted in J. Sosin, *supra* note 3, at 230.

163. *See* Chapter 5, text accompanying notes 31–40, *supra.*

164. *See* J. Sosin, *supra* note 3, at 230.

165. *See id.* at 231.

166. T. Abernathy, *supra* note 92, at 50.

167. *See* text accompanying notes 112–14, *supra.*

168. Englishmen in the early Discovery era did, however, quite frequently use appellations of royalty, such as "emperor," "king," and "prince," in referring to American Indian leaders.

169. *See* B. Bailyn, *supra* note 68, at 168.

170. *See id.* at 94.

171. The Americans relished heaping abuse on the king's slavish ministers. An assembly in Farmington, Connecticut, resolved in 1774: "That the present ministry . . . those pimps and parasites who dared to advise their masters to such detestable measures be held in utter abhorrence by . . . every American, and their names loaded with the curses of all succeeding generations" (quoted in *id.* at 125).

Bernard Bailyn has captured the discursive cant of the colonists projected at a "corrupt and prostituted ministry"; a "junto of courtiers and state-jobbers"; "court-locusts" who whispered in the king's ear, instilling in him "a divine right of authority to command his subjects." Their "detestable scheme" to destroy "the sacred liberties of the Americans" would most certainly "enslave the colonies and plunder them of their property and, what is more, their birthright, *liberty*" (quoted in *id.* at 125–26).

172. *See* J. Sosin, *supra* note 3, at 195–99.

173. *Id.* at 196.

174. *See* text accompanying notes 116–8, *supra.*

175. *See* text accompanying notes 116–7, *supra.*

176. *See* J. Sosin, *supra* note 3, at 195–99.

177. *Id.* at 232. *See* text accompanying notes 91–93, *supra.*

178. *See* text accompanying notes 156–60, *supra.*

179. J. Sosin, *supra* note 3, at 260. *See* note 122, *supra*, on Washington and Dunmore's relationship.

180. T. Abernathy, *supra* note 92, at 124.

7

The Colonists' War for America

On the eve of the colonies' Revolution, at least three competing discourses respecting the legal status and rights of the frontier Indian tribes were contending for legitimacy in American colonizing legal theory. Each was acted on in one way or another by individuals who invested fortunes on the chance that their preferred theory of Indian land rights would win out and they would profit handsomely from their perspicacity.

The British Crown's discourse of empire asserted a Norman-derived royal-prerogative right to control the disposition of Indian lands on the frontier in the Proclamation of 1763. Virginia and the other landed colonies asserted their controlling rights to the West on the basis of their Crown charters and the purer legal discourse of the natural-law-based Saxon Constitution realized by their colonies' governments. And finally, a large group of frontier speculators who cared for neither the Crown's nor the landed colonies' pretensions claimed that under natural law and natural right, the Indians themselves as sovereign princes of the soil they occupied could sell land to whomever they wished.

Of course, these divergent discourses on Indian legal status and rights were all derivative of the larger and more direct question (in the minds of the ministers at Whitehall and the colonists themselves) regarding rationalization of the land-acquisition process on the colonial frontier. As far as American colonizing legal theory during the Revolutionary period was concerned, that was virtually the only arena in which the Indians' legal status was seriously debated. Their natural rights, if any, were of only indirect concern, for they were but a supplement to the larger, manifest goals pursued by European-descended Americans on the frontier of their destiny. What directly concerned whites was the Indians' ability or inability to pass a vested title to land without the positive sanction of a European-derived sovereign entity. Only when it became apparent to Indian tribes that their own survival required a less accommodating stance toward the whites' invitations to enter the market economy for land would American colonizing legal theory directly confront the issue of the rights and status of Indians in land they did *not* desire to surrender to the whites. And that particular confrontation would not occur with notable inconveniencing frequency until after the Revolution and the adoption of a policy by the United States of simply removing the tribes by military force from their lands to make way for white settlement. Only then would American legal theory directly confront the question of whether Indians had natural rights in lands that they *refused* to sell to whites, and the answer of course was that they did not.[1]

The Patriots' Discourses

Few legislative bodies in American history have so mired themselves in corrupted self-interest parading as principle as did the Revolutionary-era American Continental Congress. In the nearly decade-long debate on the status of the western lands under the proposed Articles of Confederation, delegates from the "landed" states, particularly Virginia, continued to insist on the inviolability of their charter-based rights in the West. At the same time, numerous delegates to the Congress from the "landless" states, such as Maryland, Pennsylvania, and New Jersey, acquired or even increased their interests in various land-speculation ventures on the frontier. They hoped that the Congress would secure control of the West under the Articles of Confederation and would affirm the validity of their Indian-derived grants. Large fortunes would be determined by the answer to the question of whether the "landed" states or the central government would supervise the process of land acquisition and distribution on the frontier. And many of the largest fortunes were to be won or lost by a number of the congressional delegates themselves, entrusted with the responsibility for deciding this vital question of national interest.

By far the most powerful syndicates at the Congress, in terms of the number of delegates holding shares, were the Indiana Company and the Illinois-Wabash Company. The Indiana Company had been organized by Samuel Wharton from the ruins of the "suffering" traders–Vandalia colony project.[2] The Illinois-Wabash Company was the combination of two separate ventures resulting from the frontier land-speculation activities of the Indian traders William Murray and Louis Viviat prior to the outbreak of the Revolution.[3]

In 1773, the trader Murray had set out for the interior country with the intention of making several large purchases of land directly from the frontier tribes. Reaching the Illinois country on June 11, 1773, Murray first encountered Captain Hugh Lord, commander of the English garrison at Fort Gage at Kaskaskia. Lord was under strict orders from London to enforce the prohibition of the Proclamation of 1763 against Indian land sales to colonial speculators. Murray, however, directly challenged the captain's authority to prevent a free English subject from making purchases directly from the Indians and presented Lord with a copy of the well-traveled *Camden-Yorke* opinion. Lord described this document in a report to his superiors as an "opinion of my Lord Camden and the late Lorde Mondes [Yorke], that His Majesty's subjects were at liberty to purchase whatever quantity of lands they chose of Indians. . . ."[4] Lacking authority to arrest Murray, who like most traders would readily bring suit against any military officer who violated his "English liberties," Lord merely warned the Indian trader that he would not allow him to *settle* any of the lands, as this was expressly forbidden by royal orders.

On July 5, 1773, Murray purchased two prime tracts of land from the Illinois Indians, one at the junction of the Ohio and Mississippi rivers and the other at the Illinois and Mississippi rivers, for the combined price of $24,000. Murray's partner, Louis Viviat, then acquired two additional tracts of upper Ohio lands from the Piankeshaw Indians in 1775.[5]

These defiant purchases by Murray and Viviat on behalf of the Illinois-Wabash Company prior to the outbreak of the Revolution would later form the basis of a lawsuit, *Johnson v. McIntosh*,[6] brought in the United States Supreme Court in 1823 by the successors in interest to the land syndicate. In its refusal to recognize the validity of Murray's and Viviat's Revolutionary-era purchases from the frontier tribes, Chief Justice John Marshall's opinion in *Johnson v. McIntosh* provided Western legal thought and discourse with its single most important textual interpretation of the law governing the rights of indigenous tribal peoples in the territories they occupied.[7] Marshall's influential discourse of conquest in *Johnson*, accepted as the settlted law on indigenous peoples' rights and status in all the European-derived settler-colonialist states of the West, merely provided a *post hoc* legal rationalization for the Revolutionary-era political compromise on the frontier lands question. That compromise, embodied in a feudally derived, fictive doctrine of discovery and conquest, vested superior title to the frontier Indian lands in the United States government. Thus Marshall's decision in *Johnson*, recognizing the Doctrine of Discovery as governing the frontier land-acquisition process in the United States, had little to do with "law" as the Western legal tradition prefers to define that term. Politics and the Founders' brokered definition of "public good," which did not include the Indian tribes, determined the rights and status of American Indian nations in the lands they occupied on the frontier.

The Players and the Play

The Illinois-Wabash Company, Samuel Wharton's "suffering" traders–Vandalia syndicate, and several other lesser ventures represented at the Continental Congress had all acquired huge tracts of western land directly from the frontier tribes prior to the outbreak of revolt. The delegates who held substantial shares in these ventures worked diligently to ensure that the new Congress, despite Virginia's and the other landed states' vigorous protests and defenses of their charter rights, would assume complete control of the western frontier territories as a national domain and would recognize the validity of their Indian grants. They refused to agree to any draft of the Articles of Confederation that did not vest Congress with the authority to determine the vital western lands question.

The land-speculating delegates in Congress often voiced their opposition to the expansive frontier claims of the landed colonies in terms of the necessary balance of landholding power in a federation of supposedly equal states. However, other delegates, with less personal interest in the matter, doubted that the issue delaying agreement on the Articles of Confederation, the proposed constitution for the new federation of state sovereignties, was solely one of small states' fears of being engulfed by larger ones. John Adams commented in the spring of 1776 that the goal of a confederated union was being delayed by "that avarice of Land, which has made upon this Continent so many votaries to Mammon, that I sometimes dread the Consequences."[8] One member of the Congress voiced the fear that competition between the states for land in the West would result in wars and convulsions, tearing the continent "in pieces."[9]

Virginia, claiming the largest interest in the West under its charter, adopted the hardest line of all the landed colonies, refusing to relinquish its asserted rights under any conditions to any national governing body. On June 27, 1776, the Virginia constitutional convention resolved that no purchases of Indian lands could be made within Virginia's chartered limits without legislative approval. The state's constitution contained an amendment, which had been drafted by Thomas Jefferson, stipulating that Virginia's western boundary was to remain as it had been defined by the Crown charter of 1609. On July 4, while independence for the new nation was being declared in Philadelphia, Virginia ordered its commissioners to collect evidence against persons claiming lands acquired by Indian purchases within its chartered borders.

While Virginia pressed its all-out assault against the non-Virginia land-speculating companies, the delegates to the Continental Congress in Philadelphia debated whether or not the proposed national government should control the West, despite the claims of landed colonies under their Crown-based charters. John Dickinson's 1776 draft of the proposed Articles of Confederation gave Congress the power to enter into alliances with Indian nations, determine their boundaries, and guarantee their lands. This draft also gave Congress the authority to determine the states' geographical boundaries. No state or individual could purchase from the Indians until the boundaries of the states were established by Congress. Once those boundaries were established, only the United States could purchase Indian lands beyond the boundaries of any state. Congress would then dispose of those lands for the benefit of all the states and would set up new governments in the western territories.[10] Significantly, however, the issue of the validity of claims derived from Indian purchases made before the war was not directly addressed in the Dickinson draft.

The Dickinson draft of the Articles refuted the western claims of the states with unlimited charters, as it implicitly supported the contention of the "landless" states and their speculators that there actually were western lands lying outside the boundaries of any state. Samuel Chase of Maryland, who was intimately connected with the Illinois-Wabash Company (as were many members of the Maryland delegation), argued in support of the Dickinson draft that no state then had, had ever had, or ever could have a right to extend its boundaries to the South Sea (the Pacific Ocean). If Virginia's claims and those of other "landed states" were not limited, then the landless states would find themselves in a most vulnerable position. James Wilson, a Pennsylvanian who later became president of the Illinois-Wabash syndicate, attacked the landed states' claims to the West as unfounded, in that the original charters of states such as Virginia were based on the mistaken assumption that the South

Sea was only 100 miles from the Atlantic Ocean. He warned that Pennsylvania would not confederate unless the landed states voluntarily relinquished their extravagant claims. In support of the principles forwarded by the Dickinson draft, Wilson cited the opinion of none other than Lord Camden, given to the speculators some years earlier, that such claims could never be practical.[11]

The delegates from the landed states, particularly those from Virginia, were unmoved by the threats, counterclaims, and arguments of the speculator delegates from the landless states. Thomas Jefferson summed up the Virginians' response to the landless states' argument that they would be endangered by the growth of the large states with his famous maxim: "A man's right does not cease to be a right, because it is large."[12]

The opposition of Virginia and the other landed states blocked further consideration of the western lands question at the Congress's 1776 session. But the issue of who would control the West—Congress, for the "benefit" of all the states, or the several states that claimed the West under the charter of an enemy crown—would not go away. At the October 1777 session, three consecutive motions that would have permitted Congress under the Articles of Confederation to take steps to determine the limits of each state's territorial jurisdiction failed to garner the support of the landed states. Richard Henry Lee of Virginia, who had earlier written a letter to Thomas Jefferson expressing doubts about the legality of Virginia's claims to the West, offered the following clause to the delegates at the Congress as a compromise: "that no state shall be deprived of territory for the benefit of the United States."[13] Lee's amendment was based on the simple principle of maintaining a presently undefined status quo. It was a principle on which gentlemen could agree, given the exigencies of the moment, and over whose precise implications they could argue at a later date. There was, after all, a war to be fought against a Norman tyrant's well-drilled battalions. Lee's amendment was adopted as part of the Articles of Confederation as an interim measure, so that thirteen separate sovereignties could at least attempt to fight their common foe as a united entity.

One other important issue regarding Indian affairs was decided at this session. The Dickinson draft had originally proposed vesting the Congress with sole and exclusive control over the Indian trade and the management of Indian affairs. This centralizing clause was quickly limited by the Committee of the Whole in July 1776. A proviso was added that such powers were restricted to Indians "not members of any state." At the October 1777 session, the delegates agreed to modify this clause further. Under the Articles, Congress was given the power of "regulating the trade and managing all affairs with the Indians not members of any of the States, provided that the legislative right of any State within its own limits be not infringed or violated." This new language protecting "the legislative right" of a state within "its own limits" was designed to protect the western land claims of the landed states from congressional interference. James Madison, writing in 1784, interpreted this proviso as being intended "to save to the States their right of preemption of lands from the Indians." Madison gave the following four reasons in support of this interpretation:

1. That this was the principal right formerly exerted by the Colonies with regard to the Indians;
2. That it was a right asserted by the laws as well as the proceeding of all of them, and therefore being most familiar, would be most likely to be in contemplation of the Parties;
3. That being of most consequence to the States individually and least inconsistent with the general powers of Congress, it was most likely to be made a ground of Compromise;
4. It has been always said that the proviso came from the Virg[ini]a Delegates, who would naturally be most vigilant over the territorial rights of their Constituents.[14]

The clause in Dickinson's draft of 1776 had stated simply that Congress had the power of regulating trade with Indians who were not members of any states. This simple clause, if adopted, would have meant that the states had jurisdiction only over Indians who had been assimilated and had accepted state jurisdiction. The western tribes, of course, were still independent and had never accepted any European-derived government's jurisdiction. The Virginia delegates' added proviso protecting the state's "legislative right" within its "limits" indicates a clear intention to preserve every geographical and jurisdictional claim that Virginia might wish to assert under the Articles at a later date with respect to the unassimilated Indians of the West. As Congress had not agreed in the Articles to define the "legislative right of any state within its own limits," Virginia could lose no right by agreeing to this particular clause on Indian trade. In conjunction with Lee's amendment, stating "that no state shall be deprived of territory for the benefit of the United States,"[15] the Virginia-influenced proviso on Indian trade assured the landed states that their claims to the West remained inviolate. Until or unless they ceded their claims, the western frontier remained within their chartered limits, and Congress under the Articles lacked authority to infringe or violate their legislative rights over that territory. There was little ambiguity in these complex formulations, at least in the minds of the Virginians, who had seen to it that the Articles were structured precisely to their liking. As Merrill Jensen has stated with respect to this final draft of the Articles, "the victory for the landed states in this portion of the Articles was complete." The landed states had achieved "success . . . in seeking constitutional guarantees against attack from the landless states and the land speculators."[16]

The "Plain Facts" of the "Public Good"

The Virginians who insisted on maintaining their state's control over western lands believed that they were fighting far more than the greed of the specula-tors. To radicals such as Thomas Jefferson, the Declaration of Independence signified that the peoples of the individual states, not the British Crown, were to be the ultimate source of sovereignty. As the colonists were fighting and dying in a revolution against the potentially aggrandizing coercive power of Great Britain, the Virginians were not about to place control of the western lands in the hands of another aggrandizing central government.[17]

Many of the radicals who opposed vesting too much authority in the Congress of the new confederation firmly believed that to establish thirteen distinct centers of power was a far better method of preserving liberty than to plant a seed in one power that might grow to choke off liberty for all the citizens of the individual states. As Richard Henry Lee had written, "abridged duration, temperate revenue, and every necessary power withheld, are potent means of preserving the integrity of public men and for securing the community from the dangerous ambition that too often governs the human mind."[18] Because power corrupted, it was unwise to place too much power in one centralized body. Thus the Articles' overriding structural premise of dispersal of sovereignty represented the temporary triumph in American political theory of the radicals' distrust of centralized power.

With respect to the West, the completed version of the Articles that was passed on to the states for formal ratification in early 1778 assured that no state could be deprived of its territory for the benefit of the United States. Congress at best could arbitrate territorial disputes between states, but it could neither make nor enforce a specific decision.[19] Virginia, most contented with this proposed version of the Articles, was the only state ready to ratify without qualification or criticism by the appointed date, March 20, 1778. "Landless" Maryland, the state most discontented with the proposed Articles, presented the strongest list of objections. The Marylanders demanded that the Articles be amended to give Congress the power to determine and define the limits of the states claiming lands in the West. And Congress also had to recognize, in the words of the Marylanders, their state's right to a share of the country lying westward "of the frontiers of the United States, the property of which was not vested in individuals at the commencement of the present war."[20]

This odd formulation by the Marylanders can be better understood in light of the fact that a large percentage of Maryland's most prominent citizens had heavily invested in western land-speculating ventures based on Indian purchases prior to the "commencement of the present war." Governor Thomas Johnston, Samuel Chase, Charles Carroll, William Paca, and many other Marylanders held outright or secret shares in the Illinois-Wabash Company, and in other ventures as well. Thus Maryland's peculiar demand probably reflected the personal financial interests of controlling members in that state's delegation. Maryland's western land speculators were required to maintain that Indian nations possessed the sovereign capacity to sell their lands and "vest" a title in individual purchasers—namely, those Marylanders who held interests in Indian grants acquired prior to the "commencement of the present war."

Virginia's George Mason, himself a land speculator and close political ally of Jefferson, perceived clearly the motivation behind the Marylanders' objections and their odd formulation implicitly recognizing the natural rights of Indians to vest land titles in individual purchasers. The demand that Congress be given the right to control only those western lands not "vested" prior to the war demonstrated, in Mason's opinion, "the secret and true cause of the great opposition to Virginia's title to her chartered territory." The "cause" was the

Indian purchases held by "Governor Johnston and several of the leading men of Maryland." Mason asked sarcastically, "Do you observe the care Governor Johnston . . . has taken to save his Indian purchase?"[21]

Maryland's demands were not accepted by the Congress. The split in votes on one Maryland-submitted amendment to the proposed Articles that would have given Congress the power to appoint commissioners to ascertain state boundaries indicates the divisions in the Continental Congress on the question of western lands. Rhode Island, New Jersey, Pennsylvania, Delaware, and Maryland voted for this amendment. All were landless states with no claims in the West. New York's delegation was split on the amendment, but New Hampshire, Massachusetts, Connecticut, Virginia, South Carolina, and Georgia were solidly opposed. All these states, including New York, either had land claims in the West or were engaged in land disputes with a neighboring state. They apparently did not desire to see a national Congress with sovereign log-rolling power to override their various individual claims.

With the defeat of the Maryland amendments, Virginia moved boldly to secure its charter-based claims in the West. On November 4, 1778, the Virginia legislature disallowed every unauthorized purchase of lands from Indians within its chartered limits. Maryland responded on January 6, 1779, by declaring that it would not ratify the Articles of Confederation until Congress was given full power to fix the boundaries of the United States. The lands on the western frontier had been seized from the British Crown by the united efforts of all the colonies, and therefore all the colonies should stand to benefit from these lands.

Virginia remained unconvinced by such arguments. The Virginia House passed a set of resolutions in June 1779 declaring the state's "exclusive right of pre-emption from the Indians of all the lands within the limits of its own chartered territory."[22] Virginia's resolutions also denied the right of any individual to claim lands within the state on the basis of any past, present, or future Indian grant. In particular, all purchases made by Great Britain's king were declared the property of the commonwealth. The 1768 Fort Stanwix deed of cession to Samuel Wharton's syndicate of "suffering" traders (resyndicated as the Indiana Company) was specifically declared "utterly void, and of no effect."[23]

Within a few days of this action, Mason's bill setting up an administrative apparatus to dispose of all ungranted lands in the West was approved by the Virginia legislature, along with legislation granting preemption rights for existing Virginian settlements on the frontier. George Washington's individual claims, along with those of his men who had earned military land bounties under the Dinwiddie proclamation of 1754,[24] were finally guaranteed under the Virginia legislation. Virginia followed these actions with a formal protest to Congress drafted by Mason, denying that Congress had any jurisdiction over the state's western lands. This protest was made in response to the lobbying activities of non-Virginian speculators who were urging the Congress to take up once again the issue of control over the western lands and the validity of their Indian grants.[25]

A list of the influential politicians either directly or indirectly linked to the Continental Congress who held interests in the non-Virginian land companies reveals why that body was so hopefully looked to for aid during this period. As was noted above, the Illinois-Wabash Company's membership list in the spring of 1779 included such prominent Marylanders as Governor Thomas Johnston, Samuel Chase, Charles Carroll, and William Paca. Pennsylvania members included the merchant-financier Robert Morris and James Wilson, two of the most influential men on the continent. Other shareholders were Silas Deane of Connecticut; Conrad Gerard, France's extremely influential minister to the United States; and the Frankses and Gratzes, powerful Philadelphia merchants. The Indiana Company, of course, included the Whartons (Samuel was a delegate to the Congress), George Morgan (a congressionally appointed Indian agent), the Franklins, and Joseph Galloway.

Many of these individuals were conservative in their political outlook, so they generally favored a stronger central government with the power to constrain the feared democratic excesses of the state governments. They tended naturally to accept or cast arguments in favor of the land companies in a "constitutional" light, stressing the overriding sovereignty of the national government in the new union.[26] This sovereignty, it was argued, ought to comprehend control of the western frontier. For instance, George Morgan demanded that Congress order Virginia to close its land office until his Indiana Company's western claims could be settled before Congress "in such a manner as may tend to support the sovereignty of the United States and the just rights of the individuals therein."[27] The land companies' strategy apparently focused on asserting the superior sovereignty of Congress to override the landed states' charter claims to the West and to recognize the validity of the companies' Indian-derived grants. William Trent, Samuel Wharton's long-time partner in western land speculation, presented a memorial on behalf of the land company arguing that the Vandalia project had essentially been approved by the British government, although not formally completed by the time of the Declaration of Independence. But once the Declaration of Independence had been proclaimed, Trent theorized, "all the Rights and all the obligations of the Crown of Great Britain respecting the lands and governments herein before mentioned devolve upon the United States and are to be claimed, exercised and discharged by the United States in Congress assembled."[28]

Jefferson and the radicals preferred to think of the Declaration of Independence and the Revolution as a clean break with the mother country (a break, however, that did not diminish the supraconstitutional status of Virginia's Crown-based charter establishing its government and its western land claims). The radicals would naturally have been appalled by Trent's theory that the British Crown's disputed, feudally derived "sovereignty" over the frontier lands of America had "devolved" upon the new central government at the outbreak of revolt. According to this devolution of sovereignty argument, the colonies had declared war against one tyrannical monolith, only to see another rise like a Phoenix from the ashes to take its place. It was all so much Norman-derived feudal nonsense to Jefferson and his fellow states'-rights advocates.

But British advances in the south, combined with a Virginia currency crisis and New York's 1780 offer of cession of its western land claims to Congress, led the Virginians to reconsider their objections to a centralized government that controlled the West as part of the national domain. Joseph Jones, representing Virginia at the Congress, wrote a letter to Thomas Jefferson, then the governor of Virginia, and his close ally George Mason urging that Virginia follow New York's patriotic lead. Jones asked Mason's specific opinions on a land cession to Congress and the conditions that ought to be attached. Mason's response favored a compromise by which Congress would guarantee Virginia's title to the lands southeast of the Ohio, and Virginia would surrender its rights to the soil and sovereignty of the land northwest of the river. Certain other conditions, however, were attached to this compromise. Among the major conditions that Virginia would insist on were that at least two new states be created out of its northwest cession, that all the lands ceded by the state to the central government be considered a common fund of the Confederation, and that *all* purchases from Indians in the region be declared null and void. Mason explained this last clause, which was aimed directly at the ruination of the non-Virginian land companies, by stating that unless the speculators' scandalous actions were disavowed by Congress, the choicest territories in the West would likely end up in the hands of scheming land jobbers who cared not a fig for the interests of the nation as a whole.[29]

Congress agreed to all of Virginia's demands except one: Congress would not agree to void titles to western lands acquired directly from the Indians. Virginia responded that this vital point of principle was not negotiable. All the concerned parties recognized that principles contributed but a small part to the stalemate. Mason wrote that the Congress's decision not to void Indian-derived titles was influenced by those who sought to gratify "private interest at the public expense."[30]

The British advance up the Chesapeake had at least drawn several significant concessions from Virginia on the western lands issue. Maryland also felt the pressures of the southward British thrust and of the exhortations to union made by the ambassador of the new nation's most important ally, France. Recognizing the importance of union to its own survival, landless Maryland ratified the Articles of Confederation in early 1781.[31]

This did not mean, however, that the Marylanders and the other non-Virginian speculators had now surrendered all hopes of ever cashing in on their Indian land grants in the West. The speculators launched a massive publicity campaign. Their lobbying efforts were designed to persuade the Congress to hold firm in its decision not to deny the validity of their Indian titles and to prevail on Virginia to recognize "the Interest of the United States, in preference to the partial views of one."[32]

Among the writers who joined the fray was Thomas Paine, whose *Common Sense* pamphlet of 1776 had galvanized Revolutionary discourse and practice.[33] Paine's pamphlet on the western lands issue, which appeared in early 1781, was entitled *Public Good: Being an Examination into the Claim of Virginia to the Vacant Western Territory, and the Right of the United States to the same: to which is added proposals for laying off a new state, to be applied as a Fund for carrying on the War or Redeeming the National Debt.*[34] Soon after publishing this tract supporting the non-Virginian speculators cause, Paine was listed as owning 300 shares in the Indiana Company.[35]

Writing as an "advocate for the right of the states,"[36] Paine argued in *Public Good* that the "vacant western territory of America" should be regarded as the common right of all the citizens of all the states. "It is only till lately that any pretension of claim has been made to the contrary."[37] Paine supported this argument by citing historical evidence to refute Virginia's interpretation of its charter and its claims to the West running to the South Sea. First, at the time the charter was drafted in England, "no man there knew how far it was from the Atlantic to the South Sea . . . but believed it to be but a short distance." Second, "the uncertain and ambiguous manner in which the South Sea is alluded to (for it is not mentioned by name, but only *from sea to sea*) served to perplex the patent." Thus, "as no right can be founded on an ambiguity," the charter "can yield no service" to Virginia's claims.[38]

Paine went on to demonstrate that even if the charter had originally been valid, it no longer had the force of law behind it. The London Company, Paine noted, was the original party to the charter.[39] The Crown, however, had superseded the company when it voided the charter and assumed control over the colony. These actions effectively dissolved the charter. Thus, Paine reasoned, the rights to any vacant lands under the 1609 charter had been resumed by the Crown prior to the Americans' announcement of their independence, and by that Declaration of Independence the western lands had "devolved to the sovereignty of the United States."[40] As further proof of this argument for the devolution of sovereignty, Paine cited the Proclamation of 1763. Paine implicitly acknowledged the proclamation's grounding in the detested Crown legal discourse of prerogative. He referred to the proclamation's feudally derived prerogative as the "old remains of former arrogance."[41] Nonetheless, the proclamation had definitively established Virginia's western border at the crest of the Allegheny Mountains. As a creature of the Crown, Virginia could not deny the validity of this act. Thus beyond the proclamation's boundary the Crown might create new colonies or make grants, a sovereign power now devolved upon the United States by its assumption of sovereignty over these lands.[42] Paine was arguing, in essence, that the Crown's feudally derived sovereign claims of power over the West had been transferred to the central government of the United States, in order to rebut the arguments of the landed states. Paine had exposed the feudal logic underlying the Crown charter basis of these states' claims and had used that logic to prove that what the Norman Yoke had given to the "landed" colonies, the Norman Yoke could also take away. The detested proclamation had effectively divested Virginia of any interest it could claim in the West.

Besides attacking the *right* of Virginia's western claims, Paine attacked the *reasonableness* of one state's attempt to aggrandize such a large portion of land. An overly large state was sure to arouse the hostilities of its neighboring smaller states. Besides, the western lands represented the best source of income to pay off the debts incurred by the nation in acquiring its hard-earned independence:

Lands are the real riches of the habitable world, and the natural funds of America. The funds of other countries are, in general, artificially constructed; the creatures of necessity and continuance dependent upon credit, and always exposed to hazard and uncertainty. But lands can neither be annihilated nor lose their value; on the contrary, they universally rise with population, and rapidly so, when under the security of effectual government. But this it is impossible for Virginia to give.[43]

Spoken like a true land speculator, or at least like a true land speculator's public-relations man. Significantly, the natural-law rights of the Indians to the western lands were not discussed by Paine in his *Public Good* pamphlet. Paine's strategic resort to the devolution of sovereignty argument and its grounding feudal logic eliminated any need to discuss Indian rights. Under feudal law, with its doctrine that discovery of infidel lands vested prerogative rights of conquest in the English Crown,[44] the Crown was not required to acknowledge Indian rights in land. In the vision outlined by Paine, these prerogative rights of superior title to the Indian frontier had now devolved from the Crown to the United States. The ominous failure to include the Indian tribes within the *Public Good* implied the quiet acceptance of the feudal principle that Indians did not possess natural-law rights to the lands they occupied on the frontier.

Shortly after Paine published his propaganda effort, Samuel Wharton, the long-time speculator and central cog in the "suffering" traders–Vandalia colony syndicate (now reorganized as the Indiana Company) and a member of the Continental Congress, published an unsigned pamphlet under the short title *Plain Facts: Being an Examination into the Rights of the Indian Nations of America, to Their Respective Countries* . . . . (1781).[45] This tract was designed to persuade Wharton's fellow delegates to the Congress to affirm the validity of the Indiana Company's Indian-derived titles in the region of Virginia's proposed northwest cession.

Unlike Paine's *Public Good*, Wharton's pamphlet focused almost exclusively on Indian rights. In fact, it represents the Confederation period's most elaborate legal brief on behalf of the natural-law-based rights of sovereign Indian nations to sell their lands to whomever they pleased. In many ways, this remarkable document is perhaps the most "radical" statement on the topic of Indian rights in the Revolutionary era. Wharton was so bold as to extend the discourse of natural rights even to those peoples who, in the European mind, lived closest to the state of nature.

Wharton had spent a number of years in England advocating his speculative cause before the Ministry. The natural-rights discourse trumpeted there by the radical voices of opposition had apparently combined with Wharton's own speculative interests to radicalize his views on Indian rights and status. Citing and quoting an eclectic variety of leading English and European Enlightenment thinkers, Wharton's *Plain Facts* indicates the totalizing direction of thought that only a few individuals were inclined to follow in tracing out the full implications of Enlightenment-era natural-rights discourse and its least examined hypothesis: that even the savage Indians of America, despite their radical normative divergence, held the same rights and status in their lands as civilized Europeans.

Like many other radicals, Wharton grounded his natural-rights discourse in history, particularly in the recounting of old wrongs left unrighted.[46] *Plain Facts* related how the violations of the American Indians' natural rights commenced with Europe's first discoveries in the New World. The seizure of the Indians' lands was inaugurated by Pope Alexander's 1493 bulls of donation to Spain, by which Rome "munificently gave the whole of this vast Continent, of which but a small part was then known in Europe, to Ferdinand and Isabella."[47] This unjust action denying the American Indian's title to the New World was based on familiar papist precedents. An earlier pope had granted Africa to Portugal in 1440, "not because this Continent was uninhabited, but because the nations subsisting there were *infidels*."[48]

Wharton next attacked England's Catholic-era monarchs for adopting the popish practices of the Iberians in the infidel lands discovered by the Cabots. Even prior to the Reformation, the disposing power assumed over non-Christian "free nations" by the Roman pope was "too glaringly absurd to be regarded by Popish princes themselves" as constraining their freedom to make discoveries and trade in infidel lands. Europe's monarchs, including King Henry VII of England, himself "a zealous Catholic," blithely ignored the Spanish papal bulls and undertook discoveries and settlements in the New World. But King Henry's commissions to the Cabots, no matter how boldly stated, "could convey no territorial property, as none had been then acquired." Cabot's North American discoveries could give the Crown nothing "other than the privilege of forming establishments in these countries, with the consent of the natives, in preference to the subjects of any other state." In denying the Crown's fictive rights of conquest and title to North America acquired by discovery of already occupied territories, Wharton asserted flatly, "No man . . . can give what he has not. Whoever therefore will pretend, that the King has bestowed this property must prove that he, first, had it himself."[49]

Wharton's history lesson continued through the reigns of the Protestant monarchs Elizabeth I and James I. Both monarchs adopted the papist-inspired custom of granting rights to their subjects for discovery and conquest in America. These monarchs also found the "exploded distinction" between the rights of Christians and of infidels convenient in justifying their usurpations. Their pretense of a superior claim to America as Christians served as "the only foundation" of the English Crown's rights in the New World.

But such were the dark ages of Europe's intellectual history. According to *Plain Facts*, civilization had now been advanced by a more enlightened, "liberal" philosophy, one that extended natural rights to all peoples, Christian and non-Christian alike:

But if the princes and people of Europe, in more ignorant and superstitious ages, were so far misled by the emotions of avarice, ambition, or religious pride, as to believe it justifiable for them to cross the Atlantic, and usurp the possessions of unoffending nations . . . yet the pervading liberal influence of philosophy, reason, and truth, has since given us better notions of the rights of mankind, as well as of the obligations of morality and justice, which certainly are not confined to particular modes of faith, but extend universally to Jews and Gentiles, to Christians and infidels.[50]

Drawing on themes popularized in the writings of John Locke,[51] Wharton declared that the natives of America followed "the first immutable law of nature" in exercising their God-given rights of self-preservation—rights which necessarily included the right to acquire and hold property. No race could therefore deprive the American natives of the rightful enjoyment of their dominions as they awaited the progress of events that would bring them from their rude state of nature to "the splendid accomplishments of civilization."[52]

Besides relying on the natural-law-inspired philosophy of the European Enlightenment, *Plain Facts* appealed to the natural reason embodied in English common law to marshal support for the American Indians' land rights. Wharton noted triumphantly that the absurd opinion that Christians have a unilateral "right to heathen countries" was "ridiculed by Lord Mansfield, as of the other judges, as well as by all the council present"[53] in the famous case of *Campbell v. Hall.*[54]

Lord Mansfield's 1774 opinion for the Court of King's Bench in *Campbell v. Hall* is a central text of late-eighteenth-century English legal colonizing discourse. Like the *Camden-Yorke* opinion of the same era,[55] *Campbell v. Hall* reflected the discursive practice of a post–Glorious Revolution British politics directed toward formally inscribing the constitutional limitations on the Crown's prerogative powers.

Campbell v. Hall arose out of England's capture of the French Caribbean island of Grenada during the Seven Years' War (of which the French and Indian War in America was a component[56]). Grenada was inhabited largely by French plantation owners at the time of its surrender. The British articles of capitulation stated that the island's present laws would remain in force until His Majesty's further pleasure was made known. This course of action accorded precisely with Lord Coke's early-seventeenth-century opinion in *Calvin's Case.*[57] The king, upon the conquest of a country inhabited by Christians (French plantation owners in this case), could allow the alien Christian country's laws to remain in effect until changed by royal proclamation.[58]

The king's Proclamation of 1763, besides addressing issues of imperial management for the western North American frontier, had sought specifically to conform Grenada's government to English constitutional principles. With respect to Grenada, the proclamation, among other directives, provided for a representative assembly on the island under the Great Seal.[59] The king's letters patent establishing the Grenadians' representative assembly, as promised in the proclamation, were issued in April 1764. Following this promulgation, however, the Crown, "by virtue of our prerogative Royal," sought to impose a 4.5 percent duty on all sugar produced on the island. The date of this unilateral act was July 20, 1764, some nine months after the proclamation and four months after the formal establishment of representative assembly on the island.

Campbell, an English subject who had purchased a plantation in Grenada after the island came under British sovereignty, challenged the king's tax in a lawsuit against Hall, "a collector [for] his Majesty." Campbell's suit asserted that the king's tax had not been imposed by lawful or sufficient authority under the British Constitution. Campbell's attorneys argued that the king's Proclamation of 1763 had declared the constitutional right of assembly for Grenada's inhabitants. By this action, the king effectively surrendered his prerogative right acquired by conquest to govern the island by subsequent proclamation. Thus, constitutionally, the king could not afterward impose a tax without either an act of the Grenada Assembly or of Parliament.[60] (The North Americans, of course, denied even the right of a Parliament in which they were unrepresented to impose a tax.)

Lord Mansfield began his analysis in *Campbell v. Hall*[61] with a recitation of several basic propositions derived from Lord Coke's famous opinion in *Calvin's Case* in 1608.[62] According to Mansfield, "A country conquered by the British arms becomes a dominion of the King in the right of his Crown." The laws of that conquered country, according to Mansfield, "continue in force; until they are altered by the conqueror." These basic principles were taken straight from Coke's opinion in *Calvin's Case*.[63] Mansfield took pains to demonstrate the long-time acceptance of these principles in English common law by noting the "absurd exception as to pagans" contained in Coke's opinion. As far as Lord Mansfield was concerned, Coke's dictum in *Calvin's Case* that the king's conquest of an infidel nation abrogated its laws demonstrated the "universality and antiquity" of the more fundamental maxim that the laws of a conquered country continue in force until altered by the conqueror. For this "absurd" distinction respecting the *prima facie* invalidity of the infidel's laws, declared Mansfield, "would not exist before the Christian era, and in all probability arose from the mad enthusiasm of the *Croisades*."[64]

In European legal discourse of the Enlightenment era, words such as "universality" and "antiquity" could refer only to the ancient roman *ius gentium*, the universal Law of Nations. As Ernst Nys has explained,[65] to the Romans the term *ius gentium* "signified in the wide sense the law common to civilized peoples and included both public and private law."[66] Mansfield was thus arguing in *Campbell v. Hall* that the root principle stated by Lord Coke in *Calvin's Case*—that upon conquest, the laws of a conquered country continue in force until altered by the conqueror—originated in the "universality and antiquity" of the Roman *ius gentium*. The distinction noted by Lord Coke dealing solely with "Christian" rights in infidel lands, said Mansfield, would obviously not have existed "before the Christian era." It arose "in all probability" many centuries after the Roman *ius gentium*, and could likely be traced to, in Mansfield's carefully selected—and spelled—words, "the mad enthusiasm of the *Croisades*."[67]

By this choice of words and spelling, Mansfield employed a subtle distancing strategy. The same basic strategy can be found deployed in the many texts of the period, both English and American, that sought to limit formally the Norman-derived feudal principles of royal prerogative power.[68] In *Campbell v. Hall* the strategy is indicated by Mansfield's "French" spelling of the word "croisade." The "croisade" was the peculiar innovation of the medieval French Normans, spurred on by the influence of the papacy's sponsorship of the Norman colonizing campaigns against the infidels on the Iberian Peninsula and shortly thereafter in the Holy Land.[69] William the Conqueror invaded England under a papal banner authorizing the equivalent of a "croisade" against the English Crown's resistance to Rome's ecclesiastical authority.[70] Thus the "madness" referred to by Mansfield was the "madness" involuntarily imported into England and its common law by William the Conqueror and the Norman Yoke. Mansfield's exorcism of Lord Coke's "absurd" distinction respecting infidels thus sought to purify English legal discourse of Norman-inspired "madness." Like Jefferson in his Saxon-inspired musings,[71] Mansfield attacked the false legal consciousness imposed by the hegemonic functioning of Normal feudal discourse, to which even a figure such as Lord Coke had succumbed. Mansfield sought to return English colonizing law to a purer set of antique and universal principles founded on the natural reasoning of the Roman *ius gentium*. This return required the jettisoning of the absurd madness of Norman-imported legal discourse and its papist-inspired traditions of "croisade" directed against infidel peoples.

Mansfield's distancing strategy and its erasure of the corrupted Norman-inspired dictum of Coke's *Calvin's Case* thus provided the court in *Campbell v. Hall* with an unadulterated doctrine of kingly conquest under a British Constitution purified by the Glorious Revolution. Upon the king's conquest of a Christian *or* infidel kingdom, the laws of that kingdom continued in force until altered by the king, although of course any alterations would have to be consistent with the principles of limitation in the British Constitution.

In applying this purified legal discourse of conquest to Grenada, Mansfield specified the precise nature of the limitations on the king's prerogative to change the laws in a conquered country: once the king had promised the inhabitants the rights and liberties embodied in the English Constitution, the king's prerogative was henceforth limited by the Constitution. Mansfield reasoned that the Proclamation of 1763 had effectively guaranteed the Grenada inhabitants an established constitution. That being the case, the king was prohibited from entertaining any change in the laws that was contrary to the fundamental principles of the British Constitution, which of necessity would be incorporated into the new Grenada charter. One of these fundamental principles was the right of English subjects to have a tax imposed only by their representatives. Had the king imposed his duty (provided it was a fair one, according to Mansfield) prior to the proclamation, then Campbell would certainly have been subject to it, for the king, by right of conquest, could have immediately imposed a tax. But the king instead, by his proclamation, used his right of conquest to bestow the promised blessings of English liberties on the island. This very inducement had convinced English subjects such as Campbell to invest in Grenada prior to the formal seating of an assembly. Thus "through the inattention of the King's servants in inverting the order in which the [taxing] instrument should have passed," the king's proposed duty was "contradictory to, and a violation" of the proclamation's implied guarantee to subjects such as Campbell that any taxing legislation could subsequently be imposed only by the island's assembly or by Parliament. Because of his implied reliance on the promises of constitutional protection embodied in the proclamation, Campbell was held not subject to the tax under the British Constitution in the unanimous opinion of the King's Bench, Lord Mansfield writing for the court.[72]

The antifeudal logic of *Campbell v. Hall* contained a number of points that an American radical would have regarded as worth appropriating. Samuel Wharton apparently read Lord Mansfield's opinion for the proposition that until an English sovereign (or an English-devolved sovereign adopting the natural-law reasoning embodied in English common law) conquered an infidel nation and altered its laws, the laws of that infidel nation continued in force. The Indians of the West, reasoned Wharton, had not been conquered, nor had their laws been altered. They therefore could sell their lands under their own laws to whomever they pleased, and, under the principles of natural law, the United States and its state governments were bound to recognize the validity of land grants obtained from sovereign Indian nations.[73] In essence, Wharton argued that a decision by the United States or by a state government not to recognize the natural-law rights of sovereign Indian nations to their lands was but a perpetuation of the Norman-inspired feudal tyranny that the colonists had sought to eradicate from America by their Revolution. The doctrine that by discovery of infidel-held lands, the English Crown could claim feudal rights of conquest that allowed it to exercise prerogative powers in American lands and deny the Indians' natural-law rights to their territories was but a part of the detested Norman Yoke.

Besides appropriating Lord Mansfield's antifeudal discourse of formal limitations on the royal prerogative, Wharton's *Plain Facts* drew on the closely related opinions of Lord Camden and Yorke to support the validity of the Indiana Company's Indian grants.[74] These learned authorities, Wharton asserted, had clearly declared the East India Company's right to acquire territory from non-Christian princes by treaty or grant without the king's patent: "This most respectable opinion in favor of the absolute right of heathen Asiatics to their several territories applies directly to support the same right, as vested in Heathen Americans."[75]

The Indians, claimed Wharton, held the rights to their countries "according to the laws of nature and of nations," as "the original and first occupants and possessors of the country." Thus "no European prince could derive a title to the soil of America from discovery, because that (as old civilians, etc., agree) can give a right only to lands and things, which have either never been owned and possessed."[76] Besides the writings of "old civilians" (that is, the civil-law theorists of the Romanized Law of Nations), more modern legal theorists (Wharton cited Blackstone, Puffendorf, and Rutherforth's *Institutes of Natural Law*) all affirmed the basic proposition that England could acquire no rights to America under a theory of discovery or "conquest" because the natives, unconquered in fact, already possessed the rights to America under the natural law and the Law of Nations by their undisputed occupancy.

According to Wharton, most of the sovereigns of Europe had in fact been "compelled, by the force of truth and justice to acknowledge the Indian tribes or nations to be independent communities, and to recognize their right to the several countries inhabited by them, but also to purchase under that right." The king of England himself had frequently recognized this native right to the soil, investing various colonial proprietors with an authority to purchase territories from the native inhabitants. Wharton's summary on the Indians' rights to sell their lands to whomever they chose read as follows:

Upon the whole, therefore, as the Indian Nations of America are unquestionably entitled to all the right of "full property" in their several countries, it results as a necessary and final conclusion, that they have an undefeasible right freely to sell, and grant to any person whatsoever, and that all sales and conveyances made by any Indian tribe or nation of their lands, are in every respect, sufficient to afford the most valid and perfect title to the same.[77]

Wharton concluded *Plain Facts* with an attack on Virginia's claims to the entire Northwest. While referring his readers to Thomas Paine's *Public Good* for a "full and complete refutation," Wharton reiterated in detail Paine's argument on the devolution of sovereignty in support of Congress's right to control western land acquisition and thus, implicitly, to affirm the speculators' Indian grants acquired under natural law.[78] After the Revolution, the British government's authority to legislate for the western frontier had been transferred to "the United States in Congress assembled," according to Wharton. Thus the sovereign right to legislate over the lands ceded by the Six Nations to the proprietors of the Indiana Company had passed to Congress, not to Virginia. And Congress had the authority, as well as the duty under natural law, to recognize the Indiana Company's Indian grants.[79]

As Jefferson and the other radicals opposed to the centralizing tendencies of many of their more conservative American brethren would have been quick to point out, this argument on the devolution of sovereignty, on which the likes of Wharton and Paine relied so heavily, rested squarely on Norman-derived feudal principles. According to their Saxon-inspired notions of natural law, the Virginia radicals had always regarded the Crown's supersession of their colony's charter and claimed rights to control the western frontier as a wholly illegitimate extension of the detested Norman prerogative. Any supposed national claims to Virginia's western lands that assertedly "devolved" from the Crown's illegitimate usurpation of Virginia's rights, therefore, similarly violated Saxon-understood natural-law principles. Accepting that argument meant accepting a devolution of feudal prerogative to the United States central government. To the radicals, such a Norman-derived theory could be neither sustained nor tolerated.

The speculators' reliance on the argument regarding devolution of sovereignty, so detested by the radicals, reveals the discursive trap that confronted the land companies after the Revolutionary War. Wharton had devoted a good deal of the argument in *Plain Facts* to demonstrating the natural-law rights of the Indians to sell their lands to whomever they pleased, Virginia's charter-based claims notwithstanding. But with the final ratification of the Articles of Confederation made possible by Maryland's formal surrender on the western lands question and Virginia's continuing refusal to recognize their Indian deeds, the speculators' only avenue of appeal for the recognition of the Indians' landed natural rights lay in the lawmaking authority of Congress. Practically speaking, if the speculators desired to incorporate their Indian-derived lands into the new union, they had to appeal to Congress to recognize the validity of their grants under United States law. As Wharton clearly saw, a vision of natural law could be realized only by the positive legal and political sanction of a sovereign government that possessed the power to enforce that vision. Such were the "plain facts" of the speculator's predicament. Their discourse of natural law was powerless to enforce the Indians' rights on its own. Common sense dictated that the decision about whether or not Indian tribes could sell lands on the frontier to whomever they pleased without a European-derived governmental intermediary was an act of state. It was a decision that held profound political consequences for the future of the new nation. The public good, not natural law, therefore, would decide the Indians' rights and status in the western lands.

Thus Wharton was required to assert simultaneously the strikingly inconsistent propositions that the Indians by natural law possessed the unilateral right to alienate their territories but that the United States Congress, by assuming the Crown's Norman-derived fictive right of conquest over the West, now possessed the sovereign authority to legislate for those same territories. The speculators' arguments rested ultimately on a contradiction that could be resolved only by Congress's acknowledgment, over the strenuous objections of Virginia and the other landed states, of an essentially moral obligation to affirm the Indians' natural-law rights to sell their lands to private individuals. The Founders' sense of expediency and the "public good," however, inclined them toward accepting a compromise, rather than a troubling and divisive contradiction, on the western lands question.

The Norman Yoke Revived to Decide the Rights and Status of American Indian Tribes

The lobbying efforts of the speculators before Congress and the pamphlet-reading public continued for nearly three more years, while Virginia refused to remove its stipulation to cession of the Old Northwest demanding that Congress void Indian-derived claims of the non-Virginia land companies. Then in late 1783, a political compromise satisfactory to the Virginians and to Congress (but certainly not to the Indians or to the speculators) was finally brokered. Congress would accept Virginia's cession of its claims north of the Ohio, but it would not specifically invalidate all private land purchases from the natives in the territories, as originally demanded by Virginia. Congress however, agreed not to investigate the question of conflicting claims in the region. Given this agreement and the additional promise by Congress that the lands should be used for the common benefit of the states, the Virginians were satisfied that their cession did not require a provision against private purchases from Indians. Nor were they at all concerned about the theoretical implications of Congress's assumption of the English Crown's devolved sovereignty over the Northwest. Congress had essentially acceded to Virginia's demands, and the Virginians (aware that politics is the art of compromise) knew that national authority over the Northwest Territory had in reality devolved from Virginia, and not from some Norman tyrant.[80]

In 1784, Congress formally accepted the Old Northwest cession from Virginia, thus effectively closing the door on the land-speculating companies. At the same time, a new door opened for Congress itself, as it sought under the Northwest Ordinance of 1785, "with utmost faith . . . observed toward the Indians, their lands and property," to utilize the western lands to pay off the nation's enormous war debt.[81]

The Constitutional Convention of 1787 merely ratified the bargain struck in 1784. With little debate, the convention's new constitution for the nation vested exclusive authority in Congress to regulate trade and commerce and to make treaties with Indian tribes.[82] This was a far simpler and clearer declaration of legislative authority over Indian tribes than the superseded Articles of Confederation had contained. The Constitution's broad statement of power seemed to imply that Congress's authority over Indian tribes, and thereby Indian lands, was unlimited in scope, applying in the Old Northwest as well as elsewhere throughout the American frontier.

Significantly, however, North Carolina and Georgia did not cede their western land claims to the United States until 1790 and 1802, respectively. Georgia, in particular, extracted significant concessions from the federal government in the process—concessions that would ultimately lead to what Charles Warren has described as the most serious crisis in the history of the United States Supreme Court, the Cherokee Nation cases of the early 1830s.[83]

Furthermore, those former colonies which retained significant Indian populations and Indian-occupied lands after the Revolution, most notably Massachusetts and New York, continued their historical practice of unilaterally purchasing territory directly from Indian tribes located within their defined state borders.[84] These purchases were made despite Congress's apparently exclusive constitutional jurisdiction over Indian commerce and the series of nonintercourse acts passed soon after ratification of the Constitution, which specifically prohibited "any person or persons, or . . . state whether having the right of pre-emption to such lands or not," to purchase lands from "any nation or tribe of Indians within the United States" without the consent of the federal government.[85] Thus while the new Constitution's text implicitly sought to affirm the feudal principle that the British Crown's prerogative powers over Indian lands had *devolved* to the sovereignty of the United States, a significant faction of the American polity apparently believed that the principle applied only to that part of the western frontier ceded by the individual states to the federal government as part of the national domain. There the federal government was free to exercise its Norman-derived prerogative rights and to acquire the Indian estate by war, duress, or sometimes even peaceful purchase. The states, however, despite the Constitution and subsequent acts of Congress intended to assert the national government's unilateral control over all Indian affairs under the Constitution, continued to exercise their similarly Norman-derived, charter-based rights of preemption over Indian lands within their defined borders. The only seeming consensus on Indian rights in the decades immediately following ratification of the Constitution was that Indian tribes did not have the natural-law right to sell the lands they occupied to whomever they pleased. The Norman Yoke was revived after the Revolution to settle the law on Indian rights and status in the frontier lands. Only a European-derived government could exercise the Norman-derived rights of conquest over Indian lands devolved from the English Crown.

In time, of course, as the final state cessions were accepted by Congress and as the national domain came to comprehend an entire continent to be won from the Indian, these assertions of the states' superior rights over Indian lands lost much of their legal significance. But most significantly, of the three competing legal discourses on Indian rights and status that had been in circulation during the Revolutionary era—the centralizing feudal discourse of the Crown's right of conquest in Indian lands, the charter-based discourse of the "landed" colonies, and the natural-law-based discourse of the speculators defending the right of the Indians to own and freely sell their lands—only one had failed to retain its currency in American colonizing discourse just a decade later, when the new Constitution was signed. The notion that under natural law and natural right, the Indians themselves, as sovereign princes of the soil they occupied, could sell to whomever they wished was denied by all white men of common sense in America. This discarded discourse did not adequately address the Founders' perceptions of the new nation's public good in Indian lands. Those who had won the war for America chose instead to explain their territorial rights in America by the convenient Norman-derived fiction of a superior claim in European-derived governments to the lands of the Indians.

Thus the Norman Yoke had not been completely thrown off by the Revolution; its feudal vestiges had been preserved in United States colonizing discourse in the definition of the legal status and rights of Indian tribes in their lands. The Indians' rights, natural or otherwise, of sovereignty in their soil were to be unilaterally determined by an alien, Norman-derived tyrant.

Such was the nature of the compromised discourse of conquest respecting the western lands that was accepted by the Founders for the public good as they came to understand that term in the period between the Revolution of 1776 and the Constitution of 1787. Their discourse of natural rights, which had energized and legitimated their resistance to Norman tyranny, was compromised so as not to include the American Indians. The principal liberating thematics of the Revolutionary era, which envisaged America as a land freed of the Norman Yoke where property secured liberty and governments secured property, was restricted to Europeans by an act of state accepting the United States government's superior sovereignty over the Indian frontier in furtherance of the public good.

Johnson v. McIntosh and United States Colonizing Legal Theory

Thus in 1823, when the successors in interest to the Illinois-Wabash Company's claims based on Murray's and Viviat's Revolutionary-era frontier purchases finally had their chance to argue for the validity of their Indian-derived deeds before the Supreme Court, Chief Justice John Marshall found himself conveniently confronted by a *fait accompli*. The Indians of the Old Northwest had been forced to cede their claims to their lands to the United States during the course of various frontier military campaigns. These wars and skirmishes culminated in General Anthony Wayne's victory at the decisive Battle of Fallen Timbers in 1794. By subsequent treaty,[86] the western tribes ceded their claims to the Northwest Territory, which included the Revolutionary-era purchases of the Illinois-Wabash Company. Congress, having exercised the nation's superior Norman-derived right of conquest on the western frontier (a right acquired under the 1784 political compromise with Virginia and perfected by the treaty of cession with the western tribes), had refused numerous times to confirm the Illinois-Wabash Company's Indian deeds. In fact, in 1818 the federal government had sold the same lands described under the Illinois-Wabash Company's Indian deeds to the defendant in the company's lawsuit, William McIntosh. All that remained for the Supreme Court in *Johnson v. McIntosh*,[87] therefore, was formally to legitimate the outcome of this forty-year-old compromise by which the speculators' Indian deeds and the Indians' natural rights had been silently ignored.

Fletcher v. Peck: A Dangerous Contest Compromised

The Marshall Court, in fact, had already placed itself on record as recognizing the legal validity of the political compromise on Indian lands negotiated during the Revolutionary era. In 1810, Marshall, writing the majority opinion for the Court in the case of *Fletcher v. Peck*,[88] had held that "the nature of Indian title . . . is not such as to be absolutely repugnant to seisin in fee on the part of the state."[89] Among other questions, *Fletcher v. Peck* involved the validity of Georgia's sale in 1795 of Indian-occupied lands on its western frontier that lay within the boundaries of its original Crown charter. Chief Justice Marshall's opinion in *Fletcher v. Peck* expressly rejected the argument, earlier asserted by Thomas Paine in his *Public Good* pamphlet, that the Proclamation of 1763 excepted "the lands on the western waters from the colonies within whose bounds they would otherwise have been."[90] In rejecting this interpretation of the Proclamation of 1763, Marshall therefore also rejected the proposition that these lands, originally chartered to the colonies, had in any sense devolved from the sovereignty of Great Britain to the entire United States at the time of the Revolution. According to Marshall:

The question, whether *the vacant lands within the United States* became a joint property, or belonged to the separate states, was a *momentous question which, at one time, threatened to shake the American confederacy to its foundation. This important and dangerous contest has been compromised*, and the compromise is not now to be disturbed.[91]

Thus Marshall's opinion in *Fletcher v. Peck* recognized that the Indian territory subsequently ceded to the federal government by the Georgia legislature in 1802 was "within the state of Georgia, and that the state of Georgia had power to grant it."[92] By this holding, Marshall and the Court also recognized the Revolutionary-era "compromise" by which the "landed" states' charter claims to the West were not to be disturbed until voluntarily ceded to the United States. Significantly, Marshall's own description of the Indian-occupied interior territories as "vacant lands within the United States" also implicitly acknowledged the other side of that compromise: that the Indians were regarded as incapable of possessing natural-law rights to sell their "vacant" lands to whomever they pleased. Only a European-derived sovereign could alienate the fee-simple interest in lands occupied by Indian tribes.

The holding of *Fletcher v. Peck*, therefore, indicates that the Constitution of 1787, at least as Marshall and a majority of the Supreme Court justices understood it in 1810, had not divested Georgia of its proprietary interest in the Indian land within its original Crown-chartered borders. In 1795 Georgia could exercise its sovereign authority to patent these "vacant" Indian lands to non-Indian purchasers. The only issue on which all European-descended parties agreed prior to Georgia's 1802 cession of its Indian land claims to the federal government was that Indians did not have the natural-law right to sell their lands to whomever they pleased.

Given *Fletcher v. Peck*'s preliminary ceremonies in the legal interment of the doctrine that American Indians possessed natural rights to the lands they had occupied since time immemorial, Marshall's remaining task in *Johnson v. McIntosh*[93] was simply to pronounce the final homilies over the corpus of a no longer vital legal discourse in American colonizing theory. That discourse, long since expired, had once argued for the natural rights of the Indian nations to their tribal homelands.

Daniel Webster for the Plaintiff

Daniel Webster, the land company's lawyer in the Supreme Court case of *Johnson v. McIntosh*, reprised all the once-familiar arguments of the Revolutionary-era speculators that had lain dormant in American colonizing discourse since the Old Northwest cession of 1784 and the triumph of the theory, embodied in the Constitution, of a superior sovereignty in European-derived governments over Indian lands. In arguing that the Supreme Court ought to recognize the validity of the Illinois-Wabash Company's Revolutionary-era purchases from the tribes, Webster cited the Enlightenment-era theorists on the Law of Nations, Grotius and Puffendorf, in support of the basic proposition that the Indian "title by occupancy is to be respected, as much as that of an individual, obtained by the same right, in a civilized state. The circumstance, that the members of the society held [the land] in common, did not affect the strength of their title by occupancy." According to Webster, the issue of the case was simply whether "individuals" could purchase the Indian right to the soil "or whether that be the exclusive prerogative of the government."[94]

Webster's main point of attack on behalf of the speculators focused precisely on the government's "prerogative" powers over Indian lands. "The British king's proclamation of October 7th, 1763," Webster argued, certainly could not affect the rights of the Indians to sell. Even if it were admitted that the Indians might be British subjects, "they were still proprietors of the soil, and could not be divested of their rights of property, or any of its incidents, by a mere act of executive government."[95] The king's prerogative powers, in other words could not affect the Indians' natural-law rights to their lands.

As for the members of the company, all of whom were British subjects at the time of the transactions, Webster argued that the Proclamation of 1763 was a violation of their rights under the British Constitution if it sought to constrain them from purchasing these lands, which were within the chartered boundaries of the colony of Virginia. Webster cited Lord Mansfield's opinion in *Campbell v. Hall* as direct support for this interpretation of the limitations imposed on the Crown prerogative by the British Constitution:

And because the king had not, within the limits of that colonial government, or any other, any power of prerogative legislation; which is confined to countries newly conquered, and remaining in the military possession of the monarch . . . we have the positive authority of a solemn determination of the Court of the King's Bench, on this very proclamation, in the celebrated *Grenada* case [*Campbell v. Hall*]. . . . This country being a new conquest, and a military possession, the Crown might exercise legislative powers, until a local legislature was established. But the establishing of a government establishes a system of laws, and excludes the power of legislating by proclamation. The proclamation could not have the force of law within the chartered limits of Virginia.[96]

Having assailed the Proclamation of 1763 as an instance of illegal application of the Norman Yoke in America, Webster next attacked the speculators' second favorite target, the Virginia legislature. Virginia's act of 1779 voiding all private Indian purchases within the state's chartered boundaries[97] could not

affect the right of the plaintiffs, and others claiming under these deeds; because, on general principles, and by the constitution of Virginia, the legislature was not competent to take away private, vested rights, or appropriate private property to public laws. . . . [A]t the time the purchases now in question were made, there was no prohibiting law in existence.[98]

In other words, Webster's argument presumed that the Indians could vest a title to land in individual purchasers and that Virginia could not interfere with those vested Indian-acquired property rights. The Indians possessed the natural-law right to sell their lands to English colonists who were exercising their own natural-rights under the British Constitution, and no power on earth, be it the king, the United States government, or Virginia, could deny the validity of an Indian-obtained grant.

Defendant McIntosh's Rebuttal

Defendant McIntosh's title derived from a patent issued by the federal government. His lawyers, messrs. Winder and Murray, unashamedly relied on the feudally derived argument that the Indians lacked natural rights to the lands they occupied and that the superior title to the soil of America was vested in the European nation that had first discovered and occupied the territory claimed by the savages. Citing a long list of authorities, including Locke, Jefferson, Montesquieu, and Adam Smith, McIntosh's counsel stated that the Law of Nations as adopted by civilized European states had always "denied the right of the Indians to be considered as independent communities, having a permanent property in the soil, capable of alienation to private individuals. They remain in a state of nature, and have never been admitted into the general society of nations."[99] "Discovery," McIntosh's counsel argued, "is the foundation of title, in European nations, and this overlooks all proprietary rights in the natives." The Indians were "destitute" of the most essential rights belonging to "*citizens* in the ordinary sense of that term." They were regarded under the laws of all the colonies, and of the United States, "as an inferior race of people . . . under the perpetual protection and pupilage of the government."[100] By the law of nature, the Indians

could have acquired no proprietary interest in the vast tracks of territory which they wandered over; and their right to the lands on which they hunted, could not be considered as superior to that which is acquired to the sea by fishing in it. The use in the one case as well as the other, is not exclusive. According to every theory of property, the Indians had no individual rights to land; nor had they any collectively, or in their national capacity; for the lands occupied by each tribe were not used by them in such a manner as to prevent their being appropriated by a people of cultivators.[101]

According to McIntosh's lawyers, the rights of title belonging to "civilized nations" by virtue of first discovery of the Indians' lands thus had their basis in natural law. The English Crown adopted this law of discovery as the basis of its right in America, and therefore it was a "first principle in colonial law, that all titles must be derived from the Crown."[102]

In most of the colonies the doctrine was received, that all titles to land must be derived exclusively from the Crown, upon the principle that the settlers carried with them, not only all the rights, but all the duties of Englishmen; and particularly the laws of property so far as they are suitable to their new condition.[103]

Contrary to the radicals' history as outlined in Jefferson's by-now-forgotten pamphlet *A Summary View*,[104] McIntosh's lawyers now claimed that the colonists themselves had carried the Norman Yoke and its feudal doctrines of discovery and conquest of infidel lands with them to North America.

Thus both sides' lawyers in *Johnson v. McIntosh* had indirectly revived the major discourses on Indian land rights that had competed for dominance during the Revolutionary era. On the speculators' side, Daniel Webster raised the haunting memory of a Norman tyrant who had threatened to usurp the liberties of the freedom-loving Americans, descendants of the true Saxons. McIntosh's lawyers, on the other side, relied on a once-spurned form of discourse asserting the British monarch's right to control the lands of America to argue that the colonists had in fact been duty-bound to obey the Crown's unilateral imposition of its Norman-derived prerogative power over American frontier land purchases—a power that had devolved to the United States as a result of victory in the Revolution.

Chief Justice Marshall's Discourse of Conquest

Chief Justice Marshall, however, writing for a unanimous Supreme Court in *Johnson v. McIntosh*,[105] sought to avoid the extremes of old passions that were no longer immediately relevant to the needs and concerns of the nation in 1823. Ignoring the moral dimensions of the controversy presented by *Johnson v. McIntosh*,[106] Marshall instead focused his opinion exclusively on the need for rationalizing the process of land acquisition in a country originally inhabited by a savage people but gradually overtaken by a foreign invader. The disenchanted nature of this rationalized inquiry—its segregation of transcending questions of "justice" or "morality" from its discussion of a sovereign will driven by utilitarian concerns and expressed in positive law—is indicated by Marshall's succinct formulation of the sole issue before the Court in *Johnson v. McIntosh*: "The inquiry, therefore, is, in a great measure confined to the power of Indians to give, and of private individuals to receive, a title which can be sustained in the courts of this Country."[107]

Marshall's opinion admitted, in Lockean fashion, that this inquiry was confined by boundaries demarcated by the actual conduct of individuals in a state of nature agreeing on the rules of property acquisition for their new society.[108] The role of subsequently established courts of justice was to enforce those agreements according to the principles that "our own government has adopted in the particular case, and given us as the rule of our decision."[109] A court could not engage in speculation on the justness of those principles or their harmony with any type of hypothesized higher law. According to Marshall, "[T]he right of society, to prescribe those rules by which property may be acquired and preserved is not, and cannot be drawn into question . . . . The title to lands, especially, is and must be admitted to depend entirely on the law of the nation in which they lie."[110]

The dominant themes of Marshall's denial of Indian natural-law rights in *Johnson* are clearly established in those early evasions of judicial accountability for the positive law established by European-derived governments for acquiring lands in America. History and the decisions made and enforced by those Europeans who invaded America respecting Indian land rights determined the inescapable framework for Marshall's legal discourse. His judicial task was merely to fill in the details and rationalize the fictions by which Europeans legitimated the denial of the Indians' rights in their acquisition of the Indians' America.

Thus Marshall's opinion in *Johnson* turned immediately to the discourse of compromise which silently denied Indian natural-law land rights and which had triumphed after the Revolution—that is, the discourse of the Norman Yoke and its fiction that European monarchs acquired feudally conceived rights of conquest upon their discovery of the infidel-held territories of America. Marshall's opinion in *Johnson* held that under the "Doctrine of Discovery," assertedly recognized as part of the Law of Nations by virtually every European colonizing nation,[111] discovery of territory in the New World gave the discovering European nation "an exclusive right to extinguish the Indian title of occupancy, either by purchase or by conquest."[112] This title, which England had acquired under the Doctrine of Discovery, had devolved to the United States as a result of its victory in the Revolutionary War. Marshall's opinion in *Johnson* therefore held that the Murray-Viviat purchases of lands from the western Indian tribes without the approval or sanction of either the discovering European nation or its successor in interest, the United States, could not be recognized as valid in a United States court.[113]

Thus *Johnson*, a case involving two white litigants, effectively denied American Indian tribes recognizable full legal title to their ancestral homelands under the Doctrine of Discovery, which had been adopted by Marshall and the Court as the domestic law of the United States. Marshall described the origins of the Doctrine of Discovery and its acceptance by European colonizing governments in the following famous passage:

On the discovery of this immense continent, the great nations of Europe were eager to appropriate to themselves so much of it as they could respectively acquire. Its vast extent offered an ample field to the ambition and enterprise of all; and the character and religion of its inhabitants afforded an apology for considering them as a people over whom the superior genius of Europe might claim an ascendancy. . . . But, as they were all in pursuit of nearly the same object, it was necessary, in order to avoid conflicting settlements, and consequent war with each other, to establish a principle, which all should acknowledge as the law by which the right of acquisition, which they all asserted, should be regulated as between themselves. This principle was, that discovery gave title to the government by whose subjects, or by whose authority, it was made, against all other European governments, which title might be consummated by possession.[114]

After this historical gloss on asserted customary European imperialistic practice, Marshall analyzed the necessary legal inferences arising from the principle "that discovery gave title to the government by whose subjects . . . it was made."[115] First, the discovering European nation was held to possess "the sole right of acquiring the soil from the natives . . . a right with which no [other] Europeans could interfere."[116] Second, American Indian tribes had no theoretical, independent natural-law-based right to full sovereignty over America's soil that a European discoverer might be required to recognize under Europe's Law of Nations:

In the establishment of these relations, the rights of the original inhabitants were, in no instance, entirely disregarded; but were necessarily, to a considerable extent, impaired. . . . [T]heir rights to complete sovereignty, as independent nations, were necessarily diminished, and their power to dispose of the soil at their own will, to whomsoever they pleased, was denied by the original fundamental principle, that discovery gave exclusive title to those who made it. Those relations which were to exist between the discoverer and the natives, were to be regulated by themselves. The rights thus acquired being exclusive, no other power could interpose between them.[117]

According to Marshall, once a European nation firmly established its occupancy of territories discovered in the New World, relations with the indigenous inhabitants of that region became matters of exclusively domestic concern between the tribes and the particular invading European sovereign. As Marshall declared in another seminal Supreme Court case defining the "domestic dependent nation" status of Indian tribes within the domestic law of the United States, *Cherokee Nation v. Georgia*,[118] attempts by other European nations to "form a political connection with them would be considered by all as an invasion of our territory, and an act of hostility."[119]

Marshall drew on the history of European colonization of America to support the universality of the principles behind the Doctrine of Discovery, citing the examples of Spain, France, Portugal, and Holland, all of which, according to the *Johnson* opinion, based their territorial rights in the New World on the basis of discovery.[120] Marshall asserted that England also "gave its full assent" to the principle, grounding its rights to North America in the late-fifteenth-century voyages of the Cabots along the North American coast. "To this discovery the English trace their title."[121] Marshall stated that the charters to Sir Humphrey Gilbert and Walter Raleigh, authorizing those gentlemen "to discover and take possession of such remote heathen, and barbarous lands, as were not actually possessed by any Christian prince or people," reaffirmed the principle that discovery of infidel-held territories by the agents of a Christian monarch vested superior rights of title in the Crown.[122]

All the subsequent grants of land from the English Crown establishing colonies in North America rested on this principle of discovery, according to the *Johnson* opinion. "In all of them, the soil, at the time the grants were made, was occupied by the Indians. Yet almost every title within those governments is dependent on these grants."[123]

Marshall's historical digressions in *Johnson* thus served to demonstrate that all the colonizing European nations asserted and recognized the exclusive right of the discoverer to appropriate the lands occupied by the American Indians. Marshall next asked the question whose answer he already knew: "Have the American States rejected or adopted this principle?"[124]

Marshall's answer, that the United States had accepted the Doctrine of Discovery, simply relied on the argument on the devolution of sovereignty that had originally been advocated by the Revolutionary speculators themselves. However, Marshall's explication of the devolution in *Johnson* added an important modification. The Chief Justice reprised *Fletcher v. Peck*'s earlier acknowledgment of the lack of consensus at the time the Revolution ended as to whether the sovereignty over the lands of America had devolved to the United States or to the individual states:

By the treaty which concluded the war of our revolution, Great Britain relinquished all claim, not only to the government, but to the "proprietary and territorial rights of the United States," whose boundaries were fixed by the second article. By this treaty, the powers of government, and the rights to the soil, which had previously been in Great Britain, passed definitely to these States. . . . It has never been doubted, that *either the United States, or the several States had a clear title to all the lands within the boundary lines described in the treaty*, subject only to the Indian right of occupying, and that exclusive power to extinguish that right, was vested in that government which might constitutionally exercise it.[125]

Thus, according to *Johnson*, while the Founders may not have been able to agree on whether the several states or Congress held the title to the western frontier, they were unanimous in their agreement that the Indians' interest in their lands was inferior to that of a European-derived government. According to Marshall, Virginia's specific actions taken at the close of the Revolution to prohibit and invalidate Indian land sales to individuals evidenced Virginia's "unequivocal affirmance . . . of the broad principle which had always been maintained, that the exclusive right to purchase from the Indians resided in the government."[126] The lands purchased by the Illinois-Wabash Company were originally within Virginia's chartered bounds. Virginia ceded these lands to the United States with reservations and stipulations "which could only be made by the owners of the soil."[127] According to Marshall's analysis of the significance of this cession by Virginia of Indian-occupied territory, "The ceded territory was occupied by numerous and warlike tribes of Indians; but the exclusive right of the United States to extinguish their title, and to grant the soil, has never, we believe, been doubted."[128]

The Doctrine of Discovery's denial of "an absolute and complete title in the Indian" was recognized not only by Virginia but also by all the United States, according to Marshall. Regardless of the Supreme Court's views of the Indians' natural rights based on "abstract principles of justice,"[129] the Doctrine of Discovery was the law of the country: "We will not enter into the controversy, whether agriculturists, merchants, and manufacturers, have a right, on abstract principles, to expel hunters from the territory they possess, or to contract their limits. Conquest gives a title which the Courts of the conqueror cannot deny."[130]

Marshall's judicial abdication to the title acquired by white civilization's "conquest" of the Indians was actually an acknowledgment of the series of legal fictions supporting the Doctrine of Discovery. The rights acquired by European discovery of infidel-held lands under the doctrine were inchoate and anticipatory in nature. The Doctrine of Discovery assumed that the European discoverer would eventually establish its feudal prerogative rights of conquest over the infidel-held lands, either by wars of expulsion or by treaties of cession contracting the limits of the tribes. Thus in acknowledging "conquest" as the basis of the United States' superior title to the lands of America, Marshall specifically incorporated into United States land law the Norman-derived feudal fiction that discovery was the basis of the English Crown's original assertion of prerogative rights of conquest in America. The British government, Marshall stressed, "whose rights have passed to the United States," asserted its title and rights of conquest acquired by first discovery to all the lands occupied by Indians within the chartered limits of the British colonies. These rights, as Marshall recognized, were only claims to prerogative authority and had to be "maintained and established . . . by the sword."[131] Great Britain, in fact, did eventually succeed in perfecting these inchoate rights of discovery "as far west as the River Mississippi." As the title to a vast portion of the land now held by the United States originates in these initial Norman-derived claims of rights of conquest acquired by discovery,

[h]owever extravagant the pretension of converting the discovery of an inhabited country into conquest may appear [here Marshall is referring to the Crown's feudal right of conquest]; if the principle has been asserted in the first instance, and afterwards sustained, if a country has been acquired and held under it; if the property of the great mass of the community originates in it, it becomes the law of the land, and cannot be questioned.[132]

As for the allied principle of the Doctrine of Discovery asserting the Indians' incapacity to transfer "absolute title" to the lands they claimed by right of occupancy:

However this restriction may be opposed to natural right, and to the usages of civilized nations, yet, if it be indispensable to that system under which the country has been settled, and be adopted to the actual condition of the two people, it may, perhaps, be supported by reason, and certainly cannot be rejected by Courts of Justice.[133]

Marshall's discourse of conquest in *Johnson* settled the law on the rights and status of American Indians in the lands of the United States. Acknowledging the outcome of a political compromise that had been concluded forty years earlier, *Johnson*'s acceptance of the Doctrine of Discovery sought to absolve the Supreme Court of any injustices arising from the Founders' denial of natural rights to the American Indians. It is not surprising, therefore, that Marshall made only passing reference to the medievally derived premises supporting the Doctrine of Discovery in *Johnson v. McIntosh*—"the character and religion of . . . [America's] inhabitants afforded an apology for consider-ing them as a people over whom the superior genius of Europe might claim an ascendancy."[134] But Marshall and the other justices were well aware of the historical paternity of this bastardized principle sired by Europe's Law of Nations and legitimated by the United States Supreme Court. As was clearly recognized by Marshall's close friend and fellow Supreme Court justice, Jo-seph Story, the assumptions supporting the Doctrine of Discovery permitted European nations to claim

an absolute dominion over the whole territories afterwards occupied by them, not in virtue of any conquest of, or cession by, the Indian natives, but as a right acquired by discovery. Some of them, indeed, obtained a sort of confirmatory grant from the papal authority. But as between themselves they treated the dominion and title of territory as resulting from the priority of discovery. . . . The title of the Indians was not treated as a right of property and dominion, but as a mere right of occupancy. *As infidels, heathens, and savages, they were not allowed to possess the prerogatives belonging to absolute, sovereign, and independent nations.* The territory over which they wandered, and which they used for this temporary and fugitive purposes, was, in respect to Christians, deemed as if it were inhabited only by brute animals.[135]

The acceptance of the Doctrine of Discovery into United States law held profound implications for future relations between the federal government and the Indians. The Doctrine of Discovery's discourse of conquest was now available to legitimate, energize, and constrain as needed white society's will to empire over the North American continent. The doctrine confirmed the superior rights of a European-derived nation to the lands occupied by "infidels, heathens, and savages," encouraged further efforts by white society to acquire the Indians' "waste" lands, and vested authority in a centralized sovereign to regulate the Indians' dispossession according to national interest, security, and sometimes even honor.

Perhaps most important, *Johnson's* acceptance of the Doctrine of Discovery into United States law preserved the legacy of 1,000 years of European racism and colonialism directed against non-Western peoples. White society's exercise of power over Indian tribes received the sanction of the Rule of Law in *Johnson v. McIntosh.* The Doctrine of Discovery's underlying medievally derived ideology—that normatively divergent "savage" peoples could be denied rights and status equal to those accorded to the civilized nations of Europe—had become an integral part of the fabric of United States federal Indian law. The architects of an idealized European vision of life in the Indians' New World had successfully transplanted an Old World form of legal discourse denying all respect to the Indians' fundamental human rights. While the tasks of conquest and colonization had not yet been fully actualized on the entire American continent, the originary legal rules and principles of federal Indian law set down by Marshall in *Johnson v. McIntosh* and its discourse of conquest ensured that future acts of genocide would proceed on a rationalized, legal basis.

Like all the other great theorists and systematizers of the European legal tradition, Marshall had performed a bold and reconciling act of critical anamnesis in *Johnson.* He had articulated a conqueror's legal discourse that drew on the most ancient discursive traditions of Western legal thought but was nonetheless capable of serving the contemporary needs of his European-descended countrymen's vision of progress. The Doctrine of Discovery, the primordial mythic icon of Europe's medieval, feudal past, had been preserved and brought to readability in a modern form that spoke with reassuring continuity to a nation that was about to embark on its own colonizing crusade against the American Indians who remained on the North American continent.

NOTES

1. On the federal government's removal of the eastern frontier Indian tribes across the Mississippi River to a supposedly permanent Indian territory, *see* F. Prucha, *American Indian Policy in the Formative Years* 224–48 (1962); J. Burke, "The Cherokee Cases: A Study in Law, Politics, and Morality," 21 *Stan. L. Rev.* 500 (1969). *See also* R. Williams, "Documents of Barbarism: The Contemporary Legacy of European Racism and Colonialism in the Narrative Traditions of Federal Indian Law," 31 *Ariz. L. Rev.* 237 (1989).

2. *See* Chapter 6, text accompanying notes 116–26, *supra.*

3. Besides Murray and Viviat, the principals of the Illinois Company included the Philadelphia merchants Michael and Bernard Gratz (competitors of the Baynton, Wharton, and Morgan firm in the western Indian trade), David and Moses Franks, and Robert Callender. All were men of power and wealth; all viewed the West as a source of increase of both.

4. J. Sosin, *Whitehall and the Wilderness* at 232–33 (1961).

5. T. Abernathy, *Western Lands and the American Revolution* 122 (1959). Another active speculator, the veteran Indian trader George Croghan, had already purchased 1.5 million acres north of the Ohio country from several chiefs of the Six Nations in a private treaty. He followed up this acquisition with a purchase in July 1775, again from the Six Nations, of 6 million acres on the other side of the Ohio River. This purchase was most likely financed by a Virginia syndicate led by Dr. Thomas Walker. Numerous other deals were being pursued and brokered with the tribes throughout the western frontier on the eve of the Revolution. *See id.* at 120–21. Virginians as well as non-Virginians were covering all their bets, acquiring titles directly from the Indians in the event that a break or restructuring of relations with the mother country would render nugatory the Crown-based charter claims of Virginia and the other "landed" colonies to the West. With no law laid down on the frontier, a grant from the Indians to western lands would be as good a title as anyone could claim, given the chaos that was the American Revolutionary frontier.

6. 21 U.S. (8 Wheat.) 543 (1823).

7. *See* text accompanying notes 105–35, *infra.*

8. M. Jensen, *The Articles of Confederation* 122 (1940).

9. *Id.* at 113.

10. *Id.* at 152–53.

11. *Id.* at 154; J. Adams, "Notes of Debates in the Continental Congress in 1775 and 1776," 2 *The Works of John Adams* 492–97 (C. Adams ed. 1850). As for the previously quoted Samuel Chase, in the same week that he delivered his statement of principle on the western lands question, he delineated the following argument respecting the equally momentous issue of whether gross state population would determine the respective federal tax burden of each particular state.

> [T]he word "white," should be inserted in the eleventh Article. The Negroes are wealth. . . .
> It is the best rule we can lay down. Negroes [are] a species of property, personal estate. If
> negroes are taken into computation of numbers to ascertain wealth . . . [t]he Massachusetts
> fisheries, and navigation, ought to be taken into consideration. The young and old negroes
> are a burthen to their owners. The eastern Colonies have a great advantage in trade. This
> will give them a superiority. We shall be governed by our interests, and ought to be. [*Id.* at
> 496–97.]

12. *Id.*

13. *Id.*

14. James Madison to James Monroe (Nov. 27, 1784), in 8 *Papers of James Madison* 156–57 (R. Rutland & W. Rachal eds. 1973). *See* M. Jensen, *supra* note 8, at 156–59.

15. *See* text accompanying note 13, *supra.*

16. M. Jensen, *supra* note 8, at 160.

17. *See id.* at 162–65. *See generally* G.Wood, *The Creation of the American Republic 1776–1787* 162–96 (1969).

18. M. Jensen, *supra* note 8, at 174.

19. *Id.* at 181.

20. *Id.* at 190–91.

21. *Id.* at 205.

22. *Id.* at 207–9.

23. *Id.*

24. *Id.* at 209. *See* text accompanying notes 121–22, *supra.*

25. G. Lewis, *The Indiana Company 1763–1798* 229–36 (1941).

26. *See* M. Jensen, *supra* note 18, at 206–10.

27. *Id.* at 213.

28. *Id.*

29. *Id.* at 229–31.

30. *Id.* at 232.

31. T. Abernathy, *supra* note 5, at 245; M. Jensen, *supra* note 8, at 228–32.

32. M. Jensen, *supra* note 8, at 232.

33. The pamphlet *Common Sense* is reprinted in T. Paine, 1 *The Writings of Thomas Paine* 69–120 (M. Conway ed. 1894).

34. *Id.*, vol. 2, at 33–66.

35. A. Volwiler, *George Croghan and the Westward Movement 1741–1782* 317 (1926).

36. T. Paine, *supra* note 33, vol. 2, at 31.

37. *Id.* at 34.

38. *Id.* at 35–45.

39. *See* Chapter 5, text accompanying notes 43–45, *supra*.

40. T. Paine, *supra* note 33, vol. 2, at 46.

41. *Id.* at 52.

42. *Id.* at 52–55.

43. *Id.* at 63.

44. *See* Chapter 5, text accompanying notes 32–40, *supra*.

45. The full title of Wharton's pamphlet was as follows: *Plain Facts: Being an Examination into the Rights of the Indian Nations of America, to Their Respective Countries: and a vindication of the grant, from the Six Nations of Indians, to the proprietors of Indiana, against the decision of the legislature of Virginia, together with authentic documents proving that the territory westward of the Allegheny Mountains, never belonged to Virginia, etc.*

46. *See* the discussion of Jefferson's *Summary View*, Chapter 6, text accompanying notes 130–50, *supra*.

47. *Plain Facts, supra* note 45, at 3.

48. *Id.* Wharton decried the injustice and arrogance of the Iberian conquests that allowed Rome to spread its papist influence around the globe. He quoted the condemnatory judgment of the "illustrious Sydney," an intellectual hero to many Revolutionary-era American radicals:

> An empire . . . founded upon the donation of the Pope, which amongst those of the Romish religion, is of great importance, and the entire conquest of a people, with whom there had been no former contract, . . . degenerate[d] into a most unjust and detestable tyranny. What then shall we say of those, who pretend to a right of dominion over free nations?" [*Id.* at 4.]

49. *Id.* at 4–5.

50. *Id.* at 5–6. The Savior Jesus himself, Wharton noted, submitted to the jurisdiction and authority of "infidel magistrates," proving the proposition that heathen unbelievers could hold valid dominion.

51. *See* Chapter 6, text accompanying notes 50–63, *supra*.

52. *Plain Facts, supra* note 45, at 5–7.

53. *Id.* at 8.

54. *Campbell v. Hall*, 1 Cowp. 204 (1774).

55. *See* Chapter 6, text accompanying notes 162–68, *supra*.

56. *See* Chapter 6, text accompanying notes 1–2, *supra*.

57. *Campbell v. Hall*, 1 Cowp. 204, 209–12 (1774).

58. *See id.* 209–11.

59. *See* text of the Proclamation of 1763, reprinted in *Documents of American History* 48 (H. S. Commager 8th ed. 1968).

60. *Campbell v. Hall*, 1 Cowp. 204, 205–9 (1774).

61. *Id.* at 208–9.

62. *See* the discussion of *Calvin's Case* in Chapter 5, text accompanying notes 32–40, *supra*.

63. *Campbell v. Hall*, 1 Cowp. 204, 208–10 (1774).

64. *Id.* at 209–10.

65. E. Nys, "Introduction" to F. Victoria, *De Indis et de Iure Belli Reflectiones* 56–57 (E. Nys ed., J. Bate trans. 1917).

66. *Id.*

67. *Campbell v. Hall*, 1 Cowp. 204, 210–11 (1774).

68. For instance, the texts of Lord Camden and Yorke in their 1757 opinion on the rights of the East India Company in lands acquired by purchase from "Indian moguls" (*see* Chapter 6, text

accompanying notes 162–68, *supra*) and of Thomas Jefferson in his 1775 pamphlet *A Summary View* (*see* Chapter 6, text accompanying notes 129–50, *supra*) utilized the same basic strategy of limitation deployed in *Campbell v. Hall.*

69. *See* Chapter 1, text accompanying notes 52–76, *supra.*

70. *See* Chapter 1, text accompanying notes 55–56, *supra.*

71. *See* text accompanying notes 129–50, *supra.*

72. *Campbell v. Hall,* 1 Cowp. 204, 213–14 (1774).

73. *Plain Facts, supra* note 45, at 8–9.

74. *Id.*

75. *Id.*

76. *Id.* at 10–11.

77. *Plain Facts, supra* note 45, at 28. The opinion of attorney John Glynn of Sergeant's Inn was also included in this section. Glynn's opinion summarized the basic argument of the speculators in concise fashion:

> The property of the soil conveyed to Mr. Trent, for himself and as attorney, was certainly in the Six Nations and as incident to that property, they had a power of alienating and transferring, in any manner, on to any persons, unless they had been restrained by their own laws. In this case, the supreme power of the country resided in the sellers, who had therefore an absolute power of alienating. . . . If we suppose, that the sovereignty of the land still remains in the Six Nations, the property for the soil must be in the grantee, Mr. Trent and cannot, without violence and injustice be taken from him. . . . [T]here is no law, that restrains the subjects of England from producing in foreign dominions. [*Id.* at 38.]

78. *See* text accompanying notes 33–44, *supra.*

79. *Plain Facts, supra* note 45, at 147.

80. *See* G. Lewis, *supra* note 25, at 260–63.

81. W. Mohr, *Federal Indian Relations 1774–1788* 127 (1933); R. Horsman, *Expansion and American Indian Policy 1783–1812* 37–38 (1967).

82. *See* F. Cohen, *Handbook of Federal Indian Law* 58–62 (1982).

83. C. Warren, *The Supreme Court in United States History* 189 (1928).

84. In the case of Massachusetts, *see Joint Tribal Council of the Passamaquoddy Nation v. Morton,* 388 F. Supp. 649 (D. Me. 1975). In the case of New York, *see Oneida Indian Nation v. County of Oneida,* 414 U.S. 661 (1974).

85. 1 Stat. 138. *See generally* Cohen, *supra* note 82, at 7–9.

86. The precise events leading up to the Treaty of Greenville are described in R. Horsman, *supra* note 81, at 97–103. Maps of the land ceded by the various tribes signatory to the treaty are provided in "Indian Land Cessions in the United States," in *18th Ann. Rep. of the Bureau of American Ethnology,* Part 2, at map 49, map 19; key at pp. 654–55 (C. C. Royce ed. 1899).

87. 21 U.S. (8 Wheat.) 543 (1823). As to the sad fate of the members of Samuel Wharton's Indiana Company, *see* G. Lewis, *supra* note 25, at 271–93.

88. 10 U.S. (6 Cranch) 87 (1810). In 1795 virtually the entire Georgia state legislature was bribed by a private land-speculating company to pass an act patenting the state's unceded western territory claimed under its colonial charter to the company for nominal consideration. The next year, a new legislature, which had literally thrown the prior rascals out of office, annulled the grant to the land company. On the Yazoo land fraud, *see generally* C. Magrath, *Yazoo* (1966). The questions before the Supreme Court in *Fletcher v. Peck* were whether the 1796 legislature could annul the contract under the contracts clause of the United States Constitution and whether Georgia had the right to sell Indian-occupied territory within its original chartered boundaries to private individuals in the first place. Chief Justice John Marshall's opinion held that the 1795 legislature's grant, whether influenced by corrupt practices or not, could not be annulled, as annulment would impair the obligations of contracts in violation of the Constitution, and that any rights Indians held to those lands were not absolutely repugnant to Georgia's acts of fee ownership in alienating the lands.

89. 10 U.S. (6 Cranch) 87, 142–43 (1810).

90. *Id.* at 142.

91. *Id.* (emphasis added).

92. *Id.* at 143.

93. 21 U.S. (8 Wheat.) 543 (1823). The Illinois-Wabash Company had never entered into actual possession of the lands that William Murray and Louis Viviat had purchased directly from the tribes in 1773 and 1775. The company's members had been

> prevented by the war of the American revolution, which soon after commenced, and by the disputes and troubles which preceded it, from obtaining such possession; and . . . since the termination of the war, and before it they have repeatedly, and at various times, from the year 1781, till the year 1816, petitioned the Congress of the United States to acknowledge and confirm their title to those lands, under the purchases and deeds in question, but without success. [*Johnson v. McIntosh*, 23 U.S. (8 Wheat.) 543, 562 (1823).]

In 1818, however, the United States, after obtaining the same lands from the tribes in a treaty of cession negotiated well after the company's purchases, sold the lands described under the company's Indian deeds to William McIntosh. This action by the federal government enabled Joshua Johnson and Thomas Graham, devisees under the will of Thomas Johnson of Maryland, one of the original members of the Illinois-Wabash syndicate, to frame an action in ejectment against the government's grantee, McIntosh, challenging the validity of McIntosh's title obtained from the United States more than three decades after the Illinois-Wabash Company's purchase of the same lands from the original Indian proprietors. Under common-law property principles, the rule in such a case would normally be "first in time, first in right": the tribes having sold the lands first to the company, the subsequent cession to the United States would be void and of no effect respecting the speculators' title. Thus, the company sought to argue, the government's sale to McIntosh conveyed nothing, and the successors in interest to the company's title would be entitled to eject McIntosh from their lands acquired by Indian deeds. But the question raised by *Johnson v. McIntosh* was precisely whether the normal rules of common-law property conveyancing applied when Indian tribes sold their lands to individual purchasers rather than to the government. And the answer to that question, of course, had been long determined in American colonizing discourse. The rights of Indians to sell their lands to whomever they pleased had been denied by the Founders' acceptance of the fictions of the Norman Yoke, vesting in European-derived governments in America a superior right to the lands occupied by Indians since time immemorial.

94. *Johnson v. McIntosh*, 21 U.S. (8 Wheat.) 543, 562–67 (1823).

95. *Id.* at 563–64.

96. *Id.* at 564.

97. *See* text accompanying notes 22–23, *supra.*

98. *Johnson v. McIntosh*, 21 U.S. (8 Wheat.) 543, 564 (1823).

99. *Id.* at 565–67.

100. *Id.* at 567–71.

101. *Id.* at 567.

102. *Id.* at 570–71.

103. *Id.*

104. *See* Chapter 6, text accompanying notes 128–50, *supra.*

105. 21 U.S. (8 Wheat.) 543 (1823).

106. *Id.*

107. *Id.* at 572.

108. *Id.*

109. *Id.*

110. *Id.* at 574–77.

111. *Id.* at 573–75.

112. *Id.* at 587.

113. *Id.* at 604–5.

114. *Id.* at 572–73.

115. *Id.* at 573.

116. *Id.*

117. *Id.* at 573–74.

118. 30 U.S. (5 Pet.) 1 (1831).

119. *Id.* at 17–18. In determining whether American Indian nations could be considered "foreign nations" and therefore parties within the original jurisdiction of the Supreme Court as delimited by the United States Constitution, Marshall reasoned that

> it may well be doubted whether those tribes within the acknowledged boundaries of the United States can, with strict accuracy, be denominated foreign nations. They may, more correctly, perhaps be denominated domestic dependent nations. They occupy a territory to which we assert a title independent of their will. . . . Meanwhile, they are in a state of pupilage. Their relation to the United States resembles that of a ward to his guardian. [*Id.* at 17.]

120. *Johnson v. McIntosh*, 21 U.S. (8 Wheat.) 543, 574–75 (1823).

121. *Id.* at 576.

122. *Id.* at 577. On Gilbert and Raleigh, see Chapter 4, *supra*.

123. *Johnson v. McIntosh*, 21 U.S. (8 Wheat.) 543, 579–80 (1823).

124. *Id.* at 588.

125. *Id.* at 584–85.

126. *Id.*

127. *Id.* at 585–87.

128. *Id.* at 586.

129. *Id.* at 588.

130. *Id.*

131. *Id.* at 587–88.

132. *Id.* at 591. Having recognized the superior rights of the United States to the Indians' America by legitimizing the Norman-derived discourse of conquest and the allied Doctrine of Discovery as the settled law of the nation, Marshall concluded his opinion by exorcising any vestigial remnants of the Revolutionary-era legal discourses recognizing Indians' property rights under natural law. Specifically, Marshall denied the applicability of Lord Mansfield's famous opinion in *Campbell v. Hall* (*see* text accompanying notes 54–72, *supra*) and the opinion of Lord Camden and Yorke (*see* Chapter 6, text accompanying notes 162–71, *supra*) to the situation in America respecting Indian land rights.

Daniel Webster's argument for the Illinois-Wabash Company had placed particular emphasis on *Campbell v. Hall* and its limitation of the king's prerogative powers to countries newly conquered (*see* text accompanying notes 92–98, *supra*). Lord Mansfield's celebrated opinion, Webster claimed, demonstrated the unconstitutionality of the Proclamation of 1763 and its attempted restraints on the Indians' right to sell. Marshall distinguished *Campbell v. Hall* by admitting that while the correctness of Lord Mansfield's opinion could not be questioned, its application to the facts of *Johnson v. McIntosh* "cannot be admitted" (*Johnson v. McIntosh*, 21 U.S. (8 Wheat.) 543, 597 [1823]). Lord Mansfield's opinion held only that a tax could not be imposed on a conquered people after the king had bestowed a government upon it. *Johnson v. McIntosh* involved a question of the king's right to exercise his prerogative on what Marshall labeled as "vacant" American lands occupied by savage Indians. A tax was not at issue:

> Since the expulsion of the Stuart family, the power of imposing taxes, by proclamation, has never been claimed as a branch of the royal prerogative; but the powers of granting, or refusing to grant, vacant lands, and of restraining encroachments on the Indians, have always been asserted and admitted. [*Id.* at 597.]

Having dismissed the relevance of *Campbell v. Hall* to the question of an English-derived government's prerogative right to exercise its rights of conquest over a country not formally conquered, Marshall next turned to the opinion of Lord Camden and Yorke. This was the last meaningful appearance in American legal discourse of this well-traveled opinion of English colonizing discourse. Marshall admitted that the opinion of "those great law officers" holding that an Indian grant could convey a title to the soil without a patent emanating from the Crown "would certainly be of great authority on such a question" (*id.* at 597). In fact, Marshall disingenuously stated, the members of the Court "were not a little surprised, when it was read, at the doctrine it seemed to advance" (*id.*). The surprising doctrine embodied in *Camden-Yorke*, of course, held that Indians possessed natural-law rights to their lands. How "surprised" the members of the Court were by this doctrine is open to conjecture, but Marshall's device for denying legitimacy to *Camden-Yorke*'s doctrine of Indian rights and erasing its register from American colonizing legal theory indictates a most devious sense of historical irony. To refute the applicability of the *Camden-Yorke* opinion to the question of American Indian land rights, Marshall relied on none other than Samuel Wharton's 1781 pamphlet *Plain Facts* (*see* text accompanying notes 45–79, *supra*), which had been written in staunch defense of the natural-law rights of American Indians to sell lands to Revolutionary-era speculators. As Marshall explained:

> In a pamphlet, written for the purpose of asserting the Indian title, styled "*Plain Facts*," the same opinion [*Camden-Yorke*] is quoted, and is said to relate to purchases made in the East Indies. It is, of course, entirely inapplicable to purchases made in America. . . . [T]here is reason to believe, that the author [Samuel Wharton] of *Plain Facts* is, in this respect correct. The opinion commenced thus: "In respect to such places as have been, or shall be acquired, by treaty or grant, from any of the Indian princes or governments, your majesty's letters patents are not necessary." The words "princes or governments," are usually applied to the East Indians, but not to those of North America. We speak of their sachems, their warriors, their chiefmen, their nations or tribes, not of their "princes or governments." [*Johnson v. McIntosh*, 21 U.S. (8 Wheat.) 543, 600 (1823).]

133. *Id.* at 592. Under the Law of Nations, Marshall conceded, "humanity" (i.e., civilized nations), acting on "public opinion" (i.e., the consensus of civilized nations represented in the *ius gentium*), "has established as a general rule, that the conquered shall not be wantonly oppressed, and that their condition shall remain as eligible as is compatible with the objects of the conquest" (*id.* at 589). The usual practice under the Law of Nations was for the conquered to become incorporated with the victorious nation. "Where this incorporation is practicable, humanity demands, and a wise policy requires, that the rights of the conquered to property should remain unimpaired" (*id.*).

Marshall explained, however, that this "wise policy" could not be applied to the savages of America.

> But the tribes of Indians inhabiting this country were fierce savages, whose occupation was war, and whose subsistence was drawn chiefly from the forest. To leave them in possession of their country, was to leave the country a wilderness; to govern them as a distinct people, was impossible. [*Id.* at 590.]

Thus, according to Marshall, the European discoverers of America

> were under the necessity either of abandoning the country, and relinquishing their pompous claims to it, or of enforcing those claims by the sword, and by the adoption of principles adapted to the condition of a people with whom it was impossible to mix, and who could not be governed as a distinct society. [*Id.* at 590.]

European policy, numbers, and skill ultimately prevailed in the white man's wars for America. The Indians retreated westward as Europeans advanced from their coastal colonial communities, claiming the vacated soil under the Crown's fictive rights of conquest.

Given the actual state of relations between the two races, Marshall stated, "some new and different rule" was resorted to in rationalizing the conqueror's process of land acquisition. This rule was the Doctrine of Discovery.

134. *Johnson v. McIntosh*, 21 U.S. (8 Wheat.) 543, 572 (1823).

135. Joseph Story, *Commentaries*, §152, reprinted in M. Lindley, *The Acquisition and Government of Background Territory in International Law* 29 (1926) (emphasis added).

Conclusion

The conquest of the earth is not a pretty thing when you look into it too much. The history of the American Indian in Western legal thought reveals that a will to empire proceeds most effectively under a rule of law. In the United States, and in the other Western settler-colonized states, that rule begins with the Doctrine of Discovery and its discourse of conquest, which denies fundamental human rights and self-determination to indigenous tribal peoples.[1] For the native peoples of the United States, Latin America, Canada, Australia, and New Zealand, therefore, the end of the history of their colonization begins by denying the legitimacy of and respect for the rule of law maintained by the racist discourse of conquest of the Doctrine of Discovery. This medievally grounded discourse, reaffirmed in Western colonizing law by Chief Justice John Marshall in *Johnson v. McIntosh*, vests superior rights of sovereignty over non-Western indigenous peoples and their territories in European-descended governments. The Doctrine of Discovery and its discourse of conquest assert the West's lawful power to impose its vision of truth on non-Western peoples through a racist, colonizing rule of law.

In the United States, the doctrine has proved itself to be a perfect instrument of empire. Under the rules and principles of federal Indian law derived from the doctrine, the United States acquired a continent "in perfect good faith"[2] that its wars and acts of genocide directed against Indian people accorded with the rule of law. Supreme Court decisions interpreting the doctrine have extended to the federal government plenary power to control Indian affairs unrestrained by normal constitutional limitations. In case after case, the Supreme Court in the late nineteenth and early twentieth centuries simply refused to check Congress's free rein in matters where it was thought that broad discretionary powers were vital to the solution of the immensely difficult "Indian problem."[3] Treaties promising tribes a reserved homeland in perpetuation were wantonly violated; tribes were relocated to distant, barren regions to accommodate white expansion; and tribal lands and resources were repeatedly confiscated to satisfy the needs and destiny of a superior civilization.

Besides justifying unquestioned abrogation and unilateral determination of tribal treaty and property rights, the discourse of conquest derived from the Doctrine of Discovery has been interpreted to permit the denial of other fundamental human rights of Indian tribal peoples in the United States.[4] Violent suppression of Indian religious practices and traditional forms of government,[5] separation of Indian children from their homes,[6] wholesale spoliation of treaty-guaranteed resources,[7] forced assimilative programs,[8] and involuntary sterilization of Indian women[9] represent but a few of the practical extensions of a racist discourse of conquest that at its core regards tribal peoples as normatively deficient and culturally, politically, and morally inferior. And the United States, it is conceded, possesses one of the most "liberal" and "progressive" reputations among the Western nations respecting its treatment of native peoples under the Doctrine of Discovery.[10] For other Western colonial states, the history of indigenous peoples' fate under the West's rule of law, grounded in the Doctrine of Discovery and its denial of human rights to non-Western tribal peoples, is indeed the stuff of black legend.

For half a millennium, whether inscribed in United States Indian law and its central Doctrine of Discovery, in the Spanish jurist Victoria's Law of Nations, or in Lord Coke's English common law, Western legal thought has sought to erase the difference presented by the American Indian in order to sustain the privileges of power it accords to Western norms and value structures. Animated by a central orienting vision of its own universalized, hierarchical position among all other discourses, the West's archaic, medievally derived legal discourse respecting the American Indian is ultimately genocidal in both its practice and its intent.

The Doctrine of Discovery was nothing more than the reflection of a set of Eurocentric racist beliefs elevated to the status of a universal principle—one culture's argument to support its conquest and colonization of a newly discovered, alien world. In its form as articulated by Western legal thought and discourse today, however, the peroration of this Eurocentric racist argument is no longer declaimed. Europe during the Discovery era refused to recognize any meaningful legal status or rights for indigenous tribal peoples because "heathens" and "infidels" were legally presumed to lack the rational capacity necessary to assume an equal status or to exercise equal rights under the West's medievally derived colonizing law.

Today, principles and rules generated from this Old World discourse of conquest are cited by the West's domestic and international courts of law to deny indigenous nations the freedom and dignity to govern themselves according to their own vision. Thus as a first step toward the decolonization of the West's law respecting the American Indian, the Doctrine of Discovery must be rejected. It permits the West to accomplish by law and in good conscience what it accomplished by the sword in earlier eras: the physical and spiritual destruction of indigenous people.

The reconstruction of the West's Indian law so that it would be grounded in a vision rejecting the discourse of conquest contained in the Doctrine of Discovery could begin its search for foundations in New World soil. The principles inherent in the Gus-Wen-Tah, an indigenously articulated New World discourse of peace, suggest the beginnings of a differently oriented vision of a law to govern the relations between the West and non-Western peoples.

The principles embodied in the Gus-Wen-Tah, the Two Row Wampum,[11] were the basis for all treaties and agreements between the great nations of the

Haudenosaunee Confederacy (called the Confederated Iroquois Nations by the European colonial powers) and the great nations of Europe. These basic principles were the covenant chain linking these two different peoples by which each agreed to respect the other's vision.

When the Haudenosaunee first came into contact with the European nations, treaties of peace and friendship were made. Each was symbolized by the Gus-Wen-Tah, or Two Row Wampum. There is a bed of white wampum which symbolizes the purity of the agreement. There are two rows of purple, and those two rows have the spirit of your ancestors and mine. There are three beads of wampum separating the two rows and they symbolize two paths or two vessels, travelling down the same river together. One, a birch bark canoe, will be for the Indian people, their laws, their customs and their ways. The other, a ship, will be for the white people and their laws, their customs and their ways. We shall each travel the river together, side by side, but in our own boat. Neither of us will try to steer the other's vessel.[12]

The vision of the Gus-Wen-Tah can be found inscribed throughout the *corpora* of documents relating the American Indians' legal and political thought and discourse. At the core of this Americanized vision of law is the idea that freedom requires different peoples to respect each other's vision of how their respective vessels should be steered.[13]

The Doctrine of Discovery, with its denial of territorial and self-determination rights for indigenous peoples equal to the rights of Western peoples, works to deny respect to the Indians' visions in numerous ways. Certainly one of the most threatening is its denial of their right to an equal voice as peoples on the world stage. Under the Doctrine of Discovery, indigenous peoples' complaints of human-rights abuses and demands for territorial protection and self-determination are regarded as matters of exclusive domestic concern within the conqueror's courts and political system. Thus the West's present rule of law denies indigenous peoples an international status in their struggles for survival in the modern world. Such a status could provide indigenous peoples with ready and immediate access to international legal and political forums. Then, indigenous peoples themselves could voice their visions of their rights before the world and seek protection and preservation through means other than those provided by a conqueror's rule of law and its discourses of conquest.[14]

History records that acts of genocide are most easily concealed in a world atmosphere of complicitous silence; a people is extinguished with a whimper, not a bang. An equal voice would certainly not necessarily guarantee the continued protection and preservation of the centuries-old visions of tribal peoples. Denying that voice, however, would most assuredly assist the efforts of those in power who seek the silent liquidation of colonized tribal peoples.

Whether from cupidity or shame, those Western-derived colonial sovereignties that continue to rely on Western-derived legal discourse as a shield against tribal peoples' assertions of abuses of fundamental human rights would conveniently have the world forget that the anachronistic premises at the core of their discursive practices once unquestioningly legitimated the use of the sword against indigenous nations. That tribal nations have not forgotten the history of conquest justified by Western legal thought and discourse explains why indigenous peoples now seek to redefine radically the conceptions of their rights and status in international and domestic legal forums. Pushed to the brink of extinction by the premises inherent in the West's vision of the world and the Indians' lack of a place in that world, contemporary tribalism recognizes the compelling necessity of articulating and defining its own vision within the global community. Only then, in the free play by which a shared global discourse may evolve, can tribalism's differently oriented vision be fairly considered as something other than an anachronistic inconvenience to the West's relentless, consumption-oriented world view. But such a discourse, with its potential for broadening perspectives on our human condition, is currently suppressed by a set of medievally derived prior restraints. Discourses of conquest, grounded in archaic, racist ideas that, once revealed, could not be redeemed by those who relied on them, continue to be asserted today by the West to deny respect to the Indians' vision.

NOTES

1. *See* D. Getches & C. Wilkinson, *Federal Indian Law* 847-73 (1986).

2. *See Lonewolf v. Hitchcock*, 187 U.S. 53 (1903). Leading contemporary studies on the plenary-power doctrine include N. Newton, "Federal Power over Indians: Its Sources, Scope and Limitations," 132 *U. Pa. L. Rev.* 195 (1984); R. Clinton, "Isolated in Their Own Country: A Defense of Federal Protection of Indian Autonomy and Self-Government," 33 *Stan. L. Rev.* 979 (1981); M. Ball, "Constitution, Court, Indian Tribes," 1987 *Am. B. Found Res. J.* 1.

3. *See* R. Strickland, "Genocide-at-Law: An Historic and Contemporary View of the Native American Experience," 34 *U. Kan. L. Rev.* 713 (1986). *See also* F. Hoxie, *A Final Promise* 211-38 (1984). For a discussion of several of the more important cases, *see* C. Harvey, "Constitutional Law: Congressional Plenary Power over Indian Affairs—A Doctrine Rooted in Prejudice," 10 *Am. Indian L. Rev.* 117 (1982).

One of the more extreme examples, in that the Court had to go through a "strenuous effort" (*id.* at 121) to avoid the appearance of inconsistency, is represented by *United States v. Sandoval*, 231 U.S. 28 (1913). In *Sandoval*, the Court was asked to decide whether congressional legislation controlling the introduction of liquor into Indian country extended to the New Mexico Pueblo community. The case was complicated by the fact that in an earlier case, *United States v. Joseph*, 94 U.S. 614 (1896), the Court had found that this same group was not Indian for purposes of legislation regulating trade and intercourse between Indians and non-Indians. In effect, *Joseph* had delineated a functional test to determine which "Indians" required congressional protection as "dependent" peoples, legally regarded as wards of the federal government. According to the Court in *Joseph*, the Pueblos, who had owned land in fee simple and had adopted the language and Christian religion of the Spanish conquerors prior to coming under United States sovereignty, did not require such protection:

> They are peaceable, industrious, intelligent, honest and virtuous people. They are Indians only in feature, complexion, and a few of their habits. . . . [T]he degree of civilization which they had attained, their willing submission to all the laws of the Mexican government . . . and their absorption into the general mass of the population . . . forbid the idea that they should be classed with the Indian tribes. [*Id.* at 616-17.]

Of course, by the time they were tested again for "Indianness" in *Sandoval*, the Pueblos had been under the tutelage of the Bureau of Indian Afairs for nearly forty years. It was therefore not surprising that they passed with flying colors:

The people of the pueblos, although sedentary rather than nomadic in their inclinations, and disposed to peace and industry, are nevertheless Indians in race, customs, and domestic government. Always living in separate and isolated communities, adhering to primitive modes of life, largely influenced by superstition and fetishism, and chiefly governed according to the crude customs inherited from their ancestors, they are essentially, a simple, uninformed and inferior people. . . . With one accord the reports of the superintendents charged with guarding their interests show that they are dependent upon the fostering care and protection of the Government, like reservation Indians in general; that although industrially superior, they are intellectually, and morally inferior to many of them; and that they are easy victims to the evils and debasing influence of intoxicants. [*United States v. Sandoval*, 231 U.S. 28 (1913), at 39–41. *See also* C. Harvey, *supra*, at 120–33.]

Given the Pueblos' "Indianness," therefore, the Court concluded that Congress's plenary power did extend to them:

Not only does the Constitution expressly authorize Congress to regulate commerce with the Indian tribes, but long-continued legislative and executive usage and an unbroken current of judicial decisions have attributed to the United States as a superior and civilized nation the power and the duty of exercising a fostering care and protection over all dependent Indian communities within its borders. [*United States v. Sandoval*, 231 U.S. 28 (1913), at 45.]

4. *See*, e.g., T. Coulter, "The Denial of Legal Remedies to Indian Nations Under U.S. Law," 3 *Am. Indian J.* n. 9, at 5 (1977). *See also* F. Cohen, *The Legal Conscience* 429 (1960).

5. *See*, e.g., American Indian Policy Review Commission, 95th Cong., 1st sess., 1 Final Report, at 67–68; Federal Agencies Task Force, *American Indian Religious Freedom Act Report*, Pub. L. 95-341 (1979).

6. *See*, e.g., "Comment, American Indian Child Welfare Crisis: Cultural Genocide or First Amendment Preservation?" 7 *Colum. Human Rights L. Rev.* 529 (1976).

7. *See*, e.g., *United States v. Sioux Nation of Indians*, 448 U.S. 371 (1980); *United States v. Mitchell*, 445 U.S. 535 (1980); *United States v. Mitchell (II)*, 463 U.S. 206 (1983).

8. *See*, e.g., H. Fritz, *The Movement for Indian Assimilation, 1860–1890* (1963); *Americanizing the American Indian* (1973). *See also* C. Wilkinson & E. Biggs, "Evolution of the Termination Policy," 5 *Am. Indian L. Rev.* 139 (1977).

9. *See*, e.g., "Killing Our Future: Sterilization and Experiments," 9 *Akwesasne Notes*, no. 1, at 4.

10. *See generally* C. Wilkinson, *American Indians, Time and the Law* 5 (1987).

11. *See* "Indian Self-Government in Canada: Report of the Special Committee" (1983).

12. *Id.*

13. *See*, e.g., Chief Seattle of the Suquamish's speech in 1854 in response to a United States offer to enter into a treaty for tribal lands:

So we will consider your offer to buy our land. If we decide to accept, I will make one condition. The white man must treat the beasts of this land as his brothers.

I am a savage and do not understand any other way. I have seen a thousand rotting buffaloes on the prairie, left by the white man who shot them from a passing train. I am a savage and I do not understand how the smoking iron horse can be more important than the buffalo that we kill only to stay alive.

What is man without the beasts? If all the beasts were gone, man would die from a great loneliness of spirit. For whatever happens to the beasts, soon happens to man. All things are connected.

You must teach your children that the ground beneath their feet is the ashes of our grandfathers. So that they will respect the land, tell your children that the earth is rich with the lives of our kin. Teach your children what we have taught our children, that the earth is our mother. Whatever befalls the earth, befalls the sons of the earth. This we know. All things are connected like the blood which unites one family. All things are connected.

Whatever befalls the earth befalls the sons of the earth. Man did not weave the web of life; he is merely a strand in it. Whatever he does to the web, he does to himself. [Reprinted in *Agenda*, Sept.–Oct. 1984, at 17. *See also Basic Call to Consciousness* 1–37, 65–116 (*Akwesasne Notes* ed. 1978).]

And while whites may not realize it, this same vision at the core of American Indian legal thought served as the inspiration for their own greatest legal and political ideas and institutions in this country. *See* F. Cohen, "Americanizing the American Indian," 21 *The Am. Scholar* 183–84 (1952):

> Is it any wonder that the greatest teachers of American democracy have gone to school with the Indian?
> Were not the first common councils of the American Colonies, the Council of Lancaster in 1744 and the famous Albany Congress of 1754, councils called for the purpose of treating with the Iroquois Confederacy, whose leaders were unwilling to treat separately with the various quarreling Colonies? It was the great Iroquois Chief Canasatego who advised the Colonial governors meeting at Lancaster in 1744:
>
>> Our Wise Forefathers established Union and Amity between the Five Nations. This has made us formidable; this has given us great Weight and Authority with our neighboring Nations. We are a powerful Confederacy; and by your observing the same Methods our Wise Forefathers have taken, you will acquire such Strength and power. Therefore whatever befalls you, never fall out with one another.
>
> The advice of Canasatego was eagerly taken up by Benjamin Franklin.
>
>> It would be a strange thing [he advised the Albany Congress] if Six Nations of ignorant savages should be capable of forming a scheme for such a union and be able to execute it in such a manner that it has subsisted ages and appears indissoluble, and yet that a like union should be impracticable for ten or a dozen English colonies, to whom it is more necessary and must be more advantageous, and who cannot be supposed to want an equal understanding of their interest.
>
> The author of the American Declaration of Independence and of our first bill of rights freely acknowledged his debt to Indian teachers. Comparing the freedom of Indian society with the oppression of European society, Thomas Jefferson struck the keynote of the great American experiment in democracy:
>
>> Imperfect as this species of coercion may seem, crimes are very rare among them [the Indians of Virginia]; so much that were it made a question, whether no law, as among savage Americans, or too much law, as among the civilized Europeans, submits man to the greatest evil, one who has seen both conditions of existence should pronounce it to be the last; and that the sheep are happier of themselves, than under the care of the wolves. It will be said, that great societies cannot exist without government. The savages, therefore, break them into small ones.

14. *See generally* A. Snow, *The Question of Aborigines* 175 (1921). *See also* E. Eggleston, "Prospects for United Nations Protection of the Human Rights of Indigenous Minorities," *Aus. L.Y.B. Int'l.* 68 (1970–1973); "The Rights of Indigenous Peoples: A Comparative Analysis," 68 *Am. Soc. Int'l L. Proc.* 265 (1974); J. Ryan, "Indian Nations Compared to Other Nations," 3 *Am. Indian J.* 2 (1977); R. Barsh, "Indigenous North America and Contemporary International Law," 62 *Or. L. Rev.* 73, 99–102 (1983); G. Bennet, *Aboriginal Rights in International Law* (1978).

The controversy surrounding the so-called Belgian thesis in the United Nations following World War II provides but one well-known example of modern efforts by neocolonial European-derived governments to limit international scrutiny of their treatment of indigenous populations. Under Chapter XI of the UN Charter, entitled "Declaration Regarding Non-Self-Governing Territories," member states that have assumed responsibility for administering territories whose peoples have not yet attained a full measure of self-government must ensure just treatment of their dependent peoples. Article 73(e) of the UN Charter further mandates these member nations to submit an annual report of economic, social, and educational conditions in dependent territories to the secretary-general. The effect of these two segments of the Charter is thus to permit the UN to consider domestic matters that might normally be regarded as beyond its jurisdiction under Article 2(1) of the Charter. It is generally conceded that continued violation of Chapter XI obligations could lead to the ultimate sanction of expulsion of a member from the UN. *See* G. Bennet, *supra.*

However, when the United Nations sought to clarify the scope and substantive content of Chapter XI in the early 1950s, an intense debate erupted as to whether the chapter's protection extended to indigenous populations or was restricted to overseas colonial peoples. Belgium took the lead in arguing for the former interpretation. *See generally* "Text of Replies to the Ad Hoc

Committee on Factors," U.N. Doc. A/Ac. 67/2, May 8, 1953, at 3–31. Latin American countries vigorously opposed the "Belgian thesis," arguing that their indigenous populations had been fully integrated politically and that the Belgian position on Chapter XI could result in the dismemberment of newly independent states, converting much of the world into a colonial system. *See Official Records of the General Assembly, Seventh Session, Fourth Committee,* at 55. *See generally* G. Bennet, *supra,* at 13.

In 1960 the UN General Assembly adopted Resolution 1541 G.A. Res. 1514, 15 U.N. GAOR Supp. (No. 16), U.N. Doc. A/L 323 and Add. (1960), which essentially rejected the Belgian thesis by limiting the reporting requirements that had been designed to ensure the protections offered under Chapter XI only to territories geographically separate and culturally or ethnically distinct from the administering country. Thus Resolution 1541, which has been characterized as a "serious blow to the aboriginal cause" (G. Bennet, *supra,* at 13), stands for the proposition that indigenous peoples in the member nations of the UN are not protected by Chapter XI but are subject to the domestic law of their administering states.

Indigenous peoples today seek to heighten the level of international awareness of, concern for, and protection of their fundamental human rights in a wide variety of forums. Most significantly, within the institutional structure of the United Nations, indigenous peoples have made important strides toward securing recognition of their status as proper independent subjects of international law. In 1977, the United Nations Non-Governmental Organizations (NGO) sponsored the Conference on Discrimination Against Indigenous Populations in the Americas. The conference gave native groups their first significant opportunity to air their concerns within a recognized international institutional setting. The conference adopted the Declaration of Principles for the Defense of the Indigenous Nations and Peoples of the Western Hemisphere, representing the attending groups' consensus on the vital issues on their international agenda. Among other measures, the declaration calls for the recognition of indigenous nations as nations and proper subjects of international law, provided that the people concerned desire such recognition and meet fundamental requirements of nationhood, including a permanent population, a defined territory, and a government with the ability to enter into relations with other states. The declaration also calls for the recognition of indigenous groups that do not meet the requirements of nationhood as subjects of international law, and demands that all indigenous nations and groups "be accorded such degree of independence as they may desire in accordance with international law" (International NGO Conference on Discrimination Against Indigenous Populations in the Americas 1977, September 20–24, Geneva, *Statement and Final Documents* 4, 5 [1978]). *See* R. Barsh, *supra.*

A subsequent NGO conference, held in 1981—Indigenous Peoples and the Land—was attended by indigenous representatives from five continents. That conference adopted the 1977 declaration as a standard for all indigenous populations. Following this conference, the Subcommission on Prevention of Discrimination and Protection of Minorities issued a draft resolution urging the Human Rights Commission of the UN's Economic and Social Council (ECOSOC) to establish a Working Group on Indigenous Populations that could work toward "the evolution of standards concerning the rights of indigenous populations, taking into account both the similarities and the differences in the situations and aspirations of indigenous populations throughout the world" ("Report of the Subcommission on Prevention of Discrimination and Protection of Minorities," U.N. Doc. E/CN.4/Sub.2/495 [1981]). *See* R. Barsh, *supra.*

The Working Group was established following adoption of the subcommission's draft resolution by the Human Rights Commission and its subsequent approval by ECOSOC in 1982. The Working Group's sessions were opened to all indigenous groups. *See* Asbjorn Eide, "Study of the Problem of Discrimination Against Indigenous Populations: Report of the Working Group on Indigenous Populations on Its First Session," U.N. Doc. #/Cn.4/Sub.2/1982/33, August 25, 1982. *See generally* R. Barsh, *supra,* at 101.

In its short period of existence, the Working Group has emerged as the primary focus of international activities by both governments and nongovernmental organizations concerned with indigenous peoples' human rights. Its sessions, now regularly attended by nearly 400 persons, including representatives from over 50 indigenous organizations and observers from more than two dozen countries, are held in the same large conference room at the UN headquarters in Geneva in which the Human Rights Commission meets—just one indication of the Working Group's growing significance within the UN and the international human-rights community. *See* H. Hannum, "New Developments in Indigenous Rights," 28 *Vir. Jour. of Int'l. L.* 649 (1988).

The earlier sessions of the Working Group were focused primarily on providing a forum for indigenous and other NGOs to present oral and written interventions reporting on the human-rights violations and government practices affecting the 300 million indigenous peoples in countries throughout the world. During its more recent sessions, the Working Group has drawn on this crucial body of information as it has begun to address its mandated task of developing standards for the promotion and protection of indigenous peoples' human rights.

In 1987, the Working Group approved fourteen draft principles as the first step toward the drafting of a Universal Declaration on the Rights of Indigenous Peoples. These principles implicitly recognized the failures of existing international legal instruments and of domestic laws and policies to protect indigenous peoples' human rights. The draft principles declared the rights of indigenous peoples to be free and to be equal to all other human beings. But more significantly in terms of the development of international human-rights standards, the 1987 principles also recognized the *collective* rights of indigenous peoples to exist; to be protected against acts aimed at depriving them of their ethnic identity or forcibly assimilating them into the dominant culture; to participate fully in the economic, political, and social life of their countries; and to have their specific character as indigenous peoples reflected in the legal and political systems of their countries. In addition, the Working Group principles declared that indigenous peoples possess the right to state assistance in maintaining their indigenous identity and development, the right to special state measures for improving their social and economic conditions that reflect their priorities, the right to enjoy their traditional means of subsistence and other traditional cultural and economic activities, and the right to control health, housing, religious, educational, and other types of activities in pursuit and promotion of their own cultural development ("Report of the Working Group on Indigenous Populations on Its Fifth Session," Annex II, U.N. Doc. E/CN.4/Sub.2/1987/22 [1987]).

Drawing from these important 1987 draft principles, the Working Group prepared a full draft Declaration on the Rights of Indigenous Peoples for consideration at its sixth session, held in 1988. This draft, containing a preamble and twenty-eight sections divided into six parts, guarantees to indigenous peoples all fundamental rights and freedoms recognized in existing international human-rights instruments and important collective rights to cultural development, traditionally occupied lands, maintenance of traditional subsistence economies, and autonomy. The draft also recognizes indigenous peoples' status as subjects of international law, particularly with respect to international human-rights review and complaints mechanisms ("Report of the Working Group on Indigenous Populations on Its Sixth Session," Annex II, U.N. Doc. E/CN.4/Sub.2/1988/24 [1988]).

At its most recently completed session, in 1989, the Working Group presented the first revised text of the draft Universal Declaration on the Rights of Indigenous Peoples. This revised text reflects observations and comments received by the chairwoman/rapporteur, Erica-Irene Daes, on the 1988 draft from eleven governments, several United Nations subsidiary institutions, and a number of indigenous and other NGOs. The revised draft was expanded to contain a preamble introducing tentative language on the right to self-determination of indigenous peoples under international law, and a section specifying that the rights contained in the declaration constitute the minimum standards for the survival of indigenous peoples ("Discrimination Against Indigenous Peoples: First Revised Text of the Draft Universal Declaration on the Rights of Indigenous Peoples," U.N. Doc. E/CN.4/Sub.2/1989/33 [1989]).

Also, at the conclusion of the 1989 session, the Working Group announced that its 1990 session would focus on the crucial task of proceeding section by section through the draft declaration, with states, NGOs, and indigenous groups given an opportunity to respond both orally and in writing to the specific language to be incorporated into the final draft, which will be forwarded for ratification to the UN Subcommission on Prevention of Discrimination and Protection of Minorities and, ultimately, to the General Assembly of the United Nations.

As the Working Group enters the final, critical phase of its standard-setting activities designed to culminate in the draft Universal Declaration on the Rights of Indigenous Peoples for ultimate ratification by the UN General Assembly, indigenous peoples themselves will be presented with vital and unprecedented opportunities and challenges. The opportunities include the ability to participate directly in the process of international human-rights standard setting as the Working Group finalizes the language and principles that will be incorporated into a final draft declaration. In turn, eventual adoption by the General Assembly of this final draft will provide a unique stimulus to the contemporary global movement for recognition, protection, and promotion of indigenous peoples' human rights. A Universal Declaration on Indigenous Peoples' Rights would have implications not only within the international legal sphere, but also most certainly within domestic arenas, particularly with respect to domestic laws and policies affecting the human rights of indigenous peoples.

The draft declaration being written by the Working Group represents one of the most significant and far-reaching efforts by an international standard-setting body to specify the nature and substantive content of collective group rights under evolving notions of international human-rights law. The adoption of the declaration by the UN General Assembly would most certainly represent a significant achievement for the international human-rights movement as it addresses other conflicts involving collectivities and groups. A Universal Declaration on Indigenous Peoples' Rights will likely assume an important constitutive role in the human-rights process as institutions devoted to world public order continue to deal with crisis situations complicated by questions of ethnic and minority rights, self-determination, participation in government, and control over economic development (*see generally* H. Hannum, *supra.* at 677). The innovative use and progressive development of international human-rights norms and mechanisms by indigenous peoples can only continue to expand with the adoption of a Universal Declaration on the Rights of Indigenous Peoples. Indigenous peoples will find themselves situated to extend numerous benefits to others throughout the world who are victims of human-rights abuses.

Without question, then, the Working Group's activities present significant opportunities for indigenous peoples to participate in the development of the international human-rights standard-setting process. At the same time, indigenous peoples confront numerous challenges. As one commentator has noted, there is great "conceptual disorder" with respect to the questions, both theoretical and practical, raised by indigenous peoples' demands for recognition of their collective human rights. *See* D. Sanders, "The Re-Emergence of Indigenous Questions in International Law," 1983 *Can. Hum. Rights Y.R.* 3, 5. Much of this conceptual disorder can be traced directly to the continuing primacy of the Doctrine of Discovery in the domestic law of the European-derived settler states, and the fundamental inconsistency of this Eurocentric and racist doctrine with the most basic norms represented in contemporary international human-rights law and standards.

For example, to date in the international human-rights process, indigenous peoples have insisted on their rights to self-determination as indigenous peoples and their rights to traditionally occupied territories and subsurface resources. They have also sought a requirement that governments seek the consent of indigenous peoples before undertaking any significant actions that would affect them or the integrity of their cultures. And they want these rights protected by international human-rights law. All these demands are irreconcilable with the diminished rights and status accorded indigenous peoples under the Doctrine of Discovery. Given the primacy of the doctrine in the domestic law of the European-derived settler states, it is not surprising that international human-rights law has failed to develop adequate theories or mechanisms for protecting or promoting the types of collective group rights advocated by indigenous peoples. As indicated by state comments on the most recent Working Group draft declaration (*see* "Discrimination Against Indigenous Peoples: Analytical Compilation of Observations and Comments," U.N. Doc. E/CN.4/4 Sub.2/1989/33/Add.1 [1989]), indigenous peoples can expect continuing strong state resistance to the collective, group-oriented nature of their claims to human-rights protection.

A major challenge confronting indigenous peoples, therefore, as they seek to extend international legal recognition and protection of the collective group rights necessary for their survival, is to deprive this state resistance of its strenuously asserted legitimating foundation in a rule of law. That rule of law, of course, is maintained by the Doctrine of Discovery, which at its medievally derived and racist foundation is fundamentally at odds with the universal principles of the equality and human dignity of all peoples reflected in contemporary human-rights law and standards.

Bibliography

Abel, Annie Heloise. "The History of Events Resulting in Indian Consolidation West of the Mississippi." *Annual Report of the American Historical Association* 1, no. 235 (1906): 233–450.

Abernathy, Thomas Perkins. *Western Lands and the American Revolution.* New York: Russell and Russell, 1959.

Adams, C., ed. *The Works of John Adams,* vol. 2. Boston: Little, Brown, 1850.

Alfonso X, *Las Siete Partidas.* Translated by James Brown Scott. Castile, Chicago, New York, etc.: Published for the Comparative Law Bureau of the American Bar Association by Commerce Clearing House, Inc., Looseleaf Service Division of the Corporation Trust Company, 1931.

Alvord, Clarence Walworth. *The Mississippi Valley in British Politics: A Study of the Trade, Land Speculation and Experiments in Imperialism Culminating in the American Revolution,* vol. 1. New York: Russell and Russell, 1959.

Alvord, Clarence Walworth, and Carter, C., eds. *Illinois Historical Collections: The New Regime 1765–1767.* Springfield: Illinois State Historical Library, 1916.

Anderson, Perry. *Lineages of the Absolutist State.* London: Verso, 1979.

Andrews, Kenneth R.; Canny, Nicholas P.; and Hair, P. E. H., eds. *The Westward Enterprise: English Activities in Ireland, the Atlantic and America 1480–1650.* Detroit: Wayne State University Press, 1978.

Arber, Edward, ed. *The First Three English Books on America: [?1511–1555 A.D.], Being Chiefly Translations, Compilations, etc., by Richard Eden.* Westminister: Constable, 1895.

Bailyn, Bernard. *The Ideological Origins of the American Revolution.* Cambridge, Mass.: Belknap Press of Harvard University Press, 1967.

Ball, M. "Constitution, Court, Indian Tribes." *American Bar Foundation Research Journal,* no. 1 (1987): 23–34.

Barbour, Philip L. *The Jamestown Voyages Under the First Charter 1606–1609.* London: Published for the Hakluyt Society, 1969.

Barraclough, Geoffrey. *The Origins of Modern Germany.* 2d rev. ed. Oxford: Blackwell, 1947.

Barsh, Russell. "Indigenous North America and Contemporary International Law." *Oregon Law Review* 62 (1983): 73–125.

Barsh, Russell Lawrence, and Henderson, James Youngblood. *The Road: Indian Tribes and Political Liberty.* Berkeley: University of California Press, 1980.

Belch, Stanislaus F. *Paulus Vladimiri and His Doctrine Concerning International Law and Politics.* The Hague: Mouton, 1965.

Bennet, Gordon. *Aboriginal Rights in International Law.* London: Royal Anthropological Institute, 1978.

Benzoni, Girolamo. *History of the New World.* Translated and edited by W. H. Smyth. London: Published for the Hakluyt Society, 1857.

Berkhofer, Robert F., Jr. *The White Man's Indian: Images of the American Indian from Columbus to the Present.* New York: Knopf, 1978.

Berman, H. "The Concept of Aboriginal Rights in the Early Legal History of the United States." *Buffalo Law Review* 27 (1978): 637–67.

Bowen, Catherine Drinker. *The Lion and the Throne: The Life and Times of Sir Edward Coke.* Boston: Little, Brown, 1957.

Boxer, Charles Ralph. *The Portuguese Seaborne Empire 1415–1825.* New York: Knopf, 1969.

Boxer, Charles Ralph. *Race Relations in the Portuguese Colonial Empire 1415–1825.* Oxford: Clarendon Press, 1963.

Brundage, James A. *The Crusades: A Documentary Survey.* Milwaukee: Marquette University Press, 1962.

Brundage, James A. *Medieval Canon Law and the Crusader.* Madison: University of Wisconsin Press, 1969.

Brundage, James A. *Richard Lion Heart.* New York: Scribners, 1974.

Brundage, James A., ed. *The Crusades: Motives and Achievements.* Boston: Heath, 1964.

Bullough, Donald A. *The Age of Charlemagne.* London: Elek Books, 1965.

Burke, J. "The Cherokee Cases: A Study in Law, Politics, and Morality." *Stanford Law Review* 21 (1969): 500–31.

Burns, Robert Ignatius. *The Crusader Kingdom of Valencia: Reconstruction on a Thirteenth-Century Frontier.* 2 vols. Cambridge, Mass.: Harvard University Press, 1967.

Canny, Nicholas P. *The Elizabethan Conquest of Ireland: A Pattern Established 1565–76.* Hassocks, Sussex: Harvester Press, 1976.

Canny, Nicholas P. "The Ideology of English Colonization: From Ireland to America." *William and Mary Quarterly* 30, no. 575 (October 1973): 575–98.

Carlyle, Robert Warrand, and Carlyle, Alexander James. *A History of Medieval Political Theory in the West,* vol. 5: *The Political Theory of the Thirteenth Century.* 6 vols. Edinburgh and London: Blackwood, 1903–1936.

Clinton, Robert. "Isolated in Their Own Country: A Defense of Federal Protection of Indian Autonomy and Self-Government." *Stanford Law Review* 33 (1981): 979–1068.

Cohen, Felix S. *Handbook of Federal Indian Law.* Charlottesville, Va.: Michie/Bobbs-Merrill, 1982.

Cohen, Felix. *The Legal Conscience: Selected Papers.* New Haven, Conn: Yale University Press, 1960.

Cohen, Felix S. "Original Indian Title." *Minnesota Law Review* 32 (1947): 28–59.

Cohen, Felix S. "The Spanish Origin of Indian Rights in the Law of the United States." *Georgetown Law Journal* 31 (1942): 1–21.

Collis, J. *Christopher Columbus.* London: Macdonald and James, 1976.

Commager, Henry Steele, ed. *Documents of American History.* 8th ed. New York: Appleton-Century-Crofts, 1968.

Conway, Moncure Daniel, ed. *The Writings of Thomas Paine,* vol. 1. New York: Putnam, 1894.

Coulter, Tim. "The Denial of Legal Remedies to Indian Nations Under U.S. Law." *American Indian Journal* 3, no. 9 (1977): 5–9.

Crane, V., "Notes and Documents: Hints Relative to the Division and Government of the Conquered and Newly Acquired Countries in America." *Mississippi Valley History Review* 8 (1922): 367–73.

Craven, Wesley Frank. *The Southern Colonies in the Seventeenth Century, 1607–1689.* Baton Rouge: Louisiana State University Press, 1949.

Cronon, William. *Changes in the Land: Indians, Colonists and the Ecology of New England.* New York: Hill & Wang, 1983.

Daly, Lowrie John. *The Political Theory of John Wyclif.* Chicago: Loyola University Press, 1962.

Davenport, Frances Gardiner, ed. *European Treaties Bearing on the History of the United States and Its Dependencies,* vol. 1 (to 1648). Washington, D.C.: Carnegie Institution of Washington, 1917.

Dawson, C., ed. *The Mongol Mission: Narratives and Letters of the Franciscan Missionaries in Mongolia and China in the Thirteenth and Fourteenth Centuries.* New York: Sheed and Ward, 1955.

Deane, Herbert Andrew. *The Political and Social Ideas of St. Augustine.* New York: Columbia University Press, 1963.

Debo, Angie. *And Still the Waters Run: The Betrayal of the Five Civilized Tribes.* Princeton, N.J.: Princeton University Press, 1972.

Debo, Angie. *A History of the Indians of the United States.* Norman: University of Oklahoma Press, 1970.

Deloria, Vine, Jr. *Behind the Trail of Broken Treaties.* New York: Dell, 1974.

De Rosier, Arthur H. *The Removal of the Choctaw Indians.* Knoxville: University of Tennessee Press, 1970.

Ehler, Sidney Z., and Morrall, John B., trans. and eds. *Church and State Through the Centuries: A Collection of Historic Documents with Commentaries.* New York: Biblo and Tannen, 1967.

Elton, Geoffrey Rudolph. *The Tudor Revolution in Government: Administrative Changes in the Reign of Henry VIII.* Cambridge: Cambridge University Press, 1953.

Erdmann, Carl. *The Origin of the Idea of Crusade.* Translated by Marshall W. Baldwin and Walter Goffart. Princeton, N.J.: Princeton University Press, 1977.

Flexner, James Thomas. *Lord of the Mohawks: A Biography of Sir William Johnson.* Boston: Little, Brown, 1979.

Floyd, Troy. *The Columbus Dynasty in the Caribbean, 1492-1526.* Albuquerque: University of New Mexico Press, 1973.

Force, Peter, ed. *Tracts and Other Papers Relating Principally to the Origin, Settlement, and Progress of the Colonies in North America, from the Discovery of the Country to 1776.* New York: Smith, 1947.

Foreman, Grant. *Indian Removal: The Emigration of the Five Civilized Tribes of Indians.* Norman: University of Oklahoma Press, 1932.

Foucault, Michel. *The Archaeology of Knowledge.* New York: Pantheon Books, 1972.

Foucault, Michel. *The Birth of the Clinic: An Archaeology of Medical Perception.* New York: Vintage Books, 1975.

Foucault, Michel. *Power/Knowledge: Selected Interviews and Other Writings 1972-77.* Hassocks, Sussex: Harvester Press, 1980.

Fritz, H. *The Movement for Indian Assimilation, 1860-1890.* Philadelphia: University of Pennsylvania Press, 1963.

Getches, D., and Wilkinson, C. *Federal Indian Law, Cases and Materials.* 2d ed. St. Paul, Minn.: West, 1986.

Gibson, Charles, ed. *The Spanish Tradition in America.* New York: Harper & Row, 1968.

Gierke, Otto Friedrich von. *Associations and Law: The Classical and Early Christian Stages.* Translated by George Heiman. Toronto: University of Toronto Press, 1977.

Gierke, Otto Friedrich von. *The Development of Political Theory.* Translated by Bernard Freyd. New York: Norton, 1939.

Gierke, Otto Friedrich von. *Natural Law and the Theory of Society 1500-1800.* Translated by Ernst Barker. Cambridge: Cambridge University Press, 1934.

Gierke, Otto Friedrich von. *Political Theories of the Middle Ages.* Translated by Frederic William Maitland. Boston: Beacon Press, 1958.

Gwynn, Aubrey Osborn. *The English Austin Friars in the Time of Wyclif.* London: Oxford University Press, 1940.

Habermas, Jürgen. *Theory and Practice.* Translated by John Viertel. Boston: Beacon Press, 1974.

Hanke, Lewis. *All Mankind Is One: A Study of the Disputation Between Bartolomé de Las Casas and Juan Ginés de Sepúlveda in 1550 on the Intellectual and Religious Capacity of the American Indian.* Dekalb: Northern Illinois University Press, 1974.

Hanke, Lewis. *Aristotle and the American Indians: A Study in Race Prejudice in the Modern World.* Bloomington: Indiana University Press, 1959.

Hanke, Lewis. *The First Social Experiments in America: A Study in the Development of Spanish Indian Policy in the Sixteenth Century.* Cambridge, Mass.: Harvard University Press, 1935.

Hanke, Lewis. *The Spanish Struggle for Justice in the Conquest of America.* Philadelphia: University of Pennsylvania Press, 1949.

Hannum, Hurst. "New Developments in Indigenous Rights." *Virginia Journal of International Law* 28 (1988): 649-78.

Harvey, C. "Constitutional Law: Congressional Plenary Power over Indian Affairs—A Doctrine Rooted in Prejudice." *American Indian Law Review* 10 (1982): 117-50.

Hay, Denys. *Europe: The Emergence of an Idea.* Edinburgh: Edinburgh University Press, 1968.

Henderson, J. "Unravelling the Riddle of Aboriginal Title." *American Indian Law Review* 5 (1977): 75-137.

Hill, Christopher. *Intellectual Origins of the English Revolution.* Oxford: Clarendon Press, 1965.

Hill, Christopher. *Puritanism and Revolution.* London: Secker and Warburg, 1958.

Horsman, Reginald. *Expansion and American Indian Policy 1783–1812.* East Lansing: Michigan State University Press, 1967.

Hoxie, Frederick. *A Final Promise: The Campaign to Assimilate the Indians, 1880–1920.* Lincoln: University of Nebraska Press, 1984.

"Innocent IV, Pope." *New Catholic Encyclopedia,* vol. 7, pp. 524–525. New York: McGraw-Hill, 1967.

Jacobs, Wilbur R. *Dispossessing the American Indian: Indians and Whites on the Colonial Frontier.* New York: Scribner, 1972.

Jane, C., trans. *The Journal of Christopher Columbus.* New York: Bramhall House, 1960.

Jedin, Hubert, and Dolan, J. *Handbook of Church History,* vol. 3: *The Church in the Age of Feudalism.* New York: Herder and Herder, 1969.

Jensen, Merrill. *The Articles of Confederation: An Interpretation of the Social-Constitutional History of the American Revolution 1774–1778.* Madison: University of Wisconsin Press, 1940.

Jensen, Merrill. *The Founding of a Nation: A History of the American Revolution 1763–1776.* New York: Oxford University Press, 1968.

Jensen, Merrill. *The Making of the American Constitution.* Huntington, N.Y.: Krieger, 1964.

Kaminski, J., and Miller, H. "Jefferson Had Some Doubts, We the People: The Constitution 200 Years Ago Today." *Wisconsin State Journal,* 19 April 1987, p. S-1.

Kantorowicz, Ernst Hartwig. *Frederick the Second, 1194–1250.* New York: Ungar, 1957.

Kent, James. *Commentaries on American Law,* vol. 3, Part 6: *Of the Law Concerning Real Property, Lecture 53: Of the History of the Law of Tenure.* 5th ed. New York: Kent, 1844.

Kingsbury, S. M., ed. *The Records of the Virginia Company of London,* vol. 3: *A Justification for Planting Virginia.* Washington, D.C.: Library of Congress, 1933.

Knorr, K. *British Colonial Theories 1570–1850.* Toronto: University of Toronto Press, 1944.

Lea, H. *A History of the Inquisition of the Middle Ages.* New York: Macmillan, 1922.

Lewis, Ewart Kellogg. *Medieval Political Ideas.* London: Routledge and Kegan Paul, 1954.

Lewis, G. *The Indiana Company 1763–1798.* Glendale, Calif.: Clark, 1941.

Lindley, Mark Frank. *The Acquisition and Government of Backward Territory in International Law.* London: Longmans, Green, 1926.

Livermore, H. V. *A New History of Portugal.* Cambridge: Cambridge University Press, 1969.

Livermore, H. V., ed. *Portugal and Brazil: An Introduction.* Oxford: Clarendon Press, 1953.

Lurie, N. *Seventeenth Century America: Essays in Colonial History.* Edited by J. Smith. Westport, Conn.: Greenwood Press, 1959.

Macpherson, Crawford Brough. *The Political Theory of Possessive Individualism: Hobbes to Locke.* Oxford: Clarendon Press, 1962.

Magrath, C. Peter. *Yazoo: Law and Politics in the New Republic.* Providence, R.I.: Brown University Press, 1966.

McNickle, d'Arcy. *They Came Here First.* New York: Octagon Books, 1972.

Maitland, Frederic William. *Moral Personality and Legal Personality: The Collected Papers of Frederic William Maitland: Downing Professor of the Laws of England.* Edited by H. A. L. Fisher. Cambridge: Cambridge University Press, 1911.

Maitland, Frederic William. "English Law and the Renaissance." *Select Essays in Anglo-American Legal History,* vol. 1. Edited by the Association of American Law Schools. Boston: Little, Brown, 1907.

Mann, Horace Kinder. *The Lives of the Popes in the Early Middle Ages from 590–1304,* vol. 14. London: Kegan Paul, Trench, Trubner, 1902.

Marques, Antonio Henrique R. de Oliveira. *History of Portugal,* vol. 1: *From Lusitania to Empire.* New York: Columbia University Press, 1972.

Martin, Henry Desmond. *The Rise of Chingis Khan and His Conquest of North China.* New York: Octagon Books, 1971.

Merriman, R. B. *The Rise of Spanish Empire in the Old World and the New.* 4 vols. New York: Macmillan, 1962.

Miller, Perry. *Errand into the Wilderness*. Cambridge, Mass.: Belknap Press of Harvard University Press, 1964.

Mohr, Walter Harrison. *Federal Indian Relations 1774–1788*. Philadelphia: University of Pennsylvania Press, 1933.

Molen, Gezina Hermina Johanna van der. *Alberico Gentili and the Development of International Law*. Leyden: Sijthoff, 1968.

Morison, Samuel Eliot. *Admiral of the Ocean Sea: A Life of Christopher Columbus*. Boston: Little, Brown, 1942.

Morison, Samuel Eliot. *The European Discovery of America*. 2 vols. New York: Oxford University Press, 1971–1974.

Muldoon, James. "The Contributions of the Medieval Canon Lawyers to the Formation of International Law." *Traditio* 28 (1972): 483–493.

Muldoon, James. "*Extra ecclesiam non est imperium*: The Canonists and the Legitimacy of Secular Power." *Studia Gratiana* 9, no. 551 (1953): 572–575. Bononiae: Institutum Iuridicum Universitatis Studiorum Bononiensis.

Muldoon, James. "John Wyclif and the Rights of the Infidels: The *Requerimiento* Re-Examined." *Americas* 36 (1980): 301–16.

Muldoon, James. *Popes, Lawyers, and Infidels: The Church and the Non-Christian World 1250–1550*. Philadelphia: University of Pennsylvania Press, 1979.

Muldoon, James, ed. *The Expansion of Europe: The First Phase*. Philadelphia: University of Pennsylvania Press, 1977.

Nammack, Georgiana. *Fraud, Politics and the Dispossession of the Indians*. Norman: University of Oklahoma Press, 1969.

Nash, Gary B. *Red, White and Black: The Peoples of Early America*. 2d ed. Englewood Cliffs, N.J.: Prentice-Hall, 1982.

Nelson, William E. "The Eighteenth Century Background of John Marshall's Constitutional Jurisprudence." *Michigan Law Review* 76 (1978): 893–960.

Newton, Nell. "Federal Power over Indians: Its Sources, Scope and Limitations." *University of Pennsylvania Law Review* 132 (1984): 195–288.

Nussbaum, A. *A Concise History of the Law of Nations*. rev. ed. New York: Macmillan, 1954.

Nys, Ernst, ed. *F. Victoria, De Indis et de Iure Belli Reflectiones*. Translated by J. Bate. New York: Oceana, 1917.

O'Callaghan, Edmund Bailey, ed. *Documents Relative to the Colonial History of the State of New York*. Albany, N.Y.: Weed, Parsons, 1856.

O'Callaghan, Joseph F. *A History of Medieval Spain*. Ithaca, N.Y.: Cornell University Press, 1975.

O'Meara, John, trans. *Gerald of Wales, The History and Topography of Ireland*. New York: Penguin, 1951.

Parry, John Horace. *The Establishment of the European Hegemony 1415–1715*. 3d ed. rev. New York: Harper & Row, 1966.

Parry, John Horace. *The Spanish Theory of Empire in the Sixteenth Century*. Cambridge: Cambridge University Press, 1940.

Peckham, Howard, and Gibson, Charles, eds. *Attitudes of the Colonial Powers Toward American Indians*. Salt Lake City: University of Utah Press, 1969.

Peckman, Howard Henry. *Pontiac and the Indian Uprising*. New York: Russell and Russell, 1970.

Plucknett, T. F. T. *Studies in English Legal History*. London: Hambledon Press, 1983.

Pocock, J. G. A. *The Machiavellian Moment: Florentine Political Thought and the Atlantic Republican Tradition*. Princeton, N.J.: Princeton University Press, 1975.

Porter, Harry Culverwell. *The Inconstant Savage: England and the American Indian 1500–1600*. London: Duckworth, 1979.

Prestage, Edgar. *The Portuguese Pioneers: The Pioneer Histories*. New York: Barnes & Noble, 1967.

Prucha, Francis Paul. *American Indian Policy in the Formative Years: Indian Trade and Intercourse Acts, 1790–1834*. Cambridge, Mass.: Harvard University Press, 1962.

Purchas, Samuel. *Hakluytus Posthumus or Purchas His Pilgrimes*, vol. 19. Glasgow: MacLehose, 1906.

Quinn, David Beers. *England and the Discovery of America 1481–1620*. New York: Knopf, 1974.

Quinn, David Beers. "Ireland and Sixteenth Century Expansion." *Historical Studies* 1 (1958): 20–58.

Quinn, David Beers. "Sir Thomas Smith (1513–77) and the Beginnings of English Colonial Theory." *Proceedings of the American Philosophical Society* 89 (1945): 543–60.

Quinn, David Beers, ed. *The Roanoke Voyages 1584–1590.* 2 vols. London: Hakluyt Society, 1955.

Quinn, David Beers, ed. *The Voyages and Colonising Enterprises of Sir Humphrey Gilbert.* 2 vols. London: Hakluyt Society, 1940.

Rachewiltz, Igor de. *Papal Envoys to the Great Khans.* Palo Alto, Calif.: Stanford University Press, 1971.

Robinson, Walter Stilt. *The Southern Colonial Frontier 1607–1763.* Albuquerque: University of New Mexico Press, 1979.

Rolfe, J., trans. *A Gentili, De Iure Belli Libri Tres.* Oxford: Clarendon Press, 1964.

Royce, Charles C., ed. "Indian Land Cessions in the United States." *18th Annual Report of the Bureau of American Ethnology,* Part 2, pp. 540–643. Washington, D.C.: Government Printing Office, 1899.

Rutland, Robert Allen, and Rachel, W., eds. *Papers of James Madison,* vol. 8. Chicago: University of Chicago Press, 1973.

Schreiber, Herman. *Teuton and Slav: The Struggle for Central Europe.* Translated by James Cleugh. New York: Knopf, 1965.

Scott, James Brown. *The Spanish Origin of International Law.* Oxford: Clarendon Press, 1934.

Simpson, Lesley Byrd. *Studies in the Administration of the Indians in New Spain.* Berkeley: University of California Press, 1934.

Snow, Alpheus H. *The Question of Aborigines in the Law and Practice of Nations.* New York: Putnam, 1921.

Sosin, Jack M. *Whitehall and the Wilderness: The Middle West in British Colonial History 1760–1775.* Lincoln: University of Nebraska Press, 1961.

Strauss, Leo. *Natural Right and History.* Chicago: University of Chicago Press, 1953.

Strickland, Rennard. "Genocide-at-Law: An Historic and Contemporary View of the Native American Experience." *University of Kansas Law Review* 34 (1986): 713–55.

Sullivan, J., and Flick, A., eds. *The Papers of Sir William Johnson,* vol. 5. Albany: State University of New York Press, 1921–1933.

Taylor, E. G. R., ed. *The Original Writings and Correspondence of the Two Richard Hakluyts.* 2 vols. London: Hakluyt Society, 1935.

Thacker, J. B. *Christopher Columbus: His Life, His Work, His Remains, as Revealed by Original Printed and Manuscript Records.* New York: AMS Press, 1967.

Thorne, Samuel. "Dr. Bonham's Case." *Law Quarterly Review* 54 (1938): 545–52.

Thorne, Samuel. *Sir Edward Coke 1552–1952.* Selden Society Lecture, 1952. London: Quaritch, 1957.

Tierney, Brian. *The Crisis of Church and State 1050–1300.* Englewood Cliffs, N.J.: Prentice-Hall, 1964.

Tierney, Brian. *Foundations of the Conciliar Theory: The Contributions of the Medieval Canonists from Gratian to the Great Schism.* Cambridge: Cambridge University Press, 1955.

Trend, John Brande. *The Civilization of Spain.* London: Oxford University Press, 1944.

Ullmann, Walter. *The Growth of Papal Government in the Middle Ages: A Study in the Ideological Relations of Clerical to Lay Power.* London: Methuen, 1955.

Ullmann, Walter. *Law and Politics in the Middle Ages: An Introduction to the Sources of Medieval Political Ideas.* Ithaca, N.Y.: Cornell University Press, 1975.

Ullmann, Walter. *Medieval Foundations of Renaissance Humanism.* London: Paul Elek, 1977.

Ullmann, Walter. *Medieval Papalism: The Political Theories of the Medieval Canonists.* London: Methuen, 1949.

Ullmann, Walter. *A Short History of the Papacy in the Middle Ages.* London: Methuen, 1972.

Vaughan, Alden T. *Early American Indian Documents: Treaties and Laws 1607–1789.* Washington, D.C.: University Publications of America, 1979.

Verlinden, Charles. *The Beginnings of Modern Colonization.* Translated by Y. Freccero. Ithaca, N.Y.: Cornell University Press, 1970.

Verlinden, Charles. "Italian Influence in Iberian Colonization." *Hispanic American Historical Review* 33, no. 2 (May 1953): 199–211.

Verlinden, Charles. "The Rise of Spanish Trade in the Middle Ages." *Economic History Review* 10, no. 1 (February 1940): 44–59.

Vogel, Virgil J., ed. *This Country Was Ours: A Documentary History of the American Indian*. New York: Harper & Row, 1972.

Volwiler, Albert Tangeman. *George Croghan and the Westward Movement 1741–1782*. Cleveland: Arthur H. Clark, 1926.

Von Der Heydte, Friedrich August Freiherr. "Discovery and Annexation in International Law." *American Journal of International Law* 29 (1935): 448–71.

Wagner, H. R., and Parish, Henry Raup. *The Life and Writings of Bartolomé de Las Casas*. Albuquerque: University of New Mexico Press, 1967.

Wallace, Anthony F. C. *The Death and Rebirth of the Seneca*. New York: Knopf, 1970.

Wallerstein, Immanuel Maurice. *The Modern World-System: Capitalist Agriculture and the Origins of the European World Economy in the Sixteenth Century*. New York: Academic Press, 1974.

Walsh, Edmund, ed. *The History and Nature of International Relations*. New York: Macmillan, 1972.

Warren, Charles. *The Supreme Court in United States History*. Boston: Little, Brown, 1928.

Washburn, Wilcomb. *Red Man's Land/White Man's Law*. New York: Scribner, 1971.

Weber, Max. *The Protestant Ethic and the Spirit of Capitalism*. Translated by Talcott Parsons. New York: Scribner, 1976.

Weinreb, Lloyd. *Natural Law and Justice*. Cambridge, Mass.: Harvard University Press, 1987.

Wilkinson, Charles. *American Indians, Time and the Law*. New Haven, Conn.: Yale University Press, 1987.

Wilks, Michael. *The Problem of Sovereignty in the Later Middle Ages: The Papal Monarchy with Augustinus Triumphus and the Publicists*. Cambridge: Cambridge University Press, 1963.

Williams, Gwyn A. *Madoc: The Making of Myth*. London: Eyre Methuen, 1979.

Williams, Robert. "The Algebra of Federal Indian Law: The Hard Trail of Decolonizing the White Man's Indian Jurisprudence." *Wisconsin Law Review* (1986): 219–299.

Williams, Robert. "Documents of Barbarism: The Contemporary Legacy of European Racism and Colonialism in the Narrative Traditions of Federal Indian Law." *Arizona Law Review* 31, no. 2 (1989): 237–78.

Williams, Robert. "Jefferson, the Norman Yoke, and American Indian Lands." *Arizona Law Review* 29 (1987): 165–94.

Williams, Robert. "The Medieval and Renaissance Origins of the Status of the American Indian in Western Legal Thought." *Southern California Law Review* 57, no. 1 (1983): 1–99.

Williamson, James Alexander. *The Cabot Voyages and Bristol Discovery Under Henry VII*. Cambridge: Hakluyt Society at Cambridge University Press, 1962.

Williamson, James Alexander. *Hawkins of Plymouth*. London: Black, 1949.

Williamson, James Alexander. Sir John Hawkins: The Time and the Man. Westport, Conn.: Greenwood Press, 1970.

Wolff, R., and Hazard, H., eds. *A History of the Crusades*, vol. 2. Madison: University of Wisconsin Press, 1969.

Wood, Gordon. *The Creation of the American Republic, 1776–1787*. Chapel Hill: University of North Carolina Press, 1969.

Wood, Neal. *John Locke and Agrarian Capitalism*. Berkeley: University of California Press, 1984.

Wright, Benjamin Fletcher, Jr. *American Interpretations of Natural Law: A Study in the History of Political Thought*. Cambridge, Mass.: Harvard University Press, 1931.

Index

Abernathy, Thomas, 258
Adams, John, 246, 253, 290
Adams, Samuel, 243, 265
Adrian IV, 136–37
Africa, 59, 60, 68, 72–77, 79, 82, 121, 135, 299
Alanus Anglicus, 40–42, 45, 62, 64, 65, 90
Albert the Great, 43
Alexander II, 31
Alexander VI, 79–81, 83, 88–91, 99, 100, 133, 138, 178, 179, 180, 202, 299
Alfonso Henriques (king of Portugal), 68
Alfonso X (king of Castile), 75
Allegheny Mountains, 228, 233
Allodial tenure, 268, 269, 272
Amadas, Philip, 177
American Revolution, 233, 296
  discourses of, 228–30, 240–41, 246–55, 266–73, 279, 286n, 287, 293, 296–305
  radicals of, 227–31, 242–46, 249–55, 266, 270–73, 279, 292–93, 295
Amherst, Jeffrey (British general), 235, 236
Anastasius I (emperor of Rome), 16
Anne Archer, 157
Anti-expansionists, 234–35, 237, 259, 262, 264. *See also* Hillsborough, Lord
Appalachian Mountains, 228, 230, 233
Aquinas, Thomas, 43–45, 49, 55–56n, 64–66, 85–86, 90, 93, 96–101, 104
Arawak Indians, 78, 111n
Ards (Ireland), 143–45
Aristotle, 42, 43, 45, 64–65, 76, 211
  and theory of natural slavery, 87, 95, 174, 211
Armada, Spanish, 184
Articles of Confederation, 288–94, 96, 305, 306. *See also* Continental Congress (United States)
Augustine, Saint, 29–31, 44, 45, 51n, 63, 67, 101, 102, 196, 210
Azores, 68, 80, 82

Bacon, Francis, 176, 185, 208, 211
Bahamas, 80
Barkham's Case, 214–16
Battle of Fallen Timbers, 308
Battle of Tanneburg, 62

Baynton, Wharton and Morgan (trading house), 256, 257, 260, 262
Bellum justum (just war theory), 30, 44, 66, 67, 195–99. *See also* Augustine, Saint
Benedictine monks, 17
Berkhofer, Robert, 93
Bernard of Clairvaux, 61
Black Legend. *See Spanish Cruelties, The*
Blackstone, William, 116n, 303
Board of Trade, British, 234, 235, 238, 239, 242, 248, 259, 262–65, 277
Bologna, 26, 43
Boniface VIII, 28
Borgia, Rodrigo. *See* Alexander VI
Bracton, 38
Brant, Joseph, 258
British Constitution. *See* Constitution, British
British imperial policy. *See* Imperial policy, British
British Ministry. *See* Ministry, British
Brundage, James, 31, 36
Burgh, James, 254
Byzantium, 16, 34, 75

Cabot, John, 120–23, 156, 161, 164, 170, 178, 219, 299, 314
Caciques (Indian headmen), 82, 88
Calvin, John, 164, 217
Calvin's Case, 199, 200, 202, 204, 210, 214, 215, 217, 269, 275, 300–302
Cambridge University (England), 126, 129, 134, 163, 164, 210
Camden, first Earl (lord chancellor), 262, 263, 274–78, 288, 291, 302
Camden-Yorke opinion, 275–77, 279, 288, 300, 322n
Campbell v. Hall, 300–303, 310, 322n
Canary Islands, 68–72, 74, 78, 80, 83, 84, 105, 135
Cannibalism, 127, 128, 130, 196
Canny, Nicholas, 146
Canossa, 23
Cape Verdes Islands, 68, 80
Carleill, Christopher, 161, 162
Carrol, Charles, 293, 295
Carrol, Charles, Jr., 254

Castile, 67, 68, 85, 87, 204
Cateau-Cambresis, Treaty of, 132
Catherine of Aragon, 128
Catholic Church. *See* Church, Roman
    Catholic
Cecil, William, 140
Ceuta, 68
Charlemagne, 4, 17, 18, 35, 36, 60
Charles I (king of Spain; Charles V, Holy
    Roman Emperor), 96, 97, 123–24, 128,
    174
Charters, colonial, 230, 244–46, 249, 250, 261,
    269, 271, 272, 287–92, 297–99, 308–9, 315
Chase, Samuel, 290, 293, 295, 318n
Cherokee cases, 306
Cherokee Nation, 261, 262, 279
Cherokee Nation v. Georgia, 314
Chippewa Indians, 236
Christian Commonwealth, universal, 13, 15–
    18, 30. *See also Societas Christiana*
Christian humanism, 49–50, 56n. *See also*
    Aquinas, Thomas; Thomistic humanism
Church, Roman Catholic, 13, 16, 27, 60, 85,
    124. *See also* Papal jurisdiction, theory
    of universal; English Catholic Church
Cicero, 42
Cistercians, 61
City of God. See Augustine, Saint
Clare, Lord, 245
Clement III, 33
Clement VII, 123
Clerical marriage, 18–20
Clermont declaration, 34–37. *See also* First
    Crusade
Coke, Edward, 194, 199–202, 204, 208, 210,
    214, 215, 222n, 269, 275, 300–302, 325
College of Cardinals, 19, 20
Columbus, Christopher, 6, 49, 75–78, 80–83,
    89, 90, 99, 100, 102, 127, 128, 129, 253
Conciliarism. *See* Constance, Council of
Concordia discordantium canonum. See
    Decretum
Concubinage. *See* Clerical marriage
Congress, United States, and Indian affairs,
    230–31, 306–8. *See also* Continental
    Congress (United States)
Connally, John, 265
Connecticut, 245, 294, 295
Conquest, rights of, 199–200, 205, 229–31,
    268–70, 275–77, 289, 299–303, 305, 308,
    310–17. *See also Camden-Yorke* opinion;
    Doctrine of Discovery
Conquistadores
  English Protestant, 136, 141, 146, 163, 181,
    185, 193

Spanish, 76, 82, 85, 87, 90–93, 95, 96, 102,
    107, 123, 134, 138, 141, 143, 173, 174,
    184
Constance, Council of, 60, 62–64, 66, 69, 70,
    72, 79, 86, 90, 98
Constantine (emperor of Rome), 15
  Donation of, 57n
Constantinople, 16, 34, 75
Constitution, British, 228, 243–46, 250, 254,
    270, 275, 300, 302, 303, 310
Constitution, United States, 306, 307, 309
Constitutional Convention (United States),
    306
Continental Congress (United States), 271,
    273, 288, 290–98, 306. *See also* Articles
    of Confederation
Conway, Henry, 259
Corpus mysticum Christi, 15
Craven, Wesley, 174, 207
Crawford, William, 251
Croft, Sir James, 137
Croghan, George, 236, 256–60, 262, 277–79
Cromwell, Thomas, 123
Crusades, 13–15, 21, 26, 29–41, 44, 49, 59–62,
    66–68, 72, 73, 75, 78, 82, 98, 130, 300,
    302
  and English colonizing discourse,
    121–22, 142, 146, 161, 163, 165, 177,
    183, 185, 193, 202, 207, 212, 215, 217,
    301–2, 317
  and English conquest of Ireland, 136–38
Crusading priestly orders. *See* Teutonic
    Knights
Crusading vows, 35, 37–39, 44–45
Cuba, 80, 155

Dagge, Henry, 262, 263
Dale, Sir Thomas, 212
Davenport, Frances, 133
De Berdt, Dennys, 244
De civili domino. See Wyclif, John
De iure belli libri tres. See Gentili, Alberico
De La Warr, Lord, 212
Deane, Silas, 295
Debo, Ange, 85
Decretals, papal, 17, 44
Decretum, 26–28, 42
Dee, John, 160, 170
Delaware, 245, 246, 294
Delaware Indians, 236, 239, 260, 265
Devereux, Walter, Earl of Essex, 146
Devolution of Sovereignty. *See* Prerogative,
    English Crown's royal
Dickinson, John, 290–92
Digest, Roman, 42, 102

Dinwiddie, Robert (governor of Virginia). *See* Dinwiddie Proclamation
Dinwiddie Proclamation, 264, 294
Discovery. *See* Doctrine of Discovery
Distinctio, 27, 28
Divine law, 45, 46, 88, 93, 100, 101, 197
Divine mandate, 14, 36, 46, 131, 172, 177, 210
Doctrine of Discovery, 99, 204, 221. *See also Camden-Yorke* opinion; Conquest, rights of
and modern international law, 325–28
and modern United States law, 325–26
and United States colonizing discourse, 229, 231, 269, 289, 298, 299, 303, 309–17
Dominican order, 43, 85, 86, 88, 93–100, 102, 105, 127, 128, 167, 168, 173, 174, 180, 209
Dominium, 13, 30, 40, 41, 45, 46, 60–66, 70–72, 79, 90, 98, 100, 104, 109n, 200, 207
Donatism, 30, 63–65
Dowdall, George, 138, 139
Drake, Sir Francis, 135, 153, 154, 158, 159, 163, 177, 183, 184
Duarte (king of Portugal), 69–73, 78–84
Dublin, 137, 256
Dunmore, Lord John (governor of Virginia), 265, 274, 275, 279, 284–85n
Dunmore's War, 265, 266, 274–75
Dutch West India Company, 220

East India Company (England), 201, 210, 263, 276, 303
Ebolus of Roucy, 31
Eden, Richard, 126–31, 138–42, 147, 164, 173
Edward IV (king of England), 121
Egremont, Lord (Secretary of State), 234, 235
Eliot, John, 117n
Elizabeth I (queen of England), 132–36, 151–53, 155, 156, 158, 159, 166, 170, 171, 173, 175, 177, 180, 181, 184, 193–95, 201, 269, 299
and Irish colonial policy, 136–47
Elizabethan Renaissance, 141, 177
Elizabethan Restoration, 131, 171
Ellis, Henry, 234
Encomienda, 83–86, 88, 93–95, 112–13n, 141–43, 173
England, 121–26, 131–32, 193–94. *See also* English colonizing discourse; Imperial policy, British
and American Revolutionary-era colonial policy, 227–29, 233–45, 256, 263–65, 287
and influence of Spanish colonial theory and practice, 137–39, 143–44, 147
and Irish colonial policy, 136–47, 183

and Portuguese colonial rivalry, 121–23
and Spanish colonial rivalry, 120, 123, 126, 129, 132, 134, 136, 147, 154–56, 160, 178, 182, 193, 202–5
English Catholic Church, 122–24, 128. *See also* Recusancy laws
English Catholics, 159–60. *See also* English Catholic Church
English colonizing discourse, 120–22, 129–31, 140–41, 143–44, 156–57, 160–62, 164–74, 178–82, 184–85, 193–99, 202–4, 209–11, 214, 221, 269–70, 275–80, 300–303, 311–16. *See also* Imperial policy, British
and John Locke, 246–49
English merchants, 135, 201
English Muscovy Company, 153
English Puritanism, 164–65, 182–83
Essoin, 38
Eugenius IV, 68–72, 78, 83, 84
Eurocentrism, 46, 47, 49, 67, 73, 87, 98, 101, 104, 107, 141, 182, 195, 196, 199
Excommunication, 22–24, 37, 39, 74, 81, 153, 158, 159

Factorias, 68, 73, 82
Falcon, 157
Falkenberg, Johannes, 64, 66
Fauquier (governor of Virginia), 235, 255
Federalist Papers, 252
Ferdinand (king of Spain), 74, 77, 79–86, 88–92, 105, 129, 197
Feudalism, 18–21, 36–39, 68. *See also* Prerogative, English Crown's royal; Primogeniture
and the American Revolution, 228–31, 240, 251, 268–72, 275, 276, 279–80, 287
and English colonial theory, 121, 123, 124, 145, 177, 199–200, 207–8, 214–16, 220–21, 300–303
and Spanish colonial theory, 82, 84
and United States colonial theory, 295, 297–98, 303–4, 311–17
First Crusade, 34–37. *See also* Clermont declaration; Urban II
Fletcher v. Peck, 308–9, 314, 320n
Fort Detroit, 236
Fort Dunmore, 265
Fort Gage, 288
Fort Pitt, 260, 265, 274, 277
Fort Stanwix, Treaty of, 261, 262, 273, 278, 294
France, 133, 156, 233, 234, 235, 267, 314
Franciscan order, 85, 88
Franklin, Benjamin, 244–45, 254, 256–60, 262, 264, 265, 267, 273, 279, 295

Franklin, William, 257–60, 295
Frederick Barbarossa (emperor), 28
Frederick II (king of Sicily; Holy Roman
	Emperor), 4, 61
French and Indian War, 227–28, 233, 235,
	236, 238, 239, 241, 244, 247, 251, 256,
	258, 260, 264, 266, 267, 300

Gage, Thomas (British general), 243, 251,
	259
Galloway, Joseph, 257, 260, 295
Gates, Sir Thomas, 209, 212
Gelasius I, 16–17, 19–20. *See also* Two
	Swords, theory of
Genghis Khan, 3, 4
Genoese commerce, 75–77
	and slavery, 82
Gentili, Alberico, 169, 173, 194–200, 211
Gentili, Matteo, 194
George III (king of England), 228, 235
Georgia, 177, 294, 306, 308, 309
Gerald of Wales, 137
Gerard, Conrad, 295
Gerard, Sir Thomas, 159
Germany, colonial expansion of, 60–61. *See
	also* Teutonic Knights
Gibraltar, 68
Gierke, Otto von, 17
Gilbert, Sir Humphrey, 151–67, 175, 177, 178,
	183, 184, 193, 201, 220, 314
Giles of Rome, 109n
Glanvill, 38
Glorious Revolution (1688–1689), 176, 253,
	269, 275, 300, 302. *See also* Constitution,
	British
Gramatica, 74
Granada, 74, 80
Gratian, 26, 27, 42. *See also Decretum*
Gray, Robert, 210–11
Great Kanawha River, 261–63
Great Lakes, 233, 234, 237
Gregorio, licentiate, 87
Gregory I, 17
Gregory VII, 4, 22–27, 31–32, 33, 36, 40
Gregory IX, 37–38, 43
Gregory XI, 63
Grenada, 300–302, 310
Grenville, Lord, 242, 244
Grenville, Richard, 181
Grotius, Hugo, 13, 116n, 133, 195, 244, 309
Guanahani. *See* San Salvador
Guardianship, 70–74, 103–5
Guiscard, Robert, 20–22
Gus-Wen-Tah, 326, 327. *See also*
	Haudenosaunee Confederacy

Guyak Khan (Great Kahn of the Mongols),
	3–6, 43, 47–49

Hadrian IV, 28
Hakluyt, Richard (the elder), 156–58, 161,
	176, 181
Hakluyt, Richard (the younger), 156, 160,
	161, 163, 177–81, 183, 201
Hanke, Lewis, 87, 92, 95
Hardwicke, first Earl of (lord chancellor), 234
Harold (king of England), 31
Harriot, Thomas, 182–83
Haudenosaunee Confederacy, 234–35, 239,
	259–63, 265, 273, 277, 278, 281–82n, 304,
	327. *See also* Gus-Wen-Tah
Hawkins, John, 135, 154, 159
Hawkins, William, 135
Hayes, Edward, 157, 163–65, 167, 168
Heathens. *See* Infidels
Henderson, Richard (judge), 279
Henry II (king of England), 136, 170, 179
Henry III (Holy Roman Emperor), 18–19, 40
Henry IV (Holy Roman Emperor), 22–26
Henry VII (king of England), 77, 121–22, 156,
	170, 179, 219, 299
Henry VIII (king of England), 97, 122–26,
	128, 129, 131–32
	and Irish colonial policy, 137–38
Henry, Patrick, 243, 244, 274, 275, 279
Hildebrand-Gregory (archdeacon). *See*
	Gregory VII
Hill, Christopher, 124, 132, 175, 176
Hillsborough, Lord, 259, 262–65, 277, 278
Hispaniola, 80, 82, 83, 85, 88, 93, 135, 155
Hohenstaufen emperors, 4, 28
Holland, 220–21, 314. *See also* Dutch West
	India Company
Holy Land, 13, 15, 32–38, 40, 44, 61, 64, 302.
	See also Crusades
Holy Roman Emperor, 17, 21
Holy War. *See* Crusades
Hostiensis, 65, 66, 72, 90, 98
Huguenots, 133, 152, 175
Humanist tradition, 42–44, 47–49, 173, 174,
	195, 196. *See also* Christian humanism;
	Renaissance, humanism
	and Spanish colonial theory, 93–99, 102–4,
	166
Humbert of Silva Candida, 19–20

Iberian Peninsula, 31, 33, 67, 68. *See also
	Reconquista*
Iceland, 75
Illinois Company, 257, 258, 260
Illinois Indians, 289

Illinois River, 289
Illinois-Wabash Company, 288–90, 293, 295,
    308, 309, 315
Idolatry, 14, 46, 196
Imperial Plan of 1764, 238–41
Imperial policy, British, 227–30, 234–42, 245,
    255–56, 259, 266
Indian rights. *See* Indians; Natural law, and
    Indian rights in United States colonizing
    discourse
Indian superintendents, British imperial, 238–
    40, 255, 257, 259–61
Indian trade, 101–3, 130–31, 153, 177, 206,
    208, 233, 236, 238–39, 255, 281n, 291–92,
    306
Indiana Company, 288, 294, 295, 297, 298,
    303, 304
Indians
    and the Articles of Confederation, 290–99
    and British imperial policy during
        Revolutionary era, 227–30, 234–35, 237–
        38, 245, 255
    and *Camden-Yorke* opinion, 275–80, 288,
        303
    and English colonizing discourse, 140, 147,
        171, 180, 182, 183, 194, 211, 214–16, 219,
        220–21
    and Revolutionary land purchases, 230–31,
        233, 249–50, 255–65, 274, 277–79, 288,
        289, 290, 293–94, 296, 298–300, 304, 306,
        308–17
    and Spanish colonizing discourse, 78–79,
        88, 91–93, 98–100
    and state land purchases under the
        Constitution, 306–7
    and United States colonizing discourse,
        228–31, 246–49, 271–75, 279–80, 287,
        289, 290, 297–300, 303–17
Indians' lands. *See* Indians
Indies, 75, 78, 79, 81, 83, 88, 89, 91–98, 105,
    128, 133, 135, 139, 141, 152, 154, 155,
    157, 174, 175, 178, 179, 183, 203–5
Indulgence for sins, 34, 35, 39, 40, 44, 89. *See
    also* Crusading vows; Pilgrimage
Infidel sovereignty, 40, 41, 44, 45, 49, 60, 62,
    64–67, 69, 71, 72, 79, 80, 90, 92, 98, 104,
    105, 121, 193, 198, 200, 207, 215, 216,
    220, 229, 231, 269, 298, 301, 303, 312,
    315. *See also Barkham's Case*
Infidels, 14, 29–41, 44–47, 59, 61, 64, 65, 67–
    70, 72, 73, 75, 76, 84, 85, 90, 91, 98, 99,
    104, 106, 107
    and English colonizing discourse, 120–22,
        129–34, 152, 155–57, 165, 171–72, 183,
        195–205, 209–11, 215–20, 229, 231, 269

and rights under natural law, 44–50, 69–71,
    78–79, 230, 299, 300–303
and United States colonizing discourse, 303,
    314, 316–17
Innocent III, 44
Innocent IV, 4–6, 13–14, 43–49, 59–60, 64–67,
    69–72, 79, 86, 90, 92, 98, 104–5, 196–97,
    209
    Quod super his, 13–15, 44–47, 49, 64, 65,
        70–71, 92
Inquisition, Spanish, 85, 94, 113n, 155
Inter caetera divinae. See Alexander VI
International law, modern, 325–28. *See also*
    Law of Nations (*ius gentium*)
Investiture Controversy, 15, 18–26, 32
Ireland, 136–39, 141–44, 147, 151, 153, 156,
    159, 175, 178, 179, 211, 259, 264, 265,
    270
    Crusading-era history, 136–37
    English colonization of, 137–44, 146–47,
        152, 159, 161, 166, 179, 181, 270
    and New World colonization, 159
Irish tribes, 137, 141, 143, 146, 172, 182
    compared with New World tribespeople,
        141, 183
Irnerius, 26, 43
Iroquois Confederacy. *See* Haudenosaunee
    Confederacy
Isabella (queen of Spain), 74, 77–82, 85, 89
Ius gentium. See Law of Nations
Ius naturale. See Natural law
Ivo of Chartres, 27

Jadwiga (princess of Poland), 62
Jagiello (king of Lithuania), 62
James I (king of England), 175, 193, 201, 202,
    204, 205, 208, 209, 218, 230, 269, 299
Jamestown colony, 193, 205–7, 210, 212, 216–
    20, 230
Jay, John, 252
Jefferson, Thomas, 246, 253, 255, 266–72,
    277, 279, 290–93, 295, 296, 302, 304, 311
Jensen, Merrill, 292
Jeronymite friars, 94
Jerusalem. *See* Holy Land
John (king of Portugal), 77, 79, 80
John of Gaunt, 63
John of Plano Carpini (friar), 3–6
Johnson, Robert, 210
Johnson, Sir William, 239, 240, 257–62, 273,
    283–84n
Johnson v. McIntosh, 231, 289, 308–17, 321n,
    325
Johnston, Thomas (governor of Maryland),
    293, 294, 295

Jones, Joseph, 296
Just war theory. *See Bellum justum*

Kaskaskia, 288
Kilkenny, Statutes of, 137
King's Council of Virginia, 202. *See also*
    Virginia Company
Kumanians, 61

Lagu, 227
Land speculators, Revolutionary era, 229–31,
    249–50, 251, 255–65, 289, 292, 293, 298.
    See also Indians, and United States
    colonizing discourse
  and Indian natural rights to land, 271–80,
    304–6, 308, 314
Landabiliter, 135–36, 138, 179. *See also*
    Ireland, Crusading-era history
"Landed" colonies. *See* "Landed" states
"Landed" states, 230, 231, 246, 249, 255, 256,
    273, 279, 287–93, 295, 297, 305, 307, 308
"Landless" colonies. *See* "Landless" states
"Landless" states, 230, 231, 246, 255, 256,
    288, 290–94
Lane, Ralph, 181–83
Las Casas, Bartolomé de, 95, 128, 173, 174,
    180, 184
Las Siete Partidas (The Seven Parts), 75, 110–
    11n. *See also* Alfonso X (king of Castile)
Law, canon, 26–29, 37–40, 98
Law, civil (Roman law), 26, 39–40, 42, 98,
    102
  and the Renaissance, 42–43
Law of Nations (*ius gentium*), 13, 59, 71, 120,
    127, 132–33, 172–74, 205, 211
  Alberico Gentili and the, 195–99
  and Dutch colonizing discourse, 220
  and English colonizing discourse, 138–39,
    158–59, 167–69, 218, 220–21, 301–2
  Franciscus de Victoria and the, 96–108
  and Spain's papal title to the New World,
    133
  and United States colonizing discourse, 303,
    309, 311, 313, 316, 325
Law of nature. *See* Natural law
Laws of Burgos, 87, 88, 93, 142
Lay investiture. *See* Investiture Controversy
Lee, Arthur, 263
Lee, Richard, 246, 263, 291–93
Leo IX, 18–19, 22
Levant, 32, 35, 41, 44, 61, 75, 76, 82. *See also*
    Holy Land
"Lines of amity," 133. *See also* Cateau-
    Cambresis, Treaty of
Lisbon, 67, 68, 72, 73, 75–77, 79, 80, 135

Lithuania, 60–67, 69, 70. *See also* Teutonic
    Knights
Locke, John, 171, 211, 228–29, 244, 252, 254,
    271, 300, 311
  Second Treatise of Government, 246–49
London Company, 202, 297. *See also* Virginia
    Company
López de Palacios Rubios, Juan, 89, 90, 91
Lord, Hugh (British captain), 288
Loyal Land Company of Virginia, 261
Lurie, Nancy, 218
Luther, Martin, 89

MacLeane, Laughlin, 284n
Macpherson, C. B., 247
Madieras, 68, 76, 82
Madoc (prince of Wales), 170, 178
Maitland, Francis, 13, 208
Manifest destiny, 142, 185
Mansfield, Lord. *See Campbell v. Hall*
Manteo, 177
Marshall, John (chief justice), 231, 232n, 289,
    308, 309, 312–17, 325
Martire of Anghiera, Pietro, 127–29, 131,
    138, 183
Martyr, Peter, 93
Mary, Queen of Scots, 195
Mary Tudor (queen of England ["Bloody
    Mary"]), 128–32, 138, 139, 173, 195
Maryland, 230, 245, 246, 254, 255, 263, 288,
    290, 293–96, 305
Mason, George, 293–96
Massachusetts, 242–44, 266, 294, 306
Master of Life. *See* Neolin
Mendoza, Don Bernadino de, 158, 160, 170,
    173, 194
Mercantile colonialism, 75, 76, 82, 84, 102,
    140, 153, 233. *See also* Ministry, British
  and mercantilist thesis, British, 234
Mercer, George, 263
Merchant-Christian, 130
Mesa, Bernardo de (friar), 87
Miami Indians, 236
Milton, John, 125
Ministry, British, 233–35, 239–42, 250, 255–
    57, 260–62, 265–66, 277, 286n, 287
Minucci da Pratovecchio, Antonio, 71–72
Miller, Perry, 164
Missionaries, 14, 46, 70, 71, 80, 91, 92, 93,
    100, 105, 182, 210
Mississippi Company, 263
Mississippi River, 233, 289, 316
Mississippi Valley, 233
Mohamet. *See* Muhammad
Mongols, 3–6, 47–50

Montague, Edward, 263
Montesinos, Antonio de, 86, 88, 93
Moors, 33, 66, 67, 68, 74, 75, 91, 180. *See also* Moslems
Morgan, George, 257, 295
Morison, Samuel Eliot, 76
Morris, Robert, 295
Moslems, 13, 14, 21, 31, 33, 36, 67–68. *See also* Moors
Muhammad, 44
Muldoon, James, 66–67
Munster, 151
Murray, William, 288–89, 308, 313

Natural law, 5, 13, 14, 39, 40–43, 45–49, 59, 65–67, 70–72, 80, 86, 87, 90–93, 96–104, 129, 131, 139, 140, 166, 174, 196–99, 203, 209, 215, 218, 221
  and the American Revolution, 228, 230–31, 243, 244, 246–49, 252–54, 267, 269
  and Indian rights in United States colonizing discourse, 271–74, 280, 287, 298, 300, 303–5, 307, 309–17
Natural rights, 45, 70, 86, 90, 98, 218, 220. *See also* Indians, and Revolutionary land purchases; Indians, and United States colonizing discourse
  and the American Revolution, 228, 243–44, 246–49, 252, 254, 272, 287, 298–300, 303–7
Nebrija, Antonio de. *See Gramatica*
Necotowance, 219
Neolin, 236
New Jersey, 246, 255, 259, 288, 294
New York, 239, 242, 243, 294, 296, 306
Newfoundland, 155, 163, 220
Newport, Christopher, 207, 208
Nicholas II, 20
Nicholas V, 72, 73
Nichomachean Ethics, 42
Norman Conquest. *See* Norman Yoke
Norman Yoke, 13, 31, 228–31, 252–55, 266–73, 275, 277, 279, 289, 297, 302–4, 306, 307, 310–12
Normans, 20–21, 31, 33, 302. *See also* Norman Yoke
North Carolina, 177, 306
Northumberland, 173
Northwest Ordinance, 306
Northwest Territory, 233, 237, 238, 266, 272, 304–6, 308, 309
Nys, Ernst, 301

Ohio Company, 261, 263, 264
Ohio River Valley, 233, 234, 236, 257, 259–61, 263, 278, 289, 293, 305

Old Northwest. *See* Northwest Territory
On the Indians Lately Discovered. See Victoria, Franciscus de
On the Law of War in Three Parts. See Gentili, Alberico
O'Neill, Shane, 139
Opechancanough, 206, 213–20
"Opinio Hostiensis." *See* Vladimiri, Paulus
Otis, James, 252–53
Ottawa Indians, 236
Ovando, Nicolás de, 83, 85
Oviedo, Gonzalo Fernández de, 127, 128, 131, 138, 173
Oxford University (England), 63, 134, 194, 197, 200, 207, 211

Paca, William, 293, 295
Paine, Thomas, 296–98, 304, 308
Papacy, Roman Catholic. *See* Papal jurisdiction, theory of universal
Papal jurisdiction, theory of universal, 3–6, 13–15, 17, 20–21, 23, 27–29, 32, 39–40, 48–49, 70–74. *See also* Innocent IV; Petrine Mandate; *Unam sanctum*
  and donation of New World to Spain, 79–81, 89–91, 319n
  and Franciscus de Victoria's views on, 96–100
  and Protestant Reformation, 120
  and *Requerimiento*, 91
Paris, Treaty of, 233
Parliament, 175, 201, 240–43, 245, 250, 254, 262, 275, 301, 303
Paspahegh Indians, 206
Patents, royal, 121, 122, 156, 159, 165, 170, 177, 194, 201, 214, 219, 220. *See also* Charters, colonial
Paul, Saint, 15, 31
Paz, Matías de, 89–91
Peckham, George, 159–60, 165–73, 178, 195. *See also* English Catholics
Penn, John, 257, 263, 277
Pennsylvania, 230, 242, 244–46, 251, 255–57, 263, 273, 288, 290, 291, 294
Perestrello, 76
Perkins, William, 164, 165
Peter, Saint. *See* Petrine Mandate
Petrine Mandate, 4, 13–17, 19, 21, 22–24, 28, 29, 32–33, 40, 45, 46, 48, 49, 62, 66, 70–73, 81, 84, 89, 90, 91. *See also* Papal jurisdiction, theory of universal
Philip II (king of Spain), 128, 129, 131–33, 138, 139, 153, 154, 166, 178, 205
Piankeshaw Indians, 289

Pilgrimage, 33–40, 44. *See also* Crusading vows
Piracy, 136, 152, 154, 157, 183, 184, 197
Pittsburgh, 237. *See also* Fort Pitt
Pius II, 76
Plain Facts. See Wharton, Samuel
Plato, 211
Plenitudo potestatis, 39–41. *See also* Papal jurisdiction, theory of universal
Plymouth Company, 202. *See also* Virginia Company
Pocahontas, 206, 212
Poland, 3, 60–69. *See also* Teutonic Knights
Pontiac, 236, 237, 239
Pontiac's Rebellion. *See* Pontiac
Pope. *See* Roman pontiff
Popham, Sir John, 201
Porter, H. C., 171
Portugal, 67–74, 76, 82, 121, 267
  colonizing discourse of, 60, 70–71, 72–74
Potawatomi Indians, 236
Powhatan (Indian emperor), 177, 206–9, 211–13, 220
Prerogative, English Crown's royal, 199–200, 229, 245, 246, 250, 267–71, 272, 275–80, 287, 297, 300–304, 311–12
  as devolved to the United States, 295, 304–6, 308–10, 312
Primogeniture, 125, 134, 144
Privilegium forti, 38
Privy Council, 154, 157, 184, 237, 251, 259, 262, 263, 265, 275, 276
Proclamation of 1763, 228–31, 235, 237, 241, 242, 244, 249, 250, 254–56, 273, 277, 279, 287, 288, 297, 300–302, 308, 310
Protestantism. *See* Reformation, Protestant
Pufendorf, Samuel, 244, 303, 309
Purchas, Samuel, 218
Puritanism, 164, 165, 168, 174–76, 182–84, 210, 217–19. *See also* "Seed" of Christian faith; Perkins, William

Quebec Act, the, 266
Quinn, David, 138, 141, 142, 144, 157, 183, 205
Quod super his. See Innocent IV

Raleigh, Sir Walter, 157, 174–77, 180–85, 193, 194, 201, 211, 314
Reconquista
  Portuguese, 67–68
  Spanish, 31, 33, 67, 74
Recusancy laws, 159, 210
Reformation, Protestant, 63, 120–26, 128, 131, 132, 138, 158, 161, 183, 193, 299

Renaissance, European, 13, 15, 41–43, 55n
  humanism, 42–44, 64–65
Repartimiento, 84. *See also* Encomienda
Requerimiento, 91–93, 105, 123, 143, 173, 200
  views of Franciscus de Victoria on, 100
Rheims, Council of, 19
Rhode Island, 245, 246, 294
Richard I (king of England), 38, 121
Roanoke, 177, 181–84, 211
  lost colony of, 184
Robert the Monk, 35. *See also* First Crusade; Clermont
Rockingham, Marquis of, 245
Rolfe, John, 212
Roman Catholic Church. *See* Church, Roman Catholic
Roman law. *See* Law, civil
Roman Digest. *See* Digest, Roman
Roman emperor. *See* Rome
Roman pontiff, 16, 18, 28, 49, 61, 64, 65, 91. *See also* Papal jurisdiction, theory of universal
Romanus Pontifex, 72–74, 77, 79, 80
Rome, 15–18
Roselli, Antonio, 71, 72
Royal Council of the Indies, 93
Royal Proclamation of 1763. *See* Proclamation of 1763
Rudolf of Swabia, 23, 24
Rufinus of Bologna, 28, 45

Saint John's Harbour. *See* Newfoundland
Salamanca, University of, 77, 89, 97
San Salvador, 78, 111n
Sandys, Sir Edwin, 212
Santo Domingo, 85
Saracens, 13, 20, 21, 34, 36, 44, 71, 72, 98, 155. *See also* Moors; Moslems
Sarah Constant, 207
Saxon Constitution, 228, 253, 272, 287. *See also* Norman Yoke
Saxons, 22, 60, 227–29, 252–54, 267–72, 275, 304, 311. *See also* Norman Yoke
Scotland, 199
Second Treatise of Government. See Locke, John
"Seed" of Christian faith, 164, 165. *See also* Perkins, William
Seneca, 76
Seneca Indians, 236
Senegal River, 68
Sepúlveda, Juan Ginés de, 174
Seven Parts, The. *See Las Siete Partidas*
Seven Years' War. *See* French and Indian War

Seville, 127, 135
Sexual perversion, 14, 46, 196
Shawnee Indians, 236, 239, 265, 274
Shelbourne, Lord, 259, 262
Sidney, Sir Henry, 139–41, 143, 151, 159
Sidney, Sir Philip, 165
Silva, Guzmán de, 153
Simony. *See* Investiture Controversy
Six Nations of the Iroquois. *See* Haudenosaunee Confederacy
Slavery, 82–88, 92, 94, 95, 154, 174, 178, 180–81, 203. *See also* Hawkins, John; Hawkins, William
    English slave trade, 135
Smith, Adam, 176
Smith, John, 206–8, 211, 213
Smith, Sir Thomas, 141–46, 152, 157, 159, 162
Smith, Thomas (the younger), 210
Societas Christiana, 23, 25, 32–33. *See also* Christian Commonwealth, universal
Sosin, Jack, 261
South Carolina, 242, 294
South Seas, 290, 291, 297
Spain
    and African colonizing activities, 68, 69
    and Catholic Church influence, 75, 85
    colonizing discourse of, 60, 74, 88–89, 314
    and English colonial rivalry, 120, 123, 126, 129, 132, 134, 136, 147, 154–56, 160, 178, 182, 193, 202–5
    influence on English colonial theory and practice, 137–39, 143–44, 147
    and New World colonizing activities, 78–86
    and papal donation of New World, 79–81, 131–33
Spanish Armada. *See* Armada, Spanish
Spanish Cruelties, The, 173–74
Squirrel, 158
Stamp Act, 228, 241–45, 250, 255, 279
Story, Joseph, 316
Stuarts, 253, 268. *See also* James I (king of England)
"Suffering" traders, 256–57, 259–62, 273–75, 278, 287, 289, 294, 298
Supreme Court (United States), 231, 308–17, 325–26
Sussex, Earl of (Sir Thomas Radcliffe), 138

Talavera, Hernando de, 77, 78
Tarragona, 33, 34
Tennessee River, 261, 262
Tequinas, 128
Teutonic Knights, 60–66

Thomistic humanism, 55–56n, 93, 96–101, 104. *See also* Aquinas, Thomas; Christian humanism
Throckmorton, Francis, 173
Thurlow, Edward, 265
Tidewater Indians. *See* Powhatan (Indian emperor)
Tierney, Brian, 27
Tordesillas, Treaty of, 80
Transylvania Company, 279
Trent, William, 260, 262, 277, 295
Turks, 34, 74, 75
Two Row Wampum. *See* Gus-Wen-Tah
Two Swords, theory of, 16, 19, 28–29, 40, 53n, 54n. *See also* Gelasius I; Papal jurisdiction, theory of universal

Ullman, Walter, 40
Ulster, 138–40, 143, 146, 151
Unam Sanctum, 28–29
United States
    and Indian affairs under the Constitution, 306, 308–9, 314
    and Revolutionary-era Indian policy, 246, 287, 289–92, 294, 314–17
Universal Christian Commonwealth. *See* Christian Commonwealth, universal
Universal papal jurisdiction, theory of. *See* Papal jurisdiction, theory of universal
Urban II, 32–37, 41, 44

Vandalia colony, 263–66, 273, 274, 277, 278, 288, 289, 295, 298
Vespucci, Amerigo, 83, 102, 126, 127, 131
Victoria, Franciscus de, 13, 96–107, 127, 139, 167–69, 172, 326
    and English colonizing discourse, 167–69, 204, 209
    as "founder of international law," 114–15n, 169
Virginia, 181–84, 193, 194, 201, 204–13, 215, 220
    and cession of Old Northwest, 296, 305–6
    House of Burgesses, 242–44
    Revolutionary era, 230, 235, 242–44, 246, 249–51, 255, 256, 260–65, 271–74, 279, 287–98, 304–6, 310, 315
Virginia Company, 193, 200–202, 204, 205, 208, 210, 212, 214–17, 219–20, 230
    justification for colonizing New World, 202–4
    views on Indian sovereignty, 214–16
Viviat, Louis, 288, 289, 308, 313
Vladimiri, Paulus, 64–67, 69, 72
    "Opinio Hostiensis," 64–66

Walker, Thomas, 261
Wallerstein, Immanuel, 68
Walpole, Thomas, 262–65, 278
Walpole Company, 262–65
Walsingham, Sir Francis, 159, 161, 162, 182, 194
Wanchese, 107
Warren, Sir Peter, 258
Washington, George, 229–30, 251, 255, 263, 264, 279, 284–85n, 294
Waterhouse, Edward, 217–18
Wayne, Anthony (American general), 308
Webster, Daniel, 309–11
Wedderburn, Alexander, 265
Wends, 61

Wharton, Samuel, 257–64, 273, 277–79, 288, 289, 295, 298–300, 303–5
Wharton, Thomas, 273, 274, 295
White, John, 183, 184, 211
Whitehall. *See* British Ministry
William of Normandy, 31, 268, 269, 302. *See also* Norman Yoke
Wilson, James, 290, 295
Wyclif, John, 63–66

Yeardley, George, 213–16
York, Charles. *See Camden-Yorke* opinion
York River, 219

Zuniga, Pedro de, 204–5

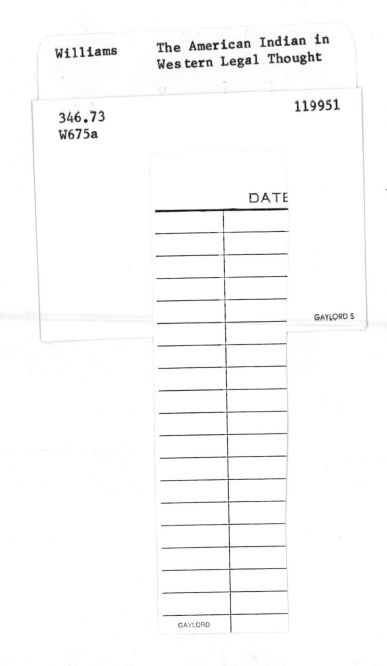

DATE DUE